T0184896

Communications in Computer and Information Science 1230

Commenced Publication in 2007
Founding and Former Series Editors:
Simone Diniz Junqueira Barbosa, Phoebe Chen, Alfredo Cuzzocrea,
Xiaoyong Du, Orhun Kara, Ting Liu, Krishna M. Sivalingam,
Dominik Ślęzak, Takashi Washio, Xiaokang Yang, and Junsong Yuan

More information about this series at http://www.springer.com/series/7899

Usha Batra · Nihar Ranjan Roy ·
Brajendra Panda (Eds.)

Data Science and Analytics

5th International Conference on Recent Developments
in Science, Engineering and Technology, REDSET 2019
Gurugram, India, November 15–16, 2019
Revised Selected Papers, Part II

Springer

Editors
Usha Batra ⓘ
GD Goenka University
Gurugram, India

Nihar Ranjan Roy ⓘ
GD Goenka University
Sohna, Haryana, India

Brajendra Panda ⓘ
University of Arkansas
Fayetteville, AR, USA

ISSN 1865-0929   ISSN 1865-0937 (electronic)
Communications in Computer and Information Science
ISBN 978-981-15-5829-0   ISBN 978-981-15-5830-6 (eBook)
https://doi.org/10.1007/978-981-15-5830-6

This Springer imprint is published by the registered company Springer Nature Singapore Pte Ltd.
The registered company address is: 152 Beach Road, #21-01/04 Gateway East, Singapore 189721, Singapore

Preface

Data science employs techniques and theories drawn from many fields within the broad areas of mathematics, statistics, information science, and computer science, in particular from the subdomains of machine learning, classification, cluster analysis, data mining, databases, and visualization. Data analytics seeks to provide operational observations into issues that we either know or do not know. Analysis is a part of any scientific research and it is the first step in building a theory. The second step is synthesis, which actually builds or creates a theory. It is also important to remember that science is not about results, but about a methodology to get them. The focus is on big data applications to tackle the problem of decision-making under uncertainty by using machine learning methods and graph theory to analyze complex structures in big data to build recommender systems and predictive models.

The 5th International Conference on Recent Developments in Science, Engineering and Technology (REDSET 2019), was held at the GD Goenka University, India, during November 15–16, 2019, in association with Springer, is our humble effort in this direction. Promotion of inquiry-based education has been the core competence of the School of Engineering at GD Goenka University since its inception and the present conference was yet another step forward. We aim to promote the interdisciplinary nature of scientific enquiry, which leads to engineering efforts to develop scientific and technologically innovative solutions so as to benefit society as a whole.

We received 353 papers and participation from 12 different countries including India, Canada, Egypt, Lithuania, Malaysia, Nepal, Nigeria, Saudi Arabia, Sweden, UAE, Vietnam, and the USA. After undergoing a rigorous peer-review process following international standards, the acceptance rate was approximately 21%. Selection was based on originality of the idea, innovation, and relevance to the conference theme and relation to the latest trends in the respective domains. We hope that the ideas and subsequent discussions presented at the conference will help the global scientific community to aim toward a nationally and globally responsible society. We also hope that young minds will derive inspiration from their elders and contribute toward developing sustainable solutions for the nation and the world as a whole.

The current proceedings contain the contributions presented during REDSET 2019. We wish to express our sincere appreciation to the members of the Technical Program Committee and the reviewers who helped in the paper selection process. We also thank the authors for their contributions that allowed us to assemble such an exceptional technical set of papers. We thank Springer for being our publication partner for this conference. Our special thanks go to the editorial staff at Springer, especially Ms. Kamiya Khatter and Ms. Alla Serikova, for their outstanding service and support.

April 2020

Usha Batra
Nihar Ranjan Roy
Brajendra Panda

Organization

Patron

Goenka Nipun   Managing Director at GD Goenka Group, India

Co-patron

Bhaskaran Suku   President of GD Goenka Group, India

Conference Program Chair

Panda Brajendra   University of Arkansas, USA

Steering Committee

Chair

Sahu Atma   Coppin State University, USA

Members

Tickoo Sham	Purdue University, USA
Klauss Raul	Technological University of Clausthal, Germany
Rauniyar S. P.	BMRD, Australia
Borana Lalit	Hong Kong Polytechnic University, Hong Kong
Mitra Shayon	Manitoba Public Insurance, Canada
Srivastava Anurag K.	Washington State University, USA
Priyadi Ardyono	Institut Teknologi Sepuluh, Indonesia
Goel Lalit	Nanyang Technological University, Singapore

Organizing Committee

Conference Chair

Batra Usha   GD Goenka University, India

Organizing Secretary

Roy Nihar Ranjan   GD Goenka University, India

Members

Agrawal Shilpy	GD Goenka University, India
Arya Vaishali	GD Goenka University, India
Banerjee Alina	GD Goenka University, India

Bashir Jasira	GD Goenka University, India
Chopra Khayati	GD Goenka University, India
Gautam Ashu	GD Goenka University, India
Gupta Niharika	GD Goenka University, India
Jindal Anita Anand	GD Goenka University, India
Kapoor Neha	GD Goenka University, India
Kataria Shipra	GD Goenka University, India
Khurana Shikha	GD Goenka University, India
Kumar Yogesh	GD Goenka University, India
Meenalochani N.	GD Goenka University, India
Mehta Deepa	GD Goenka University, India
Nagpal Arpita	GD Goenka University, India
Pankaj Manchanda	GD Goenka University, India
Priya Rashmi	GD Goenka University, India
Saini Manisha Saini	GD Goenka University, India
Sharma Ganga	GD Goenka University, India
Sharma Manka	GD Goenka University, India
Singh Jaspreet	GD Goenka University, India
Singh Ramandeep	GD Goenka University, India
Sondhi Akanksha	GD Goenka University, India

International Advisory Committee

Srivastava Anurag K.	Washington State University, USA
Priyadi Ardyono	Institut Teknologi Sepuluh, Indonesia
Panda Brajendra	University of Arkansas, USA
Goel Lalit	Nanyang Technological University, Singapore
Yorino Naoto	Hiroshima University, Japan
Kothari D. P.	GP Group of Institutions, India
Al-Rabea Adnan	Al-Balqà Applied University, Jordan
Karki Nava Raj	Tribhuvan University, Nepal
Dharshana Yapa Roshan	University of Peradeniya, Sri Lanka
Eghbal Daniel (Mehdi)	ENERGEX, Australia
Talukdar Kamarul Hasan	Kulna University, Bangladesh
Kapoor Nishal	IBM Corporation, USA
Kuswadi Son	Politeknik Elektronika Negeri, Indonesia
Chari Rama	RRCAT, India
Salazar Alvare German	Stockholm University, Sweden
Girgis Emad	National Research Centre, Egypt
Sharma Paramanand	Tohoku University, Japan
Tickoo Sham	Purdue University, USA
Rauniyar S. P.	BMRD, Australia
Hakim Lukmanul	Lampung University, Indonesia
Klauss Raul	Technological University of Clausthal, Germany
Manis Amigui Gcaro Cocotle Compa	Monterry Institute of Technology, Mexico

Victor Manuel Diez	Interconexion Electrica, Columbia
Mitra Shayon	Manitoba Public Insurance, Canada
Chhabra Amit	Pollard Banknote, Canada
Borana Lalit	Hong Kong Polytechnic University, Hong Kong
Bhalla Subhash	University of Aizu, Japan
Muhammad Akbar Hussain Dil	Aalborg University, Denmark
Abdullah Mohammad FaizLiew	University Tun Hussein Onn Malaysia, Malaysia
Beichelt Frank	University of the Witwatersrand, South Africa
Mueller Eckhard	German Aerospace Centre, Germany

Technical Committee

Yorino Naoto	Hiroshima University, Japan
Huang Miaoqing	University of Arkansas, USA
Kothari D. P.	GP Group of Institutions, India
Al-Rabea Adnan	Al-Balqà Applied University, Jordan
Garg Deepak	Bennate University, India
Raj Karki Nava	Tribhuvan University, Nepal
Dharshana Yapa Roshan	University of Peradeniya, Sri Lanka
Eghbal Daniel (Mehdi)	Energex, Australia
Talukdar Kamarul Hasan	Kulna University, Bangladesh
Kapoor Nishal	IBM Corporation, USA
Kuswadi Son	Politeknik Elektronika Negeri, Indonesia
Chari Rama	RRCAT, India
Alvare German Salazar	Stockholm University, Sweden
Girgis Emad	National Research Centre, Egypt
Vyas Abhilasha	GSFC University, India
Kumar Abhinav	Amity University, India
Kumar Singh Abhishek	BIT, India
Swaroop Abhishek	BPIT, India
Priyam Abhishek	NIT, India
Singh Abhishek Kumar	BIT, India
Elngar Ahmed	Beni-Suef University, Egypt
Kumar Ajeet	AmesGoldsmith, USA
Dureja Aman	PDM College of Engineering, India
Landage Amarsinh	Government College of Engineering, India
Singh Amit	Guru Gobind Singh Indraprastha University, India
Choudhary Amit	Maharaja Surajmal Institute, India
Upadhyay Amrita	NIT, India
Nayyar Anand	Duy Tan University, Vietnam
Garg Anjali	The NorthCap University, India
Kumar Ankit	Uppsala University, Sweden
Choudhary Ankur	Amity University, India
Vij Ankush	Amity University, India

Gupta Anuj Kumar	IKG Punjab Technical University, India
Nagpal Arpita	GD Goenka University, India
Seth Ashish	Inha University, Uzbekistan
Khanna Ashish	MAIT, India
Garg Atul	Chitkara University, India
Bhati Bhoopesh Sinigh	Ambedkar Institute of Advanced Communication Technologies and Research, India
Garg Bindu	Bharati Vidyapeeth College of Engineering, India
Panda Brajendra	University of Arkansas, USA
Shekhar Chander	Amity University, India
Banerjee Chitreshh	Amity University, India
Babu D. Veerabhadra	iNURTURE Education Solutions Pvt. Ltd., India
Mehta Deepa	GD Goenka University, India
Gupta Deepak	GGSIPU, India
Kamthania Deepali	IIT, India
Garg Deepika	GD Goenka University, India
Kumar Devendra	ABES Engineering College, India
Singh Dimple	Amity University, India
Nandan Durgesh	Accendere Knowledge Management Services Pvt. Ltd., CL Educate Ltd., India
Sharma Ganga	Guru Gobind Singh Indraprastha University, India
Rani Geeta	NSIT, India
Yadav Harikesh	NIT, India
Kumar Harish	GL Baja Institute of Engineering and Technology, India
Purohit Hemant	JIET, India
Singh Jaspreet	GGSIPU, India
Jadon Jitendra	Amity University, India
Patel Jyotirmay	Shri Ram Murti Smarak College of Engineering, Technology and Research, India
Sagayam K. Martin	Karunya University, India
Rai Kajal	Punjab University, India
Punia Kavita	JK Lakshmipat University, India
Sree Kiran	SVECW, India
Seth Kirti	Inha University, Uzbekistan
Prasad Lalit	Galgotias University, India
Kharb Latika	Jagan Institute of Management Studies, India
Sharma Lavanya	Amity University, India
Bhatia Madhulika	Amity University, India
Hooda Madhurima	Amity University, India
Goyal Manik	CDLSIET, India
Gupta Manish Kumar	Symbiosis University of Applied Sciences, India
Saini Manisha	GD Goenka University, India
Gupta Manoj	Rukmini Devi Institute of Advanced Studies, India
Singh Manu	HRIT Group of Institutions, India
Solanki Manu	Manav Rachna International University, India

Iqbal Md	Meerut Institute of Engineering and Technology, India
Nafis Md Tabrez	Jamia Hamdard University, India
Sharma Meghna	The NorthCap University, India
Vasim Baig Mirza Mustaq	Yashwant College Nanded, India
Abdul Ahad Mohd	Jamia Hamdard University, India
Thaseen Mohseena	N.E.S's Science College, India
Dawar Parul	DTU, India
Yadav Mukesh	Gurgaon Institute of Technology and Management, India
Goyal Mukta	JIIT, India
Bhatele Mukta	OIST, India
Ojha Muneendra	IIITR, India
Sharma Naresh	GD Goenka University, India
Thakur Narina	BVCOE, India
Jain Neelesh	JUET, India
Kumar Neeraj	Thapar University, India
Goel Neetu	VIPS, India
Sharma Neha	GD Goenka University, India
Gupta Neha	Manav Rachna International Institute of Research and Studies, India
Goel Neha	VIPS, India
Arora Nidhi	GD Goenka University, India
Roy Nihar	GD Goenka University, India
Patidar Nitesh	IIT, India
Malik Nitin	The NorthCap University, India
Alshorman Omar	Najran University, India
Gahlot Pallavi	IIT, India
Nand Parma	IIT, India
Nayak Pinki	Amity University, India
Thakar Pooja	Vivekananda Institute of Professional Studies, India
Sapra Pooja	WCTM, India
Ahlawat Prachi	The NorthCap University, India
Prakash Prashant	BIT, India
Johri Prashant	Galgotias University, India
Pandya Prateek	Amity University, India
Negi Prateek	IITD, India
Kumar Praveen	Amity University, India
Pappula Praveen	SR Engineering College, India
Pandey Purnendu	BML Munjal University, India
Dutta Pushan	Amity University, India
P. Raghu Vamsi	JIIT, India
Singh Rajinder	Guru Kashi University, India
Rajak Ranjit	JNU, India
Mahajan Rashima	Manav Rachna International Institute of Research and Studies, India
Priya Rashmi	GD Goenka University, India

Mishra Renu	GCET, India
Babbar Richa	Thapar University, India
Kumar Rishi	Thapar University, India
Chhikara Rita	The NorthCap University, India
Vaid Rohit	Maharishi Markandeshwar University, India
Madaan Rosy	GD Goenka University, India
Ojha Rudra Pratap	Galgotias College of Engineering and Technology, India
Goyal S. B.	City University, Malaysia
Sinha S. K.	Amity University Noida, India
Abbas Sadiqa	Manav Rachna International University, India
K. Pachalla Sameer	Mahindra Ecole Centrale, India
Mathur Sandeep	Amity University, India
Singh Sandeep	JIIT, India
Saxena Sandeep	NIT, India
Tarar Sandhya	Gautam Buddha University, India
Makkar Sandhya	LBSIM, India
Mondal Sandip	NIT, India
Gupta Sanjay	Manav Rachna International University, India
Pippal Sanjeev	MNNIT, India
Sahu Sanjib	Indira Gandhi Delhi Technical University for Women, India
Das Sanjoy	Indira Gandhi National Tribal University, India
Chauhan Sansar Singh	MNNIT, India
Vishwakarma Santosh	Manipal University, India
Juneja Sapna	BMIET, India
Varshney Sapna	University of Delhi, India
Jain Sapna	University of Petroleum and Energy Studies, India
K. Saravanan	Anna University, India
Tanwar Sarvesh	Chitkara University, India
Sharma Satendra	Yobe State University Damaturu, Nigeria
Srivastava Satyajee	Galgotias University, India
Mishra Saurabh	Chandigarh University, India
Ahlawat Savita	Maharaja Surajmal Institute of Technology, India
Jain Shaily	Chitkara University, India
Vashisth Sharda	The NorthCap University, India
Arora Shaveta	The NorthCap University, India
Suhail Sheikh	J&K Forensic Science Laboratory, India
Sachdeva Shelly	NIT, India
Agrawal Shilpy	GD Goenka University, India
Saluja Shivani	GD Goenka University, India
Sharma Shivnjali	Rajiv Gandhi Institute of Petroleum Technology, India
Mongia Shweta	Jamia Millia Islamia, India
Singh Shyamli	Indian Institute of Public Administration, India
Biswas Siddhartha	Jamia Millia Islamia, India
Menon Sindhu	KLEIT, India

Sood Smita	GD Goenka University, India
Patnaik Soma	Manav Rachna International University, India
Tanwar Sudeep	Nirma University, India
Sengupta Sudhriti	Amity University, India
Mishra Sudipta	GD Goenka University, India
Radha Suja	VIT University, India
Kumar Sumit	NIT, India
Gupta Sumit Kumar	KIET, India
Raheja Supriya	NCU, India
A. Suresh	Nehru Institute of Engineering and Technology, India
Kumar Sushil	KIET, India
Narayanan Swaminathan	QIS College of Engineering and Technology, India
Jha Swati	BML, India
Choudhury Tanupriya	UPES, India
Kumar Tapas	Lingayas University, India
Choudhary Teja Ram	JNU, India
Khatoon Thayyaba	Malla Reddy College of Engineering and Technology, India
Tewari Tribhuwan	JIIT, India
Tiwari Twinkle	JIIT, India
Batra Usha	GD Goenka University, India
Juyal Vandana	BCIIT, India
Saini Varinder	IIT, India
Arora Vasudha	GD Goenka University, India
Tayal Vijay	Amity University, India
Yadav Vijay	Bundelkhand University, India
Tayal Vijay Kumar	Amity University, India
Singh Vijendra	The NorthCap University, India
Shanmuganathan Vimal	National Engineering College, India
Jain Vishal	Bharati Vidyapeeth's Institute of Computer Applications and Management, India
Kumar Yogesh	UTU, India
Gigras Yogita	NCU, India
Kumar Yugal	Hindu College of Engineering, India

Contents – Part II

Security in Data Science Analytics

Identification of Safety and Security Vulnerabilities in Cyber
Physical Systems.   3
    Abhilasha Vyas and Usha Batra

A Walkthrough of Blockchain Technology and Its Potential Applications. . . .   14
    Sudipti Dhawan, Shubhra Shah, and Bhawna Narwal

Blockchain Technology Transforms E-Commerce for Enterprises   26
    Ankur Arora, Manka Sharma, and Suku Bhaskaran

Blockchain Secured "Smart Buildings" as Cyber Physical Systems   35
    Anupam Tiwari and Usha Batra

Iris Based Secured Newfangled System Procuring
Miniaturized Prorogation   54
    Ayesha Hena Afzal, Sherin Zafar, and M. Afshar Alam

Accessible and Ethical Data Annotation with the Application
of Gamification.   68
    Vedant Gurav, Muhanned Parkar, and Parth Kharwar

Exploring the Possibility of Sybil Attack in Position Based Routing
Protocols in VANETs: A Case Study of Greedy Perimeter Coordinator
Routing (GPCR)   79
    Nishtha and Manu Sood

CBCT: CryptoCurrency Based Blockchain Technology   90
    Rahul Johari, Kanika Gupta, Saurabh Kumar Jha, and Vivek Kumar

Fast Information Retrieval over Encrypted Outsourced Cloud Data   100
    Vasudha Arora and Shweta Mongia

Authentication of User in Connected Governance Model   110
    Ayanabha Ghosh, Tathagato Das, Sayan Majumder, and Abhishek Roy

Future of Data Hiding: A Walk Through Conventional
to Network Steganography   123
    Rohit Tanwar, Sona Malhotra, and Kulvinder Singh

Sentiment Analysis for Predicting the Popularity of Web Series   133
    Parag Kumar Garg, Mrinal Pandey, and Mamta Arora

Social and Web Analytics

An Explicit Analysis of Best Tourist Destinations 143
Satyajee Srivastava, Sonia Sharda, and Arti Ranjan

Time-Cost Solution Pairs in Multi-index Bulk Transportation Problem 154
Kuldeep Tanwar and Sudhir Kumar Chauhan

A Statistical Analysis of Various Technologies to Detect and Prevent
Fake News 164
Saurabh Singh, Shakti Vishwakarma, Sunil Kispotta,
and Akanksha Yadav

Identification of Salient Attributes in Social Network:
A Data Mining Approach 173
Ruchi Mittal

Energy Efficient Content Based Image Retrieval Recommender System
in Mobile Cloud 186
Rajalakshmi Krishnamurthi and Mukta Goyal

Semantic Web-Based Information Retrieval Models: A Systematic Survey . . . 204
Anil Sharma and Suresh Kumar

Comparative Study of Machine Learning Algorithms for Social Media
Text Analysis 223
Nidhi Malik and Saksham Jain

Spam Detection in Social Network Using Machine Learning Approach 236
Simran Chaudhry, Sanjeev Dhawan, and Rohit Tanwar

Big Data Analytics

Forecasting Movie Rating Through Data Analytics 249
Latika Kharb, Deepak Chahal, and Vagisha

Using Statistical Belief Model to Analyze Outcome Using
Bayesian Networks 258
Niharika Sanga, Jaspreet Singh, and Aniruddh Sanga

Mining Frequent Itemsets over Vertical Probabilistic Dataset Using
FuzzyUeclat Algorithm 266
Amit Rehalia, Samar Wazir, and Md. Tabrez Nafis

Comparison of Random Weight Initialization to New Weight
Initialization CONEXP 279
Apeksha Mittal, Amit Prakash Singh, and Pravin Chandra

Exploiting the Most Similar Cases Using Decision Tree
to Render Recommendation   290
   *Piyush Kolankar, Ranjeet Patel, Nitesh Dangi, Sumit Sharma,
   and Sarika Jain*

Segmentation of Breast Density Using K-Means Clustering Algorithm.   305
   Jyoti Dabass, Madasu Hanmandlu, and Rekha Vig

Automated Mucous Glands Detection and Segmentation in Colon
Histology Images Using Semantic Segmentation   316
   Manju Dabass and Jyoti Dabass

Big Data Cluster Service Discovery: A System Application for Big Data
Cluster Security Analysis.   331
   Swagata Paul, Sajal Saha, and Radha Tamal Goswami

Classification of IRIS Recognition Based on Deep Learning Techniques   342
   *Mukta Goyal, Rajalakshmi Krishnamurthi, Aparna Varma,
   and Ishita Khare*

A Decision Tree Based Supervised Program Interpretation Technique
for Gurmukhi Language.   356
   Himdweep Walia, Ajay Rana, and Vineet Kansal

Importance of Web Analytics for the Success of a Startup Business   366
   Bhavook Chitkara and Syed Mohd Jamal Mahmood

Hierarchical Bayesian Compressed Sensing of Sparse Signals.   381
   Shruti Sharma, Khyati Chopra, and Rasveen Bholan

Data Acquisition for Effective E-Governance: Nigeria, a Case Study   397
   *Ekong Edikan, Sanjay Misra, Ravin Ahuja, Fernando Pérez Sisa,
   and Jonathan Oluranti*

Smart IoT Monitoring Framework Based on OneM2M for Air Quality   412
   *Chaitanya Chauhan, Ritesh Ojha, Jain Soham Dungerchand,
   Gaurav Purohit, and Karunesh K. Gupta*

Gravitational K-Means Algorithm   420
   Mohd. Yousuf Ansari, Anand Prakash, and Mainuddin

Experimental Analysis of Convolutional Neural Networks and Capsule
Networks for Image Classification.   430
   Shweta Bali and Shyam Sunder Tyagi

Evaluation of an Efficient Method for Object Detection in Video   442
  Manoj Attri, Rohit Tanwar, Narender, and Neha Nandal

Author Index   453

Contents – Part I

Data Centric Programming

An Efficient Approach for Selection of Initial Cluster
Centroids for k-means   3
   Manoj Kr. Gupta and Pravin Chandra

Bedsore Ulcer Detection Using Support Vector Machine   14
   Anand Upadhyay, Nida Baig, and Anishka Pereira

Model Performance Evaluation: Sales Prediction.   24
   Abhishek Singh and Satyajee Srivastava

Predicting Trends of Stock Market Using SVM: A Big Data
Analytics Approach.   38
   Sneh Kalra, Sachin Gupta, and Jay Shankar Prasad

Hybrid Entropy Method for Large Data Set Reduction Using MLP-ANN
and SVM Classifiers   49
   Rashmi and Udayan Ghose

Android Smells Detection Using ML Algorithms with Static Code Metrics . . .   64
   Aakanshi Gupta, Bharti Suri, and Vishal Bhat

Parallel Solution to LIS Using Divide-and-Conquer Approach   80
   Seema Rani and Dharamveer Singh Rajpoot

US Air Quality Index Forecasting: A Comparative Study.   91
   Rishipal Singh, Vanisha Singh, and Nonita Sharma

Effect Analysis of Contrast Enhancement Techniques on Cancer
Classification in Colon Histopathology Images Using Machine Learning 103
   Manju Dabass, Sharda Vashisth, and Rekha Vig

A Novel Activation Function in Convolutional Neural Network
for Image Classification in Deep Learning 120
   Ochin Sharma

Evaluation of Nephrology Dataset Through Deep Learning Technique. 131
   Neha Dohare and Shelly Sachdeva

Prediction of Ticket Prices for Public Transport Using Linear Regression
and Random Forest Regression Methods: A Practical Approach Using
Machine Learning   140
    Aditi, Akash Dutta, Aman Dureja, Salil Abrol, and Ajay Dureja

Identification of Novel Drug Targets in Pathogenic *Aspergillus Fumigatus*:
An *in Silico* Approach   151
    Reena Gupta and Chandra Shekhar Rai

Comparing Classifiers for Universal Steganalysis   161
    Ankita Gupta, Rita Chhikara, and Prabha Sharma

Airline Prices Analysis and Prediction Using Decision Tree Regressor   170
    Neeraj Joshi, Gaurav Singh, Saurav Kumar, Rachna Jain,
    and Preeti Nagrath

ANN Based Direct Modelling of T Type Thermocouple for Alleviating
Non Linearity   187
    Ashu Gautam and Sherin Zafar

Forecasting of Literacy Rate Using Statistical and Data Mining Methods
of Chhattisgarh   203
    Aditeya Nanda, Vishwani Sati, and Shweta Bhardwaj

Recommendation System for Prediction of Tumour in Cells Using
Machine Learning Approach.   212
    Ankit Verma, Amar Shukla, Tanupriya Choudhury, and Anshul Chauhan

A Novel Mobile Based Hybrid Skin Tone Classification Algorithm
for Cancer Detection   223
    Paarth Bir and B. Balamurugan

Next Generation Computing

Detection of Lung Cancer Through Image Processing Using SVM   239
    Anand Upadhyay, Ankit Dubey, and Ajaykumar Patel

Learning Vector Quantization Based Leaf Disease Detection   246
    Anand Upadhyay, Jyoti Singh, and Rutuja Shinde

Towards Prediction of Energy Consumption of HVAC Plants Using
Machine Learning   254
    Monika Goyal and Mrinal Pandey

Ionic Concentration and Action Potential Differences Between
a Healthy and Alzheimer's Disease Person   266
    Shruti Gupta, Jyotsna Singh, and Kaushal Kumar

An Adaptive Framework for Human Psycho-Emotional Mapper
Based on Controlled Stimulus Environment   278
Ayan Chakraborty, Sajal Saha, and R. T. Goswami

Implementation of Common Spatial Pattern Algorithm
Using EEG in BCILAB   288
Tanupriya Choudhury, Amrendra Tripathi, Bhawna Arora,
and Archit Aggarwal

A Review on Enhancement of Road Safety in Vehicular
Ad-hoc Networks   301
Chiranjit Dutta, Ruby Singh, and Niraj Singhal

Intelligent Parking Using Wireless Sensor Networks: A Review   311
Ruby Singh, Chiranjit Dutta, and Niraj Singhal

Review on Computational Techniques to Identify Drug Targets
from Whole Proteome of Fungi and Bacteria   320
Reena Gupta and Chandra Shekhar Rai

Innovative Smart Hoisting Assistance   328
Anjali Garg, Vibhu Mehta, Shubham Soni, Ritika Sharma,
Himanshu Goyal, and Divyam Sachdeva

Computational Hybrid Approaches for Routing and Security
Optimization in Networks   339
Nida Iftekhar, Sherin Zafar, Samia Khan, and Siddhartha Sankar Biswas

An Empirical Analysis of Supply Chain Risk and Uncertainty
in Manufacturing Sector to Achieve Robustness   355
Surya Prakash, Gianesahwar Aggarwal, Archit Gupta, and Gunjan Soni

Preliminary Evaluation of Navigation and Timing Capability
of IRNSS/NavIC at The Northcap University   365
Kartikay Saini, Pankaj, C. D. Raisy, Preeti, Sharda Vashisth,
and Amitava Sen Gupta

Artificial Intelligence Supervised Swarm UAVs for Reconnaissance   375
Saatvik Awasthi, Balamurugan Balusamy, and V. Porkodi

Using Virtual Reality as a Cost-Effective Substitute for Engineering
Labs in Underdeveloped Countries   389
Alalade Adesoji, Sanjay Misra, and Ravin Ahuja

Distinctive Type of Fall Detection Methods Using Wearable Device Safety
and Security of Elderly Person   402
R. K. Aggrawal and Mamta Gahlan

Role of Fuzzy Set Theory and Kappa Coefficient in Urological
Disease Diagnosis.. 411
  Sunil Singh, Navin Ram Daruka, Megha Shukla, and Ashok Deshpande

Analyzing Balancing of Heterogeneous Load
on Cluster-Based Web Server....................................... 420
  Praveen Kumar, Garvit Singhal, and Seema Rawat

Author Index 433

Security in Data Science Analytics

Identification of Safety and Security Vulnerabilities in Cyber Physical Systems

Abhilasha Vyas[(⊠)] and Usha Batra

GD Goenka University, Gurgaon, India
abhilasha.cs27@gmail.com, usha.batra@gdgoenka.ac.in

Abstract. Cyber physical systems (CPS) known as a class of automated systems working as a life line of smart cities such as home automation system, power grid, automotive industry, etc. The security aspects of these systems are at high demand as these systems are involved in day to day life of people and national economy. The compromised CPS can harm day to day operations of people. CPS systems are complex in design and more prone to cyber-attacks. In this study, the safety and security deficiencies at different levels of CPS are analyzed and discussed. The systematic survey of safety and security loopholes presented in current study. In addition, this paper describes risk factors for security and techniques which can be implemented to mitigate risks. This paper also elaborated the related work done by researchers and new research focus in this area.

Keywords: CPS · Cyber-attacks · Prevention · Risk

1 Introduction

CPS known to be a unified approach to closely integrated embedded computer and communication techniques to a variety of various domains like production, civil, medical, defense, transportation, etc. the physical process in CPS managed and controlled by cyber part of the system with feedback loop to change the behavior according to demand [1]. CPS systems are known as transformation and integration of old traditional embedded devices. Integration of cyber and physical devices able to realize the real time, safe, reliable collaboration with physical processes in CPS and this makes CPS capable of collecting real time data with high accuracy. Sensors used to collect data from distributed field devices in CPS [2]. These sensors are also known as information sensing devices. RFID or infrared sensors can be used to collect and send real time data for further analysis [3]. These kind of system evolving as latest interrelated technology by the use of internet for faster response time and easier distribution. The integration of physical and cyber devices prone to number of security challenges [4]. There are number of cyber-attacks can be planned for attacking CPS. They can be insider attack or outsider attacks. The integration of cyber and physical devices raises the importance of security measures in CPS. If these physical components are compromised this will affect people livelihood. There are number attacks which can be planned on CPS can be categorized as direct and in-direct attacks (Table 1).

© Springer Nature Singapore Pte Ltd. 2020
U. Batra et al. (Eds.): REDSET 2019, CCIS 1230, pp. 3–13, 2020.
https://doi.org/10.1007/978-981-15-5830-6_1

Table 1. List the cyber-attacks planned on various physical processes.

SNo	CPS application domain	Attack	Consequences
1	Energy	Iran Bushehr nuclear power plant controlling system	Severe disorder in nuclear facilities automated operations [5]
2	Medical field	Implanted human medical devices	Attack on human planted devices by their wireless communication [6]
3	Road transportation field	Japan's control system	124 train delayed while 15 trains were suspended affecting 8.12 million people [5]
4	Air transportation system	American FAA	Shut down several air traffic control (ATC) systems in Alaska [7]

The above listed incidents provides enough clarification that attack on any layer of CPS can lead to great loss in people life & economy of nation. The security measures should be taken into consideration during design process as well as during integration and implanting process of various cyber devices [8]. The traditional security measures are not designed for CPS security [9, 10]. The security of CPS focuses on attacks which can be planned on physical part of the process and cyber pat of the process. Direct attacks can affect privacy of physical devices by tempering the temperature, wiring or batteries of the device. The outsider attacks always planned on cyber part of CPS where attacker not having any direct access to physical devices of system. This can be done by gaining access remotely, inserting malicious software, tempering security information etc. The current study provides an analysis and identification of security deficiencies of CPS at various layer. Section 2 of this paper demonstrates a layered architecture of CPS, Sect. 3 describe CPS security, Sect. 4 discusses security deficiencies and risk associated at different layers of CPS architecture, future research areas discussed in Sect. 6, Sect. 7 is conclusion.

2 Layered Architecture of Cyber Physical Systems

The CPS system is multilayered architecture. CPS is integration of computing, communication and monitoring capabilities of devices in physical process. In CPS cyber devices act as controlling part for physical devices [12]. Which are basically feedback loop networks with embedded computers. The multilayered architecture of CPS mainly divided into 3 layers. Physical, cyber and user layer. The responsibility of cyber layer is to analyze and process information and data received from physical layer. Cyber layer can be considered as divided into data layer, communication and network layer, control center. Physical layer is responsible for gathering data from various sensing information devices and execution of control signals. Physical layer further divided in sensor layer, executor layer, and perception layer. User layer is very important layer as it is responsible human computer interaction for guaranteed CPS operations (Table 2).

Table 2. Description of various layers and sub layers of CPS

Layer	Sub-layer	Role and function	Security
Physical layer: Mainly responsible for collecting and processing information from sensors and cyber devices	Sensor layer	CPS systems are combination of various sensors and cyber devices for collecting data from physical devices. The sensor layer performs analog to digital conversion of data gathered from various physical devices	Requirement of data protection, privacy of data, integrity of data, non-repudiation of data. Real time data protection
	Executor layer: execution of commands	Task layer: this sub layer is responsible for task implementation. The role of actuator is to control the devices connected to the system	Authorized actuator access
		Program layer: this sub layer is responsible for program execution. The program can be written in any low level programming and embedded programming language like VHDL, C, C++	There are number of security measures which needs to be addressed at this layer. Buffer overflow attack, direct memory access attack, authentication attack
		Implement layer: this sub layer is responsible for platform implementation and execution of program. The hardware language code is executed on X86, FGPA configuration	The basic security requirement at this layer is to maintain operating system security
	Perception layer: this layer is responsible for summarizing the results from upper layers	The perception layer is the basic hardware layer which understands the signals and produces information which can be forwarded to cyber layer	The main security requirement is to protect integrity of information. Tampering of information during transit
Information system layer: this layer is mainly responsible for processing and analyzing information gathered from physical layer	Data layer	This layer is responsible for storing the transmitted data from network communication layer. The responsibility to check data integrity before storing it into the database. If any violation or data loss then network layer resends the information	The routine security check of database is the basic security requirement at this layer. Backup of stored data is at prime importance to ensure availability of data

(*continued*)

Table 2. (*continued*)

Layer	Sub-layer	Role and function	Security
	Communication and network layer	The main task of this layer is to provide the real time communication and data transmission. This layer is also responsible all the communication between integrated devices	Require intrusion detection systems for preventing network attacks. These systems will be responsible for monitoring nature of network traffic. There is also requirement of encryption algorithms for secure data transmission between various devices
	Control layer	This is the most important layer as it receives authenticate users for secure access of system. Only authenticated users will be allowed to query database and send commands for execution	It is possible to dynamically change the properties of control layer so it is the main security requirement to protect unauthorized access to control layer. This layer is also responsible for load balancing of user queries and commands
User layer: responsible for execution of commands		This layer includes various desktop and web applications. Through this layer user is sending instruction to control layer for further execution	Unauthenticated access should be prohibited as this is the main control window of CPS

3 Security of Cyber Physical System

The secure CPS functions required to assure confidentiality, availability, integrity of data. Safety is also important to avoid any type of physical or logical threats. The security of CPS lies in CIA triad. At every layer of CPS there is a need of implementation security standards.

3.1 Importance of CPS Security

All the CPS are complex in nature and used in critical processes. So the security of CPS functions are on high priority. Smallest to smallest security compromise can result in high damage. To secure embedded physical devices there is a need of CPS monitoring system. The monitoring system will keep track of health of every embedded device. For securing cyber part that is data of CPS strong authentication and authorization techniques are required. If cyber part will be compromised then all secrete and confidential information can be used by intruder for any malicious intention. CPS systems are used in critical systems like smart grid, power generation, production, manufacturing and many more such fields. So in can of any unauthorized access to CPS can result in great loss on large scale.

3.2 Goals of Cyber Physical System Security

See Table 3.

Table 3. Security goals for cyber physical system

	Purpose	Attacks
Confidentiality	For preventing unauthorized access to information. The confidentiality can be maintained by using encryption techniques	For example: 1. healthcare CPS personal data can be used for malicious intention 2. Manufacturing CPS data can be used by competitor industry for gaining deep insight into the process
Integrity	For preventing unauthorized access for modification of data with malicious intention. This can be achieved by strong authentication process	For example: 1. Alteration of sensor traffic by DDoS flood attack 2. Alteration of healthcare CPS data for damaging patient disease record history
Availability	For uninterrupted availability of services. The term refers to availability of communication channel as well as physical devices in entire CPS network	For example: 1. DDoS attacks can be planned to block the communication channel so that services will not be available

3.3 CPS Security Requirements

CPS security require strong authenticated access for communication channel access and physical device access. CPS systems generates huge amount of sensitive data which can be used for future access. There needs to be a strong security mechanism for backup and storage of system. Encryption technique can be used for providing one level of security. Use of secure protocol require to restrict tempering of communication and network data (Figs. 1 and 2).

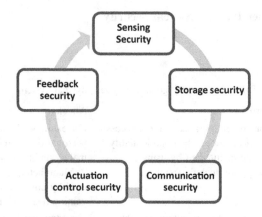

Fig. 1. Shows requirements of CPS security.

4 Security Deficiencies and Risk Associated at Different Layers of Cyber Physical System

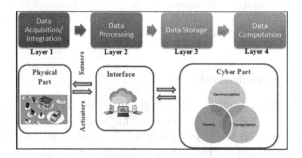

Fig. 2. Abstract layers of CPS [13]

4.1 Physical System Layer

This layer is known as backbone or foundation layer of CPS architecture. This layer contains sub layer as sensor layer, executor layer, program layer, perception layer. CPS systems are combination of various sensors and cyber devices for collecting data from physical devices. The physical devices are most of the time installed in unattended environments, sensors and network nodes with default username and password settings. This makes these devices easy target for attackers. Moreover as these devices are embedded and having very low storage capability and limited communication capacity, it is very difficult to install strong security techniques in this layer [14]. Common risk associated with this layer shown in Fig. 3.

Fig. 3. Possible attacks on physical layer

4.2   Information System Layer

This layer is known as lifeline of any CPS. This layer is responsible for storing the transmitted data from network communication layer. The CPS generated data needs to be stored for future. There is need of strong authentication and integrity check techniques to ensure the data integrity. The routine security check of database is the basic security requirement at this layer. Backup of stored data is at prime importance to ensure availability of data. However, this layer require strong intrusion detection systems for preventing network attacks. The intrusion detection system will be monitoring nature of network traffic in real time. There is also requirement of encryption algorithms for secure data transmission between various devices (Fig. 4).

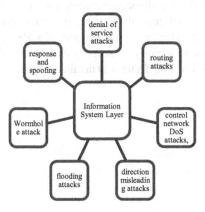

Fig. 4. Possible attacks on information system layer

4.3 User Layer

This layer is interface for managing and controlling cyber physical systems. There are number of desktop and web based interfaces for managing and monitoring CPS function. Through this layer user is sending instruction to control layer for further execution. Unauthenticated access should be prohibited as this is the main control window of CPS (Fig. 5).

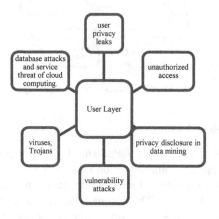

Fig. 5. Possible attacks on user layer

5 Future Research Trends

The basic challenge of cyber physical system security implementation is the lack of uniform architecture for physical devices, network and communication channels. For implementation security techniques there are significant amount of differences in security implementation at cyber and physical part of CPS [15]. We have reviewed number of research papers for identifying security challenges and attacks which can be planned at each layer of CPS. The Table 4 is detailed description of what we observed after reviewing papers.

Table 4. Detailed description of security goals, deficiencies, and required techniques

Security goals	Deficiencies	Requirement
Abstraction of protocol and pattern	• Lack of temporal semantics • Lack of standard protocol • Lack of standard computer hardware abstraction using assembling of various parts • Lack of standard programming language	• Require appropriate software and hardware abstraction model [16, 17] • Require standard protocol, scheduling, computation model [18, 19] • Require top down abstract approach for hardware abstraction [20, 21] • Require standard programming language for dynamic and static programming models [22, 23]
Scale and accuracy	• Lack of high quality monitoring control system • Lack of standard method for information processing	• Require real time event detection and prediction model [24] • Require analysis methods and distributed algorithms with low cost and energy consumption [25]
Robustness	• Lack of platform and architecture independent intrusion detection system	• Require a robust system for identifying threats and mitigating the risk to make system robust from severe threats [26, 27]

6 Conclusion

CPS is integration of physical and cyber devices. The integration leads number of security loop holes. There are various differences between traditional IT security and CPS security. Dynamic and innovative threat detection system is required to identify CPS security threats. The assessment and monitoring method is required which will be designed as per CPS architecture. We discussed detailed security loopholes at each CPS architecture layer. In future, we will propose the dynamic and smart system for identifying various threats at information system layer. As we have discussed that DDoS attack can be planned at each layer of CPS. Our next focus will be on identifying DDoS attacks in CPS.

References

1. Asare, P., Broman, D., Lee, E.A., Torngren, M., Sunder, S.S.: Cyberphysical systems (2012). http://cyberphysicalsystems.org/. Accessed 24 Dec 2016
2. Vegh, L., Miclea, L.: Enhancing security in cyber-physical systems through cryptographic and steganographic techniques. In: Automation, Quality and Testing, Robotics International Conference, pp. 1–6. IEEE (2014)

3. Zhang, B., Ma, X., Qin, Z.: Security architecture on the trusting internet of things. J. Electron. Sci. Technol. **9**(4), 364–367 (2011)
4. Nourian, A., Madnick, S.: A systems theoretic approach to the security threats in cyber physical systems applied to stuxnet. IEEE Syst. J. (2015). https://doi.org/10.1109/TDSC. 2015.2509994
5. Peng, Y., Lu, T., Liu, J., Gao, Y., Guo, X., Xie, F.: Cyber-physical system risk assessment. In: Ninth International Conference on Intelligent Information Hiding and Multimedia Signal Processing, pp. 442–447 (2013)
6. Leavitt, N.: Researchers fight to keep implanted medical devices safe from hackers. Computer **43**(8), 11–14 (2010)
7. Gervasoni, A.: Alternative funding sources for growth: the role of private equity, Venture Capital and Private Debt (2015)
8. Jalali, S.: Trends and implications in embedded systems development. Tata Consult. Serv. Limited, TCS white paper (2009)
9. Konstantinou, C., Maniatakos, M., Saqib, F., Hu, S., Plusquellic, J., Jin, Y.: Cyber-physical systems: a security perspective. In: 20th IEEE European Test Symposium, pp. 1–8 (2015)
10. Wang, E.K., Ye, Y., Xu, X., Yiu, S.M., Hui, L.C.K., Chow, K.P.: Security issues and challenges for cyber physical system. In: Proceedings of the IEEE/ACM International Conference on Green Computing and Communications and International Conference on Cyber, Physical and Social Computing, pp. 733–738 (2010)
11. Ashibani, Y., Mahmoud, Q.H.: Cyber physical systems security: analysis, challenges and solutions. Comput. Secur. **68**, 81–97 (2017)
12. Shafi, Q.: Cyber physical systems security: a brief survey. In: 12th International Conference on Computational Science and Its Applications (ICCSA), pp. 146–150. IEEE (2012)
13. Gifty, R., Bharathi, R., Krishnakumar, P.: Privacy and security of big data in cyber physical systems using Weibull distribution-based intrusion detection. Neural Comput. Appl. **31**(1), 23–34 (2018). https://doi.org/10.1007/s00521-018-3635-6
14. Peng, Y., Lu, T., Liu, J., Gao, Y., Guo, X., Xie, F.: Cyber-physical system risk assessment. In: Proceedings of Ninth International Conference on Intelligent Information Hiding and Mulitmedia Signal Processing, pp. 442–447. IEEE Computer Society (2013)
15. Giraldo, J., Sarkar, E., Cardenas, A.A., Maniatakos, M., Kantarcioglu, M.: Security and privacy in cyber-physical systems: a survey of surveys. IEEE Des. Test **34**(4), 7–17 (2017). https://doi.org/10.1109/mdat.2017.2709310
16. Padir, T., Fischer, G.S., Chernova, S., Gennert, M.A.: A unified and integrated approach to teaching a two-course sequence in Robotics Engineering. JRM **23**(5), 748–758 (2011)
17. Edwards, S.A., Lee, E.A.: The case for the precision timed (PRET) machine. In: Proceedings of the 44th ACM/IEEE Design Automation Conference (DAC), San Diego, CA, pp. 264–265 (2007)
18. Avissar, O., Barua, R., Stewart, D.: An optimal memory allocation scheme for scratch-pad-based embedded systems. ACM Trans. Embedded Comput. Syst. **1**(1), 6–26 (2002)
19. Henzinger, T.A., Horowitz, B., Kirsch, C.M.: Giotto: a timetriggered language for embedded programming. Proc. IEEE **91**(1), 84–99 (2003)
20. Berry, G.: The effectiveness of synchronous languages for the development of safety-critical systems. Technical report, Esterel Technologies (2003)
21. Lee, E.A., Neuendorffer, S., Wirthlin, M.J.: Actor-oriented design of embedded hardware and software systems. J. Circuit. Syst. Comput. **12**(3), 231–260 (2003)
22. Johannessen, S.: Time synchronization in a local area network. IEEE Control Syst. **24**(2), 61–69 (2004)

23. Tardieu, O., Edwards, S.A.: Scheduling-independent threads and exceptions in SHIM. In: Proceedings of the 6th ACM & IEEE International Conference on Embedded Software, Seoul, Korea, pp. 142–151 (2006)
24. Zhao, Y., Liu, J., Lee, E.A.: A programming model for time-synchronized distributed real-time systems. In: Proceedings of the 13th IEEE Real Time and Embedded Technology and Applications Symposium, Bellevue, USA, pp. 259–268 (2007)
25. Abdelzaher, T.: Research challenges in distributed cyber-physical systems. In: Proceedings of the IEEE/IFIP International Conference on Embedded and Ubiquitous Computing, Shanghai, China, p. 5 (2008)
26. Ahola, T., Korpinen, P., Rakkola, J., Ramo, T., Salminen, J., Savolainen, J.: Wearable FPGA based wireless sensor platform. In: Proceedings of the 29th Annual International Conference on IEEE Engineering in Medicine and Biology Society, Lyon, pp. 2288–2291 (2007)
27. Peng, Y., Lu, T., Liu, J., Gao, Y., Guo, X., Xie, F.: Cyber-physical system risk assessment, 442–447 (2013). https://doi.org/10.1109/iih-msp.2013.116

A Walkthrough of Blockchain Technology and Its Potential Applications

Sudipti Dhawan, Shubhra Shah$^{(\boxtimes)}$, and Bhawna Narwal

Indira Gandhi Delhi Technical University for Women, New Delhi, Delhi, India
sudiptidhawan@gmail.com, techieshubh@gmail.com,
bhawnanarwal@igdtuw.ac.in

Abstract. The Internet has become the hub of centralized applications. In order to give power to every member of a system, the decentralized methodology has been introduced. Blockchain is the leisure of blocks that are synchronously created on a peer to peer network. The characteristics of Blockchain such as decentralization, transparency, synchronous, and immutability provides it the power of many new applications. This paper aims to explore Blockchain and its process of working. Furthermore, it aims to elaborate on various applications keeping in mind the most recent developments.

Keywords: Blockchain · Smart contracts · Cryptocurrency · Shared resources · Internet 3.0

1 Introduction

The internet was created to give the power of common information to everyone. But ironically it gave birth to various autonomous centralized systems that gave the power only to the creator. Thus there was a requirement of creating altogether a new way to document various transactions. This is where Blockchain took birth which is a group of ledgers that can have any information e.g. transactions, identity, contracts, etc. which are added into the group only if the members are convinced hence, making the whole system decentralized. Blockchain works on peer to peer networks [1] and gives the power to every block to add another block. Block is identified by its unique hash value and when a new block is added to the chain it stores the hash value of the previous block. This block has to be added or not will depend on consensus protocols. Blockchain's foundation was laid by the name of Satoshi Nakamoto back in 2009 in [2]. It was primarily invented to be used in Crypto-Currency. Blockchain is featured in the transparency of information to everyone and at the same time keeping the same information irremovable (Fig. 1). Hence, the information once stuffed into a block and that block once added to the Blockchain would never be removed. Thus it became popular in those fields which were affected by privacy, timestamps, trust, etc.

U. Batra et al. (Eds.): REDSET 2019, CCIS 1230, pp. 14–25, 2020.
https://doi.org/10.1007/978-981-15-5830-6_2

Fig. 1. What blockchain looks like

2 Working

Blockchain is made up of a group of blocks that have three main entities. First is the header which has the hash of that block. Second is the data body which may have the transaction details or any other data that has to be kept. The third is the pre-hash value of the block that came just before it. Hence, it creates a link between the two adjacent blocks which ultimately results in a Blockchain [3]. In order to add a new block to the Blockchain the transaction must occur i.e. there must be some exchange of information that is to be recorded in a ledger of Blockchain. Once the transaction occurs the doer node adds the data respective to the transaction into a block. It further adds its digital signature and notifies every other node on the Blockchain about the same [4]. All the other nodes verify the information about the said transaction by the given clues. Once all the transactions in the block are verified the block is given a specific hash and is added to the Blockchain. The block is also saved in with the previous block's hash. This way the two blocks are interlinked. It is important to understand that Blockchain is quite heavy and that everyone wishes to add their transactions in the Blockchain. Hence, it is quite evident that there is a requirement of slowing the process of creating a block in the Blockchain. This is achieved by consensus protocols. The consensus protocol is the one that is responsible to keep all the nodes in the Blockchain network in sync with one another. That is everyone agrees to the truth, in other words, they agree to the present state of Blockchain [5]. With consensus protocols, the consensus problem arises. The first node in the Blockchain is to solve the consensus problem is the one who gets to validate the transaction and hence gets the right to create the new block in the Blockchain [6]. With this, it also gets the lucrative rewards that enhance its personal motives too. The most common consensus protocol is proof of work. Proof of work is a puzzle that is easy to solve but not so easy that everyone solves [7, 24–30]. It is important that it must be solved in a particular time period. People who are willing to work under the proof of work are called miners. The first miner, who solves the proof of work successfully first gets to validate the transaction and creates the block in a Blockchain, furthermore, at the same time receives the rewards. There are some researches that are trying to bring out new consensus protocols such as Proof of Stake, practical Byzantine fault tolerance (PBFT), proof of storage, etc.

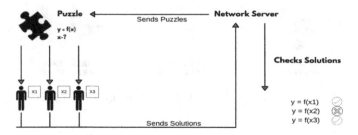

Fig. 2. Working of proof of work consensus model

3   Consensus Algorithm

It is said that the security and the robustness of a system that is based on blockchain are completely dependent upon its consensus model. But, there are three properties upon which the Efficiency of consensus protocol is measured. The consensus protocol is known as a safety protocol as all the nodes produce the same output as the node which is validating the transaction according to the rules of portable this is also known as the consistency of the shared state. A consensus protocol is said to have liveness if all the non-faulty nodes produce value. A consensus protocol is said to be fault-tolerant if it is able to recover from a failure or a node participating in consensus (Fig. 2).

3.1   Proof of Stake

A small proof of work-based networks is easy to handle because attackers would be able to gain 51% of the computing power at a much lower cost [8]. Hence the proof of the stake model was designed to overcome the disadvantages of proof of work. The proof of stake model is based on the portion of the actual holdings of the Blockchain. For example, the member who has a maximum portion of the blockchain would be allowed to make changes and mine an equivalent portion of their funds regardless of the computing power. Hence, a person who owns 20% of the blockchain would be able to mine 20% of the Blockchain transactions thus gaining 1/5 of the network power. Krypton has recently moved from proof of work to proof of stake [9].

3.2   Proof of Elapsed Time

This model is based on Intel's software guard extensions and it uses a random leader election model in other words lottery-based election model on SGS. It basically selects a random leader which will be able to finalize the block of the blockchain. When the mobile dating Road claims to be a leader and mines a block it can produce generated within the model it also has to prove that it had the shortest time and it waited for a protocol designated amount of time before it is allowed to start mining the next block. The disadvantage of this protocol is that it is dependent upon the external specialized hardware.

3.3   Practical Byzantine Fault Tolerance

This algorithm is based on broadcasting the messages across the network to understand which roads are faulty and which are not [10]. It is important to understand that all the nodes have the same state of the blockchain. After that, the message is broadcasted among all the nodes in the network and if the node is faulty in nature then it will broadcast but different messages and hence for other nodes it would be a faulty node [11]. Further, there is no need for confirmations from the nodes and there are more rewards with no variance. To enhance the quality and performance of pBFT for specific use cases and conditions, many variations were proposed and employed. Some of them are RBFT – Redundant BFT, ABsTRACTs, Q/U, HQ – Hybrid Quorum Protocol for BFT, Adapt, Zyzzyva – Speculative Byzantine Fault Tolerance, Aardvark [12].

4   Characteristics of Blockchain

The Blockchain possesses the following characteristics [13]:

4.1   Decentralization

Unlike the conventional systems on the internet which are centralized, the Blockchain is completely decentralized. In the conventional centralized systems, all the transactions are to be approved by a dominant system head. Thus it makes all the other members of the system highly dependent on the head. If for any chance the head fails or is hacked all the members of the system are affected. This, however, is not in the case of Blockchain. In a Blockchain, the new block or a transaction is conducted between peer to peer networks which means there is no requirement to check its authenticity by a central agency. Thus Blockchain not just helps in a significant reduction in the development cost but also the server and operational cost.

4.2   Persistency

The major problem faced in centralized systems is the faulty nature and various tampered policies which harm both the trust and the confidence of people in the system. This nature no more exists in the Blockchain as every block in Blockchain will be saved with the timestamp and with the hash of the previous block. In order to tamper the Blockchain, the intended member will need to change all the blocks with the new hashed beyond the particular hash, which is a very costly affair. Similarly, another way would be having more than 50% of the Blockchain with him. This again will backfire as once other members notice something like this they will start withdrawal.

4.3   Anonymity

All the members of the Blockchain communicate in the network with the help of the generated address. Every member has more than one address just to keep their identity limited from exposure. Since there is no third-party agency to keep track of the private information, privacy is maintained.

4.4   Auditability

As mentioned before every transaction is marked with the timestamp, this helps the members to validate the previously recorded transaction. By linking the two blocks and their transactions we get increased transparency and traceability.

5   Potential Applications of Blockchain Technology

The above-discussed characteristics are the main reason that blockchain has evolved its applications in the last decade. We would be summarizing various applications based on blockchains in the following section through Tables 1, 2, 3, 4, 5, 6, 7, 8, 9, 10 and 11.

Table 1. Cyber security applications.

Application	Advantages
Checking the effectiveness of software downloads/patches/updates by applying unique hashes (associates these hashes to downloads and updates)	Diminishes chances of infection through malware
Reducing DDoS (Distributed Denial of Service) attacks by making users join distributed network	Increased network security Reduced network congestion
Reducing password attacks by Use of Biometric private keys or Digital Identities and multi-step authentication	Effective information protection
Preventing hacks on IoT connected automated systems through Token platform	Convenient tracking of unauthenticated or threatening intrusion
Securing DNS (Domain Name System) through ethereum based DNS competitor	Strong decentralized security
Decentralized data storage	Mitigates honey pots formation Enhanced security interoperability
Edge devises security through multi-step identity authentication	Avoids network penetration attacks
Preventing false data inclusion into system/ledger	Higher data veracity
Firmware provenance through use of blockchain ledgers (detects who produced and where produced)	Prevents foreign intrusion attacks
Preventing password database hacking by using blockchain with public key infrastructure and multi-signature authentication	Valuable data protection (increases attacks complexity and attack frequency)

(continued)

Table 1. (*continued*)

Application	Advantages
Healthcare applications Examples: Gem, SimplyVital Health	
Patient record management by creating a hash of patient health information in the form of blocks and by collecting these blocks together constitutes the patient's identity	Keeps identity of a patient secret while sharing with third parties Single and longitudinal records are maintained
Authenticated clinical trials by storing documents as smart contractors on blockchain	Avoids usage of the humongous amount of data sets, reduces the cost incurred in audit, review of documents easy, frauds and lost file issues resolved Accountability of drug tracking increases Supply chain management ensured
Drug traceability by time stamping each transaction added to block	Ensures security, authenticity, and traceability of drugs Prevents frauds and counterfeiting
Direct service payment by Patient through cryptocurrencies instead of cash payment	Reduces overall cost and eliminates third parties from chain

Table 2. Healthcare applications.

Application	Advantages
Patient record management by creating a hash of patient health information in the form of blocks and by collecting these blocks together constitutes the patient's identity	Keeps identity of a patient secret while sharing with third parties Single and longitudinal records are maintained
Authenticated clinical trials by storing documents as smart contractors on blockchain	Avoids usage of the humongous amount of data sets, reduces the cost incurred in audit, review of documents easy, frauds and lost file issues resolved Accountability of drug tracking increases Supply chain management ensured
Drug traceability by time stamping each transaction added to block	Ensures security, authenticity, and traceability of drugs Prevents frauds and counterfeiting
Direct service payment by Patient through cryptocurrencies instead of cash payment	Reduces overall cost and eliminates third parties from chain

Table 3. Manufacturing applications.

Application	Advantages
Tracking components quality ensures efficient Supply chain management wherein certification is provided through a shared cryptographically signed ledger about the authenticity of product right from the mining of raw materials to their processing and delivery of the finished product i.e. the entire purchase cycle. Digitization all documents (for example Purchase orders, Letter of credit. invoices, etc.) is done with automatic execution based on preset triggers is done	Auditing of compliance of statutory laws/guidelines/regulations can be done easily and instantly Tracking of goods right from the source to the delivery stage can be done easily and thus recalling any defective products can be done in a cost-effective and efficient way Efficient inventory management can be achieved by employing smart contracts which will automatically send communication to the supplier when the input inventory runs low
Addresses the problem of Counterfeit products by embedding unique microcontroller on the produce and display it on a blockchain. The authenticity of the product can be verified by reading the contents of these microcontrollers, but as these microcontrollers use asymmetric cryptography, they cannot be copied and hence problems of counterfeit can be addressed	Verification of the authenticity can be done quickly and forgery/counterfeiting of products is arrested and made uneconomical Convenient tracking of the origin of the goods
Drug traceability by time stamping each transaction added to block	Ensures security, authenticity, and traceability of drugs Prevents frauds and counterfeiting
Direct service payment by patient through cryptocurrencies instead of cash payment	Reduces overall cost and eliminates third parties from chain

Table 4. Smart government.

Application	Advantages
Land Registration records are digitized and secured on a blockchain and any change in the status needs to be validated by owners	Reduce the number of intermediaries required, build trust between the transacting parties and increases process efficiency Details about the public and private property Ownership proof and property agreements and transactions are executed swiftly
Digital voting system: The vote cast by citizens shall be treated as transactions through Blockchains after authentication of voter's identity	Tamper-proof election returns Each vote can be verified and audited with no scope fraud in the voter identity

(continued)

Table 4. (*continued*)

Application	Advantages
Transparency in public expenditure and financial dealing and usage of public money. By adopting blockchain, any transaction that is performed will lead to the generation of the new block and added to the blockchain after it is validated by concerned stakeholders through an agreed cryptographic protocol	Accountability and transparency in the government budgets and expenditures and in the national banking system
Land registration records are digitized and secured on a blockchain and any change in the status needs to be validated by owners	Reduce the number of intermediaries required, build trust between the transacting parties and increases process efficiency Details about the public and private property Ownership proof and property agreements and transactions are executed swiftly

Table 5. Banking and financial services.

Application	Advantages
Fraud detection: unlike the traditional banking systems which are based on a centralized database that is vulnerable to cyber attacks, the blockchain can transform the banking sector by virtue of being a distributed ledger where each block is time-stamped holds individual transactions with links to the previous transactions. The ledger is distributed and once a transaction has been validated then the same cannot tamper	Cyber attacks could be prevented Highly secure payments process between clients
Know your customer process can be smoothened and simplified by the use of blockchain, once verification of a client has been done by an agency, the same can be accessed by others and the whole process need not be repeated	Administrative costs would be reduced significantly A check-in case of money laundering and terrorist activities ensures as a money trail can be easily identified with verification and identification of clients would be done in a jiffy
Use of smart contracts would be transforming the Insurance sector wherein automatic payments would be actuated, thus doing away with the role of intermediaries and procedural delays from the system	Increase in efficiency and reduction in cost

Table 6. Retail applications.

Application	Advantages
Blockchain is used to transform the payment system and loyalty program. It connects the buyers and sellers through a peer-to-peer network and bypasses the middleman and the associated charges	No merchant fees to be paid and no censor on the products sold and trades
The encrypted customer data, coupons, and discounts are stored in the blockchain and are made available to all stores/retailers. This data can be used by retailers to analyze the buying pattern of consumer and customize offers for them, customer incentives can be created, rewards and managed, whereas the consumers can view their loyalty information at one place	Higher customer satisfaction, more profits for stores/retailers Real-time information on loyalty points with ease of redemption and earning

Table 7. Charity applications.

Application	Advantages
Smart donations will utilize the feature of smart contracts, wherein donations are executed/money is transferred upon execution of certain trigger conditions are actuated	The open and transparent system would increase the trust level among the devotees More accountability on charities Charities can easily raise funds for their missions
Blockchain can help to create collectible which is difficult to replicate and thus can hold uniqueness value. The devotees can donate a wide range of their belongings that hold value and proof of ownership	The digital assets or collectibles offer a new revenue stream for charities The devotees can contribute to charitable causes as per their convenience

Table 8. Real estate applications.

Application	Advantages
The encrypted data related to the property will be stored in blockchain and controlled solely by the listing party	Easy access to the reliable property-related database
The digital identities of all stakeholders, i.e. buyer, seller, real estate agent, buyer's and seller's banks, authority (land registry) would be stored in the blockchain Registry application to authority would be sent digitally and verification by the officials shall be using blockchain-verified smart contracts. All transaction on the property would be time-stamped and stored in the blockchain and can be viewed by stakeholders	Transparency in all dealings and easy access to the status of the due diligence process done by authorities Check on fraudulent practices
Use of smart contracts for renting and leasing purposes	Tracing and audits of history of transactions on the property can be done efficiently

Table 9. Media applications.

Application	Advantages
Transparent payments and copyright tracking: Blockchain would empower copyright owners to track the usage of their material, enable bite-size content monetization **Reduce the role of intermediaries:** There is not much willingness to pay for the online content and the main source of revenue is through advertisements. This involves several intermediaries between the creator and consumers The creators would fix the digital copies of their content (music/video/news articles etc.) in the blockchain and could sell them directly to the interested parties	Proof of ownership Easy remunerations Easy tracking of royalties and IPRs

Table 10. Smart contracts.

Application	Advantages
Agreed contract conditions and payment conditions are submitted to the blockchain, further, any modification in the contract conditions that are agreed by the concerned parties are submitted into a new block	Addresses the concern of lost/misplaced invoices and payments of goods are released automatically when the goods (tracked and authenticated by the receiver)

Table 11. Transport and tourism.

Application	Advantages
Blockchain is a decentralized ledger that will be shared across a network of stakeholders information/transactions are stored in a transparent and verifiable way as they are time-stamped and validated by consensus by stakeholders and not a single point. Smart contracts are utilized	Blockchain can be used to streamline payments settlements across multiple parties like hotels, travel agents, aggregators by reducing intermediaries and reducing settlement period
Travelers identity management by creating a hash using passport/boarding pass/ticket and biometric identity feature say face or fingerprint and stored in the blockchain	Simplifying the traveler's identification process at various stages of the journey right from booking to boarding to check-in at the hotel and would do away with the requirement of identification process at each stage
Baggage tracking can be done as the travelers luggage changes hands from airlines to ground luggage handlers	

6 Conclusion

Blockchains are the future of the Internet industry 3.0 as it provides the common man the full power and transparency at the same time. Blockchain has come up as a major breakthrough and has the capability to fundamentally transform the existing mode of operation which can further lead to new innovations and transformation in various sectors. The characteristics of blockchain and on-time synchronous processing have evolved various applications in the past decade. This paper explored Blockchain technology and its process of working in detail along with its characteristics. Furthermore, we elaborated on various applications in detail keeping in mind the most recent developments.

References

1. Rouhani, S., Deters, R.: Security, performance, and applications of smart contracts: a systematic survey. IEEE Access **7**, 50759–50779 (2019)
2. Fu, Y., Zhu, J.: Big production enterprise supply chain endogenous risk management based on blockchain. IEEE Access **7**, 15310–15319 (2019)
3. Christidis, K., Devetsikiotis, M.: Blockchains and smart contracts for the internet of things. IEEE Access **4**, 2292–2303 (2016)
4. https://www.investopedia.com/terms/b/blockchain.asp
5. https://www.investinblockchain.com/what-is-blockchain-technology
6. https://lisk.io/academy/blockchain-basics/how-does-blockchain-work/consensus-protocols
7. Yang, Y.T., Chou, L.D., Tseng, C.W., Tseng, F.H., Liu, C.C.: Blockchain-based traffic event validation and trust verification for VANETs. IEEE Access **7**, 30868–30877 (2019)
8. Rahouti, M., Xiong, K., Ghani, N.: Bitcoin concepts, threats, and machine-learning security solutions. IEEE Access **6**, 67189–67205 (2018)
9. Baliga, A.: Understanding blockchain consensus model (2017)
10. http://www.coinfox.info/news/reviews/6417-proof-of-work-vs-proof-of-stake-merits-and-disadvantages
11. Understanding Blockchain Consensus Models. https://pdfs.semanticscholar.org/da8a/37b10bc1521a4d3de925d7ebc44bb606d740.pdf
12. Castro, M., Liskov, B.: Practical Byzantine fault tolerance. In: OSDI, vol. 99, no. 1999, pp. 173–186, February 1999
13. https://blockonomi.com/practical-byzantine-fault-tolerance/
14. Castro, M., Liskov, B.: A correctness proof for a practical Byzantine-fault-tolerant replication algorithm. Technical Memo MIT/LCS/TM-590, MIT Laboratory for Computer Science (1999)
15. Zheng, Z., Xie, S., Dai, H.N., Chen, X., Wang, H.: Blockchain challenges and opportunities: a survey. Int. J. Web Grid Serv. **14**(4), 352–375 (2018)
16. Harwick, C.: Cryptocurrency and the problem of intermediation. Independent Rev. **20**(4), 569–588 (2016)
17. Szabo, N.: Smart contracts. Virtual School (1994)
18. https://blockchainhub.net/smart-contracts/
19. https://cointelegraph.com/news/walmart-awarded-patent-for-blockchain-based-medical-records-system

20. Yue, X., Wang, H., Jin, D., Li, M., Jiang, W.: Healthcare data gateways: found healthcare intelligence on blockchain with novel privacy risk control. J. Med. Syst. **40**(10), 218 (2016)
21. https://www.ey.com/en_gl/trust/how-blockchain-could-transform-the-world-of-indirect-tax
22. https://www.blockchain-council.org/blockchain/thailand-revenue-system-to-track-taxes-using-blockchain/
23. Ainsworth, R.T., Shact, A.: Blockchain (distributed ledger technology) solves VAT fraud. Boston University School of Law, Law and Economics Research Paper, pp. 16–41 (2016)
24. Narwal, B., Mohapatra, A.K.: A review on authentication protocols in wireless body area networks. In: 2018 3rd International Conference on Contemporary Computing and Informatics (IC3I 2018), 10–12 October 2018, Amity University, Gurugram, Haryana. IEEE (2018)
25. Narwal, B.: Fake news in digital media. In: 2018 International Conference on Advances in Computing, Communication Control and Networking (ICACCCN), Greater Noida (UP), India, pp. 977–981 (2018)
26. Dhawan, S., Narwal, B.: Unfolding the mystery of ransomware. In: Bhattacharyya, S., Hassanien, A.E., Gupta, D., Khanna, A., Pan, I. (eds.) International Conference on Innovative Computing and Communications. LNNS, vol. 55, pp. 25–32. Springer, Singapore (2019). https://doi.org/10.1007/978-981-13-2324-9_4
27. Narwal, B., Mohapatra, A.K.: Performance analysis of QoS parameters during vertical handover process between Wi-Fi and WiMAX networks. In: Panda, B., Sharma, S., Roy, N.R. (eds.) REDSET 2017. CCIS, vol. 799, pp. 330–344. Springer, Singapore (2018). https://doi.org/10.1007/978-981-10-8527-7_27
28. Narwal, B., Mohapatra, A.: Energy efficient vertical handover algorithm for heterogeneous wireless networks. Int. J. Control Theor. Appl. **9**(19), 9221–9225 (2016)
29. Narwal, B., Mohapatra, A.K., Usmani, K.A.: Towards a taxonomy of cyber threats against target applications. J. Stat. Manage. Syst. **22**(2), 301–325 (2019)
30. Rani, S., Narwal, B., Mohapatra, A.K.: RREQ flood attack and its mitigation in ad hoc network. In: Panda, B., Sharma, S., Roy, N.R. (eds.) REDSET 2017. CCIS, vol. 799, pp. 599–607. Springer, Singapore (2018). https://doi.org/10.1007/978-981-10-8527-7_50

Blockchain Technology Transforms
E-Commerce for Enterprises

Ankur Arora[✉], Manka Sharma, and Suku Bhaskaran

GD Goenka University, Gurugram, India
arora.ankur.dba@gmail.com

Abstract. Blockchain is an emerging technology and gaining an attraction in businesses. The use of Blockchain technology will ease the processes of businesses and industries. It can be characterized as one of the most important predominant topics nowadays. The issues in Blockchain like privacy, security, and risk are always debatable. It has already transformed many individuals' lifestyle and companies due to inordinate influence on industries and businesses. The features of blockchain technology guarantee to be more reliable and also expedite the services. It is important to consider the privacy and security issues in this research paper. It also discusses the challenges behind the innovative technology to transform the enterprises.

There are several studies focuses on utilizing the blockchain data structure in various B2B and B2C applications. This paper includes the various aspects of trust has been examined at different dimensions. The dimensions of trust can be studied are based at different levels such as foundation, performance, process and purpose. Furthermore, It can delve the model that how the Blockchain technology can adapt in obtaining the trust level by incorporating various factors such as Security, Privacy, Brand Name, Usability, Reliability, Availability, Reputation, Third Party, Risk, Quality, Look and Feel. The use of block chain can transform ecommerce as there are many processes that can be automated and blockchain implementation can help the ecommerce application in the better way as they are working currently.

Keywords: Blockchain · Trust · Security · Privacy · Ecommerce application · Transform · Dimensions · Enterprises

1 Introduction

Blockchain technology is a decentralized electronic platform where records are maintained in an immutable fashion. The automation in business processes can be done through blockchain technology. The link can be established between two parties based on the trust rather than the goodwill or kindness. The current practices and value in influencing reviews are discussed in this paper followed by methods and benefits of using blockchain. A Blockchain is a digital record that stores a list of transactions, called "blocks", backed by a cryptographic value. Each block contains a link to the previous block, a timestamp, and data about the transactions it represents. Blocks are immutable, means that they cannot be modified once created. Trust is a foundation of any relationship in business. Success can be built on trust. There are many

© Springer Nature Singapore Pte Ltd. 2020
U. Batra et al. (Eds.): REDSET 2019, CCIS 1230, pp. 26–34, 2020.
https://doi.org/10.1007/978-981-15-5830-6_3

intermediaries that helps to create trust. Banks have trust in counterparties for their transactions they do. Relationship is created between parties; this depends on the level of trust between each party in the blockchain. Since nobody can modify a block once it was created. All the parties have to ensure that the data it contains is still valid. The conceptual model is defined using trust in terms of getting information and transaction. This will further be elaborated in perceived Usefulness (Getting Info), perceived Ease of Use (Getting Info), Intention to Getting Info, getting information behavior and finally leads to conducting transaction behavior (Sadouskaya 2017; Veuger 2018).

Similarly, Trust (Transaction) can also be elaborated in terms of perceived Usefulness (Transaction), perceived Ease of Use (Transaction), Intention to conduct Transaction and finally leads to conducting transaction behavior as shown in Fig. 1.

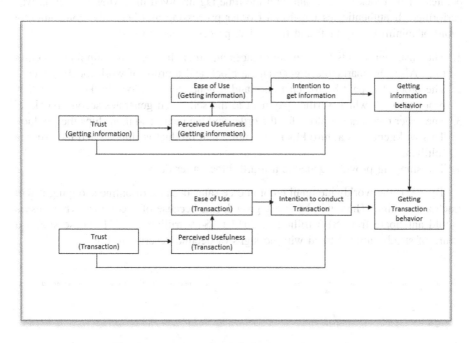

Fig. 1. Trust in getting information and transaction

Trust is the formation of getting information behavior to getting transaction behavior. Blockchain cannot be applied without trust. The concept of blockchain has been around since 1991. Bitcoin was created by creator Satoshi Nakamoto to serve as the currency's ledger called Blockchain (Hackius 2017). Blockchain uses *proof of work* that uses the data to verify the contents of a block. Proof-of work is generated for each block that is based on the content of block. Since, it is difficult to create and to modify the data without the guarantee. The guarantee will give the rights to modify the data in the blockchain. The Blockchain is defined in terms of Bitcoin as it remains decentralized while ensuring the integrity and honesty of each transaction. Since then, Blockchain technology is decentralized. It has been adapted to store medical records, events, traditional financial transactions, and even voting records. Blockchain is actually a online commerce where number of parties does react with each other. These parties may be consumers. Consumers rating plays an important role in making the purchase decision (Ramachandiran 2018; Kim et al. 2008). All popular marketplace viz. Google, e bay, Airbnb and amazon includes the reputation system that facilitates trust in many parties that they are dealing with i.e. vendors and products. This also a healthy competition between manufacturing or vendors in making products and service available for the consumers.

For example, if customer placed an order online by using blockchain-powered e-commerce site. Each cycle of the order uses the following step that is order process, placement, payment, fulfillment, and shipping. The normal ecommerce cycle incorporates a new block to the chain with the time tag involved in it when the action was performed. It authenticates the flow of order processing and helps the companies to avoid or minimize any theft and fraud. The process is as follows:

1. The customer selects the item and places an order. It enters the shipping information. Also, the marketplace generates a block and a proof of work for the order.
2. The product is paid by the customer and it generates a r block backed by another proof of work which verifies payment to the seller and generates second block.
3. The seller receives the block for the order and payment, and then ships the product. This will generates a third block indicating that product is shipped and the order is fulfilled.
4. The shipping provider generate a fourth block after delivery.

By 2021, the worldwide retail e-commerce sales because of online shopping it will reach a new high. There will be 265% growth rate because of E-commerce businesses should anticipate from $1.3 trillion in 2014 to $4.9 trillion in 2021. These shows a future of steady upward trend with no signs of decline describe in Fig. 2.

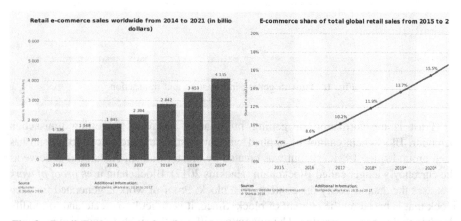

Fig. 2. Retail E-commerce sales. Source: http://beeketing.com/blog/future-ecommerce-2019/

The growth of global ecommerce over the years will leads to the involvement of blockchain technology for the ease of managing the flow and avoid theft and frauds.

The Objective of the Study is to determine the use of Blockchain technology in e-commerce enterprises. The Blockchain controllers can decide the system-wide and product/service-wide parameters to combat some of the issues in the e-commerce enterprises. The lists of objectives covered in this research paper are as follows:

1. The importance of perceived trust of blockchain technology. Trust also has a significant impact on e-blockchain acceptance.
2. The Blockchain's trusts' broad categories are foundation of trust, performance, process and purpose.

Further, parameters such as Security, Privacy, Brand Name, Usability, Reliability, Availability, Reputation, Third Party, Risk, Quality and Look and Feel are also plays an important role in evolving trust.

Blockchain in ecommerce is designed to store transactional data. This data does not need to be financial but it can be a record between two party related to payment or order fulfillment. Block chain helps the ecommerce enterprises in

a) Alternative Payment methods: Bitcoin has taken popularity and a global adoption. They will pay a bitcoin with PayPal, Stripe, or any other payment processor.
b) Faster Transaction: considering the number of parties involved in the process. The payment processors through credit card vendors, simplifying the transaction process and it has been benefited to both merchants and customers
c) More secure payments: Blockchains work well for payment processing because they balance speed, privacy, and integrity.
d) Improved payment fulfillment One of the key benefits to eCommerce platforms is that each block in the blockchain links to the previous block

Trust refers to the confidence of another person in you. The automation also requires proper calibration between the human's reliability amongst each other and the automation system reliability.

The Trust uses the control board that comprises of popular reviewers and ratings, consumer protection officials and representatives from leading companies; regardless of who is in the board the implemented actions are publicly visible, system-wide and data managed in a decentralized and incontrovertible manner. This will indicate that insights of nonrepudiation, privacy safety, and data integrity have a significant impact on trust in implications and further research directions presented. The trust in getting the information and is based on the reviewers and rating and then finally this will help the trust in transaction to carry forward the trust in getting transaction behavior.

These are some of the challenges:

• The trust in getting information and mapping it with trust in transaction will be a challenge for the blockchain implementation
• The e-commerce market is expanding and offering all sizes of different brands of products and services. E-commerce stores need to streamline the processes that are to be part of the business. For the blockchain technology it is a challenge for the implementation of business complexities (Rao 2008; Jones 2008).

- As followed in the traditional business model, the intermediaries will be removed from the transaction cycle and use of blockchain considering the smoot flow of the businesses will be the challenge for implementation.
- To get a consumer trust, the information of the consumer data has to be protected that trust has to be built. Blockchain implementation is recordkeeping is the biggest challenge for this complex business transaction.
- E-commerce enterprise is dealing with buying and selling through online platform where it deals with the different complex processes of supply chain network. IT involves supply chain logistics, payments, and more.

The challenges can be overcome by implementing the block chain technology and the following improvements can be made a) Payment Methods will be Improved b) Supply Chain Management will get Revamped c) More Transparent E-commerce

a) Payment Methods will be improved by having technology in place. blockchain will provide the identity protection. There will be freedom of transactions and Ease of Use. There will be a faster transaction and it will also reduce fraud.
b) Supply Chain network will be improved the transactions and manage the stake-holders for right time and place.
c) A transparent E-commerce facilitates in conducting transactions in a frictionless and efficient manner.

Another significant upside Blockchain offers for e-commerce businesses is that blockchain-based currencies do not exhibit personally identifiable information. Cryptocurrencies operate like cash and they do not require a user to expose sensitive data. In fact, the customer himself permits a transfer from his/her own personal "wallet" to that of the recipient.

2 Methodology Used

As part of the business problem study, the ecommerce is based on belief and convince of consumers. Because of the blockchain can be further implemented and used to facilitate the customer and the business. The following criteria used to qualify the verticals, which will form part of the detailed research study:

- Comprehensive coverage of all the constructs of Blockchain Operational Framework
- Ensure availability of Data Sources from where information can be procured to pursue the research
- Ensure a sufficient cross section of the Industry so that the results are comprehensive and can contribute significantly to Research.

The processes of any e-commerce applications are identified and considered for the ERP digitalized with the usage of Blockchain. The processes are identified for different verticals for the research study and processes are identified based in consideration of broader dimension. These verticals may be Real estate, Healthcare, Supply Chain and Logistics, Education, Internet of Things etc.

Literature Review

The business has started accepting the automation i.e. have started using robotic systems, Machine-learning to self-optimize the different processes used by the industry. The use of blockchain has already come up with the Bitcoin i.e. a solution for managing g currency. In Soon it will be sorting out the logistics in supply chain.

Over the time, logistics automation and blockchain technology will do wonder while working into a single, traceable and standardized process (Dobrovnik et al. 2018). While going through a phase of machine learning in refining the processes, there is a requirement of perceived trust. This concept has originated in 1989 but it can be flexible for applicable based on the requirement.

Perceived Trust in Automation means the human-computer interaction has been the focus of much research over the past two decades from these efforts; researchers have developed various theories that describe the development of trust in automation. The earliest machine trust theory + developed by Muir (1987) stated that trust is contingent upon a machine's predictability, its dependability, and an operator's faith that the machine will function in his or her best interest. Muir's theory proposed that in the first stage of trust development, called predictability, operators observe the machine's performance and make judgments concerning its reliability. If the operator observes inconsistencies in machine performance, trust will diminish. As the relationship matures, trust becomes dependent on attributions of performance, such as dependability.

The first dimension, the foundation of trust, represents the fundamental assumption of natural order that makes the other levels of trust possible. The second dimension, performance, reflects the expectation of consistent, stable, and desirable performance. This dimension is similar to Muir's concept of predictability. The third dimension, process, represents the underlying functioning that guides automation performance. This dimension corresponds with Muir's notion of dependability. The fourth dimension, purpose, reflects the underlying motives or intent of the machine. Purpose corresponds to faith and benevolence and reflects a positive orientation regarding a machine's future performance as shown in Fig. 3.

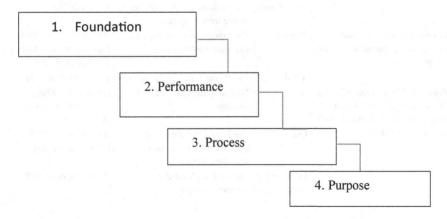

Fig. 3. Muir's model

Table 1 shows the results of our literature review: each row represents a TPM and each column a factor of trust; a cross indicates that the model has considered the factor. Authors use different terms to refer to the factors of trust, which we try to unify as follows in Table 1. Trust can be study at different levels i.e. starting from Foundation, it reflects in performance in terms of transactions, relationship etc. The process is refined and that reflects in relationships and achieving targets. There is also a purpose to study trust at each and every level. The benefit of Blockchain technology is considered to be that it establishes trust between all parties. The disputes regarding payment or order details are less likely to occur due to the decentralized and tamper-proof nature of the Blockchain. The Blockchain generates the transparency in records of all transactions. This will be providing a great help to the ecommerce businesses. The factors discussed at different dimension are shown in Table 1 are:

Table 1. Dimensions and factors used in perceives Trust

Levels	Properties	Description	Reference used
Foundation of Trust: Blockchain enables an emergent trust in the system without any individuals in the system trusting each other	Security	Once a block of data is recorded on the **blockchain** ledger, it is extremely difficult to change or remove	(Hoffman et al. 2006; Camp 2003; Suh and Han 2003)
	Privacy	Privacy in blockchain is the use of private and public keys	(Hoffman et al. 2006; Camp 2003)
	Brand name	Is a publicize name to be used again and again	(Muir 1987; Mayer et al. 1997; Madsen and Grego 2000; Sillence et al. 2007)
Performance: Blockchain activates and the performance of the system increases	Usability	Global usage of blockchain	(Madsen and Grego 2000; Hoffman et al. 2006; Suh and Han 2003)
	Reliability	More trust more reliable	(Muir 1987; Hoffman et al. 2006; Camp 2003)
	Availability	The availability of details based on the trust in system	(Camp 2003)
Process is transparent and provide the impartial justice to the individuals	Reputation	The process must be reputed and have no flaws in it	(Corritore et al. 2003; Hoffman et al. 2006; Sillence et al. 2007)
	Third party	The transparency in the process	(Corritore et al. 2003)
Purpose: The purpose of using blockchain trust is to help the system in terms of quality, look and feel and risk free	Risk	Trusted system are non-risk systems	(Muir 1987; Mayer et al. 1995; Corritore et al. 2003)
	Quality	The impressive details of the interface with the option according to use	(Corritore et al. 2003; Sillence et al. 2007)
	Look and feel	The overall pleasant aspect of the user interface	(Corritore et al. 2003)

The security has to do with protection mechanisms such as login or encryption procedures used by the website; privacy regards the safeguards of the user's personal data; brand name factor has been obtained merging the factors competence, integrity and benevolence, since these characteristics are often associated to well-known brands. The usability assesses how easy is, for the end-user, to accomplish his goals using the website. Reliability & availability is a factor representing the probability that the website will perform and maintain its functionalities. The third party seals refers to the presence of trusted third party logos on the pages of the website; reputation represents the others' experiences with the website. The risk is expresses as the probability that damages or loss can happen due to the use of a website; quality and Look Feel is the summation of characteristics such as an overall pleasant aspect of the website, and the absence of spelling and grammatical errors; finally, brand name says how well the brand behind the website known.

3 Proposed Model

The trust cannot is examined without user. The trust perception Model described in Fig. 4.

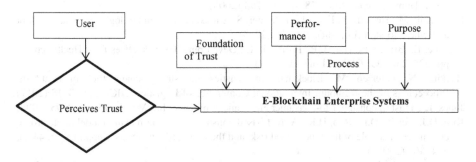

Fig. 4. Trust perception model

The user refers to the expertise and has a good knowledge about web, risk and security matters (e.g. level of knowledge about internet security, https, digital certificates, reputation system). Perceives trust can be examined in any e-Blockchain enterprise system. The dimensions and factors can be evaluated using this model (Bélanger and Carter 2008).

4 Conclusion and Implications

10% of the global GDP predictable to increase because of implementation of Blockchain technology by 2025. All around the world, the financial institutions will be experimenting with Blockchain as a platform and that will be future trade. The MasterCard have deployed its own Blockchain technology for processing payments. Justin Pinkham, MasterCard's Blockchain initiatives has foresees Blockchain as a solution which is tracking the movement of all the transactions in pharmaceuticals, luxury goods, and even diamonds industry. The concept of cryptocurrencies like Bitcoin has not grab the business but Blockchain Technology has the powers that will poised to transform e-commerce and hundreds of other industries.

Based on the upcoming and emerging area of Block chain, the trust will be definitely give a edge to this interesting area to use globally. This will definitely give a different edge to this area.

References

Kim, D.J., Ferrin, D.L., Rao, H.R.: A trust-based consumer decision-making model in electronic commerce: the role of trust, perceived risk, and their antecedents. Decis. Support Syst. **44**(2), 544–564 (2008a)

Muir, B.M.: Trust between humans and machines, and the design of decision aids. Int. J. Man Mach. Stud. **27**(5–6), 527–539 (1987)

Suh, B., Han, I.: The impact of customer trust and perception of security control on the acceptance of electronic commerce. Int. J. Electron. Commer. **7**(3), 135–161 (2003)

Corritore, C.L., Kracher, B., Wiedenbeck, S.: On-line trust: concepts, evolving themes, a model. Int. J. Hum. Comput. Stud. **58**(6), 737–758 (2003)

Dobrovnik, M., Herold, D., Fürst, E., Kummer, S.: Blockchain for and in logistics: what to adopt and where to start. Logistics **2**(3), 18 (2018)

Sillence, E., Briggs, P., Harris, P., Fishwick, L.: Developing Trust Practices for e-Health, ch. X, pp. 235–258. IGI Global, London (2007)

Hackius, N., Petersen, M.: Blockchain in logistics and supply chain: trick or treat? In: Proceedings of the Hamburg International Conference of Logistics (HICL), pp. 3–18 (2017)

Jones, K.: Trust in consumer-to-consumer electronic commerce. Inf. Manag. **45**(2), 88–95 (2008)

Kim, D.J., Ferrin, D.L., Rao, H.R.: A trust-based consumer decision-making model in electronic commerce: The role of trust, perceived risk, and their antecedents. Decis. Support Syst. **44**(2), 544–564 (2008b)

Camp, L.: Designing for trust. Trust, reputation, and security: theories and practice **35**(3), 239–251 (2003)

Hoffman, L.J., Lawson-Jenkins, K., Blum, J.: Trust beyond security. Commun. ACM **49**(7), 94–101 (2006)

Madsen, M., Gregor, S.: Measuring human-computer trust. In: Proceedings of the 11th Australasian Conference on Information Systems, pp. 6–8 (2000)

Ramachandiran, R.: Using blockchain technology to improve trust. In: e-Commerce Reviews (2018). https://doi.org/10.13140/rg.2.2.29324.00646

Sadouskaya, K.: Adoption of blockchain technology, supply chain and logistics (2017)

Veuger, J.: Trust in a viable real estate economy with disruption and blockchain. Facilities **36**(1–2), 103–120 (2018)

Bélanger, F., Carter, L.: Trust and risk in e-government adoption. J. Strat. Inf. Syst. **17**(2), 165–176 (2008)

Blockchain Secured "Smart Buildings" as Cyber Physical Systems

Anupam Tiwari[✉][iD] and Usha Batra

Department of CSE and IT, GD Goenka University, Gurgaon, India
{anupam.tiwari,usha.batra}@gdgu.org

Abstract. Blockchain, often associated with cryptocurrencies, has been lately realized to have immense potential across other domains too vide Blockchain 2.0 and futuristic Blockchain 3.0 versions. Blockchain has magnified itself beyond cryptocurrencies and has a universal appeal ranging across variety domains. Though still at inception stage, but a variegated options and choices have emerged on how blockchain can benefit and make the world better with its immutability, smart contracts and transparency features. Also we have evolving cyber physical systems (CPS), which are consolidations of new generation computing methods, physical and networking operations. In CPS, the embedded computing technologies and networks proctor and check the physical functions, with feedback loops where physical processes bear upon computing part and contrariwise. CPS incorporates the kinetics of the physical operations with software and networking, delivering abstractions and simulating, conceptions, and analysis techniques for the complete system. This paper will discuss and propose the deployment of the CPS Smart building (CPS-SB) network based on an Ethereum private blockchain system mechanized by smart contracts and also discuss inherent challenges on a IoT Simulator (Cupcarbon). The proposal allows for operation of self sustaining CPS-SB based on smart contracts to realize predictive building controls.

Keywords: Blockchain · Cyber physical systems · Internet of Things · Smart contracts

1 Introduction

Blockchain [1], the term has been abuzz across variegated domains [2] over last decade now. Such has been the power of this buzz that every domain, every corporate house, defense sectors, governance etc. all have been vying to affiliate with this buzz. Blockchain, the word first arrived in the technical arena around 2009 and onwards wherein it was first associated primarily as the mechanics and backbone for the well know cryptocurrency i.e. Bitcoin [3]. Much later around late 2013, Vitalik Buterin introduced his paper on Ethereum [4] and came up with smart contracts [5] on Blockchain. Smart contracts [9] are self-executing lines of codes subject to meeting the designed terms and condition between two parties say Buyer and a Seller. The code and the agreements contained therein exist across a distributed, decentralized blockchain network. This remains as the most advanced implementation of smart contracts [6]

© Springer Nature Singapore Pte Ltd. 2020
U. Batra et al. (Eds.): REDSET 2019, CCIS 1230, pp. 35–53, 2020.
https://doi.org/10.1007/978-981-15-5830-6_4

which unique and the firsts of its kind features like private blockchains with different consensus protocols. There are emerging and evolving alternatives to Ethereum few of which are seen in Table 1.

Table 1. Ethereum alternatives & variants

Ethereum classic (ETC)	EOS (EOS)	ARK	Cardano
Stratis (STRAT)	Lisk (LSK)	NEO	Qtum

Before proceeding ahead with associating Blockchain and CPS [7], we will briefly discuss the differences and stake clarity on few terms including Internet of things (IoT) [8], Industrial IoT (IIoT), Industry 4.0 and CPS.

1.1   IoT

IoT, first cited by K. Ashton in 1999, is a system of interconnected processing devices that are provided with unique identifiers and are enabled to share data over a network without requiring human intervention. The term "thing" in IoT can be a human with a heart monitor implant, any animal with a transponder, or an automobile that has built-in sensors to alert the driver when any desired parameters fail to meet laid down specs or any other natural or artificial object that can be assigned an IP address.

1.2   IIoT

IoT when applied specific to any industry is Industrial IoT i.e. IIoT, a term first cited by General Electric. IIoT [10] is a union of variety of technologies like big data, machine learning, sensor data, M2M communication, and automation etc. most of them which exist independently but unite vide IIoT to improve visibility, enable predictive & proactive maintenance, improve upon functional efficiency, step-up productiveness and abbreviate complexity of operations in the industry.

1.3   Industry 4.0

The term, first cited by German government in 2010, for the "High-Tech Strategy 2020", involves associating and automatically integrating things and processes to attain increased value in manufacturing with asset/resource optimization by exploiting newer technologies. Industry 4.0 [11] centers mainly on the manufacturing sector in an Industry unlike IIoT that encompasses all domains where industrial/professional instrumentation is employed.

1.4   Cyber Physical Systems (CPS)

IoT, IIoT, Industry 4.0 are not designed to reach a certain common goal while they function i.e. they do not constitute a "system" in the classical sense. The word "system" implies a set of things working together as parts of a mechanism or an interconnecting network. CPS are systems of system and are holonic in nature i.e. they are self-contained entities and a part of a larger system. CPS incorporate interfacing analogue, digital, physical, and human components machinated for operating through fusion of physics and logic. Embedded hardware through networks, superintends and checks the physical processes, usually with timed feedback schedules where physical processes influence calculations and contrariwise. These systems will render the fundament of upcoming decisive infrastructure and thus form the foundation of emerging smart services in many domains.

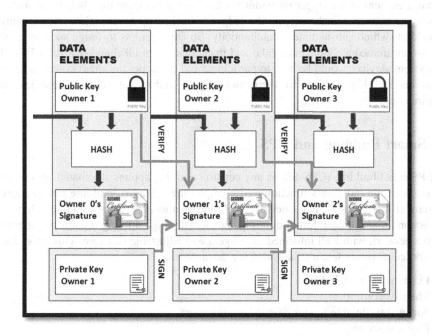

Fig. 1. Blockchain principle architecture

1.5 Blockchain (BC)

The term refers to combination of two words i.e. Block and Chain. Block constitutes of any kind of data attributes and chain refers to connecting these blocks through a consensus mechanism and forming an immutable time-stamped indexing of data which is distributed-managed by computers networked in a peer-to-peer architecture as seen in Fig. 1. BC is paving its way far beyond as it started with the Cryptocurrency Bitcoin in 2009. Today the technology is touching relatively all domains of Human Resource, Logistics, Finance, Banking, Supply chain management, Insurance, food safety, real estate, voting, Identity solutions, smart contracts etc. More simply, BC can be simplified as one giant world-wide computer made up of a number of computers i.e. nodes, that work together as a system to attain consensus.

1.6 Smart Contracts

Smart contracts are computer communications protocol which have the potential to affirm and validate pre-defined conditions in a contract that requires executing the functioning between 'things and devices'. Smart contracts allow the implementation of deemed transactions without the employment of third parties. A smart contract is a special protocol intended to contribute, verify or implement the negotiation or performance of the contract. These transactions are traceable and irreversible.

In the Smart contract system distributed ledger, a record once indexed in block, remains existent in the ledger incessantly while also at the same time being distributed across the network. Each entry in the ledger is backed up by complex cryptography algorithms which substantiate its authenticity. So any attempts to fudge such indexed entries are immediately declared fake and malicious. In an ideal and realized CPS-SB ecosystem, devices would be able to participate and act as per the smart contracts to be implemented [12], subject to their own digital authentication and identification confirmation.

2 Smart Building and CPS

A CPS smart building (CPS-SB) is any construction that applies automated operations to ascertain the building's functioning by employing actuators, building management systems (BMS), sensors, IoT gateways, real time monitoring systems and microchips to collect and manage data. Smart buildings are actually digital living organisms plugged in to a network with well informed, intelligent and adjustable software. This effort and networked environs fetches the following advantages:

- Economical with lighting
- Thermal comfort
- Air quality flexible to suit deemed environment
- Physical security
- Gain the productiveness and effectuality of the facility staff
- Better building operations
- Sanitization at compressed costs
- Positive environmental impact
- Predictive Maintenance to effect into much reduced complaints logging
- Safety and secure environs under complete monitoring

It is well appreciated that the majority of buildings are associated with greenhouse emissions which are far beyond the permissible limits. Thus smart buildings come to rescue with aim to remove this energy emission issues in the overall perspective which can be realized with predictive building controls. A smart building [13] applies technology to make dependable and salubrious environs for those inhabiting within it. It is enabled with smart sensors, intelligence based on IT, and controls for real-time dispersion of operational information for prognostic analytics and diagnostics to help manage the building and maintain it at optimal levels as seen in Fig. 2. Smart building services should be managed with the least amount of user efforts.

CPS's aim integration of computing devices, services and physical arrangements to render consistent and well-informed services. Smart buildings are essential to smart cities, but as the number of such buildings increase, so does the security risk.

2.1   Smart Building and Security

All the advantages and benefits that smart buildings offer have a deeply vulnerable side too [14]. These vulnerabilities if not deliberated right at the onset of implementation can lead to catastrophic incidents. The present day enlightened customer about multiple cyber incidents would not buy or offer himself as a product to hackers and cyber criminals.

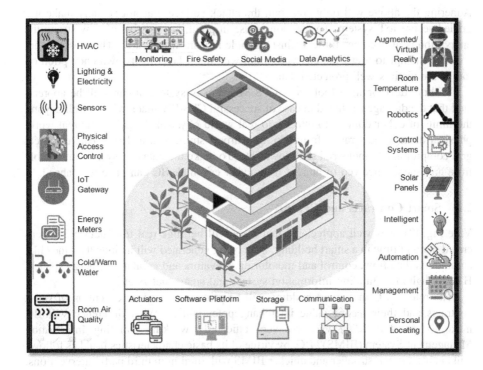

Fig. 2. Simple smart building schematic

The techniques of cyber attacks and threats are evolving by day and adding to the already complex web. Though smart buildings as CPS are still reckoned as nascent and evolving technologies, so the methodology to conceptualize any smart building ideas should also abide by *Design for security*, in addition to other deemed parameters.

The Finland DDoS attacks in 2016 [15] are just recent past, giving the world a broader picture of what may evolve and come next. In the given case, environmental control systems in the effectuated cyber attacked buildings ceased to work causing commotion and life threatening scenario for occupants.

"Hundred percent security" from an IT perspective is going to remain myth for quite some time ahead. To circumvent major part of vulnerabilities, the current architecture for a secure smart building environment is typically based on the following assumptions:

- Entire inventory of all IT devices components installed in the smart building are comprehensively accounted for and plugged.
- Updated hardware (firmware) and software with the latest patches.
- Avoiding hosting and using any vulnerability which could be exploited by cyber criminals.
- Trained operating staff on IT security aspects.
- Multiple layers of protection are in place.

Adhering the above will only constrain the attack surface, but not actually make it a graded secure IoT system. To mention a case in point, irrespective of how strong the encryption is, it becomes futile against a simple ransom ware attack. The ransom ware will not attempt to break the encryption but will add a layer of its own encryption on top of the victims well protected data.

Without developing a fool proof CPS-SB security system, it can well be appreciated that the damages inflicted in case of successful CPS-SB attack will go well beyond the limits of cyber domain to effect into real world physical damage. This real world physical damage may range from a simple airport shut down to large scale electrical grid compromise to industrial shut downs etc. To make the data and system immutable from any such conceived of attacks from cyber criminal, BC can pave way ahead.

2.2   Smart Contracts and CPS-SB

Vide Fig. (2), it is well appreciated that there will be huge real time data being generated per unit time in a smart building. Data being generated will include the kinds like automation data flow, control and monitoring, elevators and escalators, energy spends, HVAC, lighting, Building information system and smart meters etc.

The role of BC in a smart building will be primarily based on execution of smart contracts and their record value interchangepotentialities. What difference will BC make to *smart building* viz-a-viz very efficiently working Building Information Management System (BIMS)? BC, by virtue of its basic characteristics listed as follows will enable a much stronger and quicker BIMS with minimum third party interventions.

2.3   Advantages of Applying Smart Contracts in CPS-SB

- CPS-SB can work in an algorithm based trustless environment [16] without mediation of any third party or any human intervention.
- Smart contracts will enable taking decisions at a speed hitherto unthought-of without any human intervention or malicious actors.
- A permissionless blockchain would enable no limitation on connected systems and devices.
- Transparency and immutability of records and data.
- Availability of data with integrity assurance.

- Much reduced chances of compromise of data then classical ways being followed as on date.
- Duplicated storage of data at identified or all nodes improve ruggedness of CPS.

The above listed characteristics will be more percipient as we appreciate a simple maintenance issue scenario in a *smart building*.

A simple maintenance fault is reported by a occupant regarding some domestic appliance like refrigerator not cooling. In the routine scenario either the same is reported manually by the occupant and user of that appliance or it is detected by the sensor and reported to the BIMS which further activates message sending to appropriate maintaining agency. This scenario assumption works on a centralized BIMS server which might be working on a vulnerable application backend that can actually lead to either the fault not being reported only or damage to appliance. The data of any such routine faults will be based at one location as per the storage configuration backed likely in cloud.

Now, if this CPS-SB is blockchain enabled and working on smart contracts, the logic programmed in the smart contract will take care of reporting the fault to the service provider as well as enable transparency in expedited payments and closure of the fault report. Additionally, it will also ensure security of all transactions of reporting faults and payments with strong cryptography that is peculiar to BC architecture. Further all the transactions committed, in form of blocks of data, will be consistent in being replicated across all the connected nodes irrespective they are part of this particular chain or not. The BC can optionally be a permissionless or permissioned BC as per the design in place.

2.4   CPS Based Smart Building Devices and Interoperability

A CPS-SB has a prima facie assumption that all devices talk and are interoperable with each other through identified protocols. This forms the basic initial step towards attaining a "system of system" approach that necessitates automatic integration of variety sensor actor devices in the CPS-SB. The billions of envisaged CPS-SB devices will thus be a complex inventory of high and low end devices. The high end will be equipped for deemed processing requirements by virtue of aptIT resource and computational capacity while low end might not even store and process like RFID etc. The current state of communication protocols reflect islands of miscellanea protocols evolving across the globe in multiple communities while existing in isolation unconnected with each other. To add to this, all the devices are manufactured by thousands of different manufacturers with their own proprietary standards. To mention a few the range of devices in CPS-SB may be based on the traditional Wi-Fi technologies/3G/4G cellular communications to more recently seen ANT+ standard [17], Bluetooth SMART, NFC, ZigBee, Z-Wave, ZigBee, and WirelessHart, LoRa, SIGFOX etc.

The major evolving attempts in IoT device interoperability and standards across the globe include the following as seen in Fig. 3:

- **IEEE P2413**: This standard specifies an architecture model description for the IoT, which meets the international standard ISO/IEC/IEEE 42010:2011 [18].
- **IoT-A**: This standard aims to set-up an architectural model for the IoT while also determining a range of key factors to form a foundation for the IoT [19].

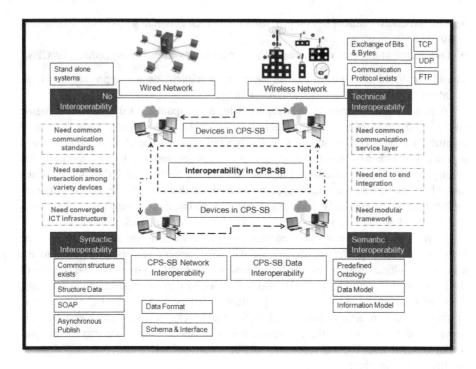

Fig. 3. Interoperability in CPS-SB

- **IoTivity**: This is an open source software model to allow seamless device-to-device connectivity to handle the egressing needs of the IoT [20].
- **Industrial Internet Reference Architecture** (IIRA): This reference standard was created in 2014 and corresponds broad industry consensus, worked up to aim IoT device interoperability and modify development of Industrial Internet systems [21].

3 Hardware and Software

To implement the testing environment of blockchain enabled smart building, the following system setup was used:

3.1 Hardware

- Laptop One: Specifications: Intel Corporation Xeon E3-1200 v6/7th Gen Core Processor Host Bridge/DRAM Registers (rev 02), Intel(R) Core(TM) i5-7200U CPU @ 2.50 GHz, Architecture x86_64, Network controller Intel Corporation Wireless 3165 (rev 79), 6xCPUs, 5.0.0-29-generic #31 ~ 18.04.1-LTS GNU/Linux, 12 GB DDR4 RAM.
- Laptop Two: Specifications: Intel Corporation Xeon E3-1500 v5/6th Gen Core Processor, 440FX- 82441FX PMC [Natoma] (rev 02), Intel(R) Core(TM) i5-7200U

CPU @ 2.50 GHz, Architecture x86_64, Network controller Ethernet controller: Intel Corporation 82540EM Gigabit(rev 02), 6xCPUs, 5.0.0-29-generic #31 ~ 18.04.1-LTS GNU/Linux, 12 GB DDR4 RAM

3.2   Software's and Applications

- **CupcarbonIoT Simulator**: IoT and Smart City and Wireless Sensor Network (SCI-WSN) simulator, part of the project PERSEPTEUR patronized by the French research agency ANR (Agence Nationale de la Recherche), tasked with funding scientific research, under the reference ANR-14-CE24-0017-01. This simulator application loaded in Laptop one. Cupcarbon version 3.8 for Linux has been used for this experiment setup.
- **Truffle Suite**: A development environment for testing framework and asset pipeline for blockchains using the Ethereum Virtual Machine (EVM). It renders support for deployments, library uniting and composite Ethereum application programs. This suite loaded in Laptop two. The following versions have been used in the suite:

  Truffle v5.0.38 (core: 5.0.38) as seen below in Fig. 4

```
smartbuilding@cyberphysical:~$
smartbuilding@cyberphysical:~$ truffle -version
You can improve web3's peformance when running Node.js v
  project
Truffle v5.0.38 - a development framework for Ethereum
```

Fig. 4. Truffle suite version

Node v8.10.0 as seen in Fig. 5 below:

```
smartbuilding@cyberphysical:~$ node -v
v8.10.0
smartbuilding@cyberphysical:~$ []
```

Fig. 5. NPM version

- **Ganache**: An open source [22] Ethereum client used for Ethereum and DAPP development, part of Truffle ecosystem. It provisions easy deployment of DAPP on any Ethereum client. This simulated public blockchain loaded in Laptop two. Ganache version 2.1.1 has been used for the setup in this paper. Ganache thus is a virtual blockchain that lays out up 10 default random Ethereum addresses. These addresses are available with private keys and public keys, and have pre-loads of 100 simulated Ethers for testing purposes. There is no "mining" involved physically and in real with Ganache. Thus it instantly substantiates any type of transaction that occurs. This allows provisioning of small codes that can be executed and tested on this simulated blockchain while also deploy smart contracts.

- **MetaMask**: is a browser extension application that allows for to access the distributed web in a browser and also permits to run Ethereum dApps [23, 24] without functioning of a full Ethereum node. This will allow in our case to connect with the BC and interact with the smart contract that is used in the CPS-SB architecture. This application was loaded in the Mozilla Firefox for Linux 69.0.1(64 bit) for Ubuntu canonical -1.0.
- **Solidity Language**: Solidity [25] is a high level programming language made to execute and implement the contract based Ethereum Virtual Machine (EVM) and possesses syntax like that of JavaScript. It is statically typed scripting language which does the process of validating and applying the restraints at compile-time as opposed to run-time. Solidity version v0.5.11 has been used in the test network made.
- **Sublime Text code editor**: A proprietary cross-platform application with a Python application programming interface. For the setup in this work, Sublime Text Build 3207, Fig. 6, is used.

```
smartbuilding@cyberphysical:~$ subl -version
Sublime Text Build 3207
smartbuilding@cyberphysical:~$ █
```

Fig. 6. Sublime version

3.3 Assumptions

- The number of sensors in a typical smart building with occupants will run into millions, but for the sake of this proposed setup, number of devices is confined to under 10.
- It is assumed that all devices, application platforms, firmware's, BC interface and platform, Ethereum application, Ganache are interoperable and are able to communicate.
- Smart contracts language solidity remains steady with its Solidity version v0.5.11.
- Ganache public blockchain has a permissionless BC and thus the transactions committed in this blockchain are publicly available for simulation purpose.
- Smart contracts being applied for simulation purpose are open source use-cases which will get specific in real life implementation cases.
- All devices have firmware and inbuilt applications and support to identify themselves with PKI.

4 Proposed Architecture

The smart building, simulated on cupcarbon simulator, will be enabled on an Ethereum blockchain, an open source, private BC and blockchain-based distributed computing platform which is duly capable of executing of smart contracts as shown in Fig. 7. The cupcarbon [26] setting is seen below in Fig. 8. The university campus in the figure is simulated with sensors and the output of these sensors and device identification is further to be enabled with BC based smart contracts as seen ahead.

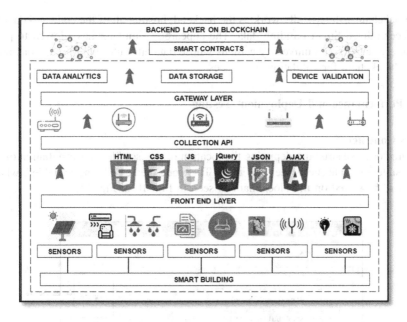

Fig. 7. BC enabled smart building

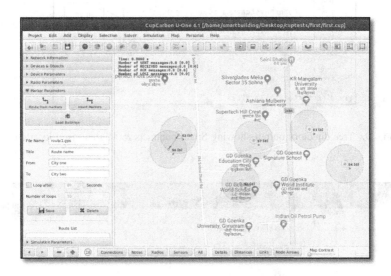

Fig. 8. Cupcarbon simulator showing sensor placements

4.1   Network Deployment

In the proposed network setup in this paper, we will access the Ganache public blockchain application with the special web browser, installed with Metamask plugin, that would be interface to a front end website that will talk directly to the blockchain.

The blockchain will basically work as the backend, hosting all of the code and data for our decentralized Smart building data. The cupcarbon simulator has allowed to place ten variety sensors in a university campus whose data attributes will be taken as input on the blockchain for validation of devices.

4.2   Performance and Deployment Testing

Smart Contract

The directory tree structure depicting the location of the .sol file after installation of the truffle suite and ganache is seen in Fig. 9. This code creates a "state variable", whose value will be stored on the blockchain as seen in Fig. 10 & Fig. 11.

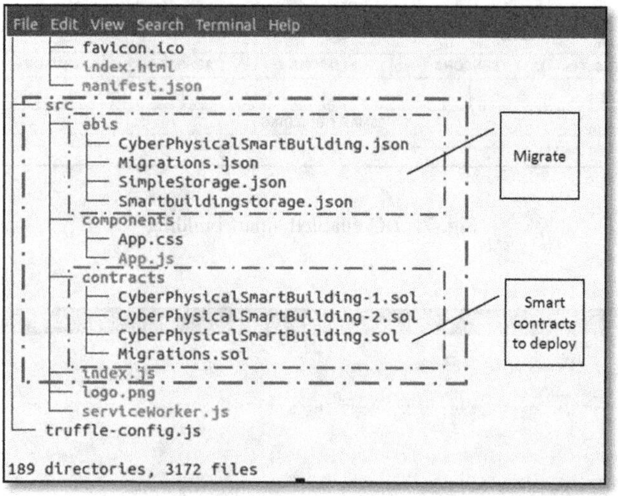

Fig. 9. Tree directory output showing Smart contracts & Migrate .json location

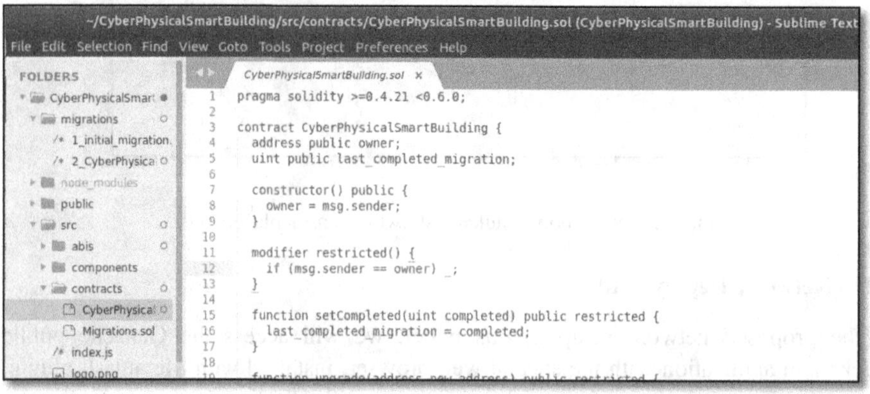

Fig. 10. CPS Generic .sol code for smart contract execution

The smart contracts deployed on the Ganache Blockchain is seen below in Fig. 11.

Fig. 11. Deployed on Ganache blockchain

The blockchain account details against which the transactions are seen indexed is seen in Fig. 12. The figure seen below shows the address ***51C6Cf with a balance of 99.98 ETH and transactions count eight which includes deployment of smart contracts and other transactions.

Fig. 12. Ganache screen showing gas expansion details

Eight blocks have been mined for the transactions with gas expended details as below in Fig. 13. In a real time scenario these blocks would contains transaction hashes or other data details as per the designed BC architecture. This mining as seen is a simulated mining and does not actually conduct a consensus algorithm run like 'proof of work' [27] or 'proof of stake' [28] etc. These options remain open for choice vide selection during design of the Blockchain architecture. However proof of work is not recommended owing to obvious heat energy expanded issues like is being faced by Bitcoin. Low energy based consensus algorithms may be used for the designs.

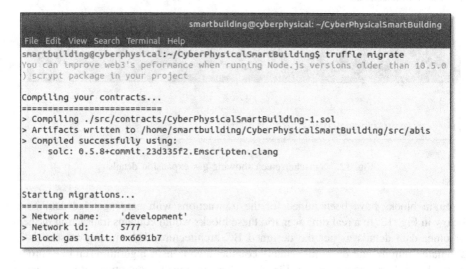

Fig. 13. Block generated details on Ganache BC

Figure 14 shows the compilation part of the smart contracts deployed on the Ganache BC. The smart contract named *CyberPhysicalBuilding-1.sol* is compiled and deployed.

```
                    smartbuilding@cyberphysical: ~/CyberPhysicalSmartBuilding
File  Edit  View  Search  Terminal  Help
smartbuilding@cyberphysical:~/CyberPhysicalSmartBuilding$ truffle migrate
You can improve web3's peformance when running Node.js versions older than 10.5.0
) scrypt package in your project

Compiling your contracts...
===========================
> Compiling ./src/contracts/CyberPhysicalSmartBuilding-1.sol
> Artifacts written to /home/smartbuilding/CyberPhysicalSmartBuilding/src/abis
> Compiled successfully using:
  - solc: 0.5.8+commit.23d335f2.Emscripten.clang



Starting migrations...
======================
> Network name:    'development'
> Network id:      5777
> Block gas limit: 0x6691b7
```

Fig. 14. Smart contracts compilation in solidity

Figure 15 below shows the generation of genesis block and effected details of transaction hash and deployment of contract address. Here the transaction reflects the deployment of the smart contract 'Smartbuildingstorage' with other details including *gas* used and *balance* remains.

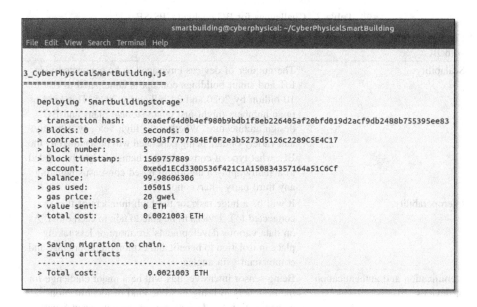

```
                    smartbuilding@cyberphysical: ~/CyberPhysicalSmartBuilding
File  Edit  View  Search  Terminal  Help

3_CyberPhysicalSmartBuilding.js
================================

  Deploying 'Smartbuildingstorage'
  ---------------------------------
  > transaction hash:     0xa6ef64d0b4ef980b9bdb1f8eb226405af20bfd019d2acf9db2488b755395ee83
  > Blocks: 0             Seconds: 0
  > contract address:     0x9d3f7797584Ef0F2e3b5273d5126c2289C5E4C17
  > block number:         5
  > block timestamp:      1569757889
  > account:              0xe6d1ECd330D536f421C1A150834357164a51C6Cf
  > balance:              99.98606306
  > gas used:             105015
  > gas price:            20 gwei
  > value sent:           0 ETH
  > total cost:           0.0021003 ETH


  > Saving migration to chain.
  > Saving artifacts
  ---------------------------------
  > Total cost:           0.0021003 ETH
```

Fig. 15. Transaction hash and smart contract deployment details.

5   Discussions

This paper has established a proof of concept to validate a simple architecture wherein a CPS-SB is enabled with Blockchain. CPS-SB, the domain is evolving fast and very few use cases are present across the globe. The Edge Building at Amsterdam, The Leadenhall Building at London, Capital Tower at Singapore, Siemens HQ at Masdar City, Al Bahr Towers at Abu Dhabi and The Crystal Building at London are few numbered SB use–case examples. These buildings mostly offer zero annual electricity bills with 100 percent rain harvested waters being used for bathing and basic washing jobs. But much remains to be realized still in terms of the actual CPS-SB envisaged. The paper is more based on near futuristic developments and evolving concepts.

The spending of ethers and gas [29] expanded on the simulated blockchain vide deployment of smart contracts reflects a conceptual implementation with loads of assumptions as bought out earlier in the paper. It is duly felt that there will be teething challenges to the technical communities working together across the globe in isolation. These key challenges may be generally bought out as below (Table 2):

Table 2. Challenges for BC enabled CPS-SB

Challenges for CPS-SB enabled with BC	Remarks
Scalability	The number of devices envisaged to be connected vide IoT and smart buildings concept is anticipated to rise to 10 billion by 2020 and 22 billion by 2025. This kind of huge numbers might just effect storage plans and BC design architecture. Whether the high velocity, veracity and variety of data being generated will be handled by the BC, what type of consensus mechanism might be needed to actually apply a algorithm based consensus negating any third party interventions
Interoperability	It will be a huge task for the high numbers of these connected IoT devices to be able to talk to each other. As on date various developments are more or less taking place in isolation to benefit and exploit on proprietary and commercial gain angles
Identification and authentication of devices	Being sensor intensive, this will be a major challenge for the designers to bring in some kind of identification-authentication for devices part of the envisaged Smart Buildings and CPS. This would entail a cryptographic based firmware that would come not only pre-loaded with each device but also is based on a globally accepted standard
Consolidation of CPS-SB products and BC platforms	If BC is envisaged to be enabled and embedded in the architecture of design of CPS-SB, then the other challenge that stands is the interoperability of data formats and application compatibility between the two
Connectivity	The billions of devices in the CPS-SB environment with even inter-intra smart buildings would certainly be challenged with the connectivity issues between devices with 100's of protocols attempting to interoperate with each other. The connectivity and then standby design between participating devices and applications monitoring in a highly scalable, multi vendor and dynamic inventory will be a key challenge
Unstructured data	The evolving numbers of billions of connected devices will step-up the challenges of addressing incoming unstructured data which will be tuned on with high volume, velocity, and variety. Not only handling the unstructured data but also how will the system identify which data is critical and which is not, will remain a challenge unless otherwise clear and exhaustive standards evolve to resolve globally

(continued)

Table 2. (*continued*)

Challenges for CPS-SB enabled with BC	Remarks
Data capturing capacities	This will be another key challenge prior to addressing the unstructured data and connectivity issuances. The system would need to capture all kinds of data related to devices as well as data being generated as a system
Ethereum alternatives	The CPS-SB once designed and in place would deem a irreversible and start from scratch effort if the BC environment needs a change in the middle of things. This need may arise owing to better options to currently available platforms like Ethereum on which the present paper is based on NEO, Stratis, Lisk, EOS etc. are fast evolving options and need to be deliberated upon as choices in near future
Evolving solidity	Solidity, the language for writing smart contracts is evolving an expedited manner for implementing smart contracts on various blockchain platforms. Till such times either solidity or any other alternatives emerge with very stable versions, it will be futile to attempt designing and investing infrastructures and efforts. Even during the work progressed during this paper in last 7 months, Solidity has upgraded from Version 0.5.6 to 0.5.11 today. Such is the good development speed and efforts by the developing communities that these all have been major version changes and are sometimes not backward compatible adding to the other challenges: 15 March 2019: Version 0.5.6 26 March 2019: Version 0.5.7 30 April 2019: Version 0.5.8 28 May 2019: Version 0.5.9 25 Jun 2019: Version 0.5.10 11 Aug 2019: Version 0.5.11

6 Conclusion

To implement BC in a CPS-SB environment, initial design will be key to successful exploitation and serving the purpose for which BC has been implemented i.e. security. Simply designing a protocol for communication between devices or devising an application to monitor and take decisions etc. will just not be enough. Ensuring that the evolving works in isolations across the global communities are put together and then benefitted as a whole is more important.

CPS-SB and BC are definitely assuring technologies evolving still and yet to mature but the union of the two has shown a still better future and a horde of advantages to explore as identified. The speculations of the joint union between the two have been discussed above and so have been the challenges which may look forward to resolves with deliberate efforts from the leading technology corporate houses and researchers. The decisive thing that evolves is the fact these technologies may keep evolving and improving in isolation but before they look forward to the union and advantages explored, the challenges need to be negated to ensure a safe and secure CPS-SB ecosystem right at design stage. The domain is highly dynamic and a plethora of research is active wherein new and better implementation frameworks are being introduced. One such alternative frameworks to Ethereum is Hyperledger by Linux Foundation, which includes projects like Indy, Sawtooth, Fabric and Burrow that can be realized to a large extent for the exploitation and realization of the union of CPS-SB and BC in near future. The future work may look to realize "proof of concepts" for such envisaged union through evolving BC platforms and CPS-SB standards of firmware's while also deliberating the aspect of "Design by Security" right at the onset stage of design and implementation. Additionally, on-chip based hardware mass production [30] is a notable contribution to the above realization but needs to be deliberated as a global standard with deemed modifications.

References

1. Ahram, T., Sargolzaei, A., Sargolzaei, S., Daniels, J., Amaba, B.: Blockchain technology innovations. In: 2017 IEEE Technology & Engineering Management Conference (TEMSCON), Santa Clara, CA, pp. 137–141 (2017)
2. Tsilidou, A., Foroglou, G.: Further applications of the blockchain. In: Conference: 12th Student Conference on Managerial Science and Technology, at Athens (2015)
3. Nakamoto, S.: Bitcoin: a peer-to-peer electronic cash system (2009)
4. Buterin, V.: A next-generation smart contract and decentralized application platform, white paper (2014)
5. Chen, G., Xu, B., Lu, M., et al.: Exploring blockchain technology and its potential applications for education. Smart Learn. Environ. **5**, 1 (2018). https://doi.org/10.1186/s40561-017-0050-x
6. Vujičić, D., Jagodić, D., Ranđić, S.: Blockchain technology, bitcoin, and Ethereum: a brief overview. In: 2018 17th International Symposium INFOTEH-JAHORINA (INFOTEH), East Sarajevo, pp. 1–6 (2018)
7. Liu, Y., Peng, Y., Wang, B., Yao, S., Liu, Z.: Review on cyber-physical systems. IEEE/CAA J. Automatica Sinica **4**(1), 27–40 (2017)
8. Dudhe, P.V., Kadam, N.V., Hushangabade, R.M., Deshmukh, M.S.: Internet of Things (IOT): an overview and its applications. In: 2017 International Conference on Energy, Communication, Data Analytics and Soft Computing (ICECDS), Chennai, pp. 2650–2653 (2017)
9. Wang, S., Yuan, Y., Wang, X., Li, J., Qin, R., Wang, F.: An overview of smart contract: architecture, applications, and future trends. In: 2018 IEEE Intelligent Vehicles Symposium (IV), Changshu, pp. 108–113 (2018)
10. Sisinni, E., Saifullah, A., Han, S., Jennehag, U., Gidlund, M.: Industrial internet of things: challenges, opportunities, and directions. IEEE Trans. Industr. Inf. **14**(11), 4724–4734 (2018)
11. Devezas, T., Leitão, J., Sarygulov, Askar (eds.): Industry 4.0. SESCID. Springer, Cham (2017). https://doi.org/10.1007/978-3-319-49604-7
12. Bajer, M.: IoT for smart buildings - long awaited revolution or lean evolution. In: 2018 IEEE 6th International Conference on Future Internet of Things and Cloud (FiCloud), Barcelona, pp. 149–154 (2018)

13. Bashir, M.R., Gill, A.Q.: IoT enabled smart buildings: a systematic review. In: 2017 Intelligent Systems Conference (IntelliSys), London, pp. 151–159 (2017)
14. Rathinavel, K., Pipattanasomporn, M., Kuzlu M., Rahman, S.: Security concerns and countermeasures in IoT-integrated smart buildings. In: 2017 IEEE Power & Energy Society Innovative Smart Grid Technologies Conference (ISGT), Washington, DC, pp. 1–5 (2017)
15. The Internet of Things Leaves Finland Cold by Jonathan Strickland. https://computer.howstuffworks.com/internet-things-leaves-finland-cold.htm. Accessed 21 Sept 2019
16. Zhang, Y., Zheng, Z., Dai, H., Svetinovic, D.: Special section on blockchain for industrial internet of things. IEEE Transactions on Industrial Informatics 15(6), 3514–3515 (2019)
17. Mehmood, N.Q., Culmone, R.: A data acquisition and document oriented storage methodology for ANT+ protocol sensors in real-time web. In: 2016 30th International Conference on Advanced Information Networking and Applications Workshops (WAINA), Crans-Montana, pp. 312–318 (2016)
18. BOG/CAG - Corporate Advisory Group. IEEE 2413-2019 - IEEE Approved Draft Standard for an Architectural Framework for the Internet of Things (IoT), 21 May 2019
19. Nati, M., et al.: Toward trusted open data and services. Internet Technol. Lett. https://doi.org/10.1002/itl2.69. Wiley
20. Lee, J., Jeon, J., Kim, S.: Design and implementation of healthcare resource model on IoTivity platform. In: 2016 International Conference on Information and Communication Technology Convergence (ICTC), Jeju, pp. 887–891 (2016)
21. Banda, G., Bommakanti, C.K., Mohan, H.: One IoT: an IoT protocol and framework for OEMs to make IoT-enabled devices forward compatible. Journal of Reliable Intelligent Environments 2(3), 131–144 (2016). https://doi.org/10.1007/s40860-016-0027-5
22. Dang, T.L.N., Nguyen, M.S.: An approach to data privacy in smart home using blockchain technology. In: 2018 International Conference on Advanced Computing and Applications (ACOMP), Ho Chi Minh City, pp. 58–64 (2018)
23. Ali, M.S., Vecchio, M., Pincheira, M., Dolui, K., Antonelli, F., Rehmani, M.H.: Applications of blockchains in the Internet of Things: a comprehensive survey. IEEE Commun. Surv. Tutorials 21(2), 1676–1717 (2019). Secondquarter
24. Cai, W., Wang, Z., Ernst, J.B., Hong, Z., Feng, C., Leung, V.C.M.: Decentralized applications: the blockchain-empowered software system. IEEE Access 6, 53019–53033 (2018)
25. Hegedus, P.: Towards analyzing the complexity landscape of solidity based ethereum smart contracts. In: 2018 IEEE/ACM 1st International Workshop on Emerging Trends in Software Engineering for Blockchain (WETSEB), Gothenburg, Sweden, pp. 35–39 (2018)
26. Bounceur, A., et al.: CupCarbon-Lab: an IoT emulator. In: 2018 15th IEEE Annual Consumer Communications & Networking Conference (CCNC), Las Vegas, NV, pp. 1–2 (2018)
27. Kumar, G., Saha, R., Rai, M.K., Thomas, R., Kim, T.: Proof-of-work consensus approach in blockchain technology for cloud and fog computing using maximization-factorization statistics. IEEE Internet Things J. 6(4), 6835–6842 (2019)
28. Nguyen, C.T., Hoang, D.T., Nguyen, D.N., Niyato, D., Nguyen, H.T., Dutkiewicz, E.: Proof-of-stake consensus mechanisms for future blockchain networks: fundamentals, applications and opportunities. IEEE Access 7, 85727–85745 (2019)
29. Kim, S., Song, J., Woo, S., Kim, Y., Park, S.: Gas consumption-aware dynamic load balancing in ethereum sharding environments. In: 2019 IEEE 4th International Workshops on Foundations and Applications of Self* Systems (FAS*W), Umea, Sweden, pp. 188–193 (2019)
30. Watanabe, H., Fan, H.: A novel Chip level Blockchain security solution for the Internet of things networks, White paper, MDPI Technologies, March 2019

Iris Based Secured Newfangled System Procuring Miniaturized Prorogation

Ayesha Hena Afzal$^{(\boxtimes)}$, Sherin Zafar, and M. Afshar Alam

Department of Computer Science Engineering,
Jamia Hamdard, New Delhi, India
Ayesha.afzal1822@gmail.com, zafarsherin@gmail.com,
aalam@jamiahamdard.ac.in

Abstract. In the present situation, various associations are totally dependent on data innovation for their survival, experiencing the negative effects of different security challenges, for example, unapproved access, physical damage and so forth. So as to maintain a strategic distance from various security breaks and concerns, a strong part for client get to that protections beneficial data and is used to create different other security applications should be received. Biometric "anchored innovation takes into account over customary security components such as password, smartcard and so on, as to take identification of data by biometric are tough in comparison with different instruments. During investigation, the "secure biometric system" is recommended for dispense with the worries related to the security of various societies and associations through the iris acknowledgment structure. Iris acknowledgment structure is a framework that perceives an individual through the breakdown of their iris design. This acknowledgment structure fuses iris picture procurement, division, institutionalization, encoding and last endorsement of iris formats. The structure for iris acknowledgment made and mimicked in this exploration study has been founded on IIT database iris pictures as wellsprings of information and for matching process parameters of hamming distance are utilize. The conclusions outline a novel and profitable philosophy which will crush distinctive unapproved gets to over the web. This iris-based recognition as the novel method system, when stood out from different iris acknowledgment is that at whatever point picked pictures are composed with database having arranged iris pictures which will result hamming distance as almost every iris acknowledgment structures clearly recognize or expel pictures and causes execution issues and gigantic clog.

Keywords: Normalization · Security challenges · Novel iris based system · Biometric · Hamming distance · Iris

1   Introduction

Nowadays Information technology security is the main concern in the present world and associations. This increasing number of attacks and dangers causes the security of data a significant test, and each association needs a safe system. Dangers to security lead to different dangerous and questionable administrations utilizing the Internet or fast wired/wireless systems network. Frameworks that are utilized.

© Springer Nature Singapore Pte Ltd. 2020
U. Batra et al. (Eds.): REDSET 2019, CCIS 1230, pp. 54–67, 2020.
https://doi.org/10.1007/978-981-15-5830-6_5

1.1 Biometric

Biometric innovation is viewed as one of the most secure and most powerful information security systems. It is utilized through its physical attributes for the confirmation reason for a person. This procedure is liked to conventional security systems, for example, secret key, keen card, and so on. Since biometric data are hard to take contrasted with different instruments. Different kinds of solid biometric are fingerprints, retinal filtering, face recognition, voice, hand geometry, penmanship are biometric and "iris" [14] is the one appeared in this paper. This current paper's examination study utilizes a solid biometric type, that i.e. iris. In light of its stronger trademark substance and high soundness rate.

1.2 Iris Recognition System

Iris is an organ with a remarkable structure and lives on. This iris quality is one of a kind, dependable and stable. Different nations use iris recuperation methods for the passage and exit of passengers in air terminals. The Iris acknowledgment framework comprises of the accompanying stages such as acquisition of image, segmentation, normalization, encoding and matching of iris images.

These steps will be discussed later in this analysis. The remainder of the paper is sorted out as follow: Literature survey is discussed in Sect. 2 which consists of work related with iris recognition and biometric. Section 3 discusses various security breaches and shortcomings. Section 4 mentions the methodology used for the iris recognition system. Section 5 consist of results and its analysis and Sect. 6 which include conclusion and future scope.

2 Literature Survey

This section depicts an extensive literature survey related to iris recognition system and biometric mechanism a through Table 1.

Table 1. Literature survey

S No.	Name of author	Results of research
1	Lin, Yu and Zhang [2]	The paper presents survey on IOT, their architecture, technologies used, privacy & security and application of IOT in the real world. They proposed the Fog/Edge computing, integrated with Internet-of-Thing (IOT) that enables the various computing services. These assistance to enhance the client's involvement and recuperation benefits if there should be an occurrence of disappointment. To build up a haze/edge based registering IOT framework, right off the bat design, empowering method, issues identified with IOT is researched and after that fog/edge figuring and IOT is set up

(continued)

Table 1. (*continued*)

S No.	Name of author	Results of research
2	Fakhr, Allam and Elsherief [3]	This paper especially discusses about these days today's protection mechanism and the way biometric is used for identification mechanism are of great interest all over. Nowadays iris based technique has become very interesting subjects for studies as nicely as realistic methods. This paper mention the painting which shows detection of iris and various steps involved in detection process
3	Silva, Monterio and Granjal [4]	In this paper, the creator increases a set of rules which help in the reputation of character by iris. This advanced iris patterns are observed and tested in diverse laboratories. At the end result with immense accuracy will be provided
4	Abomhara and Koien [6]	By deeply analyzing this research work about IOT mechanism In this paper, they mainly point out the major security issues, security threats and major open challenges in IOT. As the IOT system is available everywhere, so issues related to its security will be a major concern
5	Khaw [7]	By deeply analyzing this research work, It discusses that security of system are very important in today's world. Biometric Iris is one of the upcoming technique which provide security and authentication of the systems. Iris involves various steps for authentication like extraction of images, normalization, encoding and finally template matching

3   Gaps of Study

Following an extensive literature review, the subsequent gaps were displayed, main to the difficulty plan of the new approach such as biometric is examined, investigated, carried out and reproduced in this exploration study.

A. *Privacy Threat:* As this system assembles heaps of records for its diverse applications. These pieces of information are extremely private as well as sensitive that should be protected from being public. So for this major steps as precaution mechanism are not available at the same time for storing and sharing statistics with another provider.

B. *Security Threat:* Biometric device protection has emerged as a serious safety concern inside the gift age. One of the safety concerns is hacking such devices.

C. *Issues of Right and Legitimate Regulatory:* All across the globe there are not such potent law that can cowl this entire biometric system, so it may cause security issues.

D. *Scalability:* Scalability is one of contribution for the creation of insecure biometric devices, As various security solutions are develop with generic computing devices. But fact is that various biometric devices lack the computing power, storage capacity and even proper operating system to deploy such solutions.

4   Technique Involved

We have discussed regarding the gaps of study and literature review, this area examines the different strategies of the proposed methodology, the clarifications of the iris-based recognition system and the various techniques used to get the ideal outcomes.

In a circumstance in which a person is required or needs to perceive by iris outline, this current person's first eye is caught and afterward the design made for their iris area. As the matching procedure is done the iris designs are set inside iris database. The organizing design are matched with the designs stored in the database and result as recognized otherhand if the organizing design are not matched with the stored designs in the database and result isn't distinguished.

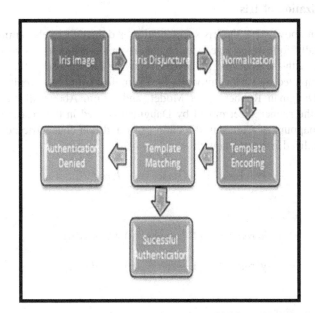

Fig. 1. Different steps for recommended iris based mechanism.

Figure 1 discusses different steps of iris based system bit by bit. To begin with, the iris image is captured and afterward, the iris recognition system makes four steps. The initial step includes iris images segmentation and normalization. After these steps, the iris template is encoded and the encoded format relates to the database layout, where the format matches. On the off chance that format is coordinated, at that point, the verification instrument is fruitful otherwise results will be rejected. The following section consists of different steps involved in iris based system. They are as follow:

4.1   Image Collection

The primary necessity for completing the iris recognition system is gathering of iris images, storage system that requires the good images obtaining component [9]. Whereas in this research work didn't procure pictures by special camera i.e. CCD camera, yet took bona fide database of IIT Delhi for obtaining iris images.

4.2   Segmentation of Iris

The initial step is to decide the real iris section from the digital picture of the eye. In iris images two circles are present the external circle which represent iris/sclera limit whereas the inner circle represent iris/pupil limit. Different mechanism are available to perform the segmentation of iris, above all these mechanism Hough Transform method is preferred because it is less affected by noise and error of eye. Hough space cast a ballot are castes as parameters from the map (focus facilitates x_c and y_c and the radius rad).

$$x_c^2 + y_c^2 - \text{rad}^2 = 0 \tag{1}$$

4.3   Normalization of Iris

As discussed in above steps the iris segmentation is done effectively on image of eye. The exceptionally following stage is to change over the acquired iris section into fix measurements, with the goal that it very well may be looked at [9]. Normalization of Iris can be completed by various process, for example, Histogram evening out, Image Registration, Daugman Rubber Sheet Model, and so on. Above all mechanism for normalization the rubber sheet model by Daugman is used in this research work. For this model remapping of Cartesian direction (x,y) and non-concentric polar portrayal which is normalized is demonstrated:

$$I(x(rad, \theta), y(rad, \theta)) \rightarrow I(rad, \theta) \tag{2}$$

With:

$$x(rad, \theta) = (1 - rad)x_p(\theta) + rad\, x_l(\theta) \tag{3}$$

$$y(rad, \theta) = (1 - rad)y_p(\theta) + rad\, y_l(\theta) \tag{4}$$

Where:
I(x, y) = image of iris section.
(x, y) = actual Cartesian coordinates.
(rad, θ) = corresponding normalized polar coordinates.
$x_p y_p$ and x_l, y_l = coordinates of the pupil and iris boundaries along the θ direction.

4.4   Iris Encoding

So as to precisely distinguish people, just the specific area of the iris section should be removed. This specific piece of the iris picture is encoded utilizing various mechanisms with the goal that format correlation is demonstrated [10]. Encoding of iris can be demonstrated through various strategies. Above all mechanism for encoding Bi-orthogonal wavelet based comer format approach of encoding is used for this research paper because this mechanism doesn't depend on Fourier transformation as well as results in quicker wavelet change.

4.5 Iris Matching

Looking at two iris layouts in the Iris matching technique is performed through passing of binary features into a function [12–15].

$$HD = 1/N_{j=1}^{N} Ca(j) + Cb(j) \tag{5}$$

Here coefficient of two iris pictures are C_a and C_b and feature vector size is represented by N. This method has Boolean operator which give 0 or 1 as results. If result is 1 that means C_a and C_b aren't same whereas if the result is 0 that point C_a and C_b are same.

For iris matching there are many mechanisms. Hamming distance mechanism is chosen for performing matching of iris images. It shows how many bits do not match two comparable Iris templates. If the two templates have hamming distance which is less than the threshold value, the two iris images are otherwise different from the same person.

5 Results

Previous section discusses various methodologies that are adopted. Now this part mainly aims for the analysis and result of proposed methodology by using MATLAB.

STEP 1: The following step associate iris images from the database of IITD are trained (Fig. 2).

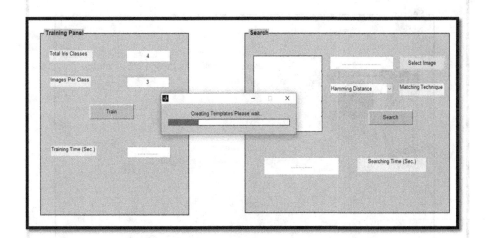

Fig. 2. Iris images training

STEP 2: The following step associate iris image selection from the database which are present or selected from different origin (Fig. 3).

Figure 4 is image of iris that refers to different databases that are untrained. Stage 2 consists of whole images of iris that are stored in a database and are trained. For these images Hamming distance methodology is used.

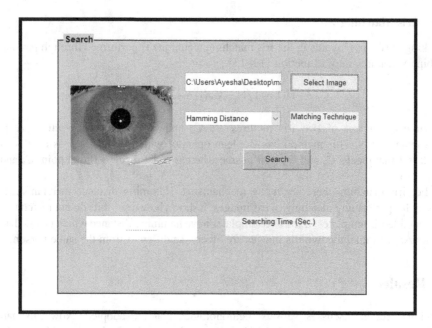

Fig. 3. Image of iris from IITD database (third image of class 3)

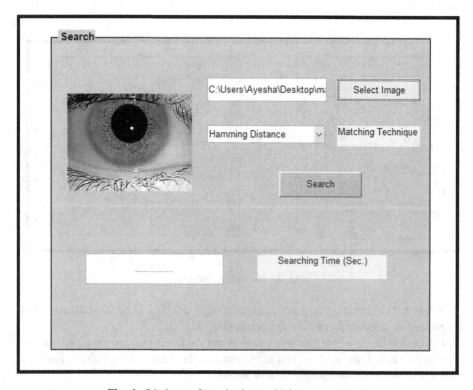

Fig. 4. Iris image from database which are not trained

STEP 3: This step involve process of searching as well as calculation of all over time which is involved for the searching methodology (Figs. 5 and 6).

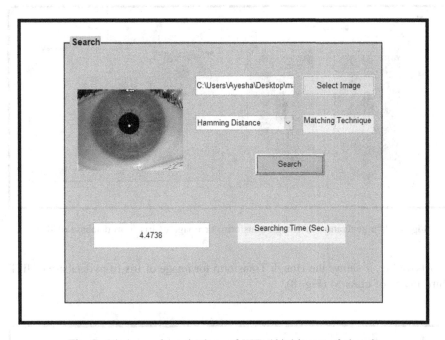

Fig. 5. Iris image from database of IITD (third image of class 3)

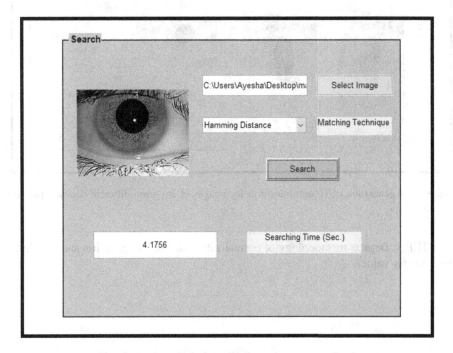

Fig. 6. Image of Iris from database that are untrained.

STEP 4: The fourth step involve Segmentation process by Hough Transform.

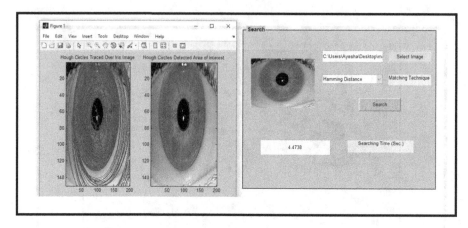

Fig. 7. Is a generation of Hough transform for image of iris from database of IITD

Above Fig. 7 shows the Hough Transform for image of Iris from database of IITD (third image of class 3) (Fig. 8).

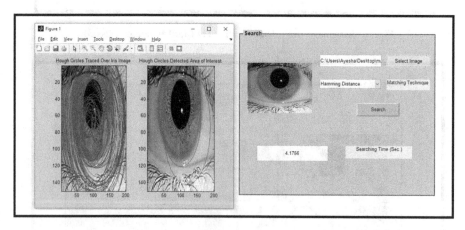

Fig. 8. Is a generation of Hough transform for images of Iris from different database that are untrained.

STEP 5: Depicts methodology of normalization for the image of iris and transform them for fix values.

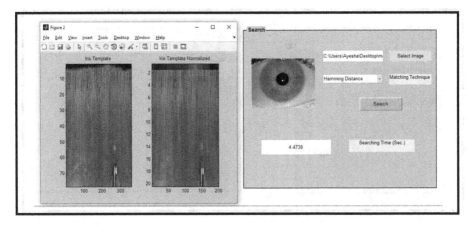

Fig. 9. Is normalization for images of Iris from database of IITD

Figure 9 represents the normalization for images of Iris from database of IITD (third image of class 3).

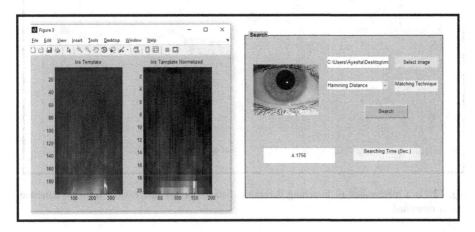

Fig. 10. Is a normalization of iris image from different database that are not trained

Figure 10 represents normalization for image of iris from some other database that are untrained.

STEP 6: In this last step mechanism of matching is performed by method of Hamming distance. In step II iris images that are selected and belong to trained database and yield the end result which is 0 otherwise non zero.

Mechanism of matching hamming distance is depicts in Fig. 11. For hamming distance result is 0 because the image of iris belongs to database of IITD (third image of class 3) that is trained.

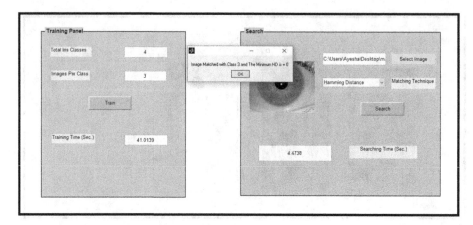

Fig. 11. Is a matching of hamming distance for image of iris from database of IITD

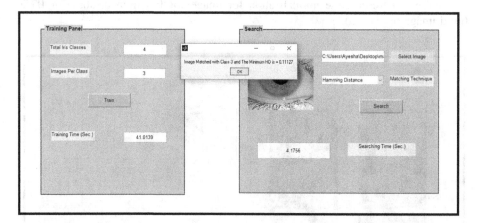

Fig. 12. Is a mechanism of matching hamming distance of iris image from different database that is untrained

Figure 12 shows the calculation of the hamming distance. Hamming distance here is not 0 (hamming distance = 0.11) because the image of iris exist to database which is untrained, as a results the particular Iris image does not match with the images of database which is trained. However, the proposed component still relates to a portion of its class3 subtleties and provides results that are the fundamental element of new iris recognition system.

Table 2. Table for images of iris matching by Hamming Distance

Serial No.	Images for query	Trained images	Class of database	Hamming distance
1	1_7	No	1	0.065
2	1_1	Yes	1	0
3	1_4	No	1	0.05
4	5_8	No	5	0.187
5	2_9	No	2	0.08
6	2_1	Yes	2	0
7	4_1	Yes	4	0
8	5_2	No	5	0.324
9	6_2	No	6	0.111
10	2_3	Yes	2	0
11	1_2	Yes	1	0
12	2_2	Yes	2	0
13	7_1	No	7	0.12
14	3_1	Yes	3	0
15	2_10	No	2	0.038
16	3_2	Yes	3	0
17	4_2	Yes	4	0
18	4_3	Yes	4	0
19	2_8	No	2	0.07
20	1_8	No	1	0.02

The above Table 2 speak about the consequences of iris images that are matching. Selected images matching mechanism is done with the trained database. In case the image which is selected and matched with the images of iris that are trained and belong to database then result for hamming distance is 0 otherwise non-zero.

6 Outcome and Future Scope

According to the current world, because of the flow of information with rapid rate which results to different security issues. Hence require a stable security solution like biometrics. A major security concern is the provision of a biometric mechanism to improve the security and privacy of the network. This proposed novel approach has therefore developed and simulated a biometric based security solution In MATLAB and validation, for the current scenario Hamming distance method has been proposed as a security solution.

Acknowledgment and dismissal with 0 and 1 as a parameter for the hamming distance can cause pointless expansions all through the system. The proposed security arrangement beats this augmentation by giving the exact 0 as a parameter to hamming distance.

Those formats that don't belong to trained database aren't dismissed. They are sent to some work job giving few coordinating hamming distance for e.g. (0.72, 0.34, 0.61) and result into a modernized iris based recognition system which is far better than other alternatives.

6.1 Future Work

- Camera for recognition of Iris (CCD camera) to capture and implement IOT-based solutions in real time.
- Comprehensive analyzes with traditional approaches.
- Explicitness, accuracy and affectability investigation should be fused.

References

1. Zafar, S., et al.: An optimized genetic stowed biometric approach to potent QOS in MANET. In: International Conference on Soft Computing and Software Engineering (SCSE) (2015)
2. Lin, J., Yu, W., Zhang, N.: A survey on internet of things: architecture, enabling technologies, security and privacy, and applications. In: INDIACom 3rd International Conference, vol. 14, no. 1 (2017)
3. Elsherief, S.M., Allam, M.E., Fakhr, M.W.: Biometric personal identification based on iris recognition. In: The 2006 International Conference on Computer Engineering and Systems (2006)
4. Granjal, J., Monterio, E., Silva, J.S.: Security for the internet of things, a survey of existing protocols and open research issues. In: International conference on ICCPEIC, Portugal (2015)
5. Sherin, Z., Soni, M.K.: Secure Routing in MANET through Crypt-Biometric Technique. In: Satapathy, S.C., Biswal, B.N., Udgata, Siba K., Mandal, J.K. (eds.) Proceedings of the 3rd International Conference on Frontiers of Intelligent Computing: Theory and Applications (FICTA) 2014. AISC, vol. 328, pp. 713–720. Springer, Cham (2015). https://doi.org/10.1007/978-3-319-12012-6_79
6. Abomhara, M., Koien, G.M.: Security and privacy in the internet of things: current status and open issues. In: International Conference in Aalborg (2014)
7. Khaw, P.: Iris recognition technology for improved authentication. SANS Institute (2002)
8. Wildes, R.P.: Iris recognition: an emerging biometric technology. Proc. IEEE **85**(9), 1348–1363 (1997). https://doi.org/10.1109/5.628669
9. Misiti, M., et al.: A biometric authentication approach for high security ad hoc networks. In: Proceedings of IEEE Workshop on Information Assistance, pp. 250–256 (2004)
10. Liu, J., et al.: Optimal biometric-based continuous authentication in mobile ad hoc networks. In: Third IEEE International Conference on Wireless and Mobile Computing, Networking and Communications, pp. 76–81 (2007)
11. Khaw, P.: Iris recognition technology for improved authentication, SANS Security Essential (GSEC) Practical Assignment, version 1.3, SANS Institute, pp. 5–8 (2002)
12. Masek, L.: Recognition of human eye iris patterns for biometric identification. University of West California (2003)
13. Daugmann, J.: High confidence visual recognition of persons by a test of statistical independence. IEEE Trans. Pattern Anal. Mach. Intell. **15**(11), 1148–1161 (1993)

14. Zafar, S., Soni, M.K.: A novel crypt-biometric perception algorithm to protract security in MANET. Int. J. Comput. Netw. Inf. Secur. **6**, 64–71 (2014)
15. Zafar, S., Soni, M.K.: Biometric stationed authentication protocol (BSAP) inculcating metaheuristic genetic algorithm. Int. J. Mod. Educ. Comput. Sci. **9**, 28–35 (2014)
16. Bazaz, T., Zafar, S.: A neoteric optimization methodology for cloud networks. Int. J. Mod. Educ. Comput. Sci. **6**, 27–34 (2018)

Accessible and Ethical Data Annotation with the Application of Gamification

Vedant Gurav$^{(\boxtimes)}$ ⓘ, Muhanned Parkar ⓘ, and Parth Kharwar ⓘ

Vidyalankar Institute of Technology, Mumbai, India
vedantgurav98@gmail.com

Abstract. Well labelled Data is paramount in Artificial Intelligence tasks and its collection is often the first step taken by Developers. Current Data Annotation methods can be controversial and ethically questionable, which is the result of large corporations innovating while also trying to reduce their costs. Gamification is the use of games and their concepts in a non-gaming context, and it has seen several creative applications in recent years. We propose a method to use Gamification to streamline and simplify the data annotation process while eradicating its ethical concerns. Our method defines three game modes that provide players with labelling tasks as part of a competitive challenge. Gamifying the data annotation process provides flexibility, scalability and reliability to the creation and improvement of labelled datasets while also improving ethicality and accessibility. Our method is catalysed by widespread adoption to deliver these benefits. With sufficient adoption, it will further the possibilities of creating relevant solutions in the domain of Artificial Intelligence.

Keywords: Training data · Gamification · Ethics · Data annotation

1 Introduction

The collection of data is often the first concern of a developer aiming to create a Machine Learning solution. The complexity of this step can vary with the problem definition, but is most likely to lean towards the difficult end of the spectrum. A simplified data collection process would drive the development of increasingly advanced AI applications, especially by organisations with limited resources to allocate to the same.

The creative Data Annotation methods that have been employed in recent times, while being great proponents of the Artificial Intelligence industry, are only accessible to and/or comprehensible by big corporations that offer services in exchange for user data. Platforms that provide a human workforce for data annotation are more open to public users, but they are chargeable, and provide limited incentive to the personnel that perform the manual data labelling. The questionable ethics of these data collection approaches must also be addressed. Rampant invasion of privacy has become the norm. Corporations feel the need to sacrifice user privacy to provide new and improved features. Manual labelling services are arguably unethical due to the low compensation provided to the personnel.

It is necessary to keep these concerns in mind and tailor our solution to mitigate them as far as possible. The concerns have been addressed in the next section.

U. Batra et al. (Eds.): REDSET 2019, CCIS 1230, pp. 68–78, 2020.
https://doi.org/10.1007/978-981-15-5830-6_6

2 Data Collection and Its Challenges

2.1 Importance of Training Data

The field of Artificial Intelligence is increasingly reliant on data. Vast datasets that are reliable and varied are of great importance in the creation of learning models. The robustness of these models, whether they are created using Machine Learning, Deep Learning or Neural Networks, is greatly influenced by the quality of the training data.

As per a study on data issues in ML and AI projects [1], collecting quality training data and ensuring that it is sufficiently suitable can prove to be a considerable hindrance in the process of the creation of ML solutions. In the next subsection, we discuss the data collection methods that are currently in use.

2.2 Existing Methods for Data Acquisition

Tech giants like Google, Facebook and Amazon have the liberty of collecting massive amounts of data through the services [2–4] they provide. These rich datasets, amongst other things, are responsible for the reliable, industry leading features that are regularly added to these services. While many corporations drive the industry forward by open sourcing their technology, Ex. Facebook [5], the fact remains that an aspiring developer may not always have the same frictionless access to vast training datasets.

Google's Quick Draw [6] experiment stands out as a creative way to collect training data. The user is prompted to doodle a specified object and the neural network makes an attempt to guess what was drawn. The application collects the drawings as well as the initial prompts and builds its labelled dataset. This training data subsequently improves the Neural Network.

This is somewhat reminiscent of the CAPTCHA service provided by Google. [7, 8] Interpreting warped text and selecting squares containing certain objects were sufficiently applicable as Turing tests. But since these tasks are performed reliably by humans, they also provided training data. Initially having provided data to aid the character recognition model used to consolidate scanned books in reCAPTCHA v1, Google's service subsequently moved on to object recognition with reCAPTCHA v2.

Tech companies and independent developers alike can take advantage of services like Amazon's MTurk [9]. While the cost of such services may be a hindrance, there are pressing concerns about their ethicality.

2.3 Ethical Concerns

Workforce Exploitation. With platforms like MTurk [9], Figure Eight [10], Clickworker [11], etc. jobs submitted by clients are presented to the people working with these companies. The workers are generally from low-wage economies. The jobs include "Human Intelligence Tasks" which leverage human abilities to label data. Common trends with these platforms include poor compensation and exploitation of the workforce.

Research performed on the Amazon MTurk platform [12, 13] found that the vast majority of workers on the platform do not make the local minimum wage. Amazon charges a considerable 20% fee on the workers' reward, resulting in the further reduction in compensation for the jobs [14].

User Privacy. Another pressing concern involves user privacy. It is now common knowledge that companies like Google and Facebook consider the user to be the product. Collection of data through free services and its use to tailor advertisements is a common practice. Google's Privacy Policy [15] states that the data Google collects may be used to maintain, improve or develop their services. This could mean that private data from services like Google Photos [2] is used to develop Google's ML solutions.

As per a news article on Facebook privacy concerns [16], Facebook's tagging feature helped train their Image Recognition models. While this feature is now turned off by default, ensuring users opting in have provided their consent, large amounts of data have been already collected and used as training data.

3 Our Proposed Solution

Our goal is the suppression of hurdles [1] that may hinder an organisation's or individual's efforts to build their own ML solutions. In our proposed method, we retain the crowd sourcing fundamentals from the Mechanical Turk like [9] services. We target a less nefarious way to provide incentives to the humans behind the labelling tasks. This will be achieved through the application of Gamification, resulting in the eradication of ethical ramifications, especially those concerning the exploitation of the workforce.

3.1 Gamification

Gamification is the application of gaming concepts in non-gaming contexts. We approach the data labelling tasks from the point of view of the labellers, with an environment that acts first and foremost as an entertainment platform. While attempts to quantitatively evaluate the engagement benefits of gamification exist, we find that approaching interface design in a game-first manner enables us to avoid the conventional embellishment of menial tasks that gamification usually brings. Instead, gamification concepts are applied to strengthen engagement in the game itself.

A research paper on the analysis and application of gamification [17] studies the psychological and social motivations of humans and maps them to common game mechanics. The ideas of autonomy, competence and relation are put forth in the study. These ideas are applied to our solution, creating a socially driven platform, with the labellers, henceforth referred to as players, competing against each other in light hearted but engaging challenges.

Autonomy. It is the freedom of choice afforded to players, which is an important factor that motivates and engages them.

Competence. It is the sense of competition that players look for in the gaming context. It is necessary even in a casual context to provide a sense of accomplishment.

Relation. It is the social factor which introduces players to a game and ensures that they return to play it periodically.

3.2 Benefits of Gamification Mapping

The mapping of gamification to the data labelling task provides flexibility and scalability to the process, as explained in the following text.

Flexibility. It is achieved through providing the players with the autonomy to choose from several types of labelling tasks referred to as game types. This enables clients to request varying types of labelling on different types of data, while providing players with variety and the choice to find game types that best suit their needs.

Scalability. It results from the social element of the game, as an increasing number of players engage with the available game types. Horizontal scalability is achieved by the addition of new labelling tasks by clients. Vertical scalability is achieved by assigning the same tasks to several players to build high support for the resultant data labels.

3.3 Benefits of Human Intelligence

An article on collaborative intelligence between humans and AI [18] highlights the importance of human intelligence in various parts of the AI workflow. Training the AI models is considered a crucial role played by humans. While the labelled data collected using our method sees high support resulting from the scalability of the process, confidence is provided through the reliability of human intelligence.

3.4 Gamification in Machine Learning

Game-powered Machine Learning [19] is an existing study on the use of gamification fundamentals to perform semantic search on multimedia. This effort in annotation of music serves as a proof of concept, demonstrating advantages including cost-effectiveness, flexibility, scalability and reliability.

3.5 Creation of Datasets

When applied to unlabelled data, our method will achieve the creation of a labelled dataset. Data will be presented to players. The client will specify the desired label classes or features and provide the unlabelled data as per their needs. The game mechanics will be crafted in such a way that the actions of the player result in the appropriate label being applied to the data. Depending on the number of features requested by the client, a single task could result in data sufficiently labelled to serve as training data to multiple unrelated learning models.

The same cluster of data (Ex. Traffic Camera Stills) can be tagged with multiple features/labels (Ex. Include Car, Car Type, Car Make, Perceived Stylishness) in such a way that multiple learning models can be created with unique capabilities. A model could be created from the Type class that can classify Cars as SUV, Sedan, Hatch, etc. The same data can be used to train a model to interpret the stylishness of a car based on the Perceived Stylishness label. Players will be effectively describing data using several features, rather than simply assigning a correct label to it. This multipurpose nature sets our solution apart from the one described in [19].

3.6 Improvement of Datasets

When applied to labelled data, our solution will improve the quality of the dataset. Improvements may include - an increased number of labels for particular features of data, improved support and confidence for existing rules, classification based on additional features that were previously ignored, etc. Benefits of the application of the process to unlabelled data may translate to labelled data applications as well.

The study [19] describes a way to use intermediate knowledge gained from the human labelled data to train models to perform the labelling tasks akin to the performance of humans. This concept is built upon by using intermediate data to actively suggest labels and strengthen pre-existing insights.

4 Description of Solution

Following is an explanation of our solution in the context of the labelling of images. Our solution consists of the following game types:

- Classification of images
  - Single Feature
  - Multiple Features (Unique Description)
- Spatial Labelling
- Chained Tasks

4.1 Classification Based on Single Feature

This game type consists of a multiplayer time trial, with players competing to quickly perform the game task. This process has been illustrated (see Fig. 1).

Task Loop:

- The game presents competing players with a set of images.
- The players are provided with goal labels. (Ex. Contains a Human)
- The player selects the images that satisfy the goal.

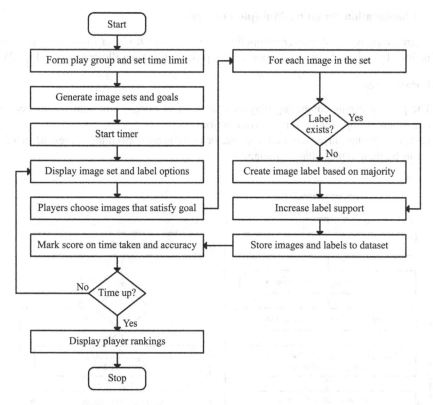

Fig. 1. Classification based on single feature – flowchart

The task loop is repeated using varying sets of images that cumulatively contribute to the game task. Players are scored based on speed and accuracy as compared to other competitors. This provides basic labelling of the objects present in the images. Applications of training data collected from this game type are as follows.

Object Detection Models. This model, similar to reCAPTCHA v2 [7], can be trained using labelled data.

Classification Based on Abstract Features. This classification, similar to Google's Image AI [20], can be performed by training models to recognise abstract qualities such as the degree to which an image looks Pleasing, the Stylishness of Cars, etc.

4.2   Classification Based on Multiple Features

This game type is a multiplayer competition, in which each player must make certain deductions by using object descriptions. This process has been illustrated (see Fig. 2).

Task Procedure:

- The game presents competing players with a set of images consisting of the same fundamental object with varying descriptions.
- Each competing player must choose one or more images from the presented image set to be their representative image.

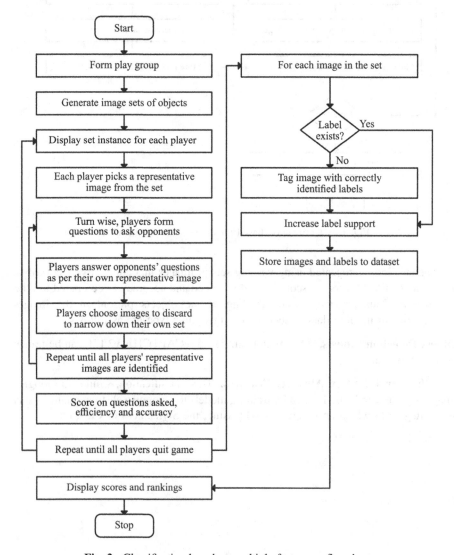

Fig. 2. Classification based on multiple features – flowchart

- Each player asks every other player to describe specific features (as per clients requirements) of the object in their representative image.
- The answers to these questions are used to narrow down the possible representative image of each player, with the goal being to correctly identify it.

Players are scored based on their questions, efficiency and accuracy of deduction as compared to other competitors. This enables the efficient labelling of multiple features and unlocks the types of models that the data can train. Applications of training data collected from this game type are as follows.

Apparel Classification. This can be achieved as described in the studies on outfit detection [21, 22] using datasets similar to [22].

Plant Life Classification. This can be achieved by training data based on features such as leaf size, petal colour and texture.

Unique Identification and Description of Objects. This is achieved within a limited set, to track objects across multiple camera views and provide accurate descriptions for Law Enforcement and Security setups. Multiple Camera Multi Object tracking has been explored in [23] by tracking similar features in the outfits worn by people in the camera views. Objects can be handed over between camera views to achieve tracking over a larger region than is visible to a single camera. This idea can be further explored to apply to other objects on which data is collected using our solution. Urban Traffic Analysis [24] can be applied to track vehicles across multiple traffic cameras. An example on collecting Vehicle Identification Datasets using this particular game type is illustrated (see Fig. 3). In this figure, the player is in the process of narrowing down the opponents representative image by posing a question pertaining to specific features of the vehicle.

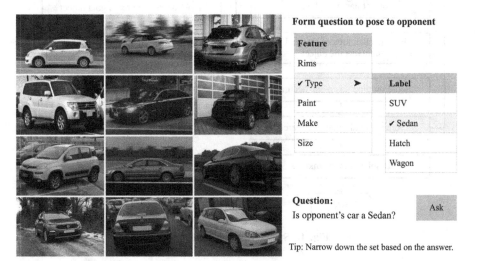

Fig. 3. Prototype of user interface for collection of vehicle unique identification and description dataset.

4.3 Spatial Labelling

This game type works similarly to the Single Feature Classification, the distinction being how the player interacts with the data. This process has been illustrated (see Fig. 4).

Task Loop:

- The game presents competing players with a set of images.
- The players are provided with goal objects. (Ex. Human, Car, Window)
- The player selects the area of the image that contains the required object.

The task loop is repeated using varying sets of images that cumulatively contribute to the game task. Players are scored based on speed and accuracy as compared to other competitors. The selections of multiple players are aggregated to apply a bounding box to the goal object. This box then used as training data for object locating models. Applications of training data collected from this game type are as follows.

Object Locating Models. Models can be trained to find bounding boxes similar to Facebook's Image Recognition [5] and reCAPTCHA [7].

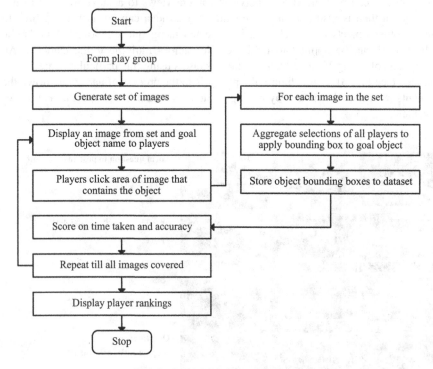

Fig. 4. Spatial labelling - flowchart

4.4 Chained Tasks

This game type includes multiple unrelated short labelling tasks that are presented to the player one after the other. This provides a variety in the gameplay and is suitable for tasks that are too simple to warrant the usage of any of the previous game types. Players are scored on speed and accuracy. This type can also be applied to perform checks on the data created by the other game types. Applications of training data collected from this game type are as follows.

Character Recognition. Achieved similarly to reCAPTCHA v1 [7].

Bounding Box Confirmation. Achieved by reinforcing the correctness of applied bounding boxes.

5   Conclusion

It is clear that data is paramount to any application of Machine Learning or Artificial Intelligence from training to implementation. Well annotated datasets are the root of an evolving intelligent world but the intrusive and unethical practices employed to obtain such data have become a rampant issue. By the use of Gamification, we can crowd source these expensive tasks in a way that circumvents the ethical issues by providing entertainment incentives to the labellers. It also ensures accurate data labels with high support and confidence by relying on human intelligence.

As shown above, there are various approaches to Gamifying data labelling. Each method has its own merits and applications. They also provide a scalable platform leveraging group entertainment and are flexible enough to meet varying customer demands. The games will provide a high level of engagement and a sense of accomplishment to users and in return build datasets without exploiting the players. These data sets would exist in the open domain allowing researchers with limited resources to utilise them for their AI solutions.

Acknowledgments. We would like to highlight the support and guidance provided to us by Prof. Mohini Kamat & Prof. Sachin Deshpande of the Department of Computer Engineering, Vidyalankar Institute of Technology, Mumbai, India.

References

1. Dimensional research survey: Artificial intelligence and machine learning projects are obstructed by data issues (2019). https://content.alegion.com/dimensional-researchs-survey. Accessed 30 Sept 2019
2. Google: offered products and services (2019). https://about.google/intl/en/products/. Accessed 30 Sept 2019
3. Facebook (2019). http://www.facebook.com. Accessed 30 Sept 2019
4. Amazon (2019). http://www.amazon.com. Accessed 30 Sept 2019
5. Shah, S.: Facebook opens up its image-recognition AI software to everyone (2016). https://www.digitaltrends.com/computing/facebook-open-source-image-ai/. Accessed 30 Sept 2019

6. Jongejan, J., Rowley, H., Kawashima, T., Kim, J., Fox-Gieg, N.: The Quick, Draw! - A.I. Experiment (2017). https://experiments.withgoogle.com/quick-draw. Accessed 30 Sept 2019
7. Google: reCAPTCHA types. https://developers.google.com/recaptcha/docs/versions. Accessed 30 Sept 2019
8. Google: reCAPTCHA v3. https://www.google.com/recaptcha/intro/v3.html. Accessed 30 Sept 2019
9. Amazon mechanical turk. https://www.mturk.com. Accessed 30 Sept 2019
10. Figure eight. https://www.figure-eight.com. Accessed 30 Sept 2019
11. Clickworker. https://www.clickworker.com. Accessed 30 Sept 2019
12. Hara, K., Adams, A., Milland, K., Savage, S., Callison-Burch, C., Bigham, J.: A data-driven analysis of workers' earnings on Amazon Mechanical Turk (v2). https://arxiv.org/abs/1712.05796 (2017)
13. Semuels, A.: The internet is enabling a new kind of poorly paid hell (2018). https://www.theatlantic.com/business/archive/2018/01/amazon-mechanical-turk/551192/. Accessed 30 Sept 2019
14. Amazon MTurk Pricing Page. https://www.mturk.com/pricing. Accessed 30 Sept 2019
15. Google privacy policy (2019). https://policies.google.com/privacy. Accessed 30 Sept 2019
16. Morris, D.Z.: Facebook is turning off facial recognition features by default, continuing its pivot to privacy (2019). https://fortune.com/2019/09/03/facebook-facial-recognition-privacy/. Accessed 30 Sept 2019
17. Aparicio, A., Vela, F.L., González-Sánchez, J., Isla-Montes, J.: Analysis and application of gamification. In: Proceedings of the 13th International Conference on Interacción Persona-Ordenador (2012). https://doi.org/10.1145/2379636.2379653
18. Wilson, H.J., Daugherty, P.R.: Collaborative intelligence: humans and AI are joining forces (2018). https://hbr.org/2018/07/collaborative-intelligence-humans-and-ai-are-joining-forces. Accessed 30 Sept 2019
19. Barrington, L., Turnbull, D., Lanckriet, G.: Game-powered machine learning. Proc. Natl. Acad. Sci. **109**, 6411–6416 (2012). https://doi.org/10.1073/pnas.1014748109
20. Djudjic, D.: The rise of the machines: Google's AI will decide if your photos are aesthetically pleasing. https://www.diyphotography.net/rise-machines-googles-ai-will-decide-photos-aesthetically-pleasing/ (2017). Accessed 30 Sept 2019
21. Jain, P., Kankani, A., Geraldine Bessie Amali, D.: A new technique for accurate segmentation, and detection of outfit using convolution neural networks. In: Satapathy, S.C., Bhateja, V., Somanah, R., Yang, X.-S., Senkerik, R. (eds.) Information Systems Design and Intelligent Applications. AISC, vol. 862, pp. 169–177. Springer, Singapore (2019). https://doi.org/10.1007/978-981-13-3329-3_16
22. Bossard, L., Dantone, M., Leistner, C., Wengert, C., Quack, T., Van Gool, L.: Apparel classification with style. https://data.vision.ee.ethz.ch/cvl/lbossard/accv12. Accessed 30 Sept 2019
23. Liu, W., Camps, O., Sznaier, M.: Multi-camera multi-object tracking (v2). https://arxiv.org/abs/1709.07065 (2017)
24. Buch, N., Velastin, S., Orwell, J.: A review of computer vision techniques for the analysis of urban traffic. IEEE Trans. Intell. Transp. Syst. **12**, 920–939 (2011). https://doi.org/10.1109/tits.2011.2119372

Exploring the Possibility of Sybil Attack in Position Based Routing Protocols in VANETs: A Case Study of Greedy Perimeter Coordinator Routing (GPCR)

Nishtha$^{(\boxtimes)}$ and Manu Sood

Himachal Pradesh University, Shimla, India
nishtha16@yahoo.com, soodm_67@yahoo.com

Abstract. Infrastructure-less Vehicular Ad hoc Networks (VANETs) in the absence of any centralized controlling authority are highly vulnerable to various types of malicious attacks. Amongst these attacks, Sybil attack is one such deadly attack that can disrupt the normal functioning of most of the VANET protocols without getting detected easily. In this attack, a legitimate vehicle with malicious intentions enters the network and can mischievously launch a few virtual vehicles camouflaging these virtual vehicles in such a way that these appear to be the legitimate vehicles for all other legitimate vehicles in the network. These superficial vehicles are known as Sybil vehicles and intend to affect the routing mechanism in a VANET by helping the malicious node to assume control of the network. In this paper, we have explored the possibility of Sybil attack disrupting the normal functioning of Position-Based category of Routing Protocols in a VANET. Our exploration here focuses only on one of the significant protocols in the category known as, the Greedy Perimeter Coordinator Routing (GPCR) protocol. With the help of the results of experimental setups, it has been shown that it is always possible for the Sybil attack to disrupt the functioning of GPCR protocol in a VANET. We are also in the process of exploring the impact of Sybil attack on other significant routing protocols for VANETs separately.

Keywords: Malicious vehicle · Sybil vehicle · Sybil launcher · Sybil attack · GPCR · Vehicle to Infrastructure (V2I) · Vehicle to Vehicle (V2V)

1 Introduction

VANET is a special category of ad hoc networks that is formed when moving vehicles equipped with On Board Unit (OBU) come in each other's radio transmission range [1, 2]. Communication among moving vehicles in VANET may be established in two different modes: one is Vehicle to Infrastructure (V2I) and the other is Vehicle to Vehicle (V2V) communication [1–6]. The V2I communication takes place through Road-Side-Units (RSUs) that are set up at predetermined distances alongside all the roads under consideration. These RSUs such as traffic lights are the infrastructure part of VANET that operate as part of the centralized authority and any communication that

© Springer Nature Singapore Pte Ltd. 2020
U. Batra et al. (Eds.): REDSET 2019, CCIS 1230, pp. 79–89, 2020.
https://doi.org/10.1007/978-981-15-5830-6_7

is to be carried out among vehicles is established through these RSU's. The V2V is an infrastructure-less mode where there is no centralized control such as RSUs. In this mode, the vehicles maintain information about their one-hop neighboring vehicles by sending packets periodically known as beacons. Beacons hold status information such as vehicle identification, destination identification, velocity, etc. in their packet headers. Every vehicle taking part in VANET stores this information in a tabular form [4].

Three different types of architectures a) pure ad hoc, b) pure cellular/WLAN and c) hybrid through which VANETs may be established differentiate these networks from other categories of ad hoc networks [7]. The pure ad hoc mode of VANET is the infrastructure-less architecture that is established without the involvement of centralized management such as an RSU. The vehicles behave in a peer to peer manner where to forward a packet from source to destination, the intermediate vehicles act as routers till the packet reaches its destination. Vehicles in this mode communicate wirelessly using a carry-forward approach. The pure cellular/WLAN mode is the infrastructure-based mode of VANET in which vehicles communicate with one another through the RSUs that acts as a central authority. The RSUs may be connected through wired connections, and vehicles communicate with the RSUs through wireless connections in this architecture. In hybrid architecture, both the V2V and V2I communications are supported by different parts of the network [2, 5–7].

Three peculiar architectures, through which VANETs may be framed, make VANET more susceptible to attacks. One of the most hazardous attacks in VANETs is the Sybil attack and as such, there exist possibilities of this attack disrupting the infrastructure-less VANETs. In Sybil attack, a malicious vehicle enters the network as a legitimate vehicle and creates an illusion of the physical presence of a higher number of vehicles than the actual number of vehicles present physically in the VANET. The superficial/virtual/illegitimate vehicles launched by the malicious vehicle to imitate the behavior of legitimate vehicles that do not actually exist are known as Sybil vehicles; and the malicious vehicle is known as Sybil launcher [8–10]. The Sybil attack implemented by the malicious vehicle may use any of the following three dimensions or their combination.

Fabricated/Stolen Identities: One of the approaches through which the Sybil vehicles are provided identity by the Sybil launcher is that the Sybil launcher creates new forged identities called fabricated identities and grant them to the Sybil vehicles. This is known as the creation of Sybil vehicles through fabricated identities. The other way by which the Sybil launcher provides identities to Sybil vehicles is by stealing a legitimate vehicle's identity (e.g. the identity of a vehicle driven out of range of the VANET) and exploit it as a Sybil vehicle's identity [9, 11–13].

Direct/Indirect: In direct communication, the Sybil launcher pretends that Sybil vehicle (s), Sybil launcher and other legitimate vehicles in VANET can communicate directly with each other. In indirect communication, malicious vehicle or the Sybil launcher does not allow its Sybil vehicles to communicate with the other legitimate vehicles and any communication with these Sybil nodes has to be routed through the Sybil launcher [9, 11–13]. This means that the Sybil launcher maintains a condition where no legitimate node is within the communication range of any of the Sybil nodes.

Simultaneous/Non-simultaneous: Under the simultaneous dimension of Sybil attack, all Sybil vehicles are launched at same instant by the Sybil launcher and all these Sybil vehicles can collectively take part in VANET. Under the non-simultaneous dimension of this attack, the Sybil launcher in the network produces Sybil vehicle(s) one after the other in fixed or variable intervals of time. Therefore, all these Sybil vehicles are not created at the same time by the Sybil launcher and consequently, all the Sybil vehicles may not take part in the communication simultaneously [9, 11–13].

Sybil attack is one of the dangerous attacks in any ad hoc network such as a VANET where a Sybil launcher by fabricating Sybil vehicle(s) may provide a false impression of the presence of non-existent vehicles to other legitimate vehicles. Not only that, this Sybil launcher as a legitimate vehicle, launches malicious activities through its Sybil nodes and may take over the control of its operations or at least, may disrupt some parts of its functioning. Since the number of vehicles entering or departing VANET at any moment is not controlled by any centralized management, it is always possible for a Sybil launcher to enter in a VANET and launch any number of Sybil vehicle(s) in the network [10]. Moreover, the Sybil launcher also enjoys the power to fabricate new Sybil vehicle(s) simultaneously at different locations or one after the other in progression or to demolish the created ones. Even the Sybil vehicle(s) created by the Sybil launcher may be shown to be placed along the same path in the direction of movement of the Sybil launcher or along a different path in a different direction(s).

Thus, a single Sybil launcher may simultaneously send messages with multiple identities and these identities give the impression of their presence at different locations at any point in time. Such situations may adversely affect routing protocols in VANET which may consequently lead to accidents, traffic jams and so on [8–10]. As a result, the presence of Sybil vehicles apart from affecting the real traffic scenario also disturbs voting mechanism, misbehavior detection, fair distribution of resources, data aggregation as well as disrupts routing mechanism in VANET [13]. In this paper, we are focusing primarily on routing protocols on which information exchange in VANETs mostly depends. Routing protocols are the standards, depending on which, the establishment of the route is carried out whenever a packet is to be delivered from a source and a destination vehicle [7]. A Sybil vehicle placed along the routing path may disrupt the routing protocol in use. The main motive of Sybil launcher is to disrupt the routing mechanism in VANET. Thus if a packet that is to be forwarded from a source vehicle to the destination vehicle in a case comes across an intermediate Sybil vehicle, then that packet is logically forwarded to the Sybil launcher. At this instance the Sybil launcher may take any of the following actions to disrupt the packet: a) the Sybil launcher may drop the entire packet and does not forward it, b) it may truncate few bits encapsulated in the packet and then forward it or c) it may entirely modify the packet information and then forward it [14].

For V2V communication in VANETs, position based category of routing protocols is of significance. In these protocols, information related to the Geographic Positioning System (GPS) obtained from On Board Unit (OBU) of every vehicle is utilized to locate vehicles in VANET. This GPS information is further utilized to make packet forwarding decisions. Therefore, these routing protocols under this specific category do not involve routing tables [7, 15].

One of the important protocols in position based category of routing protocols for VANETs is GPCR. Designed for the urban scenario, GPCR works on the concept of coordinator vehicles positioned on all the junctions of various roads. A junction is a point on the road where the road is diverted or where two or more roads from different directions meet [16]. This protocol does not involve external information like static street maps. On a straight road, to select the next intermediate hop vehicle to forward the packet from source to destination vehicle, GPCR employs a greedy forwarding strategy. To avoid signal blockage in this protocol, the data packet is traversed all along the streets and the packet is forwarded based on a pre-selected path. At junction points, instead of using the greedy forwarding strategy, the packets are forwarded to a vehicle at the junction under consideration. The vehicle at the junction is known as a coordinator node and is selected as the next hop to forward packets [16].

1.1 Research Gap

GPCR was developed as an improvement of Greedy Perimeter Stateless Routing (GPSR) that does not require a planarization algorithm. GPCR makes its routing decisions without any external information [16, 17]. The data packets are forwarded from one vehicle to another on a straight road and the data packets are forwarded to some other vehicle known as coordinator node at the intersection [16, 18]. GpsrJ+ and GeoCross were developed to improve the low PDR ratio in GPCR [19, 20]. But none of the papers discusses the possibility of disruption of the functioning of a protocol by the Sybil attack and its extent in GPCR. In this paper, we have considered the GPCR protocol from the category of Position Based Routing Protocols and explored whether it was possible to launch a Sybil attack on GPCR in a VANET. It has been shown that the Sybil attack is possible in GPCR up to the extent where it could disrupt the normal functioning of VANET.

The rest of the paper is organized as follows. Section 2 portrays the process of the occurrence of Sybil attack in a VANET using GPCR protocol. Section 3 presents the methodology followed to launch the Sybil attack on GPCR protocol and to analyze its impact. Section 4 discusses the experimental setup for simulation (using NS-2.35) for the launch of a Sybil attack on GPCR protocol. Simulation results and analysis are highlighted next followed by the conclusion and future work in Sect. 6.

2 Sybil Attack in VANET Using GPCR Protocol

To show the occurrence of Sybil attack in GPCR protocol, consider a VANET topology with fifteen vehicles. A packet from source vehicle A is to be passed to destination vehicle D as depicted in Fig. 1. Using a city scenario, we have shown that to forward the packet to D, it has to pass through two junctions J1 and J2. The dotted circle outside A denotes its communication range. A malicious vehicle has managed to enter into the VANET and is successful in launching one number of Sybil vehicles through a stolen identity in the VANET. Using a normal greedy forwarding strategy, the packet should be forwarded to vehicle L_4 because vehicle L_4 is the farthest vehicle in the direction of destination in the specified range. Using GPCR protocol, a packet is passed to a vehicle at the junction known as the coordinator node. The packet is passed to the Sybil vehicle launched by the Sybil launcher at junction J1 meaning thereby that the packet is actually forwarded to Sybil launcher vehicle, the physical location of virtual Sybil vehicle. Afterward, the packet is passed to the only vehicle L_{11} that is the coordinator node at junction J2. From J2 it directly traverses towards the destination vehicle D. According to GPCR, the route that must be followed by the packet from vehicle A to D is shown by dotted lines. As shown in Fig. 1. But due to the presence of Sybil vehicle in the network, the actual route followed by the packet due to disruption caused by Sybil attack is shown by solid lines from A to D in Fig. 1.

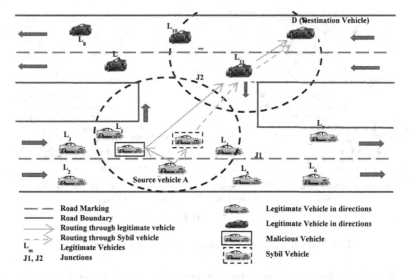

Fig. 1. Sybil attack on Greedy Perimeter Coordinator Routing (GPCR)

This shows that the presence of Sybil vehicle affects the route selection mechanism thereby, affecting the GPCR protocol which can disrupt the normal functions of the protocol. This disruption has been shown to occur through the results of the simulation experimental setup in the following section.

3 Methodology Followed

To implement the Sybil attack in GPCR in a VANET, we have considered two simulation scenarios both with the same topology. All the parameters have been kept the same with the same number of vehicles all moving at a defined speed and all of them moving toward their set destinations within this defined area in all simulation experiments. In the first simulation scenario, all the vehicles are legitimate vehicles including the malicious vehicle behaving in a normal manner, and the packets get forwarded from a source vehicle towards the destination vehicle. All the intermediate vehicles in the route are legitimate vehicles so most of the packets reach the destination smoothly without any mischievous intervention by any of the vehicles as shown in Fig. 2(a). But, in the second scenario, a Sybil launcher has entered the VANET and is successful in launching three Sybil vehicles are shown in blue color in Fig. 2(b). The Sybil launcher launches Sybil vehicles at places that have the maximum probability of acting as intermediate vehicles for packet forwarding on the route from source vehicle to the destination vehicle. Whenever the packets are routed through any of its Sybil vehicles, these packets are then logically routed to the Sybil launcher as the Sybil vehicle(s) are virtual vehicles. To disrupt the GPCR protocol, the Sybil launcher may truncate, modify or drop the packets of the message being transmitted.

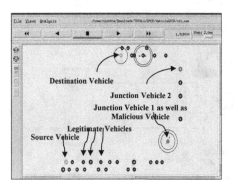
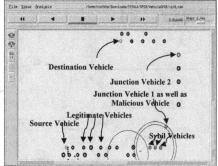

Number of mobile vehicles = 33, Simulation Time = 6 seconds, Area = 2000m *2000m, Speed of every vehicle=1 m/s, Packet Size = 1024 Bytes

(a)   (b)

Fig. 2. (a) GPCR without Sybil attack. (b) GPCR with Sybil attack.

In this work, we have considered the case where the Sybil launcher does not forward the packets and dropped all the packets at Junction J1. To analyze the impact of varying a) packet-size, b) speed and c) the number of vehicles, various simulation programs were written for both the cases: one in which all vehicles are genuine and the other that includes one Sybil launcher and three Sybil vehicles as can be seen in Fig. 2(a) and Fig. 2(b).

4 Experimental Setup

The simulations were carried out on Network Simulator (NS-2.35) installed on Ubuntu 14.04.6 LTS running as a virtual machine on VMware Workstation 10. NS2 is a discrete event simulator for the wireless environment. The transmission range of each vehicle is kept as 250 m. The number of vehicles has been varied from 15 to 33 in different sets of experiments. These vehicles have been shown to move with the discrete speeds from 1 m/s to 10 m/s (for different sets of experiments) with predefined initial and final destinations. All the simulations cover the area of 2000 m × 2000 m for all simulation scenarios. The simulation time has been set to 6 seconds. The packet size also varies from 512 to 9216 Bytes under different simulation scenarios. All other

NS2 parameters are set to their default values. Different setups for various experiments have been explained in detail in the next section. After the simulations have been conducted under the above-mentioned setup and the data thus collected has been analyzed by creating awk file(s) that use the corresponding trace file(s).

5   Simulation Results and Analysis

To evaluate the impact of Sybil attack in GPCR protocol in a VANET, different simulation programs have been written for two scenarios, one without Sybil attack and the other with Sybil attack. Three different cases have been considered under each of these categories where all other parameters were kept constant except for the following three: a) the packet-size in 1st case, b) speed of each vehicle in VANET in the 2nd case and c) the number of vehicles in the 3rd case. The following scenarios have been simulated under the categories of 'without Sybil attack' and 'with Sybil attack' for three different cases: a) Throughput & PDR Vs Packet Size, b) Throughput & PDR Vs Speed of Vehicles, and c) Throughput & PDR Vs Number of Vehicles. The performances of VANET under both the scenarios for three different cases have been compared by computing Throughput and Packet Delivery Ratio (PDR). Throughput is the number of packets delivered per unit time and Packet Delivery Ratio (PDR) is the ratio of the number of packets sent by the source to the number of packets received by the destination.

In order to analyze the impact of packet size in GPCR protocol for case 1, the following packet sizes have been implemented: 512B, 1024B, 2048B, 3072B, 4096B, 5120B, 6144B, 7168B, 8192B, 9216B for both the scenarios, one with 15 legitimate vehicles and the other also with 15 vehicles including one Sybil launcher and 3 Sybil vehicles. The corresponding results of throughput are shown in Fig. 3(a) and the PDR in Fig. 3(b).

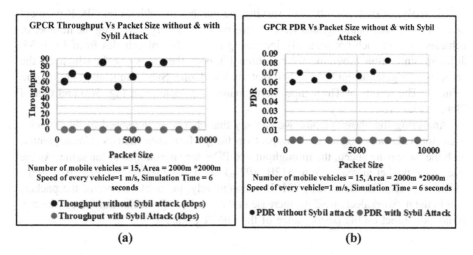

(a)   (b)

Fig. 3. (a) Throughput vs Packet Size with & without Sybil attack. (b) PDR vs Packet Size with and without Sybil attack.

The impact of change in the speed of vehicles using GPCR protocol in a VANET has been analyzed with the help of different simulation setups by increasing the speed of each vehicle by one unit from 1 to10 m/s for both the simulation scenarios. In all the scenarios that are without Sybil attack, 15 legitimate moving vehicles were simulated and 15 vehicles that included one Sybil launcher and 3 Sybil vehicles were simulated in all scenarios with Sybil attack. The performance of both the simulation scenarios is analyzed by computing Throughput as shown in Fig. 4(a) and the packet delivery ratio (PDR) as shown in Fig. 4(b).

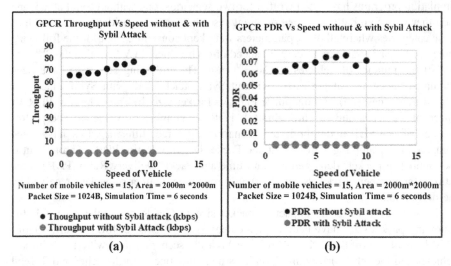

Fig. 4. (a) Throughput Vs Speed with & without Sybil Attack. (b) PDR vs Speed with & without Sybil Attack

Similarly, to study the effect of varying the number of vehicles on GPCR protocol in a VANET, different programs were written by successively increasing the number of vehicles by 2 in each program. By increasing the number of vehicles from 15 to 33, different simulation programs were written for both the cases one in which all the vehicles are genuine and the other that included one Sybil launcher and 3 Sybil vehicles. The results of Throughput performance are depicted in Fig. 5(a) and that of PDR in Fig. 5(b).

Analyzing the above graphs, we can say that change in the speed of the vehicles does not make any considerable impact on the performance metrics. Consequently, with the increasing speed, the throughput and PDR are approximately the same. As the size of the packet increases from 512B, 1024B, 512B, 1024B, 2048B, 3072B, 4096B, 5120B, 6144B, 7168B, 8192B, 9216B consecutively, the total number of the packets sent in the network decreases. An increase in the number of vehicles does not make any significant effect on the performance of the GPCR protocol.

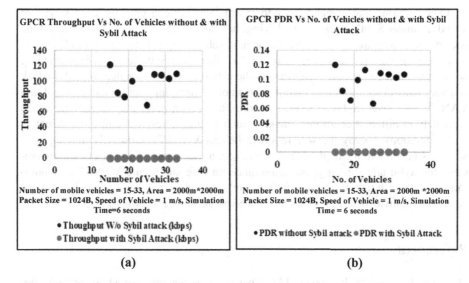

Fig. 5. (a) Throughput vs No. of Vehicles without & with Sybil Attack. (b) PDR vs No. of Vehicles without & With Sybil Attack.

From all the above simulations, it may be easily analyzed that by varying the speed or by changing the packet size, or by increasing the number of vehicles, in case a Sybil launcher has entered and launched Sybil vehicles in VANET, it is always possible for Sybil launcher to fully disrupt the communication. In all the above cases, the Sybil launcher has placed the Sybil vehicle(s) in the routing path between the source and the destination so that the data packet(s) is ultimately delivered through the Sybil vehicle(s) to the Sybil launcher. The Sybil launcher consecutively dropped all the data packets according to its desire and halted any further communication being directed towards the destination. This resulted in the values of PDR and throughput to be zero in all simulation scenarios where the Sybil attack is implemented.

In all the above cases, it has been demonstrated that throughput and PDR are directly proportional to one another.

6 Conclusion and Future Work

In this paper, we have implemented a Sybil attack in a V2V type of VANET using GPCR protocol where the Sybil launcher positioned its Sybil vehicles in such a way that these Sybil vehicles seemed to act as intermediate vehicles for packet forwarding between the source and the destination. But in fact, the packets were being forwarded to the Sybil launcher that directly discarded all incoming packets in this particular case. Therefore, all packets that came from the source vehicle were dropped by the Sybil launcher preventing any further forwarding of packets towards the destination vehicle. Therefore, such an attack makes VANETs vulnerable to disrupt the normal behaviour of the GPCR protocol.

Other options that a malicious node/Sybil launcher can exercise in this type of VANETs under Sybil attack are modifying the whole packet or a few bits/Bytes of the packet before forwarding the packet to the next vehicle. In such a case, by modifying or truncating the data packet(s) before forwarding them, the Sybil launcher is in a strong position to mislead the other vehicle(s) in the network. This shows that the Sybil attack is a very hazardous attack that disrupts the smooth functioning of GPCR protocol in a VANET. Moreover, Sybil attacker, according to its own need, may launch the attack separately in different conditions, making such an attack very difficult to be detected. Such conditions destroy the sole rationale behind VANETs, ultimately making such networks unsuitable for deployment. Therefore, a mechanism that detects and/or prevents the Sybil attack is of prime importance for safe and secure VANET communications. In our future work, the authors are working on devising a mechanism for detection, removal and/or prevention of the Sybil attack in infrastructure-less VANETs.

References

1. Singh, K.D., Rawat, P., Bonnin, J.M.: Cognitive radio for vehicular ad hoc networks (cr-vanets): approaches and challenges. EURASIP J. Wirel. Commun. Netw. **49**, 1–22 (2014)
2. Liang, W., Li, Z., Zhang, H., Wang, S., Bie, R.: Vehicular ad hoc networks: architectures, research issues, challenges and trends. Int. J. Distrib. Sens. Netw. **11**(8), 745303 (2015)
3. Eze, E.C., Zhang, S., Liu, E., Eze, J.C.: Advances in vehicular ad-hoc networks (vanets): challenges and road-map for future development. Int. J. Autom. Comput. **13**(1), 1–18 (2016)
4. Papadimitratos, P., Fortelle, A.D.L., Evenssen, K., Brignolo, R., Cosenza, S.: Vehicular communication systems: enabling technologies, applications, and future outlook on intelligent transportation. IEEE Commun. Mag. **47**(11), 84–95 (2009)
5. Singh, P.K., Nandi, S.K., Nandi, S.: A tutorial survey on vehicular communication state of the art, and future research directions. Veh. Commun. **18**, 100164 (2019)
6. Han, M.L., Kwak, B., Kim, H.K.: Anomaly intrusion detection method for vehicular networks based on survival analysis. Veh. Commun. **14**, 52–63 (2018)
7. Li, F., Wang, Y.: Routing in vehicular ad hoc networks: a survey. IEEE Veh. Technol. Mag. **2**(2), 12–22 (2007)
8. Al-Kahtani, M. S.: Survey on security attacks in vehicular ad hoc networks (VANETS). In: 6th International Conference on Signal Processing and Communication Systems, Gold Coast, pp. 1–9. IEEE (2012)
9. Vasudeva, A., Sood, M.: Survey on sybil attack defense mechanisms in wireless ad hoc networks. J. Netw. Comput. Appl. **120**, 78–118 (2018)
10. La, V.H., Cavalli, A.: Security attacks and solutions in vehicular ad hoc networks: a survey. Int. J. Ad hoc Netw. Syst. **4**(2), 1–20 (2014)
11. Sood, M., Vasudeva, A.: Perspective of sybil attack in routing protocols of mobile ad hoc network. 4th International Conference of Networks and Communications (NETCOM). LNEE, vol. 131, pp. 3–13. Springer, New York (2013). https://doi.org/10.1007/978-1-4614-6154-8_1
12. Nishtha, Sood, M.: Sybil attack on position-based routing protocols for vehicle to vehicle communication in vehicular ad hoc networks. Int. J. Control Theory Appl. **10**(40), 199–208 (2017)

13. Newsome, J., Shi, E., Song, D., Perrig, A.: The sybil attack in sensor networks: analysis & defenses. In: 3rd International Symposium on Information Processing in Sensor Networks, Berkeley, pp. 259–268. IEEE (2004)
14. Ali, L., Hassan, A., Li, F.: Authentication and privacy schemes for vehicular ad hoc networks (VANETs): a survey. Veh. Commun. **16**, 45–61 (2019)
15. Khoza, E., Tu, C., Owolawi, P. A.: Comparative study of routing protocols for vehicular ad-hoc networks (VANETS). In: International Conference on Advances in Big Data, Computing and Data Communication Systems, icABCD, Durban. IEEE (2018)
16. Lochert, C., Mauve, M., Fubler, H., Hartenstein, H.: Geographic routing in city scenario. ACM SIGMOBILE Mobile Comput. Commun. Rev. **9**(1), 69–72 (2005)
17. Karp, B., Kung, H. T.: Gpsr: greedy perimeter stateless routing for wireless networks. In: 6th Annual International Conference on Mobile Computing and Networking, Boston, pp. 243–254. ACM (2000)
18. Paul, B., Islam, M.J.: Survey over VANET routing protocols for vehicle to vehicle communication. IOSR J. Comput. Eng. **7**(5), 01–09 (2012)
19. Lee, K. C., Haerri, J., Lee, U., Gerla, M.: Enhanced perimeter routing for geographic forwarding protocols in urban vehicular scenarios. In: IEEE Globecom Workshops, Washington, USA (2007)
20. Lee, K.C., Cheng, P., Gerla, M.: Geocross: A geographic routing protocol in the presence of loops in urban scenarios. Ad Hoc Netw. **8**(5), 99–110 (2010)

CBCT: CryptoCurrency Based Blockchain Technology

Rahul Johari[1]([⊠]), Kanika Gupta[2]([⊠]), Saurabh Kumar Jha[2]([⊠]),
and Vivek Kumar[1]([⊠])

[1] SWINGER (Security, Wireless IoT Network Group of Engineering and
Research) Lab, USIC&T, GGSIP University, Sector-16C, Dwarka, Delhi, India
`swinger@ipu.ac.in`, `vivek.kul997@gmail.com`
[2] ABES Engineering College, Campus 1, 19th KM Stone, NH 24, Ghaziabad,
Uttar Pradesh, India
`{kanika.gupta, Sourabh.17bit1001}@abes.ac.in`

Abstract. With the continuous development in technology, the interest in
Blockchain Technology has been increasing since 2008. It is a data management
technology which is decentralized and mainly it is being used for Bitcoin
cryptocurrency. Blockchain technology is having certain attributes like security,
integrity and data preservation without the intervention of third party and in
resultant; it provides its usage in various applications. Blockchain is an
emerging technology in this era. Blockchain has gained prominence due to its
highly secured features. Blockchain, as the name suggests, is a chain of blocks.
Blockchain technology is made secured by incorporating the features of cryptographic hash. Each block maintains a hash value. Further, this hash value also
depends on all the previous blocks. All the blocks are connected like a linked
list. A single block contains a cryptographic hash of previous blocks, a timestamp and transaction data. A block is represented as a merkle tree root hash. All
the blocks follow the same structure, only the data varies. The major application
of blockchain due to which it has gained popularity is Bitcoin. Here, in the
proposed research work, we would like to discuss various applications of
Blockchain Technology like finance, academics, medical sciences, Intellectual
Property Rights and how it is impacting the lives of people in day-to-day life.
This paper focuses on the application of blockchain. Along with it, a comparative statistical literature review has been presented..

Keywords: Cryptography · Block chain · Tools · Cryptocurrency ·
Applications

1 Introduction

Blockchain concept was invented by Satoshi Nakamoto in 2008. It is still unknown
whether Satoshi is a single person or a group. Blockchain is a decentralized distributed
ledger. Blockchain works on proof of work timestamping scheme. [1] Table 1 lists
some common Blockchain technology tools.

U. Batra et al. (Eds.): REDSET 2019, CCIS 1230, pp. 90–99, 2020.
https://doi.org/10.1007/978-981-15-5830-6_8

Blockchain technology can be categories into three major categories [1]:

- **Public Blockchain** - Public Blockchain involved no restriction towards accessing transactions. Examples of public Blockchain are Bitcoin and Ethereum.
- **Private Blockchain** - Private Blockchain requires participants to seek permission from the network administrator to join the Blockchain network.
- **Consortium Blockchain** - This is a semi-decentralized Blockchain network. This also requires the permission from the administrators, but a number of companies operate on a collaborative mode in a network. Blockchain is used as a distributed ledger and maintains a peer to peer network. Network adheres to a set of protocols. Protocols are required for inter node connections and validate the blocks. [1] Since, blocks are dependent on each other, if any change are to be made, it requires the consensus of all the blocks which requires network protocol. Protocols also help in creating an agreement between the parties across a distributed network. It also helps in preventing the violation of the system or unauthorized use of the system. [2] Table 2 lists a set of protocols.

Table 1. Blockchain tools [3]

S. No.	Tool name	Tool description
1.	Cakeshop	• Manage a local blockchain node • Cluster setup • Works with contracts
2.	Hyperledger caliper	• Used for calculation of performance measures such as throughput, latency, success rate, and resource consumption
3.	Hyperledger cello	• Used for efficient use of blockchain network • Has a provision of customized Blockchain • Pool of running blockchain networks is maintained
4.	Hyperledger composer	• Application development framework • Builds Hyperledger fabric blockchain • Used with browser-based UI • Used as Developer Tools
5.	Multichain explorer	• MultiChain blockchain browser • Reads MultiChain block file • Transforms data into database • Loads data into database • Provides a web interface
6.	Yobichain	• Private blockchain • Includes a web server, database server, FTP server, S.A.M. (Smart Asset Management) and D.A.V.E. (Data Authentication & Verification)

Table 2. Blockchain technology protocols [7–10]

S. No.	Protocol name	Protocol description
1.	Bitcoin	• Started in November 2008 by Nakamoto • A cryptocurrency • No need of third party in transactions.
2.	Ethereum	• Public and open source platform • Features smart contracts
3.	Ripple consensus network	• Open source platform launched in 2012 • Currency termed as Ripples • Instant, safe and almost free transactions
4.	Hyperledger	• Supports financial and business transactions • Open source platform launched in 2015 by the Linux Foundation
5.	R3s corda	• Distributed ledger protocol • Used for recording, supervising and synchronizing financial agreements
6.	Symbiont distributed ledger	• Launched in October 2016 • Software development kit suitable for institutional finance • Secured high performance distributed ledger
7.	Neo	• Launched by Chinese government • Designed for a scalable network • native currency is non-divisible NEO token • Public cloud
8.	Bitshares	• fast, scalable, efficient • Smartcoin and user-issued assets are two categories of cryptocurrency in bitshare
9.	Waves	• Used to create custom tokens • Decentralized exchange in trade
10.	Qtum	• Launched by Qtum foundation, Singapore • Bitcoin based • Providing an environment for app development
11.	Proof of weight	• Based on measurable metrics
12.	Delegated proof of stake	• Proposed iteration of proof of stake • Representatives of others is selected by voting • Voting is based on trusted nodes for validation of blocks
13.	Proof of work	• Used by Bitcoin miners for mining blocks • Reward given to one who calculates block first • Relies on miners with physical rig
14.	Proof of stake	• New block is chosen depending on wealth • Network fee is collected as reward. • Energy efficient

Some of the features of block chain are [4–6] are as follows:-

- Fault tolerant
- Allows users to keep control over all transactions and data.
- Attack resistant by virtue of hashing.
- No third party involvement
- High transaction rate
- Low transaction costs
- Transparent
- Authentic
- Distributed systems

Some common applications of BlockChain Technology are [11–15] as follows:

- Financial services
- Healthcare services
- Music
- Government sector to prevent fraud
- Internet of things
- Cloud computing
- Food Industry
- Cyber security
- Digital identification
- Crypto currency
- Weapon tracking
- Smart contracts
- Supply chain
- Pay salaries
- Electronic voting

The literature survey undertaken in this research work is summarized in Sect. 2.

2 Literature Survey

A Blockchain is called state machine replication since the structure of the block remains same, only the data varies and calculations are done based upon the inputs. Further, all the working is over a secured channel. Blockchain can be classified into two types based upon where there is a controlled environment upon who participates in the Blockchain protocol and it's validation. In [16], author(s) have proposed a distributed open source framework called hyperledger Blockchain fabric. It improves the Blockchain technology by providing a distributed open platform ledger. This Linux based platform can transform how businesses are conducted nowadays and they can flourish. The proposed framework can later be extended to other domains.

In [17], author(s) have discussed how Blockchain and Internet of Things when worked upon together can benefit the Indian economy. The main focus is on digital economy. Examples of distributed applications in this context have been discussed. This work has explored the Sussex's Shared things technology.

Blockchain technology gained prominence due to its capabilities to resolve trust based transactions to trust free transactions. In [18], author(s) have demonstrated a prototype for transforming from trust based transactions to trust free transactions for a coffee shop transaction system. Author(s) also discussed the issues, challenges and the cost involved in the system. Author(s) have concluded by saying that the proposed framework can be expanded to other transaction systems and can be made more secured.

In [19], author(s) have discussed the evolution of bitcoin, it's advantages, characteristics and need. Further, author(s) explain the importance of Blockchain in the following sectors - internet of things, banking, cyber security and financial institutions.

In [20], author(s) have defined Blockchain technology in detail - history and evolution of Blockchain, it's benefits and working. Author(s) have also discussed the need of the hour for research in this emerging field. In [21], author(s) have created a peer literature review on Blockchain technology. Along with it, author(s) have explained this technology.

In [22], author(s) have presented a theoretical research paper on Blockchain. Theoretically, with examples and applications block chain has been described in detail. In [23], author(s) have discussed the importance of Blockchain in banking. Banking system faces a lot of security issues. Blockchain can resolve these issues by incorporating security and privacy. Author(s) list the challenges and propose some solution in the implementation of the Blockchain technology in the banking industry. Author(s) argue the need for the establishment of Regulatory sandbox for transforming the banking system to resolve the issues of decentralized, self-governing and permissionless systems.

In [24], author(s) have discussed the importance of adoption of Blockchain technology in modern Industry. In other words, applications of Blockchain have been taken into consideration that is, explaining where Blockchain is benefitting. In this special issue, various papers related to application of Blockchain have been collected together. In [25], author(s) have discussed the importance of adoption of Blockchain concept in the field of Internet of Things for security and privacy purposes at the cost of high bandwidth, more delays and lots of computations. Author(s) have proposed a better architecture for Internet of Things based on Blockchain which overcomes the disadvantages of the classical Blockchain architecture for Internet of Things. To achieve the same author(s) have adopted a hierarchical architecture in which they have used a private immutable ledger that is managed centrally and provides same working as a Blockchain. Secondly, a distributed architecture is preferred. Simulations prove that the proposed architecture has low packet and processing overhead.

Blockchain technology is an emerging area in every sector. It is an important subject of development. Every sector is transforming towards new technology. So, in [26], author(s) have described the use of Blockchain in education industry, that is, how Blockchain can be used to resolve issue in education department. Further, the issue and challenges in the implementation of the proposed solutions have been also listed. Blockchain technology and it's relationship with education has been discussed in detail.

In [27], author(s) presented a literature review on the various applications of blockchain other than crypto currency. It is not that crypto currency is the only one use of blockchain technology. Many other uses have been presented in this paper such as distributed storage systems, proof-of-location, healthcare, decentralized voting, et al. The papers selected for the literature review in this paper highlights different applications of blockchain.

In [28], author(s) have argued that Blockchain technology comprises of three independent concepts, that forms backbone of Blockchain - smart contracts, encryption and distributed ledger. It is these three topics that make blockchain a strong technology, hence, blockchain might be the future of technology right now. Soon, these three will become the future of blockchain.

Blockchain involves a lot of security measures. In [29], author(s) describe the importance of Blockchain in supply chain mechanism. Supply chain network is a strong mesh, if traders are involved in national as well as international trading. Hence, it becomes important to add some security measures in this trade. According to author(s), Blockchain can be an appropriate solution for this. It has the capability to enhance supply chain resilience. Author(s) have proposed a Blockchain architecture, then, author(s) describe in detail the risks associated with the supply chain mechanism and then describe how Blockchain technology can resolve this matter. The proposed solutions can be extended to other businesses too.

3   Comparison of Approaches Adopted in BlockChain Technology

Blockchain technology, heart of business 4.0 can be used in many applications, apart from it's major application of Bitcoin crypto currency. This section presents a comparison of above listed literature reviews in context of applications. Different papers discusses applications in different domain. In [16], author(s) have presented a hyperledger blockchain fabric framework in business domain. The author(s) explain how business can be transformed in a better way. In [17], author(s) showcased how blockchain and Internet of Things go hand in hand for development. Author(s) describe how Blockchain help Internet of Things in the application of Indian economy. Blockchain is no doubt beneficial in digital transactions. Blockchain in association with Internet of Things can ease digital transactions using smart devices. [18] presents a case study on coffee shop payment system.

A prototype has been proposed for transforming towards a trust free transaction system. In [19, 22, 24], all the applications have been discussed rather than focusing on a single transaction. In [23], banking application has been explored. How Blockchain can resolve the issues of banking system and the urgent need of the adoption of the proposed system based on Regulatory sandbox. In [25], author(s) have improvised the classical Blockchain model for Internet of Things using a centrally managed private immutable ledger. In [26], author(s) highlight the importance of Blockchain in education sector, different solutions have been proposed. In [27], blockchain has been used for enhancing supply chain resilience.

4 Proposed Work

A Blockchain class is implemented which can be inherited and used as a container for holding data for various applications. Efforts were made to Implement Blockchain from scratch using python programming language and following Object Oriented approach. In this particular case, Blockchain class is inherited by a Cryptocurrency class for creating a dummy cryptocurrency. Some of the Sample Snapshots are listed in Fig. 1.

Important points considered while implementing the blockchain are as follows:

4.1 Creating Blockchain Container

For cryptocurrency to reside in a block of a blockchain, Blockchain class is extended:

$$class\ Cryptocurrency\ (Blockchain)$$

4.2 Proof of Work

The proof of work for mining a block is calculated by brute forcing and finding the solution to the equation

$$target = proof_{new}^2 - proof_{previous}^2 | target \in T$$

$$T \subset SHA256(target)$$

T is subset of SHA256 hashes with 0000 as prefix.

4.3 Checking Validity of Blockchain

For checking the validity of blockchain following algorithm is used:
For each $Block \in Blockchain$

$$1.\ previous\_hash = SHA256\left(Block_{previous}\right)$$

$$2.\ target = proof^2 - proof_{previous} | target \in T$$

$$T \subset SHA256(target)$$

T is subset of SHA256 hashes with 0000 as prefix.
Time Complexity:- $O(N)$, where N is the size of the blockchain.

4.4 Providing a Command Line Interface for Interacting with Blockchain

Given a command line interface for interacting with the blockchain and performing various operations like:-

1. Initialize a blockchain:

$$Blockchain() :$$

$$create\_block(proof = 1, previous\_hash = '0')//genesis\ block$$

2. Create a block in the blockchain:

$$create\_block(proof, previous\_hash)$$

3. View the blockchain:

For each $Block \in Blockchain$

$$print\ Block_{index}$$

$$print\ Block_{timestamp}$$

$$print\ Block_{proof}$$

4. Check the validity of the blockchain.

For each $Block \in Blockchain$

$$1.\ previous\_hash = SHA256(Block_{previous})$$

$$2.\ target = proof^2 - proof_{previous}|target \in T$$

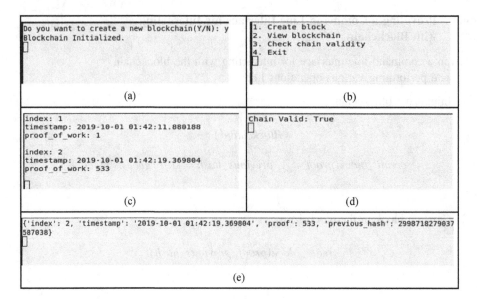

Fig. 1. (a) Initializing a Blockchain, (b) Options available in the Blockchain, (c) Viewing the blockchain, (d) Checking validity of blockchain, (e) A newly created block

5 Conclusion

Blockchain technology aims at transforming the societies. It has the power to completely change the existing systems. This literature review paper aims at focusing the importance of Blockchain in different sectors. It also brings into insight the importance of Blockchain to other researchers and inspire them to work in this emerging technology as this technology has a bright future and a lot of scope. It is high time that this technology shall be given importance.

Acknowledgement. The Author express their acknowledgement to the contribution made by Ms Samriddhi Seth towards the timely completion of this research paper.

References

1. https://en.m.wikipedia.org/wiki/Blockchain
2. https://lisk.io/academy/blockchain-basics/how-does-blockchain-work/consensus-protocols
3. https://medium.com/blockchain-blog/8-blockchain-tools-you-should-know-about-320b61652f53
4. https://medium.com/techracers/4-key-features-of-blockchain-5a4aff025d38
5. https://www.finyear.com/Eight-Key-Features-of-Blockchain-and-Distributed-Ledgers-Explained_a35486.amp.html
6. https://data-flair.training/blogs/features-of-blockchain/amp/
7. https://richtopia.com/emerging-technologies/review-6-major-blockchain-protocols

8. https://medium.com/edchain/a-comparison-between-5-major-blockchain-protocols-b8a6a46f8b1f
9. https://cryptomaniaks.com/latest-cryptocurrency-news/blockchain/blockchain-protocols-learn-them-all
10. https://masterthecrypto.com/comparison-of-major-protocol-coins/
11. https://blockgeeks.com/guides/blockchain-applications/
12. https://blockgeeks.com/guides/blockchain-applications-real-world/
13. https://www.fool.com/amp/investing/2018/04/11/20-real-world-uses-for-blockchain-technology.aspx
14. https://medium.com/technology-nineleaps/blockchain-simplified-part-2-a42161e08762
15. https://execed.economist.com/blog/industry-trends/5-applications-blockchain-your-business
16. Cachin, C.: Architecture of the hyperledger blockchain fabric. In: Workshop on distributed cryptocurrencies and consensus ledgers, vol. 310 (2016)
17. Huckle, S., Bhattacharya, R., White, M., Beloff, N.: Internet of things, blockchain and shared economy applications. Proc. Comput. Sci. **98**, 461–466 (2016)
18. Beck, R., Stenum Czepluch, J., Lollike, N., Malone, S.: Blockchain- the gateway to trust-free cryptographic transactions. In: ECIS, p. 153 (2016). Research Paper
19. Singh, S., Singh, N.: Blockchain: Future of financial and cyber security. In: 2016 2nd International Conference on Contemporary Computing and Informatics, IC3I, pp. 463–467. IEEE (2016)
20. Chatterjee, R., Chatterjee, R.: An overview of the emerging technology: blockchain. In: 2017 3rd International Conference on Computational Intelligence and Networks, CINE, pp. 126–127. IEEE (2017)
21. Seebacher, S., Schüritz, R.: Blockchain technology as an enabler of service systems: a structured literature review. In: Za, S., Drăgoicea, M., Cavallari, M. (eds.) IESS 2017. LNBIP, vol. 279, pp. 12–23. Springer, Cham (2017). https://doi.org/10.1007/978-3-319-56925-3_2
22. Nofer, M., Gomber, P., Hinz, O., Schiereck, D.: Blockchain. Bus. Inf. Syst. Eng. **59**(3), 183–187 (2017)
23. Guo, Y., Liang, C.: Blockchain application and outlook in the banking industry. Financ. Innov. **2**(1), 24 (2016)
24. Beck, R., Avital, M., Rossi, M., Thatcher, J.B.: Blockchain technology in business and information systems research. Bus. Inf. Syst. Eng. **59**(6), 381–384 (2017). https://doi.org/10.1007/s12599-017-0505-1
25. Dorri, A., Kanhere, S.S., Jurdak, R.: Towards an optimized blockchain for IoT. In: Proceedings of the Second International Conference on Internet-of-Things Design and Implementation, pp. 173–178. ACM (2017)
26. Chen, G., Bing, X., Manli, L., Chen, N.-S.: Exploring blockchain technology and its potential applications for education. Smart Learn. Environ. **5**(1), 1 (2018)
27. Miraz, M.H., Ali, M.: Applications of blockchain technology beyond crypto-currency. arXiv preprint arXiv:1801.03528 (2018)
28. Halaburda, H.: Economic and business dimensions blockchain revolution without the blockchain. Commun. ACM **61**(7), 27–29 (2018)
29. Min, H.: Blockchain technology for enhancing supply chain resilience. Bus. Horiz. **62**(1), 35–45 (2019)

Fast Information Retrieval over Encrypted Outsourced Cloud Data

Vasudha Arora[1][✉] and Shweta Mongia[2]

[1] Department of Computer Science and Engineering, GD Goenka University, Gurugram, India
vasudharora6@gmail.com
[2] Department of Informatics, UPES, Dehradun, India

Abstract. The data used in cloud applications is directly exposed to the cloud service provider, and because of the potential compromise of the cloud, could also be learned by adversaries. When encrypted data is hosted on cloud provided that there are large amount of data files, utilization of encrypted data effectively becomes a very challenging task. In a cloud computing environment, where outsourced data of organizations is shared with a large number of users. These variety of users might be interested in retrieving certain specific data files during a given session. A popular and interesting way to do so is by using keyword-based search. These search techniques facilitate users to search and retrieve data files selectively in which the users are interested. These keyword-based searches are being widely used for plaintext searches. But data encryption poses a challenge to perform keyword search using existing paintext search methods to be used for encrypted outsourced data on cloud. In this paper, we have analyzed the searchable indexes that could be used to make a fast and effective search on encrypted outsourced data and proposed a scheme that could make fast and accurate searches over encrypted outsourced cloud data. Simulation results have revealed that the proposed scheme takes much less time in generating the searchable index as compared to already existing techniques. The vector space model being used earlier for keyword based searches on encrypted data, is relatively time consuming and hence leads to very high time complexity during relevance score calculations as well as index generation for large datasets. Hence the proposed scheme achieves a fast and secure relevance scoring for large number of datasets also and in much less time as compared to the vector space model.

Keywords: Data outsourcing · Inverted indexes · Searchable encryption

1 Introduction

Data outsourcing is a service provided by a CSP to store the data of the organizations on the cloud server itself. However, such outsourcing raises some serious issues of securing the privacy of outsourced data.

© Springer Nature Singapore Pte Ltd. 2020
U. Batra et al. (Eds.): REDSET 2019, CCIS 1230, pp. 100–109, 2020.
https://doi.org/10.1007/978-981-15-5830-6_9

As a new innovation, major IT vendors such as IBM, Microsoft etc. are now incorporating the facility of data outsourcing in their service offerings. Outsourcing is an IT facility provided by cloud technology, where an individual or an organization is able to store their somewhere else using the Internet on a pay per use basis. The term 'cloud computing' as defined by NIST [1] as a "model for enabling convenient, on-demand network access to a shared pool of configurable computing resource.... that can be rapidly provisioned and released with minimal management effort or service provider interaction".

With cloud computing almost every IT facility is provided to its users over the Internet as a service which includes infrastructure including storage & servers, plat-forms, memory applications etc. Cloud is capable of offering us the private clouds as well as public clouds where we can outsource our data depending on its sensitivity. Outsourcing to a public cloud, where the provider serves multiple customers simul-taneously using resource pooling, may share many of the risks of traditional out-sourcing. These risks are difficult to alleviate using contract negotiation due to limited opportunities to customize the service delivery.

2 Inverted Index

An inverted index [10] is a data structure that is virtually used in most of IR systems. It is sometimes also known as an inverted file. In a collection C of text files, an inverted index contains the information about mapping of the terms in a file to their corre-sponding location of occurrence. In contrast to a forward index, that is used to store the information about mapping a particular document to its contents, an inverted index stores a mapping from content to its location. These are generally used for fast full text searches.

When a data user wishes to access the outsourced cloud data using queries, inverted indices are more practical for large collections. For any information retrieval problem one cannot predict the keys in advance that people will use in queries. Therefore, every word in a given document is an equally important search term and the only feasible solution is to index by all keys (words). The big advantage of inverted indexes over forward or normal indexes is that they're excellent for representing values which are appearing frequently and hence a good candidate for search engines.

The big downside of inverted indexes is their fastest implementations are hard to update, and often have to be fully rebuilt every time the database is updated. In practice, most relational databases that implement these types of indexes are columnar databases, which implement the whole table using inverted index structures to store the column values (Fig. 1).

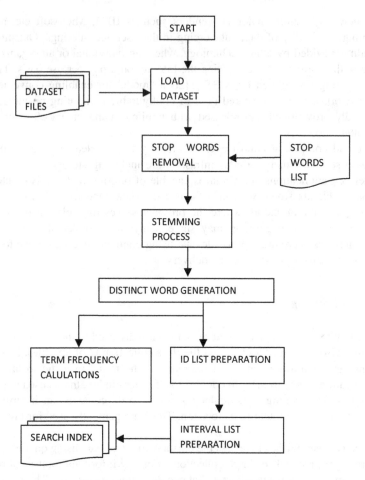

Fig. 1. Process for creating inverted index

3 Information Retrieval

Information retrieval (IR) could be stated as an activity of finding documents or contents which is unstructured (usually text) [10]. Search is a central part in information retrieval whose goal is to predict the relevant documents as per needed by the user. An Information retrieval model must encompass documents, queries by user and if possible some sort of ranking functions to rank the documents retrieved according to relevance for users.

Information retrieval from inverted indexes could be Boolean or statistical. A Boolean retrieval is based on whether the keywords entered in the search query are present or absent in the documents or statistical that applies certain rank order criteria in order to arrange the documents according to their relevance to the user.

4   Vector Space Model

In a vector space everything, such as words, documents, queries and even user preferences, is a vector in some high dimensional space. In order to understand a vector space model one should know what are the dimensions of that space, how to project words, documents and queries to that space and then finally how to compare documents and queries. In a vector space every document represents a new dimension and hence the number of dimensions is constantly growing. Therefore for m documents in the document collection we have an n dimensional vector space. The terms in the documents represent the axes of the space and documents are points or vectors in this space. When this model is applied to a web search engine a very high dimensional vector space is created consisting of tens of millions of dimensions. The vector model created is very sparse that contains a number of zeros.

If we have this vector space of documents we also represent the queries by users as vectors in the space and rank order according to their proximity, to the query in this space, where proximity refers to the similarity of vectors which can be calculated as inverse of Euclidean distance between the two vectors. This is done to come out of the Boolean model and to rank more relevant documents higher than less relevant documents. Using Euclidean distance may always not be a good idea because Euclidean distance is large for vectors of different lengths (Table 1).

Table 1. Term-document incidence matrix (Vector Space Model Information Retrieval)

Documents Terms	Research foundation F1	Network technology F2	Abstract awards F3	Cloud technology F4
Internet	0.79	0.69	0.423	0.004
Spy	0.197	0.78	0	0.645
Teaching	0.231	0	0	0.254
Beware	0.85	0	0.466	0
Domain	1.987	0	0.120	0.342

The Fig. 2 shows the vector space model for two terms Internet and Domain representing two different axes in the vector space. Here, the document vector d1 is closer to the term Network and nothing to do with Domain while d3 is closer to the term Domain and nothing to do with Network. If we want to find out a document that contain both the terms the document d2 should be the answer to the query.

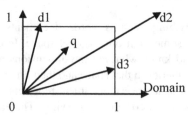

Fig. 2. Vector space model

Using Euclidean distance between q and d2 for calculating relevance of documents based on queried keywords may not be a good choice as the Euclidian distance between them is large even though the distribution of terms in the query q and distribution of terms in the document d2 are very similar. The cosine similarity between the document and the query is calculated. As a ranking function we can use tf-idf weighting scheme.

In order to retrieve information a function for ranking the documents [10] known as tf-idf rule is used. Depending on the number of times a term appears in file or a document, each term is assigned a weight. A score between the query term and the document is calculated.

Let, for any keyword in a query, a keyword t present in a file f has a term frequency denoted by $tf_{t,f}$. In order to calculate the term frequency, we ignore the exact ordering of terms in a file and we count number of times a term appears in it.

df_t the document frequency can be calculated as the total files in a collection of files denoted as C in which the keyword t appears. If in a collection of files, denoted as C, there are m files, an IDF the inverse document frequency of a term t is calculated as

$$idf_t = \log m\, df_t$$

Now tf-idf rule is used to assign the weight to a term t in a file f as

$$tf\text{-}idft, f = tft, f \times idft$$

The relevance score for file f is calculated as the sum of tf-idf weight for each term in a file. Therefore,

$$\text{Relevance Score}_{f,q} = tf - idft \quad t\varepsilon q \tag{1}$$

After calculating the scores, top-k documents with highest score are picked up and presented to the user.

5   Related Work

Before being outsourced, data is encrypted by the users. Traditional search algorithms for searching the data based on some keywords fail to search on this encrypted data and also raise a concern for privacy of keywords being searched [2].

In order to search the keywords an inverted index is created [9, 10]. An inverted index is a matrix that contains the list of all the unique terms that appear in any document in the collection, and for each term, a list of the documents in which it appears.

A VSM (Vector Space Model) was used by TRSE scheme [6] where authors represented each file in the collection as a vector and each term appearing in the file a new dimension for the vector. If a term appears in the file authors assigned a non-zero value to it otherwise a value zero is assigned for each term. Similarly, the query generated by user is represented as a vector. For each file if a term that appears in the query a non-zero value is assigned otherwise for a term present in file but not in query a zero value is assigned to it.

6   Proposed Scheme

A scheme based on rank order search is proposed for searching multiple keyword. A $O(n_t \times 3)$ order index is created. The proposed scheme [11] is described as follows: An entity data owner has a file collection containing m number of represented as $F = \{f1, f2, f3, \ldots, fm)$ that are required to be outsourced to the cloud server. The tokenization process is applied to chunk the document into terms or tokens before outsourcing. AES is used for symmetrically encrypting F. After removal of defined stop words from the file tokens are collected into an index table in sorted sequence. The sorting is done so that similar identifiers from different files with different relevance scores must be collected together in the index. This helps in reducing search time. The index table contains n_t rows and 3 columns containing the tokens, file identifiers, relevance score of each file with respect to the token. The tokens are represented as a set of n values $T = (t1, t2, t3, \ldots, tn)$. The proposed scheme creates an inverted index having file id, index term and relevance scores. In contrast to vector space matrix it creates index as shown in figure below.

Whenever a data owner uploads a new file or deletes an existing file on the cloud server the server updates the relevance scores. If there is any change or modification in an already existing file a new copy of file is created with a new file identifier and older one is automatically removed from the database (Table 2).

Table 2. Index Structure for proposed scheme

Term	File Id	Rel. Score
Network	F1	0.996
Network	F2	0.993
Network	F3	0.234
Network	F4	0.034
Species	F1	0.087
Species	F2	0.876
Species	F4	0.456
Technology	F1	0.017
Foundation	F1	0.523
Foundation	F3	0.466
Domain	F1	1.987

7 Experimental Evaluation

We created an experimental evaluation for generating the index using vector space model and our proposed scheme for overall performance evaluation on a real data set: National Science Foundation Research Awards Abstracts 1990–2003 [12]. Our experiment environment includes data owner, data users and a cloud server. We used c#. Net platform on a windows 7 machine with core i5 processor. The doubly encrypted index, I' and the encrypted collection of files F' is stored on the commercial public cloud on a virtual instance hired from Microsoft Azure. The client application was installed on a machine(with windows 7 operating system and core i5 processor) and overall scenario was simulated on c#. Net platform.

We evaluated the performance based on following parameters:

a) **Time to Generate Index**

Time taken to create the inverted index and to calculate respective relevance scores is taken into consideration here.

In a vector space model, a term document incidence matrix is created where each term represents a new dimension to the document vector. Hence, the complexity of creating such a vector is of the order $O(D \times T)$. Where D represents the number of document to be outsourced and T represents the number of tokens to be uploaded in the index. For 5 documents having 500 tokens vector space model requires 2500 elements to be uploaded. Whereas, for the inverted index created for the proposed scheme the complexity is of the order $O(nt \times 3)$, where nt represents the number of rows in the index for T number of tokens and there are 3 columns in the generated index. For 5 documents having 500 tokens, the number of terms (representing number of rows) in index is 643, the proposed scheme needs to upload 1929 elements (Fig. 3).

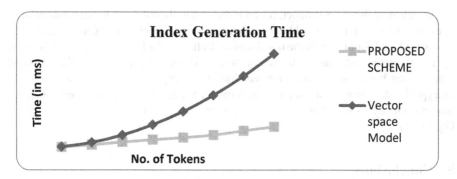

Fig. 3. Time taken to generate index on the scale of number of tokens.

For 5 documents having 500 tokens vector space model requires 2500 elements to be uploaded it takes 142 ms to generate the index. Whereas, for the inverted index created for the proposed scheme the complexity is of the order O (nt × 3). For same number of documents having same number of tokens, the proposed scheme needs to upload 1929 elements can be uploaded in 129 ms. Whereas, with D = 1,000 having approximately 20000 tokens D × T i.e. 1,000 × 20000 = 20,00,000 (approx) elements and these elements takes 1852 s for index generation. For the same set of 1000 files, with 20000 distinct tokens, having approximately 300000 terms, C = 3, nt × C = 300000 × 3 = 9,00,000 elements takes 568 s to compute an index generation in proposed scheme. Hence vector space model, index generation time is more in comparison with proposed scheme.

b) **Score Calculation on retrieval (Search Efficiency)**

In the ScoreCalculate stage, for vector space model, dot product of the query vector from the query with each row in the encrypted index I' is calculated by the cloud server (Fig. 4).

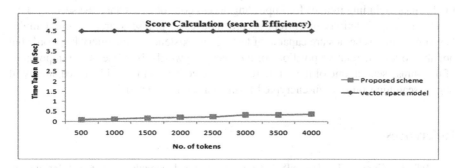

Fig. 4. Time taken to search queried keywords based on the number of tokens.

To calculate the inner product, for an n-dimensional query vector, each row needs n multiplications and n $-$ 1 additions. Hence, the complexity to calculate relevance scores is O(nm) for m files in the document collection and n keywords in the collection.

For the proposed scheme, no vector product is being generated and the proposed scheme uses binary search trees for searching the encrypted queried keywords in the encrypted index, hence for j number of terms in the encrypted request generated, the time complexity to search the required keywords and calculate the relevance scores is O(j(log nt)).

8 Conclusions

Rank ordered information retrieval in a secure way according to the relevance of documents to the users of data outsourced to the cloud is one of the major issues in cloud computing environment. A detailed survey of existing IR schemes was done. Retrieving data efficiently from cloud is one of the major issues, which makes the clients reluctant to store their data in cloud environment. Searching over encrypted data has been made possible by using vector space model and inverted indexes. For, VSM, queries and documents are converted to vectors in encrypted form and their dot product of relevance scores is calculated using the cosine similarity algorithm that provides the users with relevant documents. Number of encryption schemes could be applied such as OPE (order preserving encryption), homomorphic encryption etc. to encrypt the data and use the vector space information retrieval model. The proposed scheme creates an inverted index that makes information retrieval possible to the user comparatively faster, simpler in a secure way than using a vector space model for index generation. The proposed scheme is not only secured but has reduced the time complexity and space complexity to much larger extent. In contrast to earlier proposed schemes the proposed one can be applied to huge datasets also. The simulation results show that the vector space model for indexing does not works effectively for huge datasets and take huge time that becomes out of scope for calculations on the application created. The proposed scheme works for text files only. This could be extended to support various file formats including images for improving access control to enhance the security. One of the missing functions in current secure indexes is phrase search. Current multi-keyword search schemes are capable of testing the existence of the query keywords but not able to tell the relative positions of the query keywords. Because of the importance of the phrase search, one of the future research objectives is to provide the capability of phrase searching on data in encrypted form in a secure manner.

References

1. Mell, P., Grance, T.: The NIST definition of cloud computing, National Institute of Standarads and technology, vol. 53, no. 6, pp. 1–50 (2009)
2. Wang, C., Cao, N., Li, J., Ren, K., Lou, W.: Secure ranked keyword search over encrypted cloud data. In: Proceedings IEEE 30th International Conference on Distributed Computing Systems, ICDCS 2010, pp. 253–262 (2010)

3. Song, D., Wanger, D., Perrig, A.: Practical techniques for searches on encrypted data. In: Proceedings IEEE symposium Security and Privacy, Washington DC, pp. 44–56 (2000)
4. Wang, C., Cao, N., Ren, K., Lou, W.: Enabling secure and efficient ranked keyword search over outsourced cloud data. IEEE Trans. Parallel Distrib. Syst. 23(8), 1467–1479 (2012)
5. Wang, C., Cao, N., Li, J., Ren, K., Lou, W.: Privacy-preserving multikeyword ranked search over encrypted cloud data. In: Proceedings IEEE INFOCOM (2010)
6. Yu, J., Lu, P., Zhu, Y., Xue, G., Li, M.: Toward secure multikeyword top-k retrieval over encrypted cloud data. IEEE Trans. Dependable Secure Comput. 10(4), 239–250 (2013)
7. Arora, V., Tyagi, S.S.: Analysis of symmetric searchable encryption over encrypted cloud data. Int. J. Comput. Appl. (0975-8887) 127(12), 46–51 (2015)
8. Joy, E.C., Indira, K.: Multi keyword ranked search over encrypted cloud data. Int. J. Appl. Eng. Res. 9(20), 7149–7176 (2014)
9. Singhal, A.: Modern information retrieval: a brief overview. IEEE Data Eng. Bull. 24(4), 35–43 (2001)
10. Manning, C.D., Raghavan, P., Schutze, H.: An Introduction to Information Retrieval. Cambridge University Press, Cambridge (2008). ISBN: 0521865719. Online edition©
11. Arora, V., Tyagi, S.S.: An efficient multi-keyword symmetric searchable encryption scheme for secure data outsourcing. Int. J. Comput. Netw. Inf. Secur. 8(11), 65–71 (2016)
12. NSF Research Awards Abstracts 1990–2003 (2013). http://kdd.ics.uciedu/databases/nsfabs/nsfawards.html
13. Pallickara, S.L., Pallickara, S., Zupanski, M.: Towards efficient data search and subsetting of large-scale atmospheric datasets. Future Gener. Comput. Syst. 28(1), 112–118 (2012)
14. Raghavendra S., Geeta C.M., Buyya R., Venugopal K.R., Iyengar S.S., Patnaik L. M.: MSIGT: most significant index generation technique for cloud environment. In: Proceedings of the 2015 Annual IEEE India Conference, INDICON 2015, Delhi, India, pp 17–20 (2015)
15. Alam, B., Doja, M.N., Mongia, S.: Analysis of security issues for cloud computing. Int. J. Comput. Sci. Inf. Secur. 11(9), 117–125 (2013)
16. van Dijk, M., Gentry, C., Halevi, S., Vaikuntanathan, V.: Fully homomorphic encryption over the integers. In: Gilbert, H. (ed.) EUROCRYPT 2010. LNCS, vol. 6110, pp. 24–43. Springer, Heidelberg (2010). https://doi.org/10.1007/978-3-642-13190-5_2
17. Boldyreva, A., Chenette, N., Lee, Y., O'Neill, A.: Order-preserving symmetric encryption. In: Joux, A. (ed.) EUROCRYPT 2009. LNCS, vol. 5479, pp. 224–241. Springer, Heidelberg (2009). https://doi.org/10.1007/978-3-642-01001-9_13
18. Wang, C., Cao, N., Ren, K., Lou, W.: Enabling secure and efficient ranked keyword search over outsourced cloud data. IEEE Trans. Parallel Distrib. Syst. 23(8), 1469 (2012)
19. Gupta, B.B.: Analysis of various security issues and challenges in cloud computing environment: a survey. In: Gupta, B., Agrawal, D.P., Yamaguchi, S. (eds.) Handbook of Research on Modern Cryptographic Solutions for Computer and Cyber Security. IGI Global, Hershey (2016). https://doi.org/10.4018/978-1-5225-0808-3.ch011
20. Ibtihal, M., Driss, E.O., Hassan, N.: Homomorphic encryption as a service for outsourced images in mobile cloud computing environment. Int. J. Cloud Appl. Comput. (IJCAC) 7(2), 27–40 (2017)

Authentication of User in Connected Governance Model

Ayanabha Ghosh[1], Tathagato Das[1], Sayan Majumder[1],
and Abhishek Roy[2,3,4](✉)

[1] Adamas University, Kolkata, India
ghoshayanabha@gmail.com, tathagatodas@yahoo.com,
majumdersayan48@gmail.com
[2] Department of Computer Science and Engineering,
Adamas University, Kolkata, India
dr.aroy@yahoo.com
[3] Member (No#111299), International Association of Engineers,
Hong Kong, Hong Kong
[4] Member (No#L/0509), Cryptology Research Society of India, ISI Kolkata,
Kolkata, India
https://sites.google.com/site/diaryofaroy/

Abstract. India is striving hard to deliver Citizen centric electronic services within the affordability of populace. For this purpose, service providers have to rely upon internet as public communication medium, which is susceptible to infringement attempts of adversary. To resolve this issue, vital resources like user information should be managed in secure manner. As the state administrator, Government have to play a vital role to gain the trust of user over this electronic service delivery model. To ensure Privacy, Integrity, Non-Repudiation, Authentication (PINA) of electronic transaction, each user (i.e. Citizen) should be uniquely identified from the initial stage of transaction. This approach will prevent unauthorized access of adversary and hence services can be successfully delivered to the intended recipient only. To achieve this objective, in this paper authors have proposed a 3-level user authentication scheme during Citizen to Government to Bank (i.e. C2G2B) type of electronic transaction carried out through a Citizen centric multivariate smart card based connected service delivery model.

Keywords: User authentication · Class Diagram · Sequence Diagram

1 Introduction

Due to limited availability of amenities, developing nations like India have to strive severely for delivery of Citizen centric services within affordable budget at the doorstep of populace. Information and Communication Technology (ICT) based approaches may facilitate electronic service delivery models with enhanced effectiveness in terms of time, cost and accuracy. To implement it, identity of its user should be established with utmost security, so that adversaries are barred from their infringement attempts. This concepts becomes more user friendly in

© Springer Nature Singapore Pte Ltd. 2020
U. Batra et al. (Eds.): REDSET 2019, CCIS 1230, pp. 110–122, 2020.
https://doi.org/10.1007/978-981-15-5830-6_10

nature, if any specific instrument (like smart card) act as single window interface to deliver multivariate electronic facilities. As shown in Fig. 1 author have already proposed a Multipurpose Electronic Card (MEC) which acts as Citizen centric single window interface to access multivariate electronic services. As shown in Fig. 2 of this paper, authors have expanded the user authentication scheme using One Time Password (OTP), Username and Password and Biometric parameter (like finger print) during Citizen to Government to Bank (i.e. C2G2B) type of electronic transaction.

Section 2 states the current state of work. Section 3 describes the proposed multi level user authentication scheme. Section 4 states the conclusion drawn from this research work thereby exploring its future scope.

2   Current Status of Work

Figure 1 shows the Citizen centric multifaceted smart card [10] based Cloud Governance model, where Multipurpose Electronic Card (MEC) [1–4] serves as single window interface to transmit **SERVICE REQUEST** of user (i.e. Citizen) and receive corresponding **SERVICE RESPONSE**. Multiparty (i.e. Citizen, Government, Third Party Service provider) based Citizen to Government (C2G) type of transaction shown through Fig. 1 is further explained below:

1. **Citizen Side:**
   (a) Citizen initiates the electronic transaction using Multipurpose Electronic Card (MEC).
   (b) Citizen transmit unique parameters for verification of its identity [5].
   (c) Citizen sends SERVICE REQUEST through path - 1 of Fig. 1 to Government through Internet.
2. **Government Side:**
   (a) Government receives unique parameters and SERVICE REQUEST of citizen through Internet. At this stage of operation, Intrusion Detection System [1] may be used to prevent unauthorized attempts of intruder.
   (b) Government verifies the identity of user. As an output, any one of the following situations may arise:
      i Situation - 1 (i.e. Success): In case of successful verification [7], the electronic transaction proceeds towards next phase of operation through Step - 2c.
      ii Situation - 2 (i.e. Failure): In case of unsuccessful verification, electronic transaction is aborted and user (i.e. Citizen) is subsequently notified by system timeout through path - 2 of Fig. 1.
   (c) Cloud Server analyze the type of service requested by user (i.e. Citizen) and forward it through Firewalls to respective server of Cloud Governance [9] System. For instance, SERVICE REQUEST for banking, education, healthcare, employment will proceed towards Bank Server, Education Server, Health Server, Employment Server respectively.

3. **Third party service provider:**
   (a) The Third party service provider receives SERVICE REQUEST send by respective service server of proposed Cloud Governance model.
   (b) Finally, Third party service provider executes SERVICE REQUEST of user (i.e. Citizen) to generate desired output. For instance, as shown in Fig. 2, banking transaction will be executed by specific bank mentioned in the SERVICE REQUEST of user (i.e. Citizen).

However, the above mentioned Cloud Governance model have following scope of improvements:

- Intrusion Detection System [1] may be used to prevent illicit attempts of intruder.
- Hybrid security protocol may be proposed using One Time Password (OTP), Username and Password and Biometric [6,8] parameter to prevent infringement attempts of intruders. Authors have explained it thoroughly in Sect. 3 of this paper.
- Steganographic security protocols may be considered for transmission of sensitive information through private and public clouds.

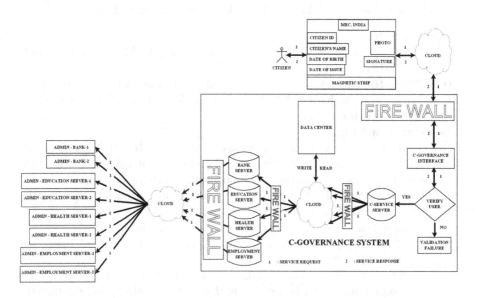

Fig. 1. Conceptual diagram of Cloud Governance model

3   Multi Level User Authentication Scheme

3 level user authentication scheme proposed for this cloud service delivery model is described through following diagrams:

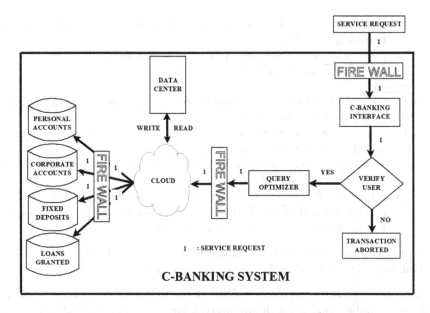

Fig. 2. Conceptual diagram for Cloud Banking model.

1. Figure 3 shows the Entity Relationship Diagram (ERD) of proposed security system to identify primary entities (i.e. Citizen, Government, C-Governance Interface, etc) and their inter-relationship.
2. Figure 4 shows the static structure of our security system through Class Diagram.
3. Figure 5 shows the sequence of operations using Sequence Diagram.

The proposed 3 level user authentication scheme is further described below:

1. **Level - 1:**
   (a) User (i.e. Citizen) transmit its unique Multipurpose Electronic Card (MEC) number to C-Governance server through public cloud.
   (b) Government verifies the unique parameter of Citizen. As an output, any one of the following situations may arise:
       i Situation - 1 (i.e. Failure): In case of unsuccessful verification the transaction is aborted.
       ii Situation - 2 (i.e. Success): In case of successful verification, Government will send an One Time Password (OTP) directly to the registered phone number of user.
   (c) User (i.e. Citizen) submits One Time Password (OTP) to Government through public cloud to proceed towards Step - 2a.
2. **Level - 2:**
   (a) User (i.e. Citizen) submit Username and Password to Government for verification.
   (b) Government verifies the unique parameters of Citizen. As an output, any one of the following situations may arise:

  i Situation - 3 (i.e. Failure): In case of unsuccessful verification the transaction is aborted.

  ii Situation - 4 (i.e. Success): In case of successful verification the electronic transaction proceed towards Step - 3a.

3. **Level - 3:**

 (a) User (i.e. Citizen) submits unique biometric parameter (like fingerprint) to Government through public cloud.

 (b) Government verifies unique parameter of Citizen. As an output, any one of the following situations may arise:

  i Situation - 5 (i.e. Failure): In case of unsuccessful verification the transaction is aborted.

  ii Situation - 6 (i.e. Success): In case of successful verification, Government permits user (i.e. Citizen) to avail desired electronic service like Cloud Banking, which is shown in Fig. 2.

Figure 2 shows the Citizen to Government to Bank (i.e. C2G2B) type of Cloud Banking transaction, which is further described below:

1. Cloud Banking Interface receives SERVICE REQUEST of user (i.e. Citizen) through public cloud from the proposed Cloud Governance model shown in Fig. 1. At this stage of operation, Intrusion Detection System [1] may be used to prevent the unauthorized attempts of intruder.

2. Bank authority verifies the identity of user (i.e. Client). As an output, any one of the following situations may arise:

 (a) Situation - 7 (i.e. Failure): In case of unsuccessful verification, the transaction is aborted.

 (b) Situation - 8 (i.e Success): In case of successful verification, the Cloud Banking transaction proceeds towards Step - 3.

3. Query Optimizer analyses SERVICE REQUEST of user in terms of Structured Query Language (SQL) to generate database queries.

4. DATA READ and DATA WRITE operations are performed over Data Center to record the banking transaction conducted so far.

5. At final stage of Cloud Banking transaction, specific bank servers like Personal Accounts, Corporate Accounts, Fixed Deposits, Loan Granted, etc executes SERVICE REQUEST of user (i.e. Client).

Figure 3 shows the Entity Relationship Diagram of Citizen to Government to Bank (i.e. C2G2B) type of transaction, which is further described below:

1. Primary entities:

 a. Citizen. b. C-Governance Interface. c. Government. d. Server. e. Database. f. Bank Server. g. Education Server. h. Employment Server. i. Health Server.

2. Interrelationship:

 (a) Citizen Interact with Government through C-Government Interface.

 (b) Government has a server.

 (c) Server can be of various types like Bank Server, Education Server, Employment Server and Health Server.

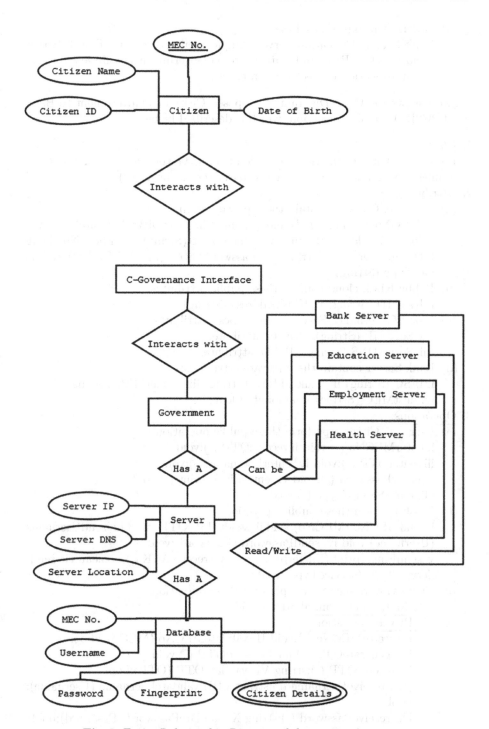

Fig. 3. Entity Relationship Diagram of the proposed system.

(d) Government has a Database.

(e) Bank Server, Education Server, Employment Server and Health Server performs Data Read and Data Write on Government Database after successful execution of electronic transaction.

Figure 4 shows the Class Diagram of proposed Citizen to Government to Bank (i.e. C2G2B) type of transaction, which is described below:

1. <u>Class:</u>
   i. User (i.e. Citizen) ii. Kiosk (i.e. Cloud) iii. C-Governance Server (i.e. Government) iv. Bank Server (i.e. Third party service provider).

2. <u>Attributes:</u>
   (a) User (i.e. Citizen) contain these private attributes:
   i. MECNo (String) ii. Name (String) iii. DateOfBirth (Date) iv. Age (Float) v. Address (String) vi. Fingerprint (String) vii. PhoneNo (Long Int) viii. Username (String) ix. Password (String) x. ACK (Bool) xi. serviceType (String)

   (b) Public Kiosk cloud contain these public attributes:
   i. KioskID (String) ii. KioskAddress (String)

   (c) Cloud Governance Server contain these attributes:
   i ServerIP (String): Private attribute.
   ii ServerDNS (String): Public attribute.

   (d) Bank Server contain these private attributes:
   i. IFSC (String) ii. bankAddress (String) iii. senderMEC (String) iv. destMEC (String) v. amount (Float)

3. <u>Operations:</u>
   (a) User (i.e. Citizen) perform these public operations:
   i. enterMECNo ( ):void ii.receiveOTP ( ):void
   iii. enterOTP ( ):void iv. enterUsername ( ):void
   v. enterPassword ( ):void vi. enterFingerprint ( ):void
   vii. enterServiceType ( ):void

   (b) Kiosk perform these public operations:
   i. sendMECNo (MECNo):void ii. sendOTP (OTP):void iii. sendUsername (Username):void iv. sendPassword (Password):void
   v. sendFingerprint (Fingerprint):void vi. receiveACK ( ):boolean vii. sendServiceType (serviceType):void

   (c) Cloud Governance Server perform these operations:
   i <u>Public operation:</u> abort ( ):void
   ii <u>Private operations:</u>
   I. receiveMECNo ( ):void II. validateMECNo (MECNo):bool
   III. generateOTP ( ):int IV. sendOTP ( ):void
   V. receiveOTP ( ):string VI. validateOTP (OTP):bool
   VII. receiveUsername ( ):string VIII. validateUsername (Username): bool
   IX. receivePassword ( ):string X. validatePassword (Password):bool

XI. receiveFingerprint ( ):void XII. validateFingerprint (Fingerprint): bool

XIII. receiveServiceType ( ):void XIV. routeToService (serviceType): void

(d) Bank Server perform these operations:

  i Public operations: a. receiveIFSC ( ):void b. validateIFSC (IFSC): bool c. receiveAmount ( ):void d. checkBalance (MECNo):bool e. showBalance (MECNo):float f. abort ( ):void g. transaction (sender-MEC, destMEC, amount):bool

  ii Private operations: a. receiveIFSC ( ):void b. receiveAmount ( ):void c. validateIFSC (bankIFSC):bool

The attributes mentioned above may be expanded further based on real time application of proposed model. Figure 5 shows the Sequence Diagram of our proposed Cloud Banking transaction, which is described below:

1. Enter MECNo ( ): As a part of **Level - 1** user authentication scheme already explained in Sect. 3, user (i.e. Citizen) enter its unique Multipurpose Electronic Card (MEC) number through public Kiosk cloud.

2. Send MECNo ( ): Public Kiosk cloud send Multipurpose Electronic Card (MEC) number of user (i.e. Citizen) to Government.

3. Validate MECNo ( ): Government verifies Multipurpose Electronic Card (MEC) number of user. As an output, any one of the following two situations may arise:
   Situation - 1 (i.e. Success): Successful validation + sendOTP ( ): In case of successful verification, Government sends One Time Password (OTP) to Citizen and transaction will proceed towards Step - 4.
   Situation - 2 (i.e. Failure): Negative Acknowledgement (NAK) + abort ( ): In case of unsuccessful verification, Government sends Negative Acknowledgement (i.e. NAK) to abort electronic transaction.

4. Request to enterOTP ( ): Public Kiosk cloud request Citizen to enter One Time Password (OTP), which was send directly by Government to the registered mobile number of Citizen during Situation - 1 of Step - 3.

5. enterOTP ( ): Citizen submit One Time Password (OTP) to Public Kiosk cloud.

6. sendOTP ( ): Public Kiosk cloud transmits One Time Password (OTP) of Citizen to Government.

7. validateOTP ( ): Government verifies One Time Password (OTP) of Citizen. As an output, any one of the following two situations may arise:
   Situation - 3 (i.e. Success): Success + Request Username and Password: In case of successful validation, Government permits electronic transaction to proceed further through Step - 8. and requests Citizen to provide Username and Password.
   Situation - 4 (i.e. Failure): NAK + abort ( ): In case of unsuccessful validation, Government will sends Negative Acknowledgement (i.e. NAK) to abort electronic transaction.

8. Request Username, Password ( ): As a part of **Level - 2** user authentication scheme already explained in Sect. 3 and on behalf of Government, Public Kiosk cloud instruct Citizen to enter Username and Password.

9. Enter Username, Password ( ): In reply, Citizen enters its Username, Password to Public Kiosk cloud.

10. Send Username, Password ( ): Public Kiosk cloud transmit username and password of citizen to Government.

11. Validate Username, Password ( ): Government verifies Username and Password of citizen. As an output, any one of the following two situations may arise:

    Situation - 5 (i.e. Success): Success+Request Fingerprint ( ): In case of successful validation, Government permits Citizen to enter its unique biometric parameter like fingerprint to proceed towards Step - 12.

    Situation - 6 (i.e. Failure): NAK + abort ( ): In case of unsuccessful validation of Username and Password of Citizen, Government will send NAK to abort the transaction.

12. Request Fingerprint ( ): As a part of **Level - 3** user authentication scheme already explained in Sect. 3 and on behalf of Government Public Kiosk cloud instruct Citizen to enter its biometric parameter like fingerprint, etc.

13. Enter Fingerprint ( ): In reply, Citizen enter its fingerprint.

14. Send Fingerprint ( ): Public Kiosk cloud transmit fingerprint of Citizen to Government.

15. Validate Fingerprint ( ): Government verifies the fingerprint of Citizen. As an output, any one of the following two situations may arise:

    Situation - 7 (i.e. Success): As a part of Citizen to Government to Bank (i.e. C2G2B) type of electronic transaction already shown through Fig. 1 and Fig. 2, Government instruct Citizen to enter destination Multipurpose Electronic Card (MEC) number and IFSC Code to identify the intended recipient to proceed towards Step - 16.

    Situation - 8 (i.e. Failure): NAK + abort ( ): In case of unsuccessful validation, Government sends Negative Acknowledgement (i.e. NAK) to abort the electronic transaction.

16. Request to enter MEC No.: Public Kiosk cloud request Citizen to enter Multipurpose Electronic Card (MEC) number and IFSC Code of the intended recipient.

17. Enter Destination MEC No, IFSC Code: In reply, Citizen enters the destination Multipurpose Electronic Card (MEC) number and IFSC Code.

18. Send Destination MEC No, IFSC Code: Public Kiosk cloud forward the destination Multipurpose Electronic Card (MEC) of recipient and IFSC Code to Government.

19. Validate Destination MEC No. ( ): Government verifies the destination Multipurpose Electronic Card (MEC) number. As the initial stage of electronic banking transaction, both Government and Bank authority performs verification of intended recipient.

20. Send IFSC Code: Government transmit destination IFSC Code to Bank authority.

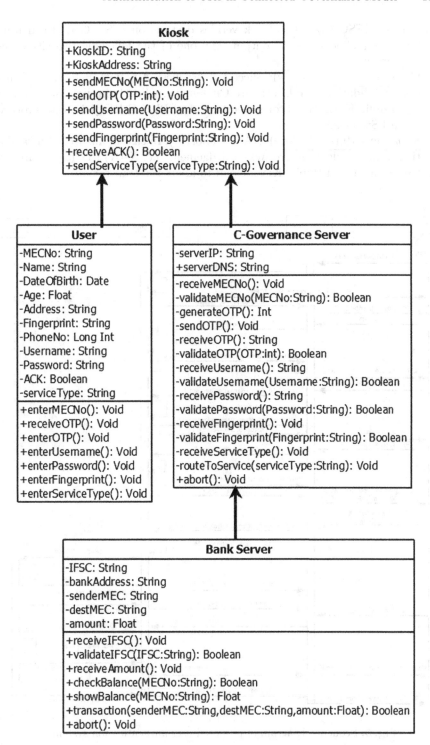

Fig. 4. Class Diagram of 3 level user authentication scheme.

21. Validate IFSC Code ( ): Bank verifies destination IFSC Code to identify intended recipient. As an output, any one of the following two situations may arise:

    Situation - 9 (i.e. Success): Success + Request Amount( ): In case of successful validation, Bank intimate Citizen (i.e. Client) through Government and Public Kiosk cloud for generation of SERVICE REQUEST to proceed toward Step - 22.

    Situation - 10 (i.e. Failure): NAK + abort ( ): In case of unsuccessful validation, Bank sends Negative Acknowledgement (i.e. NAK) to Citizen through Government and Public Kiosk cloud to abort the transaction.

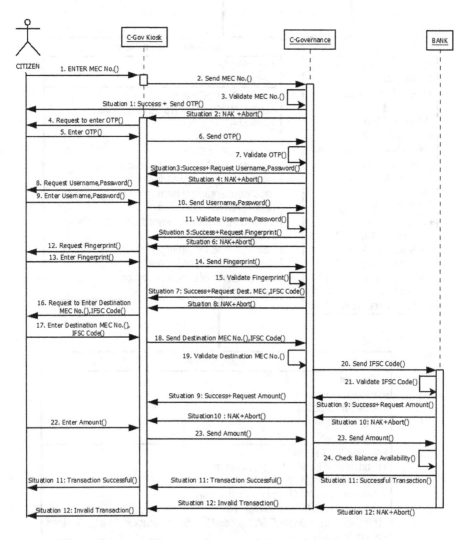

Fig. 5. Sequence Diagram of proposed user authentication system.

22. Enter Amount ( ): Citizen send SERVICE REQUEST to Public Kiosk cloud.
23. Send Amount ( ): Public Kiosk cloud transmit SERVICE REQUEST to Bank through Government.
24. Check Balance ( ): Bank verifies multiple parameters for execution of SERVICE REQUEST. At this stage of operation, any one of the following two situations may arise:

    Situation - 11 (i.e. Success): Successful transaction ( ): In case of successful verification, Citizen to Government to Bank (C2G2B) type of transaction is completed successfully, which is immediately notified to Citizen. The secured transmission of notification to Citizen may be considered as future scope of this work.

    Situation - 12 (i.e Failure): NAK + abort( ): In case of unsuccessful verification, Bank sends Negative Acknowledgement (i.e. NAK) to Citizen through Government and Public Kiosk cloud to abort Citizen to Government to Bank (i.e. C2G2B) type of electronic transaction.

As banking transaction contain multiple types of operation like loan grant, loan repay, etc, the proposed Citizen to Government to Bank (i.e. C2G2B) model have wide window open for further research work.

4   Conclusion

In order to provide prompt, reliable and budget friendly electronic services to the doorstep of populace, we have proposed this multivariate electronic service delivery model [1,2]. To enhance its security features in this paper we have explained multilevel user authentication scheme. To provide more facilities to Citizen, following aspects may be explored for future research work:

1. Internet Of Things (IoT) may be used to provide user friendly interface.
2. The concept of Distributed Database may be used to demonstrate successful database operations.
3. Block chain may be applied to track of all electronic transactions carried out by Citizen.
4. Network based Intrusion Detection System (NIDS) may be used to prevent the illicit attempts of adversaries.
5. Hardware based implementation of proposed Multipurpose Electronic Card (MEC) may be considered as future scope of work.
6. Finally, SERVICE RESPONSE should be delivered to end user (i.e. Citizen) in secure manner.

References

1. Biswas, S, Roy, A.: An intrusion detection system based secured electronic service delivery model. In: 3rd International Conference on Electronics Communication and Aerospcace Technology (ICECA 2019), pp. 1316–1321, IEEE, India, June 2019. https://doi.org/10.1109/ICECA.2019.8822016

2. Roy, A: Smart delivery of multifaceted services through connected governance model. In: 3rd International Conference on Computing Methodologies and Communication (ICCMC 2019), pp. 476–482, IEEE, India, March 2019. https://doi.org/10.1109/ICCMC.2019.8819851

3. Khatun, R., Bandopadhyay, T., Roy, A.: Data modelling for e-voting system using smart card based e-governance system. Int. J. Inf. Eng. Electron. Bus. **9**, 45–52 (2017). https://doi.org/10.5815/ijieeb.2017.02.06

4. Roy, A., Karforma, S.: UML based modeling of ECDSA for secured and smart e-governance system. In: Computer Science & Information Technology (CS & IT-CSCP 2013), National Conference on Advancement of Computing in Engineering Research (ACER13), pp. 207–222, March 2013. https://doi.org/10.5121/csit.2013.3219. ISSN 2231–5403, ISBN 978-1-921987-11-3

5. Jin, H., Debiao, H., Jianhua, C.: An identity based digital signature from ECDSA. In: 2010 Second International Workshop on Education Technology and Computer Science, vol. 1, pp. 627–630, March 2010. https://doi.org/10.1109/etcs.2010.159

6. Yahaya, Y.H., Isa, M.R.M., Aziz, M.I.: Fingerprint biometrics authentication on smart card. In: 2009 Second International Conference on Computer and Electrical Engineering (IEEE), vol. 2, pp. 671–673, December 2009. https://doi.org/10.1109/ICCEE.2009.155

7. Prabu, M., Shanmugalakshmi, R.: A comparative analysis of signature schemes in a new approach of variant on ecdsa. In: 2009 International Conference on Information and Multimedia Technology (IEEE), pp. 491–494, December 2009. https://doi.org/10.1109/ICIMT.2009.65

8. Lin, Y., Maozhi, X., Zhiming, Z.: Digital signature systems based on smart card and fingerprint feature. J. Syst. Eng. Electron. **18**(4), 825–834 (2007)

9. Nkomo, P.T., Terzoli, A., Muyingi, H., Krishna Rao, G.S.V.R.: Smart card initiative for south african e-governance - a study. In: 2006 8th International Conference Advanced Communication Technology (IEEE), pp. 2231–2232, February 2006. https://doi.org/10.1109/ICACT.2006.206443

10. Civico, F.D., Peinado, A.: Low complexity smart card-based physical access control system over IP networks. In: 12th IEEE Mediterranean Electrotechnical Conference, pp. 799–802, May 2004. https://doi.org/10.1109/MELCON.2004.1347052

Future of Data Hiding: A Walk Through Conventional to Network Steganography

Rohit Tanwar[1,2(✉)], Sona Malhotra[1], and Kulvinder Singh[1]

[1] UIET Kurukshetra University, Kurukshetra, India
rohit.tanwar.cse@gmail.com,
sonamalhotrakuk@gmail.com, kshanda@rediffmail.com
[2] University of Petroleum and Energy Studies, Dehradun, India

Abstract. In current scenario where government agencies are supporting digital communication at a heavy rate and data storage and communication time are being improved consequently, as a side effect, bad minds are getting more chances of vulnerabilities. Steganography and cryptography has been leading the front by concealing existence and meaning of the data respectively since a long time. With the promotion of packet switched networks like internet, there opens more doors towards moving to another level of steganography where instead of using traditional digital data as cover file, some network protocol or some other services plays the role of cover channel. In this paper various works recently done in the area of different categories of network security has been discussed and analyzed so as to find scope for future research.

Keywords: Internet · Network steganography · Protocol · Payload · Covert

1 Introduction

Steganography is a strategy of communicating messages securely. The strategy has turned out to be more secure on the grounds that the presence of secret data got concealed by inserting it into a suitable cover file. Based on type of cover file, steganography is classified into various kinds [1].

With regards to contemporary data and correspondence innovation, a big portion of the research work done was dedicated to strategies for concealing secret data in numerical information, text and images [2] transmitted between imparting parties. Such strategies are for the most part autonomous of the logic used in communication and mechanism — the protocols being followed in communication — which are utilized as a part of specific correspondence systems. Network steganography contrasts from such strategies in that it in view of utilizing — "controlling" — particular communication protocols' highlights to transmit secret data [3].

The majority of the data concealing strategies that might be utilized to transmit cover along with hidden data in transmission systems is designated by specific name called network steganography. K. Szczypiorski has the honor of presenting it first time in the year 2003. In opposition to run of the traditional steganographic techniques that makes use of digital media file like images file, audio file and video files as an embedding cover for securing information (steganogram) which may be considered as

© Springer Nature Singapore Pte Ltd. 2020
U. Batra et al. (Eds.): REDSET 2019, CCIS 1230, pp. 123–132, 2020.
https://doi.org/10.1007/978-981-15-5830-6_11

steganography 1.0. However, network steganography-making use of communication protocols, control components and their fundamental intrinsic functionality to hide information. Thus, such strategies are very tough to even detect and more tough to eliminate. Network steganography in this context with these additions is termed as steganography 2.0 [4].

Different network security methods can be classified as shown in figure (Fig. 1):

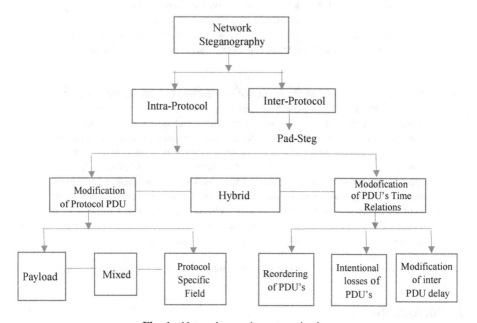

Fig. 1. Network security categorization

2 Literature Review

These are the work done by researchers as per the network security classification based on protocols specified in [3].

2.1 MLS (Multi-level Steganography) [6]

As the name suggests, two or more than two methods of steganography are combined so as to give combined and better results for data hiding problems. It can be viewed as providing secret cover to the another cover which is itself a carrier for some secret information.

2.2 HICCUPS (Hidden Communication System for Corrupted Network) [7]

HICCUPS is categorized as a steganographic method using intra-protocol approach. In this method, some specific fields or content of the frame protocol are modified. In this method, frames with wrong checksums are used intentionally to carry out secret communication. This technique is highly beneficial for Wireless Local Area Networks (WLAN's). It was the first steganographic tool recognized worldwide for wireless LAN.

2.3   LACK (Lost Audio Packets Steganography) [8]

LACK is an intra-protocol steganography technique based on hybrid approach that exploits the time relations of voice packets as well as their contents. At the transmitter end, few pre-determined voice packets are delayed intentionally in their transmission. Now as a general practice these packets having considerable delay are discarded by the general receiver who is not the intended one as a part of secret communication. The contents of these packets which are delayed intentionally are used to transmit secret data. Now only the known receivers who are aware of the technique would extract the data. For others, it will remain hidden.

2.4   PadSteg (Padding Steganography) [9]

Like as previous tools, it is also an inter-protocol steganographic method that exploits the existing relationship between the protocols of the TCP/IP suite to establish secret communication. Few examples of such protocols are ARP, TCP, UDP and ICMP protocols. This method is generally used for LANs. This technique makes use of vulnerability called Etherleak. Due to this, the padding is not always set to zero in Ethernet frames. For additional safety, PadSteg uses the mechanism of carrier-protocol hopping. Due to which, it switches among the protocols which are responsible for frame padding.

2.5   RSTEG (Retransmission Steganography) [10]

RSTEG is a network steganography method exploiting intra-protocol approach that uses hybrid technique. This method makes use of so many protocols which employs retransmission of packets. The base line of this method is to avoid sending acknowledgement of few of the packets intentionally. No receipt of the acknowledgement would lead to retransmission of the already received packet. But this time the retransmitted packet would be containing the secret data intended for particular recipient.

2.6   SCTP [11]

SCTP is a network steganography technique which is intra-protocol and based on Multistreaming method. The basic working of this approach is centered around sending subsequent chunks intentionally in between the streams specified by steganogram bits.

2.7   StegSuggest [12]

This tool makes use of Google Suggest service. This service is helpful in google search (web Search) by finding the suitable search phrase as a suggestion to the user. It does so by suggesting some popular phrases while user types which are auto complete. Steg-Suggest makes use of traffic generated through Google Suggest in the form of phrases. The technique works by inserting fresh suggestive words or phrases to the proposal forwarded to the "Google Suggest client". These freshly intruded words are carrier of steganogram bits.

2.8   TranSteg (Transcoding Steganography) [13]

It is the steganographic method making use of IP telephony. As a traditional thinking it is supposed better to compress data before embedding. However in TransSteg, The cover data is to be compressed rather so as to make space for occupying secret data. The method works by finding a codec that would ends up by providing equal voice quality better of lesser size for a given voice stream. Now the original voice sample is encoded as per the discovered codec. Now space cut down by encoding into new codec is filled by the secret data so that original voice sample and the encoded one(including hidden data) should be having same size.

The work in this area started gaining speed since first decade of 21st century. The major contributions in the area of network steganography done in last 10 years were studied and formulated as table in Table 1.

Table 1. Summary of work done in network steganography in last decade

S.N	Year of publication	Authors detail	Title of publication	Points focused
1.	2017	Al-Sharif et al. [14]	On the usefulness of information hiding techniques for wireless sensor networks security	•N/W steganography discussed from authentication as well as attacker point of view for wireless network •Sensory data image as a susceptible domain for N/W steganography applications
2.	2017	Xue et al. [15]	A new network steganographic method based on the transverse multi-protocol collaboration	•Transverse multi-protocol collaboration network steganographic method (TMPCNSM) is proposed •HTTP, FTP and DNS are used as carriers.

(continued)

Table 1. (*continued*)

S.N	Year of publication	Authors detail	Title of publication	Points focused
3.	2016	Szczypiorski and Tyl [16]	MoveSteg: a method of network steganography detection	•Given method for detecting time based N/W steganography over the network under monitoring •Less effective for heavily loaded server
4.	2016	Seo et al. [17]	Network steganography and steganalysis - a concise review	•Commented on shortcomings and novelties of existing network security.y techniques •Highlighted requirement for steganalysis techniques for network steganography
5.	2015	Jankowski et al. [9]	PadSteg: introducing inter-protocol steganography	•First information hiding technique using inter-protocol steganography •ARP, TCP are used combinedly along with the etherleak vulnerability •Approx. 32 bits/s bandwidth achieved
6.	2015	Sekhar et al. [18]	A novel approach for hiding data in videos using network steganography methods	•Use of PRNG's in network protocol for data hiding. •A fake key is used to counter the attacks if any •Min. data recovered by attacker (in case attack succeeds) because of fake key
7.	2014	Wendzel et al. [19]	Hidden and uncontrolled – on the emergence of network steganographic threats	•Highlights potential application of network security for harmful purposes •Throw light on practical use of N/W steganography and its future work

(*continued*)

Table 1. (*continued*)

S.N	Year of publication	Authors detail	Title of publication	Points focused
8.	2013	Singh, Sharma [20]	Framework for efficient secure steganographic communication over network protocols	•Data is hidden in ISN field of TCP header •Before embedding, data is compressed and encrypted first using RSA or AES-128
9.	2012	Fraczek et al. [6]	Multi-level steganography: improving hidden communication in networks	•Use of multi-level steganography •LACK used on upper layer and RTP on lower layer
10.	2011	Zander et al. [21]	Stealthier inter-packet timing covert channels	•Data hidden in inter packet times •Packet content were used for synchronization •100 bits/s data rate acheived
11.	2011	Zander et al. [22]	Capacity of temperature-based covert channels	•Data transmitted by remotely inducing and measuring the temp. of an innocent intermediate node •It was invented to attack servers but can be used in generic way as well •20.5 bits per hour max capacity achieved
12.	2010	Dhanashri et al. [23]	Steganography by hiding data in TCP/IP headers	•Data encrypted using 4th order chaotic system before embedding •Hidden in identification field of IP Header
13.	2010	Szczypiorski, Mazurczyk [24]	Toward network steganography detection	•Discussed the work done so far in N/W security •Tried to focus towards detection methods along with hiding techniques

(*continued*)

Table 1. (*continued*)

S.N	Year of publication	Authors detail	Title of publication	Points focused
14.	2009	Ciobanu et al. [25]	Steganography and cryptography over network protocols	•The tool was able to hide as well as detect. •ISN field of TCP header was used for embedding •Detection module is a linux kernel that works as steganalysis tool as well firewall
15.	2009	Desoky, Younis [26]	Chestega: chess steganography methodology	•Exploits the features of chess game for embedding •No need to employ a stego key. •Feasible to employ authenticated chess cover generated by chessmaster 8000
16.	2008	Lubacz et al. [27]	HIDING DATA IN VoIP	•Introduction to how to hide in network. •LACK,HICCUPS and SIP based VoIP protocols are proposed and described
17.	2008	Mazurczyk, Szczypiorski [8]	Steganography of VoIP streams	• Characterize existing steganography technique to use with VoIP • Proposed technique exploiting unused values and is used for IP, TCP and UDP generally • Proposed another technique called LACK exploiting delayed audio packets.

3 Motivation

Ethical utilization incorporates circumvention of web control and observation by abusive administrations, empowering network or computer scientific strategies and copyright security. It is less realized that steganographic strategies can be likewise used to enhance nature of administration (e.g. protection from packet losses in IP communication), to stretch out communication transfer speed and to give intends to anchor cryptographic key dissemination [5]

The rise of Internet, which is a system based on packet switching, has considerably changed the previously used circuit switched system worldview: The network users using the network itself, and the transport make services or applications and other parameters related to control capacities are not isolated and can be changed by the client. This difference in worldview was amongst of the fundamental reasons of the gigantic growth of the Internet. Be that as it may, these advances likewise presented surely understood issues with nature of services and with securing the network and its prime users from hurtful/undesired obstruction. It is therefore not amazing that the Internet highlighted numerous new choices for undercover correspondence. This perception might be summed up to for all fixed stationed and movable networks as well, and especially to communication protocols, that are winding up progressively differing and complex, and in this manner vulnerable to control. Network steganography methods exploit this vulnerability [3].

4 Measures of Effectiveness of Steganography

Steganography can be measured essentially by three parameters:

1. **Steganographic Bandwidth:** It can be defined as the potential throughput of the hidden messages.
2. **Resistance to Steganalysis:** It is the property by which it is hard to discover the occurrence of any hidden communication.
3. **Robustness:** It can be defined as an extent up to which a cover file can be modified such that the hidden data remain unaltered.

A decent steganographic strategy ought to be as powerful and difficult to identify as would be prudent, while at the same time offering the most elevated data transmission. The three measures are reliant: generally, the higher percentage of the steganographic data transfer capacity, the lower would be the robustness and protection from steganalysis. The protection from steganalysis is generally hard to assess in digits, as it is highly dependent not just on the complexity of the steganographic method used yet additionally on the learning and efficieny of potential observer of the transmission going on [3].

5 Conclusion

Because of the continually expanding many-sided quality of transmission protocol, there is very less uncertainty that novel, better refined steganographic procedures will be made and, as a result, the hazard of being using them for pernicious purposes will be higher. This worry adds new difficulties to the troublesome issue of giving network and data security. An in depth look of the weakness of transmission protocols to a wide range of control (not just for steganographic purposes!) turns into a critical issue.

Research focusing network steganography might be useful in this regard — may bring about helpful rules for a procedure of planning another age of vigorous communication protocol and correspondence network when all is said in done. It is emphatically trusted that the aftereffects of research on organize steganography ought not be viewed as limited to data concealing methods in essence.

References

1. Tanwar, R., Malhotra, S.: Opinion formation based optimization in audio steganography. In: Satapathy, S.C., Joshi, A. (eds.) ICTIS 2017. SIST, vol. 83, pp. 320–325. Springer, Cham (2018). https://doi.org/10.1007/978-3-319-63673-3_39
2. Bender, W., et al.: Techniques for data hiding. IBM Syst. J. **35**(3/4), 313–336 (1996)
3. Lubacz, J., et al.: Principles and overview of network steganography. IEEE Commun. Mag. **22**(5), 225–229 (2014)
4. Web Source: Network steganography and anomaly detection on stegano. https://stegano.net/
5. Huang, Y., et al.: Key distribution over the covert communication based on VoIP. Chinese J. Electr. **20**(2), 357 (2011)
6. Fraczek, W., et al.: Multi-level steganography: improving hidden communication in networks, Cornell University, New York, USA (2012). https://arxiv.org/
7. Szczypiorski, K.: HICCUPS: hidden communication system for corrupted networks. In: Proceedings of 10th International Multi-Conference on Advanced Computer System, Poland, pp. 31–40 (2003)
8. Mazurczyk, W., et al.: Steganography of VoIP streams. In: Proceedings of on the Move Federated Conference and Workshops: the 3rd International Symposium on Information Security, IS 2008, Mexico, pp. 1001–1018 (2008)
9. Jankowski, B., et al.: PadSteg: introducing inter-protocol steganography. Telecommun. Syst. **58**(1), 1011–1111 (2015). https://doi.org/10.1007/s11235-011-9616-z
10. Mazurczyk, W., et al.: RSTEG: retransmission steganography and its detection. Soft Comput. J. **5**, 505–515 (2010). https://doi.org/10.1007/s00500-009-0530-1
11. Fraczek, W., et al.: Stream control transmission protocol steganography. In: 2nd International Workshop on N/W Steganography, IWNS 2010, China (2010)
12. Białczak, P., et al.: Sending hidden data via google suggest. In: Proceedings of 3rd International Workshop on Net. Steganography, IWNS 2011, Prague, Czech Republic (2011)
13. Mazurczyk, W., Szaga, P., Szczypiorski, K.: Using transcoding for hidden communication in IP telephony. Multimedia Tools Appl. **70**(3), 2139–2165 (2011). https://doi.org/10.1007/s11042-012-1224-8
14. Al-Sharif, R., et al.: On the usefulness of information hiding techniques for wireless sensor networks security (2017). https://arxiv.org/pdf/1706.08136v1.pdf
15. Xue, P.F., et al.: A new network steganographic method based on the transverse multi-protocol collaboration. J. Inf. Hiding Multimedia Signal Process. **8**(2), 445–459 (2017). ISSN 2073-4212
16. Szczypiorski, K., et al.: MoveSteg: a method of network steganography detection. Int. J. Electron. Telecommun. **62**(4), 335–341 (2016)
17. Seo, J.O., et al.: Network steganography and steganalysis - a concise review, In: 2nd International Conference on Applied and Theoretical Computing and Communication Technology, iCATccT, Bangalore, pp. 368–371 (2016)

18. Sekhar, A., et al.: A novel approach for hiding data in videos using network steganography methods. Proc. Comput. Sci. **70**, 764–768 (2015)
19. Wendzel, S., Mazurczyk, W., Caviglione, L., Meier, M.: Hidden and Uncontrolled – On the Emergence of Network Steganographic Threats. In: Reimer, H., Pohlmann, N., Schneider, W. (eds.) ISSE 2014 Securing Electronic Business Processes, pp. 123–133. Springer, Wiesbaden (2014). https://doi.org/10.1007/978-3-658-06708-3_9
20. Singh, J., Sharma, L.: Framework for efficient secure steganographic communication over network protocols. Int. J. Adv. Comput. Res. **3**(4), 146–150 (2013)
21. Zander, S., Armitage, G., Branch, P.: Stealthier Inter-packet Timing Covert Channels. In: Domingo-Pascual, J., Manzoni, P., Palazzo, S., Pont, A., Scoglio, C. (eds.) NETWORKING 2011. LNCS, vol. 6640, pp. 458–470. Springer, Heidelberg (2011). https://doi.org/10.1007/978-3-642-20757-0_36
22. Zander, S., et al.: Capacity of temperature-based covert channels. IEEE Commun. Lett. **15**(1), 82–84 (2011)
23. Dhobale, D., et al.: Steganography by hiding data in TCP/IP headers. In: 3rd International Conference on Advanced Computer Theory and Engineering (ICACTE), Chengdu, pp. V4-61–V4-65 (2010)
24. Szczypiorski, K., Mazurczyk, W.: Toward network steganography detection. Telecommun. Syst. **49**, 161–162 (2010). https://doi.org/10.1007/s11235-010-9361-8
25. Ciobanu, R.I., et al.: Steganography and cryptography over network protocols. https://www.researchgate.net/publication/266465363_Steganography_and_Cryptography_Over_Network_Protocols
26. Desoky, A., Younis, M.: Chestega: chess steganography methodology. Secur. Commun. Netw. **2**, 555–566 (2009). https://doi.org/10.1002/sec.99
27. Lubacz, J., Mazurczyk, W., Szczypiorski, K.: Hiding data in VoIP (2008). https://www.researchgate.net/profile/Krzysztof_Szczypiorski/publication/235059356_Hiding_Data_in_VoIP/links/0c96051f26653bb57b000000/Hiding-Data-in-VoIP.pdf

Sentiment Analysis for Predicting the Popularity of Web Series

Parag Kumar Garg, Mrinal Pandey$^{(\boxtimes)}$, and Mamta Arora

Department of Computer Science and Technology, Manav Rachna University,
Faridabad, India
paraggarg33@gmail.com, {mrinal,mamta}@mru.edu.in

Abstract. With the rise of the social networking era, there is a sudden and great increase in user-generated content. Millions of people share their daily life and status by blogging on social media like Twitter. So it's a great source to analyze sentiments by simply using the text of social media and simple manner of expression. Due to the advancement of technology and easy availability of internet people are getting attracted towards the web television series due to the originality of the content and free of commercials breaks. Netflix is also one of the subscription-based videos on demand site is popularizing and got a sustainable advantage over traditional networks these days. This paper focuses on four popular comic web series and performed sentimental analysis for the prediction of the most popular web series among the four cartoon series.

Keywords: Sentiment analysis · Video-on-demand · Netflix · Web series · Social media · Prediction

1 Introduction

In the modern era of information, the Internet is widely used not only for information, entertainment but also for seeking opinions. The popularity of the social media platform is increasing exponentially. Social Media has become a common platform for sharing views and used to connect the entire world. Now a day's social media became an easy way of expressing feelings for any individuals. According to [1] the internet joins millions of people across the globe to share information and resources available on the internet. A social media platform consists of Social Networks, Bookmarking sites, Social News, Blog Comments and Forums, Media Sharing and Microblogging. The most popular social media platforms include Facebook, Twitter, Instagram, YouTube etc. (Fig. 1)

© Springer Nature Singapore Pte Ltd. 2020
U. Batra et al. (Eds.): REDSET 2019, CCIS 1230, pp. 133–140, 2020.
https://doi.org/10.1007/978-981-15-5830-6_12

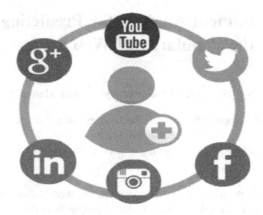

Fig. 1. Popular social media platforms

2 Sentimental Analysis

Sentimental Analysis is a branch of Machine Learning that deals with text analysis and studies the human behaviour and perception and it refers to the use of natural language processing, text analysis, Information Extraction Task and computational algorithm. Sentiments are feelings, opinion, emotions, likes or dislikes, good or bad. The text in the analysis is given the polarity to the given text, document, sentence and after that, the language is processed to figure out the sentiment related to that sentence.

Sentimental Analysis is an emerging research field that helps the industry in decision making by analyzing and scoring the opinions as negative, positive or neutral [2, 3]. The opinions, sentiments and the subjectivity of text when computationally treated is called Sentiment Analysis or opinion mining. Sentiment analysis has applications in almost every business and social domain and helps in decision making. There are three levels of sentiment analysis: Document Level, Sentence Level, Aspect level. Sentimental Analysis can be classified into two categories [3].

Lexicon based sentimental analysis and Machine learning based sentimental analysis. Lexicon based approach is the part of natural language processing which can be used for creating the bag of words related to entities, product, social problems etc. The ML-based approach is used to classify the data and for further predictions. Most of the research for sentiment analysis has used supervised ML technique very useful to identify patterns in systems, with the past work, of frequency maps and classifiers. Sentiments can be classified into three categories namely positive, neutral and negative. The focus of the research is to identify the negative segments and see if they present threats, of any real-life incidents, likely to happen in the future.

3   Literature Review

Several kinds of research are reported in the literature about sentiment analysis. According to [4] opinions can be assigned at two levels, document level as well as sentence level, still answering to the opinions is a very challenging job in natural language processing. In [4] a Bayesian classifier was used for differentiating between documents with high correctness and superiority of opinions such as editorial from news stories and describing techniques for determining opinions at the sentence level.

The sudden increase of activity in the area of opinion mining and sentiment analysis requires the computational procedure for the study of opinions, which has a linear response to the surge of interest in new methods that directly deals with opinions as a first-class object. The survey [5] includes techniques and approaches that encourage directly facilitating opinion-oriented information-seeking system.

Twitter has emerged out as a main social media platform for opinions and made huge interest in sentimental analysis researchers. Besides all of this, twitter sentiment analysis performs relatively low with less accurate results. Many institutions and researchers have noticed that important issues related to business and community may be resolved by investigating the opinion exposed in the tweets. This survey of the literature disclosed two significant motives for Twitter Sentimental Analysis research. The first is to focus on the insights into numerous business and social issues and the second one is to focus on innovation and developing improved methods for future growth [6].

With the contrast of traditional sentimental analysis data analytics techniques are being used widely to support a huge amount of data [7]. However, the objective of the sentimental analysis is to points the task of Natural Language Processing whether a part of the writing contains subjective knowledge or not and whether information behind the text can be classified as positive, negative or neutral. Figuring out the content generated by the user automatically is of great interest. Many Machine learning algorithms for sentiment classification have been employed [5, 8–11].

4   Methodology

Methodology for sentimental analysis starts with the extraction of data using twitter APIs. In this research, data has been collected as the reviews of the viewers of on-demand video subscriptions for four popular comic series available on Netflix. The English language was considered as the preferred language of tweets. Total 10000 tweets were collected for each one of the cartoon series, later duplicate tweets were removed and a unique set of tweets were considered for the experiments. The entire pre-processing was done in MOZEH tool and finally, classification and scoring were performed to get the output for each comic series (Fig. 2).

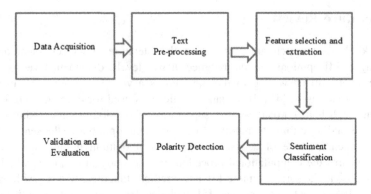

Fig. 2. Methodology

5   Experiments and Results

This section represents the results of the experiments performed on four comic web series telecast on Netflix. The results are presented in terms of graphical representation and the strengths of sentiments of the viewers in terms of positive and negative percentages of viewers. The sentiments of viewers are classified into 4 categories as very strong, strong, moderate, and weak and none. Figures 3, 4 and 5 represents the graphical view of the sentiment strengths of web series 1 to web series 4 respectively. Tables 1, 2, 3 and 4 represents the sentiment strengths in terms of positive and negative percentage. Table 5 shows the average results on 95% confidence intervals for all four web series in terms of positive and negative sentiments.

5.1   Netflix Web Series 1

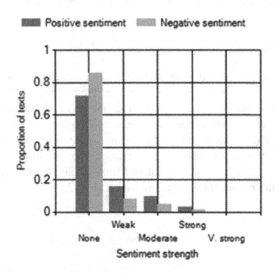

Fig. 3. Graphical representation of sentiments for web series 1

Table 1. Sentiment strength for web series 1

Score	Positive	Negative
1	71.43%	85.71%
2	15.87%	7.94%
3	9.52%	4.76%
4	3.17%	1.59%
5	0.00%	0.00%

5.2 Netflix Web Series 2

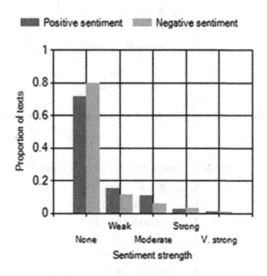

Fig. 4. Graphical representation of sentiments for web series 2

Table 2. Sentiment strength for web series 2

Score	Positive	Negative
1	71.65%	79.82%
2	14.83%	11.47%
3	10.45%	5.83%
4	2.07%	2.82%
5	0.36%	0.06%

5.3   Netflix Web Series 3

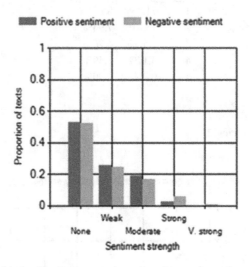

Fig. 5. Graphical representation of sentiments for web series 3

Table 3. Sentiment strength for web series 3

Score	Positive	Negative
1	52.93%	52.33%
2	25.60%	24.60%
3	19.14%	16.72%
4	2.33%	5.86%
5	0.00%	0.43%

5.4   Netflix Web Series 4

See Fig. 6

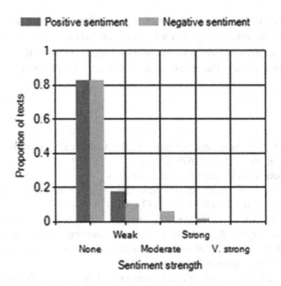

Fig. 6. Graphical representation of sentiments for web series 4

Table 4. Sentiment strength for web series 4

Score	Positive	Negative
1	82.86%	82.86%
2	17.14%	10.00%
3	0.00%	5.71%
4	0.00%	1.43%
5	0.00%	0.00%

Table 5. Average comparative sentiment strength of all four series on 95% confidence intervals

Series	Positive	Negative	Average
Web series 1	1.4444	1.2222	0.2222
Web series 2	1.4529	1.3183	0.1345
Web series 3	1.7086	1.7741	−0.0655
Web series 4	1.1714	1.2571	−0.0857

6 Conclusion

This paper presented an application of sentiment analysis for predicting the popularity of the on-demand videos like Netflix and the most popular comic web series telecasted over it. The results are based on applying sentiment analysis technique over subscriber's reviews and likes. This paper concludes that web series 3 is most popular among all. Also, the model can be modified to accommodate more web series so that it can be applied to determine the popularity of other web series. This technique can be used for different application areas of sentimental analysis as well. However, with the help of more preprocessing, the results can be improved as further work.

References

1. Gayo-Avello, D.: A meta-analysis of state-of-the-art electoral prediction from Twitter data. Soc. Sci. Comput. Rev. **31**, 649–679 (2013)
2. Totewar, A.: Data mining: concepts and techniques
3. Medhat, W., Hassan, A., Korashy, H.: Sentiment analysis algorithms and applications: a survey. Ain Shams Eng. J. **5**(4), 1093–1113 (2014)
4. Yu, H., Hatzivassiloglou, V.: Towards answering opinion questions: separating facts from opinions and identifying the polarity of opinion sentences. In: Proceeding of the 2003 Conference on Empirical Methods in Natural Language Processing, pp. 129–136. Association for Computational Linguistics (2003)
5. Pang, B., Lee, L.: Opinion mining and sentiment analysis. Found. Trends Inf. Retr. **2**(1–2), 1–135 (2008)
6. Zimbra, D., Abbasi, A., Zeng, D., Chen, H.: The state-of-the-art in twitter sentimental analysis: a review and benchmark evaluation. ACM Trans. Manag. Inf. Syst. **9**(2), 1–29 (2018). Article 5
7. Sulthana, R., Jaithunbi, A.K., Ramesh, S.L.: Sentiment analysis in Twitter data using data analytic techniques for predictive modelling. J. Phys. (2018)
8. Pang, B., Lee, L., Vaithyanathan, S.: Thumbs up? Sentiment classification using machine learning techniques. In: Proceedings of the Conference on Empirical Methods in Natural Language Processing (EMNLP), pp. 79–86 (2002)
9. Liu, B.: Sentiment analysis and subjectivity. In: Indurkhya, N., Damerau, F.J. (eds.) Handbook of Natural Language Processing, pp. 627–666. Chapman & Hall, London (2010)
10. Witten, I.H., Frank, E.: Data mining: Practical Machine Learning Tools and techniques. Morgan Kaufmann, San Francisco (2005)
11. Manning, C.D., Raghvan, P., Schutze, H.: Introduction to Information Retrieval. Cambridge University Press, Cambridge (2008)

Social and Web Analytics

An Explicit Analysis of Best Tourist Destinations

Satyajee Srivastava[1(✉)], Sonia Sharda[2(✉)], and Arti Ranjan[1(✉)]

[1] Galgotias University, Greater Noida, India
drsatyajee@gmail.com, arti.iitm@gmail.com
[2] Maharishi University, Noida, India
sharda.sonia@gmail.com

Abstract. As tourism is increasing incredible in day by day which helps in growth of GDP, Business opportunities and Job opportunities. There are countries who actually work over countries tourism growth by launching different discounts and package schemes in peak and semi peak seasons. Also review at different travel site would help people to select a best destination within the budget. Through this paper we are proposing some facts and figures of top 10 best countries of the world within the budget of $500. It also emphasize on the major criteria for travelling like Nature, Culture, Entertainment and Temperature in top best destinations countries.

Keywords: Best destination · Culture · Entertainment · Nature · Top 10 countries · Business opportunities · GDP · Job opportunities · Tourisms schemes · Budget · Growth

1 Introduction

Tourism a word is about travel pleasure of people with family or a business trip. WTO (World Tourism Organisation) defines tourism as travelling and staying in places outside the usual environment. Here we are focusing on world tourism, countries which help to increase the revenue of the country. The hospitality industries get benefit from tourism, transportation services and entertainment venues. In India government has launched Swadesh Drashan Abhiyan to promote tourism, Guidelines on safety for states for travellers, Regulations of service providers [1]. They are Ramayan Circuit, Desert Circuit, Eco Circuit, Wildlife Circuit and Rural Circuit, Buddhist Circuit, Jain Circuit and Sufi Circuit has been launched by tourism ministry to promote tourisms spirituality.

According to WTO France, US, Spain and Thailand are the highest revenue countries of the world. After launch of E-Tourist Scheme in many countries which lead to profits for many countries. Sites are classified as 'cultural', 'natural' or 'mixed' sites by UNESCO world heritage.

2 Literature Study

Literature of study act as a guide in every research some research work has already been done in the field of best tourist destination in the world, top 30 countries on revenue basis in the year of 2017, 2018 [12]. Different researcher's explored different

U. Batra et al. (Eds.): REDSET 2019, CCIS 1230, pp. 143–153, 2020.
https://doi.org/10.1007/978-981-15-5830-6_13

data in their research in aspect of travelling destinations but no researcher works done in the field of top 10 best destination countries. Few researchers collected data from online sites, User generated data using their travel details or device like GPS [1]. We can also predict tourist behaviour pattern using social media sites photographs. They also believe that competitiveness of tourist destination depend on economic, geographical, cultural and political factors [2].

One of the researcher measure, the quality of tourisms destination in emerging markets on the basis of quality of services, quality of destination features and quality of experience [9].

From the above literatures reviews and secondary data which we had collected from different sources like WTO, UNESCO India tourism statistic [12] we collected 65 countries secondary data from which, top 10 be the best destination There are several factors generally people consider while checking for holiday trip. Some of the cause are temp, possible stay, natural, cultural, entertainment, continent, country, daily budget, UNESCO culture, nature, sunny hours, protected area, environment regulations, monuments, museum, night life and restaurant [3].

Few point we should check before planning for a trip

1. Determining Goals and Desires
   a) Consider your interests.
   b) Factor in your current needs
   c) Take fellow travellers into account
   d) Research travel destinations.
2. Determine your budget.
   a) Research costs of living.
   b) Decide how much time you have to travel.
   c) Consider travel deals.
3. Considering Safety and Convenience
   a) Think about convenience.
   b) Consider the season
   c) Take special events into account.
   d) Make sure the destination is safe
4. Making the Final Decision
   a) Make your reservations for flights and accommodations
   b) Consider travel insurance.
   c) If travelling internationally, make sure your documents are in order
   d) Buy everything you'll need

Below are some of the findings depending on the budget of the person in specific weather and temp (Table 1).

Table 1. Total cost of trip in budget of $500

Country	Stay (No. of days)	Daily cost in $	Total cost approx in $
United States	5	247.35	1236.75
Spain	5	141.01	705.05
Thailand	5	72.45	362.25
Italy	5	153.72	768.6
United Kingdom	5	167.8	839
Australia	5	152.2	761
Germany	5	134.66	673.3
China	5	74.89	374.45
Japan	5	128.12	640.6
India	5	33.1	165.5

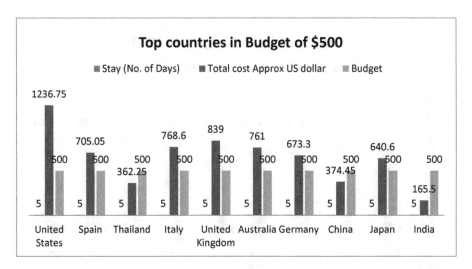

Fig. 1. Total cost of trip in budget of 500 dollar

Figure 1 shows top 10 countries total cost for 5 days if a person budget is 500 dollar. Only Thailand, China and India are the countries which a person can visit for 5 days with this budget. Daily cost per country including accommodation, food, entertainment (Table 2).

Table 2. Total cost of trip in budget of $1000

Country	Stay (No. of days)	Daily cost (US dollar)	Total cost (Approx. in $)
United States	5	247.35	1236.75
Spain	5	141.01	705.05
Thailand	5	72.45	362.25
Italy	5	153.72	768.6
United Kingdom	5	167.8	839
Australia	5	152.2	761
Germany	5	134.66	673.3
China	5	74.89	374.45
Japan	5	128.12	640.6
India	5	33.1	165.5

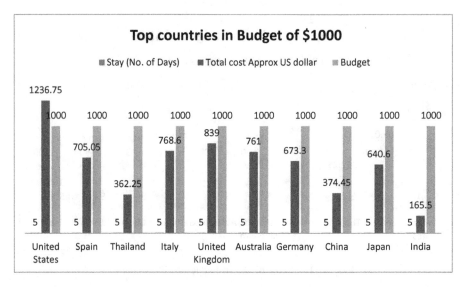

Fig. 2. Top countries expense with $1000 budget

The Fig. 2 shows that a person can stay in all 9 countries like Spain, Thailand, China, UK, Germany Japan, India, Australia except US with the budget of 1000 dollar (Table 3).

UNESCO Nature: Countries ranked by number of natural sites that are recognized as a world heritage site by UNESCO. Protected Area: Countries ranked by % of terrestrial protected areas in the total land area. Environment Regulation: Countries ranked by enforcement of environmental regulation [4, 13].

Table 3. Best nature destination

Country	Protected area ('000')	Environment regulation ('000')	UNESCO Nat ('000')
United States	39	18	2
Spain	15	23	14
Thailand	26	34	23
Italy	22	41	9
United Kingdom	13	15	11
Australia	36	10	2
Germany	4	20	14
China	29	32	1
Japan	25	10	11
India	59	16	6

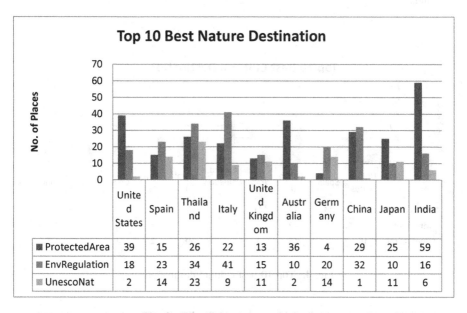

Fig. 3. Top 10 best nature destination

Figure 3 shows the top 10 best nature destination countries of the world, where nature is categorized as Protected Area, Environment Regulations and UNESCO Nature. Environment Regulations includes Air quality, Health impact, water and sanitation, forest, fisheries and biodiversity factors while considering a country [14] UNESCO Nature includes areas with exceptional natural beauty, Contains natural habitats for conservation of biological diversity. Whereas protected area defined geographical space, recognized, dedicated and managed, to achieve the long-term conservation of nature with associated ecosystem services and cultural values [8].

From the Fig. 3 Thailand and Spain are the most favorable countries in all aspects of nature sub categories (Table 4 and Fig. 4).

Table 4. Best cultural destination

Country	Monuments ('000')	Museums ('000')	UNESCO cult ('000')
United States	7	1	19
Spain	14	6	2
Thailand	29	42	48
Italy	21	3	1
United Kingdom	40	4	7
Australia	7	14	48
Germany	21	2	2
China	14	12	4
Japan	29	8	9
India	5	27	5

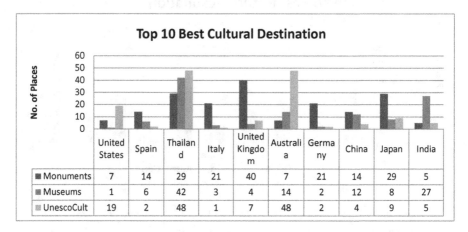

Fig. 4. Top 10 best cultural destination

In cultural category high-density of tourist attractions, museums, monuments, historical sites and rich culture make it the world's most popular tourist destination. UNESCO cult represents a masterpiece of human creative genius which exhibits an important interchange of human values [15]. UNESCO Cul: Countries ranked by number of cultural sites that are recognized as a world heritage site by UNESCO, Museums: Countries ranked by their total number of museums Monuments: Countries ranked by Average ratings of their 10 most famous monuments. Museums can be of all disciplines like arboretums, botanical gardens, nature centres; historical societies, historic preservation organizations, and history museums; science and technology centres; planetariums; children's museums; art museums; general museums; natural history and natural science museums; and zoos, aquariums, and wildlife conservation centres [11]. Figure 3 shows that Thailand, China, Australia has maximum attraction points [5] (Table 5).

Table 5. Best entertainment destination

Country	Attractions ('000')	Restaurants ('000')
United States	8	24
Spain	47	13
Thailand	47	8
Italy	27	1
United Kingdom	27	1
Australia	1	38
Germany	16	24
China	27	16
Japan	16	8
India	41	16

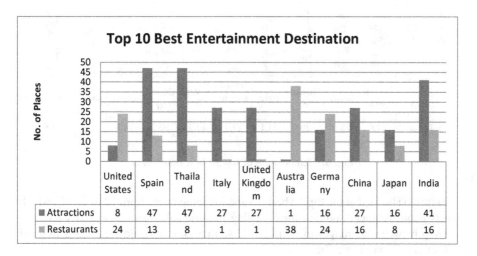

Fig. 5. Top 10 best entertainment destination

Restaurants: Majors cities of our countries ranked by Average ratings of their 10 first restaurants, attractions: Majors cities of our countries ranked by Average ratings of their 10 first attractions on various online booking sites [7]. Figure 5 represents maximum attraction places in Thailand and Spain and good number of restaurants in Australia (Table 6).

Table 6. Temperature of top 10 best destination

Country	Temp ©
United States	24.9
Spain	25.6
Thailand	29
Italy	24.1
United Kingdom	17.3
Australia	12.2
Germany	20.3
China	28.4
Japan	25
India	27.6

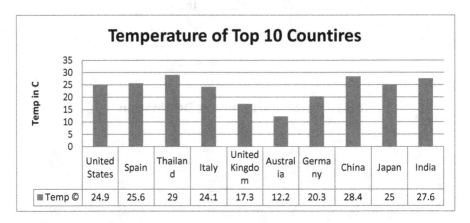

Fig. 6. Temperature of top 10 best destination

Figure 6 shows that the top 10 best destination temp range from 12 to 29 °C, which reflects good weather condition for travelling purpose [6]. Tourists generally look for the temp between the ranges of 10 to 25 °C so that they can enjoy the trip with good weather condition (Table 7).

Table 7. Top 10 countries of the world in tourism receipt

Country	2017 (US $ billion)	2018 (US $ billion)
United States	210.7	214.5
Spain	68.1	73.8
Thailand	56.9	63
Italy	49.	51.9
United Kingdom	44.2	49.3
Australia	41.7	45
Germany	39.8	43
China	34.1	41.1
Japan	38.6	40.4
India	27.3	28.56

The above Fig. 7 shows the Revenue of top 10 best countries for the year of 2017 and 2018 where Japan and India are the countries has less growth rate than other developing countries.

The increase in revenue can help in growth of GDP, Job opportunities and business options too [9]. Government can launch scheme or packages to promote tourism in low growth countries by creating more awareness in terms of historical monuments, culture of the country, entertainments and nature too [10].

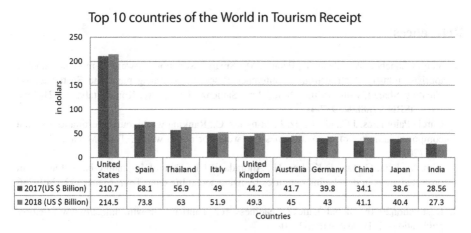

Fig. 7. Top 10 countries of the world in tourism receipt

3 Conclusion

We have considered 65 countries of the world and found the top 10 best destination on the basis of Culture, Entertainment, Nature, Temperature and Revenue growth from the last two years data.

Overall analysis show that if a person travel with the budget of 500 us dollar he can explore only few countries like Thailand, China and India in 5 days while if his budgets increase to 1000 $ the destination increase to Italy, UK, Australia, Germany, Spain, Japan.

If we consider a factor of nature while visiting a place, Thailand would be the place with good range of protected areas; Environment regulated areas and UNESCO nature. India is the country with lot of protected areas, Italy having strict environment regulation and Thailand has good rating in UNESCO nature.

People consider Entertainment as the major factor while going for vacation. China has entertainment parks, amusement parks, historical spots and many more places in comparison to other top countries. Spain and Thailand has major number of Attractions to visit for and Australia has good number of restaurants in comparison to other countries.

In culture we consider Monuments, Museums and UNESCO culture, where UK has major numbers of monuments, Thailand has Museum, Australia and Thailand are the top most in UNESCO Culture countries.

Temperature would the major factor, people generally look for 15 to 22 °C temperature while going out for a holiday.

References

1. Vargas Sanchez, A., Abate, T., Perano, M.: Smart destinations: towards a more sustainable tourism industry. In: Electronic Conference Proceedings Management and Sustainability: Creating Shared Value in the Digital Era, Sapienza University, Roma, Italy, 20–21 June 2019. ISBN 97888943937-4-3
2. García Palomares, J.C., Gutiérrez, J., Mínguez, C.: Ranking world tourist destinations with a composite indicator of competitiveness: to weigh or not to weigh? Tour. Manag. 72, 281–291 (2019)
3. Kim, Y., Kim, C., Lee, D.K., Lee, H., Andrada, R.I.T.: Quantifying nature-based tourism in protected areas in developing countries by using social big data. Tour. Manag. 72, 249–256 (2019)
4. Destination2030: Global Cities' Readiness for Tourism Growth. https://www.wttc.org/publications/2019/destination-2030/
5. City Travel & Tourisms Impact 2108, World tourism and travel council. https://www.wttc.org/media/files/reports/economic-impact-research/cities-2018/city-travel–tourism-impact-2018final.pdf
6. Li, J., Xu, L., Tang, L., Wang, S., Li, L.: Big data in tourism research: a literature review. Tour. Manag. 68, 301–323 (2018)
7. Jasroti, A., Gangotia, A.: Smart cities to smart tourism destinations: a review paper. J. Tour. Intell. Smartness 1(1), 47–56 (2018)

8. Mukherjee, S., Adhikari, A., Datta, B.: Quality of tourism destination – a scale development. J. Indian Bus. Res. JIBR **10**(1), 70–100 (2018)
9. Miah, S.J., Vu, H.Q., Gammack, J., McGrath, M.: A big data analytics method for tourist behaviour analysis. Inf. Manag. **54**(6), 771–785 (2017)
10. Vengesayi, S., Mavondo, F., Reisinger, Y.: Tourism destination attractiveness: attractions, facilities, and people as predictors. Tour. Anal. **14**, 621–636 (2009)
11. https://www.wttc.org/-/media/files/reports/2018/power-and-performance-rankings-2018.pdf
12. http://tourism.gov.in/sites/default/files/Other/ITS_Glance_2018_Eng_Version_for_Mail.pdf
13. https://earthnworld.com/most-visited-countries-in-the-world/
14. https://www.indexmundi.com/facts/indicators/ST.INT.ARVL/rankings6
15. https://www.forbes.com/sites/ericrosen/2018/09/06/new-rankings-of-the-worlds-fastest-growing-tourism-destinations/

Time-Cost Solution Pairs in Multi-index Bulk Transportation Problem

Kuldeep Tanwar[1][✉][iD] and Sudhir Kumar Chauhan[2][iD]

[1] MVN University, Palwal, Haryana, India
kuldeep.tanwar@mvn.edu.in
[2] Amity School of Engineering and Technology, Noida, Uttar Pradesh, India
skchauhan@amity.edu

Abstract. Bi-Criteria Multi-Index Bulk Transportation Problem (BCMIBTP) is the extension of single criterion multi-index bulk transportation problem. There exist works in literature, for finding cost-time solution pairs in BCMIBTP, wherein cost is given priority over time. Sometimes, transportation time is more crucial than cost. So far, no method is discussed to get efficient time-cost solution pairs in BCMIBTP, where time criterion assumes priority over cost, to the best of our knowledge. Motivated by this research gap, a method is presented to minimize time and cost simultaneously. An example is discussed to illustrate the presented method.

Keywords: Transportation problem · Multi-index · Bi-criteria · Bulk transportation · Trade-offs

1 Introduction

In the standard transportation problem, an origin can deliver units of product to any number of destinations, however; in bulk transportation problem (BTP), it is required to fulfil the need of a destination by only one origin. Maio and Roveda [1] studied the BTP through branch and bound method. Later on, Murthy [2] studied the BTP through Lexi-Search algorithm.

Haley [3, 4] introduced multi-index transportation problem (MITP) and solved the problem by extending the MODI method [5]. MITP arises when it is required to transport distinct kinds of product or when the product is transported via distinct modes of transportation. Smith [6] presented necessary and sufficient conditions for solving the MITP. Bhatia et al. [7] solved the MITP through a different approach.

Bi-criteria MITP (BCMITP) is the extension of MITP. Basu et al. [8] presented a method to solve the BCMITP by giving priority to cost over time. Initially, the all possible efficient cost-time trade-offs are found out and then trade-off ratios are used to determine the optimum transportation schedule. Bandopadhya [9] solved the BCMITP by converting the two criteria problem into single criterion.

In some situations, like fire services, ambulance services, transportation of perishable commodities etc., the transportation time is more significant than the cost. When someone is interested in minimizing the cost and time of transportation simultaneously, then the objectives conflict with each other. In situations, when time is more

© Springer Nature Singapore Pte Ltd. 2020
U. Batra et al. (Eds.): REDSET 2019, CCIS 1230, pp. 154–163, 2020.
https://doi.org/10.1007/978-981-15-5830-6_14

crucial than the cost, the decision maker may look for the options for trading off between time and cost. Bhatia and Puri [10] solved the BCMITP by giving priority to time over cost and obtained the optimum time-cost trade-offs of the problem. Gupta and Sharma [11] presented an iterative method to obtain time-cost trade-offs in MITP.

BCMIBTP having time at first priority has not been studied so far to the best of our knowledge. Motivated by this research gap, a BCMIBTP is considered in this work and a solution strategy is devised for determining the all possible efficient time-cost trade-offs of the problem.

2   Mathematical Formulation of the BCMIBTP

Suppose that there are l origins, m destinations and q modes of transportation.
   Let

y_{ijk} = the decision variable which bears value 1 or 0 accordingly the origin i fulfils the need of destination j availing k^{th} mode of transportation or not,
c_{ijk} = the bulk cost of transporting product from origin i to destination j availing k^{th} mode of transportation,
t_{ijk} is the time of transporting product from origin i to destination j availing k^{th} mode of transportation,
a_i is the quantity of product at origin i and b_j is the need of product at destination j.

The mathematical model of the considered problem is as follows:
Determine $y_{ijk} \geq 0 (i = 1, 2, \ldots, l; j = 1, 2, \ldots, m; k = 1, 2, \ldots, q)$ so as to minimize

$$\text{Min}\left(\max\{t_{ijk} : y_{ijk} = 1\}, \sum_{i=1}^{l} \sum_{j=1}^{m} \sum_{k=1}^{q} c_{ijk} y_{ijk} : y_{ijk} = 1\right) \tag{1}$$

subject to the constraints

$$\sum_{j=1}^{m} \sum_{k=1}^{q} b_j y_{ijk} \leq a_i \tag{2}$$

$$\sum_{i=1}^{l} \sum_{k=1}^{q} y_{ijk} = 1 \tag{3}$$

$$y_{ijk} = 1 \ or \ 0 \tag{4}$$

Definition: (Efficient Time-Cost Solution Pairs)
Let T_1 be the least time of BCMIBTP and C_1 be the least transportation cost at time T_1. Let Y_1 be the solution vector providing the time-cost trade-off pair $[T_1, C_1]$. Let $T_2(>T_1)$ be another time of bulk transportation and $C_2(<C_1)$ be the least cost at time T_2. Then the pair $[T_2, C_2]$ is said to be the next efficient time-cost solution pair if there exists no other solution pair $[T, C]$ s.t. $T_1 < T < T_2$ and $C_2 < C < C_1$.

3 Method

The proposed solution procedure involves two main steps. Steps 1(a) and 1(b), are to obtain the minimum time T_1 of BCMIBTP, while Step 1(c) is to obtain corresponding first cost C_1 (which is minimum for T_1). Step 2 details a procedure to obtain subsequent time-cost trade-off pairs.

Step 1

(a) Divide the given BCMIBTP into sub-problems P_k's where P_k denotes the BCBTP through k^{th} mode of transportation.
(b) Determination of minimum time of each BCBTP P_k:
   (i)   For each destination, subtract the smallest entry from the largest entry. This difference denotes the penalty.
   (ii) Select the column j for which the difference is largest and allocate 1 to the cell (i, j) which have the smallest entry. If there exists a tie among the least entry then select the cell where maximum allocation can be done. Remove the jth column from the table and reduce the quantity at the source i by b_j units. If there exists a tie among the largest difference, then choose the column that has a relatively smallest element. If again, there exists a tie then choose the cell where maximum can be allocated. In this way, either all the destinations have met their demands, otherwise, go to next step.
   (iii) Remove the last allocation and make an allocation in the cell (i, j) having next smallest entry in the column for which the penalty is largest. Repeat this step until all the destinations met their demands.
   (iv) Let $T_k^* = \max\{t_{ijk} : x_{ijk} = 1\}$. To minimize time T_k^* of each sub-problem P_k, define a time matrix $[t_{ijk}^1]$ for each problem P_k as shown below:

$$t_{ijk}^1 = \begin{cases} t_{ijk} \text{ if } t_{ijk} < T_k^* \\ \infty \text{ if } t_{ijk} \geq T_k^* \end{cases}$$

   (v)   Repeat steps (i) to (iv) to obtain minimum transportation time of each sub-problem P_k.
   (vi) Define t_j^* as: $t_j^* = \min\{t_{ijk} : x_{ijk} = 1,\}$, where x_{ijk} is the decision variable associated with minimum transportation time of sub-problem P_k.
       Then $T_1 = \max\{t_j^* : j = 1, 2, .., m\}$ gives the least time of given BCMIBTP.
(c) Determination of the cost C_1 of given BCMIBTP which is minimum for time T_1: Define a cost matrix $[c_{ijk}^1]$ as:

$$c_{ijk}^1 = \begin{cases} c_{ijk}; t_{ijk} \leq T_1 \\ \infty; t_{ijk} > T_1 \end{cases}$$

and solve the reduced cost minimizing sub-problems P_k using steps (i) to (iii) of 1 (b). Note that earlier step 1(b) was used for minimizing time of problem.

Define $C_j^* = \min\{c_{ijk}:x_{ijk} = 1\}$.

Then $C_1 = \sum_{j=1}^m C_j^*$ gives the least cost of given BCMIBTP at time T_1 and the first efficient time-cost solution pair is $[T_1, C_1]$.

Let $Y_1 = \{x_{ijk}:x_{ijk} = 1\}$ be the basic feasible solution giving the minimum cost C_1 at time T_1.

Step 2. Determination of the subsequent efficient time-cost solution pairs:

(i)   For the given cost matrix $[c_{ijk}]$, assign dual variables u_{ik} and v_{jk} to row i and column j respectively for which $x_{ijk} \in Y_1$. Determine the value of dual variables u_{ik} and v_{jk} by the following equations: $c_{ijk} = u_{ik} + v_{jk}$.

(ii) Draw horizontal and vertical lines through rows and columns respectively of each sub-problems P_k for which $x_{ijk} = 1$ and determine $\Delta_{ijk} = c_{ijk} - (u_{ik} + v_{jk})$ for all unoccupied cells (i, j, k) where the lines intersect each other.

(iii) Form a set $B_1 = \{(i,j,k) : (i,j,k) \notin S_1, \Delta_{ijk} < 0, t_{ijk} > T_1\}$ where S_1 is the set of all cells (i,j,k) s.t. $x_{ijk} \in Y_1$.

(a)   If $B_1 = \emptyset$ then Y_1 is a solution providing the minimum cost C_1 at time T_1 and hence there does not exist next best solution. In this way, the process terminates.

(b)   If $B_1 \neq \emptyset$, then let $T_2 = \min\{t_{ijk}:(i,j,k) \in B_1\}$. If there exists a tie for t_{ijk}, then choose the cell (i,j,k) for which Δ_{ijk} is numerically largest. At time T_2, determine the minimum cost $C_2(<C_1)$ as discussed in step 1(c). The second time-cost pair is $[T_2, C_2]$.

It is to be noted here that if $C_2 = C_1$ then delete the cell (i, j, k) from B_1 having time T_2 and use this reduced B_1 for further calculations in steps 2(a) and (b). It is important to also note that if $C_2 = C_1$, then by definition in Sect. 2, $[T_2, C_2]$ cannot be an efficient time-cost solution pair.

The process for determining the subsequent best solutions is repeated until $B_N = \emptyset$. On this stage, $\Delta_{ijk} \geq 0$ for all unoccupied cells (i, j, k) in which $t_{ijk} > T_N$. The minimum cost at this time T_N is C_n.

4   Numerical Problem

Consider the numerical problem studied by Singh et al. [12]. The problem has 3 origins and 5 destinations. We have $a_1 = 7, a_2 = 8, a_3 = 9$ are the quantities of commodity at the origins O_1, O_2 and O_3 respectively. Further, the needs of destinations D_1, D_2, D_3, D_4 and D_5 are 3, 5, 4, 6 and 2 respectively. In the problem, the commodity is supplied to destinations to meet their needs via two different modes of transportation. Divide the main problem into two sub-problems P_1 and P_2 where P_1 and P_2 denote the times and costs of transportation through 1st and 2nd mode of transportation respectively. The first and second entry in each cell is the time and cost of bulk transportation one-to-one. The considered BCMIBTP is represented in the following Tables 1 and 2:

Table 1. P_1 (Time and cost of BCMIBTP through 1st mode of transportation)

	D_1	D_2	D_3	D_4	D_5	$a_i \downarrow$
O_1	(6,10)	(7,9)	(4,12)	(3,7)	(4,8)	7
O_2	(3,11)	(4,10)	(6,14)	(7,14)	(5,12)	8
O_3	(5,8)	(6, 6)	(9,10)	(4,10)	(9,13)	9
$b_j \rightarrow$	3	5	4	6	2	

Table 2. P_2 (Time and cost of BCMIBTP through 2nd mode of transportation)

	D_1	D_2	D_3	D_4	D_5	$a_i \downarrow$
O_1	(5,12)	(6,10)	(5,14)	(4,8)	(5,7)	7
O_2	(4,9)	(5,12)	(4,13)	(6,16)	(7,13)	8
O_3	(6,7)	(7,5)	(8,10)	(5,12)	(6,11)	9
$b_j \rightarrow$	3	5	4	6	2	

The time matrix table associated with sub-problem P_1 is shown in Table 3.

Table 3. Representation of times of sub-problem P_1

	D_1	D_2	D_3	D_4	D_5	$a_i \downarrow$
O_1	6	7	4	3	4	7
O_2	3	4	6	7	5	8
O_3	5	6	9	4	9	9
$b_j \rightarrow$	3	5	4	6	2	

The time matrix table associated with sub-problem P_2 is shown in Table 4.

Table 4. Representation of times of sub-problem P_2

	D_1	D_2	D_3	D_4	D_5	$a_i \downarrow$
O_1	5	6	5	4	5	7
O_2	4	5	4	6	7	8
O_3	6	7	8	5	6	9
$b_j \rightarrow$	3	5	4	6	2	

Apply step 1 (b) on sub-problems P_1 and P_2, we get the decision variables $x_{211}, x_{221},$ $x_{131}, x_{341}, x_{151}$, and $x_{212}, x_{322}, x_{232}, x_{142}, x_{352}$, for sub-problems P_1 and P_2 respectively.

Define $t_j^* = \min\{t_{ijk} : x_{ijk} = 1\}$.

We get $t_1^* = \min\{3, 4\} = 3, t_2^* = \min\{4, 7\} = 4, t_3^* = \min\{4, 4\} = 4, t_4^* = \min\{4, 4\} = 4$ and $t_5^* = \min\{4, 6\} = 4$.

Then $T_1 = \max\{t_j^* : j = 1, 2, .., m\} = \max\{3, 4, 4, 4, 4\} = 4$ is the least time of BCMIBTP.

To determine the cost C_1 of given BCMIBTP which is minimum for time T_1, define a cost matrix $[c_{ijk}^1]$ as:

$$c_{ijk}^1 = \begin{cases} c_{ijk}; t_{ijk} \le T_1 = 4 \\ \infty; t_{ijk} > T_1 = 4 \end{cases}$$

The reduced sub-problems are shown in Tables 5 and 6:

Table 5. Reduced sub-problem P_1

	D_1	D_2	D_3	D_4	D_5	$a_i \downarrow$
O_1	∞	∞	12	7	8	7
O_2	11	10	∞	∞	∞	8
O_3	∞	∞	∞	10	∞	9
$b_j \rightarrow$	3	5	4	6	2	

Table 6. Reduced sub-problem P_2

	D_1	D_2	D_3	D_4	D_5	$a_i \downarrow$
O_1	∞	∞	∞	8	∞	7
O_2	9	∞	13	∞	∞	8
O_3	∞	∞	∞	∞	∞	9
$b_j \rightarrow$	3	5	4	6	2	

Solving the reduced sub-problems P_1 and P_2 shown in Tables 5 and 6, we get $C_1^* = 9, C_2^* = 10, C_3^* = 12, C_4^* = 8$ and $C_5^* = 8$. The associated solution vector is given by $Y_1 = \{x_{212}, x_{221}, x_{131}, x_{142}, x_{151}\}$ and the set of occupied cells is given by $S_1 = \{(2,1,2), (2,2,1), (1,3,1), (1,4,2), (1,5,1)\}$.

Then $C_1 = \sum_{j=1}^{5} C_j^* = 47$ is the least cost of BCMIBTP at time $T_1 = 4$ and the 1st efficient time-cost solution pair of BCMIBTP is $[T_1, C_1] = [4, 47]$.

Determination of Next Efficient Time-cost Solution Pairs

For sub-problem P_1, assigning dual variables u_{11} and u_{21} to the 1st and 2nd row respectively. Similarly, assign dual variables v_{21}, v_{31} and v_{51} to the 2nd, 3rd and 5th column respectively. For sub-problem P_2, assign dual variables u_{12} and u_{22} to the 1st and 2nd row respectively and v_{12} and v_{42} to the 1st and 4th column respectively.

Determining the value of dual variables u_{ik} and v_{jk} by solving the equations: $c_{ijk} = u_{ik} + v_{jk}$ for all cells (i, j, k) s.t. $x_{ijk} \in Y_1$. For this, we arbitrarily assign $u_{11} = 0, u_{21} = 0, u_{12} = 0$ and $u_{22} = 0$ to obtain $v_{21} = 10, v_{31} = 12, v_{51} = 8, v_{12} = 9$ and $v_{42} = 8$.

Now, computing the values of Δ_{ijk} by solving the equation $\Delta_{ijk} = c_{ijk} - (u_{ik} + v_{jk})$ for the unoccupied cells (i, j, k) where the lines intersect each other. We have $\Delta_{121} = -1, \Delta_{231} = 2, \Delta_{251} = 4, \Delta_{112} = 3, \Delta_{242} = 8$.

The set B_1 is given by $B_1 = \{(1, 2, 1)\}$. Thus, the next least time of BCMIBTP is given by $T_2 = 7$.

To determine the cost C_2 of given BCMIBTP which is minimum for time T_2, define a cost matrix $[c_{ijk}^2]$ as:

$$c_{ijk}^2 = \begin{cases} c_{ijk}; t_{ijk} \leq T_2 = 7 \\ \infty; t_{ijk} > T_2 = 7 \end{cases}$$

The reduced sub-problems are shown in Tables 7 and 8:

Table 7. Reduced sub-problem P_1

	D_1	D_2	D_3	D_4	D_5	$a_i \downarrow$
O_1	10	9	12	7	8	7
O_2	11	10	14	14	12	8
O_3	8	6	∞	10	∞	9
$b_j \rightarrow$	3	5	4	6	2	

Table 8. Reduced sub-problem P_2

	D_1	D_2	D_3	D_4	D_5	$a_i \downarrow$
O_1	12	10	14	8	7	7
O_2	9	12	13	16	13	8
O_3	7	5	∞	12	11	9
$b_j \rightarrow$	3	5	4	6	2	

Solving the reduced sub-problems P_1 and P_2 shown in Tables 7 and 8, we get $C_1^* = 7, C_2^* = 5, C_3^* = 13, C_4^* = 7$ and $C_5^* = 12$. The associated solution vector is given by $Y_2 = \{x_{312}, x_{322}, x_{232}, x_{141}, x_{251}\}$ and the set of occupied cells is given by $S_2 = \{(3,1,2), (3,2,2), (2,3,2), (1,4,1), (2,5,1)\}$.

Then $C_2 = \sum_{j=1}^5 C_j^* = 44$ is the least cost of given BCMIBTP at time $T_2 = 7$ and the 2nd efficient time-cost solution pair of BCMIBTP is $[T_2, C_2] = [7, 44]$.

Determination of next efficient solution pair:

For the given cost matrix $[c_{ijk}]$, assign dual variables u_{ik} and v_{jk} to row i and column j respectively for which $x_{ijk} \in Y_2$. Here u_{11} and u_{21} are the dual variables to the 1st and 2nd row respectively for sub-problem P_1. Similarly v_{41} and v_{51} are the dual variables to the 4th and 5th column respectively for sub-problem P_1.

For sub-problem P_2, u_{22} and u_{32} are the dual variables for the 2nd and 3rd row respectively and v_{12}, v_{22}, v_{32} are for the 1st, 2nd and 3rd column respectively.

Determining the value of dual variables u_{ik} and v_{jk} by solving the equations: $c_{ijk} = u_{ik} + v_{jk}$ for all cells (i, j, k) s.t. $x_{ijk} \in Y_2$. For this, we arbitrarily assign $u_{11} = 0, u_{21} = 0, u_{32} = 0$ and $u_{22} = 0$ to obtain $v_{41} = 7, v_{51} = 12, v_{12} = 7, v_{22} = 5$ and $v_{32} = 13$.

Now, computing the values of Δ_{ijk} by solving the equation $\Delta_{ijk} = c_{ijk} - (u_{ik} + v_{jk})$ for the unoccupied cells (i, j, k) where the lines intersect each other. We have $\Delta_{151} = -4, \Delta_{241} = 7, \Delta_{212} = 2, \Delta_{222} = 7, \Delta_{332} = -3$.

The set $B_2 = \{(i,j,k) : (i,j,k) \notin S_2, \Delta_{ijk}\langle 0, t_{ijk}\rangle T_2\} = \{(3,3,2)\}$. Then $T_3 = \min\{t_{ijk} : (i,j,k) \in B_2\} = 8$ is the next least time.

To determine the cost C_3 of given BCMIBTP which is minimum for time T_3, define a cost matrix $[c_{ijk}^3]$ as:

$$c_{ijk}^3 = \begin{cases} c_{ijk}; t_{ijk} \leq T_3 = 8 \\ \infty; t_{ijk} > T_3 = 8 \end{cases}$$

The reduced sub-problems are shown in Tables 9 and 10:

Table 9. Reduced sub-problem P_1

	D_1	D_2	D_3	D_4	D_5	$a_i \downarrow$
O_1	10	9	12	7	8	7
O_2	11	10	14	14	12	8
O_3	8	6	∞	10	∞	9
$b_j \rightarrow$	3	5	4	6	2	

Table 10. Reduced sub-problem P_2

	D_1	D_2	D_3	D_4	D_5	$a_i \downarrow$
O_1	12	10	14	8	7	7
O_2	9	12	13	16	13	8
O_3	7	5	10	12	11	9
$b_j \rightarrow$	3	5	4	6	2	

Solving the reduced sub-problems P_1 and P_2 shown in Tables 9 and 10, we get $C_1^* = 8, C_2^* = 5, C_3^* = 10, C_4^* = 7$ and $C_5^* = 12$. The associated solution vector is given by $Y_3 = \{x_{311}, x_{322}, x_{332}, x_{141}, x_{251}\}$ and the set of occupied cells is given by $S_3 = \{(3,1,1), (3,2,2), (3,3,2), (1,4,1), (2,5,1)\}$.

Then $C_3 = \sum_{j=1}^{5} C_j^* = 42$ is the least cost of given BCMIBTP at time $T_3 = 8$ and the 3rd efficient time-cost solution pair of BCMIBTP is $[T_3, C_3] = [8, 42]$.

Continuing in this way, we have $B_3 = \{(i,j,k) : (i,j,k) \notin S_3, \Delta_{ijk} < 0, t_{ijk} > T_3\} = \emptyset$. Hence, there does not exist next solution pair.

Thus, the only efficient time-cost solution pairs are [4,47], [7,44] and [8,42]. The minimum time and cost of BCMIBTP is 4 and 42 respectively. A little comparison between the cost-time method of Singh et al. [12] and presented method is shown in Table 11.

Table 11. Comparison between the existing method and proposed method

Cost-time trade-off pair by Singh et al. [12]	Time-cost trade-off pair by presented method
[43,8]	[4, 47]
[44,7]	[7, 44]
[47,5]	[8, 42]

5   Results and Discussion

The BCMIBTP is a very challenging problem directly impacting the profit making in industries. Primarily, the challenge is posed by the two objectives time and cost being of conflicting nature in the sense that minimizing time (cost) of transportation increases the cost (time) of transportation. In this study, a method is proposed which provides the decision maker efficient time-cost trade-off pairs with time criterion assuming priority over cost criterion.

The presented method of solving a BCMIBTP with time as the priority, is the first work in this direction to the best of our knowledge and hence no direct comparison with any other work is possible. However, we would like to point out the little comparisons with the cost-time method of Singh et al. [12]. By the comparative study, it is clear that the minimum cost and time of transportation by the presented method is less than the cost and time by existing method [12]. This proves the efficiency of the presented method over the existing method.

6   Conclusion

The main advantage of the presented method is that it provides better solution than the existing method [12]. Also, the presented method is easy to understand and apply on the problems. Further, it is to be noted that BCMIBTP having time at priority has not been studied so far to the best of our knowledge. This study fills the research gap in literature.

References

1. Maio, A.D., Roveda, C.: An all zero-one algorithm for a certain class of Transportation problems. Oper. Res. **19**, 1406–1418 (1971). https://doi.org/10.1287/opre.19.6.1406
2. Murthy, M.S.: A bulk transportation problem. Opsearch **13**, 143–155 (1976)

3. Haley, K.B.: The solid transportation problem. Oper. Res. **10**, 448–463 (1962). https://doi. org/10.1287/opre.10.4.448
4. Haley, K.B.: The multi-index problem. Oper. Res. **11**, 368–379 (1963). https://doi.org/10. 1287/opre.11.3.368
5. Vajda, S.: Readings in Linear Programming. Pitman, London (1958)
6. Smith, G.: A procedure for determining necessary and sufficient conditions for the existence of a solution to the multi-index problem. Aplikace Matematiky **19**, 177–183 (1974)
7. Bhatia, H.L., Swarup, K., Puri, M.C.: Time minimizing solid transportation problem. Math. Oper. Forsch. Stat. **7**, 395–403 (1976). https://doi.org/10.1080/02331887608801306
8. Basu, M., Pal, B.B., Kundu, A.: An algorithm for the optimum time-cost trade-off in three-dimensional transportation problem. Optimization **28**, 171–185 (1993). https://doi.org/10. 1080/02331939308843912
9. Bandopadhya, L.: Cost-time trade-off in three-axial sums transportation problem. J. Aust. Math. Soc. Ser. **35**, 498–505 (1994). https://doi.org/10.1017/S0334270000009577
10. Bhatia, H.L., Puri, M.C.: Time-cost trade-off in a solid transportation problem. J. Appl. Math. Mech. **57**, 616–619 (1977). https://doi.org/10.1002/zamm.19770571013
11. Gupta, A.K., Sharma, J.K.: An iterative technique for time-cost trade-off in solid transportation problems. J. Math. Phy. Sci. **21**, 133–142 (1987)
12. Singh, S., Chauhan, S.K., Kuldeep: A bi-criteria multi-index bulk transportation problem. Ann. Pure Appl. Math. **16**, 479–485 (2018). https://doi.org/10.22457/apam.v16n2a26

A Statistical Analysis of Various Technologies to Detect and Prevent Fake News

Saurabh Singh, Shakti Vishwakarma[(✉)], Sunil Kispotta,
and Akanksha Yadav

Jabalpur Engineering College, Jabalpur, India
{ssingh,shaktiv,skispotta}@jecjabalpur.ac.in,
ayadavtajm@gmail.com

Abstract. In today's life social media has special importance in almost everyone's life and it is being used as a great way to manipulate people's mind using fake news and fake articles. The topic of fake news came into vision as a serious issue in coming years. To detect and prevent fake news many technologies like blockchain, machine learning, deep learning and natural language processing have been used. This survey paper tells about novel way to compare various technologies of fake news detection and prevention from social media.

Keywords: Fake news · Blockchain · Deep learning

1 Introduction

Social media has brought to the world a platform for exchanging thoughts and ideas. Today, Social media has reached a level where everyone is free to express and share his/her opinions and publish their content. In last few years, it has become a topic of controversy as social media plays a major role in spreading of fake news. Fake news is a propaganda of spreading false news or misinformation to misguide people or influence their views. The fake news has become a major issue as the use of social media has increased a lot. It can have a large impact on people's life and specially rumors can cause a major issue like mob lynching which can ruin lives and can result in destablishing the society, it can affect brotherhood and can cause racism in the society. The main purpose of propagating it is to spread fear and violence among the people, [2]. Fake news can also affect the elections by influencing voters. It can also have negative impact on consumers as they can be misguided by the fake advertisements of fake brand. It has become very necessary to forbid the propagation of fake news. And there are solutions to this problem. As discussed in [1] prevention and detection of fake news can be done using deep neural network. Fake news can be detected using CNN (Convolutional Neural Networks), LSTM (long short-term memories) technique, Naïve Bayes Model techniques and also the problem of spreading fake news can be controlled using blockchain system as discussed in [3] which is a secured and feasible method. [4] has explained machine learning and natural language processing method to detect the propagation of fake news. The aim of this survey paper is to compare four methods (machine learning, deep learning, natural language processing, blockchain) which helps

© Springer Nature Singapore Pte Ltd. 2020
U. Batra et al. (Eds.): REDSET 2019, CCIS 1230, pp. 164–172, 2020.
https://doi.org/10.1007/978-981-15-5830-6_15

in detection and prevention of fake news. This survey paper is going to be helpful for those people also who want to select particular technology to detect fake news but are confused about which technology should be used.

2 Literature Survey

[1] discusses about fake news detection using deep neural network which involves CNN (Convolutional Neutral Networks) and LSTM (Long Short-term Memories) techniques which gives the highest accuracy of 98.3%. [2] tells how fake news has become a topic of concern in society and how social media is responsible in propagating the fake news. This paper discusses the types of fake news and how do they work and affect our lives. [3] discusses about detecting and preventing fake news through a new blockchain system. It also tells about the designing and working of blockchain system. This paper has introduced a secured, novel, effective and feasible method of stopping the spread of fake news. [4] tells about fake news detection using various algorithms of machine learning like logistic regression, support vector machine (SVM) and Naïve Bayes classification with Lidstone smoothing and among these Naïve Bayes classifier with Lidstone smoothing was found to be the most accurate algorithm with the accuracy of 83% which is also good for natural language processing (NLP) tasks. [5] introduces automatic detection of fake news by lexical, syntactic, semantic, pragmatic analysis. It gives the accuracy up to 76%. It helps to differentiate between fake and real article. [6] uses machine learning algorithms which are light gradient boosting (LGB), Catboost (CB), Neural Networks (NNets) and natural language processing (NLP) which gives the accuracy of 88.29%. [7] has built a classifier that can predict the percentage of news being real or fake on the basis of data source. The input of this method is news event. [8] discuses three methods: Naïve Bayes, Neural Network and Support Vector Machine (SVM) for detecting and preventing fake news. Naïve Bayes gives the accuracy of 96.08%, and other two methods gives the accuracy of 99.90%. In [9], Author tried to detect fake news through linguistic analysis by performing some operations like parts-of-speech tagging, named entity recognition, etc. In [10], It is shown that how the Naïve Bayes Classifier can be used to detect fake news and mathematical model of it is presented. In [11], Author used multinomial voting algorithm and tried to hybrid some algorithms of machine learning for fake news detection. In [12], author is combining the natural language processing method and machine learning method to detect fake news which reached 63.33% precision. Author used supervised learning of machine learning in it. In [13], Author used blockchain method with breadth first search algorithm to detect fake news and used rating scale to detect whether new is fake or not.

3 Methodology

We took four methods of fake news detection for statistical analysis:

1. Machine Learning
2. Deep Learning

3. Natural Language Processing (Linguistic Analysis)
4. Blockchain

Machine Learning. In Machine Learning Method, we try to classify the fake news from the real news using various type of machine learning method like Naïve Bayes, K nearest neighbors, Decision tree, Random forest and SVM, [1, 4].

Deep Learning. In Deep Learning method, we try to detect fake news from a huge collection of data using Deep Learning networks like Shallow Convolutional Neural Networks, Very Deep Convolutional Neural Network, Long Short-Term Memory Network, Gated Recurrent Unit Network, Combination of Convolutional Neural Network with Long Short-Term Memory and Convolutional Neural Network with Gated Recurrent Unit, [1].

Natural Language Processing. In Natural Language Processing, Fake news is detected using the Linguistic analysis of the article by parts of speech tagging, named entity recognition, bag of words model etc. We normally use various libraries of natural language processing through python language in this method, [9].

Blockchain. In Blockchain method, we construct a blockchain using various types of consensus protocol like Proof-of-stack, proof-of-work, proof-of-authority. Now when news is generated on social media, every node of blockchain is requested to validate its authenticity and submit the consent. Basis on the percentage of validation the news is decided that either it is fake or not. (We are saying parts of the blockchain as node here.)

In statistical analysis we provided ratings to every method based on their performance on particular property according to research papers. The rating between 4 and 5 is considered as good rating and rating between 3 and 4 is considered as medium rating and the rating below 3 is considered as substandard rating.

After analyzing all the methods, we got given table (Table 1):

Table 1. Statistical overview of various methods of fake news detection and prevention

Serial No.	Properties	Methods			
		Machine Learning	Deep Learning	NLP	Blockchain
	Positive aspects				
1	Accuracy	4.2	4.9	3.8	5
2	Variation in method	3	3	1	3
3	Ease in maintenance	3	2	3	4
4	Ease in updating	3	2	3	4
5	Multi language support	1	1	5	3
	Negative aspects				
1	Execution time	4	1	4	5
2	Hardware dependency	3	4	3	5
3	Bias factor	1	2	0	2
4	Human involvement	2	2	2	5
5	Need of previous data	5	5	4	0

3.1   Positive Parameters

Accuracy. Machine Learning takes 4.2/5 rating in accuracy. Because in [4], It gave highest efficiency of 83%. Deep Learning takes 4.9/5 rating in accuracy because in [1], It gave highest efficiency of 98.3%. In [5], Natural Language Processing reached highest accuracy of 76% so It takes 3.8/5 rating. As told in [3], Efficiency of Blockchain completely depends upon the nodes which are verifying the news so if we assume that at least 70% of nodes are honest than we will get 100% accurate news. So, the blockchain takes 5/5 rating.

Variation in Method.   [4] talks about 3 methods in machine learning. So, it takes 3/5 rating. In [1] three neural networks are given which can be used to fake news detection. So, 3/5 Rating are given to Deep learning. In [5], In Natural Language processing there is only one method so 1/5 is given. And In [3] there are 3 methods given for implementation on blockchain to detect fake news. So, it takes 3/5 rating.

Ease of maintenance. In Machine Learning, Deep Learning, Natural Language Processing. We only have to implement the algorithms and It is easy to maintain the Computers, [1, 4, 5]. But in Blockchain It is not too hard to maintain the nodes, [3]. Deep Learning requires a bit more maintenance because It uses High level graphic cards and RAM so Deep Learning got 2/5 rating, Machine Learning and Natural Language processing got 3/5 rating, Blockchain takes 4/5 rating.

Ease of Updating. In Machine Learning, Natural Language Processing, It is easy to update the system if compared with other methods, [4, 5], So Both take 3/5 rating.In Deep Learning It takes a bit more time, [1], so deep learning takes 2/5 rating and It is hard to update the Blockchain because In blockchain all the blocks are to be updated and it takes a few minutes to be updated, [3], So It takes 4/5 rating.

Multi Language Support. Natural language processing strongly supports multi languages. [5], So it takes 5/5 rating. Blockchain method can support this feature if the peers in blockchain are comfortable with multiple languages, [3], so Blockchain method deserves 3/5 rating. Machine Learning and Deep Learning can support multi languages, [1, 4] but for every language there will be need of separate model so both take 1/5 rating.

3.2   Negative Parameters

Execution time. Deep Learning takes least time to identify the fake news, [1], so it deserves 1/5 rating. Machine Learning and Natural Language Processing takes almost same time but a bit more than deep learning method, [4], [5], so they take 4/5 rating. Blockchain method need to verify the news by at least 70% of peers than it classifies the fake news, [3], so it takes highest amount of time so It takes 5/5 rating.

Hardware Dependency. Machine Learning and Natural Language Processing methods can be executed on High Quality Computers, [7, 8] So they cost least in all 4 methods so Both takes 3/5 rating. Deep Learning methods require Super Computer to be executed, [1] used Nvidia DGX-1 supercomputer, So, it takes 4/5 rating. Blockchain methods can be executed on average computers but It requires multiple computers to be connected in blockchain, [3] so it also takes 5/5 rating.

Bias Factor. It is hard in deep learning, machine learning and natural language processing methods to bias the system because they will require a lot of data set to make changes in algorithm, [1, 4, 5], but Because blockchain completely depends upon the nodes connected with it so if nodes are biased than there are high chances of being system biased, [3], So Blockchain takes 2/5 rating and NLP takes 0/5 rating because it's almost impossible to bias it, all other methods take 1/5 rating.

Human Involvement. The human involvement in deep learning, machine learning and natural language processing methods will be required to maintain the machines and algorithms, [1, 4, 5], So they take 2/5 rating, But block chain completely depends upon humans because Humans are checking the news whether it is fake or not, [3], so it takes 5/5 rating.

Need of Previous Data. The Machine Learning and deep learning requires previous data to check the news, [1, 4], so they take 5/5 rating. But in Natural Language process the data based upon mistakes in spelling and punctuations but it requires previous data to learn to classify the news, [5], so it takes 4/5 rating. In blockchain the nodes are directly connected to the official news website to check the news so they don't require the previous data to check the news, [3], so it also takes 0/5 rating.

4 Result

Based on the Table of Ratings of various methods of fake news detection we plotted Fig. 1, Fig. 2.

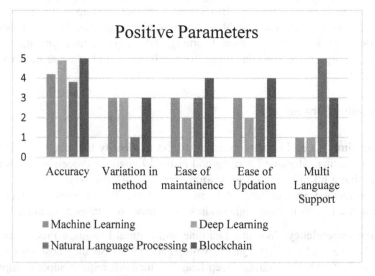

Fig. 1. Performance of various technologies based on positive factors.

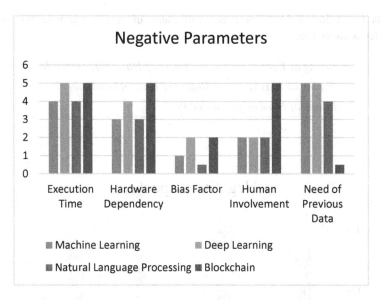

Fig. 2. Performance of various methods based on negative factors.

If we take mean of all positive properties and negative properties than we get below graph: -

Formula for rating of positive aspects or mean of positive aspects of particular technology (Fig. 3): -

$$Mean = \frac{\begin{array}{l} Rating\ of\ Accuracy\ +\ Rating\ of\ Variation\ in\ method\ + \\ Rating\ of\ ease\ in\ maintenance\ +\ Rating\ of\ ease\ in\ update\ + \\ Rating\ of\ multi\text{-}language\ support \end{array}}{5}$$

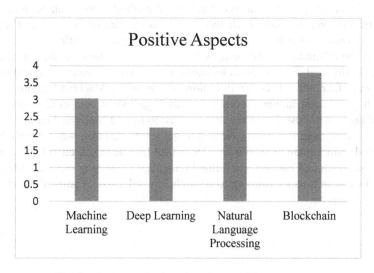

Fig. 3. Average of ratings based on positive parameters

Formula for rating of Negative aspects or mean of negative parameters of particular technology (Fig. 4): -

$$Mean = \frac{\begin{array}{l} Rating\ of\ Execution\ time\ +\ Rating\ of\ Hardware\ Dependency\ + \\ Rating\ of\ Bias\ factor\ +\ Rating\ of\ Human\ Involvement\ + \\ Rating\ of\ Need\ of\ previous\ data \end{array}}{5}$$

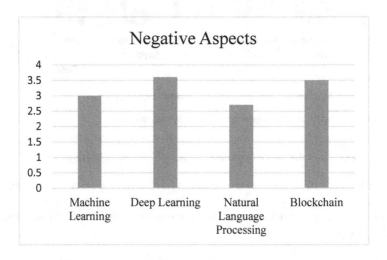

Fig. 4. Average of ratings based on negative parameters

5 Conclusion

Through this survey paper we analyzed almost all methods which can be used in fake news detection. We analyzed each technology using various positive and negative parameters. Through the Result Section We can see clearly that Blockchain Technology has highest Number of Advantages but it also has highest number of disadvantages. So, In the field of Blockchain technology some improvements can be done. The Major area of fake news detection right now is covered by Machine Learning method because it gives a bit higher accuracy than average (when compared to other technologies) but at low cost. Some researchers tried to hybrid Machine Learning method and Natural Language Processing method to get result, that also worked well. So, we can conclude Blockchain method is best for critical fake news detection but it would be better to use Machine Learning and Natural Language Processing method on Industrial Level. This research paper is going to be useful for selection of particular technology for specific purpose.

6 Future Work

After analyzing all the methods We have seen that the highest accuracy achieved in all methods is 98.3% (except blockchain) and is achieved by deep learning method and the biggest disadvantage in blockchain method is that it is completely depending on the humans because nodes are verifying the news and nodes are basically humans which are connected in blockchain through the computers, So in future if we will be able to combine both technologies that in blockchain neural networks will be verifying that either the news is correct or not that it will be highly efficient method for detection of fake news.

References

1. Kaliyar, R.K.: Fake news detection using a deep neural network. In: 4th International Conference on Computing Communication and Automation (ICCCA), Greater Noida, India (2018)
2. Khan, S.A., Alkawaz, M.H., Zangana, H.M.: The use and abuse of social media for spreading fake news. In: IEEE International Conference on Automatic Control and Intelligent Systems (I2CACIS 2019), Selangor, Malaysia (2019)
3. Saad, M., Ahmad, A., Mohaisen, A.: Fighting fake news propagation with blockchain. In: IEEE Conference on Communications and Network Security (CNS): Workshops: DLoT: 2nd International Workshop on Distributed Ledger of Things, Florida (2019)
4. Agarwalla, K., Nandan, S., Nair, V.A., Hema, D.D.: Fake news detection using machine learning and Natural Language Processing. Int. J. Recent Technol. Eng. (IJRTE) 7(6), 844–847 (2019). ISSN: 2277–3878
5. Pérez-Rosas, V., Kleinberg, B., Lefevre, A., Mihalcea, R.: Automatic detection of fake news. In: Proceedings of the 27th International Conference on Computational Linguistics, Association for Computational Linguistics, Santa Fe, New Mexico, USA, pp. 3391–3401 (2018)
6. Pham, L.: Transferring, transforming, ensembling: the novel formula of identifying fake news. In: The First-Place Entry for Fake News Classification at WSDM Cup (2019)
7. Gurav, S., Sase, S., Shinde, S., Wabale, P., Hirve, S.: Survey on automated system for fake news detection using nlp & machine learning approach, vol. 06, no. 01, January 2019
8. Aphiwongsophon, S., Chongstitvatana, P.: Detecting fake news machine learning method. In: 15th International Conference on Electrical Engineering/Electronics, Computer, Telecommunication and Information Technology (ECTI-CON), Bangkok (2018)
9. Dey, A., Rafi, R.Z., Parash, S.H., Arko, S.K., Chakrabarty, A.: Fake news pattern recognition using linguistic analysis. In: 2nd International Conference on Imaging, Vision & Pattern Recognition, Dhaka, Bangladesh (2018)
10. Granik, M., Mesyura, V., Fake news detection using naive Bayes classifier. In: IEEE First Ukraine Conference on Electrical and Computer Engineering (UKRCON), Vinnytsia, Ukraine (2017)
11. Reddy, P.B.P., Reddy, M.P.K., Reddy, G.V.M., Mehata, K.M.: Fake data analysis and detection using ensembled hybrid algorithm. In: 3rd International Conference on Computing Methodologies and Communication (ICCMC), Chennai, India (2019)

12. Traylor, T., Straub, J., Snell, N.: Classifying fake news articles using natural language processing to identify in-article attribution as a supervised learning estimator. In: IEEE 13th International Conference on Semantic Computing (ICSC), Newport Beach, CA, USA (2019)

13. Paul, S., Joy, J.I., Sarker, S., Shakib, A.-A.-.H., Ahmed, S., Kumar, A.: Fake news detection in social media using blockchain. In: 7th International Conference on Smart Computing & Communications (ICSCC), Sarawak, Malaysia (2019)

Identification of Salient Attributes in Social Network: A Data Mining Approach

Ruchi Mittal$^{(\boxtimes)}$ iD

Chitkara University Institute of Engineering and Technology,
Chitkara University, Punjab, India
ruchi.mittal@chitkara.edu.in

Abstract. Social Media is a source with tremendous volumes of data which is only growing by the day. Taking a cue from earlier studies on data generated from social media, this study is based on a dataset originally drawn from the Facebook social network page of a large multinational cosmetics company. A total of 500 out of 790 posts published on the social media page were analyzed through the data mining classification technique i.e. linear regression. Nine numeric attributes (variables) were regressed with one attribute considered as the criterion attribute and the rest eight as predictor attributes. The eight dependent variables were: V1 "lifetime post total reach", V2 "lifetime post total impressions", V3 "lifetime engaged users", V4 "lifetime post consumers", V5 "lifetime post consumptions", V6 "lifetime post impressions by people who have liked your page", V7 "lifetime post reach by people who like your page", V8 "lifetime people who have liked your page and engaged with your post"; and the independent variable was V9 "Total interactions - the sum total of comments, likes, and shares of a post". The results show that not all predictors are significant in explaining the criterion variable. Similarly, a correlation matrix was generated where the inter-attribute correlation among all nine attributes was calculated. The results of association drawn from correlation are different from regression which depicts the fundamental difference and approach of these two techniques. WEKA version 3.8 was the data mining software used to analyze the dataset.

Keywords: Social media · Data mining · Classification

1 Introduction

Social media has become an inseparable part of our lives [1] with over 80% of the global population having access to one or the other social media platform. Some popular social media sites are, in decreasing order of subscribers: Facebook, YouTube, WhatsApp, Messenger, WeChat, Instagram amongst others. For organizations, commercial and non-commercial, the use of social media for promotional purposes has a variety of advantages such as:

a) Reach
b) Low cost
c) High interactivity

© Springer Nature Singapore Pte Ltd. 2020
U. Batra et al. (Eds.): REDSET 2019, CCIS 1230, pp. 173–185, 2020.
https://doi.org/10.1007/978-981-15-5830-6_16

d) Instant communication
e) No intermediary
f) Customer feedback
g) Customer referrals

In addition another extremely useful spin-off of using social media is the data in generates. This data can we further used by organizations to analyze the hidden patterns among the data i.e. application of data mining techniques.

Social media, in terms of applications, can be categorized into 4 quadrants called the social media matrix [1] i.e. Relationship (profile-based and customized message); Self-media (profile based and broadcast media); Collaboration (content based and customized message) and Creative-outlets (content base based and broadcast message). Categorizing social media helps data scientists in deciding which data mining tools shall be more effective for which type of platform (Fig. 1).

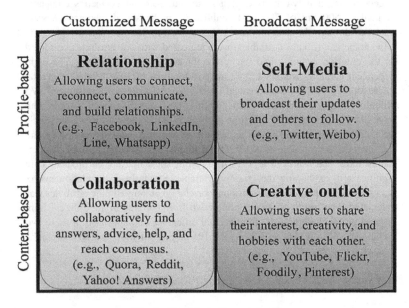

Fig. 1. Social media matrix [1]

New technologies such as social media have significantly narrowed the gap between organizations and their stakeholders, especially customers. Organizations are increasing their presence on social media as a result of which a great amount of data is being generated. This has led to the emergence of concepts such as big data and data driven business intelligence [2]. Data mining presents a viable solution to deal with this new data being generated at an immensely fast pace [3, 4]. Data mining is a popular and promising discipline for researchers to gain insights into the ever-increasing data across almost every domain of analysis. Data is the real value to the organization if it is analyzed properly to get some meaningful business knowledge. This data can be collected from various places over a period of time to be utilized in future to learn more about the organization and its important stakeholders [5, 6]. A vast amount of such data can be extracted from social media and can be run through the data mining techniques to know about the perceptions, behavior and human interactions on a specific subject related to the product, brand, or an organization [7]. One such case witnessed a massive use of social media through YouTube and Facebook as 2008 election campaigns in the United States [8] and the potential of analytical tools on such data to make future predictions at a national scale. Thus, with the rise in online social media data, the need for its analysis is also gaining attention of the researchers in the recent years.

Social media tops the agenda of many business enterprises today and firms are increasingly making their presence felt on leading social media platforms such as Facebook, Twitter, YouTube, LinkedIn etc. With the advent of technology 4.0 and technological disruption taking place in every business sector, the traditional ways of brand promotion are giving way to promotion through effective social media management. The biggest challenge with social media is the fact that it can be co-created by consumers and can get largely beyond the control of traditional marketing [9]. Given the extremely high penetration and reducing costs of internet coupled with growth in smart phone usage, social media transcends all boundaries of age, income, gender, social status and other socio-demographic indicators. Social media is both a cause and consequence of digitalization. Every individual group or organization leaves their digital imprints through the use of social media. These are a rich repository of data which can further be used in data analytics. Popular sources of extracting social data are microblogging, media sharing, social news, blog comments and forums, social networking sites, and book-marking sites [10]. While this exponential growth in data generation is known, what are scantly known are the patterns and hidden meanings within this data. Additionally, the data in addition to being humongous is also very noisy and ever-changing. One of the most effective tools available to researchers dealing with such kind of data is data mining. According to [11], social media analysis can exploit the use of data mining techniques by the researchers and business analysts to have a better understanding of data and predictive analytics involving brand management, content analysis, sentiment analysis, community or group detection [12], information diffusion [13], influence propagation [11], individual behavior analysis [14], group behavior analysis [15], and marketing research for businesses [16].

This study is based on a publicly available dataset that was originally used by Moro and others and now available in the open source data repository UCI datasets [17].

The aim of this study is to create a regression based predication model using select numeric attributes and also to analyze the inter-attribute correlation matrix. To achieve the aim, WEKA data mining software shall be applied. The data used in the study is related to posts' of a renowned cosmetics brand during the year of 2014. The study uses the data of 500 useable responses out of 790 responses due to missing data. The model shall be based on a dataset extracted from the company's official Facebook page. Facebook, as a social media platform, has been selected keeping in consideration its global unparalleled popularity. Additionally, SNS (social networking sites) – such as Facebook - are the most heavily researched social media platform among the various types of social media platforms available i.e. SNS, Blogs, Microblogs, Content communities and Forums [2].

The rest of the paper is organized as follows: Sect. 2 discusses some key previous research studies done in the field of data mining in the context of datasets drawn from social media; Sect. 3 discussed the methodology applied to achieve the aim of the study; Sect. 4 looks into the results and its analysis. The last section concludes the study and gives directions for future research. This is followed by the list of references cited in the paper.

2 Review of Literature

Using the keyword "Facebook" generated 13,30,000 entries on Google scholar from 2015 onwards; similarly "LinkedIn" generates 2,58,000 and "Twitter" generates 14,60,000 entries. This suggests the immense popularity of these terms in the world of scholarly research. Social media research has witnessed tremendous growth in the past few years with a major focus on how to make it a more effective form of communication. Social media marketing (SMM) is multidisciplinary and cross functional and managing it is a very complex affair [18]. Social media spend of organizations is increasing many fold globally making SMM a very influential sub-function within the marketing analytics domain [19]. In a study on the content analysis and a systematic review of SMM literature [20], the authors identified the firm/organization and consumer as the focus of earlier studies. Within the firm focus, the subjects analyzed were: "degree of use and facility if using social media", "Optimization, measurement, and impact of social media marketing strategies" and "abusive/unethical use". Within consumer focus, the subjects analyzed were: "increased consumption", and "use, search and share of information". In a seminal research [21] developed an evaluation model for measuring the effectiveness of a firm's investment in social media where the model consists of six stages: "setting evaluation objectives", "identifying key performance indicators (KPIs)", "identifying metrics", "data collection and analysis", "report generation and management decision making".

In a study on the comparison between Facebook and Twitter, [22] demonstrated that the marketing effectiveness is the same both the sites given that managers use the same marketing tactics in Facebook and Twitter. Various social media platforms such as Facebook, Twitter, Instagram, LinkedIn among others have been a significant subject of research in the past as far as data analytics is concerned [21–27]. As a field of science, social media marketing (SMM) is multidisciplinary and multi-faceted. It can be viewed from various perspectives such as e-commerce, data analytics, e-marketing, information systems, social media and behavioral sciences [1]. Data mining in the context of social media has been studied within a wide variety of differing perspectives ranging from fake news detection [28], adverse drug reaction [29], and emergency situation awareness [30] to the more "mundane" task of prediction of consumption patterns or other marketing sub-functions such as branding, customer satisfaction surveys, customer complaints, product feedback, sales promotion effectiveness and so on [22]. Almost all data analysis objectives can be achieved by the common strategy of using data mining, but the real task is to understand the data and identify the most relevant technique that may deliver the target objectives. In the field of data mining in marketing, for instance, one may use clustering or classification for market segmentation and customer profiling; association, clustering or topic modeling for product ontology and product reputation; regression, association or collaborative filtering for promotional marketing analysis, recommender systems, pricing strategy analysis, competitors' analysis; location based advertising and community dynamic analysis, amongst others [2]. In prior studies, social media has been the subject of the following different types of analyses: "predictive analysis", "natural language process", "effectuation analysis", "statistical analysis", "sentiment analysis", "behavioral analysis", "social media activity analysis", and "content analysis" [1, 2]. A study [31] proposes a variety of data mining methods to analyze datasets generated from social media. The prevalent use of data mining and the emerging expertise and sophistication of computing and data analytics has led to a situation where, as argued by [32], it is much more important than before to ensure that something useful is generated in terms of applications of the results. In earlier studies, authors provided clarity on how to exploit data mining techniques to uncover the interesting insights in the data obtained from social media platforms. They also recognized that in spite of many issues and challenges of security and privacy, large size of digital data, validating the results, and dynamic network arrangements, researchers are bringing in a lot of innovation in data mining tools and techniques to mine such data because of the evidential factors indicating the predictive power of data mining in the field of marketing, business, and society to have a deeper insights of customer behaviors on social media [33]. In a separate study, authors applied data mining on the data extracted from a company's Facebook page. They used SVM, one of the most popularly used technique of data mining for classification using 7 input and one output variable and they came up with two best models as "Lifetime Post Consumers" and the "Life time People who have liked a Page and engaged with a post". Authors justified their study by explaining its contribution in making the predictions to help the branding team at various stages of decision making. Further advertising and other text/sentiment analysis were also considered as a futuristic approach in the area [17]. In a different study, authors emphasized upon the importance of social media presence of the beauty brands for awareness and to engage their customers. Authors used statistical tools to perform descriptive analysis of six beauty brands in order to answer some of the business intelligence questions such as which types of posts on Facebook about the brands are likely to attract the customers; types of promotions that help to engage the customers on social media; and likelihood of the customer to respond on a Facebook posts on these brands. Such insights can help the researches in content management and customer engagement [34]. Authors analyzed blogs consisting of consumers' reactions in the form of comments, sentiments, and opinions corresponding to brands. Authors observed microblogs as a significant tool in analyzing the sentiments of consumers towards various brands and treated it as an important part of their strategy planning. They investigated 150,000 microblogs to observe the positive and negative remarks, frequency of brand mentioning, etc. These insights can help in knowing the behavioral aspects of their valuable customers and can further help in better customer relationship management [35]. Authors in a study described the growing use of social media for promotion and marketing by various companies and thereby generating a huge volume of digital data having the contents left by customers in terms of remarks, likes, comments and emotions. Various analytics can then be explored to understand these contents to know about the brand, company and their associated customers. Earlier studies applied text mining on the data generated from the social web pages of most popular brands offering pizza to unhide the behavioral patterns of customers to improve business value and enhance customer experience [36]. Authors emphasized on the concept of big data and the type of methods that can be explored for the analysis of big data. They primarily focused on the requirement of appropriate tools to analyze heterogeneous, unstructured data such as audio, video, text which is actually 95% of the big data. Authors also made the recommendations on the efficient tools and technologies for making predictions in structured big data as it gives the most valuable and reliable outcomes. They also recognized the need of real-time analysis as a future research scope [37–39].

3 Methodology

This research uses data mining techniques to further the aim of the study. Figure 2 depicts the entire process.

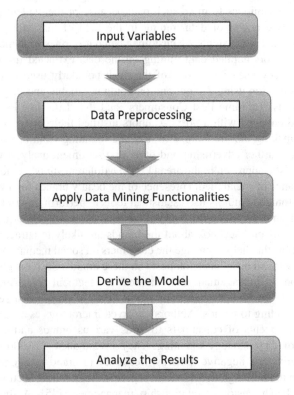

Fig. 2. Data mining process

Out of the 19 variables only those were selected as input variables which had numeric values. This left out 10 attributes and only 9 attributes were used for further processing; the details of these attributes are as per Table 1. The data mining technique used here was the linear regression method which is a type of classification technique. Linear regression predicts a range of continuous values which are captured within numeric data. This is followed by derivation of the model (Table 3) and analysis of the results (Table 4 and Table 5). In addition to linear regression, a correlation-matrix was also generated (Table 5) to contextualize the results of the regression analysis performed.

This study is based on a dataset originally drawn from the Facebook social network of a large multinational cosmetics company. A total of 500 out of 790 posts published on the social media page were analyzed. An early seminal study using the same dataset attempted to establish through data mining the impact of social media metrics on the branding strategy of the cosmetics firm [11, 17]. The dataset comprises of four classifications namely, (1) identification of individual posts; (2) the text/content is each post; (3) the features of each post; and (4) the performance based metrics which can be used to measure the impact of each post and the performance metrics to measure the impact of the page. For the purpose of this study, only the performance metrics shall be considered for further analysis. (i.e. the fourth classification).

WEKA machine learning tool version 3.8 is used for the data mining tasks in this study. Starting from 1993, WEKA is today a refined version after undergoing a number of upgrades. This tool has been very effectively used by researchers to apply data mining techniques to their data [5]. The two techniques applied to analyze the data are: "linear regression" and "correlation matrix". "Linear regression" is an approach that explains the relationship between a scalar dependent variable and one or more explanatory variables (also known as independent variables). Regression is a causal technique and linear predictor functions whose unknown model parameters are based on estimation from the data. The second technique used is the correlation matrix which essentially explains association among or between variables. It looks at how pair of variables is linearly related. The measure of the strength of the correlation is denoted in terms of Pearson's "r". In this case, the correlation matrix of n random variables $X_1,\ldots,$ Xn is the $n \times n$ matrix whose (i,j) entry is corr(X_i, X_j).

4   Results and Analysis

The data analysis in this study is based on WEKA classification data mining technique of linear regression (for model building and testing) and principal component analysis (for generating the correlation matrix output). Regression is a popular tool used by machine learning and data mining researchers [38–40].

Table 1. Variable type, performance metrics and mescription.

—
— Var X_{1-8} are independent variables
— Var X_9 shall be treated as a dependent variable
—
— "Var X_1: Lifetime post total reach - the total unique users who saw the page post
— Var X_2: Lifetime post total impressions – impressions of the post through different channels
— Var X_3: Lifetime engaged users – the total unique number of people who clicked anywhere on a post
— Var X_4: Lifetime post consumers – the total unique number of people who clicked anywhere on a post
— Var X_5: Lifetime post consumptions – the total clicks anywhere in a post
— Var X_6: Lifetime post impressions by people who have liked your page – total impressions by users who have only liked the page
— Var X_7: Lifetime post reach by people who like your page – the number of people who have seen the post
— Var X_8: Lifetime people who have liked your page and engaged with your post – the number of users who at the same time liked a page and clicked anywhere on the post
— Var X_9: Total interactions - the sum total of comments, likes, and shares of a post".

The proposed model is $X_9 = X_1 + X_2 \ldots X_8$ where $X_9 = \sum$ "comments" + "likes" + "shares". A total number of 500 instances (out of 790, with 290 being eliminated due to confidentiality issues) were used for the analysis (Table 2).

Table 2. Data characteristics.

— Attribute	— Missing Values	— Unique	— Type	— Minimum value	— Maximum value	— Mean	— Standard Deviation
— X1	— 0	— 470	— numeric	— 238	— 180480	— 13903.36	— 22740.79
— X2	— 0	— 488	— numeric	— 570	— 1110282	— 29585.95	— 76803.25
— X3	— 0	— 344	— numeric	— 9	— 11452	— 920.34	— 985.02
— X4	— 0	— 354	— numeric	— 9	— 11328	— 798.77	— 882.51
— X5	— 0	— 388	— numeric	— 9	— 19779	— 1415.13	— 2000.594
— X6	— 0	— 482	— numeric	— 567	— 1107833	— 16766.38	— 59791.02
— X7	— 0	— 438	— numeric	— 236	— 51456	— 6585.49	— 7682.01
— X8	— 0	— 290	— numeric	— 9	— 4376	— 609.99	— 612.726
— X9	— 0	— 152	— numeric	— 0	— 6334	— 212.12	— 380.23

Table 3. Results of WEKA linear regression.

— === Run information ===
—
— "Scheme: weka.classifiers. functions. LinearRegression -S 0 -R 1.0E-8 -num-decimal-places 4
— Relation: Social Media
— Instances: 500
— Attributes: 9
—   X1
—   X2
—   X3
—   X4
—   X5
—   X6
—   X7
—   X8
—   X9 (DV)
— Test mode: 10-fold cross-validation"
—
— === Classifier model (full training set) ===
—
—
— Linear Regression Model
—
— X9 =
—
—   0.015 * X1 +
—   -0.0042 * X2 +
—   -0.1548 * X4 +
—   0.0038 * X6 +
—   0.3179 * X8 +
—   -7.313
—
— === Cross-validation ===
— === Summary ===
—
— "Correlation coefficient   0.547
— Mean absolute error   141.6573
— Root mean squared error   325.4768
— Relative absolute error   84.77 %
— Root relative squared error   85.33 %
— Total Number of Instances"   500

The final model achieved is as per Table 4.

Table 4. Final regression model

—

— X_9 = -7.313 + (0.015)* X_1 + (-0.0042)* X_2 + (-0.1548)* X_4 + (0.0038)* X_6 + (0.3179)* X_8

—

— As per this model, out of the 8 attributes that were regressed 5 attributes (X_1, X_2, X_4, X_6 and X_8) were found to be significant predictors of X_9. The other attributes i.e. X_3, X_5 and X_7 were insignificant in the regression model.

Table 5. Attribute ranking and correlation matrix

"Search Method:
  Attribute ranking.

Attribute Evaluator (unsupervised):
Principal Components Attribute Transformer
Correlation matrix (correlation coefficients)"

"X1	X2	X3	X4	X5	X6	X7	X8	X9
X1	1	0.69	0.57	0.48	0.32	0.32	0.74	0.4	**0.54**
X2	0.69	1	0.37	0.32	0.23	0.85	0.65	0.32	**0.34**
X3	0.57	0.37	1	0.97	0.68	0.26	0.61	0.84	0.57
X4	0.48	0.32	0.97	1	0.71	0.22	0.5	0.81	**0.35**
X5	0.32	0.23	0.68	0.71	1	0.16	0.36	0.58	0.24
X6	0.32	0.85	0.26	0.22	0.16	1	0.58	0.31	**0.25**
X7	0.74	0.65	0.61	0.5	0.36	0.58	1	0.65	0.62
X8	0.4	0.32	0.84	0.81	0.58	0.31	0.65	1	**0.49**
X9	0.54	0.34	0.57	0.35	0.24	0.25	0.62	0.49	1"

The correlation matrix as per Table 5, was generated by the PCA functionality under the "select" attributes drop down option.

The correlation between the dependent variable (X9) and the significant attributes (X1 to X8) as per the regression output are highlighted in the table. As one can observe, out of the three dropped (insignificant) attributes namely, X3, X5 and X7, the attributes X3 and X7 show a reasonably high correlation with X9 (X3:X9 0.57; X7:X9 0.62) which is in some cases higher than the significant attributes.

The problem with the model lies in the high correlation between any two dependent variables. This is undesirable as it leads to multicollinearity which makes the regression model less precise. In this case, X2:X1, X4:X3, X7:X1, X6:X2, X5:X3, X8:X3, X5:X4, X8:X4, all have a correlation coefficient above 0.60 indicating a high degree of multicollinearity in the dataset.

5 Conclusion and Future Research

The study considered nine(one dependent and eight independent) numeric attributes out of the total of 19 in the entire dataset. WEKA version 3.8 machine learning tool [41, 42] was effectively applied for the data mining classification based on linear regression. The regression results show that five attributes namely: "lifetime post total reach", "lifetime post total impressions", "lifetime post consumers", "lifetime post impressions by people who have liked your page" and "lifetime people who have liked your page and engaged with your post" have a significant predictive or an explanatory power towards the dependent variable. The five attributes explain the attribute named as "total interactions" which is the sum total of "comments," "likes," and "shares" of a post on the cosmetics company's Facebook page. A correlation matrix was also created for all nine attributes and the correlation between the dependent variable and the individual independent variables can be observed. The strongest correlation (where 'r' is the correlation coefficient) was between the dependent variable i.e. "total interactions" and (in decreasing order; only 0.5 or more considered) were "lifetime post reach by people who like your page" (r: 0.67), "lifetime engaged users" (r: 0.57) and "lifetime post total reach" (r: 0.54). One can observe that the results of correlation are very different from regression in terms of the explanatory power of the independent attributes. This shows the basic difference between regression and correlation –while regression looks at causal relationships, correlation looks at association only. Technically, for a study like the present one, the linear regression is more appropriate as it looks at cause-effect relationships. The strength of this study lies in the effective examination of numeric attributes which in some ways are fundamentally different from categorical attributes. However, future research can look at the other attributes – including categorical attributes – and evaluate how they rate in terms of their predictive power.

References

1. Zhu, Y.-Q., Chen, H.-G.: Social media and human need satisfaction: implications for social media marketing. Bus. Horiz. **58**(3), 335–345 (2015)
2. Misirlis, N., Vlachopoulou, M.: Social media metrics and analytics in marketing–S3M: a mapping literature review. Int. J. Inf. Manage. **38**(1), 270–276 (2018)
3. Fan, S., Lau, R.Y., Zhao, J.L.: Demystifying big data analytics for business intelligence through the lens of marketing mix. Big Data Res. **2**(1), 28–32 (2015)
4. Chen, H., Chiang, R.H., Storey, V.C.: Business intelligence and analytics: from big data to big impact. MIS Q. **36**(4), 1165–1188 (2012)
5. Aggarwal, A., Mittal, R., Gupta, S., Mittal, A.: Internet of Things driven perceived value co-creation in smart cities of the future: a PLS-SEM based predictive model. J. Comput. Theor. Nanosci. **16**, 4053–4058 (2019)
6. Mittal, R.: Antecedents and consequences of massive open online courses adoption: a structural model in the Indian context. J. Comput. Theor. Nanosci. **16**, 4028–4033 (2019)
7. Mittal, R., Rattan, V.: Evaluating rule based machine learning classifiers for customer spending in a shopping mall. J. Adv. Res. Dyn. Control Syst. **11**(08)(Spl), 716–719 (2019)
8. Qualman, E.: Socialnomics. Knopf Books for Young Readers, New York (2009)

9. Kohli, C., Suri, R., Kapoor, A.: Will social media kill branding? Bus. Horiz. **58**, 35–44 (2015). https://doi.org/10.1016/j.bushor.2014.08.004

10. Aggarwal, C.C., Zhai, C.X.: A survey of text clustering algorithms. In: Aggarwal, C., Zhai, C. (eds.) Mining Text Data. Springer, Boston (2013). https://doi.org/10.1007/978-1-4614-3223-4_1

11. Agarwal, N., Liu, H.: Modeling and data mining in blogosphere. Synth. Lect. Data Min. Knowl. Discov. **1**, 1–109 (2009). https://doi.org/10.2200/S00213ED1V01Y20090-7DMK001

12. Tang, L., Liu, H., Zhang, J., Agarwal, N., Salerno, J.J.: Topic taxonomy adaptation for group profiling. ACM. Trans. Knowl. Discov. Data (TKDD) **1**, 1 (2008). https://doi.org/10.1145/1324172.1324173

13. Gruhl, D., Guha, R., Liben-Nowell, D., Tomkins, A.: Information diffusion through blogspace. In: Proceedings of the 13th International Conference on World Wide Web, pp. 491–501. ACM, New York (2004). https://doi.org/10.1145/988672.988739

14. Lauw, H., Shafer, J.C., Agrawal, R., Ntoulas, A.: Homophily in the digital world: a LiveJournal case study. Internet Comput. IEEE **14**(2), 15–23 (2010). https://doi.org/10.1109/MIC.2010.25

15. Tang, L., Liu, H.: Towards predictive collective behavior via social dimension extraction. IEEE Intelligent Systems **25**(4), 19–25 (2010). https://doi.org/10.1109/MIS.2010.36

16. Domingos, P., Richardson, M.: Mining the network value of customers. In: Proceedings of the Seventh ACM SIGKDD International Conference on Knowledge Discovery and Data Mining, pp. 57–66 (2001). https://doi.org/10.1145/502512.502525

17. Moro, S., Rita, P., Vala, B.: Predicting social media performance metrics and evaluation of the impact on brand building: a data mining approach. J. Bus. Res. **69**(9), 3341–3351 (2016). https://doi.org/10.1016/j.jbusres.2016.02.010

18. Felix, R., Rauschnabel, P.A., Hinsch, C.: Elements of strategic social media marketing: a holistic framework. J. Bus. Res. **70**, 118–126 (2017)

19. Chang, Y.T., Yu, H., Lu, H.P.: Persuasive messages, popularity cohesion, and message diffusion in social media marketing. J. Bus. Res. **68**(4), 777–782 (2015)

20. Alves, H., Fernandes, C., Raposo, M.: Value co-creation: concept and contexts of application and study. J. Bus. Res. **69**(5), 1626–1633 (2016)

21. Keegan, B.J., Rowley, J.: Evaluation and decision making in social media marketing. Manag. Decis. **55**(1), 15–31 (2017)

22. Leung, X.Y., Bai, B., Stahura, K.A.: The marketing effectiveness of social media in the hotel industry: a comparison of Facebook and Twitter. J. Hosp. Tour. Res. **39**(2), 147–169 (2015)

23. Salloum, S.A., Al-Emran, M., Monem, A.A., Shaalan, K.: A survey of text mining in social media: Facebook and Twitter perspectives. Adv. Sci. Technol. Eng. Syst. J. **2**(1), 127–133 (2017)

24. Thirumalai, C., Sree, K.S., Gannu, H.: Analysis of cost estimation function for Facebook web click data. In: 2017 International conference of Electronics, Communication and Aerospace Technology - IEEE, vol. 2, pp. 172–175 (2017)

25. Del Vicario, M., Zollo, F., Caldarelli, G., Scala, A., Quattrociocchi, W.: Mapping social dynamics on Facebook: the Brexit debate. Soc. Netw. **50**, 6–16 (2017)

26. Mhamdi, C., Al-Emran, M., Salloum, S.A.: Text mining and analytics: a case study from news channels posts on Facebook. In: Shaalan, K., Hassanien, A.E., Tolba, F. (eds.) Intelligent Natural Language Processing: Trends and Applications. SCI, vol. 740, pp. 399–415. Springer, Cham (2018). https://doi.org/10.1007/978-3-319-67056-0_19

27. Culotta, A., Cutler, J.: Mining brand perceptions from Twitter social networks. Mark. Sci. **35**(3), 343–362 (2016)

28. Gu, Y., Qian, Z.S., Chen, F.: From Twitter to detector: real-time traffic incident detection using social media data. Transp. Res. Part C Emerg. Technol. **67**, 321–342 (2016)
29. Russell, M.A., Klassen, M.: Mining the Social Web: Data Mining Facebook, Twitter, LinkedIn, Instagram, GitHub, and more. O'Reilly Media, Sebastopol (2018)
30. Shu, K., Sliva, A., Wang, S., Tang, J., Liu, H.: Fake news detection on social media: a data mining perspective. ACM SIGKDD Explor. Newsl. **19**(1), 22–36 (2017)
31. Sarker, A., et al.: Utilizing social media data for pharmacovigilance: a review. J. Biomed. Inform. **54**, 202–212 (2015)
32. Yin, J., Karimi, S., Lampert, A., Cameron, M., Robinson, B., Power, R.: Using social media to enhance emergency situation awareness. In: Twenty-Fourth International Joint Conference on Artificial Intelligence, June 2015
33. Feng, J., Barbosa, L.D.A., Torres, V.: U.S. Patent No. 9,262,517. Washington, DC: U.S. Patent and Trademark Office (2016)
34. Kennedy, H.: Post, Mine, Repeat. Palgrave Macmillan UK, London (2016). https://doi.org/10.1057/978-1-137-35398-6
35. Barbier, G., Liu, H.: Data mining in social media. In: Aggarwal, C. (ed.) Social Network Data Analytics, pp. 327–352. Springer, Boston (2011). https://doi.org/10.1007/978-1-4419-8462-3_12
36. Shen, B., Kimberly, B.: Social media, social me: a content analysis of beauty companies' use of Facebook in marketing and branding. J. Promot. Manage. **19**(5), 629–651 (2013). https://doi.org/10.1080/10496491.2013.829160
37. Jansen, B.J., Zhang, M., Sobel, K., Chowdury, A.: Twitter power: Tweets as electronic word of mouth. J. Am. Soc. Inform. Sci. Technol. **60**(11), 2169–2188 (2009). https://doi.org/10.1002/asi.21149
38. He, W., Zha, S., Li, L.: Social media competitive analysis and text mining: a case study in the pizza industry. Int. J. Inf. Manage. **33**(3), 464–472 (2013). https://doi.org/10.1016/j.ijinfomgt.2013.01.001
39. Gandomi, A., Haider, M.: Beyond the hype: big data concepts, methods, and analytics. Int. J. Inform. Manage. **35**(2), 137–144 (2015). https://doi.org/10.1016/j.ijinfomgt.2014.10.007
40. Baskin, I.I., Marcou, G., Horvath, D., Varnek, A.: Bagging and boosting of regression models. Tutorials Chemom. **28**, 249–255 (2017). https://doi.org/10.1002/9781119161110.ch16
41. Bhargava, N., Purohit, R., Sharma, S., Kumar, A.: Prediction of arthritis using classification and regression tree algorithm. In: 2017 2nd International Conference on Communication and Electronics Systems (ICCES - IEEE), pp. 606–610 (2017) https://doi.org/10.1109/CESYS.2017.8321150
42. Naik, A., Samant, L.: Correlation review of classification algorithm using data mining tool: WEKA, Rapidminer, Tanagra, Orange and Knime. Procedia Comput. Sci. **85**, 662–668 (2016). https://doi.org/10.1016/j.procs.2016.05.251

Energy Efficient Content Based Image Retrieval Recommender System in Mobile Cloud

Rajalakshmi Krishnamurthi$^{(\boxtimes)}$ and Mukta Goyal

Department of Computer Science, Jaypee Institute of Information Technology,
Noida 201307, India
k.rajalakshmi@jiit.ac.in, mukta.goyal20@gmail.com

Abstract. In current scenario, mobile devices is one of the primary sources of capturing images, due to advancement in sensors and ease of availability of digital cameras inbuilt in mobile devices. Due to high demand for content-based image retrieval applications, there is need to develop efficient methods to handle user image query, measure similarity, and response back with relevant images. But, storing large number of images in mobile device has constraints like huge memory consumption, limited computational capability, wastage of energy in storing, accessing and processing these data. In this paper, Mobile Cloud Computing based content image retrieval (MCC-CBIR) system is proposed, where images are offloaded from constrained mobile devices into resource-rich cloud server, using image compression mechanism. Recommender system is used to retrieve images based on intensity, color, and texture metrics from the cloud. The experimental results reveal less computation time, efficient image compression. Also, performance ratios like precision, relevancy, recall of the retrieved relevant images are also found to be excellent.

Keywords: Mobile cloud computing · Image offloading · Cloud computing · Compression · Content based image retrieval

1 Introduction

Mobile Computing is one of the recent high-end technology in which mobile devices are portable and capable of computing on the go [1]. Smartphones, digital cameras are examples of such predominating mobile computing device in the current scenario. Due to exponential growth in usage of mobile devices, such as smartphones, there is urging the need for mobile computing to be more enhanced. As per forecast made by ABI research, by 2020 the amount of inbuilt data traffic using a mobile device is expected to grow by 600%. In this regards to data traffic generated by mobile devices, one of the major data sources are images captured through cameras embedded with and smartphones, or standalone digital cameras. As per [2], the popular applications of these captured images are for content image retrieval, mobile visual search, mobile image search, augmented reality, mobile object recognition, etc.

© Springer Nature Singapore Pte Ltd. 2020
U. Batra et al. (Eds.): REDSET 2019, CCIS 1230, pp. 186–203, 2020.
https://doi.org/10.1007/978-981-15-5830-6_17

However, the mobile computing has a lot of limitations within its current scope [3]. The major limitations of mobile computing are battery power consumption, bandwidth consumption, computation power, wireless signal propagation, resource allocation, security, and privacy.

To address these problems, one of the well-known solutions is offloading of contents or computation from the mobile device to highly capable systems like remote servers or cloud computing servers. Cloud computing environment provides computing facility, in which large groups of remote servers are networked to allow centralized data storage and online access to computer services or resources [4].

In today's real-world application scenario, there is an immense need to get more storage out of our mobile device and laptop. Particularly, persons like people in business, office goers, professors, teachers or students use more than one device such as a mobile phone, tablet and/or a computer [5]. Storing large-scale common data in all these devices will lead to a lot of memory consumption. For example, images being a most important memory of a person's life uses most of the hard drive space, one wants to store his images to a secure private place which at the same time is easy to access.

The primary goal of the proposed system is to overcome the limitations of resource-constrained mobile computing device [6]. Next goal is to provide the users with a secure, easy and efficient platform to manage their images available on different devices, all at one place. In this work, one such efficient methodology is proposed, in which, the mobile device contents are offloaded to a cloud environment. In this proposed system, the images are stored on the resource-rich remote servers rather than on a local disk (Fig. 1).

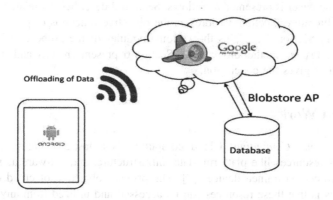

Fig. 1. Mobile content offloading using cloud computing

Any user can upload images that are captured through the camera of the user device, to personal cloud storage, and can later view them from any of user device from anywhere. This technique enhances the user accessibility and also enables the user to save a lot of memory on device and computation time of mobile device processor. Then, the contents are retrieved as per user request from the cloud. Further, to enhance the retrieval mechanism, a recommender system is also incorporated. Further, by offloading mechanism, the issues in mobile computing like memory wastage, and battery power is addressed. Hence, the proposed system is named as Mobile Cloud Computing for Content-Based Image Retrieval (MCC-CBIR).

Key contributions of this paper are

- It provides the user collect images from all user devices; store them on private cloud storage. This approach, will allow the user to store all personal images at one place, in an organized manner. The user now doesn't have to worry about personal images getting leaked, or losing them as they are always backed up to a secure private cloud.
- The user can access all of the personalized images at any time from the cloud, on the go or at home, from user's mobile, tablet or computer.
- The application will store a compressed thumbnail of every image to provide a better preview of the albums.
- For the better user experience, the application works smartly to determine the image that the user is more likely to view and start loading it beforehand.
- It provides a platform to edit the images, create albums or efficiently manage the images.

The rest of the paper is presented as follows. Section 2 describes the related works that exist in the literature. Section 3 addresses the objective functions of proposed MCC-CBIR system. Section 4 explains the various modules of the proposed system. Section 5 elaborates the methodology used. Section 6 presents results and discussions. Finally, Sect. 7 gives the conclusion.

2 Related Work

A. *Mobile Cloud Computing:* Cloud computing is a fast-growing paradigm that provides resources like platform, data, infrastructure, and software as services to the resource-constrained devices [7]. The primary objective of cloud computing resources is that these resources can be accessed and utilized from anywhere and also at any time [8]. The major role players in cloud computing are Amazon Web Services, Microsoft Azure, Google Cloud [9, 10]

The Mobile cloud computing Forum (MCCF) describes mobile cloud computing as the environment that is very simple and ease in accessibility. Where, both data storage and the processing upon data take place outside the mobile computing device connected to the remote cloud server through Internet [11–13]. There is a wide application of offloading using mobile cloud computing as stated in [14–16].

B. *Content-based image retrieval*: In literature, quite a number of work is done towards content-based image retrieval (CBIR) [17, 18] The extensive image data library can be found in personalized image collections, healthcare clinical image records, digital art gallery, mapping and geographical information systems records, digital imaging in journalism, digital legal records [19, 20]. The increased demand for digitization has proven to be needed for efficient methodology and techniques for content-based image retrieval schemes.

There are three basic types of queries used in CBIR systems to retrieve images from image repositories [21]. They are a primitive query, logical query, and abstract query. Out of these query methods, the primitive method is simple, efficient, almost primarily applied in every CBIR systems. Further, the primitive query is based on three basic features of images. The features of the image are color, shape, and texture. Next, the logical query is based on the identity of an image like label, color, size and shape attributes. The abstract query is based on similarity score of images obtained using mathematical computation.

In [22] elaborated CBIR system based on color features in the images. In this colors of images are used to generate color histograms and then images are compared for retrieval based on it. Also, in [23] authors proposed color histogram technique for content-based image retrieval. The proposed methodology is evaluated for speed and efficacy.

[24] Presented textual analysis for multi-resolution using Gabor filter. The author suggested that Gabor filter has minimized the joint two-dimensional uncertainty vectors of space and frequency. The Gabor wavelet-based image retrieval achieved accuracy and robustness. The emphasis on the texture as similarity metric is carried in [25]. In this authors focuses on naturally occurring texture and also based on structural texture. The similarly textual metrics like perception, segmentation, analysis, and synthesis are compared with other techniques to model human perception.

C. *Image Compression Techniques:* In [26], the image compression technique based Discrete Cosine transformation (DCT) is discussed. The Joint Photographic Experts Group (JPEG) images are used as input data type. The compressions of fully collared still images are verified for DCT transformation. In [27], the two techniques namely lossy and lossless transformations for image compression are discussed. In this Discrete Wavelet Transformation (DWT) and DCT are incorporated.

D. *YC_bC_r Model:* YC_bC_r is the one of the advanced representation of color space. The variable Y represents the luminance component in the image [25]. The variable C_b represents a blue difference of the chrominance component. Similarly, the Cr represents the red difference of chrominance components. Unlike the conventional RBG color space, the model has low bandwidth consumption. Also, subsampling and compression are being applied to the chrominance components of this color space.

E. *Binning Model:* The technological advancement in a digital camera has increased its popularity as essential integration with mobile devices, security systems, automobiles, etc. Further, it is important to observe that the sensor resolution of these digital cameras are highly improved than adding optical resolution using high-cost hardware enhancements like lenses. Particularly, for digital still images, the sensor resolution has shown significantly enhanced to operate even in poor lighting environment [25].

Binning methods are the process of producing superpixel by combining the electric charges of adjacent pixels. The superpixel's energy signal is then amplified and converted into digital values. The main purpose and advantages of this binning method are to suppress the noise generated through camera sensors. This noise read is suppressed by combining the charge of the adjacent pixel and convert the low pixel values to high super pixel values.

F. *Similarity measurement:* The conventional way to measure the similarity between images is to compare the features of the query image with the feature of the database images [26]. The two popular similarity measurement techniques are Euclidean distance and Cosine Angle Distance [25]. The Euclidean distance generates metrics for dissimilarities between two given vectors. Instead, to produce similarity score between two vectors, the cosine angle distance methods are used.

Consider, given two vectors V and U in N dimension space. Where vector $V = \{v_1, v2, v3...v_N\}$, and $U = \{u_1, u2, u3...., u_N\}$. Then, the similarity score (SS) is obtained using the following equation,

$$SS = \frac{\sum_{i=1}^{N} v_i u_i}{\sqrt{v_i^2}\sqrt{u_i^2}} \qquad (1)$$

3 Objective of Proposed System

The first main objective of the proposed MCC - CBIR system is to reduce the storage capacity of the mobile device. Next, the images available in the mobile devices are offloaded to the cloud. The added feature to image offloading is that the images are compressed, encoded and then stored in the cloud.

The next objective is to reduce computation power and network delay. Next, a content-based image retrieval system is proposed. Main advantages are that the proposed Recommender systems avoid the retrieval of entire images from the cloud storage. Instead, the proposed MCC - CBIR system retrieves only recommended images by the users systematically.

The third objective of the proposed MCC - CBIR system is to provide the user with an interface where the user can upload, view and manage images to cloud storage. This objective will allow the user to save a lot of memory in the mobile device, and provide easy access to view any of images from anywhere.

The fourth objective is to provide security and privacy to the user. Inorder to meet this, the user will be asked to log in to the application before accessing the personal cloud storage. To implement the verification process an XML file which contains all the username and correct password combinations.

There are several benefits of the proposed MCC-CBIR system. First, it provides one platform to store all the images. Second, it provides private cloud storage. No need to worry about losing the data anymore, always stay backed up, stay safe. Thirds, while surfing the images from the cloud, recommender system will show the next more likely to view image and load it beforehand every time to view any image. Fourth, the users can organize, personalize the images in an album. There is also image editing options available to the user.

4 Proposed System

The proposed architecture consists of three levels namely, application level, service level and cloud level as shown in Fig. 2.

First, the application level provides user interface and user authentication system. The user begins interaction with proposed MCC - CBIR system through this graphical user interface to the mobile user. In the logic interface, the user is asked to log in to his account to access the personal storage.

Next, at the service level, the user would have three different choices- upload images, view the images and manage the existing library. The application will upload users' pictures onto a secured personal online storage, delete them from your laptop or mobile, leaving the smaller resolution images to view as thumbnails, when the user selects to upload images.

Third, in cloud level, specifications and information regarding image are gathered. The information like date created, last viewed, liked or not, album name, views, etc., will also be stored in the cloud. While viewing the uploaded images, the mobile application will also recommend the more likely to view image based on the selected image. The user can also organize the images in an album.

USER INTERFACE: The user interface of the desktop application is simple and user-friendly. It is designed using the Swing API in Java.

LOGIN: Users are authenticated through a form-based login. After authentication, there is an attempt by the system to determine which storage that user should gain access to the cloud server. If the user fails to authenticate himself for more than five times, his new reset password is sent to the registered email ID.

UPLOAD IMAGES: The user is asked to select the images he wants to upload to the cloud. The original files on the computer will be deleted leaving only a compressed lower resolution thumbnail.

VIEW IMAGES: While viewing the images, the application will suggest the more likely to view image. This image will be downloaded beforehand. The description of CBIR is displayed below (Fig. 3):

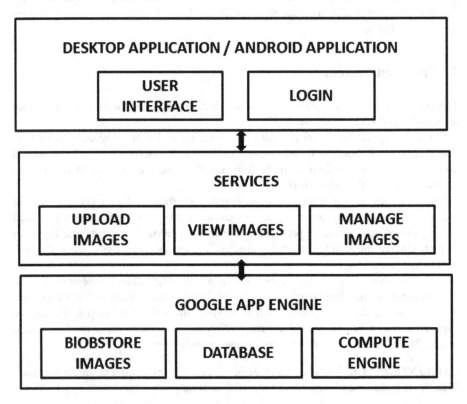

Fig. 2. Overall architecture of proposed system

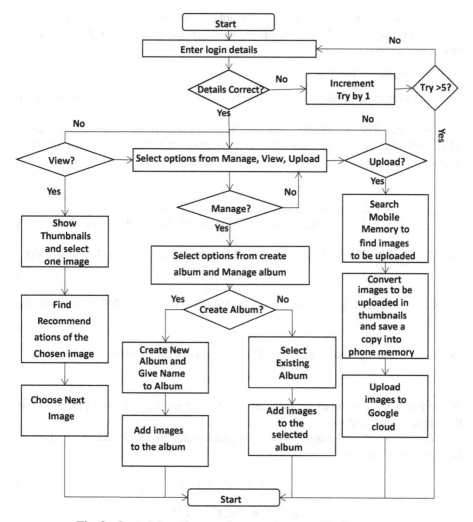

Fig. 3. Control flow diagram of proposed image offloading system

5 Methodology

Recommender system module works on content-based image retrieval and texture mapping, which shows many relevant images, which are more likely to view based on the user preferences. It won't be convenient for the user to download the images every time user surfs the image collection. A solution to this problem is to download lower resolution images rather than high definition original images.

DCT transformation and DWT transformation can be used to compress an image [8]. In this work, two procedures are proposed to work around the compressed image. First, the proposed MCC - CBIR system stores the compressed image in the cloud storage along with the original image that the user uploads. Second, the system computes the compressed image in the Google compute engine (on the cloud, data offloading) every time it is required.

A. *Compression of Images*

There are four basic modules namely preprocessing, transformation, quantization and encoding.

Preprocessing: The priliminary step is to map the red, green, blue color values to YC_bC_r selection space [9]. Here after, each component value of grayscale image is mapped to the colour space of Y, C_b, and C_r channels.

Here,

$$Est\_RedValue = RedValue/255, \ Est\_GreenValue$$
$$= GreenValue/255, \ Est\_BlueValue = BlueValue/255 \quad (2)$$

$$Est\_Y = 0.299 \cdot Est\_RedValue + 0.587 \cdot Est\_GreenValue + 0.114 \cdot Est\_BlueValue \tag{3}$$

$$Est\_C_b = -0.169 \cdot Est\_RedValue - 0.331 \cdot Est\_GreenValue + 0.500 \cdot Est\_BlueValue \tag{4}$$

$$Est\_Cr = 0.500 \cdot Est\_RedValue - 0.419 \cdot Est\_GreenValue - 0.081 \cdot Est\_BlueValue \tag{5}$$

Where Est_Y takes value in the range of 0 and 1 and Est_C_b and Est_C_r take value in the range of -0.5 and 0.5.

Next step involves the conversion of estimated value into 8-bit values based on the Eqs. (6)–(8) given below:

$$Y = 219 \cdot Est\_Y + 16 \tag{6}$$

$$C_b = 224 \cdot Est\_C_b + 128 \tag{7}$$

$$C_r = 224 \cdot Est\_Cr + 128 \tag{8}$$

Transformation: Discrete Cosine Transformation (DCT) is used for image transformation by JPEG Image Compression Standards. The DCT function is defined as the product of image block and special constant matrix.

$$F(c) = S * Block * S^T \tag{9}$$

Where, Block represents 8×8 elements obtained from pre-processed image and S represents a special 8×8 matrix.

S contains constant value for the first row based on the formula 0.5*(pi/2). Next, the cosine value is placed on every interval (0.5*(j*pi/16, j*pi − j*pi/16)) for remaining jth rows. By this way, the DCT technique places high-intensity information in top left side of the D matrix. The DCT is iteratively applied to the 8×8 block of the whole image.

Quantisation: This process involves converting the near zero value of image elements into zero and also to concatenate the remaining elements into integer value. The purpose of the quantization is to convert only larger value to zero. However, quantization is inefficient for converted small values to zero, due to lose of original value of image. In order to over this disadvantage, Huffman coding is used along with quantization. Hence, the loss of original value due to excess resolution is avoided.

Encoding: Huffman coding is used in JPEG images. First, the quantized DCT values of the images are obtained. Then elements of 8×8 blocks are amplified through constant amount of values. Then the DCT is performed to retrieve the original image.

$$B^{\wedge'} = S^{\wedge}T \, D^{\wedge'}S \tag{10}$$

Finally, the value 127 is added to each element and thus obtains the original image.

- *Image offloading into a cloud server*

The mobile computing environment on handheld mobile devices is limited by resources like memory space, computation power, battery power, network connectivity, communication capability. In order, overcome these limitations, the images are offloaded to the resource-rich cloud servers.

The service level of the proposed MCC - CBIR system provides the launching platform for offloading images into the remote cloud. In today scenario due to the almost ubiquitous nature of the Internet, it's common prevailing that, every mobile user has network connectivity either through WiFi or 4G technologies. Once the users select the upload option on the mobile application user interface, the selected images from the constrained mobile device are offloaded to the remote cloud storage.

- *Content-based Image Retrieval*

The steps involved in the content-based image retrieval are discussed below is depicted in Fig. 4.

Input: Name of Directory that contains various Images

Step 1: Read Images from the directory.

Step 2: Read Image RGB values and apply Intensity Function to each pixel of an image. Create an Intensity Matrix based on YC_bC_r Model. Store it in a file.

Step 3: Read every pixel RGB value of the Image. Extract only 7th and 6th bit of each color. Append the value of the three colors together and categorize them as per 64 Binning Model and save them to a file.

Step 4: Read every pixel value and calculate co-occurrence matrix using the same YC_bC_r model. Next step is to remove code redundancy using entropy encoding. Now, calculate energy and contrast.

Step 5: Normalize the texture matrix using above formulae and store the values into a file.

Step 6: Read all the files and map the images by key-value pairs where the key is file number and value is the linked list containing all values from all the files as a vector for every feature.

Step 7: Apply Manhattan Distance to cluster the images together.

Step 8. Normalize the vector distance using standard deviation and cosine similarity. Cluster the images with nears similarities.

Step 9: Display the recommended images to the user.

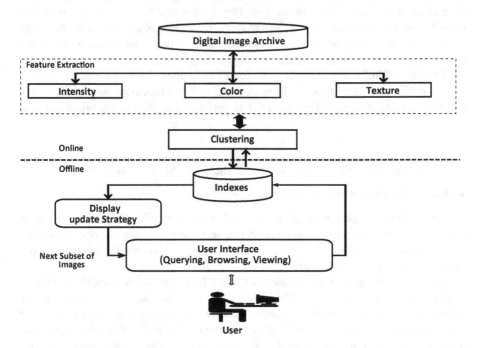

Fig. 4. Methodology for proposed MCC - CBIR recommender system in mobile cloud computing

6   Results and Discussion

To perform image offloading and retrieval in a mobile device using CBIR mechanism, 600 images are considered from Google images. There are six types of images collected namely A, B, C, D, and E. It is to be noted that, the proposed MCC - CBIR system performs the retrieval process among 600 images, irrespective of these different types of dataset. The wide range of data set is considered namely butterfly, yacht sailing, Human, Landscape, and Tourists concerning their lexicographic dataset name. Further, 100 images are considered in each dataset. The details of the images are given Table 1. The images with file format JPEG is considered, as it is the most common and popular format of images. The butterfly type images have an average size of 64 KB, Yacht Sailing with 77 KB, Human with 90 KB, Landscape 86 KB, Tourists with 103 KB.

Table 1. Details of dataset

Data set	Name	File format	No of images	Average size (KB)
A	Butterfly	JPEG	100	64
B	Yacht sailing	JPEG	100	77
C	Human	JPEG	100	90
D	Landscape	JPEG	100	86
E	Tourists	JPEG	100	103

Android platform is used to develop the mobile application. Further, the image gallery is created using android application, graphical user interface. Images are uploaded into Google App Engine Cloud using Blob store API.

A. *Discrete Cosine Transformation (DCT) transformation of images:*

DCT transformation is performed based on image compression. It is observed that average compression rate achieved is 52% at after 20 iterations as depicted in Table 2.

Table 2. Achieved compression rate using DCT technique

Data set	Size (KB)	Compression rate (%)	Number of iteration
A	30	54.7	20
B	64	44.2	20
C	124	52.2	20
D	86	57	20
E	78	54.4	20

B. *Content-Based Image Retrieval*

The content-based Image Retrieval is performed based on four parameters namely, intensity, color code, Texture and combination of Intensity and color. The snapshot of Intensity-based CBIR is given in Fig. 5 and Fig. 6. Similarly, texture based, and color retrieval is performed.

The computation time for each of the four technique (i) Intensity based, color base, Combine intensity and color based and Texture based of content-based image retrieval is depicted in Fig. 7. The average time for intensity-based is 1800 ms, with color based retrieval it took 2162 ms, combined Intensity and color based consumed 2650 ms and texture based retrieval consumed 2773 ms. Thus, the proposed image offloading and retrieval system is observed to be very effective regarding memory and computation power.

Fig. 5. Intensity-based image retrieval

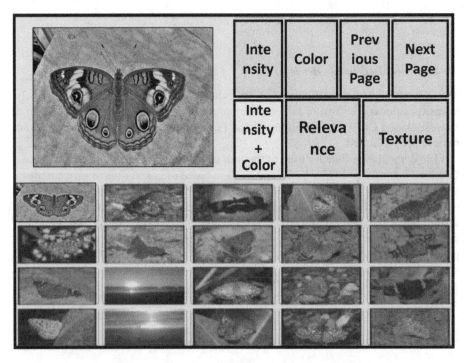

Fig. 6. Intensity + Color based image retrieval

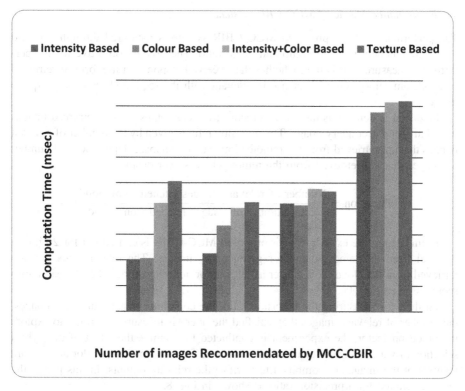

Fig. 7. Comparison of computation time in MCC-CBIR

C. *Offloading of Images from Mobile device to Cloud Server*

The main objective of mobile cloud computing is to overcome the limitations of the mobile computing like memory consumption, battery life, computation power, network connectivity, etc. Due to the advancement of Internet available through Wi-Fi or 4G in every mobile device has made convenient for the network connectivity to reach out for the resource-rich external server is very much possible. In this work, the mobile cloud computing is used as an effective solution for proposed MCC-CBIR system.

In this experiment, three types of data network connectivity are considered. First, the Internet connectivity of using broadband internet Speed of 40 Mbps, at broadband data of 150 GB using. Next, the data network connectivity through 4G mobile service provider at the data rate of 20 GB using internet speed of 15 Mbps. Third, local area network through Ethernet at the speed of 100 Mbps with a data rate of 20 GB. In all the three cases the communication cost is observed to be effectively used. The Image offloading using these networks from mobile device to the remote cloud server has been performed with ease. The user interface provides the additional facility of the user to offload images fully or partially to the cloud server. Thus, the network connectivity is up to the necessity of the proposed MCC-CBIR application to perform well.

D. *Performance Metric of MCC CBIR system*

The performance of the proposed MCC CBIR system is measured through standard parameters namely precision ratio and recall ratio. The primary objective for the performance measurement is that, whether that received response in the form of retrieved images from remote cloud database is relevant with the requested response of query image.

Precision is defined as the measurement of the correctness of the retrieved images with that of the user query image. The precision ratio is given by the number of relevant images that are retrieved from the remote cloud server database. Upon the total number of images that are retrieved from the remote cloud server database.

$$\text{Precision} = \frac{\text{Number of relevant images fetched from cloud}}{\text{Total number of images fetched from cloud}}$$

In this paper, the experiment for proposed MCC-CBIR is carried out for 20 image retrieval from the remote cloud for given query images. The total images that are retrieved from the cloud are a cluster as relevant or not relevant based on the similarity score as given Eq. (1).

Further, for measuring the precision ratio, the condition is that, out of 20 images, the number of relevant images that satisfied the query is measured. Further, to explore the precision factor, the experiment is conducted to examine the effect of the hybrid selection of various image features that extracted. That, the intensity, color and texture features of the image are combined to retrieve the relevant outputs. In this paper, the graph is plotted for a precision ratio as shown in Fig. 8.

The recall is defined as the measure of the completeness of the retrieved images with that of the user query image. Recall ratio is given by the number of relevant images that retrieved from the remote cloud server database upon the total number of actual relevant images available on the cloud server database.

$$\text{Recall} = \frac{\text{Number of relevant images fetched from cloud}}{\text{Total number of relevant images available on cloud}}$$

To estimate the recall ratio, in this experiment, 20 images are retrieved from the remote cloud server database. Similar to precision ratio, the various combinations of image extraction features like intensity, color and texture are explored.

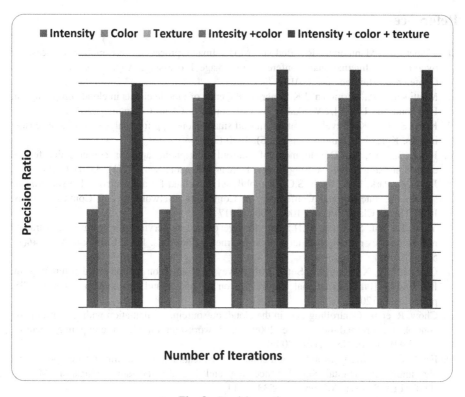

Fig. 8. Precision ratio

7 Conclusion

There is huge need to overcome the limitations of a mobile computing environment like memory, computation power, and battery power. In this work, an efficient system for image offloading and image retrieval is proposed. The proposed MCC - CBIR system uses cloud-based image offloading. The images from a mobile device are offloaded into the cloud using Blob API. Further, the offloading is made enhanced by compressing the images. The DCT transformation is performed based on YC_bC_r model. The performance of DCT is achieved to be 52% compression rate. Thus, the memory consumption is reduced in mobile devices, by this method of image offloading. Next, the relevant image retrieval from cloud based on recommender system. The CBIR is performed based on intensity, color, and texture. The future scopes of this works are offloading all the data computations onto the Google compute engine. Next, to increase the type of extensions those are supported. Further, the proposed MCC - CBIR system provides enhanced facility to upload Video and Audio files into the cloud.

References

1. Thabet, R., Mahmoudi, R., Bedoui, M.H.: Image processing on mobile devices: an overview. In: International Conference on Image Processing, Applications and Systems Conference, Sfax, pp. 1–8 (2014

2. Miettinen, A.P., Nurminen, J.K.: Energy efficiency of mobile clients in cloud computing. In: HotCloud 2nd USENIX Workshop on Hot Topics in Cloud Computing (2010)

3. Kang, S., Lee, K.: Development of android smart phone app for analysis of remote sensing images. Korean J. Remote Sens. 26(5), 1–10 (2010)

4. Kang, S., Lee, K.: Development of android smartphone app for corner point feature extraction using remote sensing image. Korean J. Remote Sens. 27(1), 33–41 (2011)

5. Jang, M., Park, M.S., Shah, S.C.: A mobile ad hoc cloud for automated video surveillance system. In: International Conference on Computing, Networking and Communications, ICNC, Santa Clara, CA, pp. 1001–1005 (2017)

6. Yang, K., Ou, S., Chen, H.H.: On effective offloading services for resource-constrained mobile devices running heavier mobile Internet applications. IEEE Commun. Mag. 46(1), 56–63 (2008)

7. Guan, L., Ke, X., Song, M., Song, J.: A survey of research on mobile cloud computing. In: IEEE/ACIS 10th International Conference on Computer and Information Science, ICIS, pp. 387–392 (2010)

8. Chow, R. et al.: Controlling data in the cloud: outsourcing computation without outsourcing control. In: Proceedings of the 2009 ACM workshop on Cloud computing security, pp. 85–90. ACM, New York (2009)

9. Ferzli, R., Khalife, I.: Mobile cloud computing educational tool for image/video processing algorithms. In: Digital Signal Processing and Signal Processing Education Meeting (DSP/SPE), Sedona, AZ, pp. 529–533 (2011)

10. Kang, S., Kim, K., Lee, K.: Tablet application for satellite image processing on cloud computing platform. In: IEEE International Geoscience and Remote Sensing Symposium - IGARSS, Melbourne, pp. 1710–1712 (2013)

11. Chun, B.-G., Ihm, S., Maniatis, P., Naik, M., Patti, A.: CloneCloud: elastic execution between mobile device and cloud. In: Proceedings of the Sixth Conference on Computer Systems, pp. 301–314 (2011)

12. Wang, S., Dey, S.: Rendering adaptation to address communication and computation constraints in cloud mobile gaming. In: Global Telecommunications Conference, IEEE, pp. 1–6 (2010)

13. Hauswald, J., Manville, T., Zheng, Q., Dreslinski, R., Chakrabarti, C., Mudge, T.: A hybrid approach to offloading mobile image classification. In: International Conference on Acoustics, Speech and Signal Processing, ICASSP, pp. 8375–8379. IEEE (2014)

14. Han, J., Mckenna, S.J.: Query-dependent metric learning for adaptive, content-based image browsing and retrieval. IET Image Proc. 8(10), 610–618 (2014)

15. Rui, Y., Hang, T.S.: A relevance feedback architecture for content based multimedia information retrieval systems. In: Proceedings IEEE Workshop on Content based access of Image and Video Libraries, pp. 82–89 (2012)

16. Stricker, M., Orengo, M.: Similarity of color images. In: Niblack, W.R., Jain, R.C. (eds.) Proceedings SPIE Conference on Storage and Retrieval for Image and Video Databases III, pp. 381–392. SPIE, Bellingham (1995)

17. Pappas, T.N., Neuhoff, D.L., de Ridder, H., Zujovic, J.: Image analysis: focus on texture similarity. Proc. IEEE 101(9), 2044–2057 (2013)

18. Kui, W., Yap, K.-H.: Fuzzy SVM for content-based image retrieval: a pseudo-label support vector machine framework. IEEE Comput. Intell. Mag. **1**(2), 10–16 (2006)
19. Krishnapuram, R., Medasani, S., Jung, S.-H., Choi, Y.-S., Balasubramaniam, R.: Content-based image retrieval based on a fuzzy approach. IEEE Trans. Knowl. Data Eng. **16**(10), 1185–1199 (2004)
20. Fadaei, S., Amirfattahi, R., Ahmadzadeh, M.R.: New content-based image retrieval system based on optimised integration of DCD, wavelet and curvelet features. IET Image Proc. **11**(2), 89–98 (2017)
21. Kundu, M.K., Chowdhury, M., Bulo, S.R.: A graph-based relevance feedback mechanism in content-based image retrieval. Knowl. Based Syst. **73**, 254–264 (2015)
22. Dubey, S.R., Singh, S.K., Singh, R.K.: Local neighbourhood-based robust color occurrence descriptor for color image retrieval. IET Image Proc. **9**(7), 578–586 (2015)
23. Sandid, F., Douik, A.: Texture descriptor based on local combination adaptive ternary pattern. IET Image Proc. **9**(8), 634–642 (2015)
24. Rashno, A., Sadri, S., SadeghianNejad, H.: An efficient content-based image retrieval with ant colony optimization feature selection schema based on wavelet and color features. In: International Symposium on Artificial Intelligence and Signal Processing, AISP, Mashhad, Iran, pp. 59–64 (2015)
25. Lee, P.Y., Loh, W.P., Chin, J.F.: Feature selection in multimedia: the state-of-the-art review. Image Vis. Comput. **67**, 29–42 (2017)
26. Lin, C.H., Chen, H.Y., Wu, Y.: Study of image retrieval and classification based on adaptive features using genetic algorithm feature selection. Expert Syst. Appl. **41**(15), 6611–6621 (2014)
27. Chandrashekar, G., Sahin, F.: A survey on feature selection methods. Comput. Electr. Eng. **40**, 16–28 (2014)

Semantic Web-Based Information Retrieval Models: A Systematic Survey

Anil Sharma[1(✉)] ⬥ and Suresh Kumar[2]

[1] USIC&T, Guru Gobind Singh Indraprastha University, Delhi, India
anilsharma.iimt@gmail.com
[2] Ambedkar Institute of Advanced Communication Technologies & Research,
Delhi, India
drsureshpoonia@gmail.com

Abstract. Effective representation of semantics in information sources has been central to Semantic Web (SW), since its inception. An information retrieval (IR) system must exploit the semantic knowledge embodied in web resources. Several attempts were made by researchers to make retrieval systems capable of utilizing web semantics. As a result, IR systems exploiting Semantic Web technologies were proposed in literature. In this paper, we have presented various intelligent models for information retrieval on SW. Our work mainly focuses on systems based on multi-agent, ontology, soft computing and concept-based paradigm employed for information retrieval on SW. Some existing surveys tried to comprehend various intelligent information retrieval models on SW, but their scope is limited. In this paper, we are providing a systematic and comprehensive elucidation of various intelligent information retrieval models with their basic approaches, key features and limitations in the context of SW. We have also provided a comparison of reviewed IR models for critical analysis.

Keywords: Information retrieval models · Semantic Web · Agent-based model · Concept-based model · Ontology-based model · Soft Computing-based Model

1 Introduction

With the proliferation of web technologies, huge amount of information is uploaded to and downloaded from the Internet every day. Due to information overload problem, users are struggling to get relevant information on the web. Search engines perform their work based on keyword search, making it difficult to tackle the problem of synonyms and polysemy. This makes the existing information retrieval methods ineffective with low precision and recall rates. This problem occurred as world wide web was not intended to be processed by machines. Although, the web page includes metadata and actions to be taken, but it does not provide interpretation of semantic of contents.

Tim Berner Lee proposed the solution of this problem in terms of the Semantic Web (SW) [1]. The word semantic simply means meaning. Meaning of data provides effective usage of data by establishing relationship and context with other data items.

© Springer Nature Singapore Pte Ltd. 2020
U. Batra et al. (Eds.): REDSET 2019, CCIS 1230, pp. 204–222, 2020.
https://doi.org/10.1007/978-981-15-5830-6_18

SW provides semantics and context to web resources, enabling machines to understand the meaning of web contents. With the advent of SW, machines can process web contents more intelligently that aid in effective information search and retrieval. Ontology is a central concept in SW. Resource Description Framework (RDF), Web Ontology Language (OWL) and SPARQL are fundamental technologies behind the success of SW.

Ontology is taxonomy of domain concepts represented in the form of entities, their attributes and the relationships between entities. It is regarded as knowledge representation tool that formulate concepts of a domain in SW [2]. For representation of ontology concepts embodied in web resources, RDF was proposed in SW framework [3–5]. Later, to generalize the process of representation, processing and inference of web contents, OWL was developed under SW framework. OWL resulted as a stronger language with better machine interoperability as compared to RDF. DAML + OIL are universal SW markup language providing machine with capability to read, interpret and infer data. In [6], DAML + OIL was used for precise knowledge representation and retrieval.

WordNet [7] represents a general purpose ontology that stores words with their synonyms. WordNet API is employed in query expansion in [8, 9]. Wikipedia is a web-based domain independent structured encyclopedia [10]. Wikipedia found to be fruitful in applications such as question answering, named entity disambiguation, text categorization and computing document similarity. Wikipedia is also employed for computing semantic similarity between query and web document concepts [11]. Jena is a semantic framework used to manipulate RDF data. RDF data is manipulated using Jena tool [3, 9]. This tool is a Java API that employs SPARQL query language for processing, retrieval and manipulation of data in RDF format [9, 12].

Development of web technologies and universal availability of web based information systems are main reasons behind the existence of web based information retrieval (IR) systems. Despite of years of research in the IR field, still there is no proposal that wins. Effective utilization of web semantics by machines was one of the ideas behind conceptualization of SW. As a result, IR systems exploiting SW technologies were proposed.

1.1 Motivation of the Survey

It has observed from literature that since last two decades researchers have been very interested in SW based information retrieval. But despite this fact only a few surveys [13–19] were published on the topic. Although these surveys contributed well in the field but were limited in scope due to lack of comprehensive approach in coverage of topic.

A survey carried out in [13] focused only on agent-based personalized semantic IR. This survey provided description of only personalized semantic search based on mining techniques, neural networks, genetic algorithm, ontology and collaborative filtering, but failed to include comparative analysis of frameworks cited in the survey. The survey in [14] concentrated on concept-based IR models on SW. Some frameworks on

WordNet, SW, conceptual indexing and Word Sense Disambiguation were also discussed in this survey, but very limited frameworks were included in this survey. The survey in [15] discussed soft computing based intelligent IR models. Further, application of probability theory, Fuzzy Logic, Genetic Algorithms and Artificial Neural Networks in context of soft web mining were also deliberated. Inclusion of few numbers of frameworks in this survey made it limited in scope. The survey in [16] explored SW and IR architecture along with some prototype systems for query expansion. Again, discussion included few frameworks mentioned without challenges and research gaps. The survey in [17] enlisted various ontology based and agent-based models for SW search along with brief description about techniques used in cited frameworks. This survey included few related frameworks that limit the scope of this survey. The survey in [18] included a brief description of agent based and ontology-based IR models on SW but failed to include research gaps for enlisted frameworks. Moreover, the survey in [19] employed classification parameters for comparison of semantic search engines approaches. A comparison of cited approaches was also presented in this survey. But only few proposals were discussed without exhaustive coverage of state-of-the-art frameworks.

It is evident that referred surveys lack comprehensive coverage of SW-based IR models. In order to understand different intelligent IR models on SW one need to refer many scattered sources. Motivated with this fact, we decided to present a systematic and comprehensive survey on intelligent IR models on SW. A comparative analysis of referred surveys with our survey based on attributes (taxonomy, comparative analysis, tabular representation, graphical representation and research directions) is presented in Table 1, where (✓) shows inclusion and (✗) denotes non-inclusion of above said attributes.

Table 1. Comparative analysis of referred surveys with present survey.

Survey Papers	Models Taxonomy	Comparative Analysis of Frameworks	Tabular Representation	Graphical Representation	Research Directions
Thangaraj et al. [13]	✗	✗	✗	✗	✓
Ali and Ahmed [14]	✗	✗	✗	✗	✗
Ahmed and Ansari [15]	✗	✗	✗	✗	✗
Singh and Jain [16]	✗	✗	✗	✗	✗
Sharma A. [17]	✗	✓	✓	✗	✗
Balan et al. [18]	✗	✓	✓	✗	✗
Ezhilarasi et al. [19]	✗	✓	✓	✗	✓
Present survey	✓	✓	✓	✓	✓

1.2 Scope and Organization of the Survey

The scope of our survey includes:

- Explanation of intelligent IR models on SW environment.
- Tabular presentation of IR models on SW for deeper understanding.
- A comparative analysis of present study with cited studies focusing on basic approach, methodology, techniques and limitations is also presented.

The present survey is organized as follows: Introduction is included in Sect. 1, while Sect. 2 discusses web-based information retrieval. Section 3 throws light on traditional information retrieval models. Section 4 discusses intelligent information retrieval models, in which we focused mainly on concept-based model, agent-based model, ontology-based model and soft computing-based model for Intelligent IR. Section 5 is about discussions and analysis. Conclusions and research directions are presented in Sect. 6.

2 Web-Based Information Retrieval

An IR system is responsible for pre-processing; organizing, storing and indexing information for retrieval of relevant documents in response to user's query, while query-document matching algorithm and relevance ranking of resultant documents being most critical activities during retrieval process. A general model of information retrieval system is discussed in [20]. With the revolutionized development of online Information Systems in every domain, web-based IR has become important area of research. Dynamic nature of Web makes web-based IR systems different from traditional IR systems in terms of knowledge representation, indexing, query expansion and interpretation, retrieving relevant documents, ranking and presentation of resultant web pages.

Information retrieval models are broadly divided into two categories i.e. Traditional IR and Intelligent IR. First, traditional IR models were based on keyword search and were mainly dependent upon syntactics of search terms. These systems suffered mainly due to two reasons: first problem of synonyms and polysemy; and second, lack of standards for information representation. Semantics of search terms were ignored in traditional search methods as they focused on syntactic properties of search words. Second in Intelligent IR, with the conceptualization of semantic web, inclusion of semantics of keywords was realized. Now, more metadata can be embodied in knowledge base regarding a keyword. Information becomes machine understandable rather than just machine readable which paved road for intelligent models in information retrieval. Literature shows that in the last two decades researchers have proposed information retrieval systems based on various models which dealt with problems of traditional IR models. In Fig. 1, hierarchal representation of IR models is shown.

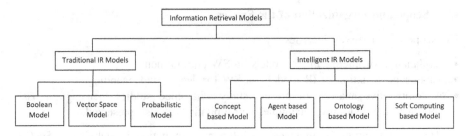

Fig. 1. Hierarchal representation of Information Retrieval Models

3   Traditional Information Retrieval Models

Traditional IR models were based on keyword search and were mainly dependent upon syntactics of search terms. Three models based on traditional IR are explained below as:

3.1   Boolean Model

In Boolean model, web pages and user's queries are denoted as index terms and Boolean expressions on index terms. This model exploits classical set theory and Boolean expressions to denote web pages and users query [21].

Limitations: Boolean Model has two major shortcomings: first, it is not able to deal with partial matching of documents with search terms as this model provides results based on exact match between web pages and user's query. Moreover, the fetched web page ranking is not considered in this scheme. Second, it's not easy to model each search query into Boolean expression.

3.2   Vector Space Model

Vector Space Model (VSM) is based on vector representation of documents and queries in multi-dimensional space. Non-binary weights based on term frequency are assigned to key terms in search query and web documents and the degree of similarity is calculated based on these weights [22].

Limitations: The problem with VSM is that it is unable to establish relationships between key terms making them unable to link with each other. Further, the relevance ranking of fetched web pages was not considered in this scheme.

3.3   Probabilistic Model

This model uses probability theory as underlying principle. Let Q represents user's query and W represents set of web pages while $S \subseteq W$ is a subset of web pages that consists of relevance information related to web pages and user's query [23, 24]. In this model, relevance ranking of fetched web pages depends upon descending order of probability of belongingness to subset S.

Limitations: Drawback of this model is that it does not incorporate frequency of key terms in relevance calculation. Also, some factors affecting relevance judgment like user preferences and score based on web page relevance to other users were not considered in this approach.

4   Intelligent Information Retrieval Models

There have been significant researches in devising intelligent methods for information retrieval on SW. Methods using various techniques like concept-based, agent-based, ontology-based and soft computing techniques etc. have been reported in literature for making machine more intelligent and web more machines readable. Following are some intelligent models used for information retrieval on SW:

4.1   Concept-Based Information Retrieval Model

Users recognize information in terms of concepts but mostly information retrieval systems employ keyword-based search mechanism. Concept can be considered as a collection of terms that together identify the clear meaning of the intended context [25]. The Concept-based IR system provides results based on conceptual relationship between web pages to the terms in user's query, rather than based on literal meaning or context found in web pages. IR system should be intelligent enough to capture the search intent and conceptual meaning of search terms in query. Conceptual Indexing and Word Sense Disambiguation (WSD) are two such approaches. Conceptual Indexing system automatically extracts conceptual information from documents and build hierarchical concept graph dynamically [26]. WSD hunt for sense implied by a term and based on that sense it assigns context to the term, whereas sense is defined by concepts. Concept-based system presents additional intelligence to IR by using ontologies.

As a result, Concept-based IR systems can fetch relevant documents even if query terms and their synonyms are not present in documents because the retrieval is guided by semantics not just by syntactic properties of terms in search query. A concept-based IR model is discussed in [27]. In this model, both information resources and user query both are represented as concepts. Word Sense Disambiguation (WSD) is employed to tackle problem of one word representing many concepts and to identify its context. Concept similarity is performed to find the conceptual match between user query and documents in information resources on Web. Knowledge repository plays an important role to facilitate concepts and their relationships with other concepts.

Limitations: The main drawback is that limited terms are incorporated in ontologies and conceptual information augmented about these terms is not complete.

In [28] authors proposed a concept-based information retrieval model that uses corpus such as Wikipedia for finding term co-occurrences and relationships between concepts. This approach employs Explicit Semantic Analysis (ESA) [29] which treats text semantics (meaning) as a combination of concepts found in knowledge resource rather than just depending upon syntactic structure of text. Feature selection works on query concepts to make it optimized for reasoning and matching. This method uses

Wikipedia as a knowledge resource to extract concepts embodied in it. So, this method cannot be deployed in very domain as it requires a pre-existing knowledge resource.

In [30] an improved concept-based IR system was presented. This model uses term clustering technique to find proximity of search term in a document. Weights and penalties were assigned to nouns using Okapi weighting scheme. Semantic frame provides matching between query and documents. Model may need significant modifications before deploying into more specialized domains like medical as concepts are overlapping in multiple clusters.

In [31] an IR system based on fuzzy formal concept analysis (FFCA), concept hierarchies and automatically built domain ontologies is proposed. Concept lattice is generated by exploiting context information from syntactic relations of a term with most frequent verbs in corpora. Fuzzy formal concept is used for relevance match between user query and search documents. Other fuzzy relations (like resemblance and tolerance) may be employed in fuzzy relational ontological modeling.

In [32] authors proposed concept-based semantic search in cloud employing Wikipedia ontology, double score weighting formula and Semantic searchable encryption scheme. Weighting scheme considered higher preference for concept associated with general meaning over concept associated with higher frequency terms of a document. Performance issue needs further investigations as encrypted search is not very efficient.

4.2 Agent-Based Information Retrieval Model

Agents are computer programs, belong to the field of Artificial Intelligence (AI) that learn the pattern and behavior of a user and act on his behalf. These agents implement the web retrieval service based on ontology [4]. Agents consider user's background, web knowledge, user's interests and searching patterns to satisfy their information need automatically. In literature, various agent-based models for information retrieval are reported. Each model used different types of agent depends specific objective. By employing ontologies, IR systems gain retrieval performance, but personalization and degree of relevance show no significant improvement [33].

A multi agent-based IR model is presented in [34]. This agent-based IR system employs multiple agents for a specific task in retrieval process. User agent consists of inference engine along with learning mechanism and environment module. Information gathering agent comprises of search strategies and optimization module. Semantic extraction module is used to extract semantics (nature, structure and relationships) of user's query and web pages. Semantic matching between user's query and web pages is performed by semantic matching agent and relevant results are forwarded to user agent.

Limitations: Building, managing and updating knowledge repositories are challenging tasks that require additional efforts.

In [4], authors proposed a multi-agent based intelligent information retrieval model in semantic web. In proposed work application of Information Collection, Storing, Reasoning, and Query Agents are reported for different task. Moreover, the proposed framework uses Resource Description Framework (RDF) model for web resources description, modeling, and web resources content representation. In the same paper, Web Ontology Language (OWL) was used to construct domain ontologies, which provide knowledge base for reasoning semantic query. This model makes use of four agents: Information Collection Agent is employed for metadata extraction from web page content description in semantic web. Storing Agent is used for storing metadata coming from information collection agent. Reasoning Agent perform semantic reasoning (semantic matching and keyword retrieval from semantic relevance). Query Agent provides the results to meet user's requirement by querying the metadata based on semantic ontology. Hence the application of multi agent improved the efficiency and precision.

In [33], authors applied intelligent agents to retrieve the information in semantic web. Further, authors exploit ontology knowledge to speedup query processing and improve accuracy. The presented model uses following agents: User Interface Agent which interact with user and make use of ontology knowledge to group user's information need. Retrieval Agent matches the user's requirement with resource description in database and collaborates with Management Agent to augment user's interest factor for arranging results in relevance of user's interest. Resource Description Agent captures the semantic description based on domain ontology from web pages captured by crawler and stores it into database. Ontology Collection Agent captures new ontologies and update existing ontologies by interaction of ontology base with www. Management Agent interacts with other agents for collaborating information of user's interest with Retrieval Agent for arranging results in user preference order. Matching module uses semantic matching algorithm for user's information request with semantic description in database.

In [35] authors proposed agent-based method for discovering web services. Semantic information related to web services plays an important role in their discovery by users. Using domain ontology and web ontology language (OWL) we can enhance the quality of representation of semantic information. Web service composition can be incorporated in the model for creating new web services by merging and reusing existing ontologies.

In [36] authors presented semantic web and agent based educational system that facilitates course contents and information in ontology form. Similarity between query concept and course resource is computed using least common super-concept (structural taxonomy based) similarity measure. A comparative analysis of Vector Space Model (VSM) and ontology-based IR indexing system is also presented in this paper. Feature-based methods for computing semantic similarity which provide additional knowledge about the concept and its relationship with other concepts were not considered in this proposal.

4.3 Ontology-Based Information Retrieval Model

Ontologies are knowledge representation tool and facilitate classification as well as mapping of concepts and their relationships in hierarchical structure. Literature shows employing conceptual knowledge (ontologies) in information retrieval process has contributed to solution of key limitations in information retrieval. An ontology-based IR system is presented in [37]. In this model, ontology vocabulary extraction is performed on query search terms. Vocabulary terms from documents are extracted based on concepts of ontology and are presented as vector space. Similarity between query and document concepts is calculated using correlation matrix between concepts.

Limitations: Relationship between different concepts, inference of semantic information from concepts, unifying semantic representations and mapping of knowledge from heterogenous ontologies. Also, supervised learning approaches can be employed to identify semantic relations between query and document concepts.

In [12], authors presented an IR system based on domain ontology. To exploit semantic relationship between ontologies query language SPARQL is used in this proposal. Ontology provides concept hierarchy and logic reasoning support, which makes it suitable tool for semantic retrieval. In this model, SPARQL query language provides extraction of information by utilizing the association between concepts defined in ontology. As a future trend, the author gives an idea about using fuzzy ontology concepts for the proposed system. In [3], search engines based on Web Ontology Language was proposed. For indexing and retrieval of semantic relationships, an algorithm based on Web Ontology Language was proposed. Proposed indexing algorithm offers better ontology maintenance and retrieving algorithm facilitate better processing of user query. This scheme consists of these components: Repository of OWL-web pages, which was prepared by semantic web crawler automatically. Here author manually created this repository by preparing ontologies with Protégé ontology editor. The objective of Ontology Analyzer tool is semantic inference from web documents written in OWL. Authors applied Pellet Reasoner and Jena tool for this purpose. Thematic Repository is developed by Ontology Analyzer Tool, which acts as input for next component of proposed model i.e. Indexer, to store the index of ontology thematic repository. Retrieval scheme is employed for determination of relevance of information to end user using precision and recall. User Interface is used to obtain input query from user and to return relevant results.

In [9], authors presented an IR system based on domain ontology. Here meaning concepts are inferred from user's query. These inferred concepts and domain ontology are used for query expansion. SPARQL query is framed and used on knowledge base to return relevant web pages. The resulted pages are ranked according to query reference. Query expansion benefits the system by considering query concepts and synonyms of these concepts as well as new concepts associated to query. Query expansion exploits field ontology for finding terms related to original query. Semantic similarity between inferred concepts and domain ontology concepts is achieved using structure based measures [25].

In [38], authors conceived the idea of an intelligent IR system based on SW. In this model, semantic relations between web pages are estimated using proposed metric. Distributed Hash Table (DHT) is used for load balancing and range queries as well as for distribution and fault tolerance. In [6], authors introduced an IR system based on Web Ontology Language exploiting semantic markup. For documents and query semantic markup DAML + OIL SW language was used thus allowing inference at the time of document indexing, query processing and result evaluation. DAML + OIL allow reading, interpretation and inference to be done over the data by machines, making machines more intelligent in processing and retrieving information over the SW.

In [5], proposed SW based intelligent IR system for solving two problems. First is how to make web resources machine understandable? And second is how to implement domain knowledge concepts for semantic search? This system utilizes ontology for organizing metadata which not only provide contents of web resources but also provide semantic relationship documents and concepts hierarchy as a basis for semantic inference. Moreover, metadata and query are encoded in RDF. The results of user's query are sorted according to user's intent and presented in a suitable format.

In [8], an intelligent Cross-Lingual Information Retrieval (CLIR) system is presented that retrieved results also from web pages written in languages other than language in which user query is written. Results are returned in original query language after translation. Spell check technique is included to facilitate user with query support. It also supplements the search by including synonyms, related words of query tokens and semantic relations. This system uses query expansion and semantic relations to determine user's search intent and context to query thus reduces irrelevant web pages to be included in results set. Universal Networking Language (UNL) was employed for cross language support. The proposed search engine is tested for agriculture domain and performance is found reasonable with retrieval of relevant results.

In [39], authors proposed a knowledge retrieval process model using semantic metadata and artificial intelligence techniques. Based on ontology, metadata inside web document is queried which provide concept base retrieval in distributed environment of e-leaning resources. Proposed system employs ontology as vocabulary for Case-Based Reasoning (CBR) and ontology was developed using RDF language. Search returns both results based on semantic term and ontology concepts. The system is tested for information retrieval in digital library.

In [40], authors presented a model for personalized search engine using query clustering technique and SW, by utilizing context of query while considering search history. The keyword based search engines uses keyword matching approach yielding low quality results. Exploitation of popular search technique for page ranking method by some commercial entities to seek people attention has thrown a challenge to researchers in IR field. ECBR algorithm [26] is applied to estimate the degree of relatedness between query and service concept keeping synonym of query into consideration. This method was tested for service retrieval in transport domain ontology.

4.4 Soft Computing-Based Information Retrieval Model

IR systems suffer due to imprecise and vague knowledge representation in user query formulation. Soft computing is an effective tool to deal with such vagueness in information representation [41]. Literature shows that soft computing techniques such as fuzzy logic [42], rough set theory [43], artificial neural networks [44], genetic algorithms [45] and evolutionary computing [46] has been successfully applied in information retrieval. In [50] authors proposed a model of soft computing-based IR model in SW. Soft computing-based IR systems vary in semantic similarity measures used to match query and document concepts. These semantic similarity measures are broadly falling into three categories: taxonomical structure, feature, and information content based semantic similarity measures. Despite of advantages of each method none of these approaches clearly emerged as a solution.

Limitations: In taxonomical structure and Feature based methods similarity computation between two terms is based on ontological hierarchical structure and function of their properties (relationship to other similar terms in corpus), which is affected by degree of coverage of input ontology. Information content semantic similarity measure exploits an additional large text corpus to compute word frequency. So, this method cannot be deployed in every scenario, because existence of such a large corpus is not feasible for every domain. In our survey, we will restrict ourselves to fuzzy logic and rough set-based IR models.

In [47], an automated approach for annotating web services-based on fuzzy rules using VSM for semantic representation was introduced. Providing semantic annotation to web services helps them to get linked with relevant service concept in domain ontology. This facilitates automatic recognition, selection, retrieval, and composition of web services by machines. Fuzzy set theory is used to computer degree of membership function for calculating similarity between a service and service concept in domain ontology.

In [2], authors introduced three-layer architecture for traffic IR system, based on fuzzy ontology on SW. Authors used fuzzy linguistic variable ontology based concept relationships for semantic query expansion.

In [48] authors discussed the problem of incapability of domain ontology to deal with uncertain information due to lack of clear-cut boundaries between concepts of domains. The solution was provided in terms Fuzzy Ontology-based Intelligent IR system was proposed. The fuzzy ontology can deal with uncertainty of relations concept hierarchy of specific domain, thus providing more accurate results. The authors claimed that with their proposal the effectiveness of IR system improved significantly.

In [49] author implemented a concept similarity method featuring formal concept analysis and type-2 fuzzy sets. The proposal employs formal concept analysis (FCA) with many-valued context to address the problem of interval valued attributes of searched concepts. Concept similarity is proposed using FCA and fuzzy sets using Information Content (IC) approach. Limitation of this method is that knowledge contained in hierarchical structure of concept lattice (level and depth of concepts) is not included in performing semantic similarity measure.

In [51] authors proposed an ontology mapping framework based on rough set theory (RST) and concept lattice. Two ontological contexts were considered for construction of concept lattice. Similarities of two ontological nodes were measured using rough set approximations. Information content (IC) of related concepts may be considered for inclusion in this proposal which could further enhance the effectiveness of retrieval system.

In [52] author's proposal was search model for SW. This model utilized fuzzy formal concept analysis for automatic construction of ontology. Rough set approximations performed the match between query and ontological concepts. Information content (IC) provides useful information regarding search concepts that may be augmented in this proposal for making system more realistic.

In [11] semantic search model using FCA and RST was proposed. This model takes advantage of Wikipedia [10] for concept similarity computation. Proposal may include YAGO [53], WordNet or any other knowledge resource other than Wikipedia. This model overcomes the limitations of existing semantic search models especially models based on Information content (IC) approach. This model works well for general domains but considered less suitable for specialized domain as Wikipedia does not ensure coverage of specific domains.

5 Discussion and Analysis

This survey presents a comparison of various techniques applied in intelligent IR models and their limitations in the context of SW. A comparative analysis of IR models surveyed is presented in Table 2. In the survey, we observed how different techniques are utilized by these models. The Fig. 2(a) shows that some of preferred techniques in IR for semantic search are query refinement (QR), use of existing corpus (WordNet and Wikipedia), formal concept analysis (FCA), explicit semantic analysis (ESA) and automatic ontology generation. Furthermore, it can be noticed from Fig. 2(b) that 41% surveyed models exploited additional corpus, while 27% models utilized FCA and 32% models used QR, ESA and automatic ontology generation.

Table 2. Comparative analysis of semantic web-based information retrieval models.

S. No.	Models	Techniques	Limitation and challenges
1	Concept-based IR model exploiting term clustering technique and Okapi algorithm [30]	Term clustering, Frequency weighted search, Okapi algorithm, proximity search, Roget's Thesaurus, WordNet	Model may need significant modifications before deploying into more specialized domains like medical as concepts are overlapping in multiple clusters
2	Fuzzy FCA and concept hierarchies-based IR model using domain ontology [31]	Fuzzy FCA, concept hierarchies, automatically built domain ontologies, concept lattice, WordNet	Other fuzzy relations (like resemblance and tolerance) may be employed in fuzzy relational ontological modeling
3	Concept-based IR model with Explicit Semantic Analysis and Wikipedia [28]	Concept extraction, Explicit Semantic Analysis, Wikipedia, feature selection	This model requires existence of knowledge domain such as Wikipedia for concept extraction and feature selection
4	Concept-based semantic search on encrypted cloud data [32]	Semantic searchable encrypted scheme, double score weighting formula, encrypted cloud data, Wikipedia	Performance issue needs further investigations as encrypted search is not very efficient
5	Concept-based search engine with cross-lingual support [8]	Cross-Lingual Information Retrieval System (CLIR), ESA, WordNet	WordNet does not assure the coverage of specialized domain concepts

(*continued*)

Table 2. (*continued*)

S. No.	Models	Techniques	Limitation and challenges
6	Multi-Agent Based IIR framework for SW [4]	Multi-Agent systems, RDF, OWL	Expansion and updating of ontology base are challenging task
7	IR system combining Semantic Web and agent paradigm [33]	Ontology, Multi-Agent systems	Lack of appropriate ontology mapping algorithm for mapping heterogeneous ontology to ontology base
8	Web service discovery method based on multiple agents [35]	Software Agent, OWL, domain ontology	Web service composition can be incorporated in this model for creating new web service by merging & reusing existing web services
9	Agent based educational system on semantic web using domain ontology [36]	Ontology, SW, software agent, least common super-concept (structure taxonomy based) similarity measure	Feature-based similarity measures can also be considered for computing semantic similarity between concept and knowledge resource
10	Search engine based on Web Ontology Language [3]	OWL, Protégé ontology editor, Jena semantic framework Reasoner, ontology analyzer tool	Ranking Algorithm can be augmented for ranking of results set in semantic search
11	Ontology based IR system for sports domain [12]	Ontology, SPARQL, semantic query language	System lacks mechanism to deal with partial match between concept and search terms
12	Semantic Web based intelligent IR system [38]	Ontology, Distributed Hash Table (DHT) for load balancing, range queries and fault tolerance	Response time varies greatly for complex and simple queries
13	SW search based on RDF [5]	Ontology, RDF, Semantic inference	Updating domain ontology whenever new one added is challenging
14	Ontology Web Language and Information Retrieval (OWLIR) framework [6]	SW, markup language: DAML + OIL, AeroText system, DAMLJessKB, Ontology	Model can be extended to include results from partial match between query and concept hierarchy
15	Personalized search engine using query clustering technique and semantic web [40]	Query clustering, web semantics, thesaurus, query expansion	Exploitation of page ranking algorithm methods by some commercial entities to seek people attention throw a challenge

(*continued*)

Table 2. (*continued*)

S. No.	Models	Techniques	Limitation and challenges
16	Enhancing semantic inter-operability in Digital Library by intelligent techniques [39]	Artificial Intelligence, Ontology, RDF, Case-Based Reasoning (CBR), Intelligent Agent	Model can be extended to integrate and use other institutional repositories and digital services. Query refinement can be augmented to extend support for user
17	Semantic IR based on query expansion using domain ontology [9]	SPARQL, Ontology, RDF, WordNet	Model needs significant changes before it can be extended to other domains
18	Fuzzy ontology based IR system for transportation domain [2]	Fuzzy ontology, RDF, RDF query languages: RDQL, RQL, SeRQL	Integration of already existing ontologies of same domain with newly created is challenging task
19	Automated annotation of web services using fuzzy set approach [47]	Extended Vector Space Model (VSM), Fuzzy techniques, WordNet	Extended VSM approach can also be applied to semantic relations such as homonyms and hyponyms
20	Automatic approach for generating fuzzy ontology for Semantic Web [54]	Fuzzy Ontology Generation Framework (FOGA), Fuzzy FFCA, Fuzzy ontology, OWL	Other soft computing techniques can also be integrated for further improving performance and effectiveness of system
21	Fuzzy ontology based intelligent IR system [48]	Fuzzy ontology, Query expansion, WordNet	Fuzzy theory and neural network techniques can be augmented to generate Fuzzy ontology automatically
22	Similarity reasoning in formal concept analysis: From one-to-many valued context [49]	Formal concept analysis, type-2 fuzzy sets, Information content approach	Knowledge contained in hierarchical structure of concept lattice is not included in performing similarity measure
23	Ontology similarity measure combining rough set and concept lattice [51]	Ontology mapping framework, Concept lattice, rough set approximations	Information Content of related concepts are not considered in this proposal
24	Rough set and fuzzy FCA based SW search [52]	RSA, Automatic ontology construction, FFCA	Information content of search terms were not considered
25	Combining FCA, RSA and Wikipedia for Semantic Web search [11]	FCA and RSA based proposal where concept similarity is computed with Wikipedia	Model is not suitable for specialized domain as Wikipedia does not guarantee coverage of specific domains

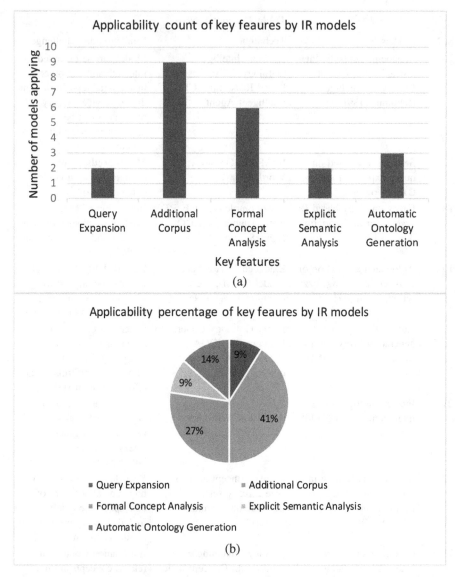

Fig. 2. (a) Applicability count and (b) Applicability percentage of key features by IR models

6 Conclusion and Research Directions

It is evident from literature that traditional IR systems were not effective due to mainly two obstacles. First, they didn't possess methods to deal with the problem of synonyms and polysemy. Second, these methods lack standards for representation, exchange and inference of knowledge encoded in web resources. The use of ontology as knowledge representation tool has overpowered the above problems. Standards like RDF, RDFS,

OWL and DAML + OIL were used to create, model and infer knowledge as domain ontology, which provided basis for intelligent information retrieval systems. This paper presents the significant research work in the field of intelligent information retrieval on SW. Our paper mainly focuses on systems based on multi-agent, ontology, soft computing and concept-based paradigm employed for information retrieval on semantic web. The purpose of this work is to highlight the limitations of these models and techniques employed for IR on SW. The aim of this survey is to focus on the challenges of IR in SW and identification of issues which were not addressed in previous studies of this topic.

IR systems were struggling with issues like dealing with imprecise and vague information, lack of standards for knowledge representation and utilization of semantic knowledge encoded in web resources etc. Researchers found solution of these problems in terms of SW. From this survey, it is observed that researchers are more inclined towards employing SW for IR tasks. Also, survey shows trends of utilization of additional corpus (WordNet, Wikipedia) and formal concept analysis as knowledge processing tool for creating an effective IR system. Application of soft computing techniques for dealing with vagueness in semantic IR systems is also observed in this survey.

References

1. Berners-Lee, T., Hendler, J., Lassila, O.: The semantic web. Sci. Am. **284**(5), 28–37 (2001)
2. Zhai, J., Yan C., Chen, Y.: Semantic information retrieval based on fuzzy ontology for intelligent transportation systems. In: Proceedings of International Conference on Systems, Man and Cybernetics, pp. 2321–2326 (2008)
3. Kumar, S., Singh, M., De, A.: OWL-based ontology indexing and retrieving algorithms for semantic search engine. In: Proceedings of 7th International Conference on Computing and Convergence Technology, pp. 1135–1140 (2012)
4. Xiao, Y., Xiao, M., Zhang, F.: Agents-based intelligent retrieval framework for the semantic web. In: Proceedings of International Conference on Wireless Communications, Networking and Mobile Computing, pp. 5357–5360 (2007)
5. Jiang, J., Wang, Z., Liu, C., Tan, Z., Chen, X., Li, M.: The technology of intelligent information retrieval based on the semantic web. In: Proceedings of 2nd International Conference on Signal Processing Systems, pp. V2-824 (2010)
6. Shah, U., Finin, T., Joshi, A., Cost, R.S., Matfield, J.: Information retrieval on the semantic web. In: Proceedings of the Eleventh International Conference on Information and Knowledge Management, pp. 461–468 (2002)
7. Miller, G.: WordNet: an on-line lexical database. Int. J. Lexicogr. **3**(4), 235–244 (1990)
8. Samantaray, S.D.: An intelligent concept based search engine with cross linguility support. In: Proceedings of 7th Conference on Industrial Electronics and Applications, pp. 1441–1446 (2012)
9. Chauhan, R., Goudar, R., Sharma, R., Chauhan, A.: Domain ontology based semantic search for efficient information retrieval through automatic query expansion. In: Proceedings of International Conference on Intelligent Systems and Signal Processing, pp. 397–402 (2013)
10. Milne, D., Witten, I.H.: Learning to link with wikipedia. In: Proceedings of 17th conference on Information and Knowledge Management, pp. 509–518 (2008)

11. Jiang, Y., Yang, M.: Semantic search exploiting formal concept analysis, rough sets, and wikipedia. Int. J. Semant. Web Inf. Syst. **14**(3), 99–119 (2018)
12. Zhai, J., Zhou, K.: Semantic retrieval for sports information based on ontology and SPARQL. In: Proceedings of International Conference on Information Science and Management Engineering, pp. 395–398 (2010)
13. Thangaraj, M., Chamundeeswari, M.: A survey of agent-based personalized semantic information retrieval. IJCST **2**(3), 448–498 (2011)
14. Ali, A., Ahmed, I.: Concept-based information retrieval approaches on the web: a brief survey. IJAIR **3**(6), 14–18 (2011)
15. Ahmed, M.W., Ansari, M.A.: A survey: soft computing in intelligent information retrieval systems. In: Proceedings of 12th International Conference on Computational Science and Its Applications, pp. 26–34 (2012)
16. Singh, G., Jain, V.: Information retrieval (IR) through semantic web (SW): an overview. In: Proceedings of CONFLUENCE2012-The Next Generation Information Technology Summit, pp. 23–27 (2012)
17. Sharma, A.: Intelligent information retrieval system: a survey. AEEE **3**(1), 63–70 (2013)
18. Balan, S., Ponmuthuramalingam, P.: A study on world wide web information retrieval and web search techniques. IJIRCCE **4**(3), 3532–3535 (2016)
19. Ezhilarasi, K., Kalavathy, G.M.: Literature survey: analysis on semantic web information retrieval methodologies. In: Proceedings of International Conference for Phoenixes on Emerging Current Trends in Engineering and Management, pp. 93–108 (2018)
20. Fernandez, M., Motta, E.: Semantically enhanced information retrieval: an ontology-based approach. J. Web Semant. **9**(4), 434–452 (2011)
21. Melucci, M.: Boolean Model. In: Liu, L., Ozsu, M.T. (eds.) Encyclopedia of Database Systems. Springer, Boston (2009). https://doi.org/10.1007/978-0-387-39940-9_917
22. Melucci, M.: Vector-Space Model. In: Liu, L., Ozsu, M.T. (eds.) Encyclopedia of Database Systems. Springer, Boston (2009). https://doi.org/10.1007/978-0-387-39940-9_918
23. Fuhr, N.: Probabilistic models in information retrieval. Comput. J. **35**(3), 243–255 (1992)
24. Jones, K.S., Robertson, S.E.: A probabilistic model of information retrieval: development and comparative experiments: Part 2. Inf. Process. Manage. **36**(6), 809–840 (2000)
25. Ali, A., Bari, P., Ahmad, I.: Concept-based information retrieval approaches on the web: a brief survey. IJCIS **3**(6), 14–18 (2011)
26. Woods, W.: Conceptual indexing: a better way to organize knowledge. Technical Report SMLI TR-97-61, Sun Microsystems Laboratories (1997)
27. Ozcan, R., Aslandogan, Y.A.: Concept based information access using ontologies and latent semantic analysis. Technical report CSE-2004-8, University of Texas at Arlington (2004)
28. Egozi, O., Markovitch, S., Gabrilovich, E.: Concept-based information retrieval using explicit semantic analysis. ACM Trans. Inf. Syst. **29**(2), 1–38 (2011)
29. Gottron, T., Anderka, M., Stein, B.: Insights into explicit semantic analysis. In: Proceedings of 20th International Conference on Information and Knowledge Management, pp. 1961–1964 (2011)
30. Henstock, P.V., Pack, D.J., Lee, Y.S., Weinstein, C.J.: Toward an improved concept-based information retrieval system. In: Proceedings of the 24th Annual International Conference on Research and Development in Information Retrieval, pp. 384–385 (2001)
31. Goyal, P., Behera, L., McGinnity, T.M.: An information retrieval model based on automatically learnt concept hierarchies. In: Proceedings of International Conference on Semantic Computing, pp. 458–465 (2009)

32. Boucenna, F., Nouali, O., Kechid, S.: Concept-based semantic search over encrypted cloud data. In: Proceedings of 12th International Conference on Web Information Systems and Technologies, pp. 235–242 (2016)

33. Cheng, X., Xie, Y., Yang, T.: Study of multi-agent information retrieval model in semantic web. In: Proceedings of International Workshop on Geoscience and Remote Sensing, pp. 636–639 (2008)

34. Luo, J., Xue, X.: Research on information retrieval system based on semantic web and multi-agent. In: Proceedings of International Conference on Intelligent Computing and Cognitive Informatics, pp. 207–209 (2010)

35. Benaboud, R., Maamri, R., Sahnoun, Z.: Semantic web service discovery based on agents and ontologies. IJIMT **3**(4), 467–472 (2012)

36. Reddy, A.B., Govardhan, A.: A novel approach for similarity and indexing-based ontology for semantic web educational system. IJIEI **4**(2), 117–134 (2016)

37. Yibing, S., Qinglong, M.: Research of literature information retrieval method based on ontology. In: Proceedings of International Conference on Multi-sensor Fusion and Information Integration for Intelligent Systems, pp. 1–6 (2014)

38. Raj, T.F.M., Ravichandran, K.S.: A novel approach for intelligent information retrieval in semantic web using ontology. WASJ **29**, 149–154 (2014)

39. Martín, A., León, C., López, A.: Enhancing semantic interoperability in digital library by applying intelligent techniques. In: Proceedings of SAI Intelligent Systems Conference, pp. 904–911 (2015)

40. Prakasha, S., Shashidhar, H.R., Raju, G.T.: Structured Intelligent Search Engine for effective information retrieval using query clustering technique and semantic web. In: Proceedings of International Conference on Contemporary Computing and Informatics, pp. 688–695 (2014)

41. Rahman, A., Beg, M.M.S.: Face sketch recognition using sketching with words. Int. J. Mach. Learn. Cybern. **6**(4), 597–605 (2014). https://doi.org/10.1007/s13042-014-0256-y

42. Zadeh, L.: Fuzzy Sets. Inf. Control **8**(3), 338–353 (1965)

43. Pawlak, Z.: Rough sets. Int. J. Inf. Comput. Sci. **11**(5), 341–356 (1982). https://doi.org/10.1007/BF01001956

44. Cohen, D., Ai, Q., Croft, W.B.: Adaptability of neural networks on varying granularity IR tasks. In: Proceedings of ACM SIGIR Workshop on Neural Information Retrieval (2016)

45. Chen, H.: Machine learning for information retrieval: neural networks, symbolic learning, and genetic algorithms. J. Assoc. Inf. Sci. Technol. **46**(3), 194–216 (1995)

46. Cordon, O., Moya, F., Zarco, C.: A new evolutionary algorithm combining simulated annealing and genetic programming for relevance feedback in fuzzy information retrieval systems. Soft. Comput. **6**(5), 308–319 (2002). https://doi.org/10.1007/s00500-002-0184-8

47. Chotipant, S., Hussain, F.K., Hussain, O.K.: An automated and fuzzy approach for semantically annotating services. In: Proceedings of International Conference on Fuzzy Systems, pp. 1–7 (2015)

48. Hourali, M., Montazer, G.A.: An intelligent information retrieval approach based on two degrees of uncertainty fuzzy ontology. Adv. Fuzzy Syst. **2011**, 11 (2011)

49. Formica, A.: Similarity reasoning in formal concept analysis: from one- to-many-valued contexts. Knowl. Based Syst. **60**(2), 715–739 (2019). https://doi.org/10.1007/s10115-018-1252-4

50. Sharma, A., Kumar, S.: Soft computing: dealing with vagueness in intelligent information retrieval. IJRECE **6**(2), 1784–1788 (2018)

51. Zhao, Y., Halang, W.: Rough concept lattice-based ontology similarity measure. In: Proceedings of the First International Conference on Scalable Information Systems (2006)
52. Formica, A.: Semantic web search based on rough sets and fuzzy formal concept analysis. Knowl. Based Syst. **26**, 40–47 (2012)
53. Suchanek, F.M., Kasneci, G., Weikum, G.: YAGO: a large ontology from wikipedia and wordnet. J. Web Semant. **6**(3), 203–217 (2008)
54. Tho, Q.T., Hui, S.C., Cheuk, A., Fong, M., Cao, T.H.: Automatic fuzzy ontology generation for semantic web. IEEE Trans. Knowl. Data Eng. **18**(6), 842–856 (2006)

Comparative Study of Machine Learning Algorithms for Social Media Text Analysis

Nidhi Malik[✉] and Saksham Jain

Amity School of Engineering and Technology, New Delhi, India
nidhimalik14@gmail.com, sakshamjn655@gmail.com

Abstract. This paper highlights the way different machine learning algorithms are used in analyzing social media text. This is the internet age. People make use of online forums, blogs posts, tweets etc. to communicate with each other. As a result of increased social networking, amount of data generated is enormous. This data is an excellent source of information in all walks of life ranging from business, marketing, trends analysis and prediction etc. Sentiment analysis refers to identification of user-generated text as positive or negative or neutral automatically. This classification of sentiments into classes can be done based on the document, Sentence, Feature or Aspect. This paper presents how machine learning techniques are used for analyzing sentiments expressed on Twitter platform. Comparative study of these machine learning techniques is done for better understanding.

Keywords: Machine learning · Twitter · Sentiment analysis

1 Introduction

The ever growing usage of social media has raised the need of analyzing its text. It is an excellent source of information in all walks of life ranging from business, marketing, trends analysis and prediction etc. According to the Oxford dictionary [1], sentiment analysis is termed as classifying opinions expressed through text to decide whether the opinion about a specific topic or product is positive or negative or neutral. Opinion Mining also stands for Twitter Sentiment Analysis, on dataset taken from Twitter, is primarily for analyzing opinions, views and conversations for various purposes like deciding the business strategy to get feedback for products, political analysis, and also for assessing public actions. Analysis of sentiment is a complex process involving 5 different steps to analyze the polarity of data. These steps are: a) Data collection, b) Text pre-processing, c) training classifier, d) Sentiment classification and e) Evaluation of Output.

Initially, it was mainly used to analyze sentiment based on long texts such as emails, letters, passages and so on. Python and R are mostly used for analysis of sentiment of a particular dataset. Machine learning approaches are used for predicting the polarity of sentiments based upon training examples and testing data-sets. Natural Language Processing, algorithms like SVM, Logistics regression, Naïve Bayes etc. are used for predicting the polarity of the sentence. There are many others factors on which sentiments may depend such as aspect, sentence, and document. It is not sufficient only to use positive and negative words for analyzing sentiment of the sentence, rather context is very significant in determining the sentiment of the text block.

© Springer Nature Singapore Pte Ltd. 2020
U. Batra et al. (Eds.): REDSET 2019, CCIS 1230, pp. 223–235, 2020.
https://doi.org/10.1007/978-981-15-5830-6_19

The paper is organized into six sections. First section introduces sentiment analysis and its need. Second section highlights the related work done and their features. In third section, we have discussed different approaches that can be used for sentiment analysis. Fourth section describes various machine learning techniques used for analyzing sentiments. In fifth section, we have evaluated different techniques and also analyzed their performance. The paper is concluded in sixth section.

2 Related Work

With the huge increase in number of Blogging and social networking sites and their user-base, sentiment and opinion analysis are becoming a new field/domain of interest for many academic-researchers as well as industry experts. Different sentimental analysis techniques have been implemented by researchers on Twitter data. For example, the work done by [2] is a real time twitter sentiment analysis for presidential elections. They have followed an approach based on crowdsourcing for sentiment annotation on in-domain political data. This data is then used for generating data for model training and testing. [3] have used labeled corpora and explained a method which automatically builds a lexicon which consists of extremely negative and positive words from this labeled corpus. Extreme reviews are then searched from the classifier which classifies based on the labeled corpora. [4] have used the IMDb dataset which contains movie reviews to further use machine learning algorithms for classification techniques using, Unigram, Bigram, Trigram, combination of unigram & bigram, bigram & trigram, and unigram & bigram & trigram. [6] discuss polarity of lexicon based sentiment analysis and semantic-orientation of words, phases, and sentences on the basis of dictionary consisting of semantic scores. And comparison of W-WSD, SentiWordNet, and Text Blob lexicon models. SMS spam filtering has been proposed by [7] by proposing a pre-processing approach for normalizing along with enhancing its performance of classifying SMS's. Text-blob is a python library for processing words which uses NLTK (natural language toolkit) for natural language processing. Large and structured set of texts known as corpora which is used for the analysis of tweets as illustrated in [12]. A novel solution to target oriented (aspect based) sentiment summarization and SA of short informal texts is described in [9]. [8] use the model for classification of tweets by using 3 approaches: Sentic-Net, Senti-WordNet and Sentis-LangNet [9]. Presents a solution to target oriented sentiment summarization as well as sentiment analysis of short informal texts mainly tweets.

3 Approaches for Sentiment Classification

While going through literature, we observed that there are two widely used approaches for detecting sentiment from text. Lexical based and Machine learning based approaches are the two main approaches used by researchers.

Lexical based approach is also termed as dictionary based approach and it relies on the use of lexicon and dictionary of words. Its performance depends on the lexical on which it is based. Techniques such as word sense disambiguation etc. can be used to enhance performance of lexical based approaches.

As discussed by [14], Machine learning is sub-divided into 2 categories- Supervised learning and Unsupervised learning. Supervised learning algorithms are probabilistic, linear, decision tree and rule based classifier, in which labeled dataset is provided as an input for training the classifier and thus model is tested on new data to get outputs. Sentiment classification in ml includes 2 steps. First includes extracting features and storing feature vector and second is to train feature vector by using classification algorithms whereas in case of Unsupervised learning, there is no category and they are not provided with the correct targets so it is dependent on the process of clustering. One of the major things to take care of while training the model is Overfitting which means that the classifier works well on your training data but on introducing it to new data its accuracy decreases or we can say it acts poorly on new data that's why machine learning experts train the models on different data then the data used of knowing the accuracy of the classifier.

4 Techniques Used

We test different classifiers: keyword-based, Naive Bayes, Logistics regression, support vector machines, random forest and finally K-nearest neighbor algorithms.

Data Description

Twitter consist of short messages, with an upper limit of 140 characters recently changed to 280 words. In micro-blogging services people often use quick and short messages, acronyms, make spelling mistakes, use emoticons along with characters that have unique meanings. Following is a brief terminology associated with tweets. For the purpose of experiments to be conducted in this paper, we have used a dataset named "Sentiment 140" which includes roughly about 1.6 million tweets labeled "1" for a positive response and "0" for a negative response. From this dataset, we need only two variables which are "Sentiment" and "SentimentText" containing polarity of tweets and the tweets respectively (Fig. 1).

A	B	C	D
ItemID	Sentiment	SentimentSource	SentimentText
1	0	Sentiment140	is so sad for my APL friend............
2	0	Sentiment140	I missed the New Moon trailer...
3	1	Sentiment140	omg its already 7:30 :O
4	0	Sentiment140	.. Omgaga. Im sooo im gunna CRy. I've been at this dentist since 11.. I was suposed 2 j
5	0	Sentiment140	i think mi bf is cheating on me!!! T_T
6	0	Sentiment140	or i just worry too much?
7	1	Sentiment140	Juuuuuuuuuuuuuuuuusssst Chillin!!
8	0	Sentiment140	Sunny Again Work Tomorrow :-| TV Tonight
9	1	Sentiment140	handed in my uniform today . i miss you already
10	1	Sentiment140	hmmmm.... i wonder how she my number @-)
11	0	Sentiment140	I must think about positive..
12	1	Sentiment140	thanks to all the haters up in my face all day! 112-102
13	0	Sentiment140	this weekend has sucked so far
14	0	Sentiment140	jb isnt showing in australia any more!
15	0	Sentiment140	ok thats it you win.

Fig. 1 Attributes of our dataset.

Data Cleaning (Pre-processing)

1) Filtering – we remove URL links (for e.g. https://Sakshamjain.me)
2) Replaces targets (e.g. "@John") with blank spaces
3) Tokenization – In tokenization long sentences are converted by using space between adjoining words and by using punctuation marks to make a collection of words called as bag of words. However, ensuring that short forms such like "don't", "I'll", "she'd" remained as a single word.
4) Stopwords– By removing articles like ("a", "an", "the", " ", "[", "{", etc.) from collection of words.
5) N-grams – By making a set of words out of adjacent words. For ex: In a Trigram system, sentence like "I do not like fish" will form three bi-grams: "I + do + not", "do + not like", "not + like fish".

Bag of Words Models

Ngrams are surprisingly powerful given their simplicity, they are fast to train and easy to understand. Even though ngram's bring some context between words, a bag of word models fails in modeling long-term dependencies between words in a sequence.

1) Word ngram: Word N-grams are described as combinations of adjacent words of length n each from the text present as the input function. we have used unigrams (n = 1) and bigrams (n = 2) as features for our classification.
2) Character ngram:
It is very similar to word ngram but instead of words, a group of character is implemented here. We used a range of 1 to 4 for getting a list of possible occurrences of the instances.
3) Word-character ngram
Basically, it is a combination of word n-gram and character ngram thus combining the list of all possible entities of word and character Ngrams. This is done so as to combine the features of each of them for getting higher accuracy by our classifier.

Evaluation of the Models

Performance metrices solely depends upon the type of problem being evaluated. Confusion matrix measures the performance such that output can be two or more classes. A table is generated which gives different combinations of predicted and actual values [13]. For better interpretation of the table, we can also see this in terms of true positives, true negative, false positive, and false negatives. Following are different parameters:

Accuracy

$$Accuracy = \frac{true\ positives + true\ negatives}{total\ examples} \tag{1}$$

Accuracy determines the correctness of training of the model and its behavior in real world. Although it will not provide any detailed information about it's application for the problem. Accuracy just tell us about the efficacy of the model trained.

Precision

$$Precision = \frac{true\ positives}{true\ positives + false\ positives} \tag{2}$$

Precision helps in determining whether the occurrence of False positives is higher than True positives. For example, in case of detecting lung cancer for an individual after analysing their test records. If model under consideration has less precision then results of the analysis can't be trusted upon as it might be a false positive. And if ration of false positives is higher than True positive then further analysis is needed to confirm the results.

Recall

$$Recall = \frac{true\ positives}{true\ positives + false\ negatives} \tag{3}$$

Recall helps when there are higher number of false negatives. When the frequency of false negatives is higher than it degrades the efficiency of our model. For example: news forecast is for rain and although seeing it you decide to carry an umbrella but incident didn't happened and later you thinking it was a bad forecast.

F1-Score

$$F1 = 2 \times \frac{precision \times recall}{precision + recall} \tag{4}$$

F1 score helps in determining the overall measure of the classifier's accuracy. F1 score combines precision and recall both. A good F1 score means that probability of both false positives and false negatives is less, therefore we can say the we can correctly classify threats in real world scenarios.

4.1   Techniques Used

We've tested different classifiers: keyword-based, Naive Bayes, Logistics regression, support vector machines, random forest and finally K-nearest neighbor algorithms.

Naive Bayes

Bayes Rule is the basis for Bayesian classifiers. Its principle is to look at conditional probabilities in a way which allows to flip the condition around in a suitable way. Conditional probability is defined as a probability that event X will occur, given the evidence Y and is normally written P(X | Y). The rearrangement of finding probability of something is based on examples of it occurring can be very useful. For example, here, given the contents, we are trying to find out the probability of a document being positive or negative. Examples of positive and negative opinions from our data set are already given so it is convenient [5]. Results of our prediction for Naive bayes model is shown in Table 1 through which we get to know that best results of naive bayes are with Word-Char ngram with an accuracy of 0.6694. And graphical representation can be seen in Fig. 2 in the form of bar-chart.

Table 1. Results of Naive Bayes model.

Type	Accuracy	Precision	Recall	F1 score
Word	0.6540	0.5334	0.7098	0.6091
Char	0.6614	0.6981	0.6548	0.6757
Word-Char	0.6694	0.6680	0.6747	0.6713

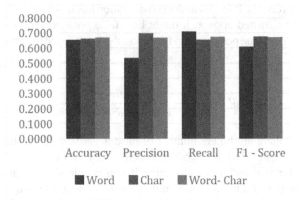

Fig. 2. Representation of Naive Bayes results

Support Vector Machine
The support vector machine algorithm is based on the principle of structural risk minimization, rather than the traditional empirical risk minimization principle. In SVM, based on the training dataset, the decision boundaries are directly determined for which the separating margins of the boundaries can be maximized in feature space. Results of our prediction for SVM model is shown in Table 2 which shows that we get best results of an accuracy of 0.7710 for Word-Char n-gram. Graphical representation can be seen in Fig. 3 in the form of bar-chart.

A separating hyperplane is written as:

$$W * X + b = 0$$

$$K(\mathbf{X}_i, \mathbf{X}_j) = \begin{cases} \mathbf{X}_i.\mathbf{X}_j & \text{Linear} \\ (\gamma \mathbf{X}_i.\mathbf{X}_j + C)^d & \text{Polynomial} \\ \exp(-\gamma|\mathbf{X}_i - \mathbf{X}_j|^2) & \text{RBF} \\ \tanh(\gamma \mathbf{X}_i.\mathbf{X}_j + C) & \text{Sigmoid} \end{cases} \tag{5}$$

Table 2. Results of Support vector machine model.

Type	Accuracy	Precision	Recall	F1 score
Word	0.7480	0.7305	0.7612	0.7456
Char	0.7692	0.7713	0.7719	0.7716
Word-Char	0.7710	0.7736	0.7733	0.7735

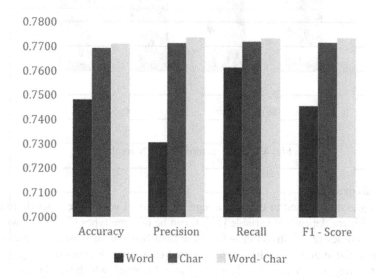

Fig. 3. Representation of SVM results

k-Nearest Neighbor

K-NN is a type of machine learning algorithm which uses feature similarity for computation of new data points. Values are assigned to the data points based on how closely it matches the points in the training set. The class assigned to an object is the most common among its k-nearest neighbours [11]. Results of our prediction for KNN model is shown in Table 3 with maximum accuracy of 0.6024 and with maximum accuracy of 0.6176. And graphical representation can be seen in Fig. 4 in the form of bar-chart.

Table 3. Results of K-NN model.

Type	Accuracy	Precision	Recall	F1 score
Word	0.6024	0.4745	0.6450	0.5467
Char	0.6118	0.6047	0.6186	0.6116
Word-Char	0.6176	0.6581	0.6450	0.6515

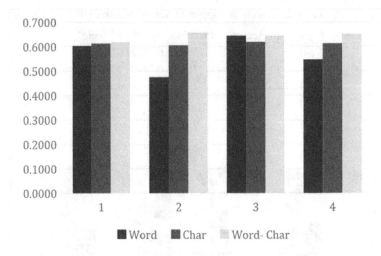

Fig. 4. Representation of K-NN results

Logistics Regression

Logistic regression is used to develop a regression model which uses logistic function to model a binary dependent variable [10]. It can be of three types (1) binary, with two possible outcomes (2) multinomial – for more than two non-ordered categories of the dependent variable and (3) ordinal – for ordered categories. Results of our prediction for Logistics Regression model is shown in Table 4 through which we can say that the maximum accuracy of approx 80%, 79.02 to be precise. And graphical representation can be seen in Fig. 5 in the form of bar-chart.

For r independent variables x1, x2 and x3.. the logistic function is:

$$\hat{p} = \frac{\exp(b_0 + b_1X_1 + b_2X_2 + \ldots + b_pX_p)}{1 + \exp(b_0 + b_1X_1 + b_2X_2 + \ldots + b_pX_p)} \tag{6}$$

where p is the probability of the event.

The goal is to obtain bi where i = 0, 1, 2..

Table 4. Results of Logistic Regression model.

Type	Accuracy	Precision	Recall	F1 score
Word	0.7554	0.8678	0.7116	0.7820
Char	0.7734	0.8615	0.7355	0.7935
Word-Char	0.7902	0.7891	0.7944	0.7917

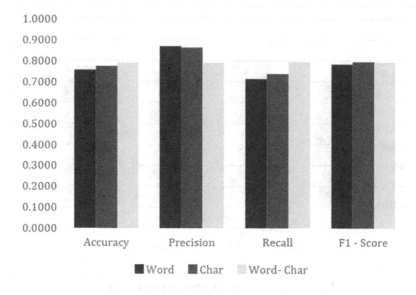

Fig. 5. Representation of Logistics Regression results

Random Forest

Random forests are constructed using the predictions of several trees. Each of these trees is trained in isolation. During Boosting, after training the base model are combined using a sophisticated weighting scheme. In this process, the trees are trained independently and the averaging is used for predictions of the trees. For construction of the random trees, there are some choices such as method for splitting the leafs, deciding which predictor should be used in each leaf and how to inject randomness into the trees [15]. Results of our prediction for Random Forest model is shown in Table 5 with an accuracy of around 73.44% with a minimum accuracy of 71.78 percentage. And graphical representation can be seen in Fig. 6 in the form of bar-chart.

$$K_k^{cc}(\mathbf{x}, \mathbf{z}) = \sum_{k_1, \dots k_d, \sum_{j=1}^d k_j = k} \frac{k!}{k_1! \cdots k_d!} \left(\frac{1}{d}\right)^k \prod_{j=1}^d \mathbf{1}_{\left[2^{k_j} x_j\right] = \left[2^{k_j} z_j\right]}, \qquad (7)$$

for all $\mathbf{x}, \mathbf{z} \in [0, 1]^d$.

Table 5. Results of Random Forest model.

Type	Accuracy	Precision	Recall	F1 score
Word	0.7178	0.7990	0.6910	0.7411
Char	0.7344	0.7831	0.7173	0.7488
Word-Char	0.7344	0.8627	0.6897	0.7665

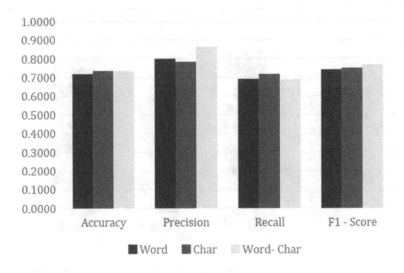

Fig. 6. Representation of Random Forest results

5   Evaluation

For word N-gram, we have validated 10000 tweets as test data and 40000 tweets as training data for different classifiers and we got an accuracy of 75.54% in Logistics regression, 65.40% in Naïve bayes, 74.80% in SVM, 71.78% in Random forest, and 60.24% in KNN.

For Char N-gram, we have validated 10000 tweets as test data and 40000 tweets as training data for different classifiers and we got an accuracy of 77.34% in Logistics regression, 66.14% in Naïve bayes, 76.86% in SVM, 72.30% in Random forest, and 61.18% in KNN.

For Word-Char N-gram, we have validated 10000 tweets as test data and 40000 tweets as training data for different classifiers and we got an accuracy of 79.02% in Logistics regression which is best amongst all of them, 66.94% in Naïve bayes, 77.10% in SVM, 73.44% in Random forest, and 61.76% in KNN.

Analysis of the prediction of tweets by our models based upon the four majorly used standards i.e. True Positive, True Negative, False Positive, and False Negative as shown in the Table 6, which depicts the comparison of different techniques- Word, Char, and Word-Char N-grams consisting of various algorithms of Machine Learning. Along with graphical representation shown in Fig. 7, the results we got by using various machine learning models corresponding with type of N-gram it was evaluated with.

Table 6. Results of Different Algorithms in terms of TP, TN, FP, FN.

Models	Type	True positive	True negative	False positive	False negative
KNN	Word	1199	1813	1328	660
	Char	1528	1531	999	942
	Word- Char	1663	1425	864	1048
Naive Bayes	Word	1348	1922	1179	551
	Char	1764	1543	763	930
	Word- Char	1688	1659	839	814
Random Forest	Word	2019	1570	508	903
	Char	1979	1693	548	780
	Word- Char	2180	1492	347	981
SVM	Word	1846	1894	681	579
	Char	1949	1897	578	576
	Word- Char	1955	1900	572	573
Logistics Regression	Word	2193	1584	334	889
	Char	2177	1690	350	783
	Word- Char	1994	1957	533	516

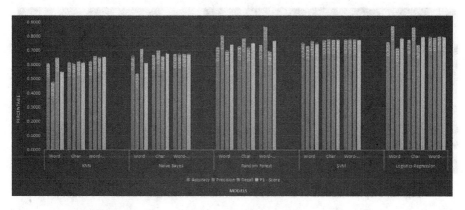

Fig. 7. Representation of Different Algorithms in terms of TP, TN, FP, FN.

Comparison of all the models along with different types of N-grams with respect to Accuracy, Precision, Recall, F1-Score also known as the four evaluation criteria is shown in Table 7. Followed by a graphical representation shown in Fig. 8, the results we got on predictions for getting the idea of which of the model works best and the model which didn't perform well.

Table 7. Results of Different Algorithms in terms of Confusion Matrix.

Models	Type	Accuracy	Precision	Recall	F1-score
KNN	Word	0.6024	0.4745	0.6450	0.5467
	Char	0.6118	0.6047	0.6186	0.6116
	Word- Char	0.6176	0.6581	0.6450	0.6515
Naive Bayes	Word	0.6540	0.5334	0.7098	0.6091
	Char	0.6614	0.6981	0.6548	0.6757
	Word- Char	0.6694	0.6680	0.6747	0.6713
Random Forest	Word	0.7178	0.7990	0.6910	0.7411
	Char	0.7344	0.7831	0.7173	0.7488
	Word- Char	0.7344	0.8627	0.6897	0.7665
SVM	Word	0.7480	0.7305	0.7612	0.7456
	Char	0.7692	0.7713	0.7719	0.7716
	Word- Char	0.7710	0.7736	0.7733	0.7735
Logistics Regression	Word	0.7554	0.8678	0.7116	0.7820
	Char	0.7734	0.8615	0.7355	0.7935
	Word- Char	0.7902	0.7891	0.7944	0.7917

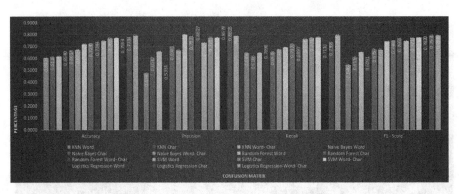

Fig. 8. Representation of Different Algorithms in terms of Confusion Matrix.

6   Conclusion

Sentiment Analysis from social media text an excellent source of information in all walks of life ranging from business, marketing, trends analysis and prediction etc. This paper presents how machine learning techniques are used for analyzing sentiments expressed on Twitter platform. In this work, upon considering F1 score we conclude that for classifying tweets using machine learning, the model word-char ngram technique combines perfectly with the model. Word-char ngram combination with our models result in getting the highest accuracy amongst all. Comparative study of all the techniques is depicted with actual results and graphical representation also for clear understanding.

References

1. https://www.linkedin.com/pulse/importance-sentiment-analysis-social-media-christine-day
2. Wang, H., Dogan, C., Kazemzadeh, A., Bar, F.: A system for real-time twitter sentiment analysis of 2012 us presidential election cycle. In: Proceedings of the ACL 2012 System Demonstrations, pp. 115–120 (2012)
3. Almatarneh, S., Gamallo, P.: A lexicon-based method to search for extreme opinions. PLoS ONE **13**, e0197816 (2018)
4. Tripathy, A., Agrawal, A., Rath, S.K.: Classification of sentiment reviews using n-gram machine learning approach. Expert Syst. Appl. **57**, 117–126 (2016)
5. Troussas, C, Virvou, M.: Sentiment analysis of facebook statuses using naive bayes classifier for language learning (2013)
6. Hasan, A., Moin, S.: Machine learning based sentiment analysis for twitter accounts. Math. Comput. Appl. **23**, 11 (2018)
7. Almeida T.A, Pontes e Silva T.B.: Text normalization and semantic indexing to enhance SMS spam filtering (2016)
8. Pandarachalil, R., Sendhilkumar, S., Mahalakshmi, G.S.: Twitter sentiment analysis for large-scale data: an unsupervised approach. Cogn. Comput. **7**(2), 254–262 (2014). https://doi.org/10.1007/s12559-014-9310-z
9. Bahrainian, S., Dengel, A.: Sentiment analysis and summarization of twitter data. In: 2013 IEEE 16th International Conference on Computational Science and Engineering, Sydney, NSW, pp. 227–234 (2013)
10. Zekic-Susan, M., Salija, N.: Predicting company growth using logistic regression and neural networks. Croatian Oper. Res. Rev. **7**, 229–248 (2016)
11. Dey, L., Chakraborty, S.: Sentiment analysis of review datasets using naïve bayes and k-nn classifier (2016)
12. TextBlob (2017). https://textblob.readthedocs.io/en/dev/
13. Skymind. https://skymind.ai/wiki/accuracy-precision-recall-f1
14. Vimalkumar, B., Vaghela, B., Jadav, M.: Analysis of various sentiment classification techniques. IJCA **140**, 975–8887 (2016)
15. Denil, M., Matheson, D.: Narrowing the gap: random forests in theory and in practice (2014)

Spam Detection in Social Network Using Machine Learning Approach

Simran Chaudhry[1], Sanjeev Dhawan[1], and Rohit Tanwar[2(✉)]

[1] UIET Kurukshetra University, Kurukshetra, India
simranchaudhry4@gmail.com, rsdhawan@rediffmail.com
[2] University of Petroleum and Energy Studies, Dehradun, India
r.tanwar@ddn.upes.ac.in

Abstract. Social network helps people to continue communication with their links. The rapidly growing network's popularity permits the users for gathering huge amount of personal details for the users. The social network offers a system through which the users usually preserve the contact with the friends. With the increment in the popularity of social networking, the users integrate huge amount of information for the users. Though, the amount of information and the ease of accessing user information can become the cause to attract malicious groups. Therefore, the networks are influenced by the spammers and lot of work has been done for identification and fixing. In research work, we have used SVM as a classification technique for detecting spam in the social network. To determine performance of the proposed work, different parameters are computed. To determine the efficiency of the proposed work, the comparison between proposed and existing work has been performed.

Keywords: Spam detection · Social networks · SVM (Support Vector Machine)

1 Introduction

In social media networks, such as Facebook, Twitter, YouTube as well as Instagram, the users of internet being active at social networks than search engine [1]. The figure for users and other institutions form pages on the social media for increasing the connection with online people. Let us consider an example of "Facebook page" that consists of more than 14 million pages from different classes like organization, business, actor, artist, sports, health, community etc. [2]. The users can see entered information along with the comments, images, and videos posted on the facebook page. The structure of a social network with different users is shown in the figure below [3].

Social media sites permit users to share their information with friends. Information can disperse frequently within the social media networks. Due to this, the social websites are affected by different malicious attacks like a spammer [4]. Thus, it has become a very critical issue in the society as well in the companies to find the solution to this problem. For long-term achievement, social media websites required to be free from spammers (Fig. 1).

© Springer Nature Singapore Pte Ltd. 2020
U. Batra et al. (Eds.): REDSET 2019, CCIS 1230, pp. 236–245, 2020.
https://doi.org/10.1007/978-981-15-5830-6_20

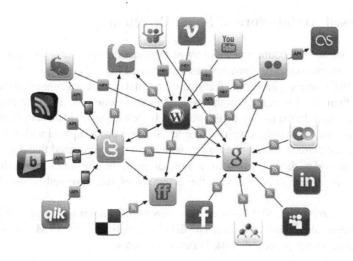

Fig. 1. Social network

Also, the organizations or brand pages need to be free from spammers, as the spammers might be damaging the reputation of the organization [5]. In this research work, we have presented a spam detection system using artificial intelligence technique. An example of Social media network model affected by spammers is shown below [6] (Fig. 2):

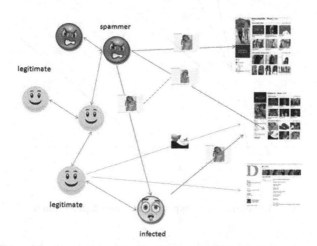

Fig. 2. An example of the social network affected by a spammer

The comments or the posts are represented by two types named Spam and legitimate post [7]. In the above figure, three kinds of users are shown namely; spammer, legitimate users and infected users. The legitimate user which is affected by the infected user is represented by green emoticons, which send spam [8]. The main aim of this research work is to detect spam post sent from spammers and another user that is affected by the virus.

2   Proposed Architecture of Spam Detection

In this section, the procedure that is followed to detect the spam in a social network is discussed. The spam detection process has been carried out in two phases: Training and testing. In the training phase, the features of the dataset are calculated as weighted values and then SVM is trained on the basis of these feature sets. The data is stored in the SVM database. In the testing phase, the data for testing spam is loaded. Features are calculated in terms of weighted values. The test features are compared with the features stored in the database. If the features are matched then it is considered that data is spam, otherwise, consider the test data as a normal post. In the end, the performance parameters are determined to depict the accuracy of the designed spam detection model.

In this research work, SVM is used as a classifier that helps to distinguish between legitimated user and the infected user. The detail description of the SVM along with the algorithm used in the proposed work is described below.

SVM (Support Vector Machine)
SVM passes a linearly differ hyperplane via dataset for the classification of data in two groups. The hyperplane is a linear differentiator for some dimension. It can be a 2D line, 3D plane or 4D+ hyperplane (Fig. 3).

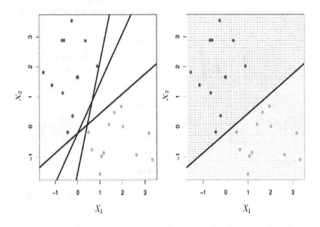

Fig. 3. Separation of hyperplanes (Color figure online)

As shown in the above figure, the blue and red objects can be separated by an infinite amount of hyperplanes. The hyperplane can be the one that can enhance the margin. The margin is known as a distance among the hyperplane with some of the secure points. The secure points are known as "support vectors" as those points control the hyper-plane. Graph 4 shows the better hyperplanes as blue and red objects.

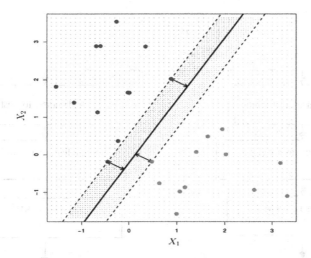

Fig. 4. Best hyperplane for the red and blue objects (Color figure online)

Above illustration is for maximum margin classifier. It enhances the hyperplane margin. It is the finest hyperplane as it lessens the generalization fault the better. If novel data would be added that the maximum margin classifier accurately classifies the novel data (Fig. 4).

SVM Algorithm

Input: Weighted value as a Training Data

Output: Classified Results

Initialize parameters   – Kernel function (Gaussian or RBF)

                       – Training Data (T)

Based on Training Data define Groups

For 1 to all Training Data

    If Training Data belongs to Spam Category

        Group 1 = 'Spam

    Else

        Group 2 = 'Non Spam

    End

End

SVMStruct = SVMTRAIN (Training Data, Group, Kernel function)

Test data = Weight of Current Data

Return; Classified Nodes = SVMCLASSIFY (SVMStruct, Test data)

End

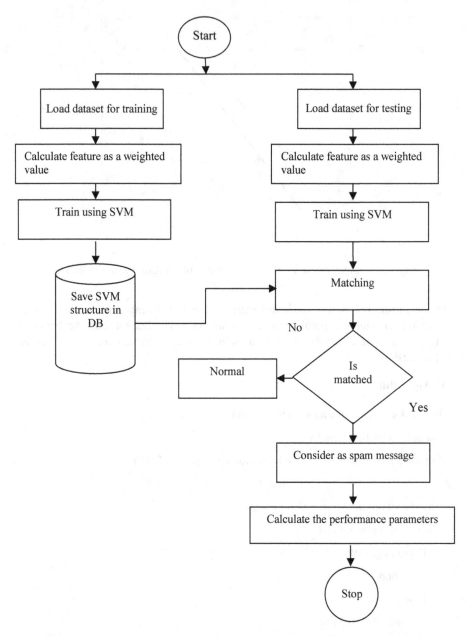

Fig. 5. Methodology of the proposed spam detection model in social networking

The above graph represents the comparison of proposed parameters with the existing parameters. The blue bar shows precision, recall and F-measure values for the proposed work whereas red bar line shows these parametric values for the existing work. As depicted in the above figure, it is concluded that the value of precision, recall, and F-measure of the research work has been increased by 2.08%, 15.24%, and 3.5% respectively (Fig. 5).

3 Experimental Results

The performance computed by simulating the proposed spam detection model in the MATLAB simulator environment are defined in this section. SVM classification algorithm is used to identify the malicious user or the user who is affected by the virus from the normal behavior of the user. The parameters used for evaluating the proposed work are, Recall, Precision and F-Measure.

A measure Recall i.e. also considered as Sensitivity is predicted by the number of actual positives which are exactly positively predicted. In this work, it is given it as a suggestion as TPR i.e. True Positive Rate [16].

Also, Precision seems to be a way which determines the positive classes predicted to the total correctly predicted classes. Although it is completely avoided in examination of ROC but the information retrieval, data mining and machine learning surrounds on these parameters only. The 2 measures i.e. True Positive Accuracy and True Positive rate and the combination of two keeps an attention on positive models. In both the cases, none of these parameters informs about handling of negative cases in the models [17].

The another measure F1-measure works with both Precision and Recall. It refers to the positive classes to the Arithmetic mean of Real and Predicted positives. It parallels to the set theoretic Dice Coefficient [19]. The G-measure is also considered to be evaluated and it's information addressed to the Arithmetic mean by Precision and Recall both [18]. The analyzed, calculated and measured Parameters in the work are elaborated in the tabular form below (Table 1):

Table 1. Performance parameters

Iterations	Precision	Recall	F-measure
1	85.23	76.28	80.5
2	88.69	77.94	82.96
3	87.26	82.45	84.78
4	90.45	79.81	84.79
5	86.94	84.53	85.71
6	85.72	84.97	85.34

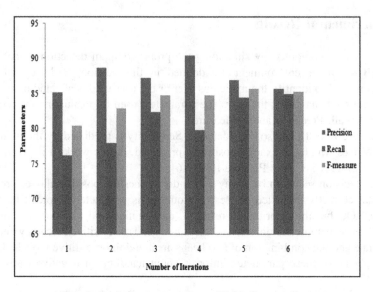

Fig. 6. Performance parameters (Color figure online)

Above figure represents the graph plotted for the measured performance parameters while detecting spam using SVM as a classifier. Here, blue color, red color, and green color represents the output of parameters measured for the proposed work. From the above graph, it is clear that the average value of precision, recall, F-measure measured for the proposed work are 87.38, 80.99 and 84.01 respectively (Fig. 6).

Comparison of Proposed Work with the Existing Work

Bhagyashri Toke and Dinesh Puri have proposed a classification algorithm (Naïve Bayes and Rule-based) to detect spammer in most commonly used social network site (Facebook). The process such as pre-processing, feature identification and then classification using Naïve Bayes and Rule-based approaches in combination has been performed (Table 2).

Table 2. Comparison of proposed with existing work

Proposed work			Existing work		
Precision	Recall	F-measure	Precision	Recall	F-measure
87.38	80.99	84.01	85.6	77.2	81.17

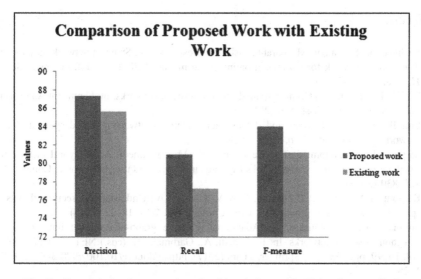

Fig. 7. Comparison of proposed work with existing work (Color figure online)

The above graph represents the comparison of proposed parameters with the existing parameters. The blue bar depicts the output of performance parameters for proposed work whereas red bar line shows the output for performance parameters for the existing work. It is concluded that the value of precision is 2.08%, recall is 15.24%, and F-measure is 3.5% of the research work has been increased by 2.08%, 15.24%, and 3.5% respectively (Fig. 7).

4   Conclusion

The usage of social media usually results in social data in unparallel form. Number, text could be the form of data that could be computed by PC. Accurate data is considered as useless when it is changed to practical information. It is mandatory to examine huge data that extracts the information from this. The users of internet on social network are more as compared to search engines. The networks of social media give an easy to access user's platform for the users that share the information with other. The information could be quickly and efficiently distributed across social networks and is now susceptible to different types of unwanted and malicious spammers/hackers. So, the security of social media and industry is crucial. The main aim of this research work is to detect spam post sent from spammers and another user that is affected by the virus. SVM classification algorithm is used to identify the malicious user or the user who is affected by the virus from the normal behavior of the user. The research has utilized parameters like precision, recall and F-measure and the resulted values for these parameters are 87.38, 80.99 and 84.01. To analyze the effectiveness of the research, the work has been computed with existing work [16] and it has been concluded that the value of precision, recall and F-measure of the research work has been increased by 2.08%, 15.24%, and 3.5% respectively.

References

1. Shehnepoor, S., Salehi, M., Farahbakhsh, R., Crespi, N.: NetSpam: a network-based spam detection framework for reviews in online social media. IEEE Trans. Inf. Forensics Secur. **12**, 1585–1595 (2017)
2. Fei, G., Li, H., Liu, B.: Opinion spam detection in social networks. In: Sentiment Analysis in Social Networks, pp. 141–156 (2017)
3. Liu, B., et al.: Analysis of and defense against crowd-retweeting based spam in social networks. World Wide Web, 1–23 (2018)
4. Sarpiri, M.N., Gandomani, T.J., Teymourzadeh, M., Motamedi, A.: A hybrid method for spammer detection in social networks by analyzing graph and user behavior. J. Comput. **13**, 823–830 (2018)
5. Kamoru, B.A., Jaafar, A.B., Murad, M.A.A., Jabar, M.A.: Understanding security threats in spam detection on social networks. Circ. Comput. Sci. **2**(5), 18–22 (2017)
6. Soliman, A., Girdzijauskas, S.: AdaGraph: adaptive graph-based algorithms for spam detection in social networks. In: El Abbadi, A., Garbinato, B. (eds.) NETYS 2017. LNCS, vol. 10299, pp. 338–354. Springer, Cham (2017). https://doi.org/10.1007/978-3-319-59647-1_25
7. Ala'M, A.Z., Faris, H.: Spam profile detection in social networks based on public features. In: 2017 8th International Conference on Information and Communication Systems (ICICS), pp. 130–135. IEEE (2017)
8. Ferrara, E.: Measuring social spam and the effect of bots on information diffusion in social media. In: Lehmann, S., Ahn, Y.-Y. (eds.) Complex Spreading Phenomena in Social Systems. CSS, pp. 229–255. Springer, Cham (2018). https://doi.org/10.1007/978-3-319-77332-2_13
9. Mahajan, S., Rana, V.: Spam detection on social network through sentiment analysis. Adv. Comput. Sci. Technol. **10**(8), 2225–2231 (2017)
10. Ezpeleta, E., Iturbe, M., Garitano, I., de Mendizabal, I.V., Zurutuza, U.: A mood analysis on Youtube comments and a method for improved social spam detection. In: de Cos Juez, F., et al. (eds.) HAIS 2018. LNCS, vol. 10870, pp. 514–525 (2018). https://doi.org/10.1007/978-3-319-92639-1_43
11. Melià-Seguí, J., Bart, E., Zhang, R., Brdiczka, O.: An empirical approach for fake user detection in location-based social networks. J. Ambient Int. Smart Env. **9**, 643–657 (2017)
12. Vishwarupe, V., Bedekar, M., Pande, M., Hiwale, A.: Intelligent twitter spam detection: a hybrid approach. In: Yang, X.-S., Nagar, A.K., Joshi, A. (eds.) Smart Trends in Systems, Security and Sustainability. LNNS, vol. 18, pp. 189–197. Springer, Singapore (2018). https://doi.org/10.1007/978-981-10-6916-1_17
13. Kamoru, B.A., Omar, A.B.J., Jabar, M.A., Murad, M.A.A., Umar, A.B.: Spam detection issues and spam identification of fake profiles on social networks. J. Theor. Appl. Inf. Technol. **95**, 21 (2017)
14. Sharmin, S., Zaman, Z.: Spam detection in social media employing machine learning tool for text mining. In: 13th International Conference Signal-Image Technology and Internet-Based Systems (SITIS), pp. 137–142. IEEE (2017)
15. Toke, P.: Spam detection in online social networks using integrated approach. Int. J. Innov. Res. Comput. Commun. Eng. (IJIRCCE) **4** (2016)

16. Powers, D.M.: Evaluation: from precision, recall and f-measure to roc, informedness, markedness & correlation. J. Mach. Learn. Technol. **2**(1), 37–63 (2011). ISSN: 2229-3981 & ISSN: 2229-399X

17. Sellke, T., Bayarri, M.J., Berger, J.: American Statistician **55**, 62–71 (2001). http://www.stat. duke.edu/%7Eberger/papers.html#p-value. Accessed 22 Dec 2007

18. Fitzgibbon, S.P.: A machine learning approach to brain-computer interfacing. Ph.D. Thesis, School of Psychology, Flinders University (2007)

19. Sokal, R.R., Rohlf, F.J.: Biometry: The Principles and Practice of Statistics in Biological Research, 3rd edn. WH Freeman and Company, New York (1995)

Big Data Analytics

Forecasting Movie Rating Through Data Analytics

Latika Kharb[1]([⊠]) [iD], Deepak Chahal[1], and Vagisha[2]

[1] Jagan Institute of Management Studies, Sector-5, Rohini, Delhi 110085, India
latika.kharb@jimsindia.org
[2] CSE, Banasthali Vidyapeeth, Newai, Rajasthan, India

Abstract. Movie prediction is an important way to predict movie revenue and performance. Through data analysis, we can find the most popular genres, performance in recent years and how it affects the reputation of the next movie. As movie production incurs huge cost and efforts, our effort is to predict the percentage of success, so that production could be managed accordingly. Throughout the paper, we will discuss about the different ways in which the data analysis used by the film gives a precise idea to each production about the best or worst chances of success and/or failure. In this paper, our goal is to focus on predicting the profitability of a film to support film investment decisions in the early stages of film production. The movie producers and directors can make use of the proposed model in various ways like: modify the movie criteria for becoming blockbusters, launch movie at particular time period to get maximum profit, predict the fan following to get a blockbuster and so on.

Keywords: Prediction · Data analysis · Blockbusters · Investment · IMDb

1 Introduction

Movie prediction is an important way to predict movie revenue and performance. Some of the criteria in calculating movie success included budget, actors, director, producer, set locations, story writer, movie release day, competing movie releases at the same time, music, release location and target audience [1]. IMDB is the most popular website for movie ratings and movie reviews. Imagine being able to analyze the reviews and understand what they liked or did not like the customers. By doing so, we can measure customer satisfaction or dissatisfaction with the movie, which can affect the revenue generated by the movie in a positive or negative way. In Fig. 1, the graph shows the genres of films by IMDB scores.

The analysis of movie data can be incredibly powerful and can make informed guesses, but cannot determine the fate of an individual project with absolute certainty. For some films, the success will be the sale of tickets, for others, the profit margin, the reviews, the social conversations, the franchise options or the Critical Awards.

© Springer Nature Singapore Pte Ltd. 2020
U. Batra et al. (Eds.): REDSET 2019, CCIS 1230, pp. 249–257, 2020.
https://doi.org/10.1007/978-981-15-5830-6_21

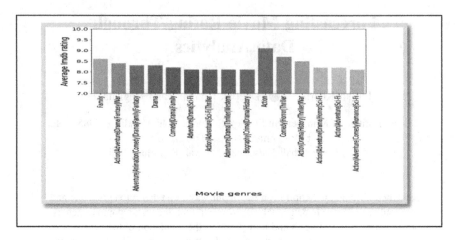

Fig. 1. Movies genres graph by IMDB score

2   Related Work

Since the analysis of movie data is such a hot topic in recent years, many articles have been published in the field of data analysis and its related field. The focus is to make the machines interdependent i.e. they don't require any kind of raw data sets to process the information [2]. In this section, we will discuss several relevant works that have been published. Prof. Junghare [3] suggested a model on the subject "Statistical analysis in reviews and ratings of films" to see how statistical analysis can be performed in reviews and ratings of films. The opinion of PEOPLE is one of the most important sources for different services. The statistical analysis of movie reviews and ratings gives users a perfect picture of what social media thinks about the movie. The movie rating information that will be generated is based on various sources such as Twitter, Facebook, IMDb and Google Trend. Federico de Gregorio [4] tackled the topic Predicting movie box office performance using, YouTube media and the database of IMDb movie data. The prediction model is primarily based on various decision key factors taken from the historical database of movies. The number of Twitter followers and the comparative analysis of comments from YouTube viewers. Postmus [5] proposed recommendation system techniques applied to Netflix movie data. This document contains the approach, the methodology, the elaboration and the evaluation of several common techniques of the recommendation system, applied to the Netflix qualifications. The data contains many user ratings on a Likert scale of 1 to 5 in different movies. The goal is to recommend movies to users who have not yet seen. SarathBabu PB [6] on the theme "Predicting the success of a movie based on the data of IMDb" points to a detailed study. Krauss [7] promoted the success of films and the awards of the academy through the analysis of feelings and social networks.

3   Background

We focus on predicting the profitability of a film to support film investment decisions in the early stages of film production. Using previous data from various sources, and using Python data analysis, this document extracts several types of features, including the theme of the movie, "when" a movie will be released, etc. [8] The results of the experiment showed that the system exceeds the reference methods by a wide margin. In addition to designing a decision support system with practical utility, this research highlights the power of predictive and prescriptive data analysis in information systems to help business decisions. For this document, we use data from Hollywood movies (2000–17). On this data, we simply perform some operations using Python to predict results. And with the help of these results, we can predict what kind of movies people liked. Artificial Intelligence involves Machine Learning and Deep Learning in which Machine learning is the subset of Artificial Intelligence, and Deep Learning is the subset of Machine Learning [9]. In this document, we chose python because python supports large libraries and data, for example, Numpy, Pandas, Scip, Matplotlib, scikit-learn, Seaborn, etc. For an effective analysis of the data.

4   Proposed Methodology

The project pipeline is organized as follows. To perform the data analysis, the data must be chosen or prepared to obtain a set of data. A number of authors tried to surface the issue but superficially, this paper seeks to rectify this omission [10].

4.1   Selecting and Importing Data

In this phase we collect information about movies and everything related. Basically, we gather all the information mainly from IMDB and part of local websites. After collecting information, we organize the data in the form of a CSV file.

We convert the data in CSV format because Python IDE, that is, the jupyter notebook supports CSV or .XLSX files. Now that the data is selected, organized and converted into a compatible format, the data is now ready to be imported into the Python IDE.

4.2   Cleaning

This first module manages the basic cleaning operations, which consist in eliminating unimportant or annoying elements for the following phases of analysis and in the normalization of some misspelled words (Fig. 2).

	director_name	num_critic_for_reviews	duration	director_facebook_likes	actor_3_facebook_likes	actor_2_name	actor_1_facebook_likes	gross
0	James Cameron	723.0	178.0	0.0	855.0	Joel David Moore	1000.0	760505847.0
1	Gore Verbinski	302.0	169.0	563.0	1000.0	Orlando Bloom	40000.0	309404152.0
2	Sam Mendes	602.0	148.0	0.0	161.0	Rory Kinnear	11000.0	200074175.0
3	Christopher Nolan	813.0	164.0	22000.0	23000.0	Christian Bale	27000.0	448130642.0
5	Andrew Stanton	462.0	132.0	475.0	530.0	Samantha Morton	640.0	73058679.0
6	Sam Raimi	392.0	156.0	0.0	4000.0	James Franco	24000.0	336530303.0
7	Nathan Greno	324.0	100.0	15.0	284.0	Donna Murphy	799.0	200807262.0

Fig. 2. Cleaning the data

4.3   Selecting and Importing Libraries for Movie Analysis

After cleaning the data, we selected and imported some libraries that would help us generate and predict the results (Fig. 3).

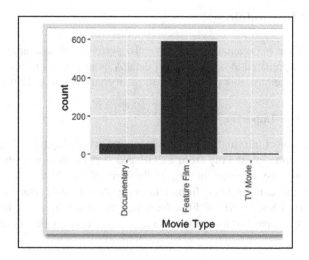

Fig. 3. Movie type selection

In Python, the Matplotlib.pyplot library helps us generate graphics [11, 12].

The panda library is used for data manipulation and analysis. In particular, it offers data structures and operations to manipulate numerical tables and time series (Fig. 4).

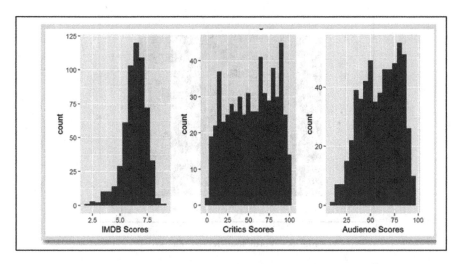

Fig. 4. Scores and count of movies

NumPy is the most basic but powerful package for scientific computing and data manipulation in Python.

The Seaborn library is used for data visualization and provides a high-level interface for drawing attractive and informative statistical graphs. The Seaborn library is based on matplotlib, the pyrotechnics library.

WordCloud is a data visualization technique used to represent text data in which the size of each word indicates its frequency or importance. You can highlight significant textual data points using a word cloud. Word clouds are widely used to analyze data from social networking websites. To generate a word cloud, we import the word cloud library in the Python IDE as shown in Fig. 5.

4.4   Implementation and Generating Results

After selecting and importing all libraries, we are ready to implement our algorithm to data for predicting the results. All the data has been sourced from secondary sources [13]. By using Matplotlib library we generated pie charts, line and bar graphs which shows us the various results, reaction of the people etc.

Seaborn library helped us to visualize the data and generate more effective graphs which helped us to analyze the data more effectively. By using we generated results as follow:

a) Which films are the best since 2000, as shown in Fig. 6. This result helped the directors and the people to choose which films are the best and direct the new version of the films, as they make a new version is a new trend in the city?

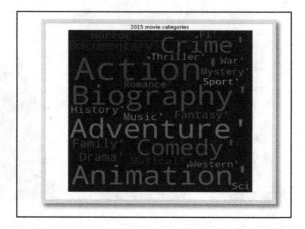

Fig. 5. WordCloud representation

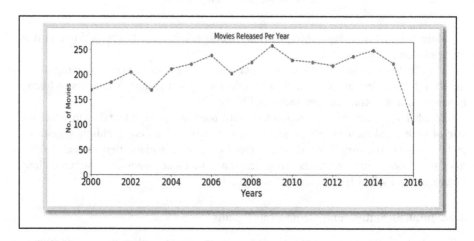

Fig. 6. Movie released per year

b) Find the best genres chosen by the viewers (according to the IMDB rating): This result helped the directors and producers to choose the best and most favorable genre so that the film can obtain a remarkable benefit

c) How many films are released per year: this result can be used by the government so that they can judge the amount of revenue generated and the amount of taxes that must be collected from the filmmakers.

d) Which language is popular among movie viewers and which country produces the most? of films: this result is used again by the producers and directors so that they can choose the language and make the film accordingly.

5   Experimental Result

In this paper, we have found the following results as follow:

a) Over the next analysis of the film we obtain the results and, according to me, the results were shocking. The film that we found the best since 2000 was "kickboxer: vengeance". According to IMDB, this movie received a rating of 9.0 out of 10.

b) According to the IMDB rating, the best genre is "Action" and your average IMDB score ranged between 9.0 and 9.5 out of 10. The second favorite genre is "thriller, comedy and horror".

c) According to the analysis, we also find that, on average, how many movies are released per year and in 2009 around 250 movies were released.

d) We also predicted the results that the language is popular among movie viewers and which country produces the maximum number of films. According to the results, we found that about 92.2% of people like English movies, 0.8% of people like Hindi movies and 7.0% of people like movies in other languages.

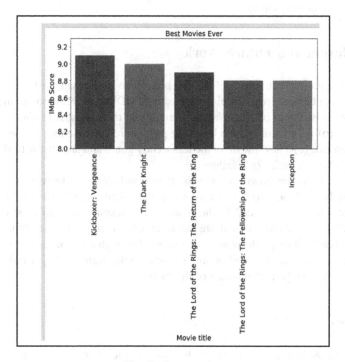

Fig. 7. Best movies

e) In addition, we discovered that countries produce more films than other countries and which country is more popular for their films, as shown in Fig. 7. We find that 74.0% like US movies. UU People love movies from other countries.

f) By film analysis we also discovered that in 2015 and 2016 how many genres and their films were produced during these years (Fig. 8).

Movie Title	Predicted Rating	95% Prediction Interval	Actual Rating
Dirty Grandpa	5.9	4.1 - 7.8	6.0
Deadpool	6.1	4.2 - 7.9	8.1

Fig. 8. Prediction of model

In this analysis, multi-variable, linear regression model was created that proved to have some capability for predicting movie popularity as indicated by IMDB movie rating score.

The prediction is rely on various decision making factors derived from historical database of movies, count of followers tweets from Twitter, and sentiment analysis of comments of YouTube viewers.

6   Conclusion and Future Work

In this article, the predictive model for the box office performance of films was represented by data derived from social networks and IMDb. According to our models, we identified the subsequent patterns: (a) the fame of the main artist is fundamental to the hit of a film, (b) the mixture of the booming past genre and a sequel movie is another guide for success, (c) a new movie in the less trendy genre and an artist with slight fame may perhaps be a sample for a failure.

Therefore, from the previous analysis, it is concluded that there is a need for a statistical analysis of the ratings and reviews of films. This would be a great and unique concept that will be introduced in the market. The results obtained after the implementation of our predictive model are better as compared to similar studies already done in this field. Although the results are not good enough for professional or business purposes, our model can be used in some online applications. A larger training set is required to enhance the performance of the model.

References

1. Ahmad, J., Duraisamy, P., Yousef, A., Buckles, B.: Movie success prediction using data mining. In: 2017 8th International Conference on Computing, Communication and Networking Technologies (ICCCNT), Delhi, pp. 1–4 (2017). https://doi.org/10.1109/icccnt.2017.8204173
2. Kharb, L., et al.: Brain emulation machine model for communication. Int. J. Sci. Technol. Res. (IJSTR), 1410–1418 (2019). http://www.ijstr.org/final-print/aug2019/Brain-Emulation-Machine-Model-For-Communication.pdf

3. Belgur, V., Karande, A., Junghare, A.M.: Statistical analysis on movie reviews and ratings. In: BE in Computer Engineering ZCOER, Pune, Maharashtra, India (2017)
4. Krushikanth, R., Jose, A.M., Supreme, M.: Prediction of movies box office performance using social media. Department of Computer Science, The University of Akron (2013)
5. Postmus, S.: Recommender system techniques applied to Netflixdata. Vrije Universiteit, Amsterdam (2018)
6. Nithin, V.R., Pranav, M.: Predicting movie success based on IMDb data. Department of CSE, National Institute of Technology Calicut (2014)
7. Krauss, J.S.: Predicting movie success and academy awards through sentiment and social network analysis. University of Cologne, Pohligstrasse 1, Cologne, Germany (2008)
8. Oghina, A.: European Conference on Information Retrieval. Springer, Heidelberg (2012)
9. Kharb, L., et al.: Implementing IoT and data analytics to overcome "vehicles danger. Int. J. Innov. Technol. Explor. Eng. 8(11), 4298–4304 (2019)
10. Kharb, L., Sukic, E.: An agent based software approach towards building complex systems. tEM J. 4(3), 287 (2015)
11. Pedregosa, F., Vanderplas, J.: Scikit-learn: machine learning in Python. J. Mach. Learn. Res. 12, 2825–2830 (2011)
12. Millman, K.J.: Python for scientists and engineers. Comput. Sci. Eng. 13(2), 9–12 (2011)
13. Kharb, L., et al.: A conjecture on the exchange rate of bitcoin. Int. J. Sci. Technol. Res. 8(10) (2019, in press). ISSN 2277-8616

Using Statistical Belief Model to Analyze Outcome Using Bayesian Networks

Niharika Sanga[1](✉), Jaspreet Singh[2], and Aniruddh Sanga[2]

[1] Accenture, Gurugram, India
niharikasanga01@gmail.com
[2] G.D. Goenka University, Gurugram, India

Abstract. In this paper we present a statistical model based on Bayesian belief Network to analyze a set of predefined outcomes based on presumptions. Using this model we use casual and diagnostic reasoning as the basis for getting new insight onto the factors shaping the positive or negative sentiments around the subject of study. As an example, we analyze the performance of first 100 days of the current Government in power. We aim to account for major factors shaping the positive or negative sentiments of people during the tenure of these 100 days. Many important factors such as the GDP growth, the new traffic policy, article 370, budget, steps towards employability generation and ease of doing business, etc. are taken into account. These factors become contributing factors in our model and based on conditional probabilities, we calculate the overall positive and negative sentiments.

Keywords: Bayesian belief network · Casual reasoning · Dependent variable

1 Introduction

Bayesian networks are graphical models to calculate probability of an event. It uses the Bayesian inference to calculate probability. Dependencies are formed between a set of identified parameters [1]. Bayesian networks can easily be adapted to model conditional dependency by showing the cause-effect relationship. It depicts the causation by forming edges in a directed graph. We use these directed edges to infer data on random variables in the graph and it can be effectively used to see causation effects.

Bayesian networks allow us to deduce conclusions with only a limited information about the subject under study. We formulate the causal relations between different factors to deduce the information. The factors determining an outcome are carefully selected and we try to derive the outcome using probabilistic model of analysis [2]. This model can be used in the absence of complete information about all parameters. The system can be calibrated even if some information is missing. The leads to incorporation of probabilistic reasoning. This model is quite flexible and can accommodate inherent uncertainty of the outcome [3]. The probabilistic Bayesian model has been used extensively to predict outcome in different domains and applications. The applications of these models are huge and they can be applied to almost any area. In [4], Jose et al. use this model to forecast election results of the 2015 Spanish Congressional Elections. Similarly, in [6], Daniel et al. tries to model a system for electoral

© Springer Nature Singapore Pte Ltd. 2020
U. Batra et al. (Eds.): REDSET 2019, CCIS 1230, pp. 258–265, 2020.
https://doi.org/10.1007/978-981-15-5830-6_22

forecasting in a complex multi-party system. Jackman applies a forecasting prediction model based on linear model to predict outcome in Germany and Sweden with quite success [12]. A similar prediction in Indian context is done in [7]. In [13], Huawei et al. propose a probabilistic model based on reinforced Poisson process to map the popularity gained by an individual. This model builds popularity by tracking individual popularity build process.

2 Methodology

We build a Bayesian model based on independent and dependent variables. Independent variables are the controlling variables, whose values have a direct bearing on the dependent variables. Values of these variables are varied and their effect are measured on dependent variables. Dependent variables on the other hand, are the variables which are affected as a result of variations in independent variables. These are experimental variables under study. In our experiment, we have identified the dependent variables and the corresponding independent variables affecting them.

Based upon the identified variables, we develop graphs based on the causal interactions between these variables. These interactions are built through our understanding of the sentimental analysis of the responses obtained from a wide spectra of sources. These sources include diverse domains such as news articles, twitter trends and social media [10]. The causal relationships of important variables are calculated by Independent variables as shown in Table 1.

Table 1. Identification of Dependent and Independent variables

Dependent variables	Independent variables		
Article 370	Religion	Population	
Budget	Occupation	Religion	Employment
Traffic rules	Population	Age	
Ease of doing business	Occupation		Employment
Traders		Occupation	
Health	Age		
Farmers	Population	Age	
Education	Occupation	Age	Employment
GDP growth rate	Employment	Occupation	

Probabilities taken are our understanding of the combination response from different cross-sections which shows the causal relationship between Independent variables for each Dependent variable. Accordingly, the probabilities have been applied for each of the important variable, and also for the Sentiment variable, to discover the related probability of interest, which is the likelihood of people in favour or against the functioning of the present government.

2.1 Dependent Variables

In our experiment, we take dependent variables as the key factors, which directly influence the popularity of Government. These key factors are the important policies and decisions of the government, shaping the perceptions of people. These dependent variables help to form positive and negative perceptions of people. We describe these dependent variables in the Table 2 [5].

Table 2. Description of Dependent variables

Dependent variables	Description
Article 370	An amendment to this article as given in the Indian constitution. This articles provided for a special status to the Jammu Kashmir citizens earlier [11]
Budget	A Description of the Government's revenue for the fiscal year, the budget launched by government in July 2019
Traffic rules	The rules, regulations and safety norms required for driving vehicles in India
Ease of doing business	Policies under the government for making business easy and flexible
Traders	The policies imposed by government for betterment of traders
Health	The Policies taken by the government for development of the health, public hospitals and health awareness programs
Farmers	The policies in terms of sops and security provided by government for Farmers
Education	The policies of the government for overall development of the Education System, which includes both public and private institutions
GDP growth rate	Gross Domestic Products (GDP) is a measure of overall market value of all goods and services produced by an economy annually [5]. It signifies the financial strength of an economy

2.2 Independent Variables

Apart from the dependent variables, we list out the Independent variables, which affect the dependent variables [8, 9]. These Independent variables have a substantial role in forming the perceptions of people towards the 100 days performance of the Government. These perceptions can be positive or negative. The identified Independent variables are as under:

Population. We classify human population living in a place as either rural or urban. This division is on the basis of the density of population. Generally urban areas include cities and towns, while rural areas include villages and countryside.

Occupation. Another Independent variable in our study is the occupation, which represents the main job or business of a person, i.e. a means of earning a living. Occupation may further be classified as Primary, secondary or tertiary.

Primary – Primary occupation includes agriculture, farming, hunting and harvesting.

Secondary – Secondary occupation includes big businesses, industry and Government offices

Tertiary – It include small businesses and trades

Reasoning. Decisive factors depend on the extent to which employment opportunities have increased or decreased. It signifies the Government policies having a direct bearing on employment generation and economic factors.

Age. We categorize age as a factor and divide citizens eligible to vote, i.e. 18 years of age or older, into the following categories:

Young – All those aged between 18–34 years
Middle-aged – All those aged between 35–55 years
Old Aged – All those with age 55 years and above

Reasoning. Age is considered as an important factor which builds perception towards Government initiatives and policies. Because of their experience, old people tend to have more rigid beliefs, while the youth are more adapt to new things and welcome any positive change. At the same time, the previous experience makes middle-aged and older people less susceptible to false or deceptive gimmicks by political parties.

Religion. Religion is factor which is a system of faith and worship. In our study, we account for the following religions:

Hindus
Muslim
Sikhs
Christians
Buddhist
Jains
Others

Reasoning. It is our belief that religion affects perceptions of people to some extent. It may not be true for all people, but to some extent, their beliefs have some role in forming their perceptions.

Employment. Employment is an Independent variable affecting the perceptions of people towards the Government. It is necessary for satisfaction of one's needs and an important factor shaping the outlook towards the Government. We classify employment by categorizing people as:

Employed
Unemployed

Reasoning. The level of satisfaction of the employed is to some extent dependent on fulfillment of his economic needs. Similarly, it can lead to distraught and mistrust in those who are unemployed.

3 Experiment

Let's come to the focal point of the analysis where we will discuss the different outcomes of the design with regard to shifts in the public response with key policies (Dependent variable). We experimented the key policies taken by the government in its first 100 days of working, after the elections in 2019. This model is presented in Fig. 1 and is used to predict the sentiment of the people over the revolutionary changes in first 100 days of government. This is the standard prediction model. This model graphically shows the relationship between the dependent and independent variables, based on the relevant factors. For each dependent variable, we extracted the relevant feature in Bayesian networks. We can see the positive and negative sentiment of people towards performance of the government during the first 100 days.

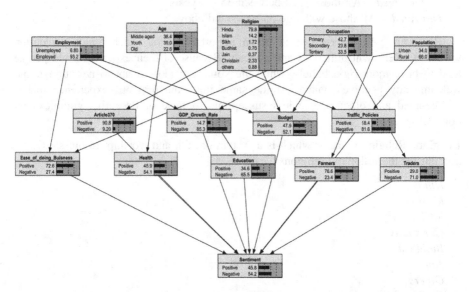

Fig. 1. Standard Scenario where we get the positive and negative sentiment of people towards the performance of government in first 100 days based on dependent and independent variables.

Figure 2 presents the second scenario where we analyse the role played by youth in overall perception forming. For this we assume an all youth population, reducing middle-aged and old population to zero. The result that we get suggests no significant change in perceptions of people, the positive perception increasing marginally by 1.2%. This scenario suggests not much significance of age in the overall perception formation.

Figure 3 presents a third scenario where we try to analyse the effect of budget, traffic rules and education together, if we take these parameters on their negative side. We see that by doing so, the negative perception grows in people.

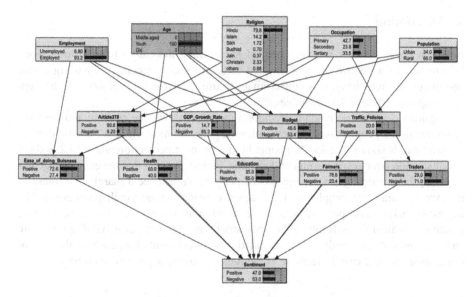

Fig. 2. Scenario 2 where we can see that youth is not having much effect on the sentiment towards the current government's working in first 100 days

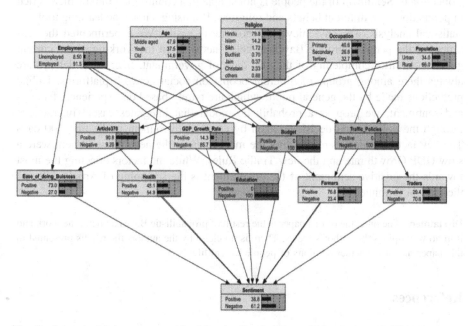

Fig. 3. Scenario 3 where we consider how the Dependent variables Budget, Traffic Rules and Education with negative values in the Bayesian network, affect the overall sentiment towards the outcome.

4 Discussion

Bayesian belief network are very helpful for learning the casual relationships. They help to better understand the problem and forecast the consequences. By using casual and diagnostic reasoning, it is consummate to use a Bayesian belief network for representing prior data and knowledge.

Figure 1 depicts the standard prediction model. It shows the positive and negative sentiment of the people based on key policies and decisions during the first 100 days of government. It shows that 45.8% people hold a positive perception while 54.2% show dissatisfaction over key government decisions. Figure 2 shows that the effect of age has little impact in shaping the perceptions of people. We can see a marginal increase in positive sentiment of people by 1.2% if we consider an all youth population. The Bayesian analysis also proposes that if the current government wants to make a strong positive statement towards the public, they strictly need to ameliorate GDP growth rate and employment. The analysis also revealed that abolishment of article 370, the ease of doing business and ease in farming is helping in making a positive sentiment.

5 Conclusion

Collection of Sentiment of the people is not simple in a country like India which is rich in population with different beliefs and religions. But using a machine learning tool and statistical analysis, we can achieve this goal fairly easily. We experimented the sentiment of the peoples through Bayesian belief network on the working of the current government after completing of the 100 days of government. Interesting debates are always there among groups of different people on social network platforms. Unlike predictions made by the general public which are purely based on experience, feelings and sentiment, we propose a probabilistic model that integrates casual interactions through the policies and decisions taken by current government in the first 100 days The key factors which were effecting the most towards the negative sentiment were a slow GDP Growth rate and the new Traffic Rules. While the factors effecting the most towards the positive sentiment of the government is the scrapping of Article 370 and the sops in farming.

Disclaimer. The outcome of this paper is the result of probabilistic Bayesian belief network and it in no way opines the author's views. There is no claim by the authors the results presented in this paper match the actual opinions of people in real life.

References

1. Aye, N.: Bayesian network probability model for weather prediction. In: International Conference on the Current Trends in Information Technology. IEEE (2009)
2. Yang, X., Li, X., Ning, B., Tang, T.: A survey on energy-efficient train operation for urban rail transit. IEEE Trans. Intell. Transp. Syst. **17**, 2–13 (2016)

3. Shubham, A., Sakshi, B.: Predicting ICC cricket world cup 2015. Int. J. Eng. Technol. Sci. Res. **2**(5), 79–89 (2015)
4. Montalvo, J.G.: Bayesian forecasting of electoral outcomes with new parties' competition. Eur. J. Polit. Econ. **59**, 52–70 (2019)
5. Piotr, B., Tomasz, K., Bartosz, W., Akhilesh, K.: Macroeconomic forecasts in models with Bayesian averaging of classical estimates. Contemp. Econ. **6**(1), 60–69 (2012)
6. Daniel, W.: Picking the winner(s): forecasting election, in multiparty systems. Electoral Stud. **40**, 1–13 (2015)
7. Deepak, K., Raj, M.: Sentiment analysis of twitter user data on Punjab legislative assembly election. Int. J. Mod. Educ. Comput. Sci. **9**, 60–68 (2017)
8. Age Structure And Marital Status. http://censusindia.gov.in/Census_And_You/age_structure_and_marital_status.aspx
9. India in Figures 2018. http://mospi.nic.in/sites/default/files/publication_reports/India_in_figures-2018_rev.pdf
10. Factors affecting. https://www.indiatoday.in/india/story/development-trust-and-big-changes-pm-defines-first-100-days-of-modi-govt-2-0-1596955-2019-09-08
11. The Constitution (Application to Jammu And Kashmir) Order (2019). The Gazette of India: http://egazette.nic.in/WriteReadData/2019/210049.pdf
12. Jackman, S.: Pooling the polls over an election campaign. Aust. J. Polit. Sci. **40**(4), 499–517 (2005)
13. Huawei, S., Dashun, W., Chaoming, S., Albert, L.: Modeling and predicting popularity dynamics via reinforced poisson processes. In: Proceedings of the Twenty-Eighth AAAI Conference on Artificial Intelligence, pp. 291–297 (2014)

Mining Frequent Itemsets over Vertical Probabilistic Dataset Using FuzzyUeclat Algorithm

Amit Rehalia[✉], Samar Wazir, and Md. Tabrez Nafis

Department of Computer Science and Engineering,
Jamia Hamdard, New Delhi 110062, India
amit.reh@gmail.com

Abstract. Data mining is the technique of extracting relevant information from large heterogeneous data sources and present in a meaningful and systematic way for users. Nowadays, data mining has become a trend and all computer-related industries are engaged with data mining. Currently, many data mining algorithms focused on computing the frequent pattern from certain and uncertain databases. In this paper, a new algorithm named FuzzyUeclat is being proposed which uses Fuzzy operators to extract frequent items from the vertical probabilistic dataset. Previously, the frequent items were computed on the basis of expected minimum support derived from the existential probability associated with items. Therefore, as the size of the database increases, the value of expected support is decreased at each level of iterations and subsequently, it approaches zero. To avoid the loss of frequent itemset, the expected minimum support is being replaced with Fuzzy min and Fuzzy max operator to compute the support for an itemset. The experimental result shows that the algorithm FuzzyUeclat increases the frequent patterns and improves the performance for the large uncertain databases.

Keywords: Data mining · Vertical probabilistic dataset · UEclat · FuzzyUeclat · Fuzzy operations · Frequent itemset mining · Association Rule Mining

1 Introduction

A few years back, "Big Data" technology and analytics have emerged and it had grabbed noticeable research in various application domains like Data Mining, E-commerce, Social Networks, Environment Science, Web Mining, etc. Data Mining now has become a trend to extract vital information from these domains and all large companies throughout the world are engaged with data mining [1]. Around 2.5 quintillion bytes data daily produced by the users and this quantity is accelerating with the growth of the Internet of Things. But we are unable to gad the rapid growth of data and sequential methods for data analysis and mining are not capable to handle such huge data [2]. These methods have being modified and empowered to handle Big Data mannerism and produce the result in the expected

---

Contribution Title.

© Springer Nature Singapore Pte Ltd. 2020
U. Batra et al. (Eds.): REDSET 2019, CCIS 1230, pp. 266–278, 2020.
https://doi.org/10.1007/978-981-15-5830-6_23

format. Data mining refers to the retrieval of interesting and useful patterns from large data sets and is being used in various applications like marketing, medical science, insurance, telecommunications, etc.

Frequent Itemset Mining (FIM) [3] is a technique in which frequent itemsets are generated from datasets (UTDB/CTDB) using minimum support value and the generated candidate which is greater than minimum support is known as frequent itemsets. Market basket analysis is the best example of FIM where the purchasing habits of the customers are analyzed. Take an example, if passenger books an air ticket, how likely he also book hotel and taxi in that destination [4].

Basically, there are two types of datasets, from where FIM is generated:

i. *Certain Transactional Dataset (CTDB):* In such type of dataset each transaction has some items connected with each other and ensures the availability of an item in a transaction. For example, if a customer purchases a computer system, with antivirus, Operating system and window's office package software.

T1 = {laptop, antivirus, operating system, office package} i.e. if someone who purchases a laptop then there is a very high probability to purchase antivirus, OS and office package.

Another example, let's assume we have a dataset transaction T1: {Sugar, Milk, Tea}. We are sure that customer purchase sugar, milk and tea during the execution of transaction T1. This dataset is called Certain Transactional Database [4]. As in this example, we can say that when the customer purchase sugar, then he also purchase milk and tea. Hence, there is some association between "Sugar", "Milk" and "Tea". The finding of these patterns is called the *Association Rule Mining* (ARM) [5], and therefore FIM is the subsets of the ARM.

ii. *Uncertain Transaction Dataset (UTDB):* In such type of datasets, transactions consist of items with existential probability with it [6, 7]. For example

T2 = {laptop: 0.60, antivirus: 0.80, OS: 0.55, office Package: 0.30}

i.e. there is a 60% chance to buy a laptop. As a laptop, antivirus, OS and office package are inter-related with each other. If someone purchases a laptop then there is an 80% chance that he will buy antivirus, 55% probability that he will purchase OS and 30% probability that he will purchase office package.

The probability (uncertainty) attached to each item is called *Existential Probability* and thus the database can be called as *Uncertain Transaction Database*.

In today's world where the database size goes on increasing day by day, for the Uncertain Transaction databases, the uncertainty [7–13] has been incorporated. For the UTDB, the occurrence of the frequency of items is computed by multiplying the existential probability and is referred to as expected support. To compute the expected support for the transaction T2 shall be:

The expected support of the laptop and antivirus will be 0.6 * 0.8 = 0.048.

Expected support of laptop, antivirus and office package is: 0.60 * 0.80 * 0.30 = 0.144.

The advantage of using the expected support is that it evaluates the probability of all the items for calculating the support. This is also called as the *existential probability*

[8, 9]. The association rule [4] exists by computing the expected support. However, there is a significant drawback to this approach. When the size of the database goes on increasing, the computed expected support of the items approaches to zero. Due to this, the items are not filtered as frequent items and hence performance degrades as the size of the database goes on increasing.

To overcome this drawback, a noble approach is presented in this paper. *Fuzzy min/max operator* [14–21] is being proposed to compute the frequent itemset mining on Fuzzy transaction datasets [22–27]. *UECLAT* [11] algorithm is being used and runs on the probabilistic dataset. UEclat is an extended form of *Eclat* [28–30] algorithm in which frequent itemsets are extracted from UTDB using the Tideset Vertical data representation, also known as vertical mining. Since it is using Fuzzy operators, hence it named as *FuzzyUeclat* algorithm. The efficiency of FuzzyUeclat is compared on the basis of the number of frequent items generated. Following steps are being performed for the execution of the proposed approach.

1) Execution of *UEclat* algorithm on the probabilistic dataset
2) Execution of the *FuzzyUeclat* algorithm on the probabilistic dataset using a fuzzy min and fuzzy max operator.
3) Comparison of *UEclat* and *FuzzyUeclat* in terms of the number of frequent items generated.

2   Related Works

Data Mining is the digging of patterns from large certain/uncertain datasets using the association rule. The goal of Data mining is digging information from datasets for further utilization of information in a comprehensible structure [31]. Data mining with given minimum support count '*S*' is called frequent Itemset Mining and out more information refers to Frequent Items [4]. There are many algorithms proposed for finding frequent itemset from certain and probabilistic databases.

A technique to retrieve the frequent itemset from a certain dataset in iterative fashion is popularized as the Apriori algorithm. In the first iteration, we analyze all size-1 items and count the existence of the number of times they appeared; items count more than the user-defined threshold value is called frequent itemsets and these frequent items combine for the next level of pruning [31]. Frequent Pattern Growth is the frequent item mining technique that persists with the computational expensive drawback, especially with a large number of patterns. To overcome this snag, Jiawei Han introduces a new technique known as Frequent Pattern Growth in which pattern fragment growth is used for mining complete set of frequent patterns [32]. FP Growth also called FP-Tree to store vital information in compressed format [33]. The Eclat is another algorithm for itemset mining. This algorithm works on a vertical database in the depth-first search technique.

The Count Distribution algorithm (CDA) is a type of data parallelism algorithm which divide a database into "n" partitions as per availability of number of processors and processors counts the candidates of relative data and broadcast their count for all other processor and conclude global counts to determine the large itemsets [31, 34].

Distribution of huge data items in a non-centralized way in data mining is known as Data Distribution and it is more beneficial when the data source is multiple sites [35].

Frequent Pattern Mining (FPM) is the technique to find attributes that occur together frequently is called frequent pattern mining. It is a complex task and computational cost is very high. To find frequent items from uncertain data sets, there exists a U-Apriori Algorithm [36]. U-Apriori Algorithm extracts the frequent items sets from uncertain data sets. The U-Apriori algorithm extends from Apriori Algorithm [1, 31]. The above-mentioned algorithms can also be termed as horizontal mining (breadth-first search) in which data is grouped into transactions to contain a set of items.

Eclat [28–30] generates the frequent itemsets in a Depth-first search (DFS) manner, where the data is represented in vertical format. To explain the same, let's consider the certain transaction database as depicted in Table 1. Consider the count = 2

Table 1. Certain transaction database

TID	Items
Txn1	3, 1
Txn2	1, 2, 4, 5
Txn3	1, 2, 3
Txn4	1, 2, 5

As per the Eclat algorithm, the database has been scanned and transferred into vertical representation as in Table 2.

Table 2. Vertical certain transaction database

Items	TID
1	{Txn1, Txn2, Txn3, Txn4}
2	{Txn2, Txn3, Txn4}
3	{Txn1, Txn3}
4	{Txn2}
5	{Txn2, Txn4}

The level 2 frequent items have been generated and defined in Table 3.

Table 3. Vertical certain transaction database at level 2

Items	TID	Items	TID
1, 2	{Txn2, Txn3, Txn4}	2, 3	{Txn3}
1, 3	{Txn1, Txn3}	2, 4	{Txn2}
1, 4	{Txn2}	2, 5	{Txn2}
1, 5	{Txn2, Txn4}	4, 5	{Txn2}

Table 4 depicts the frequent item generated for level 3.

Table 4. Vertical certain transaction database at level 3

Items	TID	Items	TID
1, 2, 3	{Txn1, Txn2, Txn3, Txn4}	2, 3, 5	{Txn2, Txn3}
1, 2, 4	{Txn2, Txn3, Txn4}	3, 4, 5	{Txn2}
1, 2, 5	{Txn2, Txn3, Txn4}	2, 3, 4	{Txn2, Txn3}

Table 5 defines the frequent items generated for level 4 items.

Table 5. Vertical certain transaction database at level 4

Items	TID
1, 2, 3, 4	{Txn1, Txn2, Txn3, Txn4}
1, 2, 3, 5	{Txn1, Txn2, Txn3, Txn4}
2, 3, 4, 5	{Txn2, Txn3}

Table 6 defines the frequent items generated for level 5 items.

Table 6. Vertical certain transaction database at level 5

Items	TID
1, 2, 3, 4, 5	{Txn1, Txn2, Txn3, Txn4}

UElcat is an extended version of Eclat to support an uncertain transaction database. Frequent items are computed on the uncertain transaction database using expected support and its formula has been defined in Eq. (1):

$$Expected\ Support(X) = \sum_{i=1}^{n} \sum_{j=1}^{k} Pi(x) \tag{1}$$

Here, X itemset consists of x1, x2, …. x|k| distinct items, n be the number of transactions in the uncertain transaction database.

3   Problem Definition

In the UEclat algorithm, the frequent itemsets are not filtered for the large databases. As the size of the database has increased, the number of frequent itemsets generated through UElcat decreases, because its probabilities are multiplied with each other and are approaches to zero. This results in the loss of the filtered item sets.

The proposed FuzzyUeclat algorithm uses the FuzzyOpr to generate number of frequent itemsets because it uses the fuzzy min or fuzzy max operations to determine the expected support.

Consider the total number of transactions in fuzzy transaction database as n, Fuzzy Max can be computed as defined in Eq. (2):

$$FuzzyOpr(X) = \sum_{i=1}^{n} max(MF(x1), MF(x2)...MF(x|K|)) \qquad (2)$$

Fuzzy Min can be computed as defined in Eq. (3):

$$FuzzyOpr(X) = \sum_{i=1}^{n} min(MF(x1), MF(x2)...MF(x|K|)) \qquad (3)$$

Here, X itemset consists of x1, x2, ..., x|k| distinct items.

4 FuzzyUeclat Algorithm

FuzzyUeclat algorithm is an extension of the UEclat [37] algorithm. FuzzyOpr (described in Eq. 2, Eq. 3) has been used to compute the expected support of the transactions. The input to the FuzzyUeclat Algorithm contains the uncertain transactional database with the operator given minimum support "minSupp" and output generates all the frequent patterns with their existential probability and is described below:

```
1. Convert the Horizontal uncertain data to vertical format.
2. for each vertical data, getting frequent 1- itemset by checking with "minSupp"
3. FuzzyUeclat(F1, minSupp)
   {
4.      F1 = F1                                    //Initialization
5.      for each Xi ∈ E &&(j > i) do
6.          for each Xj ∈ E do
7.              [R] = Xi ∪ X                       //join Xi and prefix Xj
8.              T([R] = T([Xi])∩T(Xj);
9.              P([R], Tj = FuzzyOpr(P([Xi], Tj), P([Xj], Tj)
10.             FuzzyESup([R], Tj) = ∑P([R], Tj)
11              if(FuzzyESupp([R],Tj) >= minSupp then
12                  F1 = F1 ∪ {R}
13              E = E- Xj
14          FuzzyUeclat(E, FuzzyOprSupp)
15      return F1
   }
```

The above steps of the algorithm have been explained as follows:

- Line 1 converts the horizontal uncertain database to the vertical uncertain database.
- F1 is the itemset which is obtained by 1st level of pruning with "minSupp". This is also called the prefix-pruning or initialization as defined in line 2–4.
- Line 5–8 performs all the union and intersection operations as performed in UEclat algorithm for joining and pruning of all possible candidates.

- At line 9–10, the "FuzzyESupp" is computed by using *FuzzyOpr* as defined in Eq. 2 and Eq. 3 to determine the expected support.
- At line 11–14, the "FuzzyESupp" is compared with the user-defined threshold "minSupp". The itemset is said to be frequent if the FuzzyESupp is greater than the "minSupp".

The FuzzyUeclat algorithm generates frequent itemsets with their existential probability for the uncertain transaction database using the FuzzyOpr (i.e. fuzzy min or fuzzy max operators). An example of FuzzyOpr is described in Sect. 5.

5 FuzzyOpr Example

Consider the UTDB in Table 7 for the understanding of FuzzyOpr as defined in Eq. (2) and Eq. (3).

Table 7. Vertical uncertain transaction database

Items	TID			
0	1(0.15)	2(0.23)	3(0.1)	4(0.21)
1	1(0.25)	2(0.24)	3(0.16)	4(0.18)
2	1(0.23)	2(0.17)	3(0.27)	4(0.29)
3	1(0.1)	2(0.20)	3(0.18)	4(0.30)

By using Fuzzy Max operator as defined in Eq. (2):

Value of FuzzyESupp for Tansaction$\{1,2\} = \{0.25 + 0.24\} = 0.49$
Value of FuzzyESupp for Tansaction$\{3,4\} = \{0.27 + 0.30\} = 0.57$
Value of FuzzyESupp for Tansaction$\{1,2,3\} = \{0.25 + 0.24 + 0.27\} = 0.76$

By using Fuzzy Min operator as defined in Eq. (3):

Value of FuzzyESupp for Tansaction$\{1,2\} = \{0.1 + 0.17\} = 0.27$
Value of FuzzyESupp for Tansaction$\{3,4\} = \{0.1 + 0.18\} = 0.28$
Value of FuzzyESupp for Tansaction$\{1,2,3\} = \{0.1 + 0.17 + 0.1\} = 0.37$

6   Experiments and Result Analysis

The FuzzyUEclat algorithm is being executed on various uncertain databases, and its performance is being analyzed. One such uncertain database where the algorithm is executed is shown in Table 8. The minimum support is chosen as 0.1

Table 8.   Horizontal uncertain database

TID	Items				
T1	1(0.25)	2(0.35)	3(0.2)	4(0.0)	5(0.5)
T2	1(0.0)	2(0.33)	3(0.4)	4(0.4)	5(0.0)
T3	1(0.15)	2(0.25)	3(0.0)	4(0.3)	5(0.36)
T4	1(0.25)	2(0.4)	3(0.2)	4(0.37)	5(0.24)
T5	1(0.19)	2(0.21)	3(0.57)	4(0.22)	5(0.71)
T6	1(0.11)	2(0.31)	3(0.28)	4(0.41)	5(0.56)
T7	1(0.23)	2(0.33)	3(0.09)	4(0.1)	5(0.42)
T8	1(0.14)	2(0.36)	3(0.48)	4(0.52)	5(0.06)
T9	1(0.22)	2(0.53)	3(0.31)	4(0.61)	5(0.19)
T10	1(0.53)	2(0.05)	3(0.41)	4(0.04)	5(0.18)

As per the algorithm of FuzzyUeclat, the horizontal database is converted into the vertical database as defined in Table 9.

Table 9.   Vertical uncertain database

Item	T1	T2	T3	T4	T5	T6	T7	T8	T9	T10
Item 1	1(0.25)	2(0.0)	3(.15)	4(.25)	5(.19)	6(.11)	7(.23)	8(.14)	9(.22)	10(.53)
Item 2	1(0.35)	2(.33)	3(.25)	4(0.4)	5(.21)	6(.31)	7(.33)	8(.36)	9(.53)	10(.05)
Item 3	1(0.2)	2(0.4)	3(0.0)	4(0.2)	5(.57)	6(.28)	7(.09)	8(.48)	9(.31)	10(.41)
Item 4	1(0.0)	2(0.4)	3(0.3)	4(.37)	5(.22)	6(.41)	7(0.1)	8(.52)	9(.61)	10(.04)
Item 5	1(0.5)	2(0.0)	3(.36)	4(.24)	5(.71)	6(.56)	7(.42)	8(.06)	9(.19)	10(.18)

An observation has been analyzed by executing the uncertain database (Table 9) on UEclat, FuzzyUeclat Max and FuzzyUeclat Min algorithm. The UEclat algorithm generates 10 numbers of frequent items with minimum support of 0.1. Subsequently, the FuzzyUeclat algorithm with Fuzzy min and Fuzzy max generates 99 and 175 frequent items respectively. Figure 1 and Table 10 outlines the number of frequent items generated from UEclat, FuzzyUeclat min, and FuzzyUeclat max algorithms.

Table 10. Frequent ItemSets generated

Algorithm executed	Number of frequent items (minimum support = 0.1)
UEclat	10
FuzzyUeclat with Fuzzy min operator	99
FuzzyUeclat with Fuzzy max operator	175

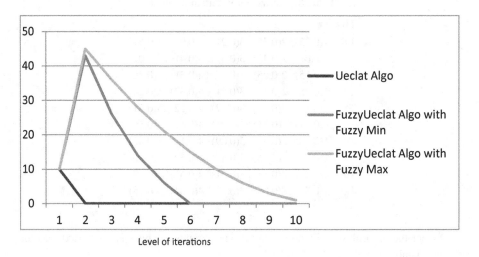

Level of iterations

Fig. 1. Number of frequent items generated on UEclat, FuzzyUeclat Min, FuzzyUEclat Max

6.1 Market Basket Dataset Example

The FuzzyUEclat algorithm is also being executed on the market basket uncertain database as shown in Table 11, and its performance is being analyzed. The minimum support is chosen as 0.2

Table 11. Horizontal uncertain database

TID	Items				
	Tooth paste	Tooth brush	Shaving cream	Shampoo	Soap
T1	0.35	0.48	0	0.33	0.12
T2	0.47	0.39	0.51	0.21	0.11
T3	0.01	0.19	0.11	0.57	0.23
T4	0.39	0.4	0	0.21	0.11

As per the algorithm of FuzzyUeclat, the horizontal database of market basket is converted into the vertical database as defined in Table 12.

Table 12. Vertical uncertain database

Item	T1	T2	T3	T4
Tooth paste	0.35	0.47	0.01	0.39
Tooth brush	0.48	0.39	0.19	0.4
Shaving cream	0	0.51	0.11	0
Shampoo	0.33	0.21	0.57	0.21
Soap	0.12	0.11	0.23	0.11

An observation has been analyzed by executing the uncertain database (Table 12) on UEclat, FuzzyUeclat Max and FuzzyUeclat Min algorithm. Figure 2 and Table 13 outlines the number of frequent items generated from UEclat, FuzzyUeclat min, and FuzzyUeclat max algorithms.

Table 13. Frequent ItemSets generated for market basket dataset

Algorithm executed	Number of frequent items (minimum support = 0.2)
UEclat	4
FuzzyUeclat with Fuzzy min operator	8
FuzzyUeclat with Fuzzy max operator	14

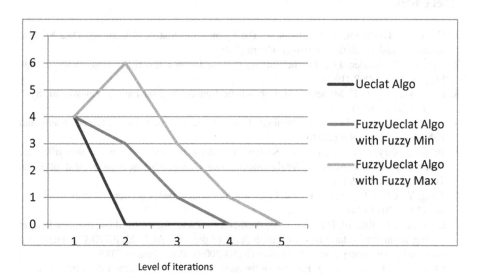

Fig. 2. Number of frequent items generated on UEclat, FuzzyUeclat Min, FuzzyUEclat Max for market basket dataset

It is clear that FuzzyUeclat performs better and generates increased frequent items in comparison to the UEclat algorithm. Usage of FuzzyMax operator performs even better in terms of frequent items because it retrieves the largest value of the item from an item sets.

7 Conclusion and Future Directions

The usage of uncertain transaction database has been progressing to analyze the behavior of the customers or their future purchasing habits or requirements. E.g. The win-loss projection of the team before the start of the match by TV channel. Therefore, the size of the database rapidly increasing from different heterogeneous sources and diverse fields. The UEclat algorithm underperforms for large uncertain databases and unable to find the interesting pattern analysis. The usage of Fuzzy min and Fuzzy max improves the performance and generates more frequent patterns for large databases, thus making the solution as feasible and efficient. However, the fuzzy min or max does not consider associations among all items but uses only one value. If the value of fuzzy min is closest to zero, then fewer frequent items are generated and vice-versa for fuzzy max. Consequently, more approaches need to be devised, which shall maintain the association rule interestingness among the frequent items.

References

1. Hastie, T., Tibshirani, R., Friedman, J.: The Elements of Statistical Learning: Data Mining, Inference, and Prediction. Springer, Cham (2009)
2. Agrawal, R., Shafer, J.C.: Parallel mining of association rules. IEEE Trans. Knowl. Data Eng. **8**(6), 962–969 (1996)
3. Bernecker, T., et al.: Model-based probabilistic frequent itemset mining. Knowl. Inf. Syst. **37**, 181–217 (2013)
4. Han, J., Kamber, M.: Data Mining: Concepts and Techniques. Morgan Kaufmann Publishers, Burlington (2016)
5. Han, E., Karypis, G., Kumar, V.: Scalable parallel data mining for association rules. In: Proceedings of the ACM-SIGMOD International Conference on Management of Data, Tucson, Arizona (1997)
6. Tong, Y., Chen, L., Cheng, Y., Yu, P.S.: Mining frequent itemsets over uncertain databases. In: VLDB 2012 (2012)
7. Bernecker, T., Kriegel, H.P., Renz, M., Verhein, F., Züfle, A.: Probabilistic frequent itemset mining in uncertain databases. In: Proceedings of the 15th ACM SIGKDD Conference on Knowledge Discovery and Data Mining (KDD 2009), Paris, France (2009)
8. Chui, C.-K., Kao, B., Hung, E.: Mining frequent itemsets from uncertain data. In: Zhou, Z.-H., Li, H., Yang, Q. (eds.) PAKDD 2007. LNCS (LNAI), vol. 4426, pp. 47–58. Springer, Heidelberg (2007). https://doi.org/10.1007/978-3-540-71701-0_8
9. Chui, C.-K., Kao, B.: A decremental approach for mining frequent itemsets from uncertain data. In: Washio, T., Suzuki, E., Ting, K.M., Inokuchi, A. (eds.) PAKDD 2008. LNCS (LNAI), vol. 5012, pp. 64–75. Springer, Heidelberg (2008). https://doi.org/10.1007/978-3-540-68125-0_8

10. Calders, T., Garboni, C., Goethals, B.: Approximation of frequentness probability of itemsets in uncertain data. In: ICDM (2010)
11. Calders, T., Garboni, C., Goethals, B.: Efficient pattern mining of uncertain data with sampling. In: Zaki, M.J., Yu, J.X., Ravindran, B., Pudi, V. (eds.) PAKDD 2010. LNCS (LNAI), vol. 6118, pp. 480–487. Springer, Heidelberg (2010). https://doi.org/10.1007/978-3-642-13657-3_51
12. Cheng, R., Kalashnikov, D., Prabhakar, S.: Evaluating probabilistic queries over imprecise data. In: SIGMOD (2003)
13. Chen, Y.L., Tang, K., Shen, R.J., Hu, Y.H.: Market basket analysis in a multiple store environment. Decis. Support Syst. **40**(2), 339–354 (2005)
14. Zadeh, L.A.: Fuzzy sets as a basis for a theory of possibility. Fuzzy Set Syst. **1**, 3–28 (1978)
15. Zadeh, L.A.: Probability measures of fuzzy events. J. Math. Anal. Appl. **23**, 421–427 (1968)
16. Yager, R.R.: Quantifiers in the formulation of multiple objective decision functions. Inform. Sci. **31**, 107–139 (1983)
17. Zadeh, L.A.: Fuzzy sets and possibility distribution. StndFuzz **195**, 47–58 (2006)
18. Zadeh, L.A.: Fuzzy Probabilities. Inf. Process. Manag. **20**, 363–372 (1984)
19. Zadeh, L.A.: Fuzzy sets. Inf. Control **8**, 338–353 (1965)
20. Zhang, Q., Li, F., Yi, K.: Finding frequent items in probabilistic data. In: SIGMOD (2008)
21. Zhang, S., Wu, X., Zhang, C., Lu, J.: Computing the minimum-support for mining frequent patterns. Knowl. Inf. Syst. **15**(2), 233–257 (2008)
22. Hong, T.P., Fournier-Viger, P., Lin, C.W.J.: A fast algorithm for mining fuzzy frequent itemsets. J. Intell. Fuzzy Syst. **29**, 2373–2379 (2015)
23. Hong, T.P., Kuo, C.S., Chi, S.C.: Mining association rules from quantitative data. Intell. Data Anal. **3**, 363–376 (1999)
24. Hong, T.P., Chen, J.B.: Finding relevant attributes and membership functions. Fuzzy Sets Syst. **103**, 389–404 (1999)
25. Hong, T.P., Kuo, C.S., Wang, S.L.: A fuzzy AprioriTid mining algorithm with reduced computational time. Appl. Soft. Comput. **5**(1), 1–10 (2004)
26. Hong, T.P., Lee, C.Y.: Induction of fuzzy rules and membership functions from training examples. Fuzzy Set Syst. **84**(1), 33–47 (1996)
27. Hong, T.P., Lin, K.Y., Wang, S.L.: Fuzzy data mining for interesting generalized association rules. Fuzzy Set Syst. **138**(2), 255–269 (2003)
28. Zaki, M.J.: Scalable algorithms for association mining. IEEE Trans. Knowl. Data Eng. **12**(3), 372–390 (2000)
29. Zaki, M., Gouda, K.: Fast vertical mining using diffsets. In: ACM KDD Conference (2003)
30. Zaki, M., Parthasarathy, S., Ogihara, M., Li, W.: New algorithms for fast discovery of association rules. In: KDD Conference, pp. 283–286 (1997)
31. Agrawal, R., Srikant, R.: Fast algorithms for mining association rules. In: Proceedings of the 20th International Conference on Very Large Data Bases, VLDB, Santiago, Chile, pp. 487–499 (1994)
32. Han, J., Pei, J., Yin, Y., Mao, R.: Mining frequent patterns without candidate generation: a frequent-pattern tree approach. Data Min. Knowl. Discov. **8**, 53–87 (2004)
33. Han, J., Pei, J., Yin, Y.: Mining frequent patterns without candidate generation. In: Proceedings of the Conference on the Management of Data, SIGMOD 2000, Dallas. ACM Press, New York (2000)
34. Dunham, M.H.: Data Mining. Introductory and Advanced Topics. Prentice-Hall (2003). ISBN 0-13-088892-3
35. Lang, R., Deng, Z.: Data distribution using time-based weighted distributed hash table. In: 2008 Seventh International Conference on Grid and Cooperative Computing (2008)

36. Wazir, S., Sufyan Beg, M.M., Ahmad, T.: Mining the frequent itemsets for a database with certain and uncertain transactions. In: Proceedings of the 21st World Multi-Conference on Systemics, Cybernetics, and Informatics (2017)
37. Yang, J., Zhang, Y., Wei, Y.: An improved vertical algorithm for frequent itemset mining from uncertain database. In: 9th International Conference on Intelligent Human-Machine Systems and Cybernetics (2017)

Comparison of Random Weight Initialization to New Weight Initialization CONEXP

Apeksha Mittal[(✉)], Amit Prakash Singh, and Pravin Chandra

University School of Information, Communication and Technology,
Guru Gobind Singh Indraprastha University, Sector-16C, Dwarka 110078, India
apekshamittal3@gmail.com, amit@ipu.ac.in, chandra.pravin@gmail.com

Abstract. Training in feedforward networks is adaptation of weights of network which makes weight initialization an important factor in determining the training speed in network. This work aims at proposing a new weight initialization technique, wherein the weights are initialized in the useful range in threshold function. It further initializes weights to each hidden node in a region which alternately contracts and expands statistically. The proposed weight initialization is compared to the conventional random weight initialization. The proposed weight initialization is expected to perform better than the random weight initialization.

Keywords: Feedforward neural networks · Weight initialization · Function approximation

1 Introduction

The universal approximation property of feedforward neural networks makes them popular choice for learning non-linearities [7,16]. A feedforward network with 1 hidden layer and non-linearity at hidden node can be used for solving almost all function approximation problems. The architecture of such network is given in Fig. 1, with I number of input, H number of hidden nodes. $z_1, \ldots, z_I$ are input to the network, y is the output of the network, $\psi_{11}, \ldots, \psi_{IH}$ denotes input to hidden layer weights, $\delta_1 \ldots \delta_H$ denotes hidden layer thresholds, $\mu_1, \ldots, \mu_H$ denotes hidden to output weights and η denotes the output layer threshold. The net output of the network is given as:

$$y = f_2 \left\{ \sum_j f_1 \left(\sum_i \psi_{ij} z_i + \delta_j \right) . \mu_j + \eta \right\} \tag{1}$$

where f_1 and f_2 are threshold functions at the hidden and output nodes respectively. Sigmoidal function (such as logistic function and hyperbolic functions) can be used as threshold functions [6]. In this work, f_1 is hyperbolic tangent and f_2 linear. Therefore, we can rewrite Eq. (1) as:

© Springer Nature Singapore Pte Ltd. 2020
U. Batra et al. (Eds.): REDSET 2019, CCIS 1230, pp. 279–289, 2020.
https://doi.org/10.1007/978-981-15-5830-6_24

$$y = \sum_j f_1 \left(\sum_i \psi_{ij} z_i + \delta_j \right) . \mu_j + \eta \tag{2}$$

Determining the initial values of weights, ψ_{ij} and μ_j and the thresholds, δ_j and η, greatly affects the speed of training of network, i.e., achieving the minimum error. A lot of work has been contributed in this area. Initial work was done by Rumelhart et al. in [15], wherein weights were initialized to random values (instead of equal values) to break the symmetry, whereas Bottou in [2] initialized weights uniformly in $(-\gamma/\sqrt{I}, \gamma/\sqrt{I})$, γ is the active range in threshold function, I is the input size. Nyugen and Widrow in [13] divided the region of interest of weight initialization in small overlapping intervals.

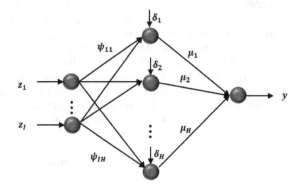

Fig. 1. Feedforward Network with 1-hidden layer.

Drago and Ridella in [5] determined an upper bound on maximum weight magnitude as $f(PNP)$, where PNP is paralyzed neuron percentage. Kim and Ra in [8] determined a lower bound on weight magnitude as $\sqrt{LRP/I}$, where LRP is learning rate parameter. Yam and Chow in [18] determined the maximum bound on hidden to output weights to be inversely proportional to net input to hidden layer node.

Sodhi and Chandra in [17] initialized weights in distinct region in interval $(-1, -1 + 2/(H - 1))$, where H is the number of hidden nodes. Qiao et al. [14] initialized weights based on useful information between input and output variables. Mittal et al. [10] initialized weights in the statistically resilient intervals in significant range of activation function. Bhatia et al. [1] initialized weights in the interval $(-3/\sqrt{I}, 3/\sqrt{I})$, where I is the number of input. Mittal et al. in [12] initialized weights with a constant magnitude.

This work aims at determining the value of weights and thresholds, ψ_{ij} and μ_j and the thresholds, δ_j and η so as to reduce the error. The weights to hidden node are initialized such that the region of interest is alternately contracted and expanded statistically. The new proposed algorithm is referred to as CONEXP in this work. CONEXP is compared to conventional random weight initialization (referred to as RNDM in this work) for 5 function approximation problems. The proposed method CONEXP is expected to perform better than RNDM.

The approach for proposed algorithm CONEXP is discussed in the next section. The functions and the network architecture used for testing CONEXP is discussed in Sect. 3. Results and discussions are presented in 4 and 5 respectively, while the conclusion is discussed in Sect. 6.

2   Proposed Work

The training of feedforward networks involve the updation of weights from the initial value close to optimal value [15]. The weight update value is dependent upon value of derivative of threshold function f_1 [6]. The useful range in f_1, $(-\gamma, \gamma)$ is the range where the value of f_1' is greater than 20% of it's maximum value, i.e., γ can be defined as:

$$\gamma = \frac{1}{5} * max \left\{ f_1'(.) \right\} \tag{3}$$

Thus the range $(-\gamma, \gamma)$ is the region of interest. Now, the minimum range $(-s, s)$ is defined where s is the $1/H$th part of the range $(-\gamma, \gamma)$, i.e.,

$$s = 2 * \gamma/H \tag{4}$$

Now, weights to each hidden node are initialized such that the region of interest is alternately contracted and expanded. The weights to first hidden node are initialized in the maximum range, i.e., region of interest $(-\gamma, \gamma)$. The weights to successive odd hidden layer nodes are initialized in the region reduced by a factor $2S$. The weights to second hidden node are initialized in the minimum range $(-s, s)$. The weights to successive even hidden layer nodes are initialized in the region increased by a factor $2S$. The weights thus initialized ensures that each hidden node has separate range in useful range of activation function. The algorithm for proposed weight initialization method CONEXP is given in Algorithm 1. I and H are the input and ψ (Input to hidden layer weights), δ (Hidden layer threshold), μ (Hidden to output weights) and η (Output layer threshold) are the output of algorithm.

3   Experiment Design

The proposed algorithm for weight initialization is tested for 5 function as discussed:

1. Fn_1: Two-dimentional function from [3, 11]:

$$y = sin(z_1 * z_2) \tag{5}$$

where z_1, z_2 is in $[-2, 2]$.

Algorithm 1. CONEXP

Input : Number of Input (I); Number of Hidden Nodes (H)
Output : ψ (Input to hidden layer weights); δ (Hidden layer threshold); μ (Hidden to output weights) and η (Output layer threshold)
1. Obtain $(-\gamma, \gamma)$, the useful range in threshold function.
2. Define s as $2 * \gamma/H$.
3. Initialize all the ψ and δ to uniformly distributed random values in (-1,1)
4. For ith hidden node
5. If i is odd
   (a) $\psi* = (G - (\lfloor i/2 \rfloor * S))$
   (b) Normalize ψ.
6. If i is even
   (a) $\psi* = (i/2) * S$
   (b) Normalize ψ.
7. Normalize δ.
8. Initialize μ and η randomly in the region (-s/2,s/2).

---

2. Fn_2: Two-dimentional function from [3,11]:

$$y = exp(z_1 * sin(\pi * z_2))$$
$\qquad\qquad$ (6)

where z_1, z_2 is in $[-1, 1]$.
3. Fn_3: Two-dimentional function from [4,11]

$$\begin{aligned}
x_1 &= 40 * exp(8 * ((z_1 - .5)^2 + (z_2 - .5)^2)) \\
x_2 &= exp(8 * ((z_1 - .2)^2 + (z_2 - .7)^2)) \\
x_3 &= exp(8 * ((z_1 - .7)^2 + (z_2 - .2)^2)) \\
y &= x1/(x2 + x3)
\end{aligned}$$
$\qquad\qquad$ (7)

where $z_1, z_2 \in [0, 1]$.
4. Fn_4: Two-dimentional function from [9,11]

$$y = (1 + sin(2z_1 + 3z_2))/(3.5 + sin(x_1 - x_2))$$
$\qquad\qquad$ (8)

where $z_1, z_2 \in [-2, 2]$.
5. Fn_5: Two-dimentional function peaks.m from MATLAB

$$y = 3 * (1 - z_1)^2 * exp(-z_1^2 - (z_2 + 1)^2) - 10 * (\frac{z_1}{5} - z_1^3 - z_2^5)$$
$$*exp(-z_1^2 - z_2^2) - \frac{1}{3} * exp(-(z_1 + 1)^2 - z_2^2)$$
$\qquad\qquad$ (9)

where $z_1, z_2 \in [0, 1]$.

The proposed algorithm CONEXP is tested on the function approximation problems using $Fn_1, Fn_2, \ldots, Fn_5$. 750 input-output discrete points are generated of which 250 input-output data points are used for training of the network and remaining 500 input-output data points are used for testing network. The network is simulated in MATLAB R2015a, 4gb ram and intel core i5 processor. Each network is trained for 1000 epochs, and for each function 30 networks are trained for RNDM and CONEXP. Thus, a total of $1000 \times 30 \times 2$ networks are trained. The network size (number of input, number of hidden nodes and number of output) is given in Table 1. The results are presented in next section.

Table 1. Network Size for $Fn_1, Fn_2, \ldots, Fn_5$

	No. of inputs	No. of hidden nodes	No. of output
Fn_1	2	15	1
Fn_2	2	15	1
Fn_3	2	15	1
Fn_4	2	15	1
Fn_5	2	11	1

4 Results

In training phase, both input-output data points are given to the network, in testing phase, only input is given to the network. The mean squared error in both cases is reported as training and testing results in Table 2. Student t-test is conducted to check whether the difference in performance of RNDM and CONEXP is statistically significant. The results for Student t-test are presented in Table 3. The train data results for 30 networks for function $f_1, f_2, \ldots, f_5$ is plotted in Figs. 2, 3, 4, 5 and 6 respectively.

5 Discussion

The training and testing results on RNDM and CONEXP are discussed:

5.1 Training Results

1. Mean: For all 5 cases, mean for CONEXP is less than RNDM.
2. Median: For all 5 cases, median for CONEXP is less than RNDM.
3. Standard Deviation: For 4 of 5 cases, St.Dev. for CONEXP is less than RNDM.
4. Maximum: For all 5 cases, maximum for CONEXP is less than RNDM.
5. Minimum: For all 5 cases, minimum for CONEXP is less than RNDM.

Table 2. Training and testing results for CONEXP v/s RNDM ($\times 10^{-3}$). Due to large data volume, summarized results (in terms of mean, median, standard deviation, maximum and minimum) of 30 networks is reported

		RNDM	CONEXP				RNDM	CONEXP
Fn_1	Mean	14.99	10.20		Fn_1	Mean	18.20	13.43
	Median	13.79	9.85			Median	16.50	12.65
	St. Dev.	4.51	2.08			St. Dev.	5.24	3.28
	Max	28.55	15.55			Max	32.71	20.11
	Min	8.45	6.47			Min	11.30	7.62
Fn_2	Mean	25.18	19.37		Fn_2	Mean	31.51	24.72
	Median	23.70	18.07			Median	28.95	22.13
	St. Dev.	7.67	5.04			St. Dev.	9.07	6.63
	Max	57.10	34.59			Max	63.38	39.62
	Min	14.66	13.55			Min	18.90	16.91
Fn_3	Mean	0.26	0.14		Fn_3	Mean	0.31	0.16
	Median	0.26	0.10			Median	0.31	0.13
	St. Dev.	0.12	0.09			St. Dev.	0.14	0.10
	Max	0.53	0.35			Max	0.63	0.45
	Min	0.07	0.03			Min	0.10	0.03
Fn_4	Mean	41.99	12.55		Fn_4	Mean	49.29	14.61
	Median	23.19	11.69			Median	23.50	13.27
	St. Dev.	58.95	3.58			St. Dev.	80.59	4.50
	Max	221.36	25.58			Max	298.31	28.56
	Min	13.53	8.52			Min	14.54	9.12
Fn_5	Mean	0.31	0.28		Fn_5	Mean	0.41	0.37
	Median	0.26	0.20			Median	0.34	0.30
	St. Dev.	0.18	0.37			St. Dev.	0.23	0.36
	Max	0.86	2.23			Max	1.09	2.19
	Min	0.11	0.10			Min	0.14	0.16

Table 3. t-test matrix

	RNDM	CONEXP
RNDM	0	0
CONEXP	4	0

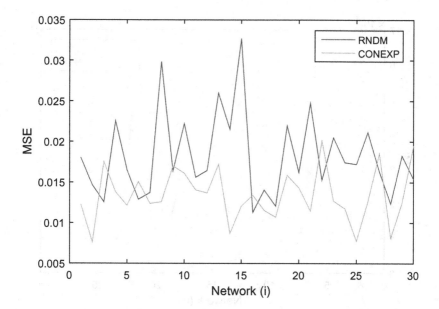

Fig. 2. Plot for MSE for 30 networks during network training for f_1.

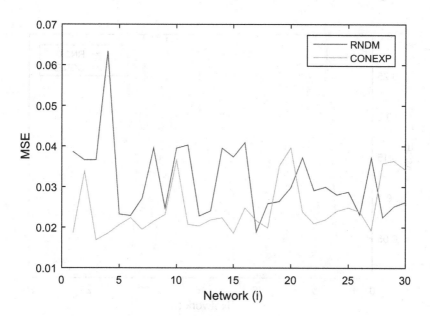

Fig. 3. Plot for MSE for 30 networks during network training for f_2.

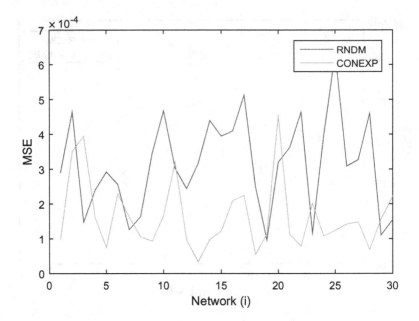

Fig. 4. Plot for MSE for 30 networks during network training for f_3.

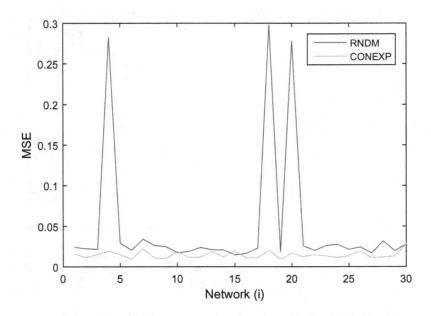

Fig. 5. Plot for MSE for 30 networks during network training for f_4.

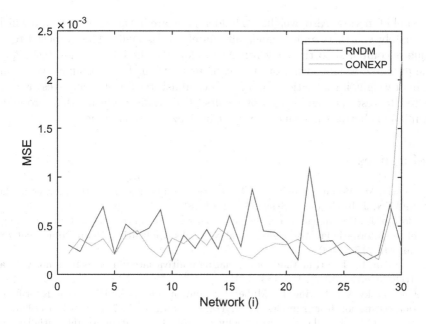

Fig. 6. Plot for MSE for 30 networks during network training for f_5.

5.2 Testing Results

1. Mean: For all 5 cases, mean for CONEXP is less than RNDM.
2. Median: For all 5 cases, median for CONEXP is less than RNDM.
3. Standard Deviation: For 4 of 5 cases, St.Dev. for CONEXP is less than RNDM.
4. Maximum: For all 5 cases, maximum for CONEXP is less than RNDM.
5. Minimum: For 4 of 5 cases, minimum for CONEXP is less than RNDM.
6. Student t-test result indicates that for 4 of 5 cases, performance of CONEXP is better that RNDM and for remaining 1 case, the performance of CONEXP is similar to RNDM. Also, it indicates that for none of the cases, performance of RNDM is better than CONEXP.
7. It is observed from Figs. 2, 3, 4, 5 and 6 that the plot of MSE for CONEXP for 30 networks is below RNDM for majority of cases.

It can therefore be concluded from the results for all statistics (mean, median, standard deviation, maximum and minimum) and Figs. 2, 3, 4, 5 and 6 that performance of CONEXP is better than RNDM. The results for Student t-test confirms the results that performance of CONEXP is better than RNDM.

6   Conclusion

A new weight initialization technique CONEXP for hidden to output layer weights is proposed in this work. The weights are initialized in the useful range in threshold function. Also, weights to hidden node are initialized in a region which alternately contracts and expands alternately statistically. The proposed technique is compared to the conventional random weight initialization technique. The proposed weight initialization technique performs better than conventional random weight initialization routine. To establish results student t-test is conducted to test the significance of results. The results indicate that proposed technique is better than random weight initialization technique.

References

1. Bhatia, M., Veenu, Chandra, P.: A new weight initialization method for sigmoidal FFANN. J. Intell. Fuzzy Syst. **35**, 1–9 (2018)
2. Bottou, L.: Reconnaissance de la parole par reseaux multi-couches. In: Proceedings of the International Workshop Neural Networks Application, Neuro-Nimes, vol. 88, pp. 197–217 (1988)
3. Breiman, L.: The II method for estimating multivariate functions from noisy data. Technometrics **33**(2), 125–143 (1991)
4. Cherkassky, V., Gehring, D., Mulier, F.: Comparison of adaptive methods for function estimation from samples. IEEE Trans. Neural Netw. **7**(4), 969–984 (1996)
5. Drago, G.P., Ridella, S.: Statistically controlled activation weight initialization (SCAWI). IEEE Trans. Neural Netw. **3**(4), 627–631 (1992)
6. Haykin, S., Network, N.: A comprehensive foundation. Neural Netw. **2**(2004) (2004)
7. Hornik, K., Stinchcombe, M., White, H.: Universal approximation of an unknown mapping and its derivatives using multilayer feedforward networks. Neural Netw. **3**(5), 551–560 (1990)
8. Kim, Y., Ra, J.: Weight value initialization for improving training speed in the backpropagation network. In: 1991 IEEE International Joint Conference on Neural Networks, pp. 2396–2401. IEEE (1991)
9. Masters, T.: Practical Neural Network Recipes in C++. Morgan Kaufmann, Burlington (1993)
10. Mittal, A., Chandra, P., Singh, A.P.: A statistically resilient method of weight initialization for SFANN. In: 2015 International Conference on Advances in Computing, Communications and Informatics (ICACCI), pp. 1371–1376. IEEE (2015)
11. Mittal, A., Singh, A.P., Chandra, P.: A new weight initialization using statistically resilient method and moore-penrose inverse method for SFANN. Int. J. Recent Res. Aspects **4**, 98–105 (2017)
12. Mittal, A., Singh, A.P., Chandra, P.: A modification to the Nguyen–Widrow weight initialization method. In: Thampi, S.M., et al. (eds.) Intelligent Systems, Technologies and Applications. AISC, vol. 910, pp. 141–153. Springer, Singapore (2020). https://doi.org/10.1007/978-981-13-6095-4_11
13. Nguyen, D., Widrow, B.: Improving the learning speed of 2-layer neural networks by choosing initial values of the adaptive weights. In: 1990 IJCNN International Joint Conference on Neural Networks, pp. 21–26. IEEE (1990)
14. Qiao, J., Li, S., Li, W.: Mutual information based weight initialization method for sigmoidal feedforward neural networks. Neurocomputing **207**, 676–683 (2016)
15. Rumelhart, D.E., Hinton, G.E., Williams, R.J.: Learning internal representations by error propagation. Technical report, DTIC Document (1985)

16. Scarselli, F., Tsoi, A.C.: Universal approximation using feedforward neural networks: a survey of some existing methods, and some new results. Neural Netw. **11**(1), 15–37 (1998)
17. Sodhi, S.S., Chandra, P.: A partially deterministic weight initialization method for SFFANNs. In: 2014 IEEE International Advance Computing Conference (IACC), pp. 1275–1280. IEEE (2014)
18. Yam, J.Y., Chow, T.W.: A weight initialization method for improving training speed in feedforward neural network. Neurocomputing **30**(1), 219–232 (2000)

Exploiting the Most Similar Cases Using Decision Tree to Render Recommendation

Piyush Kolankar[(⊠)], Ranjeet Patel[(⊠)], Nitesh Dangi[(⊠)],
Sumit Sharma[(⊠)], and Sarika Jain[(⊠)]

National Institute of Technology, Kurukshetra, Haryana, India
{Piyush_51710064, sumit_6180087, jasarika}@nitkkr.ac.in,
{Ranjeetjma2017, niteshdangi80}@gmail.com

Abstract. The Internet connects globally available large information with growing numbers of users around the world. This information is increasing at a fast pace which leads to the difficulty in finding the right user, i.e. it becomes difficult to find what exactly the user wants. To meet the user requirements, the best option is a recommendation based on the user's need. This paper provides a solution to the filtration of millions of cases stored in a prehistoric database, to generate the recommendation system for an earthquake. The algorithm presented in this paper worked on mechanism for matching similarity of input cases with stored cases. It generates a recommendation based on the similarity between the input case and the stored cases. This paper filters the cases of earthquake disaster domain to create a decision tree using the ID3 algorithm which in turn reduces the computation to match similar cases.

Keywords: Case based reasoning · Decision tree · ID3 algorithm · Recommendation

1 Introduction

Today's world is focusing on high-tech innovations and research work which helps to reduce the impact of natural disasters. We are considering earthquakes to analyze the efficiency of a recommendation system. Earthquake creates huge damage to the property and lives. Many institutes and organizations have developed systems, for the prevention of damage and causalities caused by natural disasters, which processes data of disaster and estimates its impact on the environment and human lives. The current existing system generates recommendations using the CBR approach [5]. CBR is a case-based reasoning which uses prehistoric cases stored in a database. It finds the most similar case to the input case of a post-disaster earthquake. But a recommendation generating system is considered to be optimal if it reduces the loss of causalities and helps in controlling the situation faster [11]. Humans solve problems using reasoning which is limited to the capacity of a person to remind the related things at the proper time. So an automated recommendation system is preferred over manual system. An automated recommendation system requires an artificial intelligence (AI) or expert system to deal with a real-time situation [13]. The performance of the system generally depends on the capacity of remembering similar cases encountered in the past. The

U. Batra et al. (Eds.): REDSET 2019, CCIS 1230, pp. 290–304, 2020.
https://doi.org/10.1007/978-981-15-5830-6_25

analysis of CBR illustrates that the structure of conventional CBR is very rigid as compared to the problem-solving which has the flexibility of reusing pre-historic cases [10]. CBR filters every case as tasks and matches every task with stored cases and evaluates similarity. Based on the maximum similarity, the result is a recommendation according to the query. The input information and stored cases [9] evaluated by matching the factor and similarity of each field. After making a successful evaluation of the similarity percentage, the input case similarity and the similarity of the data set are matched and a most likely equal case is the result of a CBR approach [5]. This is one of the most popular approaches for recommendation engines based on previous cases. But In this approach, matching the task and finding similarity is an expensive procedure and the current system does not fulfill the requirement of the recommendation system. The time complexity of any system plays a vital role in generation of recommendation [12]. The current mechanism of CBR is useful for a low volume of dataset, but when the system worked with large volume of datasets then system automatically slows down the system and system becomes less efficient. We proposed a recommendation system I-CBR for the earthquake which reduces existing system flaws. We have evaluated both CBR and I-CBR approaches. First, we take CBR then I-CBR with few data sets of post-earthquakes and found a major difference in their performance. I-CBR generates recommendations in optimal time.

2 Reasoning with the Case Base

Case Base Reasoning (CBR) is automated reasoning and decision-making process which solves the new problem using experience accumulated in solving problems in the past [7]. A set of rules is created by storing the conditions of problems and actions taken while solving these. The rules help in a situation when there are one or more actions to resolve it.

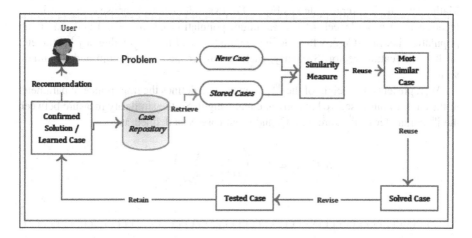

Fig. 1. Architecture of Case Base Reasoning (CBR).

The system focused on recognizing the similarity of the new problems to the existing ones and how to manage the collection of accumulated data. The architecture of CBR is shown in Fig. 1. Case base reasoning is structured as a four-step process, sometime referred to as the 4R's: retrieval, reuse, revision, and retention.

- **Retrieval:** retrieval is the process of finding a case that is similar to our current situation or state.
- **Reuse:** reuse is when we retrieve a case and propose it as a valid action to apply in our current state.
- **Revision:** revision is when we evaluate through a series of metrics or simulation how well the proposed action will perform and whether it is practical to apply it in the particular case were in.
- **Retention:** retention is applied after a successful execution by storing the result of experience this is useful when you have revised the proposed solution.

Each phase is interacting with the collection of cases, either editing this collection or retrieving action from it to make. This means the collection is constantly being edited as the system is being searched for appropriate actions based on the current situation.

In our study, we are using the earthquake information stored as a case [9]. The structure of cases and action format will be discussed later in the section. In an earthquake situation, our ultimate goal is to automate the process of estimating relief mission, to save the life and property as much as possible, which would have been done manually [4]. One optimal solution is to search for similar cases that happened in the past. Most of the time consumed in estimating the relief is finding similar cases from the past, based on the current earthquake information and stored cases [9]. The current earthquake called as a new case X, matched with all the stored cases C_i and calculate the similarity measure S_i for each case C_i. Similarity measure often acts like heuristics in classic AI search. Expert knowledge is applied to find similarity in a given problem. The similarity measure between two cases determines, how likely two cases are. Mathematically it is represented as Eq. 2. For example, lets us suppose every particular location have a bottleneck of the minimum population i.e. $\min(C_{loc})$ and maximum population i.e. $\max(C_{loc})$, which define the $\min(C_j)$ and $\max(C_j)$ value at j^{th} parameter in the case feature vector. Similarly, each parameter has its minimum and maximum value.

W_j represents the weight of the jth parameter and defines the importance of parameter in the case. In our case, we have given equal weight. So the similarity measure between the jth parameter of ith store case C_i and input case X is defined as:

$$S(C_i, X) = 1 - \left(\frac{C_{ij} - X_j}{(C_j) - (C_j)} \right) * Wj \tag{1}$$

Also, a similarity measure between the ith store case C_i and input case X is defined as a sum of all the parameter similarity of the feature vector of case C_i, mathematically represented as

$$Sim(C_i, X) = \frac{\sum_{j=1}^{N}\left(1 - \left(\frac{C_{ij}-X_j}{(C_j)-(C_j)}\right) * Wj\right)}{N} \qquad (2)$$

Where:

Sim (C_i, X) is the similarity parameter of retrieve i^{th} case, and input vector case.
N is the number of parameters in a case,
m is the total number of cases.
C_{ij} is the value of the jth parameter value of the ith case of m.
X is the input value of the parameter i.

2.1 Pseudo Code of CBR

In CBR, every case stored in the database has two vectors: feature vector and resource vector [5]. Here we are using the feature vector to compute the similarity. Algorithm of CBR has given below:

Input: In our case take the input as in the form of f_{in} = < **Location, Magnitude, injured, Date** > where the Earthquake occurred.
Output: Formulate recommendation of a most similar case.
Algorithm of CBR is as follows.
    Algorithm: CBR ()
    Step 1. Initialize maximum similarity S_{max}= 0; f_{out}= {}
    Step 2. for each case f_i to m from database
    Step 3. S_i = **Sim (f_{in} , f_i)**
    Step 4.   Check if S_{max}< S_i Then,
    Step 5. S_{max} = S_i ; Retrieve Case f_{out}= Current case f_i
    Step 6. End for
    Step 7. Check If S_{max}> 70 % then do
    Step 8.   Return the R_{case}
Algorithm for calculate similarity is given as.
    Sim(f_1, f_2)
    1. Initialized S = 0
    2. Check if location f_1 == f_2 , then
    3. S += 1.0
    4. Repeat for (j = 1 to Length (f_2) -1)
    5. S + = (|1 – [(C1j-X2j) / {Maximum_Sim (C_i) - Minimum_Sim (C_i)}] |)* W_{weight}
    6. End for
    7. Calculate average S = S/Length (f2)
    8. Return S

Note: - To analyze approaches of CBR and I-CBR we have taken data set [9].

After making a successful evaluation of the similarity percentage of each dataset by the similarity calculating formula [2] most likely equal matched case will be our result of the CBR approach.

2.2   Sample Case Analysis of CBR

The approach is focused on automated decision-making and recommendation generation in an earthquake disaster situation. Earthquake disaster case is represented as a set of pairs of the given situation called a feature vector and action called a decision [15].

For example:

Case: [feature vector | Action]
Case 1: [f_1 | Action A]
Case 2: [f2 | Action B]
Case 3: [f3 | Action C]
Case 4: [f4 | Action D]
:

Case m: [f_m | Action X]

Where f_m represents the feature vector for m^{th} case, which contains a collection of features. In our case, we are using the feature vector f_{in} that contains the feature as f_{in} = <Location, Magnitude, injured, Date> as input and generate some action as f_{out} as the outcome of CBR.

When we apply CBR on the input feature vector fin, then it will start mapping with each case stored and calculate the similarity measure with every case. The action corresponding to the case which has maximum similarity will be recommended for the new case. If the similarity measure is less than 70% then this is the new exercise and needs to be updated in the experience database with the actions taken and conditions of the case. For example, in our case, every feature vector has some minimum and maximum value, let us assume that we have

For Magnitude feature:
$\text{Max}(C_{magnitude}) = 10$; $\text{Min}(C_{magnitude}) = 0$;
For Injured People feature:
$\text{Max}(C_{injured}) = 100000$; $\text{Min}(C_{injured}) = 0$;
For Date Feature:
$\text{Max}(C_{date}) = 1000$; $\text{Min}(C_{date}) = 0$;

$N = $ Number of the parameter in the feature vector.

Also, the expert system typically has a domain model where some high-level language used to express data terminology in a set theory language. CBR does not require data to be modeled in this way and can be far more data-driven, ultimately reduces to a bunch of numbers. For the real data, calculate the similarity measure for each feature of a feature vector based on Eq. 1. If a feature in the feature vector is non-real number then follow the following procedure to calculate the similarity between y feature of ith case and feature of new case x.

$$Sim(x, y_i) = \begin{cases} Sim + 1, & if\ x = y_i \\ Sim + 0, & otherwise \end{cases} \tag{3}$$

A final similarity between the stored case and input case can be calculated by Eq. 2.

2.3 Cost Analysis of CBR

Over time collection of cases grows in size. This collection of cases allows us to build up more options for strong decision making in a given situation. In CBR, case retrieval [2] is dynamic in nature. It's the most important mechanism. To extract the most similar cases from pre-historical cases, similarity measurement computation cost is very high. For example, we are computing the similarity between the feature vector of new case fin and every case retrieve from storage. So the total computation cost to calculate the similarity is:

$$cost(Similarity\ Measure) = O(m * N) \tag{4}$$

Where,

m = Number of cases
N = Number of a parameter in the feature vector

3 The Proposed Approach for Reducing Search Space

Case-based reasoning is a high-level representation of knowledge. Dealing with millions of cases is a very difficult task. The proposed work provides a solution for filtering millions of cases stored in a prehistoric database to generate the recommendation in an earthquake situation [14]. The architecture of the proposed approach is shown in Fig. 2.

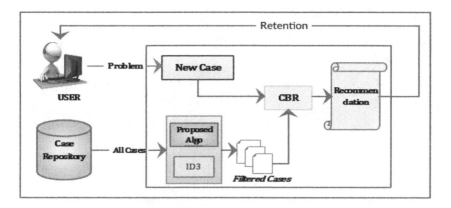

Fig. 2. Case-based reasoning using Decision Tree.

This approach is going to apply when we have a large number of cases [3]. In this process, we have filtered the cases based on the major attribute of input cases. Those cases, which are not relative to the major attributes of input case, are discarded from the process of CBR. Other cases are forwarded for the best match of input case. Following is the pseudo-code for our approach. Based on the expensive feature a decision tree is created using ID3 [6] and then selection of case has been done based on the proposed approach. The filtered cases are then passed to the CBR to find a similar case with a new problem and the corresponding solution.

3.1 Pseudo Code for the Proposed Algorithm

In the study to develop the algorithm, we used the data of an earthquake in India [9]. The system automates the recommendation process to save human life using the previous experience. The proposed algorithm is given below.

Input: Input the feature vector as our case fin = <Location, Magnitude, injured, Date> where the Earthquake occurred.

Output: Formulate recommendation of a most similar case with minimum search time.

Proposed Algorithm:

Step 1. Initialize the variable maximum similarity Smax=0; Retrieval case Cout = {}
Step 2. For each case fi from database and input fin
Step 3. Assigne_Class_Label (fi, fin)
Step 4. End For
Step 5. Construct a decision tree using the ID3 algorithm
Step 6. Filter out the case from the decision tree, which has the YES label node.
Step 7. Apply the CBR on the filtered cases.

To apply the Induction of Decision Trees (ID3) algorithm [8], assign the class label to the dataset as follow.

Assigne_Class_Label (fi, fin)
Step 1. For each feature in fi and fin
Step 2.   If the feature is non-real value
Step 3.   If fi<feature> and fin<feature> value match then
Step 4.Assign_label YES, Return
Step 5.   If the feature is a real number then
Step 6.   Assign the range of fi and fin given in the table 2
Step 7.   If both feature fi and fin belong to same range then
Step 8.Assign_label YES
Step 9.   Otherwise Assign_label NO
Step 10. End For
Step 11. If Average (Yes_Count) ≥ 50% then
Step 12.   Return Class Label YES
Step 13. Else
Step 14.   Return Class Label NO

Please note that the first paragraph of a section or subsection is not indented. The first paragraphs that follows a table, figure, equation etc. does not have an indent, either.

Subsequent paragraphs, however, are indented.

3.2   Data Generation and Pre-processing

Data have collected from Wikipedia source List of earthquakes in India the web URL is https://en.wikipedia.org/wiki/List_of_earthquakes_in_India. To apply the procedure, first of all, data will be pre-processed. Pre-processing is completed in two steps. The first step is feature selection, this is the most important to filter out the features based on the statistical measures [1]. A rank score of each feature is calculated, according to that, they are provided position in the table below. Threshold features are filtered out from the data. In our dataset after the feature selection, the remaining dataset is as shown in Table 1.

Table 1. Sample dataset after feature selection

Case no.	Location	Magnitude	Injuries
C1	Maharashtra	4.3	0
C2	Bangladesh	5.7	8
C3	Myanmar	6.7	200
C4	Nepal	7.3	3500
C5	Nepal	7.8	21952
C6	Kashmir	5.7	90
C7	Bangladesh	4.3	50
C8	Gujarat	5.1	5
C9	Kashmir	7.6	72332
C10	Maharashtra	6.6	2272

In the second step, some actions are assigned to the corresponding features and each case, like training data [2]. For example: assign an action to every case as

Case Ci: <Feature | Action>

Ci: <Location, Magnitude, Injuries, Date | humanitarian assistance, Rescue teams, Food & rations>

This is simple like rule base reasoning {if <Condition> then <Action>}. Comprehensive rule base action employed to build a powerful system that suits all the need for disaster situations. Assign action to the training dataset according to expert experience so that the recommendation generated for the new case is as per the rule.

3.3   Class Label Assignment and Create a Decision Tree

For every feature of the feature vector, appropriate class labels have assigned [6, 8]. The suitable class label will be assigned to the feature vector, f_i<Location, Magnitude, Injured, Date> of each case, when it's passed to the proposed algorithm. Class label YES or NO is assigned when the algorithm runs through step 2 to step 4. The basic range of the feature is shown in Table 2. For the date range, we consider the year when it happened. For magnitude, we take the round figure for real value.

Table 2. Range for injured people

No.	Range of injured
1	0–200
2	200–4000
3	4000–10000
4	10000–20000
5	20000–40000
6	40000–60000
7	60000–80000

The outcome of the class label assignment for the sample dataset is shown in Table 3.

Table 3. Sample dataset with the assigned class label

Case no.	Location	Magnitude	Injuries	Date	Class label
C1	Maharashtra	4.3	0	2019-03-01	N
C2	Bangladesh	5.7	8	2017-01-03	N
C3	Myanmar	6.7	200	2016-01-04	N
C4	Nepal	7.3	3500	2015-05-12	Y
C5	Nepal	7.8	21952	2015-04-25	Y
C6	Kashmir	5.7	90	2013-05-01	N
C7	Bangladesh	4.3	50	2008-02-06	N
C8	Gujarat	5.1	5	2007-11-06	N
C9	Kashmir	7.6	72332	2005-10-08	Y
C10	Maharashtra	6.6	2272	1967-12-11	Y

3.4   Calculate the Class Entropy

After class labeling, the next stage is to create a decision tree using the Induction of Decision Trees (ID3) algorithm. We are also providing a summary of the ID3 algorithm to create a decision tree that will help to recognize our work. To create a decision tree we assume class labels as the class attribute. Process of calculating entropy class and entropy for each attribute to make decision tree use the formula given in Eq. 5.

$$Entropy(Class) = -\frac{P}{P+N} log\left(\frac{P}{P+N}\right) - \frac{N}{P+N} log\left(\frac{N}{P+N}\right) \quad (5)$$

Where,

P = 4 (Number of positive response (YES) in Table 3).

N = 6 (Number of a negative response (NO) in Table 3).

Evaluate the class entropy for the sample dataset = -4/10($[log]\_2$(4/10) - 6/10($[log]\_2$(6/10) which is equal to 0.966.

Now calculate the information gain I(Pi, Ni) for each attribute of feature vector using the given formula in Eq. 6. Result shown in Table 4, 5, 6 and 7.

$$I(P_i, N_i) = -\frac{p}{P+N} log\left(\frac{P}{P+N}\right) - \frac{N}{P+N} log\left(\frac{N}{P+N}\right) \quad (6)$$

Then calculate the Entropy of each feature using the formula given in Eq. 7.

$$Entropy(Feature) = \sum_{i=1}^{N} \frac{(P_i, N_i) * I(P_i, N_i)}{P+N} \quad (7)$$

Table 4. Information gain of the location feature

No.	Location	Pi	Ni	I(Pi, Ni)
1	Maharashtra	1	1	0.966
2	Bangladesh	0	2	0
3	Myanmar	0	1	0
4	Nepal	2	0	0
5	Kashmir	1	1	0.966
6	Gujarat	0	1	0

Calculate Entropy of location feature using Eq. 7.

$$= 1 + 1/10 * (0.966) + 0 + 2/10 * (0) + 0 + 1/10 * (0) + 2 + 0/10 * (0) + 1$$
$$+ 1/10 * (0.966) + 0 + 1/10 * (0) = 0.3864$$

Similarly evaluate the information gain and the entropy of another feature i.e. magnitude feature. Result is show in the Table 5.

Table 5. Information gain for magnitude feature

No.	Magnitude	Pi	Ni	I(Pi, Ni)
1	4	0	2	0
2	5	0	3	0
3	6	1	1	0.966
4	7	3	0	0

Calculate the Entropy of magnitude feature using Eq. 7.

$$= 0 + 2/10 * (0) + 0 + 3/10 * (0) + 1 + 1/10 * (0.966) + 3 + 0/10 * (0)$$
$$= 0.1932$$

Table 6. Information gain of injured feature.

No.	Injured	Pi	Ni	I(Pi, Ni)
1	0–200	0	6	0
2	200–4000	2	0	0
3	20000–40000	1	0	0
4	60000–80000	1	0	0

Calculate Entropy for the injured feature using Eq. 7

$$= 0 + 6/10 * (0) + 2 + 0/10 * (0) + 1 + 0/10 * (0) + 1 + 0/10 * (0)$$
$$= 0.0$$

Table 7. Information gain of date feature.

No.	Date	Pi	Ni	I(Pi, Ni)
1	2019	0	1	0
2	2017	0	1	0
3	2016	0	1	0
4	2015	2	0	0
5	2013	0	1	0
6	2008	0	1	0
7	2007	0	1	0
8	2005	1	0	0
9	1967	1	0	0

Calculate the entropy of date feature using Eq. 7.

$$= 0 + 1/10 * (0) + 0 + 1/10 * (0) + 0 + 1/10 * (0) + 2 + 0/10 * (0) + 0$$
$$+ 1/10 * (0) + 0 + 1/10 * (0) + 0 + 1/10 * (0) + 1 + 0/10 * (0) + 1 + 0/10 * (0)$$

Entropy Attribute $= 0.0$

Now finally calculate the gain of each feature to decide which feature is the root node of our decision tree. An attribute with better gain value than others should be considered as root and a branch Y or N as a leaf node. A branch having different Y and N values needs further splitting.

Gain = Entropy class − Entropy attribute

The evaluated gain of each feature in a feature vector is shown in the Table 8. Select the feature with maximum gain, and tag it as the root of the decision tree [6]. The branch of the tree is the distinct value of that feature. Now find the class label of each branch if the branch of the root is labeled with a single value then nothing to do, otherwise repeat the above process for the evaluate next branch of that feature with distinct value.

Table 8. Gain of each feature

No.	Name of feature	The gain of feature attribute
1	Location	0.5796
2	Magnitude	0.7728
3	Injured	0.9660
4	Date	0.9660

4   Result Evaluation

In this section, we will show the result of our proposed algorithm and built the decision tree to reduce the cases which are unnecessary and forwarded the most appropriate cases for further CBR process.

4.1   Decision Tree

As it's clear from Table 8, "injured" and "date" are the features with maximum gain. Therefore, we have to make both as the root node and make two different decision trees, shown in Fig. 3. Both gave us the same result of filtered cases. Decision tree generated dynamically depends on stored cases and input case but the process remains the same whatever gain evaluated we just need to assign root node of maximum gain.

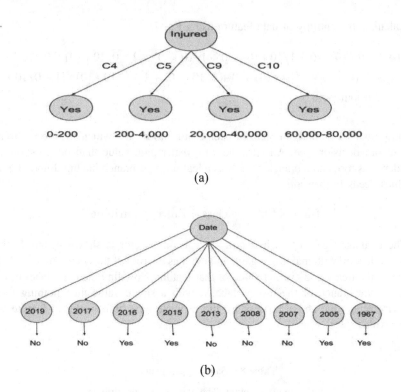

Fig. 3. Decision tree based on the gain

Once the decision tree is created, the root node is assigned. After that, we need to check the leaf node of the root node with the same data if the same data value does not have Y/N. e.g. In fig. b if year feature case in 2015 will have different Y/N then we further calculate the gain of each attribute except date feature and again assign child node to our decision tree. The whole process continues until the same case feature has a unique value of Y and N. The final decision is done to go through either Y or N.

4.2   Case Filtration Using the Decision Tree

After the creation of the decision tree, it is time to decide which case is more useful and efficient to use. Case filtration is based on the Y labeled branch of the decision tree. Select only those cases which have Y branch and no branch case have discarded, when we apply it on our sample dataset, the algorithm outputs four cases out of ten cases from sample dataset.

4.3   Case Similarity Measure of Filtered Cases

Now calculate the similarity measure of filtered cases using CBR concerning input case, which is defined in the Table 9.

Table 9. Similarity measure of filtered cases using CBR

No.	Location	Magnitude	Injured	Date	Similarity
1	Nepal	7.3	3500	2015-05-01	99%
2	Nepal	7.8	21932	1995-05-22	94%
3	Kashmir	7.6	12333	2005-12-06	56%
4	Maharashtra	6.6	2272	1967-01-02	71%

5 Comparitive Analysis of CBR and I-CBR

After analyzing both CBR and I-CBR approaches on sample data set the efficiency and reliability of a new system over the existing system provide us great results. In the CBR feature vector of each case of an earthquake estimated for every stored case. But in I-CBR most of the unnecessary cases filtered out and remaining cases proceed for further process. The existing approach works on past-historic cases and has no use of the system's evaluated results in the future. Whereas in I-CBR cases are reduced and appropriate cases estimated. Also, these results stored in the current system which enhances the system's work of efficiency and reduces the workload of the system [16]. More fast and accurate we get recommendations more likely we can make a big difference in statistics of death and live.

6 Conclusion

The requirement of a recommendation system is necessary to expedite the relief process in an earthquake disaster situation to minimize the number of injured persons, and life loss. The study of the I-CBR approach leads to the following conclusions that the I-CBR approach gives a better outcome than the standard CBR approach, which also reduces millions of cases into reduced cases. The reduce cases increase the efficiency of the recommendation system. This approach works well for the post-disaster situation based on user input features location, magnitude, injured and date in that area. In further work, we will expand the decision tree with a more efficient algorithm and add more feature to improve more efficiency and accuracy of the system. This effectively deflates the action time and saves many lives.

References

1. Jadhav, S.D., Channe, H.P.: Efficient recommendation system using decision tree classifier and collaborative filtering. Int. Res. J. Eng. Technol. **3**, 2113–2118 (2016)
2. Jain, S., Mehla, S., Agarwal, A.G.: An ontology based earthquake recommendation system. In: Luhach, A.K., Singh, D., Hsiung, P.-A., Hawari, K.B.G., Lingras, P., Singh, P.K. (eds.) ICAICR 2018. CCIS, vol. 955, pp. 331–340. Springer, Singapore (2019). https://doi.org/10.1007/978-981-13-3140-4_30
3. Cunningham, P., Smyth, B., Bonzano, A.: An incremental retrieval mechanism for case-based electronic fault diagnosis. Knowl.-Based Syst. **11**(3-4), 239–248 (1998)

4. Hamada, M.: Asian Disaster Reduction Center 2016 Annual Report. Asian Disaster ReductionCenter (2016). http://www.adrc.asia/publications/annual/16/2016_ADRC_Annual_Report.pdf. (abbrev. US State or Country if the City is not 'well known'). Accessed 17 July 2018

5. Jain, S.: Intelligent decision support for unconventional emergencies. In: Valencia-García, R., Paredes-Valverde, M.A., Salas-Zárate, M., Alor-Hernández, G. (eds.) Exploring Intelligent Decision Support Systems. SCI, vol. 764, pp. 199–219. Springer, Cham (2018). https://doi.org/10.1007/978-3-319-74002-7_10

6. Jin, C., De-Lin, L., Fen-Xiang, M.: An improved ID3 decision tree algorithm. In: 2009 4th International Conference on Computer Science & Education. IEEE (2009)

7. El-Sappagh, S.H., Elmogy, M.: Case-based reasoning: case representation methodologies. Int. J. Adv. Comput. Sci. Appl. 6(11), 192–208 (2015)

8. Ross, Quinlan, decision tree learning, ID3 (Iterative Dichotomiser 3), Wikipedia, the free encyclopedia. https://en.wikipedia.org/wiki/ID3_algorithm. Accessed 17 June 2018

9. USGS: List of the earthquake in India in the context of getting data on the web: List of the earthquake in India. https://en.wikipedia.org/wiki/List_of_earthquakes_in_India. Accessed 2 June 2018

10. Aarnio, P., Seilonen, I., Friman, M.: Semantic repository for case-based reasoning in CBM services. In: Proceedings of the 2014 IEEE Emerging Technology and Factory Automation (ETFA). IEEE (2014)

11. Adla, A., Bella, A.B.: Intelligent semantic case based reasoning system for fault diagnosis. J. Digit. Inf. Manag. 16, 1 (2018)

12. Smyth, B., Cunningham, P.: A comparison of incremental case-based reasoning and inductive learning. In: Haton, J.-P., Keane, M., Manago, M. (eds.) EWCBR 1994. LNCS, vol. 984, pp. 151–164. Springer, Heidelberg (1995). https://doi.org/10.1007/3-540-60364-6_34

13. Raj, S.D.: Automated service recommendation with preference awareness: an application of collaborative filtering approach in big data analytics. In: 2017 2nd International Conference on Communication and Electronics Systems (ICCES). IEEE (2017)

14. Thiengburanathum, P., Cang, S., Yu, H.: A decision tree based recommendation system for tourists. In: 2015 21st International Conference on Automation and Computing (ICAC). IEEE (2015)

15. Aydin, C., Tecim, V.: Description logic based earthquake damage estimation for disaster management. Anadolu Univ. Sci. Technol. Appl. Sci. Eng. 15, 93–103 (2014)

16. Jao, C. (ed.): Efficient Decision Support Systems: Practice and Challenges from Current to Future. BoD–Books on Demand (2011)

Segmentation of Breast Density Using K-Means Clustering Algorithm

Jyoti Dabass[1(✉)], Madasu Hanmandlu[2], and Rekha Vig[1]

[1] EECE Department, The Northcap University, Gurugram, India
jyotidabas91@gmail.com, rekha_vig@yahoo.co.in
[2] CSE Department, MVSR Engineering College, Hyderabad, India
mhmandlu@gmail.com

Abstract. In the contemporary world, breast tumor is the most consistently spotted neoplasm among women, that is, instigating women's transience at a higher rate. Radiologists prefer computer-aided mammography in order to detect breast cancer. Mammograms consist of many artifacts like labels, pectoral muscles whose removal is a daunting task. The presence of glandular tissues in digital mammograms plays a pivotal role in the early finding of breast cancer. This is necessary to find the radiation risk linked with screening and also to find the irregularity between right and left breasts. The proposed method focuses on pre-processing and breast density segmentation. In this method, both binarization and the modified region growing method are applied for removing the labels, background and pectoral muscles. For improving the contrast of the images bereft of the pectoral muscles, it uses the contrast limited adaptive histogram equalization with Rayleigh distribution. Next use is made of K-means clustering to segment the digital mammograms into different density regions. The proposed method is applied on a publicly accessible mini-MIAS database. Its results are validated by the expert radiologists and these compete with those of the state of the art methods.

Keywords: Breast cancer · Mammograms · Pectoral muscles · Image segmentation · Binarization · Region growing · mini-MIAS database · K-means clustering · Contrast limited adaptive histogram equalization

1 Introduction

Breast cancer is one of the most frequently scrutinized cancers in the world and accounts for 15% of cancer deaths in over 100 countries as per the reports of GLO-BOCON2018. There are approximately 2.1 million breast cancer cases detected in 2018 which amount to one among four cancer cases in women. Breast cancer has shown less in consistency in terms of the number of deaths with the highest mortality projected in Melanesia, where Fiji has the top most death rates the world over [1]. Also, 19.3 million new cancer cases are expected to be added by 2025 [2, 28]. Regarding India, the death rate is high because of patients' ignorance of the manifestation of disease, unavailability of therapeutic guidance at very perilous phases of breast cancer

© Springer Nature Singapore Pte Ltd. 2020
U. Batra et al. (Eds.): REDSET 2019, CCIS 1230, pp. 305–315, 2020.
https://doi.org/10.1007/978-981-15-5830-6_26

and inaccessibility of Medicare for large populations. In rural areas, the mortality rate is high due to scant availability of medical experts and the late discovery of breast cancer.

Medical data and biomedical engineering can help in the early detection of breast cancer. For increasing the detection accuracy it is imperative to locate the correct region of interest. This process is quite complicated due to the existence of pectoral muscles that hamper the detection.

Detection of breast cancer also gets affected due to breast tissue density which is the number of fibrous and glandular tissues. Sometimes calcifications reflecting the cancer and cancerous lump appear white in mammograms. It becomes difficult to detect cancer in case the patient's breast tissue is also dense. High tissue density affects the identification of cancerous symptoms.

The BIRAD system which is mostly used for breast density classification provides four-category classifications. The first two classes of BIRAD denote the commencement of benign stages called breast lipomas and breast cysts. BIRAD III signals the likely benign stage while BIRAD IV, the malignant phase. The BIRAD classification is applied on a mini-MIAS database which has three classes: fatty glandular, fatty and dense glandular [10].

For helping the radiologists in premature and precise detection of breast cancer, the proposed method deals with breast part removal, muscle part elimination, mammogram enhancement and its segmentation into different densities.

The proposed method is concerned with the future scope of [18] which uses morphological watershed segmentation for improving the accuracy of classification but could not provide a sub-classification into fatty and dense regions on the basis of BIRAD classification rules. Also, in [23] pectoral muscles were segmented using active contour and Hough transform and expected to work on breast density quantification after removing the pectoral muscles. This chapter tries fill up these research gaps and aims at better classification accuracy.

The chapter is organized as follows. Section 1 presents the theme of breast cancer and Sect. 2 briefs the propositioned technique. Sections 3 and 4 discuss the methods used and results obtained respectively. Section 5 gives the conclusions.

2   Related Work

This section reviews the methods in the literature utilized for removing the pectoral muscles and thus segmenting the breast into regions of different densities.

2.1   Image Segmentation

Image segmentation could be manual, semi automatic or automatic identification of the region of interest [5, 7, 8]. Automatic segmentation is prone to error in the presence of noise while manual segmentation is tedious but accurate [21]. Examples of automatic segmentation methods consist of region and graph-based methods [24, 35, 38], level set-based [37] and active contour-based [16]. No standard segmentation method exists in the literature to our knowledge. Currently, the region based convolutional neural networks (RCNNs) are suitable for segmenting the mammograms [14, 25].

2.2 Pectoral Muscle Segment

High density tissue characterized by fibro-glandular tissue type arrangement is called Pectoral muscle (PM) [23]. For an accurate early revealing of breast cancer, it is important to fragment the pectoral muscles. A survey of techniques used for segmenting the pectoral muscles is provided in Table 1.

Table 1. Methods used to remove the pectoral muscles

S. no.	Author and year	Methods involved
1.	Mustra, M. and Grgic, M., 2013 [34]	Breast skin line estimation, polynomial curvature estimation, adaptive histogram equalization
2.	Sreedevi, S. and Sherly, E., 2015 [11]	Global thresholding, grey-level thresholding, 8 connected labeling, canny edge detection
3.	Hazarika, M. and Mahanta, L.B., 2018 [29]	Seeded region growing method for removing pectoral muscles
4.	Gardezi et al. 2018 [29]	Adaptive gamma correction, binarization
5.	Esener, İ.I., et al. 2018 [9]	Region growing, line fitting, otsu thresholding for background suppression
6.	Rampun, A., et al. 2019 [27]	CNN, Modified Holistically-nested Edge Detection (HED) network
7.	Pavan, A.L., et al. 2018 [23]	Edge detection using Hough transform and pectoral muscle removal using active contour
8.	Shinde, V., & Rao, B.T, 2019 [33]	K-means clustering, thresholding and Region growing
9.	Yin, K., et al. 2019 [39]	Fitting and active contour, Iterative threshold.
10.	Shen, R., et al. 2018 [32]	Polynomial curve fitting, Genetic process and morphological medley algorithm

2.3 Breast Density Segmentation

Breast Cancer usually is observed in the bright looking fibro-glandular portion of breast tissue which appears as bright in mammograms indicating the presence of high breast density. It is an important part of a mammogram having fibrous connective tissue, ducts and lobular elements. While examining mammograms, radiologists look for the portion of fibro-glandular and fatty tissues. Their analyses vary from one radiologist to another [30]. So the fragmentation of the breast into regions of different densities is necessitated. Methods used for fragmenting the breast density are given in Table 2.

Table 2. Methods for breast density segmentation

S. no.	Author and year	Methods used
1.	Nayak, T., et al. 2019 [18]	Watershed technique, top-hat transformation, and morphological opening, the straight-line method
2.	Lee, J. and Nishikawa, R. M., 2018 [15]	Fully convolutional neural network, VGG16
3.	Kallenberg, M., Petersen, K., 2016 [12]	Sparse auto-encoder, multinomial logistic regression, and pretrained and Deep convolutional neural networks
4.	Surajudeen, A. and Zwiggelaar, R., 2017 [36]	Watershed technique and linear iterative clustering, binarization and super-pixel technique
5.	Oliver, A., Lladó, X., 2010 [19]	Principal Component Analysis (PCA), straight-line method, Linear-Discriminant-Analysis (LDA)
6.	Mohamed, A.A., et al. 2018 [17]	Convolutional neural network (CNN)
7.	Salman, N.H., & Ali, S.I. M., 2019 [31]	K- means clustering, median filter and Region growing
8.	Oliver, A., et al. 2015 [20]	Morphological and textural feature extraction, classification using supervised pixel-based
9.	Pavan, A.L et al. 2016 [22]	Fuzzy C-means clustering
10.	Zhou, C., Chan, et al. 2001 [40]	Breast boundary tracking, adaptive dynamic range compression, grey-level thresholding

3   The Proposed Method

This involves four tasks that include background removal, pectoral muscle elimination, enhancement of mammograms and segmentation of mammograms into areas of different densities. The flowchart of the proposed method which is applied on freely accessible mini-MIAS database is shown in Fig. 1. For applying the proposed method, mammogram images from the mini-MIAS database are taken as the input. Firstly the background of the mammogram images involving labels and irrelevant information is eliminated. As pectoral muscles also affect the segmentation so in the second stage these are removed using the improved region growing methods. For improving the visual quality of the mammograms, contrast limited adaptive histogram equalization is utilized with Rayleigh distribution by taking the default values for all the parameters. Finally, pre-processed images are clustered into different breast density regions using K-means clustering algorithm. For comparison, FCM clustering and texture-based techniques are used.

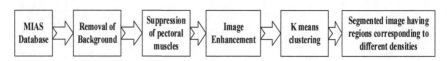

Fig. 1. Flowchart of the proposed method

3.1   Removal of Background

The background is removed in order to extract the breast profile. Threshold value of 0.1 is used to binarize the mammogram image. This approach works well for the threshold values up to 0.7. To extract the largest blobs having pectoral muscles and to extract breast profile, the connected components are arranged in the descending order from the highest to the smallest after binarization.

3.2   Suppression of Pectoral Muscle

After the removal of background, the improved region growing is used to remove the pectoral muscles. Seeded region growing being image segmentation approach is based on the selection of seed point and pixel location. Seed point is selected automatically on the basis of orientation of digital mammograms. The adjacent pixels of the seed point are scrutinized to ascertain whether the next pixel should be merged to the region or not. The procedure is repeated until the area of interest is located.

3.3   Image Enhancement

The quality of the mammogram is improved using contrast limited adaptive histogram equalization technique after removing the pectoral muscles [3, 4, 6]. In this, Rayleigh distribution is considered keeping other parameters as default. After that K-means clustering is used to fragment the breast into areas of dissimilar densities. The clustering is done in a controlled manner. Its results are verified by the expert radiologists.

3.4   K-Means Clustering

This is used to segment the breast into regions of different densities using an iterative modification that requires the input dataset and the number of clusters, K. The dataset comprises a range of structures for the individual data points. The clustering algorithm starts with the initial approximations of K centroids and then it alternates between the following two steps:

- *Data assignment step:* Each cluster will have one cluster center or centroid. In this, a data point is assigned to its adjoining centroid based on the squared Euclidean distance.
- *Centroid update step:* In this stage, each centroid is replaced with the new centroid by finding the average of all the data assigned to the cluster. The algorithm moves between the above two steps until the centroids converge.
- *Choice of K:* It must be made such that the resulting clusters are compact and separation between the cluster centroids must be large.

   K-means clustering is implemented here as it is a simple unsupervised learning that segments the breast into different densities leading to different clusters.

4 Results and Discussions

The proposed method is tested on a publicly available mini-MIAS database comprising 322 mammograms involving categories of images such as dense, glandular and fatty.

To remove the background noise binarization with threshold 0.1 is used and to extract the biggest blob the associated components are sorted out from the highest size to the lowest size. The original image is multiplied with this blob to get the best breast profile. An adaptive region growing method that selects the seed points automatically is applied on the breast profile for eliminating the pectoral muscles. The mini-MIAS database includes the right and the left-oriented images so either the right topmost or the left topmost non-zero pixel is considered as a seed point. For finding the image orientation, the image is divided into two halves and their non-zero pixels are counted. In the case of a right-oriented image, the right part will have more pixels than that of the left part. The objective of the proposed segmentation method is to dissect the mammogram into different densities (glandular, adipose, etc.) using K-means clustering technique which is matched with the ground truth provided by the expert radiologists. As per radiologists' assessment, the segmentation of mammogram results in varied tissue types such as purely dipose tissue, areas with the breast edge, highly dense tissue (homogeneous), adipose tissue with some apparent creations (curvy edifices or components of fibrous tissue), dense tissue with seeming texture structure (not homogeneous) and relatively dense tissue with roughly external conformation that may also hold more diaphanous areas (fibrotic stromal tissue, glandular tissue). For the three-category classification, segmentation accuracy of automatic regions is calculated and compared with that of the texture-based techniques as in Table 3.

There is a strong resemblance between our segmentation results and those provided by the radiologists. It can be inferred from the results that dark color signifies the lower consequent density of the categorized texture. The proposed algorithm is applied on a publicly available mini-MIAS database containing 322 images. An expert radiologist grades the segmentation in four categories: poor, good, satisfactory or very satisfactory towards the qualitative evaluation of segmentation Out of 322 digital mammograms, 4 are rated good, 8 are assessed as satisfactory and the remaining 310 are declared as very satisfactory. For comparison, we have used texture-based techniques [26] and fuzzy C-means clustering techniques (FCM) [13]. As seen from Fig. 2, K-means clustering technique provides better segmentation of breast into different densities while the texture based techniques and FCM are not able to differentiate the densities to that extent.

Table 3. Results (in percentage) showing segmentation accuracies of different regions

S. no.	Techniques	Dense	Fatty	Breast edge
1.	Texture based techniques [26]	96.7	93.8	92.8
2.	Proposed technique	98.75	95.8%	94.8%

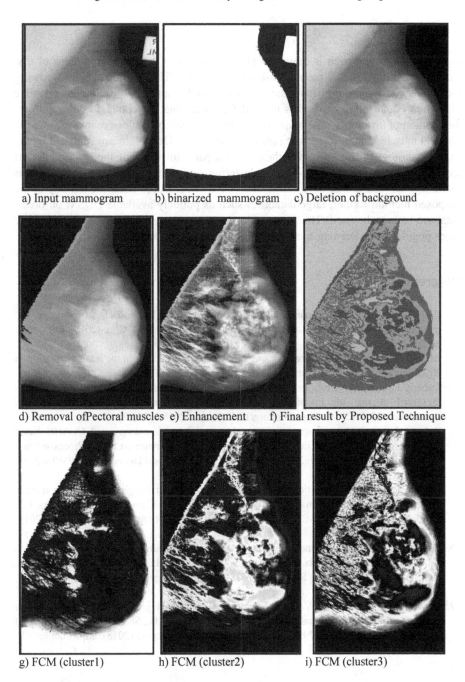

a) Input mammogram   b) binarized mammogram   c) Deletion of background

d) Removal ofPectoral muscles e) Enhancement   f) Final result by Proposed Technique

g) FCM (cluster1)   h) FCM (cluster2)   i) FCM (cluster3)

Fig. 2. Mammogram images obtained after removing the pectoral muscles followed by enhancing contrast and segmenting mammograms into regions of different density a) Input image b) Binarized image having threshold value 0.1 c) After background elimination d) Removal of Pectoral muscles e) Mammogram image enhancement f) Segmentation of digital mammograms (Proposed method g) FCM (cluster1) h) FCM (cluster2) i) FCM (cluster3) [22]

5 Conclusion

A segmentation approach is presented aimed at splitting the breast into areas of dissimilar densities using K-means clustering technique. The modified region growing method is used for eliminating the pectoral muscles and contrast limited adaptive histogram equalization method is utilized for increasing the contrast of the uniform distribution of histogram. The proposed method is found to be effective in removing the pectoral muscles and in segmenting the breast densities. Our results are validated by the expert radiologists and moreover these are on par with those of the state of the art techniques including fuzzy C-means clustering and texture-based methods. In this work, a small dataset like mini-MIAS database is used. But to show the efficacy of the proposed method further, large databases such as publicly available DDSM on breast database have to be used. The future work is to see the applicability of the currently more popular deep learning methods for the detection of breast cancer.

References

1. Bray, F., et al.: Global cancer statistics 2018: GLOBOCAN estimates of incidence and mortality worldwide for 36 cancers in 185 countries. CA Cancer J. Clin. (2018). https://doi.org/10.3322/caac.21492
2. Bray, F., et al.: Global estimates of cancer prevalence for 27 sites in the adult population in 2008. Int. J. Cancer (2013). https://doi.org/10.1002/ijc.27711
3. Dabass, J., et al.: Applications of advanced fuzzy set in medical image analysis: a review. Presented at the 4th International Conference on Computing Communication and Automation 2018 (2019). https://doi.org/10.1109/ccaa.2018.8777540
4. Dabass, J., et al.: Mammogram image enhancement using entropy and CLAHE based intuitionistic fuzzy method. In: 2019 6th International Conference on Signal Processing and Integrated Networks, SPIN 2019, pp. 24–29 (2019). https://doi.org/10.1109/SPIN.2019.8711696
5. Dabass, J., et al.: Segmentation techniques for breast cancer imaging modalities-a review. Presented at the 9th International Conference on Cloud Computing, Data Science & Engineering (CONFLUENCE 2019) (2019). https://doi.org/10.1109/confluence.2019.8776937
6. Dabass, J., Vig, R.: Biomedical image enhancement using different techniques - a comparative study. In: Panda, B., Sharma, S., Roy, N.R. (eds.) REDSET 2017. CCIS, vol. 799, pp. 260–286. Springer, Singapore (2018). https://doi.org/10.1007/978-981-10-8527-7_22
7. Dabass, M., Vashisth, S., Vig, R.: Effectiveness of region growing based segmentation technique for various medical images - a study. In: Panda, B., Sharma, S., Roy, N. (eds.) REDSET 2017. CCIS, vol. 799, pp. 234–259. Springer, Singapore (2018). https://doi.org/10.1007/978-981-10-8527-7_21

8. Dabass, M., et al.: Review of histopathological image segmentation via current deep learning approaches. Presented at the 2018 4th International Conference on Computing Communication and Automation (ICCCA) (2019). https://doi.org/10.1109/ccaa.2018.8777616

9. Esener, I.I., et al.: A novel multistage system for the detection and removal of pectoral muscles in mammograms. Turkish J. Electr. Eng. Comput. Sci. (2018). https://doi.org/10.3906/elk-1703-272

10. Gandomkar, Z. et al.: BI-RADS density categorization using deep neural networks. Presented at the Conference: Image Perception, Observer Performance, and Technology Assessment (2019). https://doi.org/10.1117/12.2513185

11. Hazarika, M., Mahanta, L.B.: A novel region growing based method to remove pectoral muscle from MLO mammogram images. In: Kalam, A., Das, S., Sharma, K. (eds.) Advances in Electronics, Communication and Computing. LNEE, vol. 443, pp. 307–316. Springer, Singapore (2018). https://doi.org/10.1007/978-981-10-4765-7_32

12. Kallenberg, M., et al.: Unsupervised deep learning applied to breast density segmentation and mammographic risks coring. IEEE Trans. Med. Imaging (2016). https://doi.org/10.1109/TMI.2016.2532122

13. Kamil, M.Y., Salih, A.M.: Mammography images segmentation via Fuzzy C-mean and K-mean. Int. J. Intell. Eng. Syst. (2019). https://doi.org/10.22266/IJIES2019.0228.03

14. Krizhevsky, A., et al.: ImageNet classification with deep convolutional neural networks. In: Advances in Neural Information Processing Systems (2012)

15. Lee, J., Nishikawa, R.M.: Automated mammographic breast density estimation using a fully convolutional network. Med. Phys. (2018). https://doi.org/10.1002/mp.12763

16. Liu, Z., et al.: A robust region-based active contour model with point classification for ultrasound breast lesion segmentation. In: Medical Imaging 2013: Computer-Aided Diagnosis (2013). https://doi.org/10.1117/12.2006164

17. Mohamed, A.A., et al.: A deep learning method for classifying mammographic breast density categories. Med. Phys. (2018). https://doi.org/10.1002/mp.12683

18. Nayak, T., Bhat, N., Bhat, V., Shetty, S., Javed, M., Nagabhushan, P.: Automatic segmentation and breast density estimation for cancer detection using an efficient watershed algorithm. In: Nagabhushan, P., Guru, D.S., Shekar, B.H., Kumar, Y.H.S. (eds.) Data Analytics and Learning. LNNS, vol. 43, pp. 347–358. Springer, Singapore (2019). https://doi.org/10.1007/978-981-13-2514-4_29

19. Oliver, A., et al.: A statistical approach for breast density segmentation. J. Digit. Imaging (2010). https://doi.org/10.1007/s10278-009-9217-5

20. Oliver, A., et al.: Breast density analysis using an automatic density segmentation algorithm. J. Digit. Imaging (2015). https://doi.org/10.1007/s10278-015-9777-5

21. Parmar, C., et al.: Robust radiomics feature quantification using semiautomatic volumetric segmentation. PLoS One (2014). https://doi.org/10.1371/journal.pone.0102107

22. Pavan, A.L.M., et al.: Breast tissue segmentation by fuzzy C-means. Phys. Medica **32**, 336 (2016)

23. Pavan, A.L.M., Vacavant, A., Alves, A.F.F., Trindade, A.P., de Pina, D.R.: Automatic identification and extraction of pectoral muscle in digital mammography. In: Lhotska, L., Sukupova, L., Lacković, I., Ibbott, G.S. (eds.) World Congress on Medical Physics and Biomedical Engineering 2018. IP, vol. 68/1, pp. 151–154. Springer, Singapore (2019). https://doi.org/10.1007/978-981-10-9035-6_27

24. Peng, J., et al.: 3D liver segmentation using multiple region appearances and graph cuts. Med. Phys. (2015). https://doi.org/10.1118/1.4934834

25. Pereira, S., et al.: Brain tumor segmentation using convolutional neural networks in MRI images. IEEE Trans. Med. Imaging (2016). https://doi.org/10.1109/TMI.2016.2538465

26. Petroudi, S., Brady, M.: Breast density segmentation using texture. In: Astley, S.M., Brady, M., Rose, C., Zwiggelaar, R. (eds.) IWDM 2006. LNCS, vol. 4046, pp. 609–615. Springer, Heidelberg (2006). https://doi.org/10.1007/11783237_82

27. Rampun, A., et al.: Breast pectoral muscle segmentation in mammograms using a modified holistically-nested edge detection network. Med. Image Anal. (2019). https://doi.org/10.1016/j.media.2019.06.007

28. Release, P.: Latest world cancer statistics Global cancer burden rises to 14.1 million new cases in 2012: Marked increase in breast cancers must be addressed (2013)

29. Safdar Gardezi, S.J., et al.: Segmentation of pectoral muscle using the adaptive gamma corrections. Multimed. Tools Appl. (2018). https://doi.org/10.1007/s11042-016-4283-4

30. Saidin, N., Sakim, H.A.M., Ngah, U.K., Shuaib, I.L.: Segmentation of breast regions in mammogram based on density: a review. Int. J. Comput. Sci. Issues 9(4), 104 (2012)

31. Salman, N.H., Ali, S.I.M.: Mammograms segmentation and extraction for breast cancer regions based on region growing. Baghdad Coll. Econ. Sci. Univ. 57, 448–460 (2019)

32. Shen, R., et al.: Automatic pectoral muscle region segmentation in mammograms usinggenetic algorithm and morphological selection. J. Digit. Imaging (2018). https://doi.org/10.1007/s10278-018-0068-9

33. Shinde, V., Thirumala Rao, B.: Novel approach to segment the pectoral muscle in the mammograms. In: Mallick, P.K., Balas, V.E., Bhoi, A.K., Zobaa, A.F. (eds.) Cognitive Informatics and Soft Computing. AISC, vol. 768, pp. 227–237. Springer, Singapore (2019). https://doi.org/10.1007/978-981-13-0617-4_22

34. Sreedevi, S., Sherly, E.: A novel approach for removal of pectoral muscles in digital mammogram. Procedia Comput. Sci. (2015). https://doi.org/10.1016/j.procs.2015.02.117

35. Sun, C., et al.: Automatic segmentation of liver tumors from multiphase contrast-enhanced CT images based on FCNs. Artif. Intell. Med. (2017). https://doi.org/10.1016/j.artmed.2017.03.008

36. Surajudeen, A., Reyer, Z.: Breast density segmentation based on fusion of super pixels and watershed transform. Int. J. Comput. Appl. (2017). https://doi.org/10.5120/ijca2017913208

37. Suzuki, K. et al.: CT liver volumetry using geodesic active contour segmentation with a level-set algorithm. In: Medical Imaging 2010: Computer-Aided Diagnosis (2010). https://doi.org/10.1117/12.843950

38. Wu, W., et al.: Automatic liver segmentation on volumetric CT images using super voxel-based graph cuts. Comput. Math. Methods Med. (2016). https://doi.org/10.1155/2016/9093721

39. Yin, K., et al.: A robust method for segmenting pectoral muscle in mediolateral oblique (MLO) mammograms. Int. J. Comput. Assist. Radiol. Surg. (2019). https://doi.org/10.1007/s11548-018-1867-7
40. Zhou, C., et al.: Computerized image analysis: estimation of breast density on mammograms. Med. Phys. (2001).https://doi.org/10.1118/1.1376640

Automated Mucous Glands Detection and Segmentation in Colon Histology Images Using Semantic Segmentation

Manju Dabass[✉] and Jyoti Dabass[✉]

The NorthCap University, Gurugram 122017, India
manjurashi87@gmail.com, jyotidabas91@gmail.com

Abstract. The most prevalent form of Colon Cancer is the Colorectal Adenocarcinoma which originates particularly in intestinal glandular structures. For its prognosis and plan of treatment, pathological tests are conducted where the morphology of intestinal glands including an architectural appearance as well as glandular formation are analyzed in samples collected during biopsies. But in modern pathology, to achieve good inter-observer along with intra-observer reproducibility of cancer grading still remains a key challenge owing to variations present in staining, sectioning and fixation procedures that also lead to artifacts introduction and variances in tissue sections and ultimately resulted in variances in gland appearances. Also, manual segmentation and classification of these glandular structures are time-consuming owing to large datasets from a single patient. Thus, in this paper semantic segmentation model for effectively detecting and segmenting the mucous glands from large size histopathological images i.e. $775 \times 552 \times 3$ is proposed which keeps the original size at the input and is the main highlight of the model. The model is trained and tested using the dataset from GlaS@MICCAI 2015 Colon Gland Segmentation Challenge.

Keywords: Glands · Deep learning · Histology image analysis · Semantic segmentation

1 Introduction

For determining the malignancy extent, the process of cancer grading is the primary criterion performed by the pathologists using the histology slides made from samples collected during the biopsy test. But the variance in structures of biological tissues sham as a challenge to both manual as well as automated investigation of histopathology slides [1]. Thus, achieving good cancer grading reproducibility still remains one of the challenges in pathological practices [2]. A viable solution to this problem can be provided by digital pathology due to the increasing ubiquitousness of histology slides [3]. Histology Image analysis enables the mining of quantitative morphological features which can make the computer-assisted cancer grading process far more objective as well as reproducible than the current processes are [4]. Thus, the demand for algorithm-development for histology image analysis has surged in recent few years.

© Springer Nature Singapore Pte Ltd. 2020
U. Batra et al. (Eds.): REDSET 2019, CCIS 1230, pp. 316–330, 2020.
https://doi.org/10.1007/978-981-15-5830-6_27

Colon Cancer according to recent studies [5] has become one of the leading death cause related to cancer in developed countries. Thus, accurate cancer grading is crucial for patients' survival. This grading can be effectively done in stained histopathological sections that are harvested during surgery or via biopsy. In [6], the authors showed that the formation along with the architecture of glands can effectively reflect the degree of aggressiveness of Colon Cancer. Thus, it is crucial to accurately do the gland segmentation from the other structures in order to have reliable different tumor/cancer classification.

In most of the organ systems, the important histological structures present are the glands that are responsible for the main mechanism for secreting carbohydrates and proteins. For Colon Cancer grading also, a key criterion is the intestinal gland morphology analysis including the architectural appearance as well as gland formation [7]. There are four types of tissue components i.e. epithelial nuclei, cytoplasm, lumen and stroma (mainly blood vessels, nervous tissues, connective tissue, etc.) that are present in glands as shown in Fig. 1. The stroma is mainly not considered as a part of the gland while the epithelial cells enclose the cytoplasm and lumen and thus, works as the gland boundary. The benign i.e. non-cancerous glands are easily analyzed using the automated segmentation algorithms owing to significant variances in size, texture, staining, shape, and location of glands. But in the malignant i.e. the cancerous cases, the gland objects significantly differ as compared to non-cancerous cases. Also, the presence of artifacts i.e. corrupted areas further makes the gland detection and segmentation task cumbersome and quite tedious. Therefore, artificial intelligence techniques like machine learning, deep learning, etc. are used to make robust models that learned to cope with the issue of tissue variability with the usage of labeled image examples.

2 Literature Review

The different works published are recapitulated in Table 1 in terms of the method implemented and limitations.

Table 1. Segmentation techniques proposed for gland segmentation in colon cancer histology images.

S. No.	Authors	Implemented method	Limitations
1	Fu et al. 2014 [8]	Here, the authors proposed an approach named 'Gland Vision' where first the images were transformed in the polar coordinate image. The aspirant gland boundaries were then located by employing a random field model and later established by using a support vector regressor. This approach demonstrated good recital for H&E and Hematoxylin-Diaminobenzidine (H-DAB) stained tissues	It required the gland boundaries to be fully intact
The validation was limited only to healthy cases

(continued)

Table 1. (*continued*)

S. No.	Authors	Implemented method	Limitations
2	Sirinukunwattana et al. 2015 [9]	This approach used the Bayesian inference approach which took account of the prior knowledge of spatial connectivity as well as neighboring nuclei arrangement present on the epithelial boundary along with the glandular structures. Here, each gland structure present in the image was treated as a polygon made up of random numbers of vertices where vertices were representing approximated locality of the epithelial nuclei. The Reversible-Jump Markov Chain Monte Carlo was used to inference the polygon	The method was slow It produced remarkable segmentation results for the entire Histologic grades with the exception of the undifferentiated grade It was stochastic in nature
3	Long et al. 2015 [10]	This technique was based on Fully Convolutional Network (FCN) where the fully-connected layers were replaced with the convolution layer, transposed convolutions performed the up-sampling and skip connections were used	The resulted segmentation maps were too coarse
4	Ronneberger et al. 2015 [11]	Here, U-Net was proposed which was the first method used for biomedical image segmentation. It was based on Convolutional Neural Network (CNN). In this approach, the up-sampled features were concatenated with higher resolution features derived from the down part which produced better gland localization while going deeper and performing up-sampling in the network	The method was unable to separate close or contiguous objects
5	Ben Taieb et al. 2016 [12]	This technique was based on topology-aware CNN. In this technique, a new-level loss function was introduced in order to take account of high-level shape priors like smoothness, complex interaction preservance between object regions	It had limited memory efficiency
6	Badrinarayanan et al. 2017 [13]	Here, Seg-Net based on CNN was proposed in which a different up-sampling technique was used in which the decoder part used the similar pooling indices that were calculated in the max-pooling step of analogous encoder part in order to do non-linear up-sampling. Thus, this technique led to more effective as well as accurate segmentation along with enhanced memory efficiency	This technique was not able to entirely unscramble the consequences of model versus solver (optimization) in attaining a scrupulous result

(*continued*)

Table 1. (*continued*)

S. No.	Authors	Implemented method	Limitations
7	Kainz et al. 2017 [14]	In this approach, two FCN networks were used in which the first network was performing object segmentation and the second network was separating close glands. The CNN predictions were then regularized by the usage of the weighted total variation for producing the final segmentation results	Several False Positives were there
8	Chen et al. 2017 [15]	This technique was based on DCAN architecture having separate object detection along with the separation CNN model like [14] but instead of performing pipelining like operations, here both these steps were performed simultaneously with each other. The first model predicts the gland object probabilities and the second model predicts the probability map for contours that separates glands. And then by the usage of threshold rule, the final segmentation masks were calculated. Also, three weighted auxiliary classifiers were used for the three deepest layers in order to strengthen the DCAN training process	The original image had to be divided into patches of size 100 × 100
9	Xu et al. 2017 [16]	Here, the idea of [14] was further modified by introducing three CNN models i.e. FCN for foreground segmentation, a faster R-CNN for object detection and in the end HED used for edge detection. These three models were fused into one while being followed by several convolutional layers in order to predict the final segmentation map and thus led to impressive segmentation accuracy	The original image had to be divided into patches of size 400 × 400 The imbalance between the edge and non-edges barriers the network training
10	Qaiser et al. 2019 [17]	This technique employed a multi-stage ensemble strategy based on the concept of persistent homology profiles (PHPs). The PHPs were developed to discriminate tumor regions from their normal counterparts by modeling the different distinctiveness of tumor nuclei. The selection of exemplary image patches was done by CNN and after this; the patch classification was done by enumerating the deviation between the PHPs of exemplars and the input image scrap	The original image had to be divided into patches of size 256 × 256

(*continued*)

Table 1. (*continued*)

S. No.	Authors	Implemented method	Limitations
11	Graham et al. 2019 [18]	Here, an FCN network-based approach was proposed that minimized the information loss rooted by max-pooling by the usage of re-introduction of the original image at different numerous points within the network. The authors also used an atrous spatial pyramid pooling having changeable dilation rates in order to preserve resolution as well as multi-level aggregation. To address uncertainty, the authors introduced random transformations during its testing-time for enhancing the segmentation results	The proposed model sometimes failed to distinguish between gastrointestinal tracts' lumen and the glandular lumen. The technique had used only small size image tiles at the input and hence, the contextual information which empowers the segmentation process is narrow

All the above approaches discussed in Table 1 were either conventional techniques applied to original image size or small patch-fed CNN based techniques. Thus, in this paper original image size fed semantic segmentation technique having a deep-layer structure similar to the VGG-16 model is used for gland detection and segmentation.

3   Quantitative Measures

The following parameters [21] are used for the qualitative assessment of the results:

1. *Accuracy:* It gives the statistical percentage of correctly identified pixels for each class. It is defined as

$$accuracy = TP/(TP + FN) \tag{1}$$

Where,
TP denote True Positives, &
FN denotes False Negatives.

2. *Intersection over Union (IoU):* It is also known as the Jaccard Similarity Coefficient and is the most commonly used statistical accuracy measurement metric that is utilized in semantic segmentation tasks to penalize the false negatives. It gives the ratio of properly classified pixels to the entire quantity of ground truth and predicted pixels i.e.

$$IoU\ Score = TP/((TP + FP + FN) \tag{2}$$

Where,
FP denotes False Positives.

Also, it can be defined as

$$IoU = \left(|GT \cap PR| \; |GT \cup PR| \right) \tag{3}$$

GT denotes the Ground Truth, &
PR denotes the Predicted Result.

3. *BF Score:* The Boundary F1 (BF) Contour matching Score indicates how well the boundary of each class aligns with the true boundary.

4 Dataset

The implemented model is assessed on the database made available by the Gland Segmentation (GlaS) Challenge held in MICCAI 2015 [19] given at [20]. This dataset consists of 165 images mostly having a size of $775 \times 552 \times 3$ and divided as eighty-five images for training part and eighty images for testing part which is further divided into sixty images as Test A and twenty images as Test B. The dataset is also provided with the help of several expert pathologists. We have used the original training dataset as well as augmented data for training the segmentation model. The gland detection and segmentation qualitative results are predicted with the help of Test A and Test B dataset. An example of a benign and malignant cancer image along with their segmented ground truth annotations from the dataset is shown in Fig. 1.

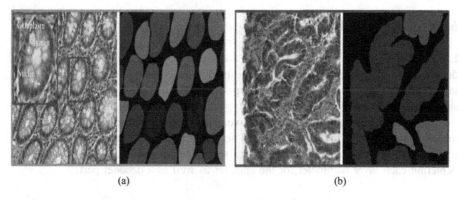

(a)   (b)

Fig. 1. GlaS challenge dataset image example: (a) benign case and it's ground truth annotation; (b) malignant case and its ground truth annotations.

5 Algorithm Used

The following algorithm is used in this paper:

1. Create Training and Testing Image Datastore using the Warwick Colon Dataset.
2. Use the 'Image Labeller' app to make the Pixel Label Datastore for the step 1 image datastore.
3. Create a Semantic segmentation network using the layer defined in Sect. 6.
4. To improve the training process, balance the classes using new class weights calculated by the following formula:

$$x = \frac{Total\ Pixel\ ccount\ in\ Pixel\ Databse}{Total\ Pixel\ Labels\ present\ in\ Pixel\ Database}$$

$$new\ class\ weights = \frac{Median(X)}{X}$$

5. Specify the new class *new class weights* in the pixel classification layer and replace the old classification layer with this *new classification layer*.
6. Specify the hyper-parameters.
7. Do the Data Augmentation.
8. Start the training process with the
9. Test the semantic segmentation with the Testing Database.
10. Evaluate the Quantitative Parameter matrix.

6 Proposed Model

In a semantic segmentation network, there are two main parts i.e. one Encoder part that do the down-sampling of the input image by the usage of convolutional and ReLU layers, and the second Decoder part that up-sample the output to counterpart the input size. This maneuver is equivalent to the typical scale-space analysis via image pyramids where a network executes the maneuvers utilizing non-linear filters optimized for the explicit deposit of classes. The CNN semantic segmentation model used for the implementation of the gland detection and segmentation results is shown in Table 2 depicting each layer parameter for the encoder as well as a decoder part.

Table 2. CNN layers for gland detection and segmentation

Layer	Used parameter description
Image Input	Image with size $775 \times 552 \times 3$
1. For Encoder part	
Convolution	64 filters with size $3 \times 3 \times 3$
Batch Normalization + ReLU	
Convolution	64 filters with size $3 \times 3 \times 64$
Batch Normalization + ReLU + Max- Pooling of 2×2 size	
Convolution	128 filters with size $3 \times 3 \times 64$
Batch Normalization + ReLU	
Convolution	128 filters with size $3 \times 3 \times 128$
Batch Normalization + ReLU + Max- Pooling of 2×2 size	
Convolution	256 filters with size $3 \times 3 \times 128$
Batch Normalization + ReLU	
Convolution	256 filters with size $3 \times 3 \times 256$
Batch Normalization + ReLU	
Convolution	256 filters with size $3 \times 3 \times 256$
Batch Normalization + ReLU + Max- Pooling of 2×2 size	
Convolution	512 filters with size $3 \times 3 \times 256$
Batch Normalization + ReLU	
Convolution	512 filters with size $3 \times 3 \times 512$
Batch Normalization + ReLU	
Convolution	512 filters with size $3 \times 3 \times 512$
Batch Normalization + ReLU + Max- Pooling of 2×2 size	
Convolution	512 filters with size $3 \times 3 \times 512$
Batch Normalization + ReLU	
Convolution	512 filters with size $3 \times 3 \times 512$
Batch Normalization + ReLU	
Convolution	512 filters with size $3 \times 3 \times 512$
Batch Normalization + ReLU + Max- Pooling of 2×2 size	
2. For Decoder part	
Max Un-Pooling layer	
Convolution	512 filters with size $3 \times 3 \times 512$
Batch Normalization + ReLU	
Convolution	512 filters with size $3 \times 3 \times 512$
Batch Normalization + ReLU	
Convolution	512 filters with size $3 \times 3 \times 512$
Batch Normalization + ReLU + Max Un-Pooling	
Convolution	512 filters with size $3 \times 3 \times 512$
Batch Normalization + ReLU	
Convolution	512 filters with size $3 \times 3 \times 512$
Batch Normalization + ReLU	
Convolution	256 filters with size $3 \times 3 \times 512$

(*continued*)

Table 2. (*continued*)

Layer	Used parameter description
Batch Normalization + ReLU + Max Un-Pooling	
Convolution	256 filters with size 3 × 3 × 256
Batch Normalization + ReLU	
Convolution	256 filters with size 3 × 3 × 256
Batch Normalization + ReLU	
Convolution	128 filters with size 3 × 3 × 256
Batch Normalization + ReLU + Max Un-Pooling	
Convolution	128 filters with size 3 × 3 × 128
Batch Normalization + ReLU	
Convolution	64 filters with size 3 × 3 × 128
Batch Normalization + ReLU + Max Un-Pooling	
Convolution	64 filters with size 3 × 3 × 64
Batch Normalization + ReLU	
Convolution	64 filters with size 3 × 3 × 64
Batch Normalization + ReLU	
Softmax Layer	
Pixel Classification Layer	

7 Results and Analysis

We implement our experiment in MATLAB 2019a Software. The 'sgdm' solver is used with 0.5 kept as momentum value. The learning rate is kept at 0.0001 throughout the training process. The minibatch size is kept as one. The optimal model is obtained after forty-seven epochs. The whole training process is summarized in Table 3 for each epoch. Figure 2 shows the accuracy and error rates during the CNN training. Figure 3 shows the original image, ground truth, and the segmented results. The pathologists from one of the esteemed cancer hospitals have verified the results and validated it for giving the précised gland morphology which is helpful to them in predicting the cancer grading effectively and in less time. The gland detection and segmentation qualitative results are summarized in Table 4.

Table 3. Parameter values during training process

Epoch	Iteration	Time elapsed (hh:mm:ss)	Mini-batch accuracy	Mini-batch loss	Base learning rate
1	1	00:00:15	61.83%	0.7699	0.1000
1	2	00:00:30	63.36%	0.7486	0.1000
1	3	00:00:45	66.20%	0.7147	0.1000
1	4	00:01:00	69.89%	0.6730	0.1000
1	5	00:01:15	73.27%	0.6343	0.1000

(*continued*)

Table 3. (*continued*)

Epoch	Iteration	Time elapsed (hh:mm:ss)	Mini-batch accuracy	Mini-batch loss	Base learning rate
1	6	00:01:33	77.54%	0.5944	0.1000
1	7	00:01:49	80.55%	0.5626	0.1000
1	8	00:02:06	83.26%	0.5305	0.1000
1	9	00:02:22	86.11%	0.5098	0.1000
1	10	00:02:37	89.64%	0.4025	0.1000
1	11	00:02:53	88.81%	0.4976	0.1000
1	12	00:03:10	88.18%	0.4116	0.1000
1	13	00:03:26	91.09%	0.4139	0.1000
1	14	00:03:41	91.46%	0.4429	0.1000
1	15	00:03:58	94.76%	0.3886	0.1000
1	16	00:04:17	93.08%	0.4355	0.1000
1	17	00:04:34	97.06%	0.4341	0.1000
1	18	00:04:51	93.51%	0.3536	0.1000
1	19	00:05:07	98.08%	0.2042	0.1000
1	20	00:05:23	94.76%	0.2934	0.1000
1	21	00:05:40	97.60%	0.1970	0.1000
1	22	00:05:57	95.69%	0.3694	0.1000
1	23	00:06:14	97.79%	0.2323	0.1000
1	24	00:06:29	97.56%	0.3346	0.1000
1	25	00:06:45	95.61%	0.2861	0.1000
1	26	00:07:00	96.46%	0.2555	0.1000
1	27	00:07:16	94.55%	0.2461	0.1000
1	28	00:07:32	96.80%	0.2225	0.1000
1	29	00:07:49	96.66%	0.2577	0.1000
1	30	00:08:06	97.13%	0.1648	0.1000
1	31	00:08:22	97.40%	0.3258	0.1000
1	32	00:08:38	99.98%	0.0736	0.1000
1	33	00:08:54	96.61%	0.2548	0.1000
1	34	00:09:09	97.85%	0.2563	0.1000
1	35	00:09:24	58.50%	0.7260	0.1000
1	36	00:09:40	96.97%	0.2427	0.1000
1	37	00:09:56	97.38%	0.2335	0.1000
1	38	00:10:12	98.35%	0.1219	0.1000
1	39	00:10:27	98.16%	0.1552	0.1000
1	40	00:10:43	98.52%	0.1711	0.1000
1	41	00:11:00	99.43%	0.0889	0.1000
1	42	00:11:16	98.25%	0.1014	0.1000
1	43	00:11:33	98.10%	0.0890	0.1000

(*continued*)

Table 3. (*continued*)

Epoch	Iteration	Time elapsed (hh:mm:ss)	Mini-batch accuracy	Mini-batch loss	Base learning rate
1	44	00:11:48	99.60%	0.0838	0.1000
1	45	00:12:04	99.10%	0.1209	0.1000
1	46	00:12:19	99.67%	0.1406	0.1000
1	47	00:12:35	99.92%	0.1828	0.1000

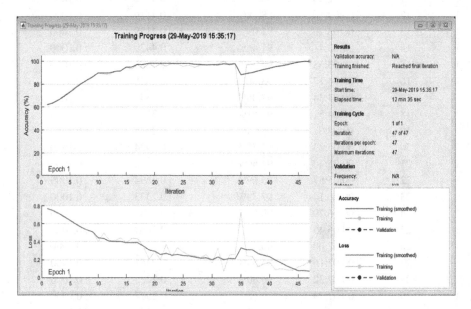

Fig. 2. Accuracy and error rate during the Semantic Segmentation model training

Table 4. The qualitative results for the gland detection and segmentation process

Dataset	Gland detection accuracy	Mean IoU	F1 score
Training	0.9982	0. 8047	0.878
Test A	0.910	0.7882	0.680
Test B	0.880	0. 7108	0.615

Original Image	Ground Truth	Segmented Result

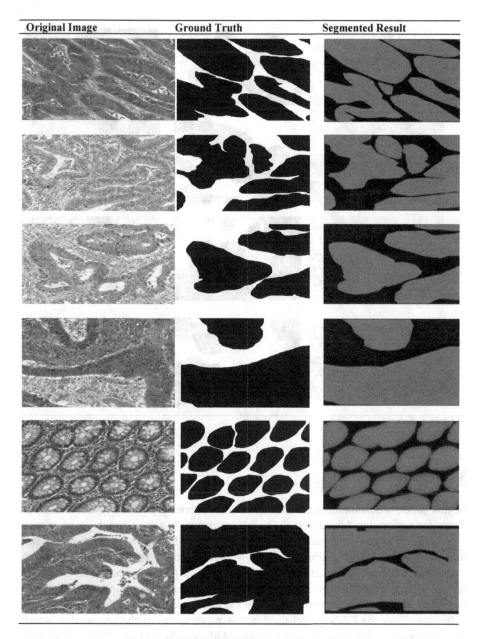

Fig. 3. Segmentation results

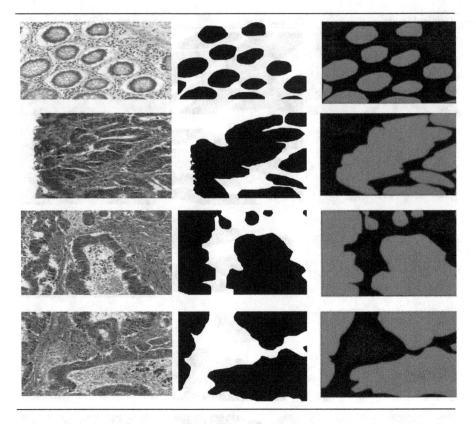

Fig. 3. (*continued*)

8 Conclusion

In this paper, a semantic segmentation network inspired by VGG-16 architecture is given for performing Gland detection and segmentation for an input image of size $775 \times 552 \times 3$. All the results were verified by the pathologists for their significance in cancer detection and grading. The segmentation model using deep learning which was earlier proposed for gland segmentation tasks were patch-size based i.e. they were first dividing the input image into small patches and then performing segmentation on them. Due to which the contextual information that could empower their segmentation is limited. Thus, the CNN model used in this paper is one of the few models which have used such a large size image at the input. Although the IoU and BF scores are low, the gland detection accuracy is quite good enough. Thus, future work will be focused on including some more databases as well as enhancing the qualitative parameters.

Acknowledgments. The authors are grateful to Dr. Hema Malini Aiyer, Head of Pathology and Dr. Garima Rawat, Pathologists at Dharamshila Narayana Superspeciality Hospital, New Delhi for their support to our research, without their help we will not be able to check the feasibility of the applied algorithm in the real-life scenario.

References

1. McCann, M.T., Ozolek, J.A., Castro, C.A., Parvin, B., Kovacevic, J.: Automated histology analysis: opportunities for signal processing. IEEE Signal Process. Mag. **32**(1), 78–87 (2014)
2. Fanshawe, T.R., Lynch, A.G., Ellis, I.O., Green, A.R., Hanka, R.: Assessing agreement between multiple raters with missing rating information, applied to breast cancer tumor grading. PLoS ONE **3**(8), e2925 (2008)
3. May, M.: A better lens on disease. Sci. Am. **302**(5), 74–77 (2010)
4. Gurcan, M.N., Boucheron, L., Can, A., Madabhushi, A., Rajpoot, N., Yener, B.: Histopathological image analysis: a review. IEEE Rev. Biomed. Eng. **2**, 147 (2009)
5. Torre, L.A., Bray, F., Siegel, R.L., Ferlay, J., Lortet-Tieulent, J., Jemal, A.: Global cancer statistics, 2012. CA Cancer J. Clin. **65**(2), 87–108 (2015)
6. Fleming, M., Ravula, S., Tatishchev, S.F., Wang, H.L.: Colorectal carcinoma: pathologic aspects. J. Gastrointest. Oncol. **3**(3), 153 (2012)
7. Bosman, FT., Carneiro, F., Hruban, R.H., Theise, N.D.: WHO classification of tumors of the digestive system (No. Ed. 4). World Health Organization (2010)
8. Fu, H., Qiu, G., Shu, J., Ilyas, M.: A novel polar space random field model for the detection of glandular structures. IEEE Trans. Med. Imaging **33**(3), 764–776 (2014)
9. Sirinukunwattana, K., Snead, D.R., Rajpoot, N.M.: A stochastic polygons model for glandular structures in colon histology images. IEEE Trans. Med. Imaging **34**(11), 2366–2378 (2015)
10. Long, J., Shelhamer, E., Darrell, T.: Fully convolutional networks for semantic segmentation. In: Proceedings of the IEEE Conference on Computer Vision and Pattern Recognition, pp. 3431–3440 (2015)
11. Ronneberger, O., Fischer, P., Brox, T.: U-Net: convolutional networks for biomedical image segmentation. In: Navab, N., Hornegger, J., Wells, W.M., Frangi, A.F. (eds.) MICCAI 2015. LNCS, vol. 9351, pp. 234–241. Springer, Cham (2015). https://doi.org/10.1007/978-3-319-24574-4_28
12. BenTaieb, A., Hamarneh, G.: Topology aware fully convolutional networks for histology gland segmentation. In: Ourselin, S., Joskowicz, L., Sabuncu, M.R., Unal, G., Wells, W. (eds.) MICCAI 2016. LNCS, vol. 9901, pp. 460–468. Springer, Cham (2016). https://doi.org/10.1007/978-3-319-46723-8_53
13. Badrinarayanan, V., Kendall, A., Cipolla, R.: SegNet: a deep convolutional encoder-decoder architecture for image segmentation. IEEE Trans. Pattern Anal. Mach. Intell. **39**(12), 2481–2495 (2017)
14. Kainz, P., Pfeiffer, M., Urschler, M.: Segmentation and classification of colon glands with deep convolutional neural networks and total variation regularization. PeerJ **5**, e3874 (2017)
15. Chen, H., Qi, X., Yu, L., Dou, Q., Qin, J., Heng, P.A.: DCAN: deep contour-aware networks for object instance segmentation from histology images. Med. Image Anal. **36**, 135–146 (2017)
16. Xu, Y., et al.: Gland instance segmentation using deep multichannel neural networks. IEEE Trans. Biomed. Eng. **64**(12), 2901–2912 (2017)

17. Qaiser, T., et al.: Fast and accurate tumor segmentation of histology images using persistent homology and deep convolutional features. Med. Image Anal. **55**, 1–14 (2019)
18. Graham, S., et al.: MILD-Net: minimal information loss dilated network for gland instance segmentation in colon histology images. Med. Image Anal. **52**, 199–211 (2019)
19. Sirinukunwattana, K., Pluim, J.P., Chen, H., Qi, X., Heng, P.A., Guo, Y.B., Böhm, A.: Gland segmentation in colon histology images: the glas challenge contest. Med. Image Anal. **35**, 489–502 (2017)
20. Warwick-QU image dataset description. https://warwick.ac.uk/fac/sci/dcs/research/tia/glascontest/about/
21. Dabass, M., Vashisth, S., Vig, R.: Effectiveness of region growing based segmentation technique for various medical images - a study. In: Panda, B., Sharma, S., Roy, N.R. (eds.) REDSET 2017. CCIS, vol. 799, pp. 234–259. Springer, Singapore (2018). https://doi.org/10.1007/978-981-10-8527-7_21

Big Data Cluster Service Discovery: A System Application for Big Data Cluster Security Analysis

Swagata Paul[1]([✉]), Sajal Saha[2], and Radha Tamal Goswami[1]

[1] Techno International New Town, Kolkata 700156, West Bengal, India
swagatapaul@hotmail.com
[2] The Assam Kaziranga University, Koraikhowa, Jorhat 785006, Assam, India
sajalsaha@kazirangauniversity.in

Abstract. A big data cluster consists of number of network connected computers offering a huge data store and processing power. Users of the big data cluster submits job to process huge amount of data stored in different computers of the cluster. All the computers works together to give the result from the data. During data processing, a number of operating system process runs on different computers and exchange data. The data exchange is done via regular protocols. During processing, one or multiple computers may not participate well due to its bad hardware or operating system issue like low disk space or memory full etc. Some computers may receive known network attack like DOS and thus slow down the performance. Some other computers may receive unknown attacks generated from the big data job itself. Therefore, the system requires a mechanism to detect such computers and isolate thereafter. To detect this, we need to know about the processes or services participating in big data computation on different computers in the cluster. In this work we describe how to discover the services active or running inside the cluster.

Keywords: Big data cluster · Service discovery · Big data security analysis

1 Introduction

Size of data is growing rapidly in the universe. Therefore, a big data cluster becomes an essence for data processing. A typical big data cluster consists of hundreds or thousands of connected computers (nodes). A big data cluster runs big data applications. Due to high data volume, the application moves to the node where data is stored. While in operation, the cluster needs to process the data in a secure way. To protect such number of nodes participating in a big data process we need to identify the attack on different processes running on them. Such attack can slow down the performance of the cluster. The processes running on big data cluster can be categorized into two set. The first set of processes creates the big data platform; we call such processes as big data service (BDS).

© Springer Nature Singapore Pte Ltd. 2020
U. Batra et al. (Eds.): REDSET 2019, CCIS 1230, pp. 331–341, 2020.
https://doi.org/10.1007/978-981-15-5830-6_28

The second set of processes are the big data jobs or big data applications, we simply call them big data process (BDP). There exists multiple similar BDS on a set of nodes and some unique BDS on other nodes. All BDSs may or may not run for BDPs. A set of BDSs engage themselves to complete a BDP. The work presented in this paper is to identify all such BDSs exists in a big data cluster and monitor their behavior and performance. Once all such BDSs are identified it will expedite the process of identifying an future attack on a big data cluster. For our experiment we have used the well known big data framework Hadoop forming a cluster of 28 nodes.

2   Related Work

To know Hadoop File System (HDFS) service 'namenode' and 'datanode' details, we need to execute the command *hadoop dfsadmin-report*. The command must be executed from a cluster node. This node must have Hadoop configuration file like core-site.xml and Hadoop client library. The details are as per the Hadoop ecosystem documentations provided by Apache Hadoop [1], hortonworks [2]. An active learner needs to know the cluster information for the purpose of attack generation or for the purpose of attack detection. Hadoop configuration and client library may not be available on the learner node. A new feature has been added in Hadoop 3.1.x called Service Discovery [3]. This works like DNS lookup and is limited to a set of BDS named YARN. Discovering active namenode of a remote Hadoop cluster is possible using Ambari API, but you need to know the ambari server login details [4]. The article [5] shows attack detection mechanism on a old version of Hadoop software which is no longer used today. The work [6] shows different known attack generation mechanism. It does not show much on how to detect such attack. The authors in [7,8] showed that MapReduce Job completion time increases with attacks. However, a Mapreduce spark streaming job, running on a hadoop cluster does not finish until it is explicitly terminated. Therefore these methods will see such spark streaming jobs as attacks. Applications on geospatial big data, biomedical signal processing, healthcare recommendation system etc. [9–14] are growing rapidly without having any knowledge of the cluster nodes. This increases the risk of attacks on the big data system. The goal is to create an application that can show which big data services running on which node and create facilities for future research on security analysis and attack detection in a big data cluster.

3   Big Data Architecture

The generalized framework of a big data cluster is shown in the Fig. 1. Though there are emerging big data platforms like Ceph, DataTorrent RTS, Disco, Google BigQuery, HPCC, Hydra [15] etc., we have used Hadoop Ecosystem as a Big Data processing framework for its well known features and advantages mentioned in Apache Hadoop Documentation [1]. The framework mainly consists of two sets of distributed components - BDPs and BDSs. A set of BDS offers a data processing component. For example, in Fig. 1, ResourceManager and a set of Slaves named NodeManagers offers a big data processing component called YARN. BDPs communicate with one or multiple BDSs to complete a data processing job.

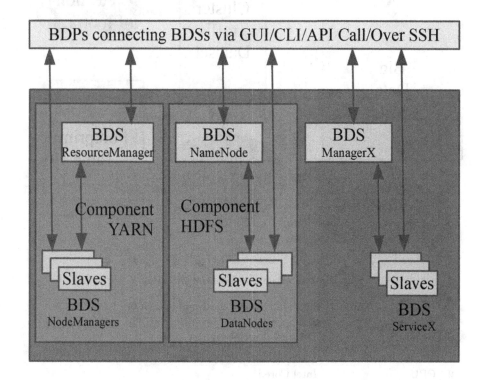

Fig. 1. Big data framework.

4   Footprint Detection Architecture

The generalized architecture is shown in Fig. 2. The cluster specification is given in Table 2. For our experiment, along with regular BDPs, we submit experimental BDPs to the cluster. While the cluster running BDPs, we capture the network traffic from all the nodes in the cluster. The capture operation is initiated from a designated node in the cluster called capture center. Capture center then collect all such network traffic. The traffic data is then merged and filtered for further investigation. The result is stored in a table. The table consists of all past records generated from earlier experiments. This table shows the footprint of the cluster, i.e. the table contains records on - which BDS is running on which node, and how they behave with the requests from BDPs.

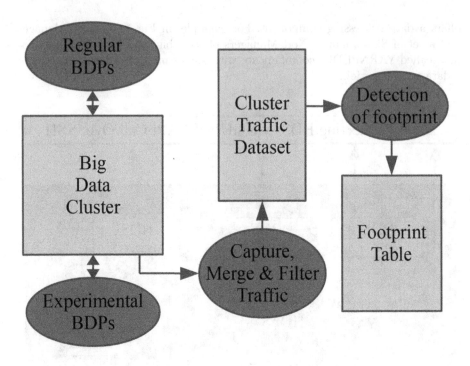

Fig. 2. Architecture for footprint detection.

Table 1. Big data cluster - hardware and NOS

Sl	Item	Detailed description
1	OS	Ubuntu 18.04 64 bits [16]
2	CPU	Intel Core i5
3	RAM	DDR3, 8 GB (6 GB allocated to the cluster)
4	Storage	1 TB SATA, a partition of 700 GB mounted on/data directory
5	LAN	1 Gbps for both LAN switch and Network Adapter
6	IP range	192.168.10.171–192.168.10.198
7	Hostnames	cseoslab001, cseoslab002, ... cseoslab028
8	Hostname:NodeName	cseoslab001:N1, cseoslab002:N2, ... cseoslab028:N28

5   Experimental Setup

The following setup was considered for our experiment to generate network traffic in all nodes of the cluster. Configuration of each part is shown in the next subsections. The designated node called capture center communicates with all other hosts via SSH to start the traffic capture, stop the capture operation and collect the traffic data.

5.1 Hardware, System and Cluster Software - Configuration

The hardware and NOS configuration of the nodes of the cluster is shown in Table 1. Configuration of basic components for the Hadoop cluster is shown in Table 2.

Table 2. Hadoop big data cluster configuration used for experiments

Sl	Item	Detailed description
1	Apache Ambari	Ver 2.7.3, on cseoslab001
2	HDFS	Ver 3.1.1, Storage Size: 13.7 TB, Block Size: 128 MB, Rep Factor: 3
3	HDFS - NameNode	cseoslab002
4	HDFS - DataNodes	25 DataNodes, cseoslab004 to cseoslab028
5	YARN	Ver 3.1.1
6	ResourceManager	One, on cseoslab002
7	NodeManagers	24 nos, on cseoslab005 to cseoslab028
8	YARN - Cluster Memory	142 GB
9	SPARK	Ver 2.3.2
10	HIVE	Ver 3.1.0 installed on cseoslab004
11	Clients	On all nodes

5.2 Software, Commands, Shell Scripts

We have used a) hping3 [17] command to launch some known attack like DOS with ICMP Flooding etc., b) code written in Java and benchmark tool named TestDFSIO to create huge file Input/Output operations, c) YARN APIs d) Loading data to HBase etc. to generate network traffic in the nodes of the cluster and capture all such traffic for further analysis for the purpose of footprint detection. Table 3 shows the details. The packets are captured as .pcapng file format [18].

6 Detection Process

Detection of each BDS was done by analyzing the captured and collected network traffic in capture center node. The traffic data is collected as .pcapng file. All such files are then merged in a way so that it is sorted by packet timestamp. Then we remove duplicate packets and filter unwanted records of type DNS lookup, ICMP, Broadcast packets etc. This merged file is then converted to .csv file containing all necessary fields for analysis. At the same time we identify all communications and its pattern among BDPs and BDSs. Detection of each BDSs are given in the following subsections.

Table 3. Packet generation

Sl	BDPs	Description
1	DOS	Packet send to YARN ResourceManager. We used hping3 command to generate packets. The command to generate the packet is *sudo hping3 -c 10010 -d 121 -w 64 -S -p 50470 --rand-source --flood cseoslab002*
2	Busy HDFS	This is an insider attack generated from a client. The attack generates huge file write operation and thus makes the system busy
3	Busy YARN	We have used YARN REST APIs via shell script to consume all possible container by running a set of Spark Streaming jobs
4	HBase data load	The command to load 1 GB data file price1gb.csv data to table price1gb is: *hbase $cls -Dimporttsv.separator=, -Dimporttsv.columns= "$k, trans_id,price, dateof_trans, prop_type, old_new, duration, town_city, dist, county, cat_type, status" price1gb spaulprice1gb.csv* [where: $cls = org.apache.hadoop.hbase.mapreduce.ImportTsv $k=HBASE_ROW_KEY]

6.1   Detection of BDSs: NameNode and DataNodes

NameNode and DataNodes are the basic BDSs in a Hadoop cluster. They represents the distributed file system of Hadoop - HDFS. Therefore it is necessary to know which one is on which node. Experiment No. 2 specified in Table 3 does large file read-write operations on HDFS. This generates huge packets on BDS namenode and BDS datanodes. At the end of the capture the generated traffic is collected and filtered on port number 8020, 50070 and 50010. These three port numbers are the default port number for namenode metadata service, NameNode WebUI and datanode Data transfer service respectively. Left side of Fig. 3 shows that node N2 works on port number 8020, 50070. Right side of Fig. 3 shows that nodes N6 to N28 works on port number 50010. Therefore N2 node is running NameNode and N6–N28 nodes are running DataNodes for HDFS component of the big data cluster. Once we detect the nodes running BDSs, we must verify their response to make sure they are the true BDSs. This is done by sending requests and checking the response received.

For all DataNodes, we further explore to find their response. The following commands are used to find the response.

curl -s http://hostname:50075/datanode.html | wc -l

curl -s http://hostname:50075/logs/hadoop-hdfs-datanode-hostname.log | wc -l

For NameNode we use *curl -s cseoslab002:50070/dfshealth.html | wc -l*

curl -s http://cseoslab002:50070/logs/hadoop-hdfs-namenode-cseoslab002.log |
wc -l to get proper response.

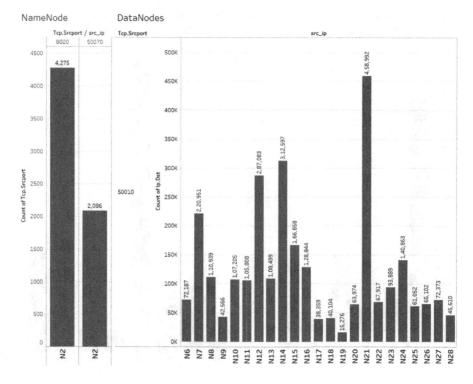

Fig. 3. NameNode and DataNodes

6.2 Detection of BDS: YARN Components

The components ResourceManager, NodeManagers, Timeline Service, Scheduler, History Server etc. are the next BDSs after HDFS. These are responsible for creating BDPs and allocating resource to BDPs. Experiment No. 3 in Table 3 is executed and the traffic is collected and analyzed is the same way. Figure 4 shows that - a) Node N3 works on port number 8188 (Timeline Service V1.5), 19888 (History Server); b) Node N2 works on port number 8088 (Resource Manager WebUI), 8025 and 8050 (ResourceManager), 8030 (Scheduler); c) Nodes - N6, N9, N11, N13, N20, N22, N23, N27 works on port number 45454 (NodeManagers). For the purpose of verification similar curl commands are used.

6.3 Detection of BDSs: ZooKeepers

Zookeepers are services that coordinate other BDSs and BDPs. They manage node configurations, implement reliable messaging, redundant services and also synchronize the execution of BDPs inside the cluster. The traffic from Experiment No. 3 in Table 3 is analyzed and the result is shown in left side of Fig. 5. It shows - a) node N4 works on port number 2888 (talk with other ZooKeepers); b) Nodes N2, N3 and N4 works on port number 2181 (talk with client BDPs). We have used ZooKeepers Java APIs to verify all of them.

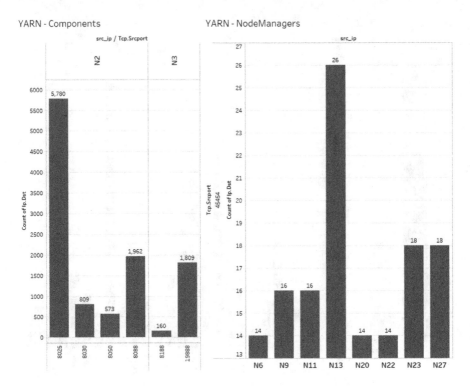

Fig. 4. YARN components

6.4 Detection of BDSs: HBase

Apache HBase [19] can be used on the top of HDFS when random, realtime and strictly consistent read or write permission is required on big data. It is capable of managing huge tables size containing million columns and billion rows. The experiment No. 4 in Table 3 uses 1 GB .csv data file. Traffic is captured when the data is being loaded on HBase table. Right side of Fig. 5 shows - a) node N4 works on port number 16000 (HBaseMaster) and 16010 (HBaseMaster info); b) node N4 and N6 works on port number 16020 (RegionServer). To verify we have used the URL - *http://cseoslab004:16010/master-status*.

7 Result and Discussion

To capture network traffic we have used command-line tools dumpcap of wireshark [20]. The impact of data capture is very low, therefore it does not consume additional resource from Hadoop. We have used Tableau version 2019.3 [21] to generate the result and the bar charts. All the outcomes of the experiments, that ensures the existence of different BDSs are recorded in a .csv file. Table 4 shows some of the results of our experiments conducted so far. We store historical data, so that in future the table can be used to detect various attack on the cluster.

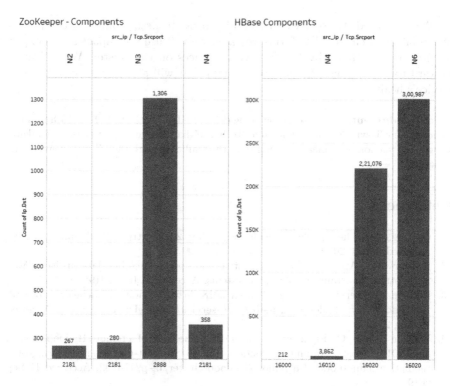

Fig. 5. ZooKeeper (Left) and HBase (Right) components

Table 4. Footprint table

Exp. no	Discover what	Result
1	NameNode	N2
2	DataNodes	N6–N28
3	YARN - ResourceManager	N2
4	YARN - NodeManagers	N6, N9, N11, N13, N20, N22, N23, N27
5	ZooKeepers	N2, N3, N4
6	HBaseMaster	N4
7	HBase RegionServer	N4, N6

8 Conclusion

In this paper, we studied the frameworks or tools available for Hadoop service detection. We introduced a system application to know about which services is running on which node. We have used Java Codes, Shell Scripts and open source or free third party tools to accomplish the job. The tool does not put significant impact on the performance of Hadoop cluster as a separate node is being used to process the network traffic.

We have used different experimental process to detect different component of the big data cluster. For future research we will use a compact single experimental process that will discover every services on the cluster. We will move forward to developing a feature-rich system that will give a clear view on each service's health.

Acknowledgment. The research is being conducted at Big Data Lab at Techno International New Town (Formerly known as Techno India College of Technology), Kolkata. We got full version of Tableau for analyzing the traffic through their Tableau Academic Programs.

References

1. Cutting, D.: The apache[TM] hadoop®, May 2019. https://hadoop.apache.org. Accessed 8 July 2019
2. Hortonworks: Apache Hadoop ecosystem and open source big data projects, May 2019. https://hortonworks.com/ecosystems. Accessed 8 July 2019
3. Hadoop, A.: Service discovery, March 2018. https://hadoop.apache.org/docs/r3.1.0/hadoop-yarn/hadoop-yarn-site/yarn-service/ServiceDiscovery.html. Accessed 10 Aug 2019
4. William Bolton, C.: Figuring out the active name node of a remote Hadoop cluster, June 2016. https://community.cloudera.com/t5/Support-Questions/Figuring-out-the-active-name-node-of-a-remote-Hadoop-cluster/m-p/174702. Accessed 17 Sep 2019
5. Aditham, S.K., Ranganathan, N.: Systems and methods for detecting attacks in big data systems, March 2019. https://patents.google.com/patent/WO201721-0005A1/en
6. Daoudhiri, K., Najat, R., Abouchabaka, J.: Attacks and countermeasures in a Hadoop cluster, August 2018
7. Glenn, W., Yu, W.: Cyber attacks on MapReduce computation time in a Hadoop cluster. In: Yu, S., Guo, S. (eds.) Big Data Concepts, Theories, and Applications, pp. 257–279. Springer, Cham (2016). https://doi.org/10.1007/978-3-319-27763-9_7
8. Huang, J., Nicol, D.M., Campbell, R.H.: Denial-of-service threat to Hadoop/YARN clusters with multi-tenancy. In: 2014 IEEE International Congress on Big Data, pp. 48–55. IEEE (2014)
9. Barik, R.K., et al.: Fog assisted cloud computing in era of big data and internet-of-things: systems, architectures, and applications. In: Mishra, B.S.P., Das, H., Dehuri, S., Jagadev, A.K. (eds.) Cloud Computing for Optimization: Foundations, Applications, and Challenges. SBD, vol. 39, pp. 367–394. Springer, Cham (2018). https://doi.org/10.1007/978-3-319-73676-1_14
10. Barik, R.K., Kandpal, M., Dubey, H., Kumar, V., Das, H.: Geocloud4GI: cloud SDI model for geographical indications information infrastructure network. In: Das, H., Barik, R.K., Dubey, H., Roy, D.S. (eds.) Cloud Computing for Geospatial Big Data Analytics. SBD, vol. 49, pp. 215–224. Springer, Cham (2019). https://doi.org/10.1007/978-3-030-03359-0_10
11. Das, H., Barik, R.K., Dubey, H., Roy, D.S.: Cloud Computing for Geospatial Big-Data Analytics: Intelligent Edge, Fog and Mist Computing, vol. 49. Springer, Cham (2018)

12. Pradhan, C., Das, H., Naik, B., Dey, N.: Handbook of Research on Information Security in Biomedical Signal Processing. IGI Global, Hershey (2018)
13. Dey, N., Das, H., Naik, B., Behera, H.: Big Data Analytics for Intelligent Healthcare Management. Academic Press, London (2019)
14. Sahoo, A.K., Mallik, S., Pradhan, C., Mishra, B.S.P., Barik, R.K., Das, H.: Intelligence-based health recommendation system using big data analytics. In: Big Data Analytics for Intelligent Healthcare Management, pp. 227–246. Elsevier (2019)
15. Gupta, B.: 10 hadoop alternatives that you should consider for big data, January 2017. https://www.analyticsindiamag.com/10-hadoop-alternatives-consider-big-data. Accessed 7 July 2019
16. Ubuntu: The leading operating system for PCs, IoT devices, servers and the cloud—ubuntu, July 2019. https://ubuntu.com. Accessed 8th July 2019
17. Sanfilippo, S.: hping3 package description, March 2019. http://www.hping.org. Accessed 11 Sep 2019
18. Wireshark: PCAPNG file format, March 2019. https://www.wireshark.org/docs/dfref/f/file-pcapng.html. Accessed 10 Sep 2019
19. Apache: Apache HBase, July 2019. https://hbase.apache.org. Accessed 8 Sep 2019
20. Wireshark: Wireshark - the world's foremost and widely-used network protocol analyzer, July 2019.https://www.wireshark.org. Accessed 10 Sep 2019
21. Tableau: Tableau, July 2019. https://www.tableau.com/. Accessed 8 Sep 2019

Classification of IRIS Recognition Based on Deep Learning Techniques

Mukta Goyal[⊠], Rajalakshmi Krishnamurthi, Aparna Varma,
and Ishita Khare

Department of Computer Science,
Jaypee Institute of Information Technology, Noida, India
{mukta.goyal,k.rajalakshmi}@jiit.ac.in,
aparnavarma123@gmail.com, khare.ishu18@gmail.com

Abstract. In this work, a man-made awareness instruct passes on an extremely profitable sort of significant making sense of how to investigate eye sickness from helpful pictures. Convolution Neural systems are significant learning computations capable of getting ready pictures and predicting the diseases. The output will be determined as either Conjunctiva and Corneal ulcer according to the decision made based on the estimated features from the image. CNNs give the best execution in model and picture affirmation issues, even outmaneuvering humans in certain aspects. An ensemble of network architecture improved prediction accuracy. An independent dataset was used to evaluate the performance of our algorithm in a population-based study. Class conjunctivitis is labeled as 0, and Corneal Ulcer is classified as 1. After extracting the features, model is classifying the image as 0 or 1. To further improve the model, this paper is used VGG-16, ResNet 152 and Alexnet to predict the disease and improve accuracy.

Keywords: Conjunctiva · Corneal ulcer · Convolution neural network · VGG · ResNet · Alexnet · Prediction · Disease

1 Introduction

Another man-made consciousness instrument conveys a very productive type of profound figuring out how to analyse eye disease from restorative pictures. Convolutional neural networks are profound learning calculations proficient at preparing pictures, yet scientists commonly need to prepare them on beyond what a million therapeutic pictures before they can test how well the calculations work. While the arrangement of illness stages is essential to understanding ailment hazard and movement, a few frameworks dependent on shading fundus photos are known. CNNs give the best execution in example/picture acknowledgment issues and even outflank people in particular. Location utilizing CNN is rough to bends, for example, change fit as a fiddle because of camera focal point, diverse lighting conditions, various postures, nearness of fractional impediments, level and vertical movements, and so forth. Notwithstanding, CNNs move invariant since a similar weight setup is utilized crosswise over space.

© Springer Nature Singapore Pte Ltd. 2020
U. Batra et al. (Eds.): REDSET 2019, CCIS 1230, pp. 342–355, 2020.
https://doi.org/10.1007/978-981-15-5830-6_29

Currently, there exists no solution for achieving the optimal accuracy on small datasets using methods based on machine learning or Deep Learning models. This paper present a robotized PC based characterization calculation. This paper examine pictures of the eye and recognize whether the eye has any malady or not. There are 2 classes to be anticipated Conjunctivitis and Corneal Ulcer. Some significant momentum issues in utilizing pictures of the eye in the malady forecast are:

- Typical convolution systems can be deceived by certain rotations. On the off chance that you didn't prepare your model for rotations of a picture it may characterize two pictures that are actually equivalent to various classes.
- CNN could be that the system searches for components being available in the picture and does not think about their relative location.
- Overfitting.

A python IDE studied about different libraries required by machine learning/deep learning models. Various data cleaning techniques have been used for cleaning the data. While playing out this undertaking authors have conquered numerous difficulties. The absolute first test was to bring the information such that images of eyes in an organized structure. This progression included the collection and organisation of images from the internet and the right use of ordinary articulations. The following work experienced the encoding target segment problem and utilizing them for the transformation into two classes. The objective of this problem is achieved using CNN techniques.

Significant Contribution of this work:

- Prediction of eye disease by just looking at the image is a well-characterized and important issue on which a few inquiries are going on to anticipate the most extreme precision.
- Normally we have seen different takes for this investigation however none of them have utilized a couple of deep learning system for order.
- This paper accomplished a great precision results while employing a number of deep models of CNN and types of CNN, additionally the profound learning models connected are commonly all around computationally costly however because of the facility of saving our deep learning models, we had the capacity to apply them on our ordinary machine.

2   Related Works

Various models of a neural network to achieve the task of classifying the diseases and the selection of the model for achieving the best accuracy. Author [1] proposed the modeling in which features are extracted hierarchically by mapping raw pixels of the input image using CNN, and further, it is classified using fully connected layers. The network parameters are intelligently tuned to obtain the highest classification performance. The deeper the network, the better it learns. It can self-learn and self-organize without any supervision. In this work, the Author [1] decided to obtain the maximum output with minimum numbers of layers by efficiently choosing the network parameters.

To perform the systematic evaluation, resizing has been done over all the input fundus images to 64 × 64 and is subjected to CNN. It has been found that to obtain optimum performance, CNN requires a maximum number of images. It is not possible to generalize the system with less number of images. Also, increasing the number of images increases the number of layers which may boost the computational time of the algorithm. Hence, the parameters of the model need to be judiciously decided to obtain the maximum performance in less time. Also, it may take more time to develop the best performing CNN model. So, to overcome this problem, the graphics processing unit (GPU) can be used.

Author [2] proposed a Deep Convolution Neural Network designed to predict saliency in the natural video for the human visual system (HVS). Author [2] used several combinations of primary (input) features such as color values and residual motion. For training of deep CNN in the two class classification problem Wooding's maps are used to select positive and negative samples. The purpose of this paper is the automatic prediction of the saliency map of normal subjects on the degraded sequence. Deep CNN requires a large amount of data for training.

Author [3] proposed an iris recognition system where the features are extracted from the pre-trained CNN model, and for the classification task, the multi-class Support Vector Machine (SVM) is used. The performance of the proposed system is investigated when extracting features directly from the segmented iris image, extracting features from the normalized iris pattern. After extraction of the features, Principal Component Analysis is used to decrease the data dimensionality and then the recognition is performed using a multi-class support vector machine.

Diagnosis of Conjunctiva and Corneal Ulcer

Intense red eye for example redness in eyes creating in 1–2 days is a typical indication of ailments of the foremost section of the eye which incorporate the conjunctiva, cornea, limbus, front and back chambers, trabecular meshwork, channel of Schlemm,

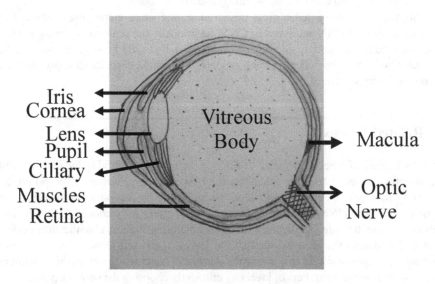

Fig. 1. Normal structure of eye

iris, focal point, zonule, and ciliary body as shown in Fig. 1. The right finding is fundamental as medications successful in one condition might be completely contraindicated in others.

Acute Mucopurulent Conjuctivitis

It is an aggravation of conjunctiva brought about by a number of microorganisms like Staphylococci, Streptococci, E. coli, N. gonorrhoeae. The clinical introduction relies upon the destructiveness and pathogenicity of the creature and the host's insusceptible reaction. Figure 2 and Fig. 3 depict the medical conditions as explained above. In beginning periods cornea, the first chamber, iris and understudy stay ordinary however, as the disease spreads it includes cornea likewise prompting kerato-conjunctivitis.

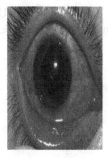

Fig. 2. Acute congestion of conjunctiva

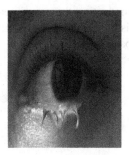

Fig. 3. Mucopurulent discharge

Corneal Ulcer

A corneal ulcer is a component of intense purulent keratitis (bacterial contamination of cornea). It is described by epithelial imperfections with invasion of the fundamental and encompassing stroma. An ulcer is because of the poison delivering living being, causing tissue passing (putrefaction) and discharge development in the corneal tissue. Purulent keratitis is almost constantly exogenous because of microscopic organisms like Pseudomonas, Staph. Aureus, Pneumococcus, N. gonorrhea, E. coli which attack the cornea from outside. If this disturbance is extreme, at that point leucocytes and polymorphs spill out from the vessels and get gathered at the base of the front chamber, where they structure the hypopyon as depicted in Fig. 4. Patients likewise whine about white spots present over the cornea as depicted in Fig. 5. The release is purulent in nature and the ulcerative spot is noticeable.

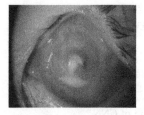

Fig. 4. Hypopyon

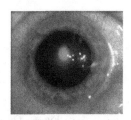

Fig. 5. Corneal ulcer

3 Modelling of the Propsoed Solution

In this proposed system two classes namely Conjunctivitis and Corneal Ulcer have been defined. Firstly this paper extracted important features using a convolutional neural network. CNN can learn relevant features from the image. An ensemble of network architecture improved prediction accuracy. The overall architecture of the proposed solution is depicted in Fig. 6 below. An independent dataset was used to evaluate the performance of our algorithm in a population-based study. Class Conjunctivitis is labeled as 0 and Corneal Ulcer is classified as 1. After extracting the features model is classifying the Image as 0 or 1. To further improve our model this paper have used VGG-16, Resnet-152 and Alexnet to predict the disease and improve accuracy.

For conducting the experiments, the computer system running Windows/Ubuntu/ Mac OS is used. Python along with dependencies namely matplotlib, scikit, nltk, keras, numpy, pandas are used.

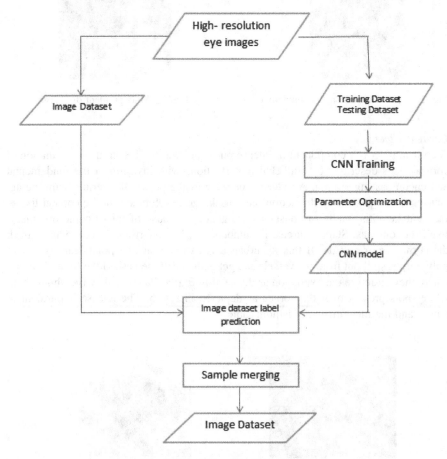

Fig. 6. Overall architecture of CNN

AIMS stands for All India Institute of Medical Science. The dataset contains eye images of patients suffering from Corneal Ulcer and conjunctivitis. We have used 100 images for training and 8 images for testing. But the Pre-processing of the dataset in our experiment is done after removing resizing and normalizing the images. Figure 7 below depicts the use case diagram of the proposed solution.

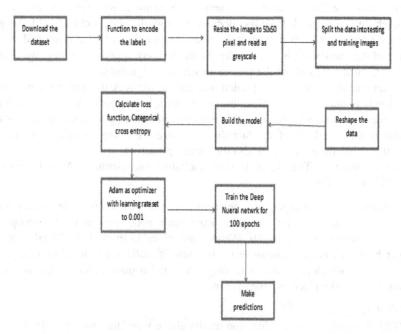

Fig. 7. Use case diagram

4   Algorithms

While performing this task we overcame many challenges [4, 5]. The very first challenge was the requirement of a huge dataset for training purposes. It is not easy for us to find the patient's eye images with specified diseases. The second challenge encountered was to recognize those parameters whose values need to be decided before training. The third challenge was the time required for training the deep learning models. And the last challenge that we had faced was a small variation in the input data leads to an extreme change in the result. Overfitting was also a serious issue while training the model.

Convolutional Neural Network for Iris Detection
There are four layers present in CNN namely Convolution, Max Pooling, Flattening, and Full Connection.

Convolution: It is done to separate the highlights from a lattice. There are many element networks (or channels) which are connected to the first picture framework to remove significant highlights from that lattice. It likewise diminishes the extent of unique picture network in this manner by keeping just the significant highlights from the picture grid. A wide range of highlight networks (or channels) is connected.

Max Pooling: Suppose a single picture is looked from changed bearings. At that point Neural systems anticipate every one of them right by utilizing a property called spatial invariance. This entire thought goes under pooling. In our undertaking we will utilize Max Pooling, for example, taking the most extreme incentive from the chose sub-network from the element framework. Max is chosen with the goal that we are as yet ready to protect the greatest highlights from the given grid and the size of the framework is additionally diminished. By applying pooling, we dispose of 75% of the data about the picture which isn't significant.

Flattening: After getting the pooled highlight framework by applying convolution and max pooling, we go for leveling the network for example changing over it into a 1-measurement, with the goal that each picture comes as one line in our dataset. This is done in light of the fact that later, we are going to include it into our Artificial Neural Network (ANN) for further preparing.

Full Connection: This layer is only including the Artificial Neural Networks (ANN) to our CNN.

In ANN we attempt to recreate the cerebrum. Along these lines, the primary test is to reproduce a neuron. The most significant thing about neuron is, they cooperate. In ANN, a neuron is only a hub. Weights are given to every hub. Weights are the manner by which neural systems learn. By them it realizes which values or signal is significant and which isn't or to what degree a signal is passed along. Now, inside the neuron 2 steps take place as given below.

STEP 1. $\sum(w_i x_i)$

STEP 2. Apply activation function on the above weighted sum, $\Phi(\sum(w_i x_i))$

Based on these steps, neuron passes this signal or value to the next neuron and so on. Activation function used is **Rectifier function**.

VGG-16: The system is described by the way that it utilizes a straightforward 3×3 convolutional layer stack, over one another in expanding profundity. The number '16' speaks to the number of weight layers of the Neural Network [6, 7]. The Keras model of the system was utilized by the VGG Team in the ILSVRC 2014 challenge, and around then, a 16 – layered neural system was viewed as profound. Amid preparing, the contribution to the CNN is a fixed size 224×224 RGB picture.

In the VGG 16 Model, the convolution walk was fixed to 1 pixel; the spatial cushioning of convolutional layer input was with the end goal that the spatial goals were safeguarded after convolution, for example the cushioning was 1 pixel for 3×3 conv. layers. Spatial pooling was done by five max-pooling layers, which pursue a portion of the convolutional layers, where not all the convolutional layers were trailed by max-pooling. Max-pooling was performed over a 2×2 pixel window, with a walk of 2. A pile of convolutional layers was trailed by three Fully-Connected (FC) layers: the initial two had 4096 channels each, the third performed 1000-way ILSVRC arrangement and in this manner contained 1000 channels (one for each class). The last layer was the delicate max layer (Fig. 8).

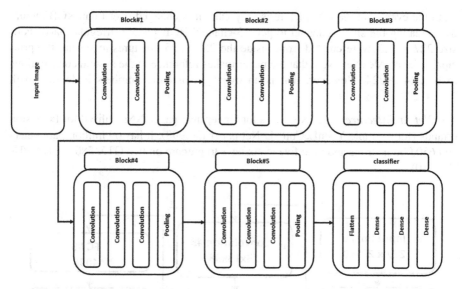

Fig. 8. VGG-16 architecture

AlexNet: In 2012, AlexNet altogether outflanked all the earlier contenders and won the test by decreasing the best 5 mistakes from 26% to 15.3%. The second spot top-5 mistake rate, which was not a CNN variety, was around 26.2%. It takes care of the issue of picture arrangement where the information is a picture of one of 1000 unique classes (for example felines, hounds and so forth.) and the yield is a vector of 1000 numbers. The ith component of the yield vector is deciphered as the likelihood that the info picture has a place with the ith class. Subsequently, the entirety of all components of the yield vector is 1. The contribution to AlexNet is an RGB picture of size 256 × 256. This implies all pictures in the preparation set and all test pictures should be of size 256 × 256. In the event that the info picture isn't 256 × 256, it should be changed over to 256 × 256 before utilizing it for preparing the system. To accomplish this, the littler measurement is resized to 256 and afterward the following picture is edited to acquire a 256 × 256 picture. Figure 9 underneath demonstrates a precedent [8, 9].

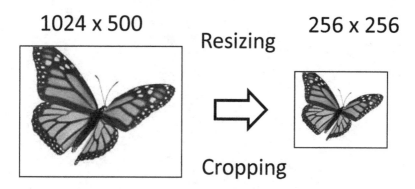

Fig. 9. Basic concept of Alex Net

In the event that the info picture is grayscale, it is changed over to an RGB picture by recreating the single channel to get a 3-channel RGB picture. Irregular harvests of size 227 × 227 were created from inside the 256 × 256 pictures to sustain the principal layer of AlexNet. Note that the paper makes reference to the system contributions to be 224 × 224. However, that is an oversight and the numbers bode well with 227 × 227.

AlexNet Architecture: AlexNet was a lot bigger than past CNNs utilized for PC vision errands (for example YannLeCun'sLeNet paper in 1998). It has 60 million parameters and 650,000 neurons and took five to six days to prepare on two GTX 580 3 GB GPUs (Fig. 10).

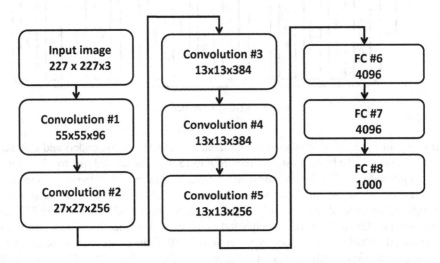

Fig. 10. AlexNet architecture

ResNet: Residual Networks (ResNet) is a great neural system utilized as a spine for some PC vision undertakings. This model was the champ of ImageNet challenge in 2015. The principal leap forward with ResNet was it enabled us to prepare amazingly profound neural systems with 150+ layers effectively.

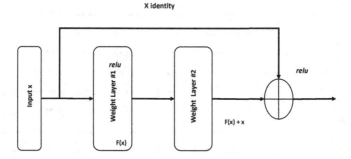

Fig. 11. ResNet architecture

For ResNet, there are 3 sorts of skip/alternate way associations when the information measurements are littler than the yield measurements.

- Shortcut performs personality mapping, with additional zero cushioning for
- The working alternate route is utilized for expanding measurements just, different easy routes are character. Additional parameters are required.
- All alternate routes are projections. Additional parameters are more than that of

The remaining module introduces skip or alternate route associations (existing before in different structures in writing). This makes it simple for system layers to speak to the character mapping. It is observed, through experiments that, it requires to skip somewhere around two layers. The Fig. 11 depicts the architecture of ResNet.

Limitation of the proposed solution are identified as computation cost is high. The biggest limitation of the deep learning modal is that it requires large amount of data for giving good result. Scalability aspects of deep learning models.

5 Results and Discussions

Following are the results of all the four models used in this work. Figure 12, 13, 14 and 15 shows the CNN result on different EPOCHs.

```
Epoch 25/50
20/20 [==============================] - 0s 20ms/step - loss: 8.0590 - acc: 0.5000
Epoch 26/50
20/20 [==============================] - 0s 17ms/step - loss: 8.0590 - acc: 0.5000
Epoch 27/50
20/20 [==============================] - 0s 18ms/step - loss: 8.0590 - acc: 0.5000
Epoch 28/50
20/20 [==============================] - 0s 17ms/step - loss: 8.0590 - acc: 0.5000
Epoch 29/50
20/20 [==============================] - 0s 18ms/step - loss: 8.0590 - acc: 0.5000
Epoch 30/50
20/20 [==============================] - 0s 18ms/step - loss: 8.0590 - acc: 0.5000
Epoch 31/50
20/20 [==============================] - 0s 17ms/step - loss: 8.0590 - acc: 0.5000
Epoch 32/50
20/20 [==============================] - 0s 17ms/step - loss: 8.0590 - acc: 0.5000
Epoch 33/50
20/20 [==============================] - 0s 17ms/step - loss: 8.0590 - acc: 0.5000
Epoch 34/50
20/20 [==============================] - 0s 16ms/step - loss: 8.0590 - acc: 0.5000
Epoch 35/50
20/20 [==============================] - 0s 17ms/step - loss: 8.0590 - acc: 0.5000
Epoch 36/50
20/20 [==============================] - 0s 16ms/step - loss: 8.0590 - acc: 0.5000
Epoch 37/50
20/20 [==============================] - 0s 17ms/step - loss: 8.0590 - acc: 0.5000
Epoch 38/50
20/20 [==============================] - 0s 17ms/step - loss: 8.0590 - acc: 0.5000
Epoch 39/50
20/20 [==============================] - 0s 16ms/step - loss: 8.0590 - acc: 0.5000
Epoch 40/50
20/20 [==============================] - 0s 17ms/step - loss: 8.0590 - acc: 0.5000
Epoch 41/50
20/20 [==============================] - 0s 17ms/step - loss: 8.0590 - acc: 0.5000
Epoch 42/50
20/20 [==============================] - 0s 17ms/step - loss: 8.0590 - acc: 0.5000
Epoch 43/50
20/20 [==============================] - 0s 16ms/step - loss: 8.0590 - acc: 0.5000
Epoch 44/50
20/20 [==============================] - 0s 16ms/step - loss: 8.0590 - acc: 0.5000
Epoch 45/50
20/20 [==============================] - 0s 17ms/step - loss: 8.0590 - acc: 0.5000
Epoch 46/50
20/20 [==============================] - 0s 17ms/step - loss: 8.0590 - acc: 0.5000
Epoch 47/50
20/20 [==============================] - 0s 16ms/step - loss: 8.0590 - acc: 0.5000
Epoch 48/50
20/20 [==============================] - 0s 16ms/step - loss: 8.0590 - acc: 0.5000
Epoch 49/50
```

Fig. 12. Accuracy results for CNN model

```
Epoch 87/100
20/20 [==============================] - 0s 224us/step - loss: 0.4279 - acc: 0.9000
Epoch 88/100
20/20 [==============================] - 0s 304us/step - loss: 0.4221 - acc: 0.9000
Epoch 89/100
20/20 [==============================] - 0s 262us/step - loss: 0.4165 - acc: 0.9000
Epoch 90/100
20/20 [==============================] - 0s 302us/step - loss: 0.4105 - acc: 0.9000
Epoch 91/100
20/20 [==============================] - 0s 256us/step - loss: 0.4046 - acc: 0.9000
Epoch 92/100
20/20 [==============================] - 0s 303us/step - loss: 0.3994 - acc: 0.9000
Epoch 93/100
20/20 [==============================] - 0s 249us/step - loss: 0.3936 - acc: 0.9000
Epoch 94/100
20/20 [==============================] - 0s 228us/step - loss: 0.3880 - acc: 0.9000
Epoch 95/100
20/20 [==============================] - 0s 314us/step - loss: 0.3823 - acc: 0.9000
Epoch 96/100
20/20 [==============================] - 0s 271us/step - loss: 0.3772 - acc: 0.9000
Epoch 97/100
20/20 [==============================] - 0s 335us/step - loss: 0.3718 - acc: 0.9000
Epoch 98/100
20/20 [==============================] - 0s 365us/step - loss: 0.3665 - acc: 0.9000
Epoch 99/100
20/20 [==============================] - 0s 269us/step - loss: 0.3615 - acc: 0.9000
Epoch 100/100
20/20 [==============================] - 0s 311us/step - loss: 0.3567 - acc: 0.9000
```

Fig. 13. Accuracy results for VGG-16

```
Epoch 87/100
20/20 [==============================] - 0s 0us/step - loss: -0.1342 - acc: 0.6500
Epoch 88/100
20/20 [==============================] - 0s 781us/step - loss: -0.1564 - acc: 0.6500
Epoch 89/100
20/20 [==============================] - 0s 0us/step - loss: -0.1850 - acc: 0.6500
Epoch 90/100
20/20 [==============================] - 0s 0us/step - loss: -0.2082 - acc: 0.6500
Epoch 91/100
20/20 [==============================] - 0s 781us/step - loss: -0.2373 - acc: 0.6500
Epoch 92/100
20/20 [==============================] - 0s 781us/step - loss: -0.2638 - acc: 0.6500
Epoch 93/100
20/20 [==============================] - 0s 0us/step - loss: -0.2917 - acc: 0.6500
Epoch 94/100
20/20 [==============================] - 0s 0us/step - loss: -0.3166 - acc: 0.6500
Epoch 95/100
20/20 [==============================] - 0s 781us/step - loss: -0.3455 - acc: 0.6500
Epoch 96/100
20/20 [==============================] - 0s 0us/step - loss: -0.3732 - acc: 0.6500
Epoch 97/100
20/20 [==============================] - 0s 0us/step - loss: -0.4009 - acc: 0.6500
Epoch 98/100
20/20 [==============================] - 0s 781us/step - loss: -0.4263 - acc: 0.6500
Epoch 99/100
20/20 [==============================] - 0s 0us/step - loss: -0.4577 - acc: 0.6500
Epoch 100/100
20/20 [==============================] - 0s 781us/step - loss: -0.4847 - acc: 0.6500
```

Fig. 14. Accuracy results for Resnet

```
Epoch 87/100
20/20 [==============================] - 0s 243us/step - loss: 0.6309 - acc: 0.7500
Epoch 88/100
20/20 [==============================] - 0s 238us/step - loss: 0.6299 - acc: 0.7500
Epoch 89/100
20/20 [==============================] - 0s 275us/step - loss: 0.6283 - acc: 0.7500
Epoch 90/100
20/20 [==============================] - 0s 275us/step - loss: 0.6280 - acc: 0.8000
Epoch 91/100
20/20 [==============================] - 0s 237us/step - loss: 0.6251 - acc: 0.7500
Epoch 92/100
20/20 [==============================] - 0s 261us/step - loss: 0.6328 - acc: 0.7500
Epoch 93/100
20/20 [==============================] - 0s 259us/step - loss: 0.6271 - acc: 0.7500
Epoch 94/100
20/20 [==============================] - 0s 288us/step - loss: 0.6211 - acc: 0.8000
Epoch 95/100
20/20 [==============================] - 0s 241us/step - loss: 0.6190 - acc: 0.7500
Epoch 96/100
20/20 [==============================] - 0s 325us/step - loss: 0.6178 - acc: 0.8000
Epoch 97/100
20/20 [==============================] - 0s 256us/step - loss: 0.6192 - acc: 0.7500
Epoch 98/100
20/20 [==============================] - 0s 256us/step - loss: 0.6140 - acc: 0.7500
Epoch 99/100
20/20 [==============================] - 0s 299us/step - loss: 0.6158 - acc: 0.7500
Epoch 100/100
20/20 [==============================] - 0s 296us/step - loss: 0.6267 - acc: 0.8000
```

Fig. 15. Accuracy result for AlexNet

It seem that VGG-16 has best accuracy on different Epoch (Tables 1, 2, 3 and 4).

Table 1. Confusion matrix for CNN model

	Predicted: Yes	Predicted: No
Actual: Yes	2	2
Actual: No	0	4

Table 2. Confusion matrix for VGG-16 model

	Predicted: Yes	Predicted: No
Actual: Yes	3	1
Actual: No	1	3

Table 3. Confusion matrix for Resnet model

	Predicted: Yes	Predicted: No
Actual: Yes	0	4
Actual: No	1	3

Table 4. Confusion matrix for Alexnet model

	Predicted: Yes	Predicted: No
Actual: Yes	1	3
Actual: No	2	2

6   Conclusion

This work is about CNN model to detect eye disease by using deep learning techniques. A hundred images have been used to train our various models like CNN, VGG-16, RESNET and ALEX-NET.CNN perform best in term of accuracy. Deep learning models learn by themselves. Stack of the layer is added to train our model to improve the performance of the system. But there are several drawbacks, also like a minute change in learning rate can affect the result drastically. Also, the Network could function spurious if there is no specification in the neural network. It gave imprecise results even when visual dissimilarity is very less. Future scope is to further bring our accuracy above 80% for all the deep learning models used in our work and feature extraction techniques.

References

1. Sasha, T., Diogo, A., Kevin, L.: ResNet in ResNet: generalizing residual architecture. IEEE Trans. Knowl. Data Eng. **30**(1), 185–197 (2018)
2. Shawn, H., Sourish, C., Daniel, P.W.E.: CNN architecture for large scale audio classification. IEEE Access **5**, 10805–10816 (2017)
3. Yunchao, W., Wei, X., Min, L.: A flexible framework for multi-label image classification. IEEE Access **6**, 13949–13957 (2018)
4. Souad, C., Francosis, T., Jenny, P., Chokri, B.A.: Prediction of visual attention with deep CNN for studies of neurodegenerative disease. IEEE Access **7**, 347–357 (2019)
5. Maram, A., Lamiaa, E.: Convolutional neural network based feature extraction for IRIS recognition. In: 2016 3rd International Conference on Systems and Informatics (ICSAI), Shanghai, pp. 062–1066 (2016)
6. Ryan, N., Keiron, T.O.: An introduction to convolutional neural network. In: 2018 International Joint Conference on Neural Networks (IJCNN), Rio de Janeiro, pp. 1–7 (2018)
7. Geetha, M., Neena, A.: An review on deep convolutional neural network. In: 2017 Sensors Networks Smart and Emerging Technologies (SENSET), Beirut, pp. 1–4 (2017)
8. Guo, T., Dong, J., Li, H., Gao, Y.: Simple convolutional network on image classification. In: 2017 IEEE International Conference on Computational Science and Engineering (CSE) and IEEE International Conference on Embedded and Ubiquitous Computing (EUC), Guangzhou, pp. 776–779 (2017)
9. Yan, K., Huang, S., Song, Y., Liu, W., Fan, N.: Face recognition based on convolutional neural network. In: 2017 IEEE International Conference on Data Science and Advanced Analytics (DSAA), Tokyo, pp. 193–202 (2017)

A Decision Tree Based Supervised Program Interpretation Technique for Gurmukhi Language

Himdweep Walia[1(⊠)], Ajay Rana[1], and Vineet Kansal[2]

[1] Amity University, Noida, India
himdweep@yahoo.com, ajayphdmba@gmail.com
[2] IET, Lucknow, India
vineetkansal@yahoo.com

Abstract. Deciphering the right context of the given word is one of the main challenges in Natural Language Processing. The study of Word Sense Disambiguation helps in deciphering the right context of the given word in use. Decision Tree is a methodology discussed under the supervised techniques used in WSD. Gurmukhi is one of the regional languages of India and much of the work done in this language is limited to knowledge-based mechanisms. The implementation of decision tree to correctly decipher the ambiguous word is new to this language and it has shown promising results with an average F-measure of 73.1%. These results will further help in Gurmukhi Word Sense Disambiguation.

Keywords: Word Sense Disambiguation · Supervised approach · Decision tree · Punjabi language · Sense-tagged corpora

1 Introduction

Word Sense Disambiguation (WSD) is given the same status in Natural Language Processing (NLP) like NP-hard problems in algorithms. WSD is the process of finding the correct sense of the word (i.e. meaning) which is being referred to in the given sentence, out of the different meanings that the word may have. By working out this problem, we will be able to work out the solution with respect to other domains of natural language processing like discourse, coherence, inference, and like wise. The humans developed the language and thus invented the many different meanings of the same word and even know in which context the given word is being used. Implementing the same wisdom in a computer is all together a tedious task, primarily because we still need to figure out how to code the entire human brain.

Consider for example, the given sentence, "The man is standing near the bank." The word "bank" is ambiguous in nature as it could mean river or financial institution. Similarly consider the word "ਉੱਤਰ", in Gurmukhi (popularly known as Punjabi). The given word can be used in four different contexts, for example, "direction", "answer", "climbing down" and "dislocation of bone". It is essential that the computer is able to decipher the correct meaning of the given ambiguous word as this alone will make the language usage by the computer intelligent. If the computer deduces wrong context of the given word in the given instance then the outcome will not be satisfactory.

© Springer Nature Singapore Pte Ltd. 2020
U. Batra et al. (Eds.): REDSET 2019, CCIS 1230, pp. 356–365, 2020.
https://doi.org/10.1007/978-981-15-5830-6_30

Machine learning comprises of various supervised and unsupervised learning methodologies which can be used to decipher the correct context of the ambiguous word. Both the methodologies have their own sets of merits and demerits and the research has yielded that supervised algorithms are more popular primarily because they are comparatively easier to implement. One of the techniques which come under Supervised is the Decision Tree Algorithm. The various components of the decision tree are root node, which is the starting point. Following this we have the internal nodes which represent the attribute value which is the outcome of application of a rule or a test on the existing node this rule or test is denoted by the branch, connecting two nodes and finally we have the leaf which denotes the result, also called class label.

Gurmukhi (or Punjabi) language is the 11th most-spoken language of the world and is one of the regional languages of India which is primarily spoken in the state of Punjab. Most of the work done in this domain for this language is mainly constricted to Knowledge-based techniques. Disambiguation of ambiguous words automatically has been a goal in computational linguistics field and there has always been state-of-art accuracy as reported by the researchers in their research papers. This paper aims to explore research on WSD for Gurmukhi language using one of the supervised techniques – Decision Tree.

2 Literature Survey

WSD has been a major research area primarily because it is imperative to understand the context in which the given word is being used in order to comprehend the information. This ability which comes naturally to humans has to be coded for the machines. In this endeavor language like English, French, German, Japanese and Chinese have had an extensive work done on them in the sphere of WSD [1, 2]. The Indian Regional Languages like Hindi, Malayalam, Tamil, Bangla, Punjabi, Urdu, etc. are mostly spoken by people in South East Asia. The majority of work done in these languages is restricted to translation, preparation of dictionary and knowledge-based techniques [3, 4]. For this paper, we are working on Gurmukhi, commonly known as Punjabi which is among the 10 most spoken language of the world. The major amount of work in this language has been limited to machine translation and building of machine readable dictionaries due to lack of sense-tagged corpora [5, 6]. For this paper, we have studied the work done in Hindi Language as Gurmukhi drives closely to this Language [10–14]. The Decision Tree algorithm has been implemented in English Language [15], which has been read for this paper. Among the Indian Regional Languages, this algorithm has been used for Assamese Language [16] and Manipuri Language [17] and those papers have been used as base papers for this study.

In the paper by Pedersen [15], the author showcases that on combining a feature set of bigrams with decision tree algorithm, fair accuracy is achieved in WSD. The approach followed starts with removing capital letters and punctuation marks from the training and test data. The paper works with bigram i.e. the given ambiguous word along with a surrounding word. This word could be either a pre or post of the ambiguous word. One more pre-condition is met which states that in the training set the bigram should have occurred more than 4 times. The test data and the training data are converted into vectors. This (training data) forms the input to the decision tree algorithm. Three classifiers were used in the experimentation – majority classifier, decision stump and Naïve Bayesian classifier, which were used to decipher the correct meaning context of the given ambiguous word. In this paper, grained scoring method has been applied where a word is counted correctly disambiguated only when the assigned sense exactly matches the true sense.

In their paper, Sarmah et al. [16], have proposed a supervised WSD system based on decision tree. The paper uses J48 which is Java implementation of C4.5 decision tree algorithm for WSD. In a decision tree we require a splitting point where the tree branches into a new node and for this purpose this paper has implemented the information gain ratio. In order to find the success rate of WSD, two evaluation processes have been implemented. The techniques of hold-out evaluation is used which helps in diving the given data into the training data and test data such that the given class is present in both the sub data sets. The other technique that has been implemented is the k-fold cross validation primarily to improve the performance.

In their paper, Singh, et al. [17] has proposed architecture for Manipuri Language. The Manipuri word sense disambiguation system contains five steps. The first is preprocessing, second is feature selection and generation, and next is training, then testing and finally performance evaluation. The given data set is processed and segregated into training and test data. In this paper, 6 features are taken to create a standard feature which includes the ambiguous word, then the normalized position of the given word, then previous word, then previous-to-previous word, then next word and lastly next-to-next word. A 5-g window is formed using the pair of the focus word and its context words which forms the context information. A focus word, based on the context may have different senses. Hence, in order to disambiguate the sense of the focused word, the contextual information is very much necessary and helps in predicting the correct one.

3   Decision Tree Method (DTM)

A decision tree is a classifier that recursively partition over the data space. Basically, it is composed of a root node, branches, internal nodes and leaf nodes. Each internal node is the decision node representing test on an attribute or a set of attributes and each branch denotes a value of the input attributes. The leaf node denotes the class label i.e. Output Value. Path searching from the root node to the leaf node forms a classification rule. Figure 1 below gives a description of a decision tree.

A decision tree is a graphical representation rather than tabular. It is a flowchart without loops and it takes comparatively more memory space. It shows the order of evaluation of the conditions. We can analyze it as an unordered set of rules and following the terminology of tree, the leaf represents a single rule and the condition is represented as the conjunction of all edges starting from the root to the given leaf. The rules are framed keeping in mind that they do not overlap each other which simply imply that any instance that we are taking covers only single rule and this constraint makes classification easier.

In the terms of WSD, the root node represents the ambiguous word and the subsequent node represent the surrounding words. the number of nodes added to the path represent the number of surrounding words added to decipher the meaning of the given ambiguous word.

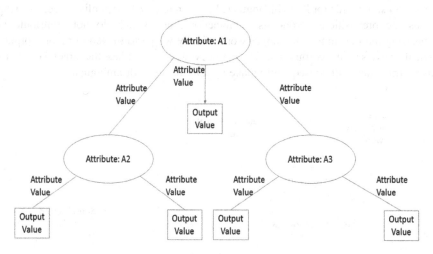

Fig. 1. Decision tree

3.1 Principle of Building a Decision Tree

Given a set of training sample with their sense category, we need to apply a mathematical function to get the best splitting attribute. Determining the best splitting attribute, the remaining training sample is partitioned into several parts. A recursive procedure is followed in each partition to form a decision tree. A recursive partitioning stops if all the tuples belongs to the same class label, or if there are no remaining attributes on which the tuples may be distributed, then majority voting is applied else if there are no tuples for a branch a leaf is created with the majority class in the sample. The edge denotes the outcome value of each test attribute node. Each branch forms a classification rule which is used to categorize test instances. The criteria used for choosing splitting attribute in our algorithm are Information Gain Ratio. This ratio helps in reducing the bias towards a multi-valued attribute.

3.2 Methodology

The approach flowchart is shown in Fig. 2. The modules proposed are systematically described step-by-step below. Starting from collection of raw data to preparing sense tagged corpus, methodology is described.

Raw Data. A total of 20 articles (with variable length) from the Punjabi Corpora [8], were sense-tagged, manually, by identifying 100 ambiguous Punjabi words.

Pre-processing. In pre-processing stage, first we remove the noisy data from the corpus. By noisy we mean, spelling mistakes, blanks, punctuation marks and unidentified symbols. After this we remove the stop words. In the study conducted by Kaur et al. [9], a list of 184 stop words for Punjabi language has been released for public usage. The stop words are prepositions, pronouns, conjunctions, etc. which do not contribute in expressing the meaning of the target word. Finally we perform stemming or morphological analysis on the corpus. This is the process where we reduce the target word to its base form which will consequently make it easier for us to disambiguate.

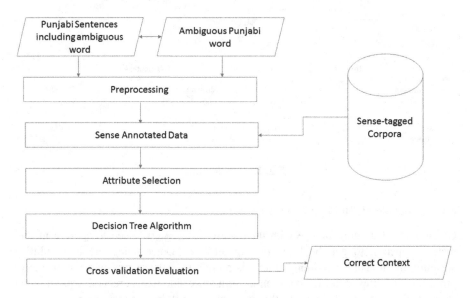

Fig. 2. Decision tree method flowchart

Sense Annotated Data. The Indo WordNet, developed by the Center for Indian Language Technology, IIT Bombay, has a repository of words of different Indian languages like Hindi, Assamese, Bengali, Gujrati, Punjabi, Tamil, Telugu, etc. [7]. The Punjabi WordNet has 23255 nouns, 2836 verbs, 5830 adjectives and 443 adverbs. Out of this 100 ambiguous words were taken from the WordNet. The Punjabi Corpora obtained contains more than 5000 ambiguous words. This corpus was then sense-tagged with 100 ambiguous words for our study.

Attribute Selection. This work considers local lexical features as clues to disambiguate the ambiguous words. These features appear on the left and right of the ambiguous word. We assign numerical values to these features (range: -2 to $+2$): ambiguous word: $\{0\}$, previous word: $\{-1\}$, previous-to-previous word: $\{-2\}$, next word: $\{+1\}$, and, next-to-next word: $\{+2\}$.

With these selected features, a 5-gram window is created using only the positional features. Based on the fact that almost all the languages have a similar syntactic and semantic structure, we rely on this positional evidence to find the correct sense of the ambiguous word.

Decision Tree Method (DTM). Machine Learning involves a classifier that learns from some sense-tagged data. The features are fed to the classifier and the algorithm identifies pattern and infer predictions from them. Decision tree is one of the popular machine learning algorithms. The reason being that a decision tree subliminally performs variable screening or feature selection. Each feature selected during the search process is represented by a node in the learned decision tree. Each node represents a choice point between a numbers of different possible values for a feature. Learning continues until all the training examples are accounted for by the decision tree. In general, such a tree will be overly specific to the training data and not generalize well to new examples. Therefore learning is followed by a pruning step where some nodes are eliminated or reorganized to produce a tree that can generalize to new circumstances. Test instances are disambiguated by finding a path through the learned decision tree from the root to a leaf node that corresponds with the observed features. An instance of an ambiguous word is disambiguated by passing it through a series of tests, where each test asks if a particular bigram occurs in the available window of context.

Cross Validation Evaluation. In this step, we partition the entire data set into 'k' subsets. Then from these subsets, one is taken as the test set and the remaining are used as the training sets. This process is repeated k times and the average error rate is calculated. The advantage of this method is that every set is used as the training as well as testing set. We have performed the k-fold cross validation evaluation on 10 Gurmukhi (Punjabi) ambiguous words with their various sense occurrences in different context.

4 Observation and Interpretation

The cross validation evaluation procedure is performed and the result is verified by using the metrics – precision, recall and f-measure. These metrics are helpful in evaluating the predictions that the model made as the results that we get can be the ones that we predicted or the ones that were not predicted. Based on this we can categorize the outputs as:

True Positive (T). They represent the case when the actual meaning of the word is same as the predicted meaning of the word.

True Negative (N). They represent the case when the word is not annotated and its meaning is also not predicted.

False Positive (t). They represent the case when the word is not annotated but its correct meaning is predicted.

False Negative (f). They represent the case when the actual meaning of the word does not match the predicted meaning.

Table 1 shows the eventuality counter of how we can segregate the data with respect to the actual meaning and predicted meaning of the given ambiguous word.

Table 1. Eventuality counter

Actual meaning	Predicted meaning		
		Correct	Not correct
	Correct	T	f
	Not correct	t	F

Precision. Precision is defined as the ratio of correctly predicted positive meaning to the total predicted positive meanings.

$$\text{Precision} = T/(T+t) \tag{1}$$

Recall. Recall is defined as the ratio of the correctly predicted positive meaning to all the meanings annotated.

$$\text{Recall} = T/(T+f) \tag{2}$$

F-measure. F-measure is defined as the weighted average of Precision and Recall.

$$F - \text{measure} = 2 \times (\text{Precision} \times \text{Recall}/(\text{Precision} + \text{Recall})) \tag{3}$$

The testing was done with 10 ambiguous words, each having 3 or 4 different contexts in which they can be used. The precision, recall and f-measure of each ambiguous word are listed as percentage in Table 2.

Table 2. Result analysis

Ambiguous Words	Context	Precision (in %)	Recall (in %)	F-measure (in %)
ਉੱਤਰ	4	76.4	75.8	75.5
ਸੰਗ	3	72.4	72.2	72
ਸਹੀ	3	69.8	68.8	68
ਹਾਰ	4	72.4	70.8	71
ਕੱਚਾ	3	76.2	76	76
ਘੱਟ	3	53.6	52.4	53.5
ਚੱਕ	4	72.6	71.8	71.5
ਜੋੜ	4	76.2	75.5	75.5
ਵਾਰ	4	90.1	88.8	89
ਵਿਚ	3	83.4	83.4	83

The above table is shown in graphical representation (Fig. 3) to show implication of using a decision tree to decipher the meaning of an ambiguous word. The precision represents the percentage of correct meaning deciphered whereas recall represents the percentage of sensitivity as it represents all meaning(s) of the given ambiguous word, whether correct or not correct. The result shows that decision tree gives a good disambiguation percentage.

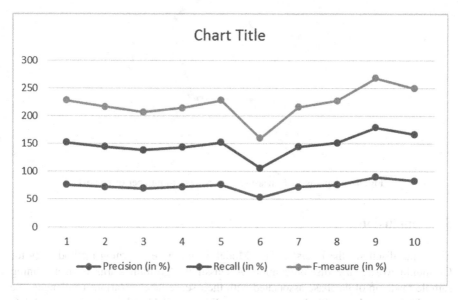

Fig. 3. Graphical representation of precision, recall and F-measure

On further analysis of the results shown, it was seen that the ambiguous word having more different contexts gave a better predicted value. The graph (Fig. 4) shows the mapping of F- measure with respect to the number of context i.e. different meanings of the given ambiguous word. The sample of 10 (ten) Gurmukhi words that we took had 5 (five) words with 3 (three) different contexts and 5 (five) with 4 (four) different contexts. The graph clearly displays that the ambiguous words having more contexts have a better F-measure.

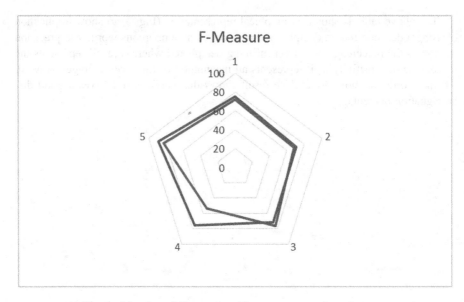

Fig. 4. Mapping of F-measure with respect to number of context

5 Conclusion

The paper discusses the Decision Tree Model, a supervised learning methodology for Gurmukhi word sense disambiguation. A classifier algorithm learns from a training sample made up of database associated with their sense labels. Various challenges like sense-inventory along with their senses were discovered. Also the sense-annotated data as a training sample was manually prepared. Cross validation evaluation was performed and Precision, Recall and F-measure were used as the metrics for the proposed WSD work. Gurmukhi is a less computational aware language and WSD task using a supervised approach – decision tree with cross validation evaluation is the first initiative towards Gurmukhi Language. This will provide a helpful contribution to Natural Language Processing.

Acknowledgments. The author expresses gratitude towards the guides for helping and directing this research. The author acknowledges Amity University Uttar Pradesh, Noida where the author is registered as scholar for providing with extensive online and off-line resources for research.

References

1. Navigli, R.: Word sense disambiguation: a survey. ACM Comput. Surv. **41**(2), 1–69 (2009). Article 10
2. Kumar, R., Khanna, R., Goyal, V.: A review of literature on word sense disambiguation. Int. J. Eng. Sci. **6**, 224–230 (2012)
3. Bansal, M.: Word sense disambiguation: literature survey for Indian languages. Int. J. Adv. Res. Comput. Sci. Softw. Eng. **5**(12), 605–607 (2015)

4. Walia, H., Rana, A., Kansal, V.: A study on different word sense disambiguation approaches and their application on Indian regional languages. In: Proceedings of International Conference on Technology and Trust, pp. 28–29 (2017)
5. Kumar, R., Khanna, R.: Natural language engineering: the study of word sense disambiguation in Punjabi. Int. J. Eng. Sci. 230–238 (2011)
6. Walia, H., Rana, A., Kansal, V.: Different techniques implemented in Gurumukhi word sense disambiguation. Int. J. Adv. Technol. Eng. Sci. 5(6), 40–46 (2017)
7. Punjabi WordNet. http://tdil-dc.in/indowordnet/index.jsp
8. Punjabi Corpora. Obtained from Evaluations and Language Resources Distribution Agency. Paris France
9. Kaur, J., Saini, J.R.: Punjabi Stop Words: A Gurmukhi, Shahmukhi and Roman scripted chronical. In: Proceedings of the ACM Symposium on Women in Research, pp. 32–37 (2016)
10. Singh, S., Siddiqui, T.J.: Role of Karaka relations in Hindi word sense disambiguation. J. Inf. Technol. Res. 8(3), 21–42 (2015)
11. Singh, S., Siddiqui, T. J.: Role of semantic relations in Hindi word sense disambiguation. In: Proceedings of the International Conference on Information and Communication Technologies, vol. 46, pp. 240–248. Elsevier Procedia Computer Science (2015)
12. Singh, S., Singh, V.K., Siddiqui, T.J.: Hindi word sense disambiguation using semantic relatedness measure. In: Ramanna, S., Lingras, P., Sombattheera, C., Krishna, A. (eds.) MIWAI 2013. LNCS (LNAI), vol. 8271, pp. 247–256. Springer, Heidelberg (2013). https://doi.org/10.1007/978-3-642-44949-9_23
13. Singh, S., Siddiqui, T.J.: Utilizing corpus statistics for Hindi word sense disambiguation. Int. Arab J. Inf. Technol. 12(6A), 755–763 (2015)
14. Singh, S., Siddiqui, T. J.: Evaluating effect of context window size, stemming and stop word removal on Hindi word sense disambiguation. In: Proceedings of the International Conference on Information Retrieval & Knowledge Management, pp. 1–5. IEEE Xplorer (2012)
15. Pederson, T.: A Decision Tree of Bigrams is an accurate predictor of word Sense. In: Proceedings of the Second Meeting of the North American Chapter of the Association for Computational Linguistics on Language Technologies (2001)
16. Sarmah, J., Sarma, S.S.: Decision tree based supervised word sense disambiguation for Assamese. Int. J. Comput. Appl. 141(1), 42–48 (2016)
17. Singh, Rl, Ghosh, K., Nongmeikapam, K., Bandyopadhyay, S.: A decision tree based word sense disambiguation system in Manipuri language. Adv. Comput. Int. J. 5(4), 17 (2014)

Importance of Web Analytics for the Success of a Startup Business

Bhavook Chitkara(✉) and Syed Mohd Jamal Mahmood

GD Goenka University, Gurgaon, India
bhavook.chitkara@gdgu.org,
smjamalmahmood1208@gmail.com

Abstract. Businesses today are discovering the significance of an online presence. However, only a handful of them, know the importance of identifying what users are doing on their blog or business website. Here Web Analytics plays a critical role. Web Analytics, also known as Web data analytics, help boost website traffic & provide the website visitors' data. This study shows how web analytics help in collecting the important information of users behaviours, age, demographics, gender, conversions & source of traffic details. Startups & small businesses can optimise their content based on users' interest & take productive decisions. India which has become a hub of the startups in the world. Studies have showed that 90% of the startups get failed, in this paper it has been tried to find out how can Web Analytics play the role of catalyst for the success of the startup business. The sooner businesses embrace web analytics, the better.

Keywords: Web analytics · Google analytics · Startup · Web analytics tool · Startup success

1 Introduction

1.1 Startups and Web Analytics

The surge in the activity of Startup is due to the current set up that had its roots in the post-liberalisation economic activities [12]. The funding picture looks upbeat as the startup investments are reaching more than the US $10 billion. The insight unleash that the heightened competition were cost-effectiveness, reliability, and skilled professionals that are always a service bank to foreign companies [2, 9]. And this is the reason for continuous growth where some of the well-known companies in the market are of vital importance in the Indian market.

The thriving ecosystem has three major flourishing elements that included - a high-quality talent hub, a large market, and financial access. These parameters are the productive indicators of entrepreneurship activities and offer engaging studies [3, 7].

Startups are the youthful organisations that have several tasks running parallel with such a fast pace that people acquire the background of a multi-tasker. Being controlled by the inside as well as outside factors, India is the 4th destination of promoting startups biologically after the UK, US, and Israel [7, 10]. The inside factors include the organisation's idea and its execution, whereas the outside factor is the Indian government.

© Springer Nature Singapore Pte Ltd. 2020
U. Batra et al. (Eds.): REDSET 2019, CCIS 1230, pp. 366–380, 2020.
https://doi.org/10.1007/978-981-15-5830-6_31

India is the third largest startup economy in the world, India is a land where 3000+ new startups incorporated every year. Startups have given employment to around 300K individuals. 70% of the startups started in Delhi/NCR, Bangaluru and Mumbai regions. Bangaluru is also known as the Silicon Valley of India which has witnessed as the biggest investment destination in the previous years. Bangaluru itself accounts for more than 40% of the fundings [20].

Expanding step-by-step, the government also is focusing on improving methodologies and bringing changes to enhance the ease of doing business [15, 17].

Web Data Analytics is the study of web patterns and trends of the performance of the website at a specific or any region. It is a technique which is used to measure and analyse the performance of the website by collecting and analysing the website data in the form of reports [6, 8].

Web analytics is used to analyse the primary metrics and user's activity with traffic flow and pattern on the website.

Web analytics can be considered as a data analysis process which involves:

- Collection of patterns of visitors' data (website data)
- Analysing of the collected data and generating reports
- Generating insights by Understanding the reports
- Optimising the website
- Importance of Web Analytics

1.2   Why Web Analytics Is Needed?

Web Analytics is needed to determine the success rate of a business website and the brand associated with this [11, 13]. Following activities can be achieved by Web Analytics:

- Assess of web content problems
- Insight of website trends
- Monitoring of web traffic and users' pattern
- Demonstration of goals acquisition
- Figuring out of potential keywords
- Identifying the segments which needed the improvement

2   Web Analytics Process

Web Analytics Process gets completed in six steps; whenever a user visits the website, it gets recorded by the webserver. This data is then processed with Web Analytics, generating an in-depth report in tabular & chart form. The very first step of Web Data Analytics' process is to determine your goals. It is the most crucial step of any Web Analytics Process as all other levels revolve around this only. To get the desired outcome, the Goals need to be defined clearly. After defining the Goals, the next process will be to track the Goal's achievements and that can be tracked by KPI (Key Performance Indicators) - considered as the second step of the process. On the behalf of

Key Performance Indicators, the data is accumulated and then this "Collect Correct and Suitable Data" is the Third step of the process. Once correct and suitable data is found, it is analysed and this "Analyse Data" is considered as Web Analytics process' Fourth step. Fifth Step of the Process is "Test Alternatives" and it's done on the behalf of Analysed data. Last but not least is the Sixth Step of the Web Analytics Process which is Implementation of the insights [1, 5]. So the Web Analytics Process can be represented in Six Steps:

- **Goals** (Set the required business goals)
- **Important Performance Indicators** (to track the goal achievement)
- **Accumulate correct and suitable data**
- **Analyse data** (to get the insights)
- **Test alternatives** (Based on analysed data)
- **Implement insights** (Fig. 1).

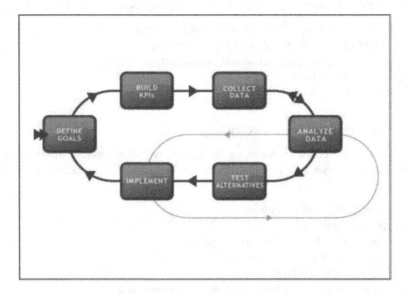

Fig. 1. [24] A fig showing Web Analytics Process

3   Web Analytics Tools

There are several tools available to undergo the Web Analytics of a website. These tools can be used to analyse and generate the customised report as per the requirement. They provide the overall performance of the website [13, 16]. There are tools which also provide the in-depth lacking details by analysing the On Page and Off Page Search Engine Optimisation parameters [18]. Following are the tools which are mostly used for the Web Analytics purpose:

- Google Analytics Tool
- KISSmetric

- Adobe Analytics Tool
- SEMRush Tool
- Hubspot Analytics Tool

Google Analytics Tool: Google Analytics is probably most reliable web analytics tool which offers a detailed statistic of your online traffic. It's used by more than 60% of the total startups. Google analytics tool also helps in the tracking and measuring website visitors, traffic sources, goals, conversion, along with other metrics (as you can see in the above image).

Google Analytics Tool generates reports on –

3.1 Audience Analysis

Audience analysis provides a detailed report of the visitors, following useful parameters can be tracked under the Audience Analysis:

- Demographics (Age and Gender of the website visitors)
- Geo (location and preferred Language of the visitor)
- Interests (affinity reach and market segmentation of the website visitor
- Behaviour (New and consistent visitors, their visiting frequency, and engagement)
- Technology (Browsers, OS, and networks of audience)
- Device (Mobile, laptops, iPads & Desktops)
- Benchmarking
- Users flow (User flow activity) (Fig. 2).

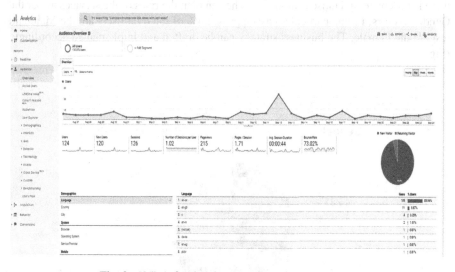

Fig. 2. [25] A fig showing overall Audience Analysis

Age Analysis: With the help of Age Analysis, the website owner can identify the age group of users who are visiting the site; accordingly, the looks and feel of the website can also be designed. As in this specific case, it has been noticed that the age group of 33.50% of the Total visitors is 25–34. It can easily be noticed that max user for this specific products/service are under the 50 years of the age group (Fig. 3).

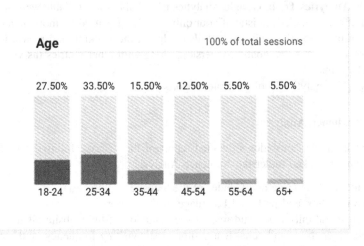

Fig. 3. [25] A fig showing Age Analysis

Gender Analysis: With the help of Gender Analysis, business owner can determine the Gender percentage and can plan his business strategies accordingly [1]. Let's say if there is a website of a unisex saloon, then he can plan the rates of the services as per the Gender visitors. In this particular case approx. 54% of the total users are the Male and rest are the Female. The business strategy can be drafted and implemented accordingly (Fig. 4).

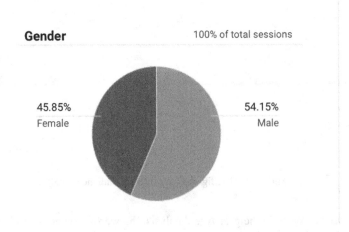

Fig. 4. [25] A fig showing Gender Analysis

Audience Interest Category Analysis: This analysis provide the details of the Interest categories of the visitors. This is very useful analysis for the business owners who are planning to start a new venture parallel with their existing one. It helps make the decisions basing on the audience Interest Category Analysis (Fig. 5).

Interest Category   100% of total sessions

5.49%   ▇▇▇   Sports/ Individual Sports/ Running & Walking

3.94%   ▇▇   Computers & Electronics/ Consumer Electronics/ Electronic Accessories

3.05%   ▇▇   Sports/ Individual Sports/ Cycling

2.96%   ▇▇   Food & Drinks/ Cooking & Recipe/ Soups & Stews

2.45%   ▇   Travel/ Tourist Destinations/ Historical Sites & Buildings

Fig. 5. [25] A fig showing Interest Category Analysis

Active User Analysis: This type of analysis helps the business owner in determining the Active Users or visitors of the site. This is tracked any time, and helps the owner to determine the number of users that appear usually at a time of the day. Thus, the Ad words can be set up accordingly (Fig. 6).

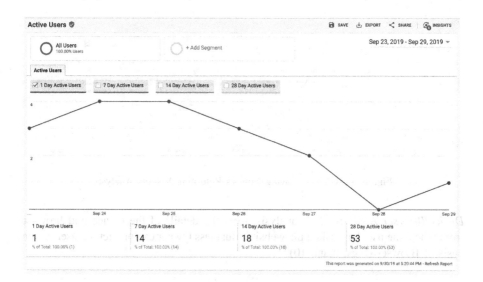

Fig. 6. [25] A fig showing Active User Analysis

Location Analysis: The location analysis lets the website owner know visitors' geographic location when they visits the website. Location Analysis also gives the detailed report on the basis of country as well as on respective state of that country [13]. In this case it has been noticed that out of 14 users 8 came from United States, 3 came from and 1 each from Argentina, Australia and China. Out of 14 Users the 10 are the New Users and out of these 10, 4 users visit from United States, 3 from Japan and 1 each from Argentina, Australia and China (Fig. 7).

Secondary dimension ▾ | advanced

Country	Acquisition: Users ↓	New Users	Sessions	Behavior: Bounce Rate	Pages / Session	Avg. Session Duration	Conversions (Goal 1: Create an Account Goal): Create an Account Goal (Goal 1 Conversion Rate)	Create an Account Goal (Goal 1 Completions)	Create an Account Goal (Goal 1 Value)
	14 % of Total: 100.00% (14)	10 % of Total: 100.00% (10)	21 % of Total: 100.00% (21)	42.86% Avg for View: 42.86% (0.00%)	5.14 Avg for View: 5.14 (0.00%)	00:08:58 Avg for View: 00:08:58 (0.00%)	0.00% Avg for View: 0.00% (0.00%)	0 % of Total: 0.00% (0)	$0.00 % of Total: 0.00% ($0.00)
1. United States	8 (57.14%)	4 (40.00%)	15 (71.43%)	40.00%	4.40	00:04:31	0.00%	0 (0.00%)	$0.00 (0.00%)
2. Japan	3 (21.43%)	3 (30.00%)	3 (14.29%)	33.33%	12.67	00:40:08	0.00%	0 (0.00%)	$0.00 (0.00%)
3. Argentina	1 (7.14%)	1 (10.00%)	1 (4.76%)	0.00%	2.00	00:00:13	0.00%	0 (0.00%)	$0.00 (0.00%)
4. Australia	1 (7.14%)	1 (10.00%)	1 (4.76%)	100.00%	1.00	00:00:00	0.00%	0 (0.00%)	$0.00 (0.00%)
5. China	1 (7.14%)	1 (10.00%)	1 (4.76%)	100.00%	1.00	00:00:00	0.00%	0 (0.00%)	$0.00 (0.00%)

Show rows: 10 Go to: 1 1 - 5 of 5

Fig. 7. [25] A fig showing Location Analysis

New vs Retuning Visitors Analysis: This report is very useful for any business owner, as it gives the analysis of the new and returning visitors. In this specific case, it can be noticed that out of 14 users; 10 are the new Visitors and 5 are the Returning visitors. The business strategy for the returning visitors can be drafted accordingly. It is very useful analysis for the startups which majorly runs on mobile app [23] (Fig. 8).

Plot Rows | Secondary dimension ▾ | Sort Type: Default ▾ | advanced

User Type	Acquisition: Users ↓	New Users	Sessions	Behavior: Bounce Rate	Pages / Session	Avg. Session Duration	Conversions (Goal 1: Create an Account Goal): Create an Account Goal (Goal 1 Conversion Rate)	Create an Account Goal (Goal 1 Completions)	Create an Account Goal (Goal 1 Value)
	14 % of Total: 100.00% (14)	10 % of Total: 100.00% (10)	21 % of Total: 100.00% (21)	42.86% Avg for View: 42.86% (0.00%)	5.14 Avg for View: 5.14 (0.00%)	00:08:58 Avg for View: 00:08:58 (0.00%)	0.00% Avg for View: 0.00% (0.00%)	0 % of Total: 0.00% (0)	$0.00 % of Total: 0.00% ($0.00)
1. New Visitor	10 (66.67%)	10 (100.00%)	10 (47.62%)	70.00%	4.60	00:12:04	0.00%	0 (0.00%)	$0.00 (0.00%)
2. Returning Visitor	5 (33.33%)	0 (0.00%)	11 (52.38%)	18.18%	5.64	00:06:09	0.00%	0 (0.00%)	$0.00 (0.00%)

Fig. 8. [25] A fig showing New vs Returning Visitors Analysis

Device/Browser Analysis: This analysis gives the details of the device and browser from where the user has visited the website. Business Owner can predict the user on the basis of Browser (Figs. 9 and 10).

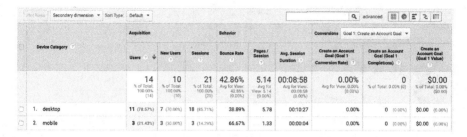

Fig. 9. [25] A fig showing Device Analysis

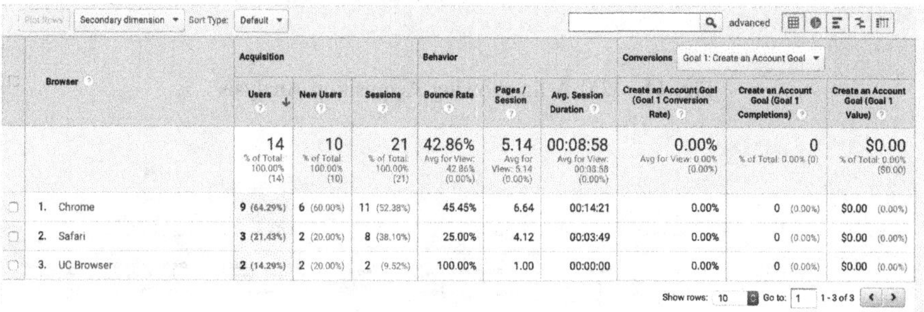

Fig. 10. [25] A fig showing Browser Analysis

Acquisition Analysis: Acquisition analysis is done to explore the web traffic origin sources [11, 13]. It provides us the ability to:

- Capture traffic from different channels (especially from the source or from the referrals)
- Have a look at the built campaigns
- Trace traffic using Adwords [2]
- Track social media traffic
- Analyse the traffic from search engines (triggered landing pages and geographical summary)
- See which plug-ins gave you traffic [13] (Figs. 11 and 12).

Fig. 11. [25] A fig showing Acquisition Analysis

	Acquisition			Behavior				Conversions Goal 1: Create an Account Goal ▼		
Source	Users	New Users	Sessions	Bounce Rate	Pages / Session	Avg. Session Duration	Create an Account Goal (Goal 1 Conversion Rate)	Create an Account Goal (Goal 1 Completions)	Create an Account Goal (Goal 1 Value)
	3 % of Total: 21.43% (14)	2 % of Total: 20.00% (10)	6 % of Total: 28.57% (21)	33.33% Avg for View: 42.86% (-22.22%)	2.33 Avg for View: 5.14 (-54.63%)	00:02:31 Avg for View: 00:08:56 (-71.87%)	0.00% Avg for View: 0.00% (0.00%)	0 % of Total: 0.00% (0)	$0.00 % of Total: 0.00% ($0.00)
1. baidu.com	2 (66.67%)	2 (100.00%)	2 (33.33%)	100.00%	1.00	00:00:00	0.00%	0 (0.00%)	$0.00 (0.00%)
2. foundationapi.com	1 (33.33%)	0 (0.00%)	4 (66.57%)	0.00%	3.00	00:03:47	0.00%	0 (0.00%)	$0.00 (0.00%)

Fig. 12. [25] A fig showing Referral Sources under Acquisition Analysis

Tree Map Analysis: This Analysis give the overall view of the source of all the users. As in this specific case there are 11 Direct users which means they come directly through the url. Then it shows there are Referral Users which mean these users come through the referral of any another url and 1 entry is through Organic Search (Fig. 13).

Behaviour Analysis: The Behaviour analysis observes visitors' activities on an online platform [18]. Behavioural data are generally found under the given segments:

- **Site Content:** It provides the details of the pages viewed. It provides the information of the page which the users visit and the page where the user exits from the website [16].
- **Site Speed:** It provides the information of page load time, execution speed, and performance data.
- **Site Search:** It provides the information of how the visitor search across any specific website. It can be analysed what the visitor searched for or how did they land on a particular landing page of the site.
- **Events:** The events are visitors' actions along with content (for example, downloads, sign up, & log-in, etc.). It can be analysed easily (Figs. 14 and 15).

Fig. 13. [25] A fig showing Tree Map Analysis under Acquisition Analysis

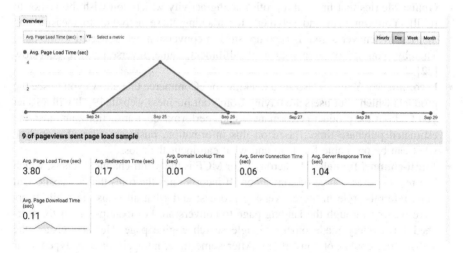

Fig. 14. [25] A fig showing Behaviour Analysis

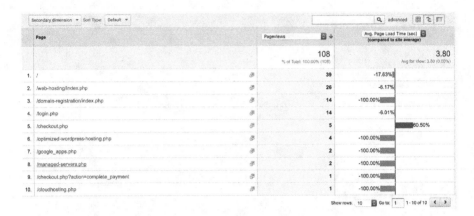

Fig. 15. [25] A fig showing Page Load under Behaviour Analysis

Conversion Analysis: Conversion is a goal completion (download, checkout, buy, etc.) by a user on a website.

- **Goals:** Metrics that find out a profit-making activity which you wish the visitor to fulfill. You can plan and set them for tracking these activities to measure the metrics. Whenever a goal is accomplished, a conversion gets reflected to the data. Thereby, you can observe your goal fulfillment, value, reverse path, & goal flow [22].
- **E-commerce:** You can also set a tracking for eCommerce that allows you to see the products which your users are buying from your business website [9]. It will also let you find out the product performance, sales performance, transactions, and also the estimated purchase time. Based on this information, businesses can also analyse what can be profitable for them and what can incur their loss.
- **Multi-channel funnels:** The acronym for MCF is the Multi-channel funnels, which is a report of the source of conversion. It incorporates the roles that a website will play, referrals' role in the conversion process; and what all slabs did while users were passing through the landing page to conversion. For example, a visitor searched for a query made on the Google search engine page. He then visited the website but could not convert [8]. After some time, he again directly typed your website's name and made a purchase; all these activities get traced by MCF.
- **Attribution:** The attribution modelling supports credit sales or conversions to touch-points in the process of tracking of conversions. Attribution also allows you to decide the platforms, strategies, and modules that are great for your business. Say, an individual stumbled on your site via AdWords ad but did not make any purchase. A month later, he again visits your website through a social platform but again doesn't buy. However, the third time, when he visits your site directly and gets converted. In such a case, the last interaction model can credit directly for the conversion. Whereas the first interaction model offers credit to a paid medium. Hence, you will analyse which module should be credited for the conversion (Fig. 16).

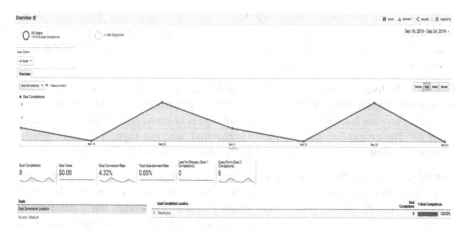

Fig. 16. [25] A fig showing Conversion Analysis

4 Importance of Web Analytics for the Startups

A startup is a new business venture either with a new idea or of an existing idea, in today's digital era all the companies want to register their existence online. They want to market & advertise their products and services online. One of the studies shows 60% of the budget of the marketing goes to the digital marketing [18]. For that every entrepreneur wants to mark his business online through the websites. Web Analytics plays a critical role in understanding the performance of a website.

Following are the parameters which a website owner always keen to improve:

- Bring the website on the Top Searches
- Best ranking for the target keywords
- Ability to track the demographic details of audience
- Ability to track the behaviour of audience
- Ability to track the device and browser used by the audience
- Ability to track the website performance and lacking parameters

The above parameters can be tracked and improved by using the Web Analytics Tool like Google Analytic Tool. The success rates increase for those who successfully can get mark their presence online.

5 Challenges Faced by the Startups

Data Security in Web Analytics: Privacy & data security are raising concern in the world of online marketing and analytics. Especially after the GDPR act, there's a fear in the consumer world about data security. Certain countries have even more stringent rules about the usage of its citizen's personal data by the companies. Non-compliance to data security could cost the organizations dearly. Brands like Google and Facebook faced tough time handling data privacy and security of their users [14]. It's a big challenge for the startups too, have will they manage the users' data. They will have to draft and implement the tough policies for their employees, being it developers, analysts and marketing team members and will have to make sure that no data of the users should be leaked/used for any purpose.

Failure to Deliver Action Items: Web analytics reports are just tables & graphs with metrics and dimensions. All a tool can offer is to provide you with 'how much' depending on your business [5]. The real challenge is to answer- "So? What should I do about it?" The proper data analytics team is required, who can suggest the management the required strategy which need to be implemented as per situation and requirement.

Troubles in Integration: Each Web analytics tool, at some point, should be joined with some other data source. For instance, the offline sales data, competitor data, third party data, or API. At this point, every major player of the market has a standardised procedure to pull it off. But it's still a challenge for many customised implementations.

Insufficient Knowledge: Web data analytics has been around for 10 plus years now. However, the exact implementations, the best and proven practices, and deriving actionable insights – all are still the mystery. I am quoting it confidently as I've worked with Sr. Account Managers & Support Engineers with almost every primary web analytics tool in the world! – One common thing I can say is that none of them are 100% confident on the way their devices work.

Difficulty in Accessing Content: Users of regional demographics found it difficult to use the English Keyboard also there is less content available for the users in the regional languages. This is the one of the mainstream challenge faced by the website owner, as it has been seen that mostly websites are in Languages, though provision of translating the content into another languages available but it doesn't provide the correct record of the visitors in translated format [6].

Low Data Speed: Websites run on internet and to allow the server to load good animations, video and good quality images good internet speed is required. Having fast internet is a challenge for almost all developing countries including India. Out of 122 countries, India ranked 109 for mobile internet speed.

6   Conclusion

Small businesses and startups should not check their website traffic/data occasionally. It won't just hurt their online reputation, but also draws a negative impact on the revenue and customer interaction. The study made clear that web traffic is not a separate task from its operations. In fact, Web Analytics is a critical process that can help businesses (mainly startups) improve their website traffic drastically. Web analytics helps small, mid-sized business and brands to analyse the key metrics, and visitors' activity along with user's traffic flow and pattern on the website. As about 90% of the startups fail in 5 to 10 years of span, [17, 19] this failure can be avoided [4, 21] if the businesses make a proper strategy of on the basis of the reports generated by Web Data Analytics. With the help of Google Analytics and other Web Analytics tools, the small business & startup owners can easily track down the age, gender, interest, and location of the visitors [10, 11]. It makes it easy for such companies and brands that have an online presence to observe the user behaviour, know what people are or aren't responding well to, which posts are going well for targeted audience, which keywords to target, which ads to run, and then chalk-out their strategies for success accordingly. Though there are certain challenges that come along with the web analysis process such as the need for fool-proof security, integration hazards, failing in delivering action items, difficulty is accessing content, and low data speed for that matter, Web Analytics practice is much critical for small businesses. Apart from this, the Web Analytics is required to assess the success rate of a site or business that is associated with it. For the startups which run their business majorly online for them it is very beneficial to know the data of the Returning and the New visitors. Coupons, offers and special discounts on the services can also be decided accordingly. With proper Web Analysis process that completes in six steps, and potent web analytics tools such as Google Analytics Tool, Adobe Analytics Tool, SEMRush Tool and more discussed in details in the study, online success seems attainable. Thus, by applying the tactics, advanced practices & in-depth knowledge from this detailed study, startups as well as enterprise companies can achieve all their online business goals, beast their competition, & avoid strategic assumptions or actions that can leave revenue on the table.

References

1. Alsos, G., Isaksen, E., Ljunggren, E.: New venture financing and subsequent business growth in men- and women-led businesses. Entrep. Theory Pract. **30**(5), 667–686 (2006)
2. Bhati, V.S., Bansal, J.: Social media and Indian youth. Int. J. Res. Anal. Rev. (IJRAR) **7**(1) (2019). E-ISSN 2348-1269. P- ISSN2349-5138
3. Busenitz, L., Barney, J.: Differences between entrepreneurs and managers in large organizations: biases and heuristics in strategic decision-making. J. Bus. Ventur. **12**(1), 9–30 (1997)
4. Cope, J.: Entrepreneurial learning from failure: an interpretative phenomenological analysis. J. Bus. Ventur. **26**(6), 604–623 (2011)
5. Eggers, J., Song, L.: Dealing with failure: serial entrepreneurs and the costs of changing industries between ventures. Acad. Manag. J. **58**(6), 1785–1803 (2015)
6. Fang, W.: Using Google analytics for improving library website content and design: a case study. Libr. Philos. Pract., 1–17 (2007)
7. Huang, X., Brown, A.: An analysis and classification of problems in small business. Int. Small Bus. J. **18**(1), 73–85 (1999)
8. Kaushik, A.: Web Analytics: An Hour a Day. Wiley, Hoboken (2007)
9. Kaushik, R.: Digital marketing in Indian context. Int. J. Comput. Eng. Manag. **19**, 2230–7893 (2016)
10. Kropp, F., Lindsay, N., Shoham, A.: Entrepreneurial orientation and international entrepreneurial business venture startup. Int. J. Entrep. Behav. Res. **14**(2), 102–117 (2008)
11. Macmillan, I., Zemann, L., Subbanarasimha, P.: Criteria distinguishing successful from unsuccessful ventures in the venture screening process. J. Bus. Ventur. **2**(2), 123–137 (1987)
12. Mathews, B.: Think Like A Startup: a white paper to inspire library entrepreneurialism (2018). Vtechworks.lib.vt.edu. http://vtechworks.lib.vt.edu/handle/10919/18649. Accessed 7 Sept 2018

13. Malacinski, A., Dominick, S., Hartrick, T.: Measuring Web Traffic, Part 1 (2001). www-106. ibm.com/developerworks/web/library/wa-mwt1/. Accessed 18 Nov 2019
14. Malhotra, B.: E-Business: issues & challenges in Indian prespective. Global J. Bus. Manag. Inf. Technol. 4(1), 11–16 (2014)
15. Mazzarol, T., Volery, T., Doss, N., Thein, V.: Factors influencing small business start-ups. Int. J. Entrep. Behav. Res. 5(2), 48–63 (1999)
16. Najjar, L.J.: Handbook of Human Factors in Web Designing, e commerce user interfaces. http://lawrence-najjar.com/papers/Designing_e-commerce_user_interfaces_2011.pdf/. Accessed 19 Sept 2019
17. Osborne, R.: Why entrepreneurs fail: how to avoid the traps. Manag. Decis. 31(1) (1993). https://doi.org/10.1108/00251749310023139
18. Paramasivan, C., Selladurai, M.: Emerging trends in new start-up technopreneurs. J. Bus. Manag. 2(7) (2016). https://ssrn.com/abstract=3067536
19. Peña, I.: Intellectual capital and business start-up success. J. Intellect. Cap. 3(2), 180–198 (2002)
20. Rani, M.A.: Startup India: opportunities & challenges "Startup India stand up India". ACADEMICIA Int. Multidiscip. Res. J. 7(1), 104–113 (2017)
21. Ucbasaran, D., Shepherd, D., Lockett, A., Lyon, S.: Life after business failure. J. Manag. 39 (1), 163–202 (2012)
22. Valentine, E.L., Stewart, G.: The emerging role of the board of directors in enterprise business technology governance. Int. J. Discl. Gov. 10(4), 346–362 (2013). https://doi.org/ 10.1057/jdg.2013.11
23. Yeadon, J.: Web site statistics. Vine 31(3), 55–60 (2001)
24. Google Image
25. https://analytics.google.com/ (aoptraininginstitute@gmail.com)

Hierarchical Bayesian Compressed Sensing
of Sparse Signals

Shruti Sharma[✉], Khyati Chopra[✉], and Rasveen Bholan[✉]

GD Goenka University, Gurugram, India
shruti_sml@yahoo.com, khyatichopra134@gmail.com,
rasveen@gmail.com

Abstract. Compressed sensing (CS) is a new concept in signal processing where one seeks to minimize the number of measurements to be taken from signals while still retaining the information necessary to approximate them well. Conventional approaches to sampling signals or images follow Shannon's celebrated theorem: the sampling rate must be at least twice the maximum frequency present in the signal. Compressed Sensing theory asserts that one can indeed recover certain signals and images from far fewer samples or measurements than traditional methods used, provided signal has some sparse representation in some transform domain. In this paper, we have explored two types of framework to formulate CS problem from Bayesian perspective, i.e., MAP Estimation Framework (Type-I) and Hierarchical Bayesian Framework (Type-II). It has been deduced from the results that Bayesian methods perform very well for the recovery of sparse signals as compared to Greedy Algorithms.

1 Introduction

Most of the data acquisition systems firstly collects the data of interest and after exploiting redundancies compress the data. When the signal has sparse representation in some basis, then acquisition and compression processes can be combined, reducing the required number of measurements to be acquired [1]. This is exactly done in compressed sensing. Sometimes this paradigm is also termed as *Sampling and Compression* paradigm. However, in 2006, David Donoho in his seminal work proposed a mathematical framework for combining acquisition and compression stage [2]. In phenomenal work of Emmanuel Candes, Romberg and Terence Tao, they showed that with few random linear frequency measurements, original sinusoidal signal can be reconstructed with an assumption that signal is sparse in frequency domain [2].

Compressed sensing theory's is a mathematical framework for acquiring few information rich measurements rather than many information poor measurements. Underlying theory of compressed sensing builds on the various branches of mathematics which include Linear Algebra, Real Analysis, Topology, graph theory, Wavelet theory etc. [3].

Bayesian methods make appropriate statistical assumption on the solution of (4) and (5). Unknowns are treated as stochastic quantities with assigned probabilities and various estimation techniques identify the required sparse solution. Thus, CS problem from Bayesian perspective can be seen as a sparse regression problem. In this paper, we

© Springer Nature Singapore Pte Ltd. 2020
U. Batra et al. (Eds.): REDSET 2019, CCIS 1230, pp. 381–396, 2020.
https://doi.org/10.1007/978-981-15-5830-6_32

have explored two types of framework to formulate CS problem from Bayesian perspective, i.e., MAP Estimation Framework (Type-I) and Hierarchical Bayesian Framework (Type-II).

2 Compressive Sensing as Sparse Recovery Problem

Let ψ be the space in which N × 1 dimensional signal **b** can be sparsely represented by N × 1 dimensional signal **w**. In other words, **b** lies in the sparse space of ψ:

$$b = \psi w \tag{1}$$

Let **y** be M × 1 measurements of **b** with M × N measurement matrix **A**

$$y = Ab = (A\psi)w = \phi w \tag{2}$$

Therefore, $y = \phi w$ is solved in compressed sensing assuming that **w** is sparse. However in real life, measurements are always noisy.

$$y = \phi w + n \tag{3}$$

Since, M<<N, **w** can't be obtained directly from measurements as the inversion is ill posed problem. By exploiting sparsity of **w** reconstruction problem can be formulated as:

$$\hat{w} = \arg\min_{\hat{w}} \left\{ \|y - \phi w\|^2 + \tau\|w\|_0 \right\} \tag{4}$$

Where $\|w\|_0$ denotes the number of non-zero components of **w**. However, such problem is NP hard and a more relaxed sparsity constrained problem can be formulated as:

$$\hat{w} = \arg\min_{\hat{w}} \left\{ \|y - \phi w\|^2 + \tau\|w\|_1 \right\} \tag{5}$$

Where $\|w\|_1$ denotes the $l1$ norm of **w**.

Equation (5) can be solved by a number of algorithms including linear programming and other greedy algorithms like Matching Pursuit, Orthogonal Matching Pursuit, by providing point estimates of the weights **w**. Bayesian methods include Maximum a Posteriori estimation (MAP) and Hierarchical Bayesian framework deals with a prior belief on **w** and provides posterior belief.

2.1 Bayesian Methods

Bayesian methods make appropriate statistical assumption on the solution of (4) and (5). Unknowns are treated as stochastic quantities with assigned probabilities and various estimation techniques identify the required sparse solution. Thus, CS problem from Bayesian perspective can be seen as a sparse regression problem. Two types of framework to formulate CS problem from Bayesian perspective are:

- MAP Estimation Framework (Type-I)
- Hierarchical Bayesian Framework (Type-II)

2.1.1   MAP Estimation Framework (Type-I)

MAP Estimation Framework for Bayesian compressed sensing is as shown in Fig. 1. MAP estimator aims at finding w that maximizes the posterior probability of $p(w|y)$ given the prior on $p(w)$ i.e.

$$\hat{w}^{MAP} = \arg\max_{\hat{w}}\{p(w|y)\} \tag{6}$$

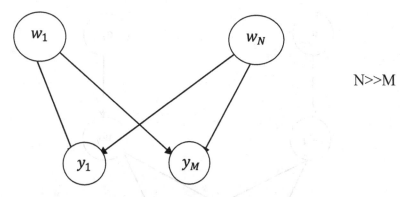

N>>M

Fig. 1. Framework in MAP estimation

According to bayes theorem:

$$p(w|y) = \frac{p(y|w).p(w)}{p(y)} \tag{7}$$

Since $p(y)$ is not function of w, from (6) and (7)

$$\hat{w}^{MAP} = \arg\max_{\hat{w}}\{p(w|y)\} = \arg\max_{\hat{w}}\{p(y|w).p(w)\} \tag{8}$$

Where, $p(y|x)$ is known as likelihood function.

Thus, in MAP estimation framework, based on the measurements y we try to figure out what weights should be, given the prior on solution and conditional distribution of measurements y given unknowns w. However, MAP based methods provide point estimates of the solution in which point of interest is the mode of posterior distribution and hence, limits its use.

2.1.2 Hierarchical Bayesian Estimation Framework (Type-II)

Hierarchical Bayesian estimation provides full posterior density function over all the possible values of w and also provides estimate of noise variance which is encountered while modelling compressive measurements. In hierarchical Bayesian framework, new random variable α_i is introduced which controls the variable w_i. Various methods are studied in machine learning for example Markov Chain Monte Carlo (MCMC) or Relevance Vector Machines (RVM) which models this dependence or control of α and w. RVM with type-II maximum likelihood (ML) procedure is one of the highly efficient algorithm which provides considerably sparse solution while still preserving the accuracy of results. Thus, instead of solving a MAP problem in w, with this framework one solves for the estimates of hyper-parameters α leading to an estimate of the posterior distribution for w. The framework is as shown in Fig. 2.

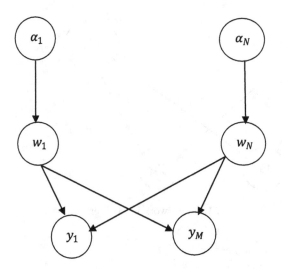

Fig. 2. Hierarchical framework for MAP Type-II estimation

3 Hierarchical Bayesian Modelling

In Hierarchical Bayesian modelling, all the variables are treated as stochastic quantities with assigned probability distributions. The unknown signal w is assigned a prior distribution and the observation y is assigned with conditional distribution which further depends on the parameters called *hyper-parameters*. Hyper-parameters are assigned with distribution and thus called *hyper-priors*. Two widely used hyper-priors are Gaussian hyper-priors and Laplacian hyper-priors. Bayesian Compressive Sensing (BCS) using both hyper-priors are studied throughout the report.

3.1 BCS Using Gaussian Hyper-Priors

a) *Measurement Noise Model* (n)

The measurement noise n (in Eq. (3)) is independent of measurements and Gaussian with zero mean and variance β^{-1}. (β is precision parameter)[**]

$$p(n|0, \beta) = \mathcal{N}(0, \beta^{-1}) \tag{9}$$

[**]We can place a prior on β but for simplicity it is taken as uniform distribution here however considered in Laplacian hyper-prior treatment.

b) *Measurement Model* (y)

From Eq. (3), it can be inferred that

$$p(y|w, \beta) = \mathcal{N}(y|\phi w, \beta^{-1}) = \prod_n p(y_n|w^t \varphi(x_n), \beta^{-1}) \tag{10}$$

c) *Signal Model* (w)

To model w, hierarchical structure is introduced and the following Gaussian prior α is employed on w (Prior on α is considered to be uniform for simplicity):

$$p(w|\alpha) = N(w|0, \alpha) = \prod_i \mathcal{N}(w_i|0, \alpha_i^{-1}) \tag{11}$$

Figure 3 shows graphical model for Bayesian compressive sensing employing Gaussian hyper-priors.

3.2 Evidence Approximation

By combining various stages of hierarchical Bayesian model, joint distribution can be defined as

$$p(w, \alpha, \beta, y) = p(y|w, \beta) \cdot p(w|\alpha) \cdot p(\alpha) \cdot p(\beta) \tag{12}$$

Now,

$$p(w, \alpha, \beta|y) = p(w|\alpha, \beta, y) \cdot p(\alpha, \beta|y) \tag{13}$$

Here,

$$p(w|\alpha, \beta, y) \propto p(w, \alpha, \beta, y) \tag{14}$$

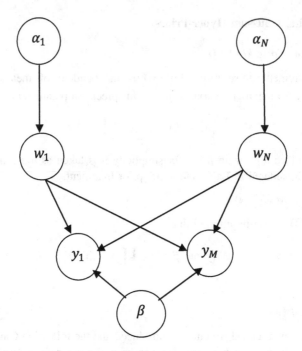

Fig. 3. Graphical model for Bayesian compressive sensing employing Gaussian hyper-priors

From theory of conditional Gaussian distributions and partitioned Gaussian distribution, it is easy to verify that given $p(y|w, \beta)$ and $p(w|\alpha)$,

$$p(w|y, \alpha, \beta) = \mathcal{N}(w|m, \Sigma) \tag{15}$$

$$m = \beta\Sigma\phi^t y \text{ and } \Sigma = \left(\mathbf{A} + \beta\phi^t\phi\right)^{-1} \tag{16}$$

Where $A = diag(\alpha_i)$ and $\phi : N \times M$ design matrix.

$$p(\alpha, \beta|y) = \frac{p(y, \alpha, \beta)}{p(y)} \propto p(y, \alpha, \beta) = \int p(y|w, \beta^{-1}).p(w|\alpha).p(\alpha).p(\beta)dw \tag{17}$$

Thus,

$$\max p(w, \alpha, \beta|y) \equiv \max p(y, \alpha, \beta) \tag{18}$$

Values of α_i and β are determined using type-II maximum likelihood (Evidence Approximation) in which we maximize marginal log-likelihood function over w.

3.3　Evaluation of Evidence Function

$$J = p(y, \alpha, \beta)$$

$$= \int \left(\prod_{n=1}^{N} \sqrt{\frac{\beta}{2\pi}} \exp\left(-\frac{\beta(y_n - w^t \varphi(x_n))^2}{2} \right) \cdot \prod_{i=1}^{M} \sqrt{\frac{\alpha_i}{2\pi}} \exp\left(-\frac{w^t A w}{2} \right) \right) dw$$

$$= \left(\frac{\beta}{2\pi} \right)^{N/2} \left(\frac{\prod_{i=1}^{M} \alpha_i}{2\pi} \right)^{M/2} \int \exp(-E(w)/2) dw$$

Where $E(w) = \beta \|y - w^t \phi(x)\|^2 + w^t A w$
Solving $E(w)$

$$E(w) = \beta y^t y + w^t \Sigma^{-1} w - 2\beta w^t \phi(x) y - m^t \Sigma^{-1} m + m^t \Sigma^{-1} m$$
$$= \beta y^t y + w^t \Sigma^{-1} w - 2\beta w^t \Sigma^{-1} \Sigma \phi(x) y - m^t \Sigma^{-1} m + m^t \Sigma^{-1} m$$
$$= \beta y^t y - m^t \Sigma m + (w - m)^t \Sigma^{-1} (w - m)$$
$$= E(y) + gaussian$$

Where $E(y) = \beta y^t y - m^t \Sigma^{-1} m$

$$J = p(y, \alpha, \beta) = \left(\frac{\beta}{2\pi} \right)^{N/2} \left(\frac{\prod_{i=1}^{M} \alpha_i}{2\pi} \right)^{M/2} \frac{1}{\sqrt{2\pi . \det(\Sigma)}} \int \exp(-E(y)) dw \quad (19)$$

$$\ln J = \frac{N}{2} \ln\beta + \frac{1}{2} \sum_i \alpha_i - \frac{1}{2} \ln|\det(\Sigma)| - \frac{N}{2} \ln 2\pi + E(y) \quad (20)$$

Goal is to maximize Eq. (20) w.r.t. α and β

i) *Maximization w.r.t α*

$$\frac{\partial J}{\partial \alpha_i} = \frac{1}{2\alpha_i} - \frac{1}{2} \Sigma_{ii} - \frac{1}{2} m_i^2 = 0$$

$$\alpha_i = \frac{1 - \alpha_i \Sigma_{ii}}{m_i^2} \quad (21)$$

ii) *Maximization w.r.t β*

$$\frac{\partial J}{\partial \beta} = \frac{N}{2\beta} + \frac{1}{2} \|y - w^t \phi(x)\|^2 - \frac{1}{2} Trace(\Sigma \phi^t \phi) = 0$$

$$\frac{1}{\beta} = \frac{||y - w^t \phi(x)||^2}{N - \sum_i \gamma_i} \tag{22}$$

where $\sum_i \gamma_i = Trace(\Sigma \phi^t \phi)$

From Eq. (15), $p(w|y, \alpha, \beta)$ can be found out by iteratively updating values of m and Σ with noise variance given in Eq. (22).

4 Fast BCS

Equation (17) can be seen as convolution of two Gaussians which is again a Gaussian:

$$\ln(p(y, \alpha, \beta) \propto \ln(\mathcal{N}(y|0, C))$$

In the formulation of (20), $E(y)$ is the only observation dependent term. Thus solving for $E(y)$ yields:

$$E(y) = \beta y^t y - \beta^2 y^t \phi \Sigma^t \Sigma^{-1} \Sigma \phi^t y$$
$$= y^t C^{-1} y$$

Where

$$C = (\beta^{-1} I + \phi A^{-1} \phi^t) \tag{23}$$

Hence,

$$\ln(p(y, \alpha, \beta) \propto -\frac{1}{2}\left[N ln 2\pi + ln|C| + y^t C^{-1} y \right] = \mathcal{L}(\alpha)$$

Equation (23) can be decomposed as

$$C = \beta^{-1} I + \sum_{m \neq i} \alpha_m^{-1} \phi_m \phi_m^t + \alpha_i^{-1} \phi_i \phi_i^t \tag{24}$$

$$C = C_{-i} + \alpha_i^{-1} \phi_i \phi_i^t \tag{25}$$

Here, C_{-i} is C without the contribution of ith basis vector.
Applying woodbury identity to Eq. (25)

$$C^{-1} = C_{-i}^{-1} - \frac{C_{-i}^{-1} \phi_i \phi_i^t C_{-i}^{-1}}{\alpha_i + \phi_i^t C_{-i}^{-1} \phi_i} \tag{26}$$

$$det(C) = det(C_{-i}).det(1 + \alpha_i^{-1} \phi_i C_{-i}^{-1} \phi_i^t) \tag{27}$$

$$\mathcal{L}(\boldsymbol{\alpha}) = -\frac{1}{2}[Nln2\pi + \ln(\det(\boldsymbol{C}_{-i}).\det(1 + \alpha_i^{-1}\boldsymbol{\phi}_i\boldsymbol{C}_{-i}^{-1}\boldsymbol{\phi}_i^t))$$
$$+\boldsymbol{y}^t\left(\boldsymbol{C}_{-i}^{-1} - \frac{\boldsymbol{C}_{-i}^{-1}\boldsymbol{\phi}_i\boldsymbol{\phi}_i^t\boldsymbol{C}_{-i}^{-1}}{\alpha_i + \boldsymbol{\phi}_i^t\boldsymbol{C}_{-i}^{-1}\boldsymbol{\phi}_i}\right)\boldsymbol{y}] \tag{28}$$

Equation (28) can be written as

$$\mathcal{L}(\boldsymbol{\alpha}) = \mathcal{L}(\boldsymbol{\alpha}_{-i}) + \lambda(\alpha_i) \tag{29}$$

Where

$$\lambda(\alpha_i) = \ln\left(1 + \alpha_i^{-1}\boldsymbol{\phi}_i\boldsymbol{C}_{-i}^{-1}\boldsymbol{\phi}_i^t\right) - \frac{||\boldsymbol{\phi}_i^t\boldsymbol{C}_{-i}^{-1}\boldsymbol{y}||^2}{\alpha_i + \boldsymbol{\phi}_i^t\boldsymbol{C}_{-i}^{-1}\boldsymbol{\phi}_i} \tag{30}$$

Equivalently Eq. (30) can be written as

$$\lambda(\alpha_i) = \ln(\alpha_i) - \ln(\alpha_i + s_i) + \frac{q_i^2}{\alpha_i + s_i} \tag{31}$$

Where $s_i = \boldsymbol{\phi}_i^t\boldsymbol{C}_{-i}^{-1}\boldsymbol{\phi}_i$ and $q_i = \boldsymbol{\phi}_i^t\boldsymbol{C}_{-i}^{-1}\boldsymbol{y}$.
s_i is called sparsity and q_i is called quality of $\boldsymbol{\phi}_i$.
The stationary points of marginal likelihood w.r.t α_i occurs when

$$\frac{d\lambda(\alpha_i)}{dx} = \frac{\alpha_i^{-1}s_i^2 - (q_i^2 - s_i)}{2(\alpha_i + s_i)^2} = 0$$

$$\alpha_i = \begin{cases} \frac{s_i^2}{(q_i^2 - s_i)}, & s_i < q_i^2 \\ \infty, & s_i \geq q_i^2 \end{cases}$$

4.1 Sequential Bayesian Learning Algorithm for Gaussian BCS

i) Initialize noise variance β^{-1}.
ii) Initialize α_i using one basis function $\boldsymbol{\phi}_i$ as

$$\alpha_i = \frac{||\boldsymbol{\phi}_i^t\boldsymbol{y}||^2}{||\boldsymbol{\phi}_i^t||^2}$$

and remaining $\alpha's$ as infinity so that only $\boldsymbol{\phi}_i$ can be included in the model.
iii) Compute Σ and $\boldsymbol{m}$ (which are scalars initially), s_i and q_i for all M bases $\boldsymbol{\phi}_i$.

$$m = \beta\Sigma\phi'y$$

$$\Sigma = (A + \beta\phi'\phi)^{-1}$$

iv) Select a candidate basis vector ϕ_i from the set of all M.

v) Compute $\theta_i \triangleq q_i^2 - s_i$.

vi) If $\theta_i > 0$ and $\alpha_i < \infty$ i.e. ϕ_i is in the model, *re-estimate* α_i.

vii) If $\theta_i > 0$ and $\alpha_i = \infty$ i.e. ϕ_i is not in the model, *add ϕ_i to the model.*

viii) If $\theta_i < 0$ and $\alpha_i < \infty$, i.e. ϕ_i is in the model, *delete ϕ_i from the model and set* $\alpha_i = \infty$.

ix) Update β

$$\frac{1}{\beta} = \frac{||y - w^t\phi(x)||^2}{N - \sum_i \gamma_i}$$

x) If converged terminate, otherwise goto 3.

4.2   BCS Using Laplacian Hyper-Priors

Laplacian hyper-priors model unknown signal effectively and enforce sparsity to a large extent. Figure 4 shows graphical model for Bayesian compressive sensing employing Laplacian hyper-priors and is 2 layer hierarchical model.

a) *Measurement Noise Model (n)*

On measurement noise, gamma prior is placed on β as follows:

$$p(\beta|a^\beta, b^\beta) = \Gamma(\beta|a^\beta, b^\beta) = \frac{(b^\beta)^{a^\beta}}{\Gamma(a^\beta)} \beta^{(a^\beta-1)} \exp(-\beta b^\beta) \tag{32}$$

Here,

β denotes hyper-parameter (inverse variance of noise)

b^β denotes scale-parameter

a^β Denotes shape parameter

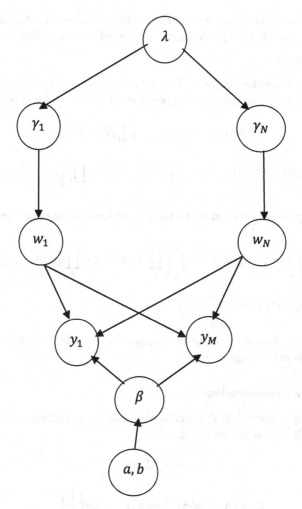

Fig. 4. Graphical model for Bayesian compressive sensing employing Laplacian hyper-priors

Gamma prior on β is generally chosen as it is conjugate to itself. *Conjugate priors lead to posterior distributions having same functional form as the prior and thus simplifies the analysis.*

b) *Measurement Model* (*y*)

Laplace prior on *w* can be written as:

$$p(w|\lambda) = \frac{\lambda}{2}\exp\left(-\frac{\lambda}{2}\sum_i|w_i|\right) \tag{33}$$

Laplace priors enforce sparsity to a large extent. However, Laplace distribution is not conjugate to observation $p(y|w, \beta)$. So, we model it in hierarchical manner.

c) *Signal Model* (w)

To model w hierarchically, firstly Gaussian hyper-prior γ is employed on w given by Eq. (33) and on γ Laplacian hyper-prior is employed given by (34).

$$p(w|\gamma) = N(w|0, \gamma) = \prod_i \mathcal{N}(w_i|0, \gamma_i)$$

$$p(\gamma|\lambda) = \Gamma(\gamma|1, \lambda/2) = \prod_i \Gamma(\gamma_i|1, \lambda/2) = \prod_i \frac{\lambda}{2} exp(-\frac{\lambda}{2}\gamma_i) \tag{34}$$

Therefore, $p(w|\lambda)$ can be written by Eq. (35) which is of the same form of Eq. (33).

$$p(w|\lambda) = \int p(w|\gamma,).p(\gamma|\lambda)d\gamma = \int \left(\prod_i \mathcal{N}(w_i|0, \gamma_i) . \prod_j \frac{\lambda}{2}exp(-\frac{\lambda}{2}\gamma_j) \right) d\gamma$$

$$= \frac{\lambda^{N/2}}{2^N} exp\left(-\sqrt{\lambda}\sum_i |w_i|\right) \tag{35}$$

The prior distribution on λ can be assumed to be uniform as it just provide us flexibility in choosing range of λ.

4.3 Evidence Approximation

It can be seen that $p(w|\gamma, \lambda, \beta, y)$ is multivariate Gaussian distribution $\mathcal{N}(w|m, \Sigma)$ and $p(y, \gamma, \beta, \lambda)$ will be maximized; where

$$m = \beta\Sigma\phi^t y$$

$$\Sigma = \left(\Lambda + \beta\phi^t\phi\right)^{-1} with \ \Lambda = diag\left\{\frac{1}{\gamma_i}\right\}_{i=1}^N$$

Joint distribution of all the stochastic variables is given by Eq. (36) and marginalized joint distribution w.r.t w is given by Eq. (37)

$$p(w, \gamma, \lambda, \beta, y) = p(y|w, \beta).p(w|\gamma).p(\gamma|\lambda).p(\lambda).p(\beta) \tag{36}$$

$$p(y, \gamma, \beta, \lambda) = \int p(y|w, \beta^{-1}).p(w|\gamma)p(\gamma|\lambda).p(\lambda).p(\beta)dw \tag{37}$$

Similar to the analysis done for BCS using Gaussian hyper-priors, Eq. (37) can be written as:

$$p(y, \gamma, \beta, \lambda) = \left(\frac{1}{2\pi}\right)^{\frac{N}{2}} . |C|^{-\frac{1}{2}} . \exp\left(-\frac{1}{2} y^t C^{-1} y\right) . \prod_i \frac{\lambda}{2} exp(-\frac{\lambda}{2} \gamma_i) . p(\beta) \qquad (38)$$

Where $C = (\beta^{-1} I + \phi \Lambda^{-1} \phi^t)$ and $y^t C^{-1} y = \beta ||y - w^t \phi(x)||^2 + w^t \Lambda w$
Instead of maximizing Eq. (38) directly, we maximize $\mathcal{L} = \ln(p(y, \gamma, \beta, \lambda))$

$$\mathcal{L} = -\frac{1}{2} \left[N ln2\pi + \ln|C| + y^t C^{-1} y \right] + N ln\frac{\lambda}{2} - \frac{\lambda}{2} - ln\lambda + (a^\beta - 1)ln\beta - b^\beta \beta \qquad (39)$$

Maximizing $\mathcal{L}$ w.r.t. γ yields γ_i given in Eq. (41)

$$\frac{\partial \mathcal{L}}{\partial \gamma_i} = \frac{1}{2} \left[\frac{\Sigma_{ii} + m_i^2}{\gamma_i^2} - \frac{1}{\gamma_i} - \lambda \right] = 0 \qquad (40)$$

$$\gamma_i = \frac{-\lambda + \sqrt{\gamma_i^2 - 4\lambda(\Sigma_{ii} + m_i^2)}}{2} \qquad (41)$$

Maximizing $\mathcal{L}$ w.r.t. λ yields λ given in Eq. (42)

$$\frac{\partial \mathcal{L}}{\partial \lambda} = \frac{N}{\lambda} - \frac{1}{2} \sum_i \gamma_i - \frac{1}{\lambda} = 0$$

$$\lambda = \frac{N-1}{\frac{1}{2} \sum_i \gamma_i} \qquad (42)$$

Maximizing $\mathcal{L}$ w.r.t. β

$$\frac{\partial \mathcal{L}}{\partial \beta} = 0$$

$$\frac{1}{\beta} = \frac{\frac{||y - w^t \phi(x)||^2}{2} + b^\beta}{N/2 - a^\beta} \qquad (43)$$

4.4 Fast Laplacian BCS

Similar to Eq. (23) to Eq. (29), Eq. (39) can be written as

$$\mathcal{L}(\gamma) = \mathcal{L}(\gamma_{-i}) + \ell(\gamma_i) \qquad (40)$$

Where

$$\ell(\gamma_i) = -\lambda \gamma_i - \ln(1 + \gamma_i s_i) + \frac{q_i^2 \gamma_i}{1 + \gamma_i s_i} \qquad (41)$$

The stationary points of marginal likelihood w.r.t γ_i occurs when

$$\frac{\partial \ell(\gamma_i)}{\partial \gamma_i} = -\lambda - \frac{s_i}{(1+\gamma_i s_i)} + \frac{q_i^2}{(1+\gamma_i s_i)^2} = 0$$

$$\gamma_i = \begin{cases} 0, & q_i^2 - s_i < \lambda \\ \dfrac{-\left(s_i^2 + 2\lambda s_i\right) + \sqrt{\left(s_i^2 + 2\lambda s_i\right)^2 - 4\lambda s_i^2\left(\lambda + s_i - q_i^2\right)}}{2\lambda s_i^2}, & q_i^2 - s_i \geq \lambda \end{cases}$$

4.5   Sequential Bayesian Learning Algorithm for Laplacian BCS

i)   Initialize $\lambda = 0$.

ii)   Initialize γ_i using one basis function ϕ_i as

$$\gamma_i = \frac{\left\|\phi_i^t\right\|^2}{\left\|\phi_i^t y\right\|^2}$$

  and remaining $\gamma's$ as 0 so that only ϕ_i can be included in the model.

iii)   Compute Σ and m.

iv)   Select a candidate basis vector ϕ_i from the set of all M.

v)   Compute $\theta \triangleq q_i^2 - s_i$.

vi)   If $\theta > \lambda$ and $\gamma_i > 0$ i.e.ϕ_i is in the model, *re-estimate* γ_i.

vii)   If $\theta > \lambda$ and $\gamma_i = 0$ i.e. ϕ_i is not in the model, *add* ϕ_i *to the model.*

viii)   If $\theta < \lambda$ and $\gamma_i > 0$, i.e. ϕ_i is in the model, *delete* ϕ_i *from the model and set* $\gamma_i = 0$.

ix)   Update β by Eq. (43), λ by Eq. (42).

x)   If converged terminate, otherwise goto 3.

5   Results and Discussions

It can be inferred from the results (Fig. 5 and Fig. 6) corresponding to noisy as well as noiseless measurements, Bayesian methods perform very good for the recovery of sparse signals as compared to Greedy Algorithms. It is because of the fact that a priori information of unknown signal will reduce the entropy of system and hence improves the performance of the algorithms.

For BCS employing Laplacian Hyper-priors, performance was found to be better as compared to the BCS employing Gaussian hyper-priors especially at low sparse levels for noisy as well as noisy measurements [4–7]. It is due to the fact that Laplacian Hyper-priors models the system and solve the optimization problem corresponding to Eq. (5) whereas Gaussian Hyper-priors solve the optimization problem Eq. (4) which is quadratic in nature and thus provides less sparse solution with effective accuracy.

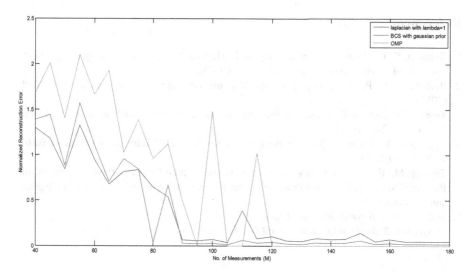

Fig. 5. Reconstruction error v/s no of measurements for noisy systems

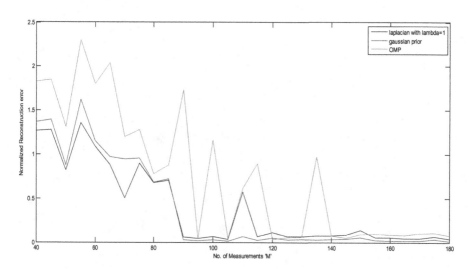

Fig. 6. Reconstruction error v/s no of measurements for noisy systems

6 Conclusion

We have investigated two types of framework to formulate CS problem from Bayesian perspective, i.e., MAP Estimation Framework (Type-I) and Hierarchical Bayesian Framework (Type-II). It has been deduced from the results that Bayesian methods perform very well for the recovery of sparse signals as compared to Greedy Algorithms. For BCS employing Laplacian Hyper-priors, performance was found to be better as compared to the BCS employing Gaussian hyper-priors especially at low sparse levels for noisy as well as noisy measurements.

References

1. Babacan, S.D., Molina, R., Katsaggelos, A.K.: Bayesian compressive sensing using laplace priors. IEEE Trans. Image Process. **19**(1), 53–64 (2010)
2. Bishop, C.M.: Pattern Recognition and Machine Learning. Springer-Verlag, New York (2013)
3. Tipping, M.: Sparse Bayesian learning and the relevance vector machine. J. Mach. Learn. Res. **1**, 211–244 (2001)
4. Ji, S., Xue, Y., Carin, L.: Bayesian compressive sensing. IEEE Trans. Signal Process. **56**(6), 2346–2356 (2008)
5. Tipping, M., Faul, A.: Fast marginal likelihood maximisation for sparse Bayesian models. In: Bishop, C.M., Frey, B.J. (eds.) Proceedings 9th International Workshop Artificial Intelligence and Statistics (2003)
6. Sparselab. http://sparselab.stanford.edu/
7. http://www.dbabacan.info/software.html (for fast laplcaian BCS)

Data Acquisition for Effective E-Governance: Nigeria, a Case Study

Ekong Edikan[1], Sanjay Misra[1(✉)], Ravin Ahuja[2],
Fernando Pérez Sisa[3], and Jonathan Oluranti[1]

[1] Covenant University, Ota, Nigeria
edikan.ekong@stu.cu.edu.ng, {sanjay.misra,
jonathan.oluranti}@covenantuniversity.edu.ng
[2] Shri Vishwakarma Skill University, Gurgaon, India
ravinahujadce@gmail.com
[3] Universidad Central del Ecuador, Quito, Ecuador
fjperez@uce.edu.ec

Abstract. Implementation of e-government system as a means of administering government services promotes efficiency and effectiveness in governance. E-government provides a platform for adequate information exchange between the government, who deploys the system and its users which comprises of its citizens. Involving citizens in the decision making process highlights one of the qualities of good governance. Accurate data acquisition is required for developing a competent model for distribution of available resources. This paper examines different platforms that can be used for communication with the government in Nigeria and the awareness that these platforms exist by collating data gotten from 120 interviewees. A more efficient information exchange model is developed after analysis of the acquired data using a statistical software.

Keywords: E-government · Data acquisition · Awareness platforms · Statistical software · E-government services

1 Introduction

The integration of adequate technology in various sectors of a nation's economy has become one of the essential requirements for its development. It is believed to provide a means for increasing effectiveness, productivity, efficiency and transparency [1, 23]. Integrating the right technology in all possible areas of a citizen's everyday life and activities and a proper information retrieval system can aid in improving the communication between citizens and the government. It can also help the government in knowing what move to make in order to improve the standard of living of its citizens [2, 24]. Most developed countries have succeeded in making efficient use of different technologies for effective governance. E-government is a term generally used to represent the utilization of information and communication technologies in administering governance.

© Springer Nature Singapore Pte Ltd. 2020
U. Batra et al. (Eds.): REDSET 2019, CCIS 1230, pp. 397–411, 2020.
https://doi.org/10.1007/978-981-15-5830-6_33

A major function of any government is the ability to make decisions and allocate resources based on these decisions made. Most developing and underdeveloped countries employ assumption as a means of making these decisions, giving room for inaccuracy in the distribution of available resources. An enormous amount of data is generated each day from individuals, companies and other subcomponents that make up a country's economy, and its improper analysis conceives the use of assumption in the decision making process. These data has become so much that performing analysis with conventional technology is next to impossible leading to wastage of useful data. Big data technology provides a means for processing these huge amounts of data and its deployment in the developmental process of a country can prove beneficial. In a bid to ensure maximum levels of democracy, a government must be in continuous communication with its citizens and make them a core part of the decision making process. Data from citizens can be gathered through various social media outlets, press media, emails, calls/SMS, etc. Big data provides a platform for processing and analyzing these unstructured data and also offers access to a variation of large volumes of data which proved inaccessible at an earlier stage. Any government can be termed "good", if it makes effective and efficient use of new and valuable data [3, 22].

This paper examines numerous articles on e-government, and an analysis is carried out on the various models developed by each author. The model presented in this paper is geared towards ensuring a further increase in the efficiency and effectiveness in e-governance. This is done by developing a model which will include creating awareness through a variety of platforms frequently utilized by each individual (citizens) that media for exchange of information with government exist. This model also fosters real time interaction between government and citizens for real time data gathering.

1.1 Defining Problem

Data is a key element of any government's administration needed for efficient planning and decision making. Acquiring data is one thing, but for it to aid effectiveness and efficiency, accuracy and being up-to-date becomes a priority. There are various means of gathering data but direct communication between citizens and a government can prove a near accurate means of gathering data needed for correctly allocating resources. After preliminary review on e-governance, results show that most developed countries of the world employ e-governance as a means of increasing effectiveness and efficiency in administering government services to citizens. [4, 7] and [20] examined e-government services in local governments in Nebraska (United States), Netherlands and Turkey respectively. E-government provides a means of fostering direct communication between the government and its citizens. In order to successfully implement these services in Nigeria and enable direct communication between her and its citizens, various means of communicating with the different government bodies must first be made known to the citizens. To aid this research, the following research question and sub-question were developed;

This question arises from the citizen's knowledge of the existing means of communicating with the government: Are you as a citizen aware of the various means of communicating with the government?

Sub-question:
What are the best possible means of creating awareness for these communication means, for you as an individual?

The paper focuses on the data acquisition aspect of e-government deployment in Nigeria leading to improved relationship between the government and its citizens which are also users of the e-government framework [10].

2 Related Works

Developed and some developing countries of the world utilize e-government as a tool in governance. [3], defines E-government as "the use of resources such as internet, mobile etc., to improve the functioning of government". Gao and Lee [4], improves on this definition by adding that E-government is "the utilization of information and communication technologies to foster a better government and improve its quality of services, majorly through the application of internet and web technologies". These definitions portray e-government as a necessary tool for a country's development. A major driving force for effective e-governance is the acquisition of data from various areas of an economy. According to [3] Many E-government platforms are designed to harness only structured data which is mostly used for statistical purposes and not in providing critical solution for problems that can improve quality of services rendered by government. The authors developed a model which was aimed at implementing big data in e-government for maximum efficiency and effectiveness in services rendered by e-governance and involving citizens in the decision making process [3]. Gasova and Stofkova [2], reiterated that information and communication technology has had an effect on the need for information, mode of working and communication, and behavior of citizens which in-turn has affected various structures of an economy: cultural, social, commercial and public structures. This is linked with E-government and a model which aims to improve quality in services rendered by e-government is developed for the Slovak republic. The authors named the model the ICTI e-government business model and partitioned it into four different models: Information, communication, transaction and integration business models. The function of each partition is as follows:

Information Business Model: This model was designed to provide required and optional information and highlight the arrays of e-government services that can be accessed by citizens and businesses. It fostered adding of informational value to its user and aids in solving user issues and enhance convenience by utilizing a single e-government portal in the provision of an array significant information.

Communication Business Model: This model is based on supporting communication between public administration and users. The authors sectioned this model into interactive and automated. The interactive section is designed to support a two way communication system while the automated section is designed to support two way system but can also provide communication in one direction.

Transactional Business Model: Aims to introduce a backbone system or erase the existing offline services by focusing on the utilization of administrative protocols using the platform of e-government.

Integration Business Model: Designed to include citizens, business, government and other bodies present in an economy in the creation of value.

Nigeria is a country rich in culture with diverse tribes, languages and way of living. Adopting e-government in the Nigerian economy would involve examining these cultural factors and different working practices to understand how it would affect this adoption. [1], examines the effects of cultural perceptions and working practices in adopting e-government in Lagos state.

In a bid to fully a understand the variety of data sources and its application in social and economic analysis, [5] developed a big data architecture model. This model utilizes non-conventional data sources and data analysis procedures in its design and is aimed at predicting social and economic traits, trends and changes. [5], Classified the non-conventional data sources of social and economic data on the basis of user purpose for generating data: Information search, transactions, information diffusion, social interaction and non-deliberate (generation of data without intent). The authors highlighted the fact that most of these social and economic data gotten from non-conventional means require the internet to function. They stated that "The increasing penetration and importance of the internet in almost every social and economic activity has positioned it as a basic means for the generation of such kind of data". The paper further highlights non-conventional procedures for analyzing these social and economic data. The analyzed data gotten from deployment of the big data architecture model promotes efficient decision making but is influenced by certain factors which are discussed in [11].

[6] Examines the need for big data in effective governance stating that data analysis and its predictive characteristics can give better insight into development strategies that can be realized in the future. Application of big data analytics in the public sector, healthcare sector and in drug discovery, all important aspects to be analyzed in relation with economic development, was discussed, and also its benefits were highlighted. Matthias finger's proposed model for e-governance with the emergence of new information and communication technology (NICT) and an action model which highlights procedures of steps to take when reports from big data analytics have been procured and its benefits is examined. The benefits of the action model according to the paper includes; predictive policing, increased operational efficiency, better consumer services and identification new market. The authors also listed techniques applied in data analysis; data mining, text analysis, machine learning, predictive modeling, cluster analysis, and classification. Only the first three of the listed techniques were discussed in the paper. The paper concluded by analyzing the challenges concerned with big data analytics and reiterates that effective services and effective ideas can be conceived by the government if these analytics are applied in deployment of its plans and strategies for economic development.

[4], developed a theorem which analyzes various e-government services and their response to two selected social media platforms used in minute local governments in Nebraska; Facebook and twitter. An analysis on how this social media platforms are being used by the local government is performed and the authors divide the e-governments

services into two main services; transaction and information services and also its asso-ciation with the utilization of these two platforms. Results gotten shows that, Transaction services are a function of utilization of the Facebook platform while information services are associated with the twitter platform. A model called "the conceptual model of social media adoption" was developed. After examining the characteristics of these two social media platforms, the researchers concluded that twitter, being a more interactive tool compared to Facebook, may be preferable to small local governments (in Nebraska) in terms of information propagation to not just occupants of the local government, but also individuals in much bigger geographical areas who are keen on having relations with small local governments for either business purposes or other activities that could prove beneficial to both parties. The research carried out by [4] was focused on e-government's response to two social media platforms (Facebook and twitter) while [10], examined the adoption of social media in the implementation of e-government in the public health sector by analyzing and reviewing different publications related to the research.

In [7], obstacles facing the adoption of e-government and approach for tackling these obstacles is examined. The author developed an analytical model of the e-government concept that features three aspects; (i) stages in the e-government inno-vation process, (ii) Obstacles created by government and citizens, (iii) structural and cultural obstacles. The research presented two major approaches for dealing with obstacles to e-government innovation which are given as "fixing" and "framing". A case study of the deployment of a technological structure aimed at fostering coop-eration between Netherlands' police and its citizens was examined by the developed model. According to the paper, officials of government and citizens are not inspired by the promises that comes with technology but by structures that relate opportunities created by technology to the generation of public value. It concludes by saying the issues facing the innovation of e-government in not just tackling structural obstacles by fostering development of robust technologies, but also to structure and make desirable technological practices.

"Information systems success-based approaches" from the view of government officials was used as a basis for analyzing the success of the e-government framework in [8]. Serbia was used as a case study and the authors applied structural equation modelling (SEM) procedures in examining data gotten from questionnaires distributed to 154 e-government framework employees. After much analysis and study carried out on other research works related to this research, the conceptual model created (an update to the DeLone and McLean IS success model) had the following features which are measured by its corresponding listed trait; Quality of system, quality of informa-tion, quality of service, satisfaction derived from usage, user intention, and net benefits. The traits used to measure these features in the paper include;

– Quality of system: is measured by user friendly nature of e-government system, easy usage of system and e-government framework ability to provide good services to user.
– Quality of information: this is measured using precision, reliability, usefulness and sufficiency of information provided by the framework. It also utilizes "how current the information is" as an attribute for measuring quality of information.

- Quality of service: attributes for measurement are system's readiness to provide required service, framework's ability to ensure secure user transactions, availability of services at any time it is required, attending to system users individually and ability of system to understand user needs and act accordingly.
- Satisfaction derived from usage: Is measured by user satisfaction with e-government framework, e-government system has met user expectations and services provided by system are of high quality.
- User intention: measured by user dependency on system, frequent usage of system, user's inclination to use system in future and how regular system in sued in future.
- Net benefits: this is measured by e-government system's ability to make user jobs easier, save user time and usefulness of system in user jobs.

As part of the conclusion, the research stated that the developed model proffered further confirmation that quality of service is critical for the developing stages of an e-government framework. Further analysis on the quality of e-government services is carried out in [9]. The research fosters quality of services by highlighting major factors that need to be taken into consideration by e-government platforms when mapping out web service portals with its employees as users. Gathering of data for this purpose was done by examining the viewpoint of 30 quality management professionals in a university setting and designing of questionnaires. The research results enumerated four aspects which must be acknowledged in the measurement of quality of service provided by the e-government system; information quality, technical efficiency (encompasses design of system to foster availability, accessibility and easy usage), confidentiality (security, reliability and privacy levels) and smoothness of information exchange (communication) with the employee. The authors also classified e-government based on its activities and relation with its users;

- Relations that have been set up between government and business.
- Relations that are fostered through government and its citizens (who are also tagged as customers of the e-government services). This focuses on seamless information exchange between the two parties.
- Relations established between government and its employees. This promotes communication between various government parastatals and their employees leading to an improved productivity level through management of human resources.
- Government to Government relations which involves promoting communication between the various government parastatals for increased performance efficiency.
- Intra-government relationship fosters information dissemination and flow within the government.

The research reiterates the provision of improved quality services is a function of the government and utilization of online routes fosters increased efficiency and clarity in provision of these services and effective communication with its citizens.

[12], reveals the factors that prove influential in the employment of e-government in Mauritius, a developing state. After a survey of 247 citizens, the authors stated that developing states should attach more priority to citizens between the ages of 18–39 in promoting awareness of services through educating of citizens on how to use these services provided by the e-government framework. The paper reiterated the need to

ensure quality of information in the framework by focusing on security and privacy. This in turn promotes trust and reduces inability to adapt to change. The issue of privacy alongside transparency remains a thriving issue when it comes to data acquisition. [13], examines this issue in relation to the government while [14], analyzes the trends in the e-government structure and the ample opportunities it provides. Inadequate framework structure and gaps in its design were outlined as two major factors that account for failure in projects developed by e-government. [15], was aimed at developing approaches that will associate these projects with more achievability and less susceptibility to failure. Reduction of failure enhances success of the services provided by the framework. [16], proposes the "integrative model of e-filing continuance usage" as a measure for determining success of the services e-government provides. These services are deployed based on different factors (such as geographical, socio-demographic and economic) and [17] examines these factors with aim of finding out which of them envisions the adoption of e-government services by collating data from the survey of 612 individuals in Finland. The paper also analyzes the relationship between adoption of the framework and the internet.

[18], proposes a model which employs multimedia data as medium for increasing efficiency of information structures which support e-government frameworks and adopts related procedures for developing structured data from unstructured documents. [19], analyzes implementation of e-government cloud in government bodies in China and examines mechanism that determines and affects it, while [20] examines the mechanisms involved in citizens' choice to utilize the services provided by e-government in Turkey.

From the studies reviewed, it was found out that most of the models are developed with the assumption that the citizens are already aware of the various means of exchanging information with the government. This paper examines these gaps and proposes a model to bridge the gaps.

3   Methodology and Framework of Research

For the purpose of this research, given its qualitative nature, a total of 150 people were approached but 120 were willing to take part in the research. 120 individuals (citizens of Nigeria) were interviewed (on the field) and in order to get near accurate data due to difference in taste for different age groups, the 120 individuals interviewed were divided into three age groups (20–35, 36–50 and 51-above). The research questions served as the interview questions and was explained to each individual one after the other and their corresponding answer to each question asked was recorded. Lagos and Ogun states were used as the field of survey and the interviewees were selected at random. 47.5% of the interviewees fell within the age bracket of 20–35, 42.5% within the bracket of 36–50 and the remaining 10% fell within 51 and above. The research methodology was aimed at interviewing respondents from almost all works of life: University setting – staff/students, (20%), Small business owners (20%), Security personnel (5%), Information technology personnel (10%), pastors (5%), Bankers (10%), Firm employees (12.5%), Graphics designers (5%), restaurant managers (2.5%) and hawkers (10%). Table 1 shows descriptive analysis of the respondents and Fig. 1 shows the research framework which emulates the framework developed by [21].

Table 1. Descriptive analysis

Interviewees	Number	Percentage (%)
Age bracket		
20–35	57	47.5
36–50	51	42.5
51-above	12	10
Occupation		
University staff/student	24	20
SMEs	24	20
Security personnel	6	5
Information technology	12	10
Pastors	6	5
Bankers	12	10
Firm employees	15	12.5
Graphics designers	6	5
Restaurant managers	3	2.5
Hawkers	12	10

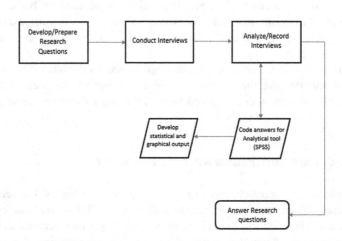

Fig. 1. Research framework

3.1 Results and Data Analysis

The data gathered from interviews with the respondents was analyzed using the SPSS statistical software. Each data set was assigned a code and a graphical output was generated. Analysis of graphical output is carried out in the following subsections.

3.1.1 Awareness

The Awareness question, which inquires if the interviewees are aware of the existing platforms for communicating with the government, required a Yes or No answer. Each answer was then compared to the selected age brackets. Figure 2 shows that 90% (108 interviewees) of the 120 interviewed were not aware that platforms for direct communication with the various Nigerian government agencies existed. The 10% (12 respondents) which are aware have never utilized the platforms. Further analysis show that 8 of the 12 respondents fell within the age bracket of 36–50 and 4 within 20–35. No individual in the age bracket of 51-above knew about the existing information exchange platforms.

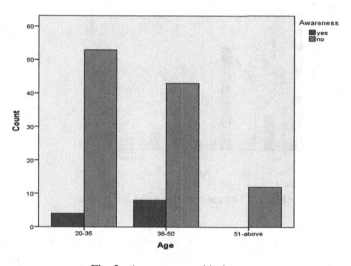

Fig. 2. Awareness graphical output

3.1.2 Awareness Platforms

The Interviewees were also asked the best possible platforms for creating awareness that the information platforms exist. This section selected a variety of known communication mediums for this sub-question: Emails, Social media (Facebook, YouTube, instagram, twitter, blogs, Whatsapp), Television, SMS/Telemarketing (use of calls fall in this category), Newspaper/Magazines and Radio. Analysis of Fig. 3, 4 and 5, show that Social media, e-mails and SMS/telemarketing record the highest percentages for creating awareness. According to Fig. 3. Use of Social media and emails as creating awareness platforms is more popular among the age brackets of 20–35 and 36–50 with a total of 44 individuals preferring social media in both age brackets and 28 of the 120 preferring the email platform. SMS/telemarketing record highest percentage for 36–50. In relation to occupation, Fig. 3 and 4 show that social media cuts across all occupations. Use of emails is familiar with all occupations except Hawkers and restaurant managers. A general cumulative results in Newspapers/magazines and radio recording the least percentage in both age bracket and occupation analysis.

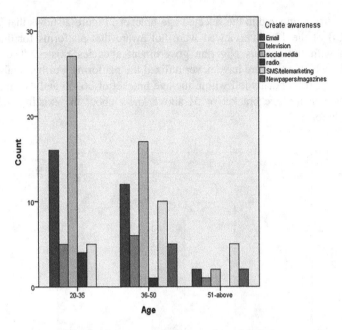

Fig. 3. Awareness platform and age brackets

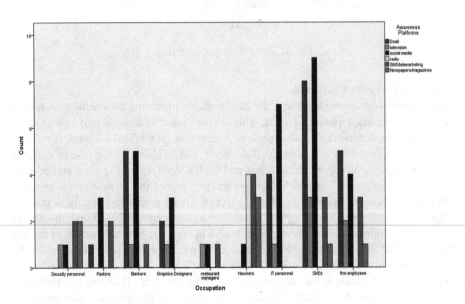

Fig. 4. Awareness platforms and occupations

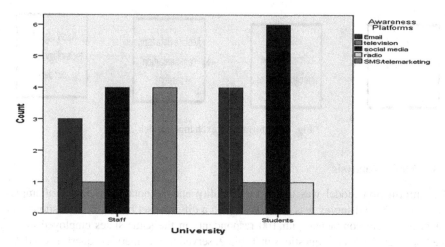

Fig. 5. Awareness platforms and occupations (university and students)

3.2   Information Exchange (Communication) Model

As earlier stated, e-government fosters direct communication between government and its citizens. Two major means of direct information exchange and real-time interaction between the Nigerian citizens and the government, from the analysis carried out above, would be through the use of emails, social media and calls/SMS. The government should have dedicated phone numbers, e-mail address and secure social media accounts (on different influential social media platforms) which should be made known, through the awareness creation platforms, to its citizens. A feedback model would promote good relationship between the government and its citizens as this would encourage the latter to keep using the communication platforms. Through this process, a near-accurate data for effective resource allocation and efficient governance, can be acquired. The information exchange model emulates the communication model developed by [2] with little adjustments:

– Awareness creation of e-government services through selected awareness platforms.
– Use of e-mails, SMS/calls and social media to establish communication which includes interactive session with a designated government employee.
– Data acquisition through interactive session.
– Application of big data technology to structure enormous amounts of data generated each day through the millions of citizens who make use of the platforms.
– Relay feedback information to citizen after allocation resources using sorted data (Fig. 6).

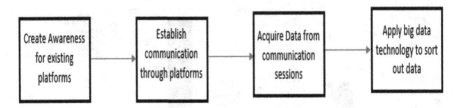

Fig. 6. Information exchange model

3.3   Model Analysis

The information model was tested for usability and acceptance as forms of implementation. A field survey was carried out with a different set of outlined questions and interviews were conducted with 100 respondents in the same states employed in the methodology. The set of questions in Table 2, served as the interview questions and the framework of this analysis also follows that of Fig. 1.

Table 2. Usability and acceptability questions and corresponding options

S/N	Interview questions	Measurement scale
1	Would you like to be made aware of the platforms that exist for communicating with the government?	Yes/No
2	Will you use these platforms to communicate with the government if made aware?	Yes/No
3	How often would you use these platforms if made aware?	Scale (1–10)
4	Would you like a feedback from the government?	Yes/No
5	How convenient do you think you would be using these platforms for communication?	Scale (1–10)
6	Do you think these existing platforms are a good means of data collection for government?	Yes/No
7	Would you like to be attended to by a skilled government employee for adequate information exchange?	Yes/No

The interview questions were explained to the interviewees and the corresponding answers recorded. Questions 3 and 5 were used to test usability (i.e. acceptance of the system) which is determined by two criteria: usage of the system and convenience of the system both rated on a scale of 1–10. In the analysis of data recorded, 1–4 is tagged as "poor", 5 is "average" and 6–10 is "good". Table 3 gives a descriptive analysis of the result. For acceptance levels, 73% of the 100 interviewed fell on the scale (6–10), 17% on 5 and 10% on the scale (1–4). For the convenience criteria; 77% was recorded in scale (6–10), 13% in 5 and 10% in scale 1–4. A critical review of these results reveal that percentage of acceptance levels of the information exchange model are at high due to high percentage levels recorded in scale 6–10 for both criteria.

Table 3. Descriptive analysis of Questions 3 and 5 from Table 2

	Results		
Usage scale			
	1–4 (Poor)	**5 (Average)**	**6–10 (Good)**
Interviewees	10	17	73
Convenience scale			
Interviewees	10	13	77

Testing of the developed model revealed that 10% of the 100 interviewed picked the scale 1–4. This is due to certain factors and when asked, the respondents attributed it to inadequate access to the internet for social media and email platforms. This is caused by lack of finances to purchase data for accessing the internet due to expensive nature of network data, and poor network access services provided by the network providers in Nigeria. For the case of call/SMS, the respondents advised that calling/SMS charges should either be reduced or scrapped off when communicating with government for data collection.

4   Conclusion and Recommendations

This research analyzed communication between the government and its citizens as a medium for a near accurate data acquisition procedure. Awareness of various mediums for communicating with the government in Nigeria and best possible mediums for creating awareness were criteria used in developing research questions. A comprehensive field survey (Lagos and Ogun states) was carried out with 120 individuals interviewed and the recorded data was collated and examined using SPSS. The Results showed that for the first research question, 90% of the 120 respondents were not aware of the existing platforms whole 10% were aware. For the sub-question, from the data gotten, the three major means of creating awareness for each individual included emails, social media and calls/SMS. A model which is aimed at creating a more efficient communication relationship between the parties involved (government and citizens) was developed using the results gotten from the survey. This model was then tested for usability levels which also denotes acceptance of system by the citizens. Results show that the system has a high percentage of usability and convenience which connotes a high level of acceptance. Citizens encouraged the idea of creating awareness of government information exchange platforms and recommended it as a good means of data acquisition. Inadequate trust levels can affect proper data acquisition and In order to encourage citizens to keep using this platform, a good feedback model, which will show that the information passed by the citizen was taken into consideration, is necessary. Also employment of government officials with required skills for good interaction is tantamount to ensure frequent usage of the platforms. This satisfies the characteristic of a user friendly e-government system.

Acknowledgment. The authors wish to appreciate the Center for Research, Innovation, and Discovery (CU-CRID) of Covenant University, Ota, Nigeria, for partly funding of this research.

References

1. Choudrie, J., Zamani, E.D., Umeoji, E., Emmanuel, A.: Implementing E-government in Lagos State: understanding the impact of cultural perceptions and working practices. Gov. Inf. Q. **34**(4), 646–657 (2017)
2. Gasova, K., Stofkova, K.: E-government as a quality improvement tool for citizens' services. Procedia Eng. **192**, 225–230 (2017)
3. Rajagopalan, M.R., Solaimurugan, V.: Big data framework for national e-Governance plan. In: Eleventh International Conference on ICT and Knowledge Engineering (2013)
4. Gao, X., Lee, J.: E-government services and social media adoption: experience of small local governments in Nebraska state. Gov. Inf. Q. **34**, 627–634 (2017)
5. Blazquez, D., Domenech, J.: Big Data sources and methods for social and economic analyses. Technol. Forecast. Soc. Chang. **130**, 99–113 (2018)
6. Agnihotri, N., Sharma, A.K.: Big Data analysis and its need for effective governance. Int. J. Innov. Adv. Comput. Scie. **4**(2347–8616), 219–224 (2015)
7. Meijer, A.: E-governance innovation: barriers and strategies. Gov. Inf. Q. **32**(2), 198–206 (2015)
8. Stefanovic, D., Marjanovic, U., Milan, D., Culibrk, D., Lalic, B.: Assessing the success of e-government systems: an employee perspective. Inf. Manag. **53**(6), 717–726 (2016)
9. Janita, S.M., Miranda, J.F.: Quality in e-Government services: a proposal of dimensions from the perspective of public sector employees. Telematics Inform. **35**(2), 457–469 (2018)
10. Tursunbayeva, A., Franco, M., Pagliari, C.: Use of social media for e-government in the public health sector: a systematic review of published studies. Gov. Inf. Q. **34**(2), 270–282 (2017)
11. Janssen, M., Van Der Voort, H., Wahyudi, A.: Factors influencing big data decision-making quality. J. Bus. Res. **70**, 338–345 (2017)
12. Lallmahomed, M.Z., Lallmahomed, N., Lallmahomed, G.M.: Factors influencing the adoption of e-government services in Mauritius. Telematics Inform. **34**(4), 57–72 (2017)
13. Janssen, M., Van Den Hoven, J.: Big and open linked data (BOLD) in government: a challenge to transparency and privacy? Gov. Inf. Q. **32**(4), 363–368 (2015)
14. Joseph, R.C.: A structured analysis of e-government studies: trends and opportunities. Gov. Inf. Q. **30**(4), 435–440 (2013)
15. Guha, J., Chakrabarti, B.: Making e-government work: adopting the network approach. Gov. Inf. Q. **31**(2), 327–336 (2013)
16. Veeramootoo, N., Nunkoo, R., Dwivedi, Y.K.: What determines the success of an e-government service? Validation of an integrative model of e-filing continuance usage. Elsevier (2018). https://doi.org/10.1016/j.giq.2018.03.004
17. Taipale, S.: The use of e-government services and the internet: the role of socio-demographic, economic and geographical predictors. Telecommun. Policy **37**(4–5), 413–422 (2013)
18. Amato, F., Colace, F., Greco, L., Moscato, V., Picariello, A.: Semantic processing of multimedia data for e-government applications. J. Vis. Lang. Comput. **32**, 35–41 (2016)
19. Liang, Y., Qi, G., Wei, K., Chen, J.: Exploring the determinant and influence mechanism of e-government cloud adoption in government agencies in China. Gov. Inf. Q. **34**(3), 481–495 (2017)

20. Kurfali, M., Arifoglu, A., Tokdemir, G., Pacin, Y.: Adoption of e-government services in Turkey. Comput. Hum. Behav. **66**, 168–178 (2017)
21. Pusatli, T.O., Misra, S.: Software measurement activities in small and medium enterprises: an empirical assessment. Acta Polytechnica Hungarica **8**(5), 21–42 (2011)
22. Popoola, S.I., Popoola, O.A., Oluwaranti, A.I., Atayero, A.A., Badejo, J.A., Misra, S.: A cloud-based intelligent toll collection system for smart cities. In: Bhattacharyya, P., Sastry, H., Marriboyina, V., Sharma, R. (eds.) NGCT 2017. CCIS, vol. 827, pp. 653–663. Springer, Singapore (2018). https://doi.org/10.1007/978-981-10-8657-1_50
23. Oduh, I.U., Misra, S., Damaševičius, R., Maskeliūnas, R.: Cloud based simple employee management information system: a model for african small and medium enterprises. In: Rocha, Á., Guarda, T. (eds.) ICITS 2018. AISC, vol. 721, pp. 115–128. Springer, Cham (2018). https://doi.org/10.1007/978-3-319-73450-7_12
24. Jonathan, O., Ogbunude, C., Misra, S., Damaševičius, R., Maskeliunas, R., Ahuja, R.: Design and implementation of a mobile-based personal digital assistant (MPDA). In: Mandal, J.K., Mukhopadhyay, S., Dutta, P., Dasgupta, K. (eds.) CICBA 2018. CCIS, vol. 1031, pp. 15–28. Springer, Singapore (2019). https://doi.org/10.1007/978-981-13-8581-0_2

Smart IoT Monitoring Framework Based on OneM2M for Air Quality

Chaitanya Chauhan[1], Ritesh Ojha[1], Jain Soham Dungerchand[1],
Gaurav Purohit[2], and Karunesh K. Gupta[1(✉)]

[1] EEE Department, Birla Institute of Technology and Science (Pilani Campus),
Pilani, India
kgupta@pilani.bits-pilani.ac.in
[2] CEERI, Pilani, India

Abstract. Generally, Pollution estimations are performed utilizing costly hardware at settled areas or committed portable hardware research centers. This is a coarse-grained and costly approach to estimate pollution. In this paper, we present a portable approach for estimating fine-grained air quality continuously. We propose practical information acquisition model for indoor and outdoor air quality monitoring which can be carried anywhere as a portable device. It consists of gas detection circuitry for CO, CO_2, PM2.5, PM10 and humidity sensor. Array of gas sensors are connected to microcontroller after signal conditioning circuit. This data is sent to a cloud service platform which provides facility of accessing the data in the form of real-time graph. An android app has been developed for the easy access of the air quality data on mobile phones. Data can be collected from many such Active Queue Management (AQM) blocks. We present fundamental models and examine its execution challenges.

Keywords: Air quality prediction · ONEM2M · Real-time communication · Data publishing app · Cloud upload · Sensor array

1 Introduction

Internet of Things (IoT), where every physical device is said to be smart and is equipped for interfacing with machines, computers or even human beings. Using IoT one can sense and control objects remotely across existing network setup, creating possibilities for direct amalgamation of the physical world into computer-based systems, and enhanced benefits when IoT is interfaced with sensors and actuators [1]. IoT is the integration of reality and technology [2]. IoT technology involves feeding (or introducing) an IP address to an unconnected device (such as refrigerator, ACs and so on) for internet connectivity. This facilitates connection between a network-connected object and other internet-enabled devices or systems [3, 4].

OneM2M is a worldwide initiative and partnership project which involves 8 different SDOs (Standard developing organizations) and 200 different Industry partners. It is a very recent technology as it started in 2012 as a partnership project and had 2 interoperability events in 2015 and 2016 [5]. The purpose and goal of oneM2M is to develop technical specifications which address the need for a common M2M Service

© Springer Nature Singapore Pte Ltd. 2020
U. Batra et al. (Eds.): REDSET 2019, CCIS 1230, pp. 412–419, 2020.
https://doi.org/10.1007/978-981-15-5830-6_34

Layer that can be readily embedded within various hardware and software, and relied upon to connect the myriad of devices in the field with M2M application servers worldwide. A critical objective of oneM2M is to attract and actively involve organizations from M2M-related business domains such as: telematics and intelligent transportation, healthcare, utilities, industrial automation, smart homes, etc. The produced standardized specifications enable an Eco-System to support a wide range of applications and services, and one such application is addressed and focused in the present paper is air quality monitoring.

Air is constituted by 99% oxygen, nitrogen, water vapors and inert gases. It is polluted due to rise in urbanization, human and industrial activities. Vehicular emissions are also a major contributor to amount of nitrogen oxide, carbon monoxide, carbon dioxide in air. Air quality monitoring refers to the continuous, structured and long-term assessment of toxicity in air by measuring the concentration of certain pollutants such as carbon monoxide, carbon dioxide, PM10 & PM2.5. The temperature and humidity is also an important measure of the state of surroundings.

In this paper AQM nodes has been designed and developed to monitor the level of pollutants present in the air at any given location. This will enable us to monitor state of air in real-time. The accessibility to real-time data would make us better informed about the pollution pattern and the ways in which it impacts the environment and increases contamination. Better knowledge and vehicles controls would lead to reduced pollution. Informed citizens would also take healthier routes. Industries would also benefit from such real-time analysis and can monitor the processes and equipments which contribute more to the air contamination.

The data collected by the sensor is accessible to authorized people through the cloud. The cloud services would graphically represent the data. A mobile application has also been made which will enable users to get real-time air quality wherever they travel. Data from multiple channels can also be accessed through the app which will enable is us to compare air quality at different locations.

2   The Proposed Architectural Model

The Fig. 1 shows the layered model of OneM2M architecture. On the grass-root level, the application layer includes Sensors, devices, MEMS etc. which generally acquires the data and send to Smartphone application which uses it [6, 7]. Then on the top of that we have Common service layer which allows application layer or Network layer to use common service functions. Network layer provides an underlying network to assist the CSE in case it needs some data or updates [8]. The OneM2M framework supports various nodes. Nodes are logical entities that are individually identifiable in the oneM2M System. Nodes are either Common Service Entity CSE-Capable or Non-CSE-Capable: CSE capable contains one or more CSE in it. In nutshell it is a software layer which sits between M2M applications and communication HW/SW that provides data transport. It normally rides on top of IP and provide functions that M2M applications across different industry segments commonly need. Those functions are exposed to Applications via developer friendly APIs and allows for distributed intelligence like device, gateway, and cloudapps.

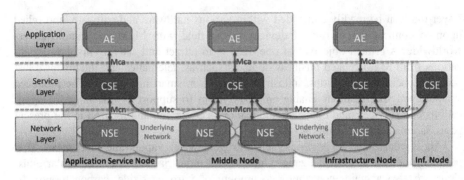

Fig. 1. The general structure of OneM2M framework

AE - Application Entity
API - Application Programming Interface
NSE - Network Services Entity
CSE - Common Service Entity

The monitoring system is divided into 4 units, namely M2M Device, M2M Gateway, M2M Server and M2M application. M2M Device is a set of sensors including six sensors including PM and CO using microcontroller and light weight power supply. The node has equipped with Bluetooth 4.0 and WIFI 802.11ac shield for data communication (Fig. 2).

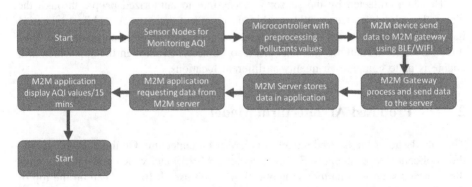

Fig. 2. System flowchart

In the first phase, sensor nodes acquire the concentration of all the pollutants. The concentration/data acquire using microcontroller from sensor data. The data is then changed into $\mu g/m^3$ and mg/m^3 as per the Indian standard and can be depicted from Table 1.

Table 1. Breakpoints of different pollutants in IND-AQI (CPCB, 2014).

AQI category (Range)	$PM_{2.5}$	NO_2	O_3	CO	SO_2
	24-h	24-h	8-h	8-h	24-h
Good (0–50)	0–30	0–40	0–50	0–1.0	0–40
Satisfactory (51–100)	31–60	41–80	51–100	1.1–2.0	41–80
Moderate (101–200)	61–90	81–180	101–168	2.1–10	81–380
Poor (201–300)	91–120	181–280	169–208	10.1–17	381–800
Very poor (301–400)	121–250	281–400	209–748	17.1–34	801–1600
Severe (401–500)	250+	400+	748+	34+	1600+

Note: While CO concentrations are expressed in mg m^{-3}; the other pollutants are expressed in μg m^{-3}.

Using Table 1 the overall AQI i.e. IND-AQI, can be estimated only if the concentrations of minimum three pollutants are available by sensor node, with at least one of them being either PM2.5 or PM10. The IND-AQI is then taken as the maximum AQIi of the constituent pollutants, denoted as dominating pollutant. Once the data is acquired the node preprocess and average AQI reading. Then based on IND-AQI categories namely good, satisfactory, moderate, poor, very poor and severe depending on whether the AQI falls between 0–50, 51–100, 101–200, 201–300, 301–400 or 401–500, respectively updates the data to server. The application then fetch the data and display the final reading of AQI at refresh rate of 15 min.

3   Results and Discussion

The system is tested with the sensor nodes on different days in CEERI-Pilani. It collects and updates results in every 1 min and 19 s. The accessibility to real-time data would make user better informed about the air quality pattern and the ways in which it impacts the environment and increases contamination. The cloud services would graphically represent the data. A mobile application has also been made which will enable users to get real-time air quality wherever they travel. The graphical representations of air quality parameters are shown in Fig. 3.

AQM nodes are providing real-time data of six sensors for air quality monitoring. The sensors are shown in Fig. 4(a). A high precision static and a low precision participatory node has been built as shown in Fig. 4(b). Further an android mobile application is built to visualize real time AQI (air quality Index). An android-based application is shown in Fig. 5 which connects with sensory nodes using either WIFI or Bluetooth Low power protocol. Menu selection page for different channels is provided which shows the collect data from different nodes installed at different place. The numbers of AQM nodes are installed which will be collected and fetched from the cloud after every 1 min and 19 s. The required time is calculated in accordance six parameters which are connected to AQM node.

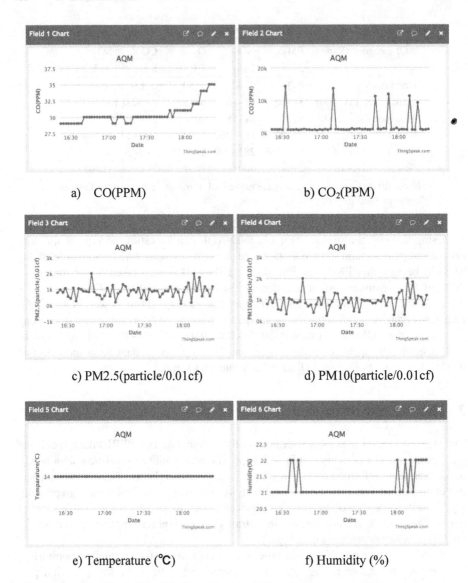

a)   CO(PPM)   b) CO$_2$(PPM)

c) PM2.5(particle/0.01cf)   d) PM10(particle/0.01cf)

e) Temperature (°C)   f) Humidity (%)

Fig. 3. Graphically represent of air quality parameter [9]

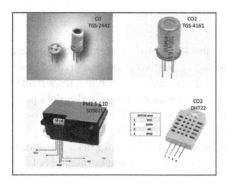

Fig. 4. (a) Typical sensors used for node development (b) Static (Yellow) node & participatory node [10]. (Color figure online)

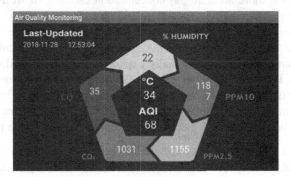

Fig. 5. Mobile application (Version 1.0) with different panel views

4 Conclusion

This paper describes the execution of an Air Quality Monitoring System. The proposed architecture in the paper presents mobile (Dynamic) platforms for fine-grained real-time air pollution estimation which can be deployed anywhere like public transport, etc. using BLE/WIFI as communication protocol between sensing nodes and a data publishing app. Considering the increasing number of low-cost WIFI and capability of distributed sensing nodes, diverse area can be monitored with the help of data publishing app. The Air quality Index is generated in app using different sensor parameter like temperature and humidity, PM 2.5/10, CO and CO_2 for accurate estimations of the air especially.

The fundamental novelties of this paper are given as follows:

The improvement of an air quality observing framework that utilizes sensors in a remote system.

The embedding of data publishing app and cloud framework for monitoring data coming from different channel which will then be used with neural network for anomaly detection.

The advancement of micro-control programming for propelled information handling, information storage, and Web and App publishing program related with air quality monitoring design. Exceptional consideration was conceded for pragmatic low power execution of sensing nodes.

The proposed dynamic air quality monitoring presents the following focal points:

It gives stretched out capacities to air quality monitoring for indoor and outdoor conditions along with long-range.

It can provide more accurate gas concentration estimates if we implement neural network to remunerate the temperature and humidity impacts.

It presents client-side data visualization for keeping check on environmental condition especially for asthma patients, patients with cardiovascular diseases, etc. Health aware people can additionally exploit these types of facility for safer route navigation. People utilizing our framework will turn out to be more educated about the degree of air contamination and will be inspired to pursue better for environment. Separated from these applications at an individual dimension, this information could be utilized as an extra contribution to extensive scale policymaking.

The impact of cross factors on the performance of system can be estimated by utilizing neural network systems. We will address this issue in a future work.

Acknowledgements. We wish to express our sincere thanks to Director, CEERI and BITS Pilani for providing us this wonderful opportunity to learn and develop our skill set. We are extremely grateful and indebted to him for his expert, sincere and valuable guidance extended to us. We thank him for inspiring us to dive into the core of the subject and for his efforts to help me understand the subject.

References

1. Indoor Air Quality. The Inside Story: A Guide to Indoor Air Quality, March 2015. http://www.epa.gov/iaq/pubs/insidest.html
2. Due, R., Santi, P., Vasilakos, A.V., Carlo, S.: The sensable city: a survey on the deployment and management for smart city monitoring. IEEE Commun. Surv. Tut. **21**(2), 153–1560 (2019). Second Quarter
3. Budde, M., Berning, M., Busse, M., Miyaki, T., Beigl, M.: The TECO Envboard: a mobile sensor platform for accurate urban sensing — and more boulder. In: 9th International Conference on Networked Sensing Systems (INSS), pp. 11–14 (2012)
4. Postolache, O.A., Pereira, J.M.D., Girao, P.M.B.S.: Smart sensors network for air quality monitoring applications. IEEE Trans. Instrum. Meas. **58**(9), 3253–3262 (2009)
5. Chae, M.J., Yoo, H.S., Kim, J.Y., Cho, M.Y.: Development of a wireless sensor network system for suspension bridge health monitoring. Autom. Construct. **21**, 237–252 (2012)
6. Kim, Y., Evans, R.G., Iversen, W.M.: Remote sensing and control of an irrigation system using a distributed wireless sensor network. IEEE Trans. Instrum. Meas. **57**, 1379–1387 (2008)
7. Bertocco, M., Cappellazzo, S., Carullo, A., Parvis, M.: Virtual environment for fast development of distributed measurement applications. IEEE Trans. Instrum. Meas. **52**(3), 681–685 (2003)
8. Wang, J., Gao, X., Gao, Q.: The design of wireless testing system for concrete rigidity based on virtual instrument. In: Proceedings of the CECNet, 1994, pp. 2968–2971 (2012)
9. Kumar, P., Agarwal, A., Purohit, G., Raju, K.S.: Intelligent home with air quality monitoring. In: Proceedings of International Conference on Sustainable Computing in Science, Technology and Management, vol. 1, pp. 1583–1587, June 2019
10. Kumar, P., Purohit, G., Tanwar, P., Gautam, C., Raju, K.S.: Real time, an IoT-based affordable air pollution monitoring for smart home. In: Luhach, A.K., Kosa, J.A., Poonia, R. C., Gao, X.-Z., Singh, D. (eds.) First International Conference on Sustainable Technologies for Computational Intelligence. AISC, vol. 1045, pp. 837–844. Springer, Singapore (2020). https://doi.org/10.1007/978-981-15-0029-9_65

Gravitational K-Means Algorithm

Mohd. Yousuf Ansari[1]([✉]), Anand Prakash[2], and Mainuddin[3]

[1] Defence Scientific Information and Documentation Centre,
DRDO, Delhi, India
md_ya@yahoo.co.in
[2] Institute for Systems Studies and Analyses, DRDO, Delhi, India
adprakash2006@gmail.com
[3] Department of Electronics and Communication, Faculty of Engineering
and Technology, Jamia Millia Islamia, New Delhi, India
mainuddin@jmi.ac.in

Abstract. The technologies of the present era produce large amount of spatiotemporal data related to various fields. Clustering is a tool to extract useful information from the large repository of data and helps in data analytics. We propose a Gravitational K-Means clustering algorithm as an extension of K-Means algorithm to exploit the idea of relative importance of one object to other objects in a phenomenon. The notion of relative importance can be realized by the concept of mass and gravity. Therefore, we employ the concepts of gravitational laws in the formation of clusters. We propose a function to map an intrinsic attribute of the object to mass of the object. The mass function is used to calculate center of mass of a cluster in place of geometry-based centroid. We further propose to use gravitational force as a measure of dissimilarity in place of Euclidean distance. Silhouette index is used to select the value of input parameter and also for measurement of quality of obtained clusters. The proposed algorithm is applied on a real fire dataset. The result reveals that the proposed algorithm produces more natural clusters. We also perform the comparative study with K-Means algorithm and found that the proposed algorithm outperforms K-Means algorithm in terms of convergence and semantics.

Keywords: Clustering · K-Means · Mass function · Center of mass of a cluster · Gravitational force

1 Introduction

The present technologies have capability to generate spatiotemporal data pertaining to different types of phenomenon. There are five types of spatiotemporal data [1] and events are one of its type. The examples of events include seismic events, fire events, crime events, and disease cases. To extract and analyze useful information from large amount of spatiotemporal data, the data mining techniques can be used.

Clustering is the one of the category of data mining, which group datasets based on some concept of similarity [2]. Clustering has capability to transform a spatiotemporal data into useful information that, in turn, can be used to get some meaningful conclusion about the phenomenon under study. The clustering algorithms can be mainly

© Springer Nature Singapore Pte Ltd. 2020
U. Batra et al. (Eds.): REDSET 2019, CCIS 1230, pp. 420–429, 2020.
https://doi.org/10.1007/978-981-15-5830-6_35

categorized into five types. One of the types is partitional. The K-means algorithm is a partition-based clustering algorithm in which partitions are based on crisp set. The K-means clustering algorithm has applications in numerous fields. For example, it can be used to make predictions on likelihood of forest fires in a specific area in relationship to the season of the year. This would allow to effectively understand how season and the occurrences of forest fires are related, through which decisions can be made by the local fire authorities to reduce state expenses by proper planning.

The K-Means algorithm is robust; however, its performance depends on initialization conditions including instance order [3]. The outcome of K-Means algorithm depends on the randomly selected initial clusters [4]. The traditional K-Means algorithm produces good results only when the initial chosen centroids are close to final centroids of the clusters [5].

We observed that the relative importance of one object in phenomena like fire events, crime events, and seismic events affects the occurrence of other events under same phenomenon. The notion of relative importance can be realized by the concept of mass and gravity. The more important object has more gravity in comparison to less important objects. The idea is source of inspiration for the development of proposed algorithm.

The proposed Gravitational K-Means algorithm, however, doesn't solve the initialization problem but it finds out weighted means of the cluster by utilizing 'mass function' in finding center of masses of clusters as per Definition 2 and 3. The idea of calculating center of masses instead of geometry-based centroids gives a sensible guidance to reach final centers of clusters. The traditional K-means algorithm makes use of the Euclidean distance to assign data objects to the closest cluster. The proposed approach uses the gravitational force between data objects and center of masses as per Definition 4 for assigning data objects to the closest cluster. The concept of gravitational force seems to be more natural than Euclidean distance in the context of center of mass. Critical attribute in a data object acts as mass of the object and helps in forming meaningful clusters. The proposed approach has been applied on a real fire dataset of USA. We employed the silhouette index [6] to measure the quality of clusters for a particular value of K. The proposed approach is compared with the traditional K-Means algorithm. The results reveal that our approach outperforms the K-Means algorithm.

The organization of the paper is as follows. Section 2 provides the overview of related work. Section 3 describes background of K-Means algorithm. Section 4 describes our proposed algorithm along with terms and definitions. Section 5 discusses the experimentation done with the proposed algorithm using a real fire dataset. Finally, the conclusion and future work is explained in the Sect. 6.

2 Related Work

Clustering is a process in which objects are grouped in a manner such that objects of the same group have similar properties and objects belonging to different group have dissimilar properties. Various clustering algorithms are proposed by researchers to analyze spatiotemporal data. Kamat et al. [7] employs K-means algorithm for analyzing earthquakes occurred in India. The authors show that K-Means can be utilized for analysis of seismic data and interpretation of their results. Martino et al. [8] propose an algorithm for clustering spatiotemporal data. The algorithm is based on Extended Fuzzy C-Means algorithm. The authors apply the algorithm to earthquake epicenters that occurred in Southern Italy from 2001 to 2014.

Mayorga et al. [9] propose a spatiotemporal clustering algorithm for the analysis of crime events by extending Fuzzy C-Means algorithm. Further, to analyze criminal directionality a cluster reorganization algorithm is also proposed. Hu et al. [10] propose a spatiotemporal method for crime analysis, which is based on kernel density estimation method. The proposed approach is applied on residential burglaries in Louisiana in 2011. Ansari et al. [11] proposed an approach based on Fuzzy C-Means algorithm for detection of crime spot. The authors apply the method on a real-world crime dataset of County of Montgomery in the US state of Maryland and show that it effectively discovers spatiotemporal crime clusters of good quality.

Adin et al. [12] propose a two-step method in both spatial and spatiotemporal domain for estimation of disease risk maps. The proposed method addresses the problem of local discontinuity in spatial pattern. The approach is applied to stomach cancer mortality and brain cancer incidents in Spain.

Hudjimartsu et al. [13] employs spatiotemporal clustering approach with Kulldorff's Scan Statistic (KSS) to identify fire hotspots. The authors implemented KSS method by employing circular window for scanning and likelihood value on scanned result. The likelihood ratio for each window is calculated by using Poisson model. Monte Carlo approach is used for testing statistical significance. The approach is applied to fire data pertaining to Riau Province. Oliveira et al. [14] propose an approach based on Shared Nearest Neighbor (SNN) algorithm that has capability to integrate space, time and semantic attributes in the clustering process. The authors apply the approach on a synthetic dataset and fire dataset. The authors also performed experimentation on fire dataset by including semantic attribute (burnt area) in addition to spatial and temporal dimensions and demonstrate that inclusion of semantic attribute helps in the identification of better results in terms of semantics.

Liu et al. [15] propose a spatiotemporal clustering algorithm based on permutation tests to address the problem of parameter sensitivity. The method makes use of statistical information of the data to determine cluster and their significance. The proposed approach makes it easy for the selection of optimum clustering parameter values. Husch et al. [16] propose a spatiotemporal clustering algorithm by computing empirical correlations of spatial neighbors over time. The authors also show that the proposed clustering algorithm can be extended for large scale parallelization.

Velden et al. [17] study various distance-based clustering methods for mixed data. The mixed data comprises of continuous and categorical data. The authors suggested different steps such as data preprocessing, specific distance measure usage, and data reduction for mixed data. The authors observe that no single method performs satisfactorily on all datasets.

J. Gomez et al. [18] and P. Binder et al. [19] propose gravitational clustering algorithms which are robust to noise and outliers.

As mentioned in the above paragraphs several approaches have been proposed to deal with spatiotemporal data. To the best of our knowledge, none of the approaches exploits the idea of relative importance of one object to other objects and realizes it with the concept of mass and gravity. The Sect. 4 describes our proposed algorithm with the definition of the concepts.

3 K-Means Algorithm Background

Traditional K-Means clustering algorithm (shown in Fig. 1) is based on geometry-based centroids. Given a dataset $X = \{x_1, x_2, ..., x_n\}$ that contains n data points, the algorithm aims to partition the dataset into a set of K number of clusters, $C = \{c_1, c_2, ..., c_K\}$ having centroids $v = \{v_1, v_2, ..., v_K\}$.

The centroid vi of a cluster ci is calculated as per Eq. (2)

$$v_i = (1/n_i) \times \sum (Spatiotemporal\ Coordinates) \tag{1}$$

where n_i is number of objects in cluster c_i.

Input: Dataset $X = \{x_1, x_2, ..., x_n\}$ containing n objects and number of clusters i.e. value of K

Output: A set of clusters $C = \{c_1, c_2, ..., c_K\}$

Algorithm
1. Initialize: Randomly select K centroids in the dataset.
2. Iterate:
    a. Assign data objects to the closest cluster
    b. Update centroid of each cluster as per equation (1)
3. Halt: Stop when centroids remain unchanged

Fig. 1. K-Means algorithm

In order to know the actual value of K in the dataset, we have to execute K-Means algorithm several times for different values of K. Moreover, it produces good results only when the initial chosen centroids are close to final centroids of the clusters.

By analyzing K-Means algorithm, it is evident that we require some kind of initial guidance to reach final centroids to achieve better clusters and convergence. We can alleviate this problem by introducing the concept of gravitational mass for relative importance of an object in the dataset; because we know that a bigger mass attracts a smaller mass according to gravitational force. Therefore, we propose gravity-based K-Means to achieve better clusters and convergence of the K-Means algorithm and is explained in next section.

4   Gravitational K-Means Algorithm

In some natural phenomenon like fire events, seismic events, crime events, and others, the intrinsic attribute of objects play a vital role in the formation of the clusters. Hence it is sensible to make clusters based on the critical attribute to make semantically better clusters. The proposed algorithm uses a mass function, mentioned in Definition 2, to map a critical attribute of the object to define mass of the object. The algorithm computes the center of mass, mentioned in Definition 3, in place of geometry-based centroid of a cluster. The traditional K-Means clustering algorithm employs a distance-based metric as a measure of dissimilarity to form clusters. The proposed algorithm uses mass-based metric as a measure of dissimilarity in the formation of clusters. The mass-based dissimilarity is calculated by gravitational force which is mentioned in Definition 4. For example, in the fire dataset, we can use burn area attribute of a fire event as mass to form clusters. By adopting this idea, we propose to extend the traditional K-Means algorithm as follows:

Definition 1. Clustering is a process of partitioning a given dataset $X = \{x_1, x_2, ..., x_n\}$ that contains n number of data objects into a set of K number of partitions called clusters $C = \{c_1, c_2, ..., c_K\}$ such that $c_i \neq \phi$, $(i = 1, 2, ..., K)$ and $c_i \cap c_j = \phi$, $(i \neq j)$ and $c_i \cup c_j = X$, $(i \neq j)$.

Definition 2. A mass function is a real valued function that quantifies j^{th} attribute of the ith object $x_i \in X$ i.e. $M_i: A_{ji} \rightarrow R$, where $A_{ji} \in x_i$.

Definition 3.   Center of mass μ_i of a cluster c_i is calculated as per Eq. (2)

$$\mu_i = \sum (M_i \times \text{Spatiotemporal Coordinates}) / \sum M_i \qquad (2)$$

Definition 4. A gravitational force F, between two mass M_1 and M_2, separated at Euclidean distance d, is defined as follows:

$$F = G \times (M_1 \times M_2)/d^2 \qquad (3)$$

where G is gravitational constant.

Our proposed algorithm (shown in Fig. 2), accepts two parameters, a dataset (X) and number of clusters (K) as input and produces K number of clusters as output. The algorithm has three phases namely initialization, iteration and halt. In initialization phase, we generate K random center of masses by choosing critical attributes of K data objects in the dataset. In iteration phase, we assign a data object to a cluster which has largest value of gravitational force between the center of mass of the cluster and the object. The calculation of gravitational force is based on Eq. 3, mentioned in Definition 4. We update center of masses of the clusters in subsequent iterations. In halt phase, we use a stopping criteria to converge the algorithm finally; one of the criteria can be when center of masses in i^{th} and $(i + 1)^{th}$ step do not change.

Input: Dataset X = {x₁, x₂, ..., xₙ} containing n objects and number of clusters i.e. value of K

Output: A set of clusters C = {c₁, c₂, ..., c_K}

Algorithm
1. Initialize: Randomly select K center of masses.
2. Iterate:
    a. Assign data objects to the closest cluster on the basis of gravitational force between data objects and center of masses as per definition 4.
    b. Update center of masses of each cluster as per definition 3.
3. Halt: Stop when center of masses remain unchanged.

Fig. 2. Gravitational K-Means

5   Experiment

The proposed algorithm is applied to fire data set [20], which was prepared by Department of Agriculture, USA. The data pertains to the frequency, extent and magnitude of all wildland fires of different parts of USA from 1984 to 2014. Each fire event is having 18 attributes. We select the relevant attributes such as latitude, longitude, date, fire type and burnt area. The dataset contains 21,673 events of fire, on which our proposed algorithm is applied.

To execute the proposed algorithm on the fire dataset, selection of parameter K is critical. For the selection of parameter K, we use silhouette validity index. Silhouette Index [6] is based on two things, measure of cohesion and measure of separation. Cohesion is how similar a point is to its own cluster and separation is how dissimilar a point is to all other points belonging to other clusters. The value of silhouette Index ranges from −1 to +1. High value of silhouette index is indicative of good quality clusters.

We start the experimentation dataset by taking K = 2, 3, 4, 5, 6, 7, 8, 9 and 10 because we don't have precise knowledge about number of clusters to be formed in the dataset. For every K value, the obtained clusters are validated by the silhouette index. We found that at K = 4, the silhouette index has the maximum value as shown in the Fig. 3, therefore we chose K = 4, executed the algorithm and obtained four clusters. The 3D view of obtained spatiotemporal clusters is shown in Fig. 4 and its 2D view on world map is shown in Fig. 5. As depicted in Fig. 4, the first cluster contains 2927 fire events which occur during winter season depicted in blue color, the second cluster contains 7421 fires during the season of spring shown in cyan color, third cluster has 8700 fires that occur during summer season which contains highest number of fire events shown in yellow color and finally fourth cluster contain 2625 fire events during autumn season shown in dark red color.

The obtained result reveals that there is a pattern of the occurrence of forest fires in a particular season of a year in a specific region. After analyzing the result of our proposed algorithm, we found that the maximum number of fire events occurs during summer season. Moreover, the temperature profile of USA [21] reveals that chances of fire events are more likely to fall in the month of June, July and August that is during summer season and also supports the result of the proposed algorithm. From the obtained result we claim that in case of fire events the attribute 'burn area' plays critical role in obtaining semantically better clusters. Hence, our proposed algorithm can be used in phenomenon where intrinsic attribute plays an important role in the formation of clusters.

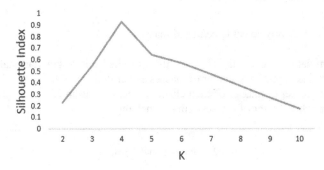

Fig. 3. Silhouette index vs. K

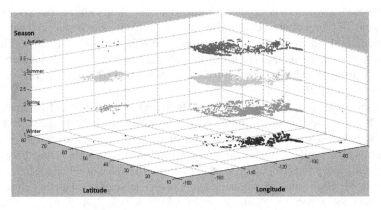

Fig. 4. Spatiotemporal clusters in 3D (Color figure online)

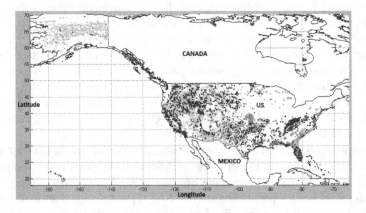

Fig. 5. Spatiotemporal clusters in 2D

For the comparative study, we also executed K-Means algorithm on the fire dataset by taking same parameter values i.e. K = 4. The silhouette index is used for comparing the quality of clusters obtained by both algorithms. We found that the proposed algorithm achieves higher value of the silhouette index that K-Means algorithm for same parameter values. This indicates that our algorithm outperforms K-Means in terms of quality of clusters. Moreover, it has been also observed that proposed algorithm takes fewer numbers of passes to converge in comparison to K-Means algorithm. The performance graph is shown in Fig. 6.

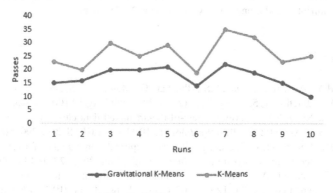

Fig. 6. Performance graph

6 Conclusion and Future Work

The current technologies have capability to produce huge amount of spatiotemporal data pertaining to various fields. Clustering can be used as an efficient technique in data analytics. We have used notion of relative importance of objects by introducing the concept of mass and gravity to develop Gravitational K-Means clustering algorithm, by extending K-Means algorithm, to produce semantically better clusters.

K-Means is one of the notable partition-based clustering approaches. The K-Means algorithm is robust; however, its performance depends on initialization conditions including instance order. The proposed algorithm, however, doesn't solve the initialization problem of K-Means but it finds out weighted means of the cluster by utilizing 'mass function' in finding center of masses of clusters. The traditional K-means algorithm makes use of the Euclidean distance to assign data objects to the closest cluster. The proposed approach uses the gravitational force between data objects and center of masses for assigning data objects to the closest cluster. Silhouette index is found to be useful for selection of input parameter values and also for the measurements of obtained quality of clusters. In addition, the silhouette index is used to compare K-Means and our proposed algorithm. We apply the proposed algorithm on a real fire dataset for experimentation purpose. Result reveals that the proposed algorithm produces more natural clusters. We also perform the comparative study with K-Means algorithm and found that the proposed algorithm outperforms K-Means algorithm in terms of convergence and semantics. Hence, our proposed algorithm can be used in phenomena where intrinsic attribute plays an important role in the formation of clusters.

As part of future work, the proposed algorithm can be extended to sense noise data using sophisticated gravitational concepts. The validity index catering mass of object is also need to be developed to better assess quality of obtained clusters. Some heuristic approach needs to be developed to select input parameter value K. The proposed algorithm needs to be compared with other clustering algorithms. Moreover, the proposed algorithm needs to be applied on a greater number of real datasets where intrinsic attribute plays an important role in formation of clusters.

Acknowledgments. This work is supported by Ministry of Electronics and Information Technology, Government of India under the Visvesvaraya Ph.D. scheme.

References

1. Ansari, M.Y., Ahmad, A., Khan, S.S., Bhushan, G., Mainuddin: Spatiotemporal clustering: a review. Artif. Intell. Rev. **53**, 2381–2423 (2020). https://doi.org/10.1007/s10462-019-09736-1
2. Ahmad, A., Khan, S.S.: Survey of state-of-the-art mixed data clustering algorithms. IEEE Access **7**, 31883–31902 (2019). https://doi.org/10.1109/ACCESS.2019.2903568
3. Pena, J.M., Lozano, J.A., Larranaga, P.: An empirical comparison of four initialization methods for the K-means algorithm. Pattern Recogn. Lett. **20**, 1027–1040 (1999)
4. Khan, S.S., Ahmad, A.: Cluster center initialization algorithm for K-means clustering. Pattern Recogn. Lett. **25**(11), 1293–1302 (2004). https://doi.org/10.1016/j.patrec.2004.04.007
5. Jain, A.K., Dubes, R.C.: Algorithms for Clustering Data. Prentice Hall, Englewood Cliffs (1988)
6. Rousseeuw, P.: Silhouettes: a graphical aid to the interpretation and validation of cluster analysis. J. Comput. Appl. Math. **20**(1), 53–65 (1987)
7. Kamat, R.K., Kamath, R.S.: Earthquake cluster analysis: K-means approach. J. Chem. Pharm. Sci. **10**(1), 250–253 (2017)
8. Martino, F.D., Pedrycz, W., Sessa, S.: Spatiotemporal extended fuzzy C-means clustering algorithm for hotspots detection and prediction. Fuzzy Sets Syst. **340**, 109–126 (2018)
9. Mayorga, D., Melgarejo, M.A., Obregon, N.: A fuzzy clustering based method for the spatiotemporal analysis of criminal patterns. In: IEEE International Conference on Fuzzy Systems (FUZZ-IEEE), pp. 738–744 (2016)
10. Hu, Y., Wang, F., Guin, C., Zhu, H.: A spatio-temporal kernel density estimation framework for predictive crime hotspot mapping and evaluation. Appl. Geogr. **99**, 89–97 (2018)
11. Ansari, M.Y., Prakash, A., Mainuddin: Application of spatiotemporal fuzzy C-means clustering for crime spot detection. Def. Sci. J. **68**(4), 374–380 (2018). https://doi.org/10.14429/dsj.68.12518
12. Adin, A., Lee, D., Goicoa, T., Ugarte, M.D.: A two-stage approach to estimate spatial and spatio-temporal disease risks in the presence of local discontinuities and clusters. Stat. Methods Med. Res. **28**(9), 2595–2613 (2019)
13. Hudjimartsu, S.A., Djatna, T., Ambarwari, A., Apriliantona: Spatial temporal clustering for hotspot using Kulldorff scan statistic method (KSS): a case in Riau Province. IOP Conf. Ser. Earth Environ. Sci. **54**, 012056 (2018). http://iopscience.iop.org/article/10.1088/1755-1315/54/1/012056
14. Oliveira, R., Santos, M.Y., Pires, J.M.: 4D+ SNN: a spatio-temporal density-based clustering approach with 4D similarity. In: IEEE 13th International Conference on Data Mining Workshops (ICDMW) (2013)

15. Liu, Q., Liu, W., Tang, J., Deng, M., Liu, Y.: Permutation-test-bed clustering method for detection of dynamic patterns in spatiotemporal datasets. Comput. Environ. Urban Syst. **75**, 204–216 (2019). https://doi.org/10.1016/j.compenvurbsys.2019.02.007
16. Husch, M., Schyska, B.U., Bremen, L.V.: CorClustST - correlation-based clustering of big spatio-temporal datasets. Future Gener. Comput. Syst. (2018). https://doi.org/10.1016/j.future.2018.04.002
17. van de Velden, M., D'Enza, A.I., Markos, A.: Distance-based clustering of mixed data. WIREs Comp. Stats. (2018). https://doi.org/10.1002/wics.1456
18. Gomez, J., Dasgupta, D., Nasraoui, O.: A new gravitational clustering algorithm. In: Proceedings of the 2003 SIAM International Conference on Data Mining (2003). https://doi.org/10.1137/1.9781611972733.8
19. Binder, P., Muma, M., Zoubir, A.M.: Gravitational clustering: a simple, robust and adaptive approach for distributed networks. Sig. Process. **149**, 36–48 (2018). https://doi.org/10.1016/j.sigpro.2018.02.034
20. Data.gov. https://catalog.data.gov/dataset. Accessed 09 Apr 2019
21. Climate of the United States. https://en.wikipedia.org/wiki/Climate_of_the_United_States. Accessed 08 Oct 2019

Experimental Analysis of Convolutional Neural Networks and Capsule Networks for Image Classification

Shweta Bali[(⊠)] and Shyam Sunder Tyagi

Manav Rachna International Institute of Research and Studies, Faridabad, India
bali82.shweta@gmail.com, shyam.fet@mriu.edu.in

Abstract. Deep Learning neural networks with the help of Convolutional neural networks (CNNs) have succeeded to find solution to a large diversity of problems related to images. The success is credited to their capacity to learn hierarchical features directly from images and then feeding the feature vectors for classification. Subsampling in CNNs loses the spatial relationships between the features which is essential to determine the correct class of objects. CNNs also fail to handle rotation invariance. To address this concern, capsule networks which are group of neurons use two main algorithms namely dynamic routing algorithm and route by agreement algorithm to model the spatial and pose variability. These networks can address the problem of rotational and spatial variance, deal with reduced quantity of labeled data and handle imbalanced classes in the given dataset. In this paper convolutional neural network is compared with capsule network using augmented CIFAR-10 dataset.

Keywords: Convolutional neural network · Capsule network · Deep learning · Image classification

1 Introduction

Image Classification is the task of label assignment to a new image from predefined set of classes. The goal of deep learning algorithm is to discover the underlying pattern from the dataset and classify the new data based on the trained data. Given an image, for the machine to understand the contents of the image need to be quantified. The process is called feature extraction where feature vectors are extracted by applying algorithm to the input image. Traditional machine learning techniques used hand engineered features such as histogram of oriented gradients (HOG) [1], local binary patterns (LBP) [2] to extract feature vector whereas the process of feature extraction is automated in case of deep learning algorithms for image classification. There are a numerous number of challenges faced by image classification algorithms. Some of them are viewpoint and scale variations, deformations, occlusions, changes in illumination, background clutter, intra-class variations. The classifier needs to be developed considering these challenges. Convolutional Neural Networks (CNN) [3] are special type of deep learning algorithms that have made a major breakthrough in face recognition. CNN's worked well for image classification task, but they have some limitations and drawbacks. One of the downsides

© Springer Nature Singapore Pte Ltd. 2020
U. Batra et al. (Eds.): REDSET 2019, CCIS 1230, pp. 430–441, 2020.
https://doi.org/10.1007/978-981-15-5830-6_36

of CNN is max pooling which limits them to capture spatial and pose related information in the images. They are also not robust to affine transformation and to improvise their generalizability they need large amount of training samples with a number of rotations and transformations that is difficult to achieve for real world applications. To overcome this drawback Capsule networks were first introduced by Geoffrey Hinton's paper [4] where they introduced a capsule network architecture as shown in Fig. 1 [4] that has reached state-of-the-art performance on MNIST dataset. Capsule networks require less amount of training examples and preserves pose related information in the images. Capsule network is built on the notion of inverse graphics. The network consists of a number of capsules which represent functions that predicts the presence and instantiation parameters of specific objects present at a particular location in the image. The activations in the network map hierarchy of parts.

This paper is systematized as follows: Sect. 1, we discuss the need of capsule networks. Section 2 gives literature review. Section 3 examines capsule networks. Section 4 represents experimental setup, performance measures and the results achieved on augmented CIFAR-10 dataset. Section 5 presents the conclusion and the areas for further study.

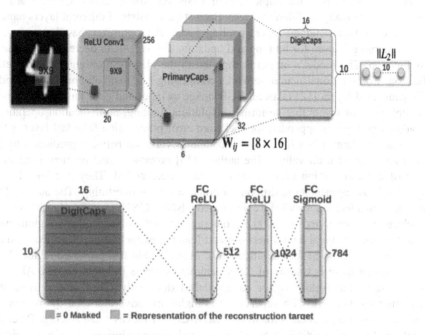

Fig. 1. Architecture of capsule network [4]

2 Literature Review

Extensive research has been done by the researchers for classifying the images. Earlier approaches that included a number of algorithms and techniques proposed by different researchers relied on the techniques such as Histogram of oriented gradients (HOG) which was initially developed to detect pedestrians. SIFT (Scale variant feature transform) [5] which was also one of the representative techniques used for detection as well as classification. With the advent of machine learning a number of algorithms such as Support Vector machines [6], Random forests and kd-trees [7], boosting classifiers [8], bag of features [9]. Support Vector machines classify the data with the help of hyperplane that is capable of separating linear as well as non-linear data by transformations using linear and non-linear kernels respectively. The machine learning techniques [10] were unable to handle variation in the image size, occlusions, deformations etc. It was difficult to develop a generic algorithm that could work for different problems. To overcome the drawbacks of the earlier techniques, deep learning algorithms evolved due to emergence of GPUs (Graphical Processing Units) and availability of standardized datasets in different domains. Convolutional Neural Networks have achieved good performance in different image-related tasks. LeNet-5 [11] multilayer network is used for implementing CNN on Arabic digits. CNNs learn the features automatically in different stages. Each stage consists of different layers namely convolutional layer, hidden layer, pooling layer. An optimizer based on gradient descent learning is used for training and updating the weights to decrease the value of loss function. The model's output is supplied to the classification algorithm for classification. Convolutional neural networks comprising of 5 convolutional layers and 3 fully connected layers [12] takes an RGB image as input and goes through a series of different types of layers that perform convolution, pooling, normalization operations. An additional layer is appended for backward error propagation. The last layer is loss layer that calculates a loss function that computes variation between prediction by the model and ground truth values. The authors [13] proposed GPU efficient implementation of 2D convolution process, new features were added. They considered techniques such as augmentation, dropout in order to reduce overfitting. The authors [14] came up with a technique called Region-based CNN(R-CNN) used the algorithm based on selective search to extract 2000 regions present in the images. These regions were fed to the convolutional neural network and features extraction is performed on these regions and fed to SVM for classification of object within that proposed region. They concluded that there is sharing of CNN parameters across different classes. Also, the dimensions of the feature vector have reduced drastically. They also showed that pretraining the network with supervision is highly effective and then the network is fined tuned for the target class for small data. R-CNN achieves mean Average Precision (mAP) on PASCAL VOC07 58.5%. A new visualization technique [15] was developed to find problems on how to obtain better results by providing details of intermediate layers and classifier. It used multi-layered deconvolutional network (deconvnet). ImageNet trained model performed well on datasets such as Caltech-101, Caltech-256 whereas for trained models built using smaller datasets such as PASCAL, these models generalize less but the performance can be enhanced by using various different types of loss functions that are used to detect multiple objects per image. The authors [16] investigated the impact of depth of a network on the accuracy of recognition task. They proposed a network architecture which used 3 * 3 filter and achieved significant improvement by using the depth of 16–19 layers. The architecture used smaller receptive fields of size 3 * 3 throughout the whole network with stride of 1. The implementation allows performing training as well as evaluation on multiple GPUs in which batches of training images are split and processed on parallel GPUs. The experiments are performed on ILSVRC-2012 dataset and top-1 and top-5 errors are computed for evaluating the performance. The authors found that increasing the depth from 11 to 19 layers causes decrease in the classification error. The VGG-Net based network surpassed the previous techniques, that produced top results in ILSVRC-2012 and ILSVRC-2013 competitions. The major drawback of CNNs is that they are poor in capturing spatial information, deformations and pose related information in the images. These drawbacks were overcome by the capsule networks.

3 Capsule Networks for Image Classification

Capsule network [17] architecture is based on neural network that has shown improvement in performance of image related tasks such as semantic and instance segmentation, classification [18–20], localization, object detection in comparison with convolutional neural networks. In classifying the handwritten digits of MNIST dataset [21] the architecture consists of capsules and the output from each capsule is a vector of 8-dimensions and its length symbolizes expected probability of presence of the object and orientation encodes pose parameters related to the object. The capsules exhibit the property of equivariance where in case the object makes any transformations in the form of translation, scaling or rotation then capsule will output same length vector but with slightly different orientation. In [22] the capsule networks for classifying the histological images of breast cancer. They found that architecture can be optimized by varying the quantity of convolutional layers, primary and capsule layer's dimensions, regularization. They noticed that the cross-validation results of capsule networks are comparable with results of convolutional neural networks. In [23] the authors performed sentiment analysis by using capsule networks and Recurrent Neural Network (RNN). The authors [24] proposed a framework using multilevel capsules that make use of hierarchical representations for learning spatial information and densely connected convolutions are used. The network achieved accuracy of 96.90% on SVHN dataset and also there was decrease in the count of parameters used by ensemble model created from seven CapsNet models for CIFAR-10 dataset.

Capsules are collections of neurons whose activity vectors represent pose parameters and the length of these vectors represent the probability of existence of a specific object. Capsule networks work on the concept of routing by agreement based on which the outputs are sent to all parent capsules in the next layer. Each Capsule tries to predict the output of the parent Capsules.

Consider the "capsule i", the output of the capsule is u_i, the prediction for parent j is calculated as $\hat{u}_{j|i} = W_{ij}u_i$, where W_{ij} is the weight matrix. Coupling coefficients c_{ij} are computed as $c_{ij} = \exp(b_{ij})/\sum_k \exp(b_{ik})$ where b_{ij} is the log probability which tells the coupling ability of "capsule i" can be coupled with "capsule j". The input vector to the parent capsule j is calculated as follows $s_j = \sum_i c_{ij}\widehat{u}_{j|i}$. The output vectors v_j of the capsules have values greater than one so a non-linear squashing function is applied so that the values are less than one which is calculated as $v_j = (\|s_j\|^2)/(1 + \|s_j\|^2) \cdot (s_j/(\|s_j\|^2))$. The log probabilities are updated based on the agreement a_{ij} between two vectors $v_{j|i}$ and $\widehat{u}_{j|i}$ where $a_{ij} = v_j.\widehat{u}_{j|i}$.

4 Experiments

4.1 Datasets

Experimentation is performed on dataset named Canadian Institute for Advanced Research (CIFAR)-10 (Fig. 2) [26]. The dataset consists of 32 * 32 colored images divided into 10 different classes. 50,000 images will be used for training and testing will be performed on 10,000 images.

Fig. 2. Sample images from CIFAR-10 dataset

4.2 Preprocessing

The training set is augmented using transformations such as rotation, horizontal flip, vertical and horizontal shift of 20%. Different rotation angles (20, 40, 60, 80°) are used in different augmentation techniques. Augmentation helps avoid overfitting of the model.

4.3 Architecture of Capsule Network

Capsule Networks architecture is made up of number of layers. The capsule network architecture that is adopted for experimentation comes from [25] where the authors discussed the capsule network as follows: The architecture is as follows:

1) **Input layer:** This layer comprises of input training images. In case of CIFAR-10 dataset, the input images are 32 * 32 colored images. In case the images are of large size, they are down sampled so that the model is trained on reduced number of parameters and training time is also reduced drastically.

2) **Convolutional layers:** The initial layer uses 256 filters of kernel size 9 with stride value of 1 and activation function as RELU to generate feature maps. The second layer uses reshape function to convert the feature maps into vectors. The output from the first layer is passed to 256 filters of kernel size 9 with stride value of 2 which gives an output of dimensions 6 * 6 * 256.

3) **Primary Capsule Layer:** In this layer the output from the above layers is reshaped to 8-dimensional vector. Also, this output needs to be squashed which means that length of output vector should be between 0 and 1. The output is 32 primary capsules with 6 * 6 * 8 capsules each. These capsules are fed to higher layers.

4) **Image Capsule Layer:** This layer takes the input from primary capsule layer and results in 10 capsules that represent the class of the 16-dimensional vector and with a total output of size 10 * 16. Further, lambda layer is used to predict the output class by converting these 10 capsules into single value.

4.4   Reconstruction

A network called as decoder network is appended to the capsule network for tuning the output of the capsule network as well as for reconstruction of the images. It makes the model generalizable. The network consists of two components mask and decoder. The main function of mask is to mask the output which is not desired. Masking is performed using one-hot encoding function. The decoder consists of three fully connected layers with 512, 1024 and 3072 nodes that is used for reconstruction of original images of size 32 * 32. The count of pixels in last fully connected layer is equal to the count of pixels in input image.

4.5   Loss Functions

There are two types of losses in the capsule network [4]. Margin loss predicts if certain object of a class is present in the particular image or not. It is equal to the value computed by squaring length of output vector associated with an object. For an object to be present margin loss should be greater than or equal to 0.9. From margin loss is calculated as follows:

For each image capsule "k" the margin loss is computed as

$$L_k = T_k \max(0, m^+ - \|v_k\|)^2 + \lambda(1 - T_k)\max(0, \|v_k\| - m^-)^2 \tag{1}$$

The value of the parameter T_k equals 1 in case the object of a particular class k is present, $m^+ = 0.9$, $m^- = 0.1$.

Reconstruction loss is the square difference between the input image and the reconstructed image.

$$\text{Final loss} = \text{Margin Loss} - \lambda(\textit{Reconstruction Loss}) \tag{2}$$

4.6 Results

The experimentations are achieved on the augmented CIFAR-10 dataset. Augmentation is performed by rotating the images by horizontal flipping, vertical and horizontal translation of 20% and rotating by 20° (CapsNet-20, CNN-20), 40° (CapsNet-40, CNN-40), 60° (CapsNet-60, CNN-60), 80° (CapsNet-80, CNN-80) respectively. Figure 3 depicts the results of training accuracy of the capsule network and shows that accuracy drops with the increase in the rotation angle from 20° towards 80°. It can be due to complexity of the dataset as well as complex backgrounds.

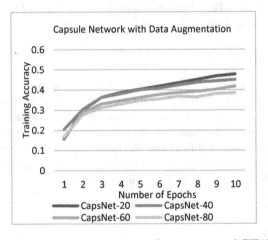

Fig. 3. Training accuracy results of Capsule networks on augmented CIFAR-10 dataset for 10 epochs

The data augmentation results on a baseline CNN is shown in Fig. 4. The training accuracy of the baseline CNN also reduces with the increase in the angle from 20° to 80°. It also shows that the accuracy is better than the capsule networks. The capsule networks require more time to train the network as compared to the convolutional neural networks as shown in the Fig. 5. It may be attributed to the computational complexity and also due to routing by agreement algorithm.

In the Fig. 6 the margin loss for the capsule networks for different data augmentation showed that the margin loss increases by small amount with the increase in the angle of rotation which indicates that if some tweaks such as increasing the count of convolutional layers, capsules in the primary capsule layers can be applied to the model to see the improvements. Figure 7 depicts that convolutional neural network loss increases with the increase in the amount of angle of rotation. This shows that performance of convolutional neural networks deteriorates with increase in the angle of rotation.

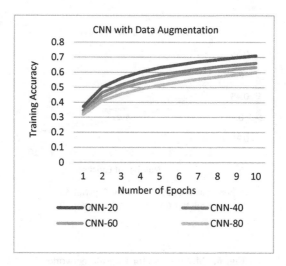

Fig. 4. Training accuracy results of Convolutional neural network (CNN) on augmented CIFAR-10 dataset

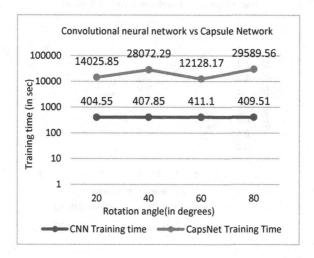

Fig. 5. Training time results for Convolutional neural network and Capsule network with rotation angles

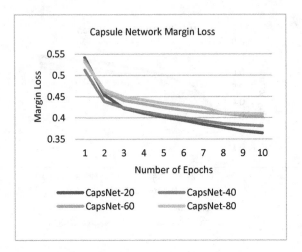

Fig. 6. Margin loss for Capsule networks

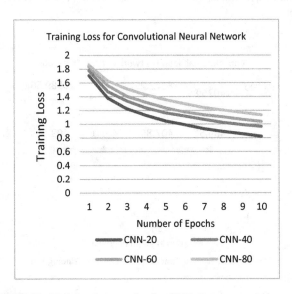

Fig. 7. Training loss results for CNN data augmentation

4.7 Testing Results

The results of the model are evaluated on 10,000 testing images of the CIFAR-10 dataset. Accuracy is calculated as the ratio of correctly identified images by the total number of the images [29].

$$Accuracy = \Sigma \; Correctly \; identified \; images \div Total \; number \; of \; images \qquad (3)$$

Table 1. Comparison of accuracy and loss for CNN and Capsule networks

No. of epochs	Convolutional neural network		Capsule network	
	Accuracy (%)	Training time (sec)	Accuracy (%)	Training time (sec)
10	72.90	499.41	75.50	8734.40
25	80.25	1240.79	79.03	21891.58
50	80.50	2410.18	81.21	20010.30
75	83.31	3426.85	83.51	25678.12

Keras and Tensorflow deep learning libraries are used for implementation. The experiments are performed on Intel(R) Core (TM) i7-6700 CPU@3.40 GHz 3.40 GHz (32.0 GB RAM). From Table 1 we can conclude that the accuracy of capsule network [4] is comparable to that of the baseline convolutional neural networks.

5 Conclusion

Image classification for complex datasets such as CIFAR-10 is a challenging task. The main drawback of the convolutional neural networks is the problem of pooling which causes lot of spatial information to be lost. Capsule networks solved this problem with the help of routing by agreement [4] algorithm. From the experiments it is found that capsule networks take lot of time for training in comparison to the convolutional neural networks. The accuracy is also low and comparable to convolutional neural network which may be attributed to the complex background present in the images. Some tweaks are required either the number of the layers or primary capsules or the number of epochs or optimizers can be explored so as to improve the performance of capsule networks. Further the experiments can be performed on distorted and blurred images.

References

1. Dalal, N., Triggs, B.: Histograms of oriented gradients for human detection. In: Proceedings of IEEE Computer Society Conference on Computer Vision and Pattern Recognition (CVPR), vol. 1, pp. 886–893 (2005)
2. Heikkilä, M., Pietikäinen, M., Schmid, C.: Description of interest regions with local binary patterns. Pattern Recognit. **42**(3), 425–436 (2009)

3. Lawrence, S., Giles, C.L., Tsoi, A.C., Back, A.D.: Face recognition: A convolutional neural-network approach. IEEE Trans. Neural Netw. **8**(1), 98–113 (1997)
4. Sabour, S., Frosst, N., Hinton, G.E.: Dynamic routing between capsules. In: Advances in Neural Information Processing Systems, pp. 3856–3866 (2017)
5. Zhou, X., Yu, K., Zhang, T., Huang, T.S.: Image classification using super-vector coding of local image descriptors. In: Daniilidis, K., Maragos, P., Paragios, N. (eds.) ECCV 2010. LNCS, vol. 6315, pp. 141–154. Springer, Heidelberg (2010). https://doi.org/10.1007/978-3-642-15555-0_11
6. Liu, J., Zhang, S., Deng, S.: A method of plant classification based on wavelet transforms and support vector machines. In: Huang, D.-S., Jo, K.-H., Lee, H.-H., Kang, H.-J., Bevilacqua, V. (eds.) ICIC 2009. LNCS, vol. 5754, pp. 253–260. Springer, Heidelberg (2009). https://doi.org/10.1007/978-3-642-04070-2_29
7. Zaklouta, F., Stanciulescu, B., Hamdoun, O.: Traffic sign classification using kd trees and random forests. In: The 2011 International Joint Conference on Neural Networks, pp. 2151–2155. IEEE (2011)
8. Korytkowski, M., Rutkowski, L., Scherer, R.: Fast image classification by boosting fuzzy classifiers. Inf. Sci. **327**, 175–182 (2016)
9. Nowak, E., Jurie, F., Triggs, B.: Sampling strategies for bag-of-features image classification. In: Leonardis, A., Bischof, H., Pinz, A. (eds.) ECCV 2006. LNCS, vol. 3954, pp. 490–503. Springer, Heidelberg (2006). https://doi.org/10.1007/11744085_38
10. Mogelmose, A., Trivedi, M.M., Moeslund, T.B.: Vision-based traffic sign detection and analysis for intelligent driver assistance systems: perspectives and survey. IEEE Trans. Intell. Transp. Syst. **13**(4), 1484–1497 (2012)
11. El-Sawy, A., EL-Bakry, H., Loey, M.: CNN for handwritten arabic digits recognition based on LeNet-5. In: Hassanien, A.E., Shaalan, K., Gaber, T., Azar, A.T., Tolba, M.F. (eds.) AISI 2016. AISC, vol. 533, pp. 566–575. Springer, Cham (2017). https://doi.org/10.1007/978-3-319-48308-5_54
12. Wu, J.: Introduction to convolutional neural networks. National Key Lab for Novel Software Technology. Nanjing University, China, 5, p. 23 (2017)
13. Krizhevsky, A., Sutskever, I., Hinton, G.E.: ImageNet classification with deep convolutional neural networks. In: Advances in Neural Information Processing Systems, pp. 1097–1105 (2012)
14. Girshick, R., Donahue, J., Darrell, T., Malik, J.: Rich feature hierarchies for accurate object detection and semantic segmentation. In: Proceedings of the IEEE Conference on Computer Vision and Pattern Recognition, pp. 580–587 (2014)
15. Zeiler, Matthew D., Fergus, R.: Visualizing and understanding convolutional networks. In: Fleet, D., Pajdla, T., Schiele, B., Tuytelaars, T. (eds.) ECCV 2014. LNCS, vol. 8689, pp. 818–833. Springer, Cham (2014). https://doi.org/10.1007/978-3-319-10590-1_53
16. Simonyan, K., Zisserman, A.: Very deep convolutional networks for large-scale image recognition. arXiv preprint arXiv:1409.1556 (2014)
17. Xi, E., Bing, S., Jin, Y.: Capsule network performance on complex data. arXiv preprint arXiv:1712.03480 (2017)
18. Afshar, P., Mohammadi, A., Plataniotis, K.N.: Brain tumor type classification via capsule networks. In: 25th IEEE International Conference on Image Processing (ICIP), pp. 3129–3133. IEEE (2018)
19. Kumar, A.D.: Novel deep learning model for traffic sign detection using capsule networks. arXiv preprint arXiv:1805.04424 (2018)

20. Jiménez-Sánchez, A., Albarqouni, S., Mateus, D.: Capsule networks against medical imaging data challenges. In: Stoyanov, D., et al. (eds.) LABELS/CVII/STENT -2018. LNCS, vol. 11043, pp. 150–160. Springer, Cham (2018). https://doi.org/10.1007/978-3-030-01364-6_17

21. Hinton, G.E., Krizhevsky, A., Wang, S.D.: Transforming auto-encoders. In: Honkela, T., Duch, W., Girolami, M., Kaski, S. (eds.) ICANN 2011. LNCS, vol. 6791, pp. 44–51. Springer, Heidelberg (2011). https://doi.org/10.1007/978-3-642-21735-7_6

22. Iesmantas, T., Alzbutas, R.: Convolutional capsule network for classification of breast cancer histology images. In: Campilho, A., Karray, F., ter Haar Romeny, B. (eds.) ICIAR 2018. LNCS, vol. 10882, pp. 853–860. Springer, Cham (2018). https://doi.org/10.1007/978-3-319-93000-8_97

23. Wang, Y., Sun, A., Han, J., Liu, Y., Zhu, X.: Sentiment analysis by capsules. In: Proceedings of the 2018 World Wide Web Conference, pp. 1165–1174. International World Wide Web Conferences Steering Committee (2018)

24. Phaye, S.S.R., Sikka, A., Dhall, A., Bathula, D.R.: Multi-level dense capsule networks. In: Jawahar, C.V., Li, H., Mori, G., Schindler, K. (eds.) ACCV 2018. LNCS, vol. 11365, pp. 577–592. Springer, Cham (2019). https://doi.org/10.1007/978-3-030-20873-8_37

25. Understanding Capsule Network Architecture. https://software.intel.com/en-us/articles/understanding-capsule-network-architecture

26. CIFAR-10 and CIFAR-100 datasets. https://www.cs.toronto.edu/~kriz/cifar.html

27. Johnson, J.M., Khoshgoftaar, T.M.: Survey on deep learning with class imbalance. J. Big Data 6(1), 27 (2019)

28. Perlich, C.: Learning curves in machine learning. In: Encyclopedia of Machine Learning, pp. 577–580 (2010)

29. Park, J.-G., Kim, K.-J.: Design of a visual perception model with edge-adaptive gabor filter and support vector machine for traffic sign detection. Expert Syst. Appl. 40(9), 3679–3687 (2013)

Evaluation of an Efficient Method for Object Detection in Video

Manoj Attri[1], Rohit Tanwar[2(✉)], Narender[1], and Neha Nandal[3]

[1] Manav Rachna University, Faridabad, India
{manoj,narender}@mru.edu.in
[2] University of Petroleum and Energy Studies, Dehradun, India
r.tanwar@ddn.upes.ac.in
[3] St. Martin's Engineering College, Hyderabad, India

Abstract. In this real world, many public or open areas are facilitated with cameras at multiple angles to monitor the activities of human for safety of people or infrastructure. The object detection is a fundamental concept of computer vision that focused on the detection of instances of objects of a certain class (such as person, animal, ghost, buildings, or vehicles) in videos. This manuscript presents a method for object detection using background subtraction and morphology. The core of the proposed work is the simple background subtraction method. In the first step we developed a background model based on some video frames that only consists of static background without any moving object. A suitable scheme is applied for updating the background model so that the challenges like camera shake, dust and fog particles in air should be resolved. The scheme uses the "learning rate" for the entire frame. In the second step we extract the foreground pixels which are in motion. After the initial foreground extraction, the morphological operators are applied for noise cleaning.

Keywords: Object detection · Object tracking · Basic background subtraction · Mathematical morphology · Learning rate

1 Introduction

In today's technical world, the motion oriented object detection is considered as an hot area of research currently in trend that attracts lots of attention of research community like computer vision, video processing, automation analysis, object representation etc. The moving object detection focused on finding out the instances of semantic objects of a various classes like as animal, human, satellites, building, crops, vehicle, geographical region or anything which can be identified in video frames, while object tracking is considered as the task where the trajectory of either single or more than one objects is followed in frames [1, 2]. The detected object can be represented in the form of point, contour, skeleton or boundary of object using segmentation etc. [3]. In the current era, the video cameras such as IP camera, CCTV camera, or some other kind of surveillance cameras are installed everywhere for surveillance. At some places, flying

U. Batra et al. (Eds.): REDSET 2019, CCIS 1230, pp. 442–451, 2020.
https://doi.org/10.1007/978-981-15-5830-6_37

cameras like drone are available for the surveillance of mob, busy places, hilly areas, deep zones etc. It enhances the development of the intelligent video surveillance system which is used for the estimation of the moving person or object.

Since, the motion oriented object detection technique involved in various real-time applications such as image analysis, image automation, auto-annotation, scene recognition and scene understanding [4–7]. But in real-time, it is still an open challenge due to the complexity of the system. It is one of the key problems in image processing and computer vision, which has received continuous attention since the birth of the field. We, as a human being, easily "detect" various objects such as car, flower, people, buildings, and automobiles etc.

In the literature, we found some challenges that needed to be faced during the detection of moving object in video frames [4–6]:

- There may be some illumination changes like sudden or gradual change due to lighting effect or due to sunlight in water.
- There may also some distracting motions like camera-shake, moving elevator, motion in water, weaving tree leaves etc.
- Facing environmental effects like dust particles in air, rain, fog in the environment etc.

The image processing provides various techniques for object detection but one that is used in this paper is basic background subtraction (BBS). This technique mainly used to model the background from initial few frames and then it identifies the moving pixels from each frame by computing the difference from current image with an effective threshold. This technique extracts the meaningful pixel more accurately. The objects not in background are also get detected by this technique however they are not in motion. The main drawback of existing BBS methods enlists that they are sensitive to the environmental change such as sudden or gradual illumination variation. Most of the existing methods applied the static background for modelling but there is requirement to update the background model along with current frames. Here, the updation of the background model is again a serious challenge for background subtraction technique. Even after updating the model, experimental results were not up to the mark. So for noise cleaning morphology was used. Mathematical morphology (MM) is a branch of science based on set theory. In such situation, the post processing plays a crucial role where the morphology is used for extracting image components or geometrical features which is used for description and representation of region shape, such as skeletons, boundaries etc. [7–11]. The morphological operators are used to remove the noisy pixels or outliers from the detected pixels [9, 12, 13]. Our goal in this research is to develop a method for automatic object detection. Two morphological operators are used i.e. erosion and dilation.

2 Literature Review

Background subtraction is a straightforward way to deal with identify moving articles in video sequences. The essential thought is to subtract the present edge from a foundation picture and to order every pixel as closer view or foundation by contrasting the distinction and an edge [18]. Morphological tasks pursued by an associated part examination are utilized to register every single dynamic district in the picture. By and by, a few troubles emerge: the foundation picture is undermined by clamor because of camera developments and vacillating articles (e.g., trees waving), light changes, mists, shadows. To manage these challenges a few techniques have been proposed [19].

A few works utilize a deterministic foundation model, e.g., by portraying the allowable interim for every pixel of the foundation picture just as the most extreme pace of progress in sequential pictures or the middle of biggest interframes supreme distinction [20, 21]. Most works anyway depend on measurable models of the foundation, accepting that every pixel is an irregular variable with a likelihood circulation evaluated from the video stream. For instance, the Pfinder framework ("Person Finder") utilizes a Gaussian model to portray every pixel of the foundation picture [22]. An increasingly broad methodology comprises of utilizing a blend of Gaussians to speak to every pixel. This permits the portrayal of multi modular appropriations which happen in common scene (e.g., on account of shuddering trees) [23].

Another arrangement of calculations depends on spatio–fleeting division of the video signal. These strategies attempt to distinguish moving districts considering not just the worldly development of the pixel forces and shading yet additionally their spatial properties. Division is performed in a three-dimensional (3-D) district of picture time space, thinking about the fleeting development of neighbor pixels. This should be possible in a few different ways, e.g., by utilizing spatio–fleeting entropy, joined with morphological activities [24]. This methodology prompts an improvement of the frameworks execution, contrasted and customary edge distinction techniques. Different methodologies depend on the 3-D structure tensor characterized from the pixels spatial and transient subordinates, in a given time interim [25]. For this situation, identification depends on the Mahalanobis separation, expecting a Gaussian appropriation for the subsidiaries. This methodology has been executed progressively and tried with PETS 2005 informational index. Different options have likewise been considered, e.g., the utilization of a district developing strategy in 3-D space–time [26].

A critical research exertion has been done to adapt to shadows and with nonstationary foundations. Two sorts of changes must be considered: show changes (e.g., because of the sun movement) and quick changes (e.g., because of mists, downpour or unexpected changes in static articles). Versatile models and limits have been utilized to manage moderate foundation changes [27]. These systems recursively update the foundation parameters and edges so as to follow the advancement of the parameters in nonstationary working conditions. To adapt to sudden changes, various model procedures have been proposed [27] just as prescient stochastic models (e.g., AR, ARMA [28, 29]).

Another trouble is the nearness of phantoms [30], i.e., bogus dynamic areas because of statics objects having a place with the foundation picture (e.g., vehicles) which all of a sudden begin to move. This issue has been tended to by joining foundation subtraction with outline differencing or by elevated level activities [31, 32].

3   Background Subtraction

Background subtraction is a process that extracts foreground objects from the image frames more accurately as compared to others. As mentioned in [8] many other traditional object detection methods follow same value of "learning rate" for complete frame but the proposed method make use of different "learning rate" for every pixel as per given parameters. As found in the literature many object detection methods face environmental changes they can be sudden or gradual change. Because of these changes one requires to update the background model using the given "learning rate". According to [8], background subtraction process is further classified in three parts:

Background Model Initialization
Initially the requirement is to estimate the background model. There is an assumption that few initial frames are used for modeling of the background and also the sequence of frame begins with the non-presence of an object. In [8, 10], the selective averaging technique is used to construct the model.

$$BM_N(x,y) = \frac{\sum_{m=1}^{N} I_m(x,y)}{N},$$

BMN(x, y): It is specified as the intensity value of the pixel (x, y) of the technique, $I_m(x, y)$ represents the intensity value of pixel (x, y) of the mth frame. The total count of frames are taken to be N.

Background Subtraction
After constructing the background model, the difference is being find out among the existing frame and the background frame to detect the object [2, 10, 11, 14],

$$D_t(x,y) = |I_t(x,y) - BM_{t-1}(x,y)|,$$

$BM_t(x, y)$: represents the intensity value of pixel (x, y) at time some time t, and $I_t(x, y)$ represents the intensity value of pixel (x, y) in the existing frame at an instant t. The variation is then compared to the threshold Thad for background and foreground pixel classification.

$$(x,y) = \begin{cases} foreground \ if \ D_t(x,y) \geq Th_{ad} \\ background \ if \ D_t(x,y) < Th_{ad} \end{cases}$$

Background Model Update
Due to environmental changes the model can be updated iteratively for each frame. Hence in [8], updation is done in pixel-by-pixel fashion with learning rate, αad, t(x, y) for each pixel. The rate of change of background dynamics is directly proportional to the rate of updating the model. The rate of updating the model is used through the learning rate. An increase in value of background dynamics will subsequently increase then the learning rate in context of the model in order to reduce the false alarms. The model is updated according to the following equation:

$$BM_t(x,y) = \alpha_{ad,t}(x,y)I_t(x,y) + (1 - \alpha_{ad,t}(x,y))BM_{t-1}(x,y),$$

Such that $0 \leq \alpha_{ad}$ and $t(x, y) \leq 1$. Here, the value of learning rate i.e. α_{ad}, $t(x, y)$ is highly dependent on two parameters and their weights, α_1 and α_2 where w_1 and w_2 are weights and $w_1 + w_2 \leq 1$.

$$\alpha ad, t(x, y) = w1\ \alpha1 + w2\ \alpha2$$

The learning rate is assigned as per the values of following two parameters [9, 10].

1. The first parameter is greatly affected by the difference *i.e.* $D_t(x, y)$. The large value for α_1 is assigned for a smaller $D_t(x, y)$ and σ_1 is $Th_{ad}/5$ where σ_1 is a function of Th_{ad}.

$$\alpha_1 = \begin{cases} e^{-\frac{1*D_t(x,y)^2}{2*\sigma_1^2}} & if\ D_t(x, y) < Th_{ad} \\ 0 & otherwise \end{cases}$$

2. The another parameter α_2 depends on temporal duration of a pixel in the background [10]. The reliability and stability are calculated by finding the temporal count C_{bg}, using the equation:

$$\alpha_2 = \begin{cases} e^{-\frac{1*(\zeta_{max}-C'_{bg})^2}{2*\sigma_2^2}} & if\ C_{bg} \geq \zeta_{min} \\ 0 & otherwise \end{cases}$$

where $\sigma_2 = 15$, $\zeta_{max} = 150$ and $\zeta_{min} = 30$ are assumed and $C'_{bg} = min(\zeta_{max}, C_{bg})$. In case a pixel is supposed to remain as background pixel and counted for greater than ζ_{min} frames then α_2 attains a non-zero value. The α_2 parameter increases with an increase in Cbg.

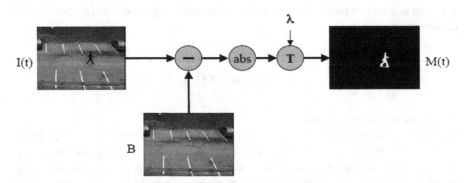

Fig. 1. Basic Steps for Background Subtraction [9] method

4 Morphological Operators

The morphological operators focused on the shape of features and used to reduce the outliers or noisy pixels. The morphological operations are applied to remove unwanted pixels after classification of pixels [10–14] (Fig. 2).

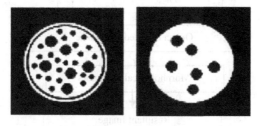

Fig. 2. Result before and after morphology [10]

- Erosion- The erosion is reduction of the objects size and removal of the small anomalies especially by doing subtraction of objects having their radius smaller as compared to the structural element [12, 14–16].
- Dilation- Dilation is a technique which expands the area of objects along the boundary, by filtering the broken areas, holes or connected regions that are separated through the structure element [13–16].

5 Methodology Used

In this work, the background subtraction based scheme is developed for dynamic background scenes that also have shadow issues.

The proposed work is completed in two steps: (i) Model the background and then compute a suitable threshold for each pixel classification, (ii) Pixel classification. The working steps of the suggested work is shown in Fig. 1. This paper mainly focuses on moving object to detect the object. As shown in Fig. 3 the colored video frame is taken as input and then result is being provided with background subtraction. But the results was not clear then after morphological operators are applied for noise cleaning.

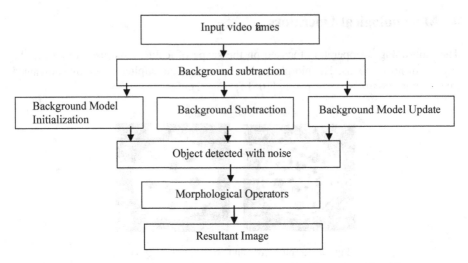

Fig. 3. Showing Block Diagram of Proposed Object Detection Algorithm

6 Experimental Results

This work is carried out on Windows XP OS with Intel Pentium (R) 4-processor having 2.46 GHz of speed and 2 GB RAM. Implementation of this research work is done with Matlab-2011 tool. The proposed work suggests significant improvement in terms of qualitative results which clearly depicts the strength in reducing the moving shadow, and other changes occurred in the background. The visual results of this experimental work depicts that the proposed results are better as shown in Fig. 4.

In the given Fig. 4, first column shows the original video frames. Second column represents the proposed results without post processing. Third column depicts the proposed results which are computed using post processing. The classified results are having some outliers which are considered as noisy pixel. So, this work has applied morphological operator to reduce the outlier or noisy pixel. Hence, the result shown in the third column are much better than the second column. So, the overall qualitative results of the proposed method using post processing is much better than results without post processing.

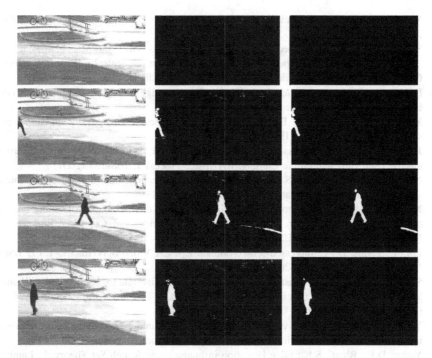

Fig. 4. Object detection results using background subtraction then applying morphology

7 Conclusion

In this paper, the object is detected using the background subtraction method and detected results have been improved using morphological operators. These operators reduced the misclassification rate. After morphological operation as exhibited in experimental results, the proposed method performs better in terms of qualitative results. This work deals with grayscale images. To resolve the wrongly classified pixel's, the purpose morphological operators are applied for noise cleaning. The proposed method produces good results as compared to other as shown in Fig. 4. The overall quality of proposed results is much better. In future, this work may be extended using GUI based application and cloud. It may be compared with [12, 17] on the basis of various parameters.

References

1. Kuralkar, P., Gaikwad, V.: Human object tracking using background subtraction and shadow removal techniques. IJARCSSE **2**(3), 79–84 (2012)
2. Yadav, D., Singh, K.: A combined approach of Kullback-Leibler divergence method and background subtraction for moving object detection in thermal video. Infrared Phys. Technol. **76**, 21–31 (2015)

3. Yilmaz, A., et al.: Object tracking: a survey. ACM Comput. Surv. **38**(4), 1–45 (2006). Article no. 13
4. Sharma, S., et al.: Cloud based emerging services systems. Int. J. Inf. Manag. 1–12 (2016)
5. Zhuang, L, Tang, K.: Fast salient object detection based on segments. In: IEEE International Conference on Advanced Video and Signal Based Surveillance (2009)
6. Davies, E.: Computer and Machine Vision: Theory, Algorithms, Practicalities, 4th edn. Elsevier, Amsterdam (2012). ISBN: 978-0-12-386908-1
7. Mahmoud, A., Walaa, M.: Fast and accurate approaches for image and moving object segmentation, pp. 252–259. IEEE (2011)
8. Jia, Z., et al.: Visual information fusion for object-based video image segmentation using unsupervised Bayesian online learning. IET Image Process **1**, 168–181 (2007)
9. NagaRaju, C., NagaMani, S.: Morphological edge detection algorithm based on multi-structure elements of different directions. IJICTR **01** (2011)
10. Ng, K.K., Delp, E.J: Background subtraction using a pixel-wise adaptive learning rate for object tracking initialization. VIPER, School of Electrical and Computer Engineering, Purdue University, Indiana USA (2011)
11. Liu, Y., Pados, D.: Compressed-sensed-domain L_1-PCA Video Surveillance. IEEE Trans. Multimed. **18**(3), 351–363 (2016)
12. Sharma, L., Yadav, D.K.: Histogram based adaptive learning rate for background modelling and moving object detection in video surveillance. Int. J. Telemed. Clin. Pract. **2**(1), 74–92 (2017)
13. Yadav, D., Singh, K.: Adaptive background modeling technique for moving object detection in video under dynamic environment. Int. J. Spat. Temporal Data Sci., 1–13 (2017)
14. Yadav, D.K., Bharti, S.K.: Edge Detection in Image Using Rough Set Theory. L. Lambert Academic Publishing, Germany (2015)
15. Jain, A.K.: Fundamentals of Digital Image Processing, 1st edn. Pearson-Education, New Jersey (2011)
16. Rafael, C., Richard, E.: Digital Image Processing. Tata McGraw-Hill Publication, New Delhi (2008)
17. Sharma, L., et al.: Fisher's linear discriminant ratio based threshold for moving human detection in thermal video. Infrared Phys. Technol. **78**, 118–128 (2016)
18. Gonzalez, R.C., Woods, R.E.: Digital Image Processing. Prentice-Hall, Englewood Cliffs (2002)
19. Cucchiara, R., Grana, C., Piccardi, M., Prati, A.: Detecting moving objects ghosts and shadows in video streams. IEEE Trans. Pattern Anal. Mach. Intell. **25**(10), 1337–1342 (2003)
20. Haritaoglu, I., Harwood, D., Davis, L.S.: W4: who? when? where? what? a real time system for detecting and tracking people. In: IEEE International Conference on Automatic Face and Gesture Recognition, pp. 222–227, April 1998
21. Haritaoglu, I., Harwood, D., Davis, L.S.: W4: real-time surveillance of people and their activities. IEEE Trans. Pattern Anal. Mach. Intell. **22**(8), 809–830 (2000)
22. Wren, C.R., Azarbayejani, A., Darrell, T., Pentland, A.P.: Pfinder: real-time tracking of the human body. IEEE Trans. Pattern Anal. Mach. Intell. **19**(7), 780–785 (1997)
23. Stauffer, C., Eric, W., Grimson, L.: Learning patterns of activity using real-time tracking. IEEE Trans. Pattern Anal. Mach. Intell. **22**(8), 747–757 (2000)
24. Ma, Y.-F., Zhang, H.-J.: Detecting motion object by spatio-temporal entropy. In: IEEE International Conference on Multimedia and Expo, August 2001
25. Souvenir, R., Wright, J., Pless, R.: Spatio-temporal detection and isolation: results on the PETS2005 datasets. In: Proceedings of the IEEE Workshop on Performance Evaluation in Tracking and Surveillance (2005)

26. Sun, H., Feng, T., Tan, T.: Spatio-temporal segmentation for video surveillance. In: IEEE International Conference on Pattern Recognition, vol. 1, pp. 843–846, September 2000
27. Boult, T., Micheals, R., Gao, X., Eckmann, M.: Into the woods: visual surveillance of non-cooperative camouflaged targets in complex outdoor settings. Proc. IEEE **89**, 1382–1402 (2001)
28. Monnet, A., Mittal, A., Paragios, N., Ramesh, V.: Background modeling and subtraction of dynamic scenes. In: Proceedings of the Ninth IEEE International Conference on Computer Vision, pp. 1305–1312 (2003)
29. Zhong, J., Sclaroff, S.: Segmenting foreground objects from a dynamic textured background via a robust Kalman filter. In: Proceedings of the Ninth IEEE International Conference on Computer Vision, pp. 44–50 (2003)
30. Siebel, N.T., Maybank, S.J.: Real-time tracking of pedestrians and vehicles. In: Proceedings of the IEEE Workshop on Performance Evaluation of Tracking and Surveillance (2001)
31. Cucchiara, R., Grana, C., Prati, A.: Detecting moving objects and their shadows: an evaluation with the PETS2002 dataset. In: Proceedings of the Third IEEE International Workshop on Performance Evaluation of Tracking and Surveillance (PETS 2002) in conj. with ECCV 2002, pp. 18–25, May 2002
32. Collins, R.T., Lipton, A.J., Kanade, T., Fujiyoshi, H., Duggins, D., Tsin, Y., Tolliver, D., Enomoto, N., Hasegawa, O.: A System for Video Surveillance and Monitoring: Vsam Final Report Robotics Institute, May 2000

Author Index

Abrol, Salil I-140
Adesoji, Alalade I-389
Aditi I-140
Afshar Alam, M. II-54
Afzal, Ayesha Hena II-54
Aggarwal, Archit I-288
Aggarwal, Gianesahwar I-355
Aggrawal, R. K. I-402
Ahuja, Ravin I-389, II-397
Ansari, Mohd. Yousuf II-420
Arora, Ankur II-26
Arora, Bhawna I-288
Arora, Mamta II-133
Arora, Vasudha II-100
Attri, Manoj II-442
Awasthi, Saatvik I-375

Baig, Nida I-14
Balamurugan, B. I-223
Bali, Shweta II-430
Balusamy, Balamurugan I-375
Batra, Usha II-3, II-35
Bhardwaj, Shweta I-203
Bhaskaran, Suku II-26
Bhat, Vishal I-64
Bholan, Rasveen II-381
Bir, Paarth I-223
Biswas, Siddhartha Sankar I-339

Chahal, Deepak II-249
Chakraborty, Ayan I-278
Chandra, Pravin I-3, II-279
Chaudhry, Simran II-236
Chauhan, Anshul I-212
Chauhan, Chaitanya II-412
Chauhan, Sudhir Kumar II-154
Chhikara, Rita I-161
Chitkara, Bhavook II-366
Chopra, Khyati II-381
Choudhury, Tanupriya I-212, I-288

Dabass, Jyoti II-305, II-316
Dabass, Manju I-103, II-316

Dangi, Nitesh II-290
Daruka, Navin Ram I-411
Das, Tathagato II-110
Deshpande, Ashok I-411
Dhawan, Sanjeev II-236
Dhawan, Sudipti II-14
Dohare, Neha I-131
Dubey, Ankit I-239
Dungerchand, Jain Soham II-412
Dureja, Ajay I-140
Dureja, Aman I-140
Dutta, Akash I-140
Dutta, Chiranjit I-301, I-311

Edikan, Ekong II-397

Gahlan, Mamta I-402
Garg, Anjali I-328
Garg, Parag Kumar II-133
Gautam, Ashu I-187
Ghose, Udayan I-49
Ghosh, Ayanabha II-110
Goswami, R. T. I-278
Goswami, Radha Tamal II-331
Goyal, Himanshu I-328
Goyal, Monika I-254
Goyal, Mukta II-186, II-342
Gupta, Aakanshi I-64
Gupta, Amitava Sen I-365
Gupta, Ankita I-161
Gupta, Archit I-355
Gupta, Kanika II-90
Gupta, Karunesh K. II-412
Gupta, Manoj Kr. I-3
Gupta, Reena I-151, I-320
Gupta, Sachin I-38
Gupta, Shruti I-266
Gurav, Vedant II-68

Hanmandlu, Madasu II-305

Iftekhar, Nida I-339

Jain, Rachna   I-170
Jain, Saksham   II-223
Jain, Sarika   II-290
Jha, Saurabh Kumar   II-90
Johari, Rahul   II-90
Joshi, Neeraj   I-170

Kalra, Sneh   I-38
Kansal, Vineet   II-356
Khan, Samia   I-339
Kharb, Latika   II-249
Khare, Ishita   II-342
Kharwar, Parth   II-68
Kispotta, Sunil   II-164
Kolankar, Piyush   II-290
Krishnamurthi, Rajalakshmi   II-186, II-342
Kumar, Kaushal   I-266
Kumar, Praveen   I-420
Kumar, Saurav   I-170
Kumar, Suresh   II-204
Kumar, Vivek   II-90

Mahmood, Syed Mohd Jamal   II-366
Mainuddin   II-420
Majumder, Sayan   II-110
Malhotra, Sona   II-123
Malik, Nidhi   II-223
Mehta, Vibhu   I-328
Misra, Sanjay   I-389, II-397
Mittal, Apeksha   II-279
Mittal, Ruchi   II-173
Mongia, Shweta   II-100

Nafis, Md. Tabrez   II-266
Nagrath, Preeti   I-170
Nanda, Aditeya   I-203
Nandal, Neha   II-442
Narender   II-442
Narwal, Bhawna   II-14
Nishtha   II-79

Ojha, Ritesh   II-412
Oluranti, Jonathan   II-397

Pandey, Mrinal   I-254, II-133
Pankaj   I-365
Parkar, Muhanned   II-68
Patel, Ajaykumar   I-239
Patel, Ranjeet   II-290

Paul, Swagata   II-331
Pereira, Anishka   I-14
Porkodi, V.   I-375
Prakash, Anand   II-420
Prakash, Surya   I-355
Prasad, Jay Shankar   I-38
Preeti   I-365
Purohit, Gaurav   II-412

Rai, Chandra Shekhar   I-151, I-320
Raisy, C. D.   I-365
Rajpoot, Dharamveer Singh   I-80
Rana, Ajay   II-356
Rani, Seema   I-80
Ranjan, Arti   II-143
Rashmi   I-49
Rawat, Seema   I-420
Rehalia, Amit   II-266
Roy, Abhishek   II-110

Sachdeva, Divyam   I-328
Sachdeva, Shelly   I-131
Saha, Sajal   I-278, II-331
Saini, Kartikay   I-365
Sanga, Aniruddh   II-258
Sanga, Niharika   II-258
Sati, Vishwani   I-203
Shah, Shubhra   II-14
Sharda, Sonia   II-143
Sharma, Anil   II-204
Sharma, Manka   II-26
Sharma, Nonita   I-91
Sharma, Ochin   I-120
Sharma, Prabha   I-161
Sharma, Ritika   I-328
Sharma, Shruti   II-381
Sharma, Sumit   II-290
Shinde, Rutuja   I-246
Shukla, Amar   I-212
Shukla, Megha   I-411
Singh, Abhishek   I-24
Singh, Amit Prakash   II-279
Singh, Gaurav   I-170
Singh, Jaspreet   II-258
Singh, Jyoti   I-246
Singh, Jyotsna   I-266
Singh, Kulvinder   II-123
Singh, Rishipal   I-91
Singh, Ruby   I-301, I-311

Singh, Saurabh II-164
Singh, Sunil I-411
Singh, Vanisha I-91
Singhal, Garvit I-420
Singhal, Niraj I-301, I-311
Sisa, Fernando Pérez II-397
Soni, Gunjan I-355
Soni, Shubham I-328
Sood, Manu II-79
Srivastava, Satyajee I-24, II-143
Suri, Bharti I-64

Tanwar, Kuldeep II-154
Tanwar, Rohit II-123, II-236, II-442
Tiwari, Anupam II-35
Tripathi, Amrendra I-288
Tyagi, Shyam Sunder II-430

Upadhyay, Anand I-14, I-239, I-246

Vagisha II-249
Varma, Aparna II-342
Vashisth, Sharda I-103, I-365
Verma, Ankit I-212
Vig, Rekha I-103, II-305
Vishwakarma, Shakti II-164
Vyas, Abhilasha II-3

Walia, Himdweep II-356
Wazir, Samar II-266

Yadav, Akanksha II-164

Zafar, Sherin I-187, I-339, II-54

Printed in the United States
by Baker & Taylor Publisher Services

Printed in the United States
by Baker & Taylor Publisher Services